ENCYCLOPEDIA OF SPORTS SCIENCE

Volume 1

ENCYCLOPEDIA OF **Sports** SCIENCE

Volume 1

John Zumerchik

EDITOR

MACMILLAN LIBRARY REFERENCE USA
Simon & Schuster Macmillan
NEW YORK

Simon & Schuster and Prentice Hall International
LONDON · MEXICO CITY · NEW DELHI · SINGAPORE · SYDNEY · TORONTO

Simon & Schuster Macmillan
1633 Broadway, New York, NY 10019

Printed in the United States of America

printing number

10 9 8 7 6 5 4 3 2 1

LIBRARY OF CONGRESS CATALOGING-IN-PUBLICATION DATA
Encyclopedia of sports science / John Zumerchik, editor.
       p. cm.
    Includes bibliographical references and index.
      ISBN 0-02-897506-5 (set : alk. paper). — ISBN 0-02-864665-7 (v. 1 : alk. paper). — ISBN 0-02-864666-5 (v. 2 : alk. paper)
      1. Sports sciences—Encyclopedias. 2. Sports—Physiological aspects—Encyclopedias. I. Zumerchik, John.
GV558.E53 1997
613.7' 1—dc21   96-47502
                                                      CIP

The paper used in this publication meets the minimum requirements of American National Standard for Information Sciences—Permanence of Paper for Printed Library Materials, ANSI Z39.48-1984.

Contents

List of Contributors   vii
Preface   ix

PART ONE: SPORTS

Acrobatics   3
Balancing Skills, 4
Fluidity and Summation of Forces, 6
Inertia and Angular Momentum, 9
Using Sensory Clues, 18
Body Size Advantages, 19

Archery   26
The Basics, 28
Bow and Arrow Energy , 30
Bow Dynamics, 32
Arrow Dynamics, 35
Shooting Aids, 37

Baseball   39
Pitching Phases, 40
Types of Pitches, 43
Bat and Ball Collision, 48
Hitting Theories, 54
Base Running, 57

Basketball   62
Shooting Mechanics, 63
The Physics of Shooting, 68
Hang Time and Shot Blocking, 77
Raise the Basket to Twelve Feet? 79
Passing, 80
Defense, 82

Bowling   85
The Basics, 86
Throwing the Ball, 88
The Path of the Ball, 91
Pin Collisions, 100

Boxing   108
Punching Power, 109
Head Movement and Concussions, 112
Forces on the Brain, 113
Boxing Gloves, 117

Catching Skills   122
Judging a Fly Ball, 122
Catching Technique, 126
Lacrosse: A Unique Catching Sport, 128

Cycling   130
Frame Geometry, 131
Frame Materials, 132
Stability, 133
Forces Acting on Bike and Rider, 135
Biomechanics, 143

Equipment Materials   153
Selecting Materials, 154
Bicycles, 162
Golf, 167
Athletic Shoes, 172
Other Sports, 175

Field Athletics: Jumping   178
Takeoff Speed and Center of Gravity, 178
Muscle Forces and Jumping Ability, 181
High Jump, 182
Long Jump, 185
Triple Jump, 189
Pole Vault, 191
Environmental Factors in Jumping, 196

Field Athletics: Throwing   201
Environmental Considerations: Forces, 202
Dynamics of Field Throwing, 208

Football   230
Collision Dynamics, 231
Throwing, 235
Punting, 237
Placekicking Dynamics, 239
Sprinters as Receivers? 243
The Dynamics of Collision Injuries, 244

Gliding and Hang Gliding   252
The Physics of Flight, 254
Sources of Energy, 260
Gliding as a Sport, 265

Golf   269
Swing Power, 270
Sidehill Lies, 279
Putting, 279
Golf Clubs, 280
The Golf Ball, 281

Hockey   292
The Hockey Puck, 293
Sticks and Shooting, 297
Skating Power and Power Skating, 307

Karate   311
Balance and Base of Support, 312
Generation of Force, 313

Paddle Sports   321
Basics of Watercraft, 323
Dynamics of Oars and Paddles, 330
Physique and Paddle Sports, 335
Paddle Sport Techniques, 335

Running and Hurdling   340
Basics of Running, 341
Aerodynamics of Running, 344
Sprinting, 346
Distance Running, 353
Tuned Tracks, 360
Hurdling, 361

Sailing   369
Air Forces on the Sail, 370
Directional Sailing, 374
Hull Design: Stability and Resistance, 381
Importance of Weight Distribution, 383
Match Racing: Wind and Weather, 386

Skating   390
The Ice, 392
Figure, Hockey, and Speed Skating: A Comparison, 398
The Physics of Skating, 401
Mechanics of Speed Skating, 407

Skiing   419
Surface Conditions: Physics of Snow, 420
Resistive Forces in Skiing, 421
The Mechanics of Alpine Skiing, 427
Nordic Skiing Techniques, 434

Soccer   439
The Soccer Ball, 440
Soccer Technique, 446

Statistics   **453**
Statistical Issues, 454
Issues of Probability, 461
Prediction: Trends in Future Athletic
    Performance, 467

Strength Training   **471**
Background, 472
Principles of Strength Training, 473
Guidelines for Training, 476
Aids for Strength Training, 478
Types of Strengthening Exercises, 480
Physiological Adaptations, 484
In Conclusion, 487

Swimming   **488**
Science and Swimming Records, 488
The Body in Water, 490
Buoyancy and Flotation, 491
Drag: Resistance and Swimming Speed,
    494
Propulsion in Water, 498
Sweep Actions, 503
Breaststroke: Velocity Fluctuations, 505
Dive Starts, 507

Tennis   **510**
Tennis Rackets, 511
The Strings, 516
Tennis Shots, 519
Surface Effects, 528
Biomechanics, 529

Volleyball   **534**
Aerodynamics and the "Floater," 535
The Jump Serve: Endline "Spiking,"
    539
The Spike, 541
Passing, 544
Setting: What Is a Legal Set? 546

Weight Lifting   **549**
Principles of Weight Lifting, 550
Olympic Weight Lifting, 557
Power Lifting, 561

Wrestling   **567**
The Basics of Wrestling, 568
Sumo Wrestling, 573

PART TWO: THE BODY

Aging and Performance   **583**
Biological Theories of Aging, 584
Age-Related Changes and Exercise,
    584
Psychological Effects of Exercise, 594
Does Disuse Accelerate Aging? 595

It's Never Too Late, 597
Older Adults Who Become Athletes,
    597
Aging Athletes, 598
Do Athletes Live Longer? 599
Which Sports Promote Longevity? 600

Ankle, Foot, and Lower Leg   **603**
Functional Anatomy, 603
Overuse Injuries, 608
Prevention, 611

Body Composition   **616**
Typical Fat and Nonfat Components, 617
Measuring Body Composition, 618
Desirable Weight, 623

Energy and Metabolism   **625**
Chemistry: The Basis of Change, 626
Cellular Metabolism: Breaking Down
    Fuels for Energy, 629
Whole-Body Metabolism, 641

Female Athletes   **651**
Body Composition and Strength, 652
Physiological Functions, 655
Reproductive Function, 657
Eating Disorders, 663

Heart and Circulatory System   **667**
Circulation: The Basic Pattern, 667
The Heart, 670
The Arteries, 677
The Capillaries, 683
The Veins, 684
Bleeding, 685

Knee   **688**
Functional Anatomy, 688
Pathophysiology and Treatment, 691
Prevention of Injuries, 693

Motor Control   **700**
Theories of Motor Control, 701
The Nervous System, 701
The Central Nervous System and
    Motor Control, 706
Sensation and Motor Control, 709
Development and Motor Control, 714
In Conclusion, 718

Nutrition and the Athlete   **720**
Terminology, 720
The Caloric Nutrients, 722
Vitamins and Minerals, 732
Water, 739
Weight Control, 746

Pelvis, Hip, and Thigh   **752**
The Pelvis and Athletics, 753

Functional Anatomy, 754
Pathophysiology and Treatment, 757
Prevention of Injuries, 759

Rehabilitation   **763**
Responses to Tissue Injury, 764
Phase 1 of Rehabilitation: Acute, 766
Phase 2 of Rehabilitation: Subacute, 769
Phase 3 of Rehabilitation: Resuming
    Full Activity, 772
Phase 4 of Rehabilitation: Maintenance
    and Prevention, 775

Respiration   **777**
Physics of Respiratory Gases, 777
Physiology of Respiration, 782
Respiratory Diseases, 791
Sports at High and Low Air Pressure:
    Mountaineering and Scuba Diving,
    794

Shoulder, Elbow, and Wrist   **808**
Mechanics of Throwing and Swinging,
    808
Functional Anatomy, 811
Pathophysiology and Treatment, 820
Preventing Arm Injuries, 822

Skeletal Muscle   **825**
Control of Contraction, 825
Structure of Skeletal Muscle, 828
Stimulation of Skeletal Muscle, 830
Contraction of Skeletal Muscle, 831
Relaxation of Skeletal Muscle, 834
Types of Skeletal Muscle Fibers, 835
Effects of Exercise, 837

Skeletal System   **842**
Bone, 843
Joints, 860
Preventing Injury to the Bones and Joints,
    866

Spine   **871**
Anatomy and Function of the Spine, 872
Back Injuries, 875
Prevention and Therapy, 881

Vision   **887**
The Physiology of Vision, 888
Processing Visual Information in
    Sports, 894

Index   907

Contributors

ANGELO ARMENTI
California University of Pennsylvania

TOMMY BOONE
Department of Exercise Physiology
College of Saint Scholastica

THOMAS H. BRAID
Argonne National Laboratory
Argonne, Illinois

SIDNEY BROADBENT
Ice Skate Conditioning Equipment
Littleton, Colorado

ROBERT J. DALEY
MacNeal Hospital
Berwyn, Illinois

MICHAEL FOLEY
Louisiana Therapy Services
Slidell, Louisiana

STEVE R. GEIRINGER
Department of Physical Medicine and
Rehabilitation
Wayne State University

DAVID E. HARRIS
Lewiston-Auburn College
University of Southern Maine

BRUCE HAUGER
Department of Physical Therapy
College of Saint Scholastica

JAMES R. HOLMES
Orthopedic Surgery Associates
Ypsilanti, Michigan

FRED HOLMSTROM
Department of Physics
San Jose State University

DON C. HOPKINS
Department of Physics
Hamline University

DAVID H. JANDA
Institute for Preventative Sports Medicine
Ann Arbor, Michigan

JAMES A. KOEHLER
Department of Physics
University of Saskatchewan

BARBARA LELLI
Lisbon Falls, Maine

DON B. LICHTENBERG
Department of Physics
Indiana University

DAVID A. LIND
Department of Physics
University of Colorado

ERNIE MCFARLAND
Department of Physics
University of Guelph

ALAN E. MIKESKY
School of Physical Education
Indiana University

MICHAEL R. NOTIS
Department of Material Science and
Engineering
Lehigh University

ANGELA ROSENBERG
Department of Psychology
College of Saint Scholastica

NANCY ROWLAND
National Institute for Fitness and Sport
Indianapolis, Indiana

HARVEY G. SCHNEIDER
Concord, Massachusetts

JEAN SZILVA
Department of Anatomy and
Neurobiology
University of Vermont College of
Medicine

ARJUN TAN
Department of Physics
Alabama A&M University

DAVID A. THOMAS
Department of Material Science and
Engineering
Lehigh University

ARKADY VOLOSHIN
Department of Mechanical Engineering
and Mechanics
Lehigh University

JAMES D. WHITE
Department of Physics
Baldwin-Wallace College

ELLEN J. ZEMAN
Department of Molecular Physiology
and Biophysics
University of Vermont College of
Medicine

CHERYL A. ZUMERCHIK
Boulder, Colorado

DAVID L. ZUMERCHIK
Southwest Urology Associates
Evergreen Park, Illinois

Preface

The *Encyclopedia of Sports Science* aims to answer two types of questions about sports. The first type includes questions such as: What makes a skate slide across the ice? What makes a curveball spin? Is there an explanation for Michael Jordan's incredible "hang time"? These are questions about the physics of sports. The second kind of question concerns such issues as: Will weight lifting hurt the knees? How does exercise affect the aging process? Why do many young female gymnasts attempt to "stay small," and what are the physical consequences? These are questions about how the body functions when participating in sports. Both of these areas can be summed up in the purpose of this Encyclopedia: to help widen our knowledge of science as it pertains to sports.

As the many illustrations show, in many sports a seemingly simple movement is often ruled by a complicated law of physics. These pictures also show how an understanding of the underlying principles can result in an improved athletic performance.

This Encyclopedia, therefore, has many uses. A student interested in improving her tennis game will find a description of the biomechanics of the serve. The college rowing team learns in the entry on paddle sports why racing shells have sliding seats. The high school football coach and the physics teacher both will find material to illustrate the principle of linear momentum. And even the spectator will be pleased to understand why a golf ball behaves the way it does.

The Encyclopedia has been divided into two main parts: Sports and The Body. In the first part, each entry deals with a particular sport (e.g., Archery) or a subject common to several sports (e.g., Catching Skills). Each begins with an introduction that provides historical information, after which the basic science concepts are presented. Every attempt has been made to integrate as many stories from the annals of sports as possible, so that the reader can easily relate to the material. For readers seeking additional information, the bibliography at the end of the entry provides titles for further reading.

Many concepts of physics apply to more than one sport. Rather than repeating explanations, we have restricted ourselves to describing certain phenomena once. In related sports, the reader will find *See also* references to a fuller explanation of basic principles of physics. For example, the main explication of aerodynamic forces can be found in the entries on Gliding and Field Athletics: Throwing. The treatment of wind and Coriolis effects is, not surprisingly, a part of the entry on Sailing.

Part Two deals with the physiology of sport. Here entries such as Heart and Circulatory System, Knee, and Respiration provide information about how the body works under stress, what type of damage or trauma might be incurred in certain sports, and, most important, how injuries can be prevented.

The articles in both parts are arranged alphabetically for easy access. Cross-references within entries guide readers to related articles.

Not all sports have been included here. For example, the English sport of cricket does not have its own entry, but included in the article on baseball is an essay entitled "Who's Tougher to Hit: A Cricket Bowler or a Baseball Pitcher?" Information about scuba diving can be found in the entry on Respiration in Part Two. Other sports received no attention because there is minimal scientific research. The index at the end of Volume 2 provides quick access to all concepts and names of athletes cited.

Unlike sports medicine, the field of sports physics is a fairly young discipline. This Encyclopedia provides data not previously published and does so in language that appeals to the student and to interested laypeople.

Part One

Sports

Acrobatics

TUMBLING, TWISTING, and somersaulting surely were among the earliest human skills—useful for the hunter as well as the hunted. The combination of strength, flexibility, and balance needed to perform acrobatic moves certainly would have improved the chances of survival. Interest eventually grew beyond survival skills, and warriors, as well as town clowns and court jesters, took pleasure in showcasing their acrobatic agility.

Structured acrobatics originated well before today's major sports, such as football, basketball, or even baseball. What is today called gymnastics began in Germany around 1810. Friederich Ludwig Jahns intent was to develop a physical education movement based on natural outdoor activity. Jahn and his associates invented games and then hung ropes and constructed supporting apparatus to broaden the range and dynamics of the games. He is credited with inventing at least three pieces of modern gymnastic apparatus: the horizontal bar, the parallel bar, and the rings.

Several of Jahn's protégés came to the eastern United States in the 1820s and shortly thereafter set up a *Turnverein*, or gymnastic association, in the Boston, Massachusetts, area. The movement slowly grew and spread around the United States.

Yale was one of the first universities to construct a gymnasium similar to Jahn's *Turnplatz*, or "gymnastics place." In the 1860s the school built a larger gymnasium that contained much of the gymnastic apparatus that can be found in today's gymnasium: horizontal bar, parallel bars, vaulting horse, springboard, trapezes, flying rings, and landing mats.

The influence of Jahn's movement goes well beyond gymnastics, for acrobatic skills are essential to many sports and forms of entertainment. Acrobatic acts are the cornerstone of most circuses. On the tenth of July 1982, when the circus star Miguel Vasquez performed the first quadruple back somersault while moving from one trapeze to another, he accomplished an acrobatic feat of uncanny timing and strength. It took incredible timing and skill for him to rotate so quickly, knowing just when to come out of his tuck, and it also took incredible strength on the part of the trapeze artist who caught Miguel, his brother Juan, as he pulled out of a tucked rotation moving at approximately 113 kilometers per hour (70 MPH) (Brancazio, 1984).

From the raw athleticism of the trapeze artist to the grace of an accomplished figure skater, the wide range of acrobatic sports captures the imagination of many. And new acrobatic sports continue to gain in popularity. Diving, roller blading, skydiving aerobatics, and snowboarding are a few of the many relatively new sports that are heavily dependent on acrobatic skills.

A frequently asked question is whether acrobatics should be considered a sport, an art, or a circus act; the ramifications of this question are quite significant. First, while a circus performer attempts to make easy skills appear difficult, an artist attempts to make the difficult look easy. Second, for a circus performer, form is not paramount, whereas for an artist, form and body lines are crucial. Finally, there is the question of perspective: is the performance for the audience or for judges? For divers, gymnasts, figure skaters, and freestyle skiers, these questions are more than philosophical ponderings. These athletes compete neither head-to-head, nor against a clock, but instead are evaluated in a highly subjective way: they are judged. Assessment is based on biomechanical and aesthetic factors, weighing difficulty, efficiency, and artistry. Visual qualities, such as pleasing lines and motion, rhythm, and design of routine all are important criteria. More subjective qualities, such as difficulty, originality, creativity, and impression of personality contribute to what is called aesthetic movement. Other criteria, such as grace, apparent effortlessness, efficiency, control, fluidity, continuity, and dynamics, are also significant because they affect artistic perception.

Criticism abounds because of the subjective nature of the judging process. Scores are the focus of constant controversy. It is unrealistic to expect to mollify all the critics, yet there is room for improvement in making competitions fairer. Critics contend that competitions should be judged on objective scientific principles, rather than subjective ones.

Unfortunately, this is not easily accomplished. Pushing the body's range of motion (ROM) to the limit, and performing bodily manipulations in many planes and around several axes, does not easily lend itself to simple scientific explanations. Many of these skills require subtle movements that are very difficult to describe, more difficult to coach, and harder yet to judge. This article will not give an exhaustive presentation of all the physical principles involved in acrobatic maneuvers, but will present a basic overview of the key concepts.

Overcoming Fear

Athletes participating in acrobatic sports usually have a high threshold of fear, for it takes courage to place one's body in very precarious airborne, off-balanced positions. For instance, most of the cliff divers of Acapulco, Mexico, learned by watching their forebears and through plenty of practice. Dispelling fear and instilling confidence are usually the two primary goals of an acrobatics coach. Once a young athlete gets over her initial fear, most skills can be refined purely by trial and error. As a gymnast masters the basics, subtle adjustments can be made to fine tune her skills, giving her movements an aesthetically pleasing. fluidity. An experienced coach possesses a bag of teaching tricks to accomplish this, so that with the proper equipment, children quickly learn skills that once took many months to master.

Balancing Skills

Whatever acrobatic movement is being attempted, its proper execution depends on an understanding of balance. It requires a full awareness of where one's center of gravity rests. The term *center of gravity* (COG) refers to the geometric center of mass distribution, which can, depending on position, lie either inside or outside the body. It is the

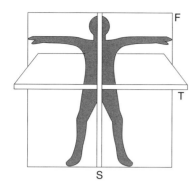

Figure 1. *The center of gravity (center of mass) is the point where the gravitational force can be considered to act on the body as a whole, and the point about which all torques on the body can be calculated to determine rotations. The force of gravity is actually distributed throughout the body; not one atom escapes the gravitational force. The center of gravity is the three-dimensional intersection of the frontal (F), transverse (T), and sagittal (S) planes.*

Figure 2. *The center of gravity is a point that can be inside or outside the body. The dots indicate the approximate center of gravity for different body positions. It varies by body type and is usually higher for men than women.*

point where the gravitational force can be considered to act on the body as a whole, and the point about which all forces on the body can be calculated to determine rotations (*see Figure 1*).

Because of differences in physical structure, the COG varies among individuals. Using a simple experiment, it is possible to figure out if one has a high or low COG. Take three steps back from a wall, with a chair positioned between oneself and the wall. Lean over so that the head rests against the wall (legs about 45° to torso) and lift the chair up against the chest. Next, try to stand up. If one has a low COG, the weight of the chair will not prevent one from standing up; with a high COG, one will be unable to stand.

Almost everyone's center of gravity lies somewhere between hips and mid-body. A person with heavy thick, legs and relatively small trunk, shoulders, and arms will usually have a COG that lies around the lower hips. Someone with thin legs and buttocks, yet a heavily muscled torso, neck, and arms, will have a higher COG, closer to the abdomen.

Pair figure skaters and cheerleaders know from experience that everyone has a different COG. Knowing a partner's COG is essential for the stability necessary to effectively perform lifts, throws, and catches. The most stable position is that in which the COG lies directly over the supporting hands.

For example, the jump into a high front swan on a partner's hands (held directly overhead) would be nearly impossible unless the lifter lifts from the jumper's COG. The jumper starts by standing as close to her partner as possible, placing her hands on his shoulders; simultaneously, her partner places his hands on her hips (at her COG). As she jumps directly upward, he bends his knees to begin lowering himself directly under her rising COG. At a minimum, she exerts a force equal to, or greater than, her weight. How much greater the force is than her weight determines the velocity at which she rises to a balancing point directly over her partner's head.

In any acrobatic move, the COG always must be directly over the center of support. If a perpendicular line is drawn from the center of the base of support during a handstand, the weight is divided equally on each side of the line. Should a move require that a greater proportion of body mass rest to either side of the perpendicular, the limbs on the lighter side must be extended outward to compensate for the imbalance. For example, in the one-handed handstand pictured in Figure 3, most of the gymnast's mass rests to his right, so his left leg remains close to perpendicular, yet his right leg must be extended away from the perpendicular to counter the greater body mass that rests to his left.

Balance is also highly dependent on response times. If a person begins to fall, there is only a small window of opportunity in which he or she can take corrective action to prevent a fall. Response times can be broken down into two components: recognition time and reaction time. Response time may be just the recognition time, or it may be recognition time plus reaction time. (Reaction time encompasses the

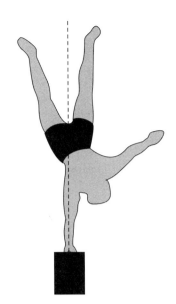

Figure 3. *During a handstand, the gymnast's mass lies equally to the left and right of his center line of gravity. While balancing in a one-handed handstand, the right leg must be extended perpendicularly outward to counter the greater body mass to the left. Although the right leg and left arm are both extended, movement of the leg has a much greater effect on balance, not only because of its greater mass but also because of its greater moment of inertia (a function of its distance from the balancing point at the hand).*

additional time necessary to trigger the body to move, say, an arm to execute the required corrective movement.)

For reasons related to both genetics and training, response times vary tremendously among individuals. The range varies from a lightning-fast 0.15 second to a slow 0.5 second (Lind, 1995). Because of the number of physiological factors involved (sight, hearing, brain function, body structure, muscle makeup, neurological structure), definitive conclusions about the causes of the differences have yet to be established.

The handstand is perhaps the most common acrobatic skill requiring balance. Many consider it the foundation skill of gymnastics because it forms an integral part of routines on apparatus as well as of floor exercises. Straight-line body alignment is achieved by locking the arms, trunk, neck, and legs in a straight line with the shoulders depressed. Handstands performed off the floor or on different apparatus require slightly different adjustments to compensate for the different support positions of the hands. In any routine, a handstand usually serves as a stopping point from which to launch a maneuver in the opposite direction.

It is remarkable to watch a gymnast generate tremendous rotational velocity, yet bring that velocity to a stop as she rises into a handstand. The force necessary to create linear or angular movement requires a force of an equal amount to stop the movement. Therefore, most giant swings into a handstand show a gymnast placing her hands apart to create a wider base of support, which aids both stability and the amount of force that can be generated to create angular rotation.

During a floor ascent to a handstand, the body's COG moves through a 90-degree arc. In coming to a balanced handstand position, the arms are angled about 20 degrees beyond the horizontal, but as the legs rise upward over the head and the shoulders shift backward, the arms assume a vertical position. By using a 20-degree lean to start, the gymnast keeps the COG more closely over the center of support throughout the movement into a handstand.

Of course, a gymnast can begin with her arms in a more vertical position, but the push-off and spring must be much more forceful. Using a more forceful ascent, however, jeopardizes balance because the arms usually need to be quickly angled backward to counter the greater force used in the ascent.

Fluidity and Summation of Forces

From years of practice, athletes know what they need to do from a mechanical perspective and what it should feel like. Most athletes do not try to concentrate on the mechanics because usually far too many steps are involved. It is a distraction that takes away from their concentration on timing and a smooth, flowing movement. They hope that sufficient muscle memory develops through hours upon hours of practice so that when performance time comes, they can perform without thinking.

Doing it right usually requires a summation of joint forces. Muscles act upon bones so that each force exerted adds to the previous force to propel the athlete in the intended direction. Simultaneous firing of muscles limits the force generated to transfer energy from the bigger, slower muscles to the smaller, faster ones. For example, the height reached during a dismount depends on the amount of force exerted by the gymnast that actually gets exerted about the axis of rotation, which, in this case, is the bar. If bad timing decreases the force exerted, the body loses velocity, thereby decreasing the velocity as the gymnast releases from the bar.

Although continuity of joint forces is basic to generating maximum power, it also is vital in developing a fluid motion. In sports that depend on the interpretation of judges, for example, like diving, gymnastics, and figure skating, the subjective nature of scoring places a great deal of emphasis on fluidity. To achieve continuity of joint forces, the swinging gymnast must begin a motion with a coordinated pull with her upper body, which is then "overlapped" by the motion of the lower body. There must be no pause in the motion between upper and lower body: it must be continuous. If this principle is violated, not only will the force generated be less, but a poor "feel" results from the improper timing, which makes performing a smooth, fluid dismount all the more difficult.

Summation and continuity of joint forces become particularly important for divers taking off from a springboard or gymnasts taking off from a Reuther springboard. Depending on the event, gymnasts approach the springboard with varying degrees of velocity, usually their maximum controllable velocity. This gives them the greatest linear momentum (mass × velocity), so that when they strike the springboard, the higher and farther their linear momentum will carry them in the horizontal and vertical planes. This is important because the best scores are achieved by those with the highest and longest trajectory.

Divers, on the other hand, take a slower, more measured approach to the end of the board. They can do this because their springboard has much greater elasticity than the Reuther board used by gymnasts. The diver's major concern rests with the vertical jump component, as only a small amount of horizontal momentum is necessary to execute twisting and somersaulting maneuvers.

Despite their different objectives, the takeoff mechanics for divers and gymnasts are quite similar. As the arms and shoulder drive upward, the back extends upward and back, followed by hip extension, then knee extension, and finally a flexing of the feet. Whatever the jumping surface, the jumper compresses herself by exerting as much downward motion as possible so that the muscular forces generated during extension may act for the maximum time during extension.

What complicates the springboard jumping process is the need for the elastic energy of the springboard to work in conjunction with the summation and continuity of the body's joint forces. If the springboard jump occurs with the athlete leaving the board still in a crouched position—body positioned to generate additional force, but the feet no longer in contact with the surface to generate force—the vertical and horizontal distance is limited by the inability to fully exert muscle force (*see also FIELD ATHLETICS: JUMPING*).

Once the body is airborne, there is nothing that can be done to counter an off-course trajectory. Airborne trajectory, in this case the body's COG, is one of the few factors that are predetermined the instant the diver or gymnast takes off from the springboard. The COG follows a parabolic curve, with the descent following the same curved pathway as the ascent.

Although springboard divers cannot make adjustments after takeoff, they can adjust the springiness of the board by adjusting the center support pin prior to their attempt. Rolling it forward toward the water increases springiness; rolling it backward toward the base decreases springiness. Adjusting the pin affects not only the springiness of the board but also the timing of the diver. The upward energy represents energy of motion, kinetic energy, which in turn determines the height at which the diver (or gymnast) flies. Angle of takeoff and takeoff velocity are the primary determinants of the time the athlete will remain airborne.

According to the principle of conservation of energy, at maximum height all the kinetic energy generated at takeoff is converted to gravitational potential energy because the diver or gymnast has no kinetic energy left. An adjustment to the bounce of the springboard allows the diver to generate an initial impulse (force × time), which gets stored in the elastic board during the initial downward motion. A second impulse of energy, from the musculoskeletal extension in conjunction with the board recoiling upward, gets added to the initial impulse of energy.

To repeat: adjusting the pin affects both the springiness of the board and the timing of the diver. The diver attempts to optimize the takeoff time so that she can compress to her maximum extent and then recoil before her feet leave the board. Thus, in order to maximize the kinetic energy at takeoff, the diver must maximize the work done by the body's musculoskeletal system. In other words, the time of reaction of the board must be adjusted to match the bioreaction time of the diver. A perfect match between the body's summation of forces and the elasticity of the board at one adjustment will be undone by a readjustment of the pin.

For both divers and gymnasts, a powerful controlled thrust against the board or floor is essential at takeoff. Not only is this thrust the sole determinant of elevation; it is also the major factor in establishing rotation. Because most rotation movements are established at takeoff, the acrobat must decide whether to emphasize elevation at the expense of rotation, or rotation at the expense of elevation. Of course, the greater the overall thrust generated, the more can be achieved in both regards.

Inertia and Angular Momentum

The term *acrobatics* refers to a seemingly endless variety of body movements. The essence of most acrobatic moves is jumping, for execution of most routines depends on achieving adequate air time to complete the aerial maneuver. Without adequate hang time, the athlete forfeits his margin for error in completing airborne maneuvers. He ends up landing or entering the water in an unbalanced position, unable to finish off the maneuver or nail the landing.

Of equal importance is the fluidity of movement. Gymnasts move effortlessly from feet to hands, from feet to feet, and from hands to feet. These movements are what physicists refer to as dynamic; that is, a relationship exists between changes in motion and the forces that produce them. The motions and forces become quite complicated in three dimensions, especially for the nonfixed shape of the human body. There exist three changes-in-motion forces exerted by, and acting on, the athlete: muscle, gravity, and contact. Muscular forces are internal and change the shape of the body. Gravity and contact forces are external and change the motion of the center of gravity and the angular momentum of the body. Rarely do these forces occur in isolation. The acceleration of the COG in the intended direction is always proportional to the net external force applied. For instance, a doubling of the force applied results in a doubling of acceleration.

Because muscle forces are internal, the manner in which they make an athlete move is not immediately apparent. It is clear, however, that without something to push against, it is impossible for someone to change her state of motion, whether to start, stop, or even turn a corner. For example, the person in a canoe floating freely in water will always lose a tug-of-war with a person standing on a shore, regardless of which one is stronger, and the football player trying to make a quick change of direction on wet turf slips and falls down. The principles of physics behind these occurrences is contained in Newton's third law: forces always occur in equal, opposite, and simultaneous pairs. Sometimes these forces are called "action" and "reaction," but since it is not possible to tell which comes first, it is best to avoid such terms. The strong man in the canoe cannot outpull the weak man on shore because the canoe cannot push against the strong man even if he tries with all his might to push against the canoe. The football player slips and falls because the wet turf cannot push hard enough against him to sustain his desire to change direction.

The use of muscle forces thus depends on contact forces. A jumper uses muscle force to extend his legs, causing his feet to push against the floor as the floor simultaneously pushes against his feet.

Figure 4. *In executing a back flip, divers and gymnasts bring their arms downward and forward after their feet have left the ground so that the lower body can swing forward and upward.*

Figure 5. *Because of the added mass of the skis—a mass extending far from the axis of rotation—rotations are much tougher for an acrobatic skier than a gymnast or a diver. Acrobatic skiers wisely choose short skis. Snowboards are even shorter, and many avid snowboarders easily execute complete airborne rotations called helicopters.*

This contact force of the floor upward overcomes the downward pull of gravity, causing the jumper's COG to accelerate upward. Without contact with the floor, the jumper would accelerate downward at 9.8 meters per second^2 (32 ft./sec.^{2}) like every other piece of matter in free-fall. The free-falling gymnast cannot change his COG motion by muscular exertion, since there is nothing to make contact with and push against.

Despite the value of linear momentum to describe many actions, the anatomical makeup of the human body limits its usefulness. Bones, or levers, move in a rotational manner, not a linear one. Angular movements are the means to the end, which is linear motion. Through a series of angular movements, linear motion of the total body becomes possible. Although the human body easily executes rotational motions, its inconsistent axes of rotation makes it inefficient. In comparison, a Ferris wheel is an ideal example of rotational motion because its center, or axis of rotation, remains stationary as the radius of the wheel moves around it. Unlike the human body, it does not change shape as it rotates. If the Ferris wheel could be articulated to change its shape, the motion would become very complicated, much like that of the human body.

Rotational motion is analogous to linear motion. What sets the two apart is torque. Any force that results in rotational movement is called a torque. Torque, or moment of inertia, depends upon the magnitude of force and its distance from the axis of rotation. Rotational or angular motion requires a force couple, that is, two equal and opposite forces acting on the body. A common force couple resulting in angular motion occurs as a diver or gymnast becomes airborne. For example, as the right foot pushes backward, the left foot plants firmly (pushing forward), so that the springboard diver rotates, or twists, from right to left about his longitudinal axis. The external forces of the springboard on the diver's feet, the actual cause of the motion, are of course equal and opposite to the direction the feet are pushing (*see Figure 4*).

In the same way that angular motion is analogous to linear motion, angular momentum is analogous to linear momentum. Anything that rotates possesses angular momentum. Once a Ferris wheel, or any object, is set in rotation, it tends to continue to rotate. Of course, a Ferris wheel will eventually stop due to friction in the bearings and air resistance, yet there is momentum associated with all rotational motion. Rotational velocity, mass, shape, and mass distribution all affect the amount of angular momentum.

The product of a turning body's moment of inertia and its angular velocity determines its angular momentum. According to the law of conservation of angular momentum, excluding external forces, a turning body has a constant angular momentum, which means that the product of moment of inertia and angular velocity about the axis of rotation is constant. However, the moment of inertia for each person is different. It depends on the body's mass and how that mass is distributed relative to the axis of rotation.

The farther the mass rests from the axis of rotation, the greater the moment of inertia. A gymnast or diver who heads out to the ski slopes to replicate the same acrobatic somersaults and twists she perfected in the gym and pool is in for a rude surprise: the added mass of the skis, at an extreme position from their axis of rotation, means the athlete must use much greater torque to begin rotating. If she does not, she certainly will crash-land. The smaller moment of inertia of the shorter snowboard makes it easier to rotate, and this is in large part responsible for its growing popularity (*see Figure 5*).

If no torque is exerted to change an athlete's angular momentum around an axis of rotation, the angular velocity still can be increased by changing the way mass is distributed around the axis of rotation. Many routines in gymnastics and figure skating are based on this principle of changing the moment of inertia (*see Figure 6*). Because a gymnast can reposition her body in a number of configurations—bending her arms or legs—the moment of inertia can be continually altered. By moving the body toward and away from her axis of rotation, and without exerting any additional torque, a conscious effort can be made to increase or decrease the rate of spin. This principle is most evident when a figure skater moves from a slow spin to a fast spin. She may start out with her arms extended in a loose spin, but then she brings them in snugly against the body for a tight, high-velocity spin. Because the moment of inertia with arms extended is approximately three times as great, rotational velocity is increased

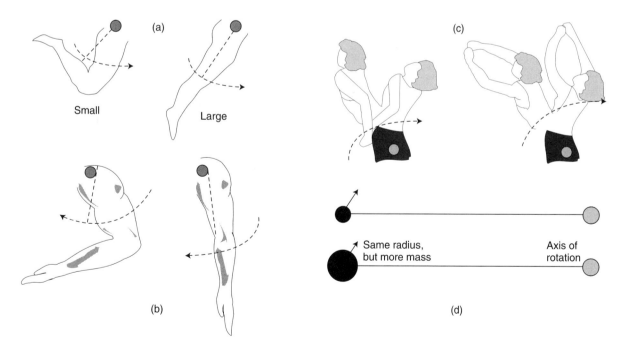

Figure 6. *The moment of inertia to move a body part is highly dependent on the body part's weight, and the distance of mass from the axis of rotation. In examples (a), (b), and (c), the importance of mass distribution is the difference between a large and small moment of inertia. In (d) mass itself is the difference: the more a body part weighs, the more force it takes from the muscles to move it and to stop it.*

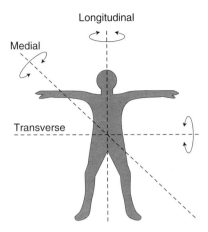

Figure 7. *The human body can rotate along three different axes: transverse (flips), longitudinal (twists), and medial (cartwheels).*

threefold by pulling the arms and hands in toward the body for a tight spin.

Figure 7 shows the three different axes around which athletes can rotate: longitudinal, transverse, and medial. The longitudinal axis is the vertical head-to-toe axis that is used for twisting motions by divers and gymnasts, and for spinning motions by figure skaters. It is the easiest rotating motion to perform because it has the lowest moment of inertia of the three rotations. The transverse axis, running horizontally through the body's COG, is the rotational axis used for flips and somersaults. The medial axis is a back-to-front axis that is commonly used by gymnasts in performing cartwheels.

A free rotation around any axis occurs around the COG as center. The cartwheel is not quite a free rotation, since the gymnast is momentarily in contact with the floor. It occurs with the arms and legs of the gymnast acting like the spokes of a wheel with the COG as its axle. In a well executed cartwheel, the gymnast's COG moves in a straight line at constant speed and her hands and feet are at rest as they touch the floor. A giant swing on the high bar is not a free rotation. The axis of rotation in this case is the bar itself. The gymnast's COG moves in a circle around the bar as the gymnast's body rotates at the same angular velocity about its COG.

Somersaults and Twists

Surefooted experiences with the force of gravity make most people quite confident and secure walking and running around the planet. The most gifted athletes test, stretch, and even attempt to defy gravity. Basketball players, long jumpers, and ski jumpers go airborne with a very good idea of how high and far they will travel and how to control their flight paths. Few of these athletes, however, show any desire to engage in the free-flowing airborne acrobatics of a gymnast or diver.

Airborne end-over-end somersaulting is an inherently unsettling experience for anyone making his first attempt. There are probably two reasons for this feeling. First, the athlete has lost contact with the ground. Once he has left the ground, he is committed to a trajectory; and the manner in which he has left the ground heavily influences his spinning and twisting. Second, being head over heels for the first time, he may tense up or panic because he has yet to learn how to control the very different airborne motion.

Airborne maneuvers are very difficult, in part because the gymnast must control her angular momentum while she is airborne; and the greater the number of somersaults and twists involved, the greater the angular momentum. Somersaulting is a difficult maneuver for humans because weight is not equally distributed from the COG, which also acts as the center of rotation. In other words, the body rotates more like a thrown ax than a Ferris wheel. Twisting, on the other hand, is a much simpler maneuver, because weight is equally distributed to the left and right of the body's vertical center, and body weight is very close to the axis of rotation (*see Figure 8*).

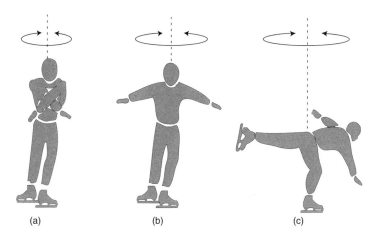

(a)   (b)   (c)

Figure 8. *The rate of rotation can be much faster about the longitudinal axis than about the transverse axis. Position (a), like that used by a spinning figure skater, speeds up the rate of rotation, (b) slows it down and (c) not only slows it down but is difficult to control because of the unbalanced (nonsymmetric) position. Figure skaters can complete three or four airborne spins, more than twice as many as a gymnast, because they are converting more of their significant linear motion into vertical motion. This means greater jumping height and more time aloft to execute spins.*

Many gymnastic events require athletes to use a running start and launch themselves from a springboard. The takeoff foot or feet are subjected to a much greater braking force at ground contact than during the run-up because of the much longer foot-board contact time. This creates rotational motion as the feet come to a stop while the body carries forward at a faster rate. The force exerted by the board against the acrobat's body is so strong that rotation is initiated despite any attempt of the athlete to counter this force while airborne. An exaggerated example of rotational motion occurs when a runner trips over a protruding tree root. Momentum keeps the body moving forward, but the foot stops in its tracks, creating a torque about the COG. In a split second, the rotational motion is so great that the runner lands flat on his face.

Rotational force is a torque, or the product of the force on the stubbed toe times the distance to the runner's COG, which is, on average, a yard or meter high. Because of this tremendous rotational force, many acrobatic maneuvers "go with the flow," using the rotation generated at takeoff to start the somersaulting maneuver.

Whenever a step is taken in running or walking, a braking force results as the foot contacts the ground. In walking or running, the braking and thrusting force cause the body to rotate alternatively about the one or the other foot. Smooth uniform motion demands that the average force at the feet must be vertically upward and equal to the weight. A walker or runner does not fall flat on her face because the braking force is limited and is countered by the following stride. Without a follow-up step, the countering braking or thrusting interaction does not take place; therefore, a gymnast experiences a

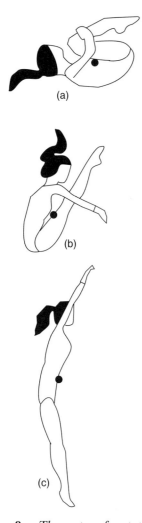

Figure 9. *The rate of rotation around the transverse axis depends on the moment of inertia, which in turn depends on the distance of the body's mass from the axis of rotation (center of gravity). The tucked position (a) is the fastest, followed by the pike (b), and then the layout (c).*

rotational force as the takeoff foot or feet launches her into an airborne trajectory.

Despite the very natural way somersault rotation occurs, the speed of rotation is heavily dependent on the position assumed by the athlete. There are three means of executing a somersaulting maneuver: layout, pike, and tucked (*see Figure 9*). The layout is the slowest rotational maneuver. Because the body fully stretches out lengthwise, weight is distributed far from the axis of rotation. The tucked position is at the other extreme: the fastest rotation. In the tight tuck, because the head is down and the knees are up to the chin, body mass gets squashed tightly around the axis of rotation. Physicist Peter Brancazio calculated that the moment of inertia is the smallest in a tuck position, 1.5 times larger in a tight pike, 3 times larger in a loose pike, and 5 times larger in the layout position (Brancazio, 1984).

Most of the airborne rotations can be attributed to angular momentum. A diver does not require as much trunk flexion as a trampolinist in executing airborne maneuvers because the diver's flight always has some horizontal velocity (he must clear the board). He can use a full-body lean to displace his COG in front or behind his base of support (*see Figure 10*). It should be noted that changes in momentum are not all-or-nothing propositions. In other words, not all the horizontal momentum need go to vertical momentum, nor all the vertical into horizontal.

Change in momentum is not restricted to the body as a whole but can be broken down into body segments. The momentum of one part of the body can be transferred to another part of the body, and certain body segments contribute more to angular momentum than others. In a cinematic study of the two-time Olympic gold medalist Greg Louganis, it was reported that body segment contribution to rotation fell in the range of 7 to 21 percent (Miller, 1985). And of all the body segments responsible for airborne rotations, the trunk, because of its large mass, accounts for at least 80 percent of the nontakeoff angular momentum (Adrian, 1989). For example, the arm swinging across the body certainly generates nontakeoff angular momentum, but it is minor in comparison with the action of the upper body swinging the arm across the body.

Twisting adds an additional wrinkle to any somersaulting maneuver. The primary method of twisting is accomplished by the feet, pushing laterally as well as downward against the supporting surface. The arms and torso thrust in the direction of the twist, which causes the feet to push off the surface in the opposite direction. A surface force is exerted in the opposite direction and of equal magnitude to that created by the thrust of the arms and torso against the surface.

Once the turn has started, the arms and hands are held as tightly to the body as possible to decrease the moment of inertia by shortening the radius of rotation, which in turn accelerates the speed of rotation. If a slow twisting motion is desired, the arms are extended to increase the moment of inertia and the radius of rotation. Further,

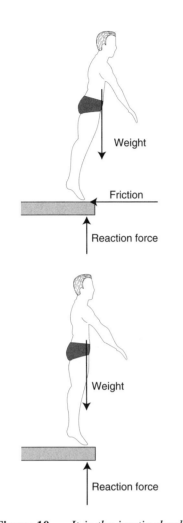

Figure 10. *It is the inertia developed from the run-up and gravity that creates a force couple against the reaction force of the friction of the feet, which allows divers to create the torque and angular momentum about the transverse axis to execute a somersault. From a standing position weight and reaction force are in line, which makes it much more difficult to somersault.*

if a diver held dumbbells in each hand, the moment of inertia for the twist would be even greater, making the spin ever slower.

It was long believed that the only way that airborne twisting could be accomplished was by beginning the twisting motion while still in contact with the ground. But this is not so. In fact, most twisting maneuvers of world-class gymnasts and divers are accomplished primarily after the feet leave the ground or springboard.

Airborne twisting occurs because the body maintains angular momentum once the athlete becomes airborne. The body uses the angular momentum generated at the horizontal (somersault) axis to begin rotating at the longitudinal (twisting) axis. Although angular momentum must remain constant, it can be redirected from the horizontal to the longitudinal axis. Not all the angular momentum in the horizontal axis can be converted to the vertical axis, so the body continues to somersault as it begins to twist.

It should be noted, however, that an airborne gymnast can achieve a stable rotation around only those axes for which the moment of inertia is a maximum or minimum. Rotation around any other axis causes a change in the rotation axis even though the direction of the angular momentum remains constant. Thus, the angular velocity is directed along different axes as the airborne maneuver takes place. During a twisting and somersaulting maneuver, it is always easier to twist than somersault because the body is much longer than wide—mass is closer to the longitudinal axis than the transverse axis. Athletes combat this natural tendency by emphasizing the somersault rotation at takeoff, leaving the twisting motion until most of the somersaulting motion finishes.

Note: Zero angular momentum turns. In the above examples, all angular momentum is generated during takeoff when the reaction force of the springboard is directed off-center from the body's COG. If the reaction force is directed through the COG, the body goes airborne without any rotation. There is still a way to initiate twisting in these cases: the action-reaction method. In the action-reaction method, what takes place is called a zero angular momentum twist.

The most adept zero angular momentum twister on earth is probably the cat. When a cat is dropped in an upside-down position, it can quickly execute a zero angular momentum turn and land on its feet. According to the principle of conservation of angular momentum, and given that no external torques act on the body, the total angular momentum must remain zero. If a part of the body rotates one way, the remainder (of the body) rotates with equal and opposite angular momentum. Both parts rotate, but in opposite directions. Thus, the cat's tail jerks (rotates) in one direction while the rest of the body rotates in the opposite direction.

Although the physiology of the cat greatly assists it in making these twists, sky divers and astronauts train so that they can execute these twists, too. They can reorient their bodies in any direction while floating through air or space. Trampolinists jump straight up and down, so they also must rely upon zero angular momentum rotations.

To execute a zero angular momentum twist to the right, two movements must occur in rapid succession. First, the action of the right arm across the body and twisting from the waist is quickly followed by a natural reaction of the lower body swiveling to the left (in the opposite direction). Second, there is an immediate follow-up rotation of the lower body to the right that naturally creates counterrotation of the upper body to the left. The real trick is to perform these maneuvers so that action is a stronger force than reaction; otherwise the two cancel each other out. This can be accomplished because in the first movement, the legs are fully extended to increase their moment of inertia, limiting their counterrotation force. And in the second movement, the arms rely on limited extension to limit the magnitude of their counterrotating force (*see Figure 11*).

How do athletes learn to execute the subtle movements necessary to perform these conceptually complex zero angular momentum turns? Only through trial-and-error practice, and by increasing their range of motion, can athletes learn to execute zero angular momentum turns. Astronauts and sky divers spend endless hours trying to develop the double action movements to execute these twists adeptly.

Giant Swings and Dismounts

Gymnasts and divers all try to achieve as much height as possible in order to extend the time "window" for completing their airborne acrobatics. Gravity forces airborne acrobats to hurry things up. All dismounts and dives require the performer to get out of the tucked or piked position quickly so that she can nail the landing. Once she comes close to finishing her spins and twists, she extends her arms upward or outward to increase the moment of inertia. This significantly slows down the spin rate so that she can position her body for the landing.

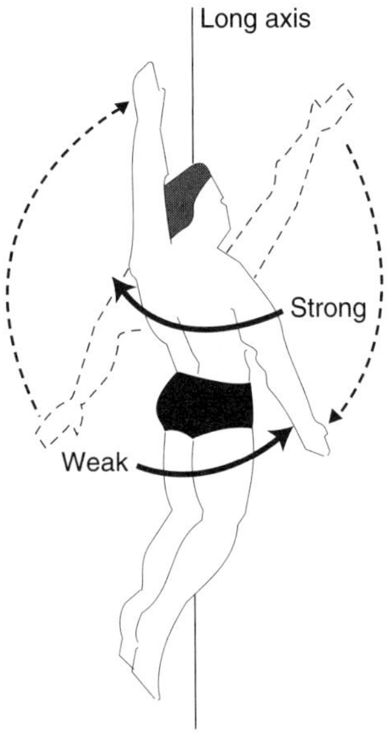

In addition to using the Reuther board to initiate somersaults and twists, gymnasts also develop "flyaway" dismounts from gymnastic apparatus. Execution of a flyaway requires a giant swing. A centripetal force (inward and toward center) must be present to cause the gymnast's COG to move in a circle rather than a straight line, as it would in the absence of all forces. Except for the minor force of friction from the hands sliding on the bar, three major forces come into play: muscle, gravity, and the bar pulling on the hands (the other half of the force of the pair of hands pulling on the bar). To move in a circle, the total external force of gravity and the bar on the gymnast must be toward the axis of rotation. This total force is proportional to the square of the speed of the gymnast. At the bottom, where speed is maximum and gravity is pulling in the wrong direction, the force that the bar exerts must be the greatest, not only to overcome gravity, but to provide the maximum acceleration. It is at this point that the bar bends the most, and the gymnast has to hold on the tightest. Remember that the bar cannot pull on the gymnast if the gymnast

Figure 11. *To execute a zero angular momentum backward somersaulting twist from an arched position, the diver swings both arms in an arc in one direction to create a stronger twisting impulse in the upper body to counter the twisting motion in the other direction by the lower body.*

does not pull on the bar. At the top of the circle, gravity is operating in the same direction as the acceleration, and if the gymnast is going slowly enough, he may have to push rather than pull just to support his weight. In most high bar routines, the gymnast comes to rest at the top and holds a handstand for a few seconds before continuing.

Figure 12 shows how the giant swing is accomplished. To generate additional velocity, energy from the muscles must be transformed into the kinetic energy of the swing by doing work. Stated simply, the strategy is to flex the muscles when it is hardest to do so and to unflex them when it is easiest. The gymnast starts pulling his COG toward the bar near the bottom of the swing when the force is greatest and extends to the fullest near the top when the force is least. The work does not have to be done by the arms; they merely have to hold on. It is efficiently accomplished by flexing at the hips and depressing the shoulder girdle.

This pumping action generates additional kinetic energy and the subsequent additional velocity. For the same reason, a child on a swing lays out—extends the legs straight out from the body—at the point of highest velocity and tucks—curls the legs up—at the point of zero velocity. Gymnasts attain even greater height when they time their dismount with the flexing of the bar. Additional kinetic energy is generated from the muscular forces exerted by the gymnast and the elastic energy of the bar, a trampoline effect as the bar bends and straightens.

The interesting problem facing the gymnast in attempting fly-aways from a horizontal bar is deciding just when to let go of the bar. By circling around the bar at an ever increasing rate, a gymnast increases his rotational momentum so that he maximizes velocity upon release. Naturally, the greater his velocity, the higher and farther from the bar he will travel. From years of practice, world-class gymnasts know exactly when to release from the bar. They gain an understanding of the dynamics of free flight.

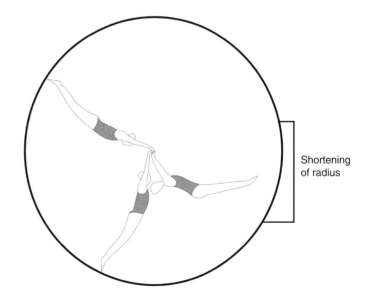

Shortening of radius

Figure 12. *Utilizing gravitational acceleration and changing the moment of inertia makes a giant swing on the high bar possible. The moment of inertia is increased on the downswing by lengthening the radius of rotation and decreased on the upswing by shortening the radius of rotation.*

In the giant swing, a gymnast generates tremendous angular momentum about her transverse axis. Upon release, her COG will follow the smooth arc of a parabola—just like a thrown ball—while she continues to rotate about her transverse axis. Most dismounts are backward somersaults because the natural rotation at the point of hand release is from the bottom to top, as opposed to top to bottom when the feet leave a supporting surface. Because the body is fully extended during a giant swing, the moment of inertia is very large. Thus, when a gymnast comes out of a giant swing into a tucked or piked position, she can easily complete two or three somersaults before landing.

The force exerted by the bar on the gymnast toward the center of the circle of rotation is tremendous, about four to five times the weight of the gymnast; not surprisingly, one will not find many two-hundred-pound gymnasts doing the giant swing. The moment after the dismount, however, this force disappears, and the gymnast continues in the direction she was going at a tangent to the circular motion. Anyone who has jumped off a fast-moving swing understands what happens during a dismount. If one jumps off the swing at the bottom of the arc, one flies away horizontally. If one jumps off when the swing reaches its horizontal peak, one flies off in a nearly vertical flight path. A gymnast wants to maximize the height she reaches to give her the greatest amount of time to complete her dismount move; therefore, she releases just before reaching her horizontal peak so that she attains good height and has a trajectory that carries her away from the apparatus.

Using Sensory Clues

A beginning diver who attempts a 1½ somersaulting dive, only to belly flop, experiences a double insult. She not only alerts everyone near and far by the splattering sound of her body slapping across the water's surface, but she also experiences excruciating pain. Back flops or belly flops usually occur because the diver lost track of her relative position while airborne.

Far more so than in most sports, divers and gymnasts need to use all their senses to execute many movements successfully. Some visual clues are very simple and assist in both static and dynamic movements. Every maneuver should be attempted with some predetermined specific points of eye contact in mind. For example, a world-class gymnast on the balance beam never looks straight down to see that her feet are indeed centered on the beam. Instead she focuses on and aligns herself with the end of the beam. The end of the beam acts as the point of reference as she executes movements. Coaches recommend that a gymnast concentrate on the initiation of each movement before looking toward the landing or next maneuver. If a gymnast prematurely

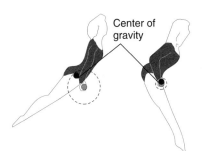

Center of
gravity

Figure 13. *By slightly piking at her hips, the gymnast shifts her center of gravity to a position outside of her body and very near the bar, making rotation around the bar much easier. The dotted line shows the radius of her center of gravity as she rotates about the bar in either a back hip circle or a forward hip circle.*

looks beyond the initiation phase, to the spin or landing phase, chances are the takeoff will be less than optimal.

These guidelines are fine for most situations, but sometimes a direct line of sight to a reference point is impossible. For instance, when executing a triple somersault with a 1½ twist, it is no longer feasible for a diver to judge distance solely by relying on eyesight to figure out his position in space. Spinning or twisting at a high rate makes it impossible to focus clearly upon anything, yet a diver retains enough focus to count seeing the water surface three times, with the third sighting bringing him out of the tucked or piked position. With the water surface far below, many divers listen closely to the rebounding sound they make leaving the board. From this sound, they can accurately estimate just when they will hit water.

The sense of touch also plays a part. As gymnasts and divers leave a springboard, the touch or feel experienced through their feet is the earliest cue they receive as to the vertical height and horizontal distance they most likely will attain. With this information, they can make very early adjustments in the movement planned to compensate for an extra strong or weak takeoff.

In addition to the equilibrium functions of the head as the carrier of the eyes and the ears, by its placement it is also the focus of orientation. Watching the head of a gymnast or diver gives visual clues that can alert viewers to intent. In a backward somersault, if the head is held in line with the body as the diver leaves the board, this suggests that her major focus is on takeoff elevation. In comparison, when the diver's head is thrown back, the diver is more concerned about backward rotation. For single rotation maneuvers, however, often the backward thrust of the head suggests insecurity or a way to compensate for poor technical execution. It indicates poor technical execution because the head is far less biomechanically effective in bringing about rotation than the arms and legs.

Body Size Advantages

Many amateur and professional athletes have been frustrated by what they perceive to be limitations due to body size and shape. At times, complaints about body size advantages are little more than an excuse for limited talents or skills. But in some sports, these concerns are justified. For example, shorter basketball players, lighter football players, and shorter-legged hurdlers are all at a disadvantage. While some athletes can overcome size disadvantages to excel, it is true that stardom in such sports depends, in part, on body size. Acrobatic sports, unlike most others, actually favor those who are small in stature. Over the last few decades, the most obvious quality of all the top world-class gymnasts—Olga Korbut, Nadia Comaneci, Mary Lou Retton, and Shannon Miller—is that they have petite frames.

The Vestibular System: Mechanical Determinant of Balance

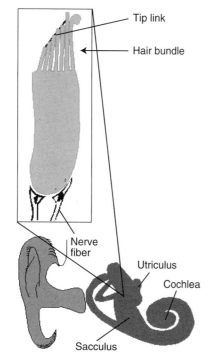

Tip link

Hair bundle

Nerve fiber

Utriculus

Cochlea

Sacculus

The internal ear contains over 60,000 acceleration-sensitive hair cells. The vertically oriented sacculus hair cells primarily detect up-and-down accelerations, the utriculus hair cells primarily detect horizontal plane accelerations, and the cochlea detects transverse plane accelerations.

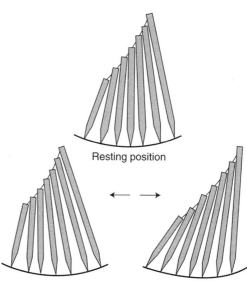

Resting position

Negative displacement

Positive displacement

Hair bundles remain straight but pivot about their base when stimulated by the motion of the body. They shift back and forth like falling dominos.

Without balance, neither the graceful movements of a trained gymnast nor the everyday movements of life would be possible. In any sport, it would be impossible to compete without a sense of equilibrium. The equilibrium and balance demands posed by somersaults and twists in acrobatic sports make the need for a sense of balance ever more acute. Yet balance is something often taken for granted.

Balance is a function not of the brain per se, but of nervous system mechanisms of sensory feedback. Equilibrium and balance are controlled by sensory cells of the body's nervous system that detect pressures within the body's hollow organs, such

The average height of women in the United States is about 5 feet 6 inches, and it is immediately apparent that world-class female gymnasts are far shorter than average. In fact, most world-class female gymnasts average around 4 feet 10 inches in height, and the median height continues to decline. In the all-around women's competition at the 1992 Olympics in Barcelona, U.S. gymnast Shannon Miller

as blood vessels, bladder, and stomach. The most sensitive detectors are the hair cells located in the vestibular apparatus within the bony canals of the inner ear, which consists of a series of semicircular canals (fluid-filled tubes) that connect with each other and the cochlear duct. Hair cells within these semicircular canals are responsible for the body's sensitivity to sound, detect linear accelerations (including those caused by gravity), and discern angular acceleration (for example, from flips and twists).

Detection of angular acceleration during rotation of the head occurs along three different axes. First, the vertically oriented sacculus detects the north-south angular acceleration from nodding the head up and down. Second, the horizontally oriented utriculus is sensitive to east-west angular acceleration from shaking the head side to side. And third, the cochlea, in combination with the sacculus and utriculus, detects transverse angular acceleration, for example, when the head tips sideways so that the ear touches the shoulder.

The vestibular system is a complex microscopic wonder of mechanics and physiology. Until something goes wrong, it is very much taken for granted. Motion sickness is a striking example of a disoriented vestibular apparatus. Many who venture out on a small boat in rough seas know firsthand the gut-wrenching sickness caused by the unpredictable linear and rotational accelerations that occur as the boat gets tossed about.

The nervous system is in total havoc because the vestibular apparatus is unable to interpret linear and angular accelerations.

The vestibular labyrinth operates something like this: Receptor cells, which contain hairs, are found within the semicircular canals. Whenever the head turns, the semicircular canals and the hair cells turn with the movement (*see figure*). The fluid within the canals, however, tends not to move. A construction level demonstrates a similar principle. Fluid within the tubes of the level remains stationary as it is tilted up and down, but the position of the air bubble changes, as determined by the tilt of the instrument. In essence, while the instrument tilts, the fluid is left behind. In the ear, balance is maintained by the stationary fluid bending the hair cells, which in turn activates the nerve fibers. The hair cells act as receptors of the hydraulic and mechanical stimulus and encode this information in the form of an electrical response that is forwarded to the brain by nerve impulses.

Hair cells are stimulated only with changes in the rate of motion—accelerations and decelerations of the head. One of the major functions of vestibular information is to help the brain control eye motion. As the head turns from side to side, the eyes can remain sharply focused on the same point. To maintain this fixed line of sight, the eyes must rotate at the same rate that the head rotates, but in the opposite direction. The vestibular system makes this possible. When a fig-

ure skater rotates very quickly around a vertical axis, it is the vestibular system that allows her eyes to remain fixed on one point despite the fact that her head is spinning around at great speed. A figure skater fixes on an object as long as possible, then quickly flips her head around and refocuses on the same object again. She keeps a fixed reference point, no matter how many spins she happens to make.

Another use of vestibular information is reflexive; it helps keep the body in an upright position. Although the vestibular system is vital for movement and reflexes during activities such as running and jumping, it is usually not the primary postural reflex, but a collaborative reflex (*see also CATCHING SKILLS*). Vestibular feedback takes on greater importance when it relays information to the brain to provide conscious awareness of the position and acceleration of the body. An experienced diver, in a tightly tucked somersault, is in no position to look for visual clues regarding his position. His vestibular system plays a vital part in signaling just when to pull out of a tight tuck to "knife" into the water as he finishes a forward 3 ½ somersault.

If a diver's vestibular system were somehow turned off, it is unlikely he would be able to pull out of a tuck at the right moment during the rotation. A diver who can execute ten near-perfect 3½ somersault dives in a row would be lucky to "nail" one out of ten dives without a functioning vestibular labyrinth (Figures adapted from Hudspeth, 1994).

(4 ft. 7in., 71 lbs.) and her equally small Russian counterpart, Tatiana Goutsou, captured the silver and gold medals. (Male gymnasts also tend to be shorter than average, yet the difference is less dramatic because they do not compete in events such as the uneven parallel bars and the balance beam.)

There are several reasons for this phenomenon, some obvious,

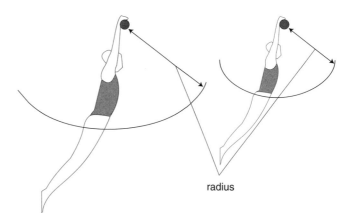

radius

Figure 14. *A shorter gymnast can more easily execute giant swings because of her smaller moment of inertia (smaller radius of rotation).*

The Tragedy of Trying to be Small

In July 1994, Christy Henrich, once ranked among America's best gymnasts, died at the young age of 22. Just prior to the 1988 Olympics, a judge commented on her size. At 4 feet 11 inches and 95 pounds, she was, he said, too fat to make the Olympic team. She began to starve herself. She went on to place fourth in the uneven parallel bars at the 1989 world championships in Stuttgart, but eventually dropped out of competition as her health faded. At the time of her death, she weighed only 52 pounds, and the official cause of death was multiple-organ system failure. Gymnastic officials now educate coaches and judges about the effects of anorexia and bulimia, advising them to not comment on the weight of a gymnast.

others quite subtle. Before a short gymnast even makes her first move, she has a built-in advantage: scale. For all airborne maneuvers, upon which much of gymnastics is based, judges appear to grant shorter gymnasts favorable treatment. When a 5-foot gymnast executes a 15-inch (37.5 cm) vertical jumping maneuver on the beam or during a floor exercise, it looks very impressive. She reaches a vertical height that is one-fourth her body height. In comparison, the same 15-inch vertical jump by a 6-foot-tall gymnast is only about one-fifth her body height. To the judges, the lasting impression is that the shorter person jumped higher.

There are several advantages in having a petite frame. First, a petite, short gymnast has a smaller mass than her taller counterparts, so the moment of inertia for rotational movements about a horizontal bar is smaller. Assuming the small gymnast puts the same amount of work into a maneuver, the rotational energy for the large and small person will be the same, but the angular velocity will be greater for the smaller person. Therefore, when bar release occurs, angular velocity remains constant, so the smaller gymnast somersaults more rapidly because of the greater angular velocity developed during rotation.

The difference in distance from the COG to the axis of rotation is another advantage smaller gymnasts have over their larger peers. As shown in Figure 14, a short gymnast's COG is much closer to the bar (which is the axis of rotation). This may be compared to a yo-yo at the end of a string. If the string is short, the moment of inertia is small. It is easy to rotate the yo-yo in a complete vertical circles around the axis of rotation at the hand. But if the string is long, the moment of inertia is large, so it takes much more force to get the yo-yo rotating in circles around the hand axis. It is easier for a short gymnast not only to swing, but also to swing in a smoother, more graceful motion. A taller gymnast not only has her COG farther from the bar and thus moves at slower angular velocities, just as a long pendulum takes longer to swing back and forth than a short one. The angular speed may be slower, but the velocity of the tall gymnast's COG is actually greater than the velocity of the short gymnast. The forces involved are also much larger. In the giant swing, an 80-pound gymnast appears to move more rapidly, even though the speed of her COG is actually slower, and the force she exerts on the bar is only 400 pounds as compared with the 160-pound gymnast's 800 pounds. This latter force causes a very noticeable bend in the bar that may detract from the grace of the performance.

For twisting and turning motions, shorter gymnasts have considerable advantages. As with swings, the force required to produce a given turning rate is proportional to the body's moment of inertia. Kenneth Laws, dancer and physicist, determined that the moment of inertia for a 6-foot athlete executing a turn is twice that for a 5-foot-3-inch athlete (Laws, 1984). The 15 percent difference in linear dimensions results in the doubling of the moment of inertia. The largest contributor to a large moment of inertia for horizontal movement, which limits the ability to rotate, is wideness at the hips. Perhaps that is why most world-class female gymnasts excel at a very young age, before their hips widen in the postpuberty years.

Though the old proverb "the bigger they are, the harder they fall" may hold true, the taller athlete is less likely to fall in the first place. In terms of balance, shorter gymnasts are at a disadvantage. A short stick pivoting at one end falls faster from side to side than a long stick. For example, it is much harder to balance a pencil at the end of one's finger for any extended period than a yardstick. This difference in balancing ability holds true regardless of foot size. Even when a short and a tall person have the same size feet, a short person still has more difficulty balancing on one foot than a tall person.

The mass of a gymnast plays less of a role than height, yet the distribution of mass is a major consideration. When a smaller gymnast stands on the beam, less of her body extends over both sides of the bar. This makes balance and execution of movements easier. When falling to one side, the gymnast must quickly rotate her nonsupporting leg in the direction that she is falling to get the rest of the body to move in the opposite direction—more directly over the center of the beam. Keeping the body balanced over the center of the beam is easier for the slender-bodied individual because a greater proportion of her total mass lies directly over the beam. The more an individual's body extends over both sides of the bar, the more likely it is that an unbalanced position will develop.

The uneven bars give additional advantages to the shorter gymnast. To account for the difference in body length, competitors are allowed to precisely position the two uneven parallel bars at an optimal distance apart. Moves like the back hip circle require the body to wrap around the bar, so it is essential that the bars are positioned correctly to avoid impact trauma. Nevertheless, taller women competitors need to continually pike and spread (their legs) during swings to avoid ground contact. This makes their already slower rotation around the bar even slower. Shorter gymnasts, on the other hand, need neither to tuck nor to spread their legs to clear the lower bar or ground when swinging past. This allows them to swing more smoothly and quickly.

In addition to distinct biomechanical advantages, the shorter gymnast requires far less strength for support and movement. Body weight is the force of gravity acting on body mass. The greater the mass, the more pronounced the effects of gravity. Through evolution, human structure is ideally suited to meet the demands of the forces of earth's gravity. Gravity is nondiscriminating; it affects everyone equally. Thus, impact forces and accelerating forces are directly related to body mass. Accelerating a person of larger mass requires far more force than that necessary to accelerate a smaller mass person at the same rate. The additional force necessary is not readily apparent because, as a rule, larger people generate more force through their larger muscles.

When scientists estimate the amount of force exerted by muscle, they consider the total muscle mass; more specifically, the total cross-sectional fiber content in any particular muscle. Research by Kenneth Laws shows that a person whose muscle mass is twice the linear size of another person would have four times the cross-sectional muscle area. This means that the former, with twice the linear muscle size, can exert four times the force of the latter. It is necessary, however, to consider proportion. For example, a tall individual with great muscle mass yet a fairly high percentage of body fat is far less apt to perform strength maneuvers on, say, the rings, than a smaller person with moderate muscle mass and a low percentage of body fat. The rings, like most gymnastic events, favor those individuals with a petite, lightweight frame, low body fat, and great muscle mass.

Although those small in stature are at a disadvantage in many sports, acrobatics is not one of them. Their advantages are many. In reality, the great majority of people, by the nature of their averageness, are at the greatest disadvantage. The nature of the term *average* itself connotes no advantage. Average-sized people find themselves caught in the middle: too small to excel in sports like basketball and football, yet too large to excel in sports like gymnastics and diving. The average-sized athlete must be that much more athletically proficient to compete against the inherent advantages of taller and shorter peers.

John Zumerchik

Risk of Injury

A smaller gymnast usually suffers fewer injuries because force impacts with the ground and apparatus are less severe. She also experiences less stress and pressure on the joints because her body's levers are shorter.

References

Adrian, M., and J. Cooper. *The Biomechanics of Human Movement*. Indianapolis: Benchmark Press, 1989.

Baker, W. "Swinging as a Way of Increasing the Mechanical Energy in Gymnastic Maneuvers." In H. Matsui (ed.), *Biomechanics*. Champaign, Illinois: Human Kinetics Publishers, 1983.

Brancazio, P. *Sports Science*. New York: Simon and Schuster, 1984.

Brink, D., and G. Satchler. *Angular Momentum*. New York: Oxford University Press, 1994.

Duck, T. "Biomechanics of Twisting." In L. Sinclair (ed.), *Gymnastics: Everything You Wanted to Know*. Toronto: Canadian Gymnastics Federation, 1980.

Eaves, G. "The Falling Cat and the Twisting Diver." *New Scientist* 8 (1960): 249.

Edwards, M. "Zero Angular Momentum Turns." *American Journal of Physics* 54, no. 9 (1986): 846–847.

Frohlich, C. "Do Springboard Divers Violate Angular Momentum Conservation?" *American Journal of Physics* 47, no. 7 (1979): 583–592.

Hudspeth, A., and V. Markin. "The Ear's Gears: Mechanoelectrical Transduction by Hair Cells." *Physics Today* 47, no. 2 (1994): 22–28.

Laws, K. "The Dancer as Athlete." In C. Shell (ed.), *1984 Olympic Scientific Congress Proceeding*. Champaign, Illinois: Human Kinetics Publishers, 1986.

Laws, K. "The Physics of Dance." *Physics Today* 38 (1985): 24.

Laws, K. *The Physics of Dance*. New York: Schirmer, 1994.

Lind, D. *The Physics of Skiing*. Woodbury, New York: American Institute of Physics, 1996.

Miller, D. "Greg Louganis' Springboard Takeoff: Linear and Angular Momentum Considerations." *International Journal of Sports Biomechanics* 1, no. 4 (November 1985): 288–307.

Rackham, G. "The Fascinating World of Twist: Twist by Somersault Transfer." *Swimming Times* 47 (1970): 263.

Pepe, M., and C. Phinizy. *Book of Diving*. Philadelphia: J. B. Lippincott, 1961.

Smith, T. *Gymnastics: A Mechanical Understanding*. London: Hodder and Stoughton, 1982.

Tonry, D. *Tumbling*. New York: Harper and Row, 1983.

Yeadon, M., et al. "The Production of a Sustained Aerial Twist During a Somersault without the Use of Asymmetrical Arm Action." In D. Winter (ed.), *Biomechanics*. Champaign, Illinois: Human Kinetics Publishers, 1985.

Archery

ARCHERY is perhaps the most ancient and intriguing sport in the history of the world. It was used in hunting and for war, and its origins predate recorded history. Homer, the Greek poet of the eighth century B.C.E., glorified numerous feats of archery in his epics the *Iliad* and the *Odyssey*. On the basis of archeological evidence, some scholars date the origins of archery as far back as 15,000 years ago; more conservative estimates place its beginnings 7,000 to 8,000 years ago.

Ancient archery equipment has been discovered on all the continents and no conclusive archeological link has established one population as the first to use the bow and arrow. Instead, much evidence suggests the contrary: that archery developed independently at locations throughout the world.

The bow and arrow, though first used for hunting, developed as a weapon of war. Some historians date the Egyptians' implementation of the bow and arrow as weaponry to around 5000 B.C.E. The arrow offered definite strategic advantages over the primary weapons of the time, the slingshot and the spear. Whereas the slingshot had a maximum range of about 43 meters (141 ft.) and the spear 53 meters (177.1 ft.), the arrow could be shot over 90 meters (295.2 ft.). It is believed that the Egyptians secretly equipped and trained their troops with bows and arrows, while their enemies remained armed primarily with spears. The Egyptian army thus gained a definite edge.

This was just one of many pivotal roles for the bow and arrow throughout history. The nomadic Huns, as well as the Mongolian armies of Genghis Khan and his sons Ögödei and Chagataix, were ruthlessly effective empire builders and, not surprisingly, masters of archery. Historians attribute much of Genghis Khan's empire building (1206–1227 C.E.)—from the Pacific Ocean west to the Volga River, and from the northern extremes of Siberia south to the Caspian Sea—to his soldiers' ability to use their bows from horseback (Arkanc', 1954). Almost all of his soldiers were mounted, which meant they outranged their adversaries (shooting from a higher position allows the arrow to travel farther) and more easily kept out of harm's way.

Around the same time, far to the west, the English monarchy also realized the need for an army of skilled bowmen. From the thirteenth to seventeenth centuries, English rulers issued decrees that made archery compulsory for all able-bodied men. Officials regularly inspected homes to ensure that every man had a bow in good working order and ready for use.

On the battlefield, the English longbow was superior even to the gunlike crossbow because the longbow allowed a good bowman to aim and shoot six shots per minute at a range of 182.9 meters (200 yd.). This proved to be a significant advantage over the crossbow, which not only had a shorter range, but also required a slower, more painstaking reloading and shooting process.

The size and shape of bow construction varied greatly among different regions and continually evolved through time. The ancient Egyptians employed one of the shortest bows, only about 1.3 meters (4.5 ft.) in height. Japanese archers in the sixteenth and seventeenth centuries wielded what were perhaps the largest bows, about 2.4 meters (8 ft.) in height. The longer the bow, the greater the firing range, but a 2.4-meter-tall bow posed some significant problems. It proved unwieldy on horseback, and a man's arms were neither long enough nor strong enough to fully draw the bowstring. A desire to match the bow to body size and physique may partially explain why the African Pygmy tribes used meter-long bows.

It is historically unclear when interest in archery as a sport surpassed its original function as a means of survival. Nevertheless, it flourishes today as a sport. In the United States alone, more than 10 million amateurs participate in some form of archery. As a sport, archery consists of four major classifications: target, the most popular; field archery, mostly for hunting; flight shooting, for distance; and

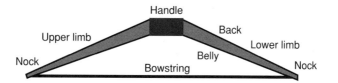

All bows are basically a two-armed spring, spanned and held under tension by a bowstring. They consist of two limbs, or bending portions, connected by a handle or riser. The belly is the face of the limbs closest to the archer when in use; the back is farthest away. The limbs terminate in nocks that provide a secure point of attachment for the bowstring.

A few inches down from the nocks the limbs can be either straight or recurved. Recurved limbs are bent in an opposite arch, back toward the bow handle. Recurvature effectively "shortens" the bow by increasing early draw stiffness (resistance). Recurves can be either working or static. In a working recurve, the curved portion of the limb partially unwinds or straightens out during the last half of the draw. The limb tips of a static recurve are inflexible.

Figure 1. *The anatomy of a bow. Ancient bows were constructed of yew, ash, and oak. Modern bows are primarily lightweight composites—foam, carbon, and fiberglass—with more resilient Dacron and Kevlar replacing linen as the primary material for bowstrings. The two primary types of bows—longbow and recurve—are shown here.*

crossbow shooting. The bow used in the early modern Olympics (1900–1908) resembled the very plain and simple English longbow. But the longbow had a number of deficiencies, and the target shooter and bow hunter of the 1990s used equipment far superior to that used by these early Olympians (*see Figure 1*).

The following sections explain some of the basics of archery: how the bow works, the dynamics involved in bow-arrow interaction, and the basics of arrow flight. Examples are drawn from the very old as well as the very new, so that the reader can develop an appreciation for the evolution of materials and designs.

The Basics

Shooting an arrow consists of four phases: (1)nocking, (2)drawing, (3)anchor point, and (4)release (*see Figure 2*). These four steps seem simple and straightforward, but there are subtleties involved.

In the nocking phase (positioning the arrow's tail on the bowstring), the archer assumes a stable base of support—feet about shoulder width apart—perpendicular to the target. Although it seems counterintuitive, one should never grip the handle too firmly with the bow hand. A looser grip minimizes the torque (rotational force about a fixed axis) upon arrow release, which can cause erratic flight. Modern bow design and shooting aids have reduced much of the torque problem but have not eliminated it, so instructors still recommend a looser grip.

In the drawing phase, the archer, with a fully extended bow hand, should draw back the bowstring toward her head, rather than allow her head to move toward the bowstring. Pressure exerted by the fingers on the arrow nock should be kept to a minimum prior to drawing. To maximize arrow velocity, it is important that the arrow be brought back to full draw. Each inch of draw near full draw contributes much more to the total stored energy than an inch of draw near the beginning. Nevertheless, an archer should not choose a bow that requires a straining effort to bring to full draw; straining is detrimental to accuracy. A proper bow is one that propels an arrow at high speed, yet requires minimal effort and energy on the archer's part to create that speed.

One of the most prevalent causes of inaccuracy is the inability to hold the bow at full draw before release. Called creeping, this flaw is significant because small changes in draw length result in large changes in arrow velocity. To avoid creeping, the archer must select a bow at the proper bow weight.

Bow weight and *mass weight* are two different terms that archers use in characterizing a bow. Mass weight is the actual weight of the bow. A good target archery bow (equipped with a stabilizer) usually weighs 1.4 to 2.7 kilograms (3–6 lb.). Of course, modern materials allow manufacturers to design even lighter bows, but a certain amount of mass weight helps the archer hold the bow steady, improving shooting accuracy. Bow weight, on the other hand, refers to the pounds of force required to draw the bowstring a given distance, usually about 71 centimeters (28 in.). Bow weight generally varies between 11 and 35 kilograms (25–75 lb.), with most falling between 14 and 23 kilograms (30–50 lb.). How far the archer draws also alters the standard bow weight categorization. If the archer draws more than 71 centimeters—say, 76 centimeters (30 in.)—the bow weight increases in pounds, and likewise, if the archer draws less, the bow weight decreases.

Obviously, an archer's strength is a paramount concern in selecting a bow weight. The archer should have adequate strength to draw and hold the bowstring without strain or fatigue. Generally, most men feel comfortable with a bow of 14 to 23 kilograms (30–50 lb.), most women with a bow of 11 to 16 kilograms (25–35 lb.). Beginners should select a bow weight lighter than the maximum they are able to handle because there is no proportionality between bow weight and arrow velocity. In other words, doubling the bow weight does not result in a corresponding doubling of arrow velocity. In fact, an arrow launched from a 41-kilogram (90-lb.) bow has an increased arrow velocity of only about 20 to 25 percent over an arrow launched from a 20-kilogram (45-lb.) bow.

The anchor point is the third phase. At this stage, with the bow at full draw, the archer places his bow hand against his jaw. Aiming is an experiential skill because, unlike a rifleman who looks down the barrel of a gun, the archer does not sight down the shaft; accurate aiming is thus more difficult. The archer's line of sight lies in the same vertical plane as the arrow, but a different horizontal plane (*see Figure 3*).

The archer sights by looking over the tip of the arrow at some fixed point, called the point of aim. To determine this point, one must figure out the point where the line of sight intersects the line along which the arrow is aimed. When a target is a moderate distance away, the convergence of these two lines is "point-blank" range (archery

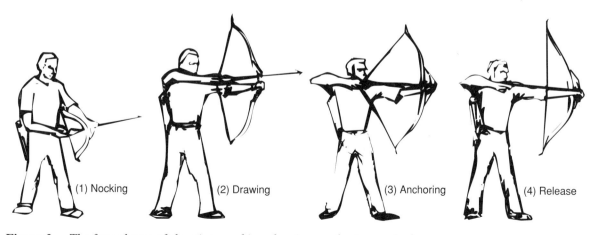

(1) Nocking   (2) Drawing   (3) Anchoring   (4) Release

Figure 2. *The four phases of shooting: nocking, drawing, anchoring, and release.*

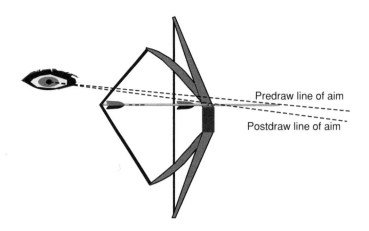

Figure 3. *The difference in angles between predraw and postdraw sighting makes aiming a very experiential skill. The postdraw line of aim is well below the spot toward which the arrow is actually pointing. Some believe aiming should be taken predraw because the angle between the line of sight and the arrow's point of aim is smaller. This is true because the arrow's tip lies farther forward of the eye.*

jargon being the origin of this common idiom). When the target is a short distance away, the point of aim is in front of the target; for long distances, it is above the target (*see also VISION*).

The release point and follow-through make up the final phase of shooting. Much as in shooting a rifle, or even a basketball, it is important to hold the release position until the arrow embeds into the target. Remaining motionless until arrow impact helps develop and recall the "muscle memory" or "feel" to consistently shoot with accuracy from that given distance. Furthermore, if there is movement after release, it usually is an indication of an earlier flaw—movement that probably started prior to release and continued afterward.

Bow and Arrow Energy

When early man threw a spear, the distance it traveled was a result of release velocity and release angle. Quite predictably, the big and strong usually proved better spear throwers than the small and weak. They could accelerate their longer arms forward at greater speed. With the introduction of the bow and arrow, this clear-cut distinction between the weak and strong no longer existed. Great strength was not a requirement of a skilled archer. Because the bow released stored muscular energy very quickly and only moderate strength was necessary to store this energy, it quickly replaced the spear as the weapon of choice.

The key to the great ability of the bow to store energy lies within the bow's limbs. Bow designers from antiquity onward relied upon flexible limb materials to improve bow performance by adhering to principles of effective elastic energy storage. Energy is the capacity to do work (force × distance), and energy is characterized as either potential or kinetic. Potential energy is the energy an object possesses because of its position. For example, a car parked on a hill has potential energy: when the brake is released, the potential energy begins to decline as the car picks up kinetic energy—the energy of motion—as it makes its way down the hill.

Almost any event or process, natural or man-made, involves a transformation of energy from one form to another. When a material absorbs the impact of a collision with another object, its elastic strain potential energy (ESPE) determines the way the material responds. When two pool balls collide, there is a large ESPE; when two sponge balls collide, there is a small ESPE. This transformation of energy is of critical importance in archery. As the archer does work in drawing the bowstring back, this work results in ESPE. However, a bow's ESPE is unique in that energy is put into the bow very slowly, and upon bowstring release, energy releases very rapidly. And—as with a ball dropped from greater and greater heights—the farther the archer draws back the bowstring, the more energy is put into the bow. This energy is stored in the bow (potential energy) until the bowstring is released, and the potential energy is then transformed to the kinetic energy of the arrow.

According to the principle of conservation of energy, energy can be neither created nor destroyed; energy output must equal energy input. However, not all the energy expended by the archer results in useful work—arrow kinetic energy. Some of it gets wasted, or dampened, within the mechanical apparatus of the bow itself: the bowstring, bow limbs, and the wave movement or oscillation of the arrow.

An efficient bow delivers most of its stored energy to the arrow, limiting energy loss due to dampening effects. Efficiency is measured as the ratio of kinetic energy of the arrow as it leaves the strings to the energy imparted to the bow to bring it to full draw. As mentioned above, some stored bow energy is lost as kinetic energy of the limbs, bowstring, and oscillations of the moving arrow. Limb kinetic energy loss is minimized by selecting arrows that are matched to the bow. Bowstring waves—like those of a guitar string when it is plucked—are minimized by using synthetic bowstrings made of resilient, low-stretch, high-strength fibers such as Dacron and Kevlar.

The efficiency of the bow-to-arrow energy transfer can be best judged at the point of arrow release. An efficient bow is one in which, at the time the arrow leaves the bowstring, the limbs and bowstring quickly reach a very slow velocity. If the bow-to-arrow mass ratio is great, there will be a significant amount of energy retained in the bow, part of which is felt as bow recoil. Recoil energy eventually dampens or dissipates, either in the bow or in the archer himself. Bow recoil is greatest when the bowstring is released at full draw without an arrow, and least when a very heavy arrow is released from a partial draw.

Experienced archers know that the heavier the arrow, the more energy the bow transfers to it. But a more efficient transfer of energy does not necessarily result in greater arrow velocity. Table 1 shows that a lighter arrow will always leave the bow at a higher velocity, and the velocity will increase only incrementally, not double, when bow weight and bow mass are doubled.

Arrow velocity is not always of primary concern. A more massive arrow actually has a slightly lower launch velocity, but it penetrates

ARROW VELOCITIES FOR TWO DIFFERENT BOWS

Arrow mass (m) (lb.)	Bow 1: 45-lb. weight; 0.035-lb. mass			Bow 2: 90-lb. weight; 0.07-lb. mass			Difference in vel. (%)
	$m + K$	vel. (ft./sec.)	kin. energy	$m + K$	vel. (ft./sec.)	kin. energy	
0.05	0.085	168	1,411	0.120	200	2,000	19
0.06	0.095	159	1,516	0.130	192	2,212	21
0.07	0.105	151	1,596	0.140	185	2,396	23
0.08	0.115	144	1,659	0.150	179	2,563	24
0.09	0.125	139	1,738	0.160	173	2,694	25

Table 1. *The weight of bow 2 is twice that of bow 1. Here mass K is the mass that would have exactly the same kinetic energy as the bowstring and limbs at the time the arrow leaves the bowstring. When the bow weight and mass are doubled, the arrow velocity increases by only 19 to 25 percent. But as the arrow mass increases, so does the difference between arrow velocities. (Adapted from Klopsteg, 1943)*

farther into a target because it has greater kinetic energy from its greater mass (*see also FOOTBALL*). Therefore, for greater flesh penetration, hunters use heavier arrows than their target shooting counterparts.

Bow Dynamics

As the archer draws the arrow, the force created by her muscles is transmitted by the bowstring to the bow itself, resulting in deformation or strain of the bow's limbs as they bend back. The back or outside curve of the bow is under tensile stress (pulling apart), and the belly or inside curve is subjected to compressive forces (pushing together). The limbs themselves act much like a two-armed spring.

According to Hooke's law, an applied force or stress results in a proportional deformation or strain ($F = -kx$). One way to understand Hooke's law is to visualize a spring: As one stretches a spring to greater lengths, it exerts a greater force in the opposite direction, pulling the spring back to its original, compressed position. This means that the stiffer the spring—in this case the limbs—the greater the restoring force exerted, in this case by the string (via the bow limbs) on the arrow. A bow is actually more complex. As the bowstring is drawn back, different parts of the bow are subject to different degrees of strain. Generally, there is far less strain at the handle and the tips than at the midsection of the limbs.

Another important factor is the inherent stiffness of the material of the bow, known as Young's modulus of elasticity, E. For a spring of a given size, the spring constant is Hooke's law (k [in the equation $F = -kx$] is greater if E is greater). For example, the Young's modulus of a material like spring steel is over 20 times that of the wood yew (commonly used for bows). This means it would take 20 times more

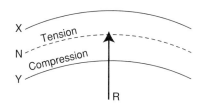

Figure 4. *An unstrung limb of a given length and thickness being bent in a circular arc of radius R. The back (X) experiences tension, and the belly (Y) experiences compression. Line N is the neutral plane, where tension and compression are equal.*

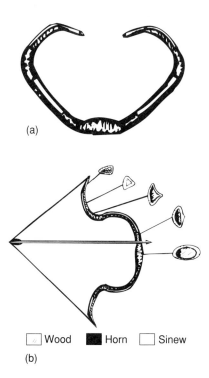

Wood   Horn   Sinew

(b)

Figure 5. *The ancient recurve is shown (a)unstrung and (b)strung. The genius behind the recurve is its composite construction. It combined a superior recurve design with sinew that was effective against tensile forces and horn that resisted compressive forces. The result was a bow that allowed a long draw length for a relatively small bow. (Adapted from McEwen, 1991)*

force to bend a strip of steel 1 inch (2.5 cm) than it would to bend yew 1 inch.

Figure 4 shows an unstrung limb (tip to handle) of a given length and thickness being bent. Consider a bow made up of a number of long, thin strips glued together. The strips that lie toward the inside of the neutral plane shorten when the bow is arched (compression) and those on the outside lengthen (tension).

Longitudinal layers of the bow parallel to the median plane lengthen or shorten by amounts proportional to their distance from the neutral plane. This means that the longitudinal planes of material stretch or compress depending on their distance to the back or the belly of the bow, with the maximum stress occurring at the outermost fibers. Hooke's law makes it possible to calculate the stresses or forces at work inside the bow. The potential energy stored in the bent bow is the sum total of the energy stored in each successive layer, which means that each layer can be considered a spring unto itself.

Most materials exhibit springlike behavior only as long as their deformation or strain is small. When the strain exceeds a certain amount, the material ceases to behave elastically and either breaks or exhibits plasticity. Plasticity occurs when a material undergoes a permanent change in its shape or size. When material becomes "plastic," it no longer springs back to its original shape if stretched or compressed. At this point, the yield value, the material is considered permanently deformed; moreover, the resistance of the material to further strain rapidly declines. Intelligent bow construction prevents the material from reaching its yield value—the point beyond which it loses elasticity or breaks.

A material with a large permissible strain and high Young's modulus will store the most elastic strain potential energy. Of all the types of wood used to construct ancient bows, bows constructed of yew provided the highest maximum permissible strain. High-weight bows made of woods other than yew must be made wider and thicker.

Although the material chosen for bow construction is important, the bow design is of equal or greater importance. While the English longbow became legendary, the Turks proved the practicality of a more compact bow. Turkish bowmakers made composite bows with highly reflexed limbs, the first recurves. Though relatively small, these bows had long draw lengths.

Eventually Asian bowmakers (Turkish and Tartar) arrived at a superior composite design consisting of a layer of wood forming the median plane of the bow with a strip of animal horn—usually from a water buffalo—glued against its belly for compressive strength. Along the back of the bow, long fibers of animal sinew were glued to it in a thick layer, enhancing its ability to withstand tensile stress (*see Figure 5*). The sinew was put on wet and shrank as it dried, further stretching the belly, which resulted in highly reflexed limbs (a C shape unstrung). This material combination enhanced the elastic energy so much that, when strung, such a bow strained its belly and back as much as a wooden bow at full draw. Sinew-reinforced

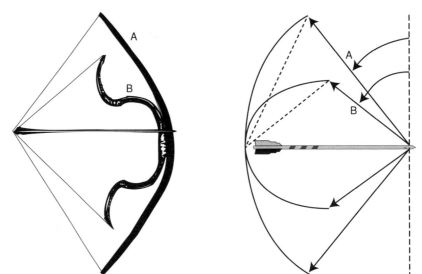

Figure 6. *Right: The ratio of draw length to bow length for the shorter composite recurve (B) is greater than for a typical longbow (A). The limb extremes of both bows are kept as light as possible. Greater mass toward the tips requires more energy to move the limbs and more energy loss as the limbs recoil and are stopped by the string.*

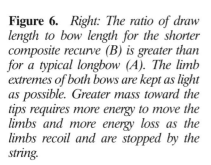

Figure 7. *Above: Limb sections of a traditional longbow design (a) and a trapezoidal design (b). The horizontal line shows the relative distance of the outermost fibers from the median plane. The traditional longbow design put excessive stress in sections least able to withstand it. It overworked the bow in compression and underworked the bow in tension. The trapezoidal design (b) more nearly matches the strength characteristics of wood. This is why the limbs of the modern recurve are wide, and the handle is thick. If the limbs were thick instead of wide, only the most Herculean of men could bring the bow to full draw. And if the grip were as thin as the limbs, the archer would receive the brunt of the shocking recoil of the limbs. As a general rule, most grips are at least twice as thick as the limbs because it makes them eight times as resistant to bend and less likely to deliver a punishing recoil.*

reflexed bows put the limbs under greater tension when strung, which meant that they possessed much more potential energy fully drawn than a conventional longbow. Moreover, sinew relieved some of the strain from the back and prevented splintering. Because wood tends to break and splinter on the tension side (the back) rather than the compression side (the belly), sinew added considerable time to the lifespan of a bow.

The Turkish bows had a high ratio of draw length to bow length, meaning that the limbs could be drawn much farther back relative to the overall length of the bow (*see Figure 6*). Thus, much more power was achieved without resorting to an unwieldy bow like the 2.4-meter Japanese longbow. Sinew reinforcement of the short, flexible, and lightweight reflexed limbs of the composite bow made it capable of storing large amounts of energy under tension. This composite could shoot an arrow farther and faster than any wooden longbow of equal draw weight. The recurve bow is also more efficient than the longbow. Longbows waste a great deal of energy in the material itself from a higher limb and string velocity after the arrow leaves the string.

Despite its many advantages over the longbow, stringing the reflexed bow was a precarious task. Even for men of considerable strength, recurved bows with ears were quite dangerous to string. They often sprang back into the face of the stringer.

Most ancient bows, including longbows, were immediately unstrung after use to prevent plasticity. The horn that ancient Turks added to their composite reflexed bows helped maintain their material integrity, preventing warp. Turkish warriors benefited mightily from this technological advance. They kept their bows strung for prolonged periods, continually ready for use, without adversely affecting the bows' performance.

What is surprising is not the demise of the English longbow in the twentieth century, for most technology eventually reaches a point of obsolescence, but the incredible lasting power of the Turkish recurve.

The 1990s version of the working recurve—consisting of composite materials—is the bow of choice for target archery. This should not come as a surprise, for a 45-pound working recurve sends an arrow off at a velocity nearly 20 percent greater than a longbow of comparable weight (McKinney, 1990).

Arrow Dynamics

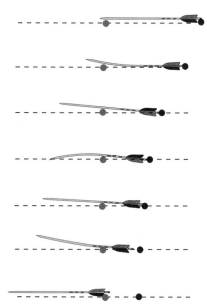

Figure 8. *The path of the arrow from the point of release to the point of clearance from the bow. (The handle is represented by the gray circle, the string by the dark circle, and the median plane by the dotted line.) The archer's paradox occurs: the arrow takes a straight-line course and does not veer sideways as it bends and vibrates about 5° to 7° from the median plane upon release. It is important that the spine of the arrow is "tuned" to the bow weight and draw length used by the archer. If an arrow is too stiff or too flexible, accurate shooting is nearly impossible.*

Because an arrow is guided along only one side of the bow, rather than through the bow's center, it may seem amazing that the arrow travels in anything close to a straight line. At full draw, the axis of the arrow is in direct line to the target, but as the bowstring is gradually drawn down and the arrow approaches the undrawn position, its tip moves to the left of where it is aimed (*see Figure 8*). Upon a typical fully drawn release, it seems the arrow should be deflected off to the side and veer severely along the undrawn axis position. Because it does not, this has been called the archer's paradox: the arrow first deflects to the left (if the archer is right-handed), but stabilizes itself in flight to travel directly to the intended target.

Once the string is released, the arrow bends and vibrates because the bow, in effect, pushes against the arrow as it passes by the handle. This arrow movement allows the tail end of the arrow to cleanly clear the bow despite the fact that the string drives the arrow nock directly toward the center of the bow. This pushing lateral force of the bow on the arrow starts the arrow oscillating (flexing back and forth).

The arrow oscillates not only while it passes by the bow, but for an appreciable number of cycles after leaving the string. An arrow properly matched to the bow is said to snake or slither its way around the handle, and once it has completely cleared the handle, it continues to oscillate. Each oscillation causes a collision with the handle that will deflect the arrow to the left of the line of aim (assuming a right-handed archer).

When archers speak of matching an arrow to the bow, they usually refer to the spine of an arrow (its oscillation frequency or deflection). Young's modulus is used to measure the spine. Archers determine the Young's modulus of an arrow by measuring the deflection of the shaft when depressed by a 0.68-kilogram (1.5-lb.) weight. For example, an arrow spined to 30-kilogram (65-lb.) recurve deflects about 1 centimeter (0.40 in.) under the 0.68-kilogram weight.

For an arrow of a given length, the shaft must be a certain diameter to be correctly spined. The measure of oscillations or deflection depends on both the Young's modulus of the material and the size (diameter) of the arrow. This means, for any arrow material, the greater the shaft's diameter, the stiffer the spine. For example, because aluminum has a much greater Young's modulus than wood, aluminum arrows can have smaller diameters.

An archer must also consider the physiological factor of drawback length. What is a properly spined arrow for a 30-inch draw ends up being out of tune—improperly spined—if the draw is only 26 inches.

A properly spined arrow tends to stabilize itself rapidly so that it follows a straight-line path to the target. It completes one full oscillation from release until it leaves the string so that it heads off in a direct line toward the target. If the spine is too stiff, the arrow experiences several oscillations before clearing the bow, brushing against the handle each time it passes. The shaft of the arrow or fletching (feathers) brushing against the bow changes the arrow's direction and reduces its velocity. The resulting shot will end up low and to the right of the intended target. If the spine is too weak and flexible, the arrow may never stabilize and follow its intended trajectory, instead flying consistently to the left of the target. The tail end strikes the handle because it fails to move leftward as it makes its way around the handle.

For better aerodynamics, often a smaller-diameter arrow will be preferred to a larger diameter arrow. A smaller-diameter arrow requires the archer to select an arrow made from materials with a high Young's modulus to achieve the correct spine.

Up until the 1960s, arrows were made only of woods like birch, spruce, and cedar. Because of the nature of wood and the limitations of the manufacturing equipment, it was extremely difficult to achieve uniformity. Accurate target archery is heavily dependent on arrow uniformity. Target archers in the 1990s are far more accurate than their predecessors due to high-precision manufacturing equipment. Aluminum-tube arrows have a very high degree of uniformity, more than was ever possible with wooden arrows.

Because of greater velocity with better accuracy, aluminum remains the material of choice for arrows. Aluminum has a much higher Young's modulus than wood, which allows manufacturers to reduce the arrow's diameter. This makes aluminum arrows more aerodynamic, and they thus attain greater velocities; yet their high Young's modulus allows them to achieve the same precision—correctly spined—as the larger-diameter wooden arrows. The latest innovation, tapered aerodynamic arrows, constructed of aluminum and wrapped with carbon/graphite fibers, has shown signs of even better performance. These arrows have an even higher Young's modulus, so they can be made with a small diameter for aerodynamic efficiency yet can still achieve the correct spine for accuracy.

Fletching

Fletching (commonly known as feathers) is as vital to the flight of an arrow as the airfoils found on aircraft wings, performing the same drag, lift, and stability functions. Fletching stabilizes the arrow so that it can maintain a high-velocity rotation around the longitudinal axis along the shaft. Previously, all fletching was made of turkey feathers. In the 1990s, because of durability concerns, vinyl and other plastics began to replace feathers.

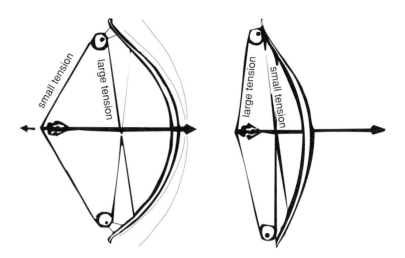

Figure 9. *Because two strings are pulling instead of one, only about half the force is necessary to pull a compound bow back to full draw, compared with a standard recurve of the same weight. Further, the eccentric pulleys of a compound bow allow it to be held in a cocked position with very little tension in the bowstring (left). Unlike conventional bows, tension increases after bowstring release (right). The compound bow has replaced the recurve for hunting purposes because it is easier to bring to, and hold at, full draw. It also produces greater arrow velocity and thereby greater penetration into targeted prey.*

Shooting Aids

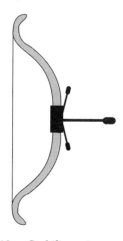

Figure 10. *Stabilizers increase the moment of inertia of the bow—that is, they increase the force necessary for the bow to twist and turn in the archer's hand.*

Since the invention of the compound bow in 1966 (*see Figure 9*), there have been many advances in archery equipment, perhaps more than during the preceding 400 years. Most of the advances have come in the form of the fine-tuning accessories, for added convenience as well as accuracy. Draw release aids, bow sights, clickers, sight windows, arrow rests, and stabilizers are just some of the many innovations.

Bows in the 1990s often come with a sight window, which also includes an arrow rest. The sight window is a cutaway section located above the handle. Its primary purpose is to minimize the typical 5- to 7-degree arrow deflection characteristic of bows of the past. It minimizes this deflection because the arrow moves past the bow in a relatively closer path to the bowstring from the moment of full-drawn release to the undrawn position. It also allows the archer a direct line of sight to the target.

Important additional tools that are widely used by world-class target archers include stabilizers and bow sights (which use the same principle as rifle sights). Stabilizers are metal rods that come in a variety of lengths and weights. An archer usually screws three stabilizers into the back of the bow handle (one extending forward and one to each side) to negate some of the ill effects of faulty bow arm technique (*see Figure 10*). She stabilizes the bow for the same reasons that a tightrope walker holds a long stick horizontally for stability. It

Traditional Archery

Despite the numerous technological advances in archery equipment since the 1960s, thousands of archers are rediscovering the charm and simplicity of "old archery," a return to the "bent stick." Archery traditionalists classify as traditional any bow whose basic design has remained unchanged for centuries. Although use of modern materials, like fiberglass, is acceptable, some stricter traditionalists handcraft their own wooden recurves or longbows from osage orange or yew and fletch their wooden arrows with wild turkey feathers. Some archers handcraft bows similar to the ancient Turkish recurve, using the same combination of natural materials: wood, sinew, and horn. A properly handcrafted bow is a highly capable weapon, capable of downing an elk, a moose, or a bear.

increases the moment of inertia, which means that it increases the force necessary for the bow to twist and turn in the archer's hand. As a result, the archer is able to hold the bow more steadily. Archery instructors recommend that one practice without the aid so that one can correct any faulty bow arm technique and thus shoot more accurately both with and without the aid of stabilizers.

Bow sights are different from rifle sights in that the archer does not look down the shaft of the arrow as a rifleman looks down the barrel of a gun. The bow sight, mounted about 4 or 5 inches (10–12.5 cm) above the arrow, is aligned to the archer's line of vision. Bow sights have a large range of adjustments, not only to match each individual, but also for each specific shooting distance.

Bow sights, sight windows, and stabilizers incrementally improve the accuracy of all archers. Many believe that these devices have removed much of the skill from the sport. A growing cadre of traditionalists have shunned shooting aids and all modern technology to return to the old-fashioned ways. Handcrafting their own bows and arrows, these traditionalists take special pride in constructing their own equipment as did their forebears. It is yet to be seen whether this movement will continue, but it perhaps bodes well for the sport, widening the realm of options.

John Zumerchik*

Special thanks to David Thomas for his assistance in the material science sections of this article.

References

Arkanc', G. *History of the Nation of Archers*. R. Blake and R. Frye (trans.). Cambridge, Massachusetts: Harvard University Press, 1954.

Bruce, E. *The History of Archery*. New York: William Morrow, 1957.

Foley, V., et al. "The Crossbow." *Scientific American*, 252, no. 1 (January 1985): 104–110.

Hickman, C., et al. "Archery: The Technical Side." *National Field Archery Association of the United States*, 1947.

Klopsteg, P. "Physics of Bows and Arrows." *American Journal of Physics* 11 (1943): 175–192.

Klopsteg, P. *Turkish Archery and the Composite Bow*, 3rd ed. Manchester, England: Simon Archery Foundation, 1987.

Locke, L. *The Name of the Game: How Sports Talk Got That Way*. White Hall, Virginia: Betterway Publications, 1992.

McEwen, E., R. Miller, and C. Bergman. "Early Bow Design and Construction." *Scientific American*, 264, no. 6 (June 1991): 76–82.

McKinney, W., and M. McKinney. *Archery*. Dubuque, Iowa: W. C. Brown, 1990.

Schaar, J. *Modern Archery Ballistics*. Tempe, Arizona: Grand Slam Archery, 1986.

Baseball

THE MODERN GAME of baseball emerged in the United States in the 1840s and was played by a fraternal network of associations and clubs. When professional teams were formed in the 1860s and 1870s, baseball began to evolve into the America's first large-scale professional sport. Perhaps professional baseball teams grew in popularity because they provided fledgling cities and towns with a shared experience, or perhaps the colorful personalities of early ballplayers contributed to baseball's expansion. Whatever the reason, by the early twentieth century Americans were flocking to ballparks to catch a glimpse of such early baseball legends as Ty Cobb, "Shoeless" Joe Jackson, and Babe Ruth.

As baseball's popularity grew, cities built expensive ballparks to showcase their players. Unlike most sports, which require standard playing fields, ballparks come in a variety of dimensions, each possessing its own character and presenting different challenges to ballplayers. In Yankee stadium, for example, with its short right field and cavernous center field (440 ft. deep, or 133 m), pitchers tried to force sluggers like Babe Ruth to hit toward center field and away from the "short porch" in right field by pitching low and outside. In Wrigley Field, on the other hand, the shallower center-field wall (400 ft.) and the strong Chicago wind meant that pitchers would have to pitch high and tight to the same batter to minimize the number of home runs. For many baseball fans, the variability of ballpark dimensions and the conditions to which players must constantly adjust only adds to the charm of the game.

In addition to adjusting to the different settings, a player must continuously adjust to maximize his strengths and minimize his limitations. Even before the multimillion-dollar annual salaries common in the mid-1990s, many professional ballplayers explored both legal and illegal means of improving their performances to increase their salaries or to lengthen their careers. In the early 1960s the Detroit Tiger Norm Cash tried to improve his hitting by hollowing out his bat and filling it with cork to "juice it up." Beginning in the 1960s the Hall of Fame pitcher Gaylord Perry baffled hitters with his spitball, which bobbed and weaved its way to the plate. Management has been involved in advantage-seeking of its own. For instance, the owners and management of weak-hitting teams have been known to seek an

Strategy

Teams and players often vary their strategy from day to day and from ballpark to ballpark, depending on the ballpark's dimensions and on field and weather conditions.

edge by keeping the infield grass high, softening the dirt in front of home plate, and storing game balls in a freezer (to get lower bat-ball rebound velocity). While some of these strategies were ethically dubious, many were founded on a learned understanding of the scientific principles behind baseball. This article will separate the science from the folklore.

Pitching Phases

An excellent pitching staff—including power pitchers such as Nolan Ryan—is one of the most important advantages a team can have. Players and fans alike widely believe that good pitching can always stop good hitting and that a team simply cannot win without good pitching. Thus, a ball club's first priority is to acquire and to develop a strong, healthy pitching staff.

However, the enormous stress pitching places on the muscles, ligaments, tendons, and joints in the throwing arm is a major cause of injury. Major league ball clubs try to evaluate their pitchers' physiological capabilities to estimate the length and quality of a pitcher's career. But predicting a pitcher's longevity is no simple task, as a number of factors must be considered: his size, strength, physical fitness, conditioning, genetics, and efficiency of body motion during the delivery.

A successful evaluation of a pitcher requires a thorough consideration of mechanics. A pitcher's muscles function optimally when exerted in a specific sequence and with proper timing, enabling each muscle to contribute maximally to the pitching motion: stride, hip rotation, torso rotation, and arm movement. A high-velocity pitch, for example, requires a fluid motion to achieve maximum hand (and ball) velocity and is therefore more a function of proper mechanics than brute strength.

Windup.   The windup is the slow-motion preparation stage that allows the pitcher to attain the proper balance and position to deliver the pitch. The pitcher uses many joints—finger, wrist, elbow, shoulder, hip, knee, and ankle—to produce several torques (rotational forces around an axis) during the delivery. Proper balance and position are necessary to maximize torque as the pitcher transfers energy from the legs to the hips, to the torso, to the arm, and, finally, to the ball (*see Figure 1*).

Cocking.   During the second, cocking stage, the pitcher applies maximum tension to all the muscles. Forward motion begins with the pelvis rotating and the opposite leg kicking forward and planting in front of the body as the pelvis, the chest, and the shoulder move forward. Hip rotation must start before torso rotation so that the torso muscles stretch, allowing them to contract more forcefully. The lagging torso "loads up" the pitching arm with greater potential energy

Figure 1. *In the windup stage, pitchers use a combination of angular (forward and down) and rotational (twisting) momentum.*

Figure 2. *The cocking stage is the "loading up" process prior to acceleration.*

(energy based on position) prior to release. Rotating the hips before the torso fully utilizes the slower, more forceful muscles in the lower body to add strength to the weaker, more explosive muscles in the shoulder and arm (*see Figure 2*).

Pitchers and coaches disagree on whether a high leg kick or twisting of the torso during the cocking stage adds power to the delivery. Biomechanically, it is unlikely that these motions add power. Luis Tiant, a dynamic right-hander who pitched in the 1970s, would kick high and twist clockwise (away from the plate and toward second base) to generate more power as his body unwound a moment later. These contortions may have had a largely psychological effect because they caused him to take his eyes off the batter, enabling him to vary his delivery angle and disguise the ball from the batter a bit longer. Tiant's twisting motion has not been imitated by many other pitchers, however, as the loss of control and balance that results from the new movements offsets the marginal increase in pitch velocity.

Acceleration. In the acceleration stage, potential (loaded-up) energy is converted to kinetic (movement) energy. As the driving leg propels first the body and then the arm forward, the spring begins to unload and the pitcher plants his front foot pointing forward. As the knee then bends forward in the same direction as the pitch, the pitcher delivers maximum lower-body torques. The forward momentum of the body transfers energy from the lower body to the following shoulder and elbow. As in the hip- and torso-energy transfer, the arm lagging behind the shoulder helps the shoulder muscles to stretch and contract more forcefully, facilitating arm acceleration.

The large transfer of energy at the end of the pitching motion requires very quick acceleration followed by rapid deceleration, placing tremendous stress on the arm. A disproportionate amount of the energy is transferred through the shoulder and elbow, and the elbow joint experiences an extension (straightening) force toward the end of the acceleration phase. The elbow has a natural tendency to extend fully, potentially hyperextending; therefore, the extension must be smooth, with the elbow slightly bent, "shortening the arm," to maintain fluidity of the deceleration forces affecting the elbow. The manner in which the pitcher allows his elbow to extend affects the amount and type of spin imparted on the ball as it leaves his fingertips. Contorting the elbow's motion in an attempt to get a little bit more spin can lead to injury.

Length of stride is not critical, but a good pitcher keeps his front leg flexible for fluidity. The Hall of Fame pitcher Tom Seaver, an advocate of this technique, had such an exaggerated leg-bend that his uniform's right knee was permanently dirt-stained. He explained, "it is always a good sign to me that I am driving down when I release the ball and am incorporating the powerful muscles of my lower body" (Seaver, 1984). Seaver's exaggerated leg-bend maximized his lower body's deliverable energy and relieved the strain on his arm and shoulder.

Figure 3. *Midway through the acceleration stage, the hand no longer accelerates the ball and instead travels with the ball until the point of release.*

Wrist Snap

Hard throwers are often said to have a powerful wrist snap, but studies show that the ball is actually released from the pitcher's hand before most of the wrist snap (flexion) occurs. Wrist snap is an important final component of the pitching motion, but its importance has been overrated by many coaches. (Vaughn, 1992)

Figure 4. *During the release and deceleration stage, good balance is imperative, as deceleration forces are approximately twice as great as acceleration forces. According to one study, 46.9 percent of pitch velocity comes from step and body rotation, with the remainder coming from arm action. (Toyoshima, 1974)*

Many believe the acceleration phase distinguishes professional from amateur pitchers. A study carried out by doctors at Centinela Hospital Medical Center found that professional pitchers primarily use the subscapularis muscle (which lies in front of the shoulder blade), whereas amateurs tend to use all the rotator cuff muscles (Gowan, 1987). The professional's coordinated, fluid motion of torso, body, and elbow requires less effort from the rotator cuff and biceps, the muscles on which amateurs rely for power. Using the subscapularis—along with the pectoralis major (upper chest), serratus anterior (ribs), and latissimus dorsi (back)—the professional throws the ball with greater velocity and uses a shorter acceleration phase, requiring him to rely on a wider range of muscle groups (*see also SHOULDER, ELBOW, AND WRIST*).

Release and Deceleration.   During the release and deceleration stage, the arm accelerates past the body and weight is transferred to the leg opposite the throwing arm. At the moment of release, the ball leaves the thumb first while the index and middle fingers remain to impart the desired spin. Deceleration of the body and arm begins as soon as the ball is released. The arm must be decelerated quickly to keep the humeral head (top of arm bone) from separating from the glenoid cavity (socket). Because deceleration forces are approximately twice as great as acceleration forces, most throwing-arm injuries occur from improper mechanics in the deceleration stage. Proper arm mechanics reduce the forces applied to the shoulder and relieve rotator cuff tension. The planted opposite leg helps by maintaining balance and by allowing for a smooth transition; without correct balance, the risk for joint hyperextension at one of the torque points is increased. The pitcher must therefore apply enormous force to the muscles around the shoulder to decelerate the arm and to hold the humerus in the glenoid cavity as the arm accelerates past the body. The body is so loaded up with energy before release that, unless there is a smooth transfer of energy as the throwing-arm motion comes to rest, there is a great probability of injury (*see Figure 4*).

Delivery Angle

Delivery styles vary—from the almost directly overhand throw of Jim Palmer, to the sidearm delivery of Dennis Eckersley, to the underhand pitch of Dan Quisenberry, to the three-quarters delivery of most major league pitchers. While there is no single best way to throw a baseball, all pitchers need proper mechanics. Delivery should never be rushed. Observable signs of a rushed delivery are opening the lead shoulder too soon, extending the glove hand, and lifting the back foot too early. These poor mechanical techniques, particularly prevalent among Little League sidearm pitchers, let pitchers use a whipping (snapping) motion to deliver more velocity.

A study by Dr. James Albright of Little League and college pitchers showed some of the disastrous effects of poor mechanics, or whipping (Albright, 1978). Seventy-three percent of starting pitchers with

Sidearmers

While sidearm delivery is not inherently more conducive to injury, the style is more difficult to master and is frequently executed improperly, particularly by young pitchers.

Pitchers' Longevity

Most professional pitchers try to throw a variety of pitches, not only to keep hitters guessing, but to relieve some of the repetitive strain on the throwing arm.

poor mechanics had injury symptoms, as opposed to 21 percent of those with good mechanics. Injury is uncommon with a three-quarters or overhand delivery, even when the poor mechanics that injure sidearm pitchers are used. A sidearm pitcher is no more prone to injury, but the delivery style is much more difficult to master.

Dead Arms

A pitcher may lose speed on his fastball due to injury, age, or the strain caused by muscle fatigue. During the acceleration phase, the shoulder and elbow lead the wrist and ball, and energy is stored in the stretched arm's tendons. The "spring" energy of these stretched tendons releases as the wrist and ball accelerate past the shoulder and elbow. The elasticity of the arm's tendons determines the speed of acceleration. Arms go "dead" as age and injury reduce the spring, or elasticity, of the tendons in the arm. With this loss of elasticity comes a decrease in arm acceleration and a subsequent decrease in maximum pitch velocity.

There are, of course, exceptions. At the age of 46 and in his final season (1993), Nolan Ryan had his fastball clocked at over 95 miles per hour (MPH; 152 KPH). His contemporaries—Seaver, Carlton, and Palmer—had all retired many years earlier. Not only did Ryan avoid a "dead" arm, but he remained among the league leaders in strikeouts. Over the course of his career, from the 1960s to the 1990s, he accumulated over 5,500 strikeouts, 7 no-hitters, and over 50 major league records. Ryan's longevity is partly attributable to his impeccable year-round conditioning and to the fact that he was careful not to overthrow or to continue pitching when he was tired. But even his arm finally gave out, when a tendon snapped in a late September game in 1993.

To ensure long careers and to prevent injury, major league pitchers vary their pitches. Even the best pitchers, like Nolan Ryan, throw off-speed pitches, such as the change-up, to relieve some of the continual repetitive strain on their throwing arm and "mix up" their pitches to better fool the batter (*see also SHOULDER, ELBOW, AND WRIST*).

Types of Pitches

Pitching involves a psychological as well as a mechanical element. Pitchers and batters often try to intimidate and outguess each other. The pitcher concentrates on deceiving the batter, while the batter concentrates on subtle changes in the pitcher's technique that offer clues to the pitcher's intentions. To maximize the chances of fooling the hitter, the pitcher tries to use the same motion for every type of pitch.

There are many types of pitches, and many ways to throw them. Variations in grips and pressure points among major league pitchers reflect subtle differences in their motions and hand and finger sizes.

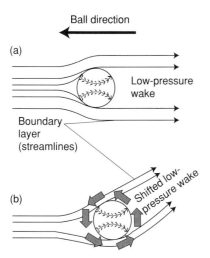

Figure 5. *Air moves uniformly past a spinless baseball (a) from an area of high pressure (in front of ball) to an area of low pressure. The rapidly spinning curveball (b) shifts the low-pressure wake behind the ball so that the ball curves sharply in the direction that it is spinning. The deflection arises because of this extra force—the Magnus effect. If a baseball were perfectly smooth and seamless, the Magnus effect would cause the ball to curve in the opposite direction.*

Curve Dynamics

An effective curveball must break vertically as well as horizontally; a curve that breaks only horizontally will just hit a different part of the long, narrow bat.

Curveball

The curveball is not an illusion: it really does curve. By creating a whirlpool of rotating air around itself, the curveball deflects toward the direction of the rotation. Any projectile, such as a thrown ball, encounters 14.6 pounds per square inch of air pressure (normal) pushing it sideways, for example, toward first base, but it also encounters an equal and opposite force pushing it toward third base. In such a case, the ball travels in a straight-line trajectory (except for the sinking caused by gravity). Once spin is applied, as in the case of a curveball, pressure is no longer equal on each side of the ball, and there is an imbalance of drag (air resistance) forces. This extra force, called the Magnus force, is created by the spin and occurs at a right angle to the direction of the air velocity and to the axis of spin. The Magnus force is at a maximum if the axis of spin and the direction of flow are at right angles. As the spin axis and direction of airflow converge, the Magnus force declines until it reaches a zero value where the two axes coincide. Cross breezes, headwinds, and trailing winds all alter the axes of spin versus airflow and, consequently, the magnitude of the Magnus force (*see also SOCCER*).

The Magnus force acts in a complex manner. Although the rough surface and the asymmetrical seams of the baseball allow the spin to curve the ball in the direction of the spin, a seamless, smooth-surface racketball, imparted with equal spin, curves in the opposite direction. Figure 5 shows the effect of spin on the protruding, asymmetrical baseball seams, which creates greater air pressure on the side of the ball opposite from the side where the spinning initiates (from the right-handed pitcher's perspective, from the third-base side of the ball to the first-base side). The air pressure on the third-base side of the ball, which is traveling relatively faster through the air than on the first-base side, creates greater pressure on the ball to deflect it toward first base. If the difference between the pressure on the third-base side of the ball and the first-base side is as small as 1½ ounces, a curveball thrown at a velocity of 75 MPH will deflect, or curve, a little more than 1 foot (Adair, 1990).

Although the curveball may be released with as much velocity as the fastball, rotation is the sole determinant (except for wind) of the amount of sideward deflection. A rapidly spinning ball creates much more turbulence (nonstreamlined airflow) than a slowly spinning ball. Turbulence affects both the ball's speed and direction. As the rotation speed increases, the increased turbulence causes a proportional decrease in velocity. A curveball with less speed will curve more because it takes longer to get to the plate, and consequently has more time to deflect. For example, a pitch thrown at 95 MPH and rotating at 1,700 revolutions per minute (RPM) will not curve as much as a pitch thrown at 75 MPH and rotating at 1,700 RPM. The pitch thrown with more velocity will rotate fewer times per foot traveled than the slower pitch thrown with the same rate of spin.

An effective curveball has to break both horizontally and vertically. Because the hitting area of a bat is approximately 2.5 to 2.75

Two-seam

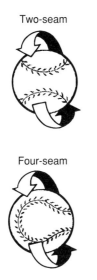

Four-seam

Figure 6. *The two-seam fastball (above) rotates with the seams, while the four-seam fastball (below) rotates across the seams.*

The Rising Fastball

The rising or hopping fastball is actually an illusion. The fastball thrown with considerable backspin simply sinks less than the typical fastball—by as much as 4 inches.

inches (6.25–6.9 cm) wide and 7 to 9 inches (17.5–22.5 cm long, a ball that breaks only horizontally will simply hit a different part of the bat. A baseball that breaks vertically is about three times harder to hit than a baseball breaking horizontally. Dodger pitcher Sandy Koufax was difficult to hit because his curveball dropped as if it had rolled off the end of a table, leaving batters swinging at air.

Fastball

A well-placed fastball is the most important pitch for pitchers at all levels. Figure 6 shows the two most common ways to throw the fastball: with four seams or with two seams. The two-seam grip rotates with the seams; the four-seam grip rotates across the seams. Because the seams create boundary-layer turbulence (nonstreamlined airflow around the contour of the body with which it is in contact) and because four seams create more turbulence than two seams, the four-seam fastball creates greater ball movement. When released with backspin, the four-seam fastball creates the illusion of rising. Although the two-seam fastball creates less movement, many pitchers find its movement is more unpredictable and continue to throw both the two-seam and the four-seam fastball.

Every pitch has a natural downward curve caused by gravity. Because gravity exerts a downward force on the ball from the moment of release, it is impossible to throw the ball in a straight line, that is, parallel to the ground without sinking (unless it could be thrown at 18,500 MPH, or 29,600 KPH, putting it into a low-altitude earth orbit). Fastballs thrown with backspin rotate up and back toward the pitcher. Whereas the curveball has a horizontal Magnus effect, the backspin fastball has a vertical Magnus effect. Backspin forces create greater pressure underneath the ball than on top, creating an upward Magnus force that lessens the force of gravity.

Rising, then, is largely a matter of perception. The ball does not actually rise; it simply sinks less than the typical fastball. To the hitter it appears as if the ball rises and hops over the bat. Psychologist Michael McBeath concluded that when a batter underestimates the ball's initial velocity, it appears lower during the middle trajectory stage and appears to accelerate and rise as it crosses home plate. The hop is perceived due to difficulties in gauging the velocity of the approaching ball. For batters, the hopping illusion seems more exaggerated when, as they level off to hit the ball, they squat and further lower their body and line of vision (McBeath, 1990). This illusion is further compounded when a pitch is thrown with considerable backspin, causing the ball to rise—that is, sink less than a pitch with no backspin—by as much as 4 inches (10 cm). The distance is considerable given that major league bats can be no larger than 2.75 inches in diameter (*see also CATCHING SKILLS*).

The split-finger fastball, a downward-deflecting fastball, is a very effective pitch that increased in popularity in the early 1990s. By 1996, however, its popularity began to decline as it became associated with more frequent arm injuries. Like a slider, the split-finger fastball

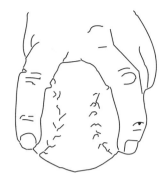

Figure 7. *The split-finger fastball is thrown with topspin, causing it to drop.*

breaks late, but downward. The index finger and middle finger grip the ball so that as the wrist snaps through the delivery, the fingers impart a slow topspin that causes the ball to drop (*see Figure 7*).

The same dynamics apply to the fly ball. A long fly ball hit with substantial backspin can turn a routine warning-track fly ball into a home run by adding 15 to 20 feet to what would otherwise be a flight distance of 325 feet (98 m). Given the same spin rate, the lower the line drive, the greater the Magnus force. The Magnus force is always perpendicular to the ball's velocity, so the lower-angle flight path means that the force is more vertical (greater lift).

Knuckleball

The knuckleball is held either with the fingernails or by the knuckles right above the fingernails (*see Figure 8*). During the acceleration stage and as the ball is released, finger extension counters the natural backspin caused by the pitcher's elbow extension and wrist snap. The ball is released with little or no spin. As a result, the knuckleball moves very erratically as it approaches home plate.

Laces on the ball act as a roughened surface to create the turbulence necessary to generate ball movement. The nonsymmetrical location of the laces causes nonsymmetrical lateral forces, a large imbalance in the forces at a right angle to the airflow around the ball. In flight, a ball's seam should be positioned in the boundary layer (air moving along ball surface) to create ball movement.

By manipulating the seams in different ways, the pitcher can alter the way the knuckleball reacts; no two pitches will react in the same way. Unlike the curveball, the knuckleball's slow rotation changes the location of the seams in relation to the airflow, causing a pressure imbalance. A smooth surface on one side and a rough surface on the other, for example, create an asymmetrical drag force that is larger on the smooth side, deflecting the ball toward the rough side.

Figure 10 shows a pitch in which a smooth section of the ball is on top and a seam is positioned across the bottom. The bottom seam causes turbulence that delays the air passing across that part of the ball; at the same time, the lack of seam at the top allows air to pass quickly. As a result, the wake shifts, or redirects airflow, upward, forcing the ball downward. Because a pitcher cannot accurately predict the airborne position of the seams, the knuckleball is an extremely difficult pitch to control and is often challenging for the catcher to glove.

Sometimes a spinless knuckleball will not deflect, or break, at all because the seams are not positioned to affect the boundary-layer flow around the ball, and the ball is very easy for the batter to hit. When the seams are positioned where the boundary-layer separation begins, however, air current moves back and forth along the seams, causing the wake behind the ball to shift laterally and vertically as the seams vary the airflow around the ball. Because the position of the seams in relation to the boundary layer determines the ball's direction, and because the seams' interaction with the bound-

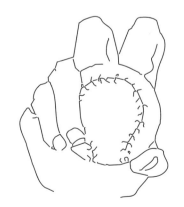

Figure 8. *The knuckleball's grip accounts for its unpredictability.*

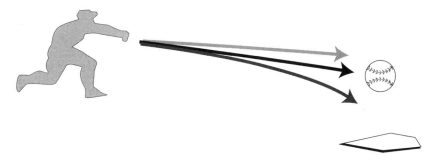

Figure 9. *The effect of gravity on different pitches: backspin, little or no spin, and split-finger (topspin). The top arrow shows the hypothetical trajectory of an excessively backspinning fastball, in the middle is the typical fastball, and below is the slowly topspinning split-finger fastball.*

ary layer is continually changing, the ball's trajectory is extremely unpredictable. As a result, a good knuckleball is perplexing to judge and very difficult to hit because batters must make split-second eye-hand adjustments.

Spitball

Illegally modified balls, called spitballs, are also difficult for batters to hit but are much easier for pitchers to master. Gaylord Perry, an above-average pitcher throughout his twenties and thirties, is one pitcher who used the spitball to considerably prolong his career. Between the ages of 24 and 34—the years associated with a pitcher's best work—Perry pitched an impressive 2,294 innings and compiled 134 wins. But as the speed of his fastball decreased, he relied increasingly on his spitball—successfully extending his career until the age of 45 and pitching 3,057 additional innings for 180 wins, more than during his first decade as a major league pitcher. Although Perry went on to enter the Hall of Fame, he is best remembered for using the illegal spitball to such an extent that on two occasions (in 1968 and 1973) major league rules were changed in an attempt to limit his ability to modify a ball's surface.

The major league first restricted the use of spitballs in 1920, when each team was allowed to retain only two spitball pitchers. The next year, seventeen pitchers were named spitball pitchers and allowed to throw the pitch for the remainder of their careers. In the 1990s, baseball insiders agree that more pitchers still throw the illegal spitball than the legal knuckleball. The ball is secretly modified by the pitcher (or, occasionally, the catcher) in one of two ways: by applying moisture such as Vaseline, saliva, hair gel, or sweat to the pitcher's fingers and then onto the ball; or by scuffing or scraping the ball's leather cover to create an unsmooth surface.

Lubrication allows pitchers to throw the slowly rotating spitball by enabling the finger pressure points on the ball to control the amount of spin—much the way the grip controls the knuckleball's spin. The slippery grip allows the pitcher to apply greater elbow extension and wrist snap during the release because the ball slides, or is squeezed, out between the fingers and thumb (as a bar of soap squirts out of one's hand in the shower). The extra elbow extension

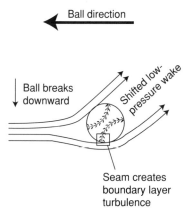

Figure 10. *In this knuckleball model, the air crosses the top of the ball unimpeded while the air crosses the bottom slightly impeded. This bottom-side slowing of the airflow causes the ball to break downward.*

Pitch Characteristics

Pitched ball	Speed (MPH)	Spin rate (RPM)	Rotations enroute to plate
Fast	85–95	1600	11
Curve	70–80	1900	16
Knuckle	60–70	25–50	1/4–1/2

Table 1. (Source: Adair, 1990)

and wrist snap provide greater velocity, so batters have little time to react as the ball flutters, drops, and breaks.

By scuffing or by applying foreign substances to the ball, pitchers also alter its aerodynamic properties. Smooth balls, especially at low wind speeds, deflect in the direction opposite the Magnus effect. The spitball, with its altered, unsmooth surface, is very unpredictable and, as a result, extremely difficult to hit (*see also FIELD ATHLETICS: THROWING*). Some believe that spitballs, which are often considered "more lively," were an important factor in the dramatic increase in home runs in the 1920s.

Bat and Ball Collision

The increased frequency of home runs has fueled considerable debate about the extent to which new, more "lively" balls are responsible. Figure 11 illustrates the increase in home runs per game per team over the years. Certain periods appear to be home-run "booms," as in the 1920s and during the 1987 season.

The liveliness of a baseball can be scientifically tested. When scientists address the speed and distance of rebound from collisions, they describe these phenomena using what is known as the coefficient of restitution—the ratio of the relative speeds of two bodies immediately before and after a collision between them. For an official major league baseball, the required coefficient of restitution is 0.546 ± 0.032. When a ball hits a wall, for example, its speed as it bounces off the wall is reduced by roughly half. The physicist Robert Adair calculated that the 0.032 variation means that the distance two identically hit baseballs travel can vary by 15 feet (4.5 m; Adair, 1990). Because modern baseball manufacturing and testing methods better

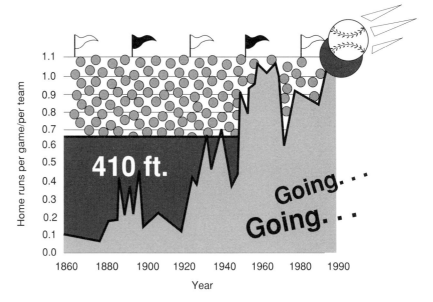

Figure 11. *The number of home runs has increased over the years, with many peaks following expansion years, when pitching talent was diluted.*

ensure a uniform coefficient of restitution, the actual variation among regulation baseballs is much less than 0.032.

Prior to 1950, however, baseball production was not subject to regular quality control. Despite repeated claims by Spaulding, the manufacturer of official major league baseballs, never to have changed the specifications for baseballs, the U.S. National Bureau of Standards found that baseballs had a coefficient of restitution of 0.41 in 1943, much lower than those produced by modern machines. In other words, the 1940s ball could lose almost 60 percent of its speed after collision, whereas a 1990s ball loses less than 50 percent. The lower coefficient is reflected in the low home-run total in the early 1940s.

The home-run boom of 1987 spurred many independent tests of the coefficient of restitution, but no statistically relevant change was found. If anything, the tests showed that the coefficient may even have decreased slightly from 0.546 from the mid-1980s to the mid-1990s. Consequently, scientific evidence indicates that new, live balls were not responsible for the 1987 home-run boom. One theory is that the increase in home runs is a long-term probably attributable to the better diet, off-season conditioning, and strength training of modern players. In the 1990s, the average baseball player is larger and stronger than his predecessors, so an increase in home runs should be expected. And as home-run hitters command some of the largest salaries in major league baseball, players understandably strive to increase their home-run potential.

Major league baseball officials test the coefficient of restitution by launching balls into a wall of the same ash used to construct bats. Although launching a ball into a wall provides consistent results, in bat-ball collisions the coefficient of restitution varies depending on the site of contact on the bat. At or near the "sweet spot" of the bat, the coefficient of restitution is highest; near either end, it is lowest. When the ball rebounds off the end of the bat (or off the "fists," the portion of the bat near the handle), most of the energy is absorbed as vibrational energy, rather than as rebound energy. The coefficient of restitution also varies with impact velocity—the greater the impact velocity, the lower the coefficient of restitution (*see also STATISTICS*).

Bat Selection

The optimum bat weight is based on a hitter's strength, on his type of swing, and on pitch speed. Many players, in the belief that the bigger the bat, the farther the ball will travel, choose the heaviest piece of lumber they can lift. A well-hit ball, however, depends more on the speed of the swing than on the weight of the bat. Greater bat speed results in a higher coefficient of restitution and increased postimpact velocity. Bat weight is important, however, when a strong hitter can swing a heavier bat at the same speed as a lighter bat.

A study by the physicist Paul Kirkpatrick illustrates why bat speed is of greater significance than bat weight (Kirkpatrick, 1963). Assum-

Juiced Balls?

Despite a popular misconception, the coefficient of restitution (rebound ability) of major league baseballs has remained fairly consistent since the early 1950s.

Who Is Tougher to Hit: A Cricket Bowler or a Baseball Pitcher?

While cricket and baseball share a number of similarities, it is the differences that determine whether it is more difficult to hit against a cricket bowler or a baseball pitcher. The game of cricket is very popular in England, Australia, West Indies, South Africa, India, Pakistan, New Zealand, and Sri Lanka and has gained popularity in American communities where large numbers of immigrants from these countries live. Cricket fans are as passionate about their sport as Americans are about baseball. For instance, the "body-line" tactics (in which the ball is aimed directly at or near the batsman) used by the visiting English team against the Australians during the 1932–1933 cricket season strained relations between the two nations so severly that members of the Australian parliament—then a self-governing dominion under the British Commonwealth—called for Australia to sever its relations with its mother country.

One clue to the different challenges posed to baseball and cricket hitters is evident simply by looking at the scoreboard. In cricket, each side plays a maximum of only two innings; however, several hundred runs are usually scored in each innings (always plural in cricket). An individual batsman may score a century (100 runs), a double

century (200 runs), or even a triple century (300 runs) in a single innings before he is out. The objective of the batsman is to remain at bat as long as possible and to pile up as many runs as possible. In the annals of the game, two batsmen remained at bat for over 16 hours in a single innings spanning several days in which they both piled up over 300 runs. In baseball, on the other hand, the total number of runs seldom reaches double digits. As the number of runs illustrates, it is far more difficult for a batter to hit a pitcher in baseball than for a batsman to hit a bowler in cricket.

Among the most important factors are the differences in the size and the shape of the baseball and cricket bats. The cricket bat is 4.25 inches in width, considerably wider than the diameter of

a baseball bat, which at its widest is 2.75 inches. Except for the edges, the hitting surface of the cricket bat is nearly flat, whereas the baseball bat is round. The effective hitting surface of the baseball bat is thus further reduced, as balls hit "uncleanly," or at large angles, will either pop up or be grounded.

The sizes of the strike zones are also quite different. The baseball strike zone is determined by the batter's stature and stance as well as by the judgment of the umpire. The strike zone is also wider than the cricket bowler's fixed target—the wicket, which is only 9 inches wide, just twice as wide as the cricket bat. Thus, it is more difficult for the bowler to get the batsman out than for a pitcher to strike out a batter. Game rules also favor the cricket batsman over the baseball hit-

Comparison Table

Mode	Baseball	Cricket
Throw distance	60.5 ft.	66.95 ft.
Throw motion	Nonrestricted	Restricted
Throw run-up	Not permitted	Permitted
Ball arrival	Airborne	Bounced
Ball movement	Extreme	Significant
Ball diameter	9.25 in.	9 in.
Ball color	White	Dark red
Bat width	2.75 in.	4.25 in.
Strike/wicket	17 in. × 24 in.	9 in. × 24 in.

ing that a major league hitter could double the weight of his bat without losing speed, postimpact velocity would also double. If he could double his bat speed (with the bat weight unchanged), the postimpact velocity would increase fourfold. Therefore, a hitter's optimal bat weight should not compromise bat speed. Aware of this fact, Jeffrey C. Di Tullio, an aeronautics professor at Massachusetts Institute of Technology, came up with a novel solution: dimpling the surface of the bat, much like the surface of a golf ball. For any given bat weight, he discovered that the speed of a dimpled bat is 3 to 5 percent greater than that of a standard, nondimpled bat. This is because "roughen-

ter, since he can (and most often does) block the ball and is not forced to advance in doing so.

While in baseball the ball is thrown directly at the strike zone, the cricket ball is "pitched," or bounced, in front of the bat. For the batsman, an error in the lateral adjustment of the bat is at that moment the greatest, as is the chance that the ball may nick the edge of the bat and be caught by a fielder or the wicketkeeper. A ball may also pass under the bat and hit the wicket. A ball with a lot of spin will "break," or turn, significantly upon bouncing. This aspect of cricket has no counterpart in baseball. Slow-ball bowlers, or "spinners," have a much greater role in cricket than the slow-ball "knucklers" in baseball.

The top speeds of the fastballs are almost exactly the same in both sports. The fastest recorded pitch in baseball and the fastest recorded ball in cricket are both around 100 MPH (160 KPH). But while a baseball can be thrown in

any manner, the cricket ball must be "bowled"—with a straight arm and smooth action—and not "thrown." This restricted arm motion robs the bowler of some of the pace off the ball, which is compensated for in part by the fact that the bowler is allowed to run at full speed to deliver his ball. There is also a significant difference in distance between the pitcher and the batter: 60 feet 6 inches for baseball compared with nearly 67 feet for cricket. The 8 percent shorter distance between the baseball pitcher and the batter gives the pitcher a greater advantage than the cricket bowler. For a 95 MPH or faster fastball, the flight time of the baseball is at the threshold of the reaction time of most hitters. In cricket, the slightly longer distance allows the batsman a crucial fraction of a second longer to focus on and to react to the approaching ball.

The comparative size and weight of the balls further disadvantage the baseball batter. The cricket ball is

fractionally smaller than the baseball (9 in. versus 9–9.25 in. in circumference) but is slightly heavier (5.5–5.75 oz. versus 5–5.25 oz.). As a result, the Magnus effect is greater for the larger, lighter baseball, which may shift more as it travels through air. Furthermore, since the wicket is vertical, the batsman uses a golf swing rather than a level swing, worrying only about the lateral movement of the ball (called the "swing" in cricket). The baseball hitter, on the other hand, must watch for both horizontal and vertical movement of the ball.

The visibility of the ball is one area that favors the baseball hitter over the cricket batsman. The slightly smaller cricket ball is dark red and more difficult to see, particularly when thrown as a fastball near the end of the day or in fading light. Cricket games are sometimes suspended for the day when the batsman appeals on account of visibility problems.

Who is harder to hit: the baseball pitcher or the cricket bowler? The answer is the baseball pitcher. If a top cricket batsman tried to hit against top major league pitchers, he would probably perform better against off-speed pitchers than against fastball pitchers, owing to the longer reaction time to which he is accustomed. On the other hand, top baseball hitters such as Pete Rose and Wade Boggs (rather than the big-swinging home run hitters) would probably do well against even the fastest bowlers.

Arjun Tan

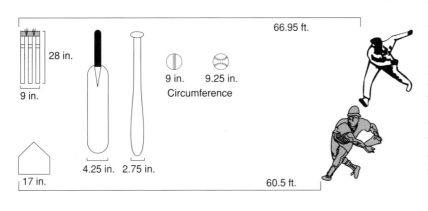

ing" the smooth surface of the bat by adding dimples improves the bat's aerodynamics (*see also GOLF*).

Regardless of skill level, optimal bat weight declines as the speed of the pitch decreases because bat speed will play a greater role than potential energy transfer. More energy comes from bat speed for slower pitched balls because less energy is supplied by the pitch. Robert Watts, a professor of mechanical engineering at Tulane University, demonstrated that the optimal bat weight for major league players is between 30 and 34 ounces (0.8–0.9 kg). For Little Leaguers, the optimal bat weight is about 21 ounces (0.6 kg), though most Lit-

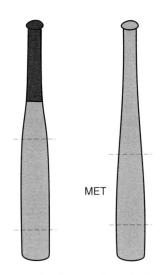

Figure 12. *The enlarged "sweet spot" of an aluminum bat (left) is located closer to the handle. MET= maximum-energy-transfer point (sweet spot).*

tle Leaguers use much heavier bats. Slow-pitch softball players also tend to use bats that are heavier than the optimal weight.

Aluminum versus wooden bats. Although studies show that balls hit in the "sweet spot" (the middle) of an aluminum bat do not travel farther than balls hit similarly with wooden bats, aluminum bats perform much better for off-center hits. Figure 12 shows the sweet spot of an aluminum bat and of a wooden bat. Aluminum bats are stiffer and have a much broader sweet spot. Balls hit off the fists of an aluminum bat (up the handle, away from the sweet spot) generate less vibrational energy and travel much farther. Most pitchers consider an inside pitch very effective when a batter hits the ball off the fists. If the pitch does not split the bat in two, the ball is put into play only weakly and can be easily fielded.

Allowing aluminum bats in the major leagues would drastically change the game. The strategy of pitchers, particularly those who pitch with too little velocity to accumulate strikeouts, would need to change. With the batter holding an aluminum bat, the pitcher cannot expect to gain an out by throwing a pitch that forces the batter to hit off the fists. With its added stiffness, the aluminum bat might allow batters to hit such a pitch over the infielders' heads for an easy single. The center of mass for an aluminum bat is closer to the handle, and aluminum is much denser and stronger than ash. When a ball is struck away from the maximum-energy-transfer (MET) point, or sweet spot, the firmer aluminum bat absorbs much less of the resulting vibrational energy than the ash bat.

The aluminum bat also has a broader curve than the wooden bat, giving it a greater coefficient of restitution for most contact points along the bat (that is, the ball bounces off the aluminum bat with greater speed). The bat-to-ball rebound velocity varies between aluminum and wooden bats at a number of different points from the barrel of the bat. In and around the sweet spot, performance is about equal; for contact points farther from the sweet spot, aluminum bats hold a decided advantage over wooden bats (*see Figure 13*).

The difference is apparent when the ball rebounds farther up the

Figure 13. *Batted-ball velocity is a function of the site of impact and the composition of the bat. The broader curve for the aluminum bat illustrates that its effective hitting surface is larger and closer to the handle than that of a wooden bat. (Adapted from Watts and Bahill, 1990)*

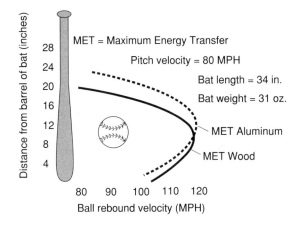

bat handle. The graph illustrates a pitch velocity of 80 MPH (128 KPH). For a speed of 100 MPH (160 KPH), the curve would show an even larger difference in the coefficient of restitution between the wooden and the aluminum bats, especially for balls hit farther up the handle.

Another advantage of the aluminum bat over the wooden bat is its lightness, so it can be accelerated more quickly by the hitter, resulting in a higher rebound velocity as compared with that of a ball hit with a heavier, wooden bat of the same size (*see also EQUIPMENT MATERIALS*).

Grip Firmness

In addition to bat composition and impact location, grip firmness affects ball velocity. Historically, baseball coaches have taught their players to maintain a tight grip on the bat. One study concluded that postimpact velocity improves by 22 percent with a tight grip when an aluminum bat is used (Weyrich, 1989). A tight grip also increased postimpact velocity with a wooden bat, but the difference was only 4 percent.

The effects of grip firmness on postimpact velocity may be attributed to the speed at which vibrational energy travels along the bat. At the moment of impact, vibrational waves travel down the bat quickly, reaching the batter's hands while there is still bat-ball contact. A firm grip enables the hitter to lessen the vibrational energy of the bat, increasing the energy transferred to the ball and, consequently, the postimpact velocity. Figure 14 shows the difference in vibrational energy between a vise-held and handheld bat. The difference is attributable to the effectiveness of the body's muscles, joints, and tendons in absorbing vibrational energy. The difference in physical properties of the two materials is the reason that a tight grip has a greater effect on the postimpact velocity. Because aluminum is denser than wood and because aluminum bats are hollow, vibrations travel more quickly in aluminum bats than they do in wooden bats. Vibrational energy, which cannot be transferred effectively to the ball, travels to the hands more quickly with an aluminum bat, making the hands more effective at dampening the wasteful vibrational energy. The

Figure 14. *Oscillation traces of vibration measurements from a vise-held bat collision is shown above; the trace for a handheld bat is shown below. The handheld bat dampens out vibrations more quickly because of the ability of muscles, joints, and tendons to absorb vibrational energy. (Adapted from Brody, 1990)*

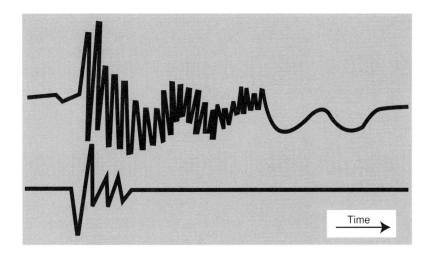

energy of the swinging bat is thus more efficiently transferred to the ball, increasing postimpact velocity. In the millisecond of bat-ball contact, the batter's hands can do little to dampen the vibrational waves that shake a wooden bat because the ball is gone by the time the vibrational waves reach the hands.

Illegal Bats

For decades major league players have tinkered with their bats to increase their hitting percentages. Modifications—intended to increase the coefficient of restitution of the bat and, consequently, the postimpact velocity of the ball—usually involve drilling out the end of the bat and filling the hollow portion with cork or rubber balls. Many players believe that if the bat is filled with an elastic, "springy" substance, the ball will travel farther. Norm Cash was one player accused on several occasions of illegally modifying his bat. The principles of physics demonstrate that such efforts do very little to increase the distance the ball can travel.

During the millisecond of bat-ball collision, energy cannot be effectively transferred from the bat to the ball because the moment of impact is too short. In fact, a ball hit by a modified bat might even lose distance if bat speed decreased because the added material was heavier than ash.

Hitting Theories

Hitting a baseball has been described as the toughest skill to master in any sport. Because even the best hitters fail seven of every ten trips to the plate, major league teams employ a hitting coach to improve hitters' chances against the odds (*see also STATISTICS*).

Many different theories of hitting have developed due to the physiological variability among humans and the numerous factors at work. The best known is the Charlie Lau style, which emphasizes a head-down, top-hand release and has been used by great hitters such as George Brett (Royals) and Frank Thomas (White Sox). Other theories include the wait-and-react (minimized stride) style of Paul Moliter (Blue Jays) and the attack-the-ball (decide to swing then explosively move) style emphasized by hitters such as John Kruk and Dave Winfield. No single style is clearly superior to the others, though numerous players in each camp point to examples of its style's superiority. Some of the greatest Hall of Fame hitters used what hitting coaches of the 1990s consider poor mechanics. Ty Cobb held his hands apart on the bat, thus retarding the axis of rotation yet he won 10 batting titles. Left-hander Mel Ott lifted his right foot in the air before taking his stride and therefore limited his ability to make midswing adjustments; he also led the National League in home runs six times.

Both the Lau style and the wait-and-react style use reduced stride, emphasizing slow feet and quick hands. Because pitches are

Figure 15. *Many coaches believe that the best hitting style is the one using a short stride forward with the hitter's center of gravity shifting back over the rear foot as the front leg comes forward. This allows the hitter to delay his swing as long as possible while still developing forward inertia for power.*

thrown at different speeds and look remarkably similar at the point when hitters must decide whether to swing, a short stride allows for the greatest timing adjustment by allowing the weight to shift backward at the same time the batter steps forward. Forward inertia is created without committing the body to the pitch. The hitter delays his swing as long as possible. By separating the stride and swing components, the hitter improves his timing through the lengthened adjustment period. Longer-stride hitters, on the other hand, generate more power but start to swing sooner. In their case, the body's weight often shifts forward too quickly for slower pitches, prematurely releasing the power generated by the hips and legs. Hitters may look off-balance and foolish as they try to slow their swings and may miss the ball completely or put it weakly into play.

In addition to variations in hitting styles, hitters use different paths of swing. Figure 16 illustrates the swings of three players. Player A has a level swing without wrist eversion (cocking and breaking, or flexing, the wrists during the swing). A level swing in baseball means that the hitter swings upward from horizontal by 8 to 10 degrees to counter the ball's similar downward path. Player B has an uppercut swing with great wrist eversion. He swings up by as much as 20 degrees. Player C, usually a larger man with long arms and a long stride, uses a long, level, arc swing with little wrist eversion. His swing-rotation center covers a longer-than-average span. Although he must begin his swing earlier, with the longer span he generates more power than player A, yet requires less precise timing and accuracy than player B, who uses a sweeping, quick swing with wrist eversion. Player C drives the throat of the bat forward (rather than rotating on a fixed axis, like player B). The long-arc technique allows player C to hit toward center field and toward the opposite field with great power.

The arc of the swing does not necessarily affect the velocity of the ball as it leaves the bat, but it does affect the average angle of the ball's postimpact flight. Player B's uppercut swing is more likely to project the ball at the optimal angle for distance (45°). It is also more likely to undercut the ball slightly (a full undercut of the ball pops it up), which can increase the distance the ball is carried by as much as 50 feet (15.24 m). Undercutting creates backspin which, similar to a rising fastball, creates a lifting force that carries the ball farther (same dynamics as a curveball).

According to the engineer Robert Watts, if a hitter could hit the ball wherever he pleased, he would use a slight undercut to hit the

Figure 16. *Bat and ball trajectories are shown for three different types of swings: level, uppercut, and long-arc. (Adapted from Adair, 1990)*

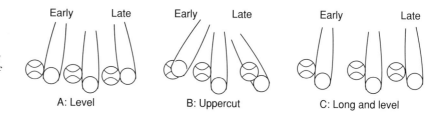

Early　Late　　Early　Late　　Early　Late

A: Level　　B: Uppercut　　C: Long and level

ball with optimal backspin, sending the ball much farther than a perfectly centered bat-ball collision (Watts and Baroni, 1989). A 0.39-inch undercut—still a very solid collision—gives the ball greater lift and less drag. A ball hit with a perfectly centered collision would travel about 377 feet, while one hit with only a slight (0.39-in.) undercut would travel about 443 feet. Hitters like player B who use the big wrist eversion swing not only generate more power, they are more likely to bat the ball farther owing to their slight undercut. This explains in part why home-run hitters seldom have a high batting average. Figure 16 illustrates the difficulty facing player B: he has little room for error if he takes an early or late swing. When he swings early, he is more likely to ground out to first base. When he swings late, he is more likely to pop up to third base. Because player B swings closer to the optimal angle for distance, he is more likely not only to hit home runs, but to pop up and ground out as well.

For all types of swings, strong wrists are important to maintain the bat's horizontal position and to generate bat speed during the final, force-producing stage. Nearly all uppercut hitters use an exaggerated wrist eversion to deliver additional torque to the swing. Although wrist eversion increases bat speed, it also usually causes a loss of bat control. Exaggerated wrist eversion makes it more difficult to maintain correct bat position and timing. Although hitters who do not use much wrist eversion must also maintain correct bat position, their timing need not be perfect for good contact. Player A's swing, for example, shows how a level swinger may make good contact even when the swing is early or late. When he swings early, player A is likely to drive the ball past the first and second basemen. When he swings late, he is likely to hit the ball over the third baseman's head. Overall, hitter A has a much larger margin for error than hitter B.

A good hitter, regardless of hitting style, tries to keep his center

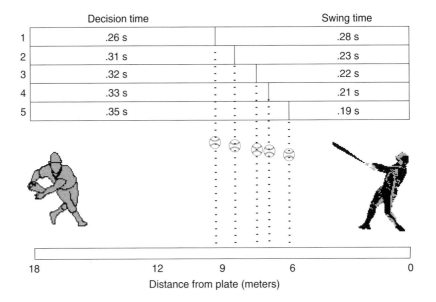

	Decision time		Swing time
1	.26 s		.28 s
2	.31 s		.23 s
3	.32 s		.22 s
4	.33 s		.21 s
5	.35 s		.19 s

18   12   9   6   0

Distance from plate (meters)

Figure 17.   *The ability to wait—the difference between decision time and swing time—is one of the key attributes separating average hitters from great hitters. For a curveball that takes .54 seconds from first sighting until the ball crosses the plate, the decision times for Ted Williams (2), Hank Aaron (3), Mickey Mantle (4), and Stan Musial (5) are considerably greater than for the average, sub-.300 hitter (1). (Adapted from Hay, 1985)*

of gravity in a level plane as he strides forward, in order to limit the need for vertical adjustments. The lead arm remains nearly straight to increase the radius of the arc of the swing, allowing an increase in bat velocity without a corresponding drop-off in bat control.

Base Running

Stealing a base requires good timing, speed, and sliding technique. Table 2 shows a breakdown of the average pitcher, catcher, and runner times for high school players attempting a steal of second base (Southworth, 1989).

The pitcher and catcher have an average of 0.25 second to throw out a runner. Despite the large time cushion, runners continue to try to steal. Players who run faster than average have a significantly higher chance of stealing successfully. Other factors may make the base runner's attempt to steal worthwhile, including a large lead, a good jump, and choosing the right slide. The lead and jump are skills developed and refined through trial and error. Although sliding is also an experience-related skill, the runner may consider one of three types of slides, depending on the situation: straight-in, hook, and headfirst. The hook slide was for many years preferable to the straight-in slide because it occurs a few feet farther from the oncoming ball, thus presenting a smaller, more difficult target for the baseman to tag, especially if the throw is slightly off target.

Led by pioneer Pete Rose, nicknamed "Charlie Hustle," most major league base stealers have abandoned the hook slide in favor of the headfirst slide because they believe it gets them to the base more quickly. Because the surface area of the chest (on which the runner lands for the headfirst slide) is much larger than that of the legs (which scrape the ground for the straight-in slide), will decelerate more quickly during a headfirst slide, allowing him to begin his slide later and much closer to the base. The runner's additional step saves a valuable fraction of a second that may mean the difference between arriving safely and being tagged out.

The headfirst slide has a biomechanical advantage as well. Positive acceleration requires runners to use a pronounced forward lean to balance their center of gravity. By changing the angle of the body, they

Base Running

Defense (Battery)	sec.	Offense	sec.
Pitch	= 0.90		
Catcher's hesitation	= 0.30		
Catcher's throw	= 1.75	Runner's time	= 3.20
Total	= 2.95	Total	= 3.20

Table 2. (Southworth, 1989)

Better Equipment: Breakaway Bases

Whether a base runner resorts to the feetfirst or headfirst slide, impact with a fixed base poses an enormous injury risk. Sliding is a very difficult skill to master and may cause knee and ankle injuries for the feetfirst slider and finger, hand, and wrist injuries for the headfirst slider. Field conditions, poor stride judgment, faulty technique, and inadequate conditioning all contribute to sliding injuries.

The distance at which players begin to slide varies widely. Even for Rickey Henderson, an all-time stolen-base leader, every slide is different. The grooming of the playing surface is one factor to consider. On a hard clay surface the runner may need to begin his slide three feet from the base. On a sandy, well-groomed surface—which creates much less friction—4 or 5 feet may be more appropriate.

With anchored bases, a runner trying to avoid the tag collides with the immovable base at a high velocity. The impact is similar to a high-speed automobile striking a massive, nondeformable object, such as a tree or a rock. Because the object does not move, the car absorbs the impact and suffers all the collision damage. Similarly, throwing a small snowball at a large tree will flatten the snowball, while throwing a small rock at a large snowbank leaves the rock undamaged. In each case, kinetic (movement) energy must be absorbed. The rock hitting the snowbank, unlike the car

hitting a rock, may extend impact and reduce the force of impact by a factor of 100. To reduce the force of impact, one must extend the time of impact. Sliding into a base causes many injuries because the runner must reach the base as quickly as possible and then stop as quickly as possible. This is further complicated because the slider must come to a stop while maintaining contact with the base. A similar hazard existed in hockey until anchored goalposts were replaced with breakaway goalposts.

One can estimate the forces, or twisting moments (torques), that a runner will sustain when sliding into a base by calculating of the average force needed to stop the mass of the runner. The velocity with which the runner launches himself is limited to the maximum speed a human can run. Top base stealers reach their maximum speed (25–30 ft./sec.) prior to sliding. High-speed running diminishes the deceleration effect from the distance of surface touchdown to

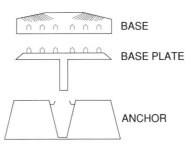

BASE

BASE PLATE

ANCHOR

base contact (about 5 ft.). At the moment of foot-base or hand-base contact, most of the deceleration necessary to stop the runner has already taken place. The average force (F) times the distance traveled (S) determines the amount of work required to remove the kinetic (motion) energy of the runner ($F \times S = 1/2$, or mass $\times$ velocity^2)

When the runner uses a toe-hook slide, the body slides past the base with the knee flexing to decelerate the horizontal momentum of the runner. If the sliding distance traveled upon base contact is 2 feet and the runner's velocity is 30 feet per second, the force of impact is seven times the runner's weight. If the runner makes a drastic misjudgment, such as coming too quickly on the bag and then stopping within only 6 inches, the force of impact increases to 28 times the runner's weight. The worst injuries occur when the runner's cleat catches the bag in such a way that the foot and ankle twist. In that case, the ankle or knee could be badly damaged from the combined twisting and compression forces. Using a toe-hook slide and oversliding the base significantly decrease risk of injury because the margin for error is increased. However, there still remain significant risks of knee ligament damage when the knee flexes beyond 90 degrees between the lower and upper legs.

can continually adjust their center of gravity in relation to the foot that is doing the driving. Because efficient running mechanics require the body to lean forward, the base runner need only further lower his body—maintaining the center of gravity ahead of the striding foot—in order to dive forward for the headfirst slide (*see Figure 18*).

In comparison, the feetfirst slide requires a relaxing phase as the body inefficiently straightens, becomes airborne, and kicks the legs

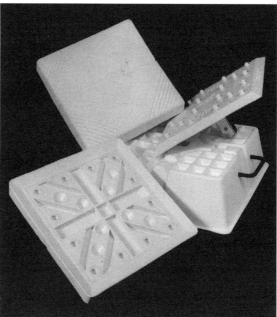

Breakaway bases are anchored by receiving holes for the protruding nobs on the top of the fixed, rubber-mat base. Research suggests that wider use of these bases would prevent numerous injuries. (Photo courtesy of Rogers Sports Corporation)

Breakaway bases diminish the risk of injury, particularly if the force needed to release the base is modest, for example, 150 pounds of force (a release point of 700 ft./lb. of energy). Similar to force-sensitive release settings on downhill ski bindings, the grommets on breakaway bases come in a variety of sizes, with earlier release (at 75 lb. of force) for lighter Little Leaguers and later release (at 150 lb.) for adults. Critics argue that runners may kick out or overslide the base and get tagged out, but others feel this is a small concession considering the likely significant reduction in injuries. Many senior leagues realized the danger of base-related injury and began allowing the over-running of all bases years ago. Doctors at the Institute for Preventative Sports Medicine sought to determine the effectiveness of breakaway bases in preventing injuries (Janda, 1993) and provided seven minor league teams and seven college teams with breakaway bases to use on their home fields. Injuries declined dramatically. In the 498 away games played with traditional bases, ten players were sidelined due to sliding injuries. Three could not play for more than a month and two needed surgery. In comparison, for the 486 home games played with breakaway bases, only two runners were injured sliding—a significant, 80 percent reduction.

Given these findings as well as the number of games that professional baseball players miss due to sliding injuries, one might be surprised that major league baseball still does not use breakaway bases to protect its multimillion-dollar investments in star players. Given the widespread participation of Americans in baseball and softball—Little League, high school, college, and recreational leagues—the U.S. Centers for Disease Control has estimated that 1.7 million injuries per year would be prevented if breakaway bases were universally used, saving $2 billion per year in acute medical costs—quite a payback for a small, preventive investment.

David Lind and John Zumerchik

Figure 18. *In a headfirst slide, the body shifts from a 70-degree lean to a 30-degree lean. The hand hits the ground first, followed by the knee, chest, and thigh.*

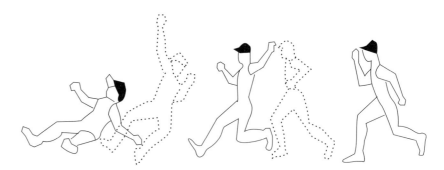

Figure 19. *In a feetfirst slide, the body moves from a 70-degree lean to an erect upright position, a move that is inefficient for forward acceleration. Other inefficiencies result from the fact that the body is being airborne and the arms are moving back rather than forward. When the runner begins his slide too close to the base, the likelihood of injury to the ankle and knee increases because the foot jams into the base.*

out in front. An erect or back-leaning position moves the center of gravity backward, resulting in a deceleration force (*see Figure 19*). Similarly, a track sprinter leans his torso forward to maximize acceleration throughout the race but leans backward to slow down after breaking the tape.

With practice, the headfirst slide offers distinct advantages. However, the abrupt sliding stop into the anchored base increases the chances of a wrist sprain or jammed finger (*see the box "Breakaway Bases"*). But as the paramount concern of most base stealers is high speed and a quick stop, the popularity of the headfirst slide probably will continue to grow.

John Zumerchik and Angelo Armenti

References

Adair, R. *The Physics of Baseball*. New York: Harper and Row, 1990.

Adair, R. "The Physics of Baseball." *Physics Today*, May 1995: 26–31.

Albright, J., et al. "Clinical Study of Baseball Pitchers: Correlation of Injury to the Throwing Arm with Method of Delivery." *American Journal of Sports Medicine* 6 (1978): 15.

Brancazio, P. "How Do You Throw a Curveball?" *Cenco Physical Sports Series*, 1991.

Briggs, L. "Effect of Spin and Speed on the Lateral Deflection (Curve) of a Baseball; and the Magnus Effect for Smooth Spheres." *American Journal of Physics* 27 (1959): 589.

Brody, H. "Models of Baseball Bats." *American Journal of Physics* 58 (1990): 756.

Corson, R., et al. "The Biomechanics of Head-First versus Feet-First Slide." *American Journal of Sports Medicine* 12 (1984): 229.

Dyson, G. *The Mechanics of Athletics*. London: University of London Press Ltd., 1973.

Gowan, I., et al. "A Comparative Electromyographic Analysis of the Shoulder during Pitch." *American Journal of Sports Science* 15 (1987): 586.

Hay, J. *Biomechanics of Sport Techniques*. Englewood Cliffs, New Jersey: Prentice-Hall, 1985.

Janda, D. "An Analysis of Preventative Methods for Baseball-Induced Chest Impact Injuries." *Clinical Journal of Sports Medicine* 2 (1992): 172.

Janda, D. "Sliding Injuries in College and Professional Sports." *Clinical Journal of Sports Medicine* 3 (1993): 78.

McBeath, M. "The Rising Fastball: Baseball's Impossible Pitch." *Perception* 19 (1990): 545.

Seaver, T. *The Art of Pitching*. New York: Heart, 1984.

Southworth, H. *High Percentage Baserunning*. Champaign, Illinois: Leisure Press, 1989.

Toyoshima, S., et al. "Contribution of the Body Parts to Throwing Performance." *Biomechanics IV*. Baltimore, Maryland: University Parks, 1974.

Vaughn, R. "Mechanics of the Baseball Throw." In *Gatorade Sports Science Institute Report*. Chicago, Illinois, 1992.

Ward, J. "The Art of Hitting." *New York Times*, 27 March 1994, Sports Sunday section, p. 2.

Watts, R., and S. Baroni. "Bat-Ball Collisions and the Resulting Trajectories of Spinning Balls." *American Journal of Physics* 57 (1989): 40.

Watts, R., and T. Bahill. *Keep Your Eye on the Ball: The Science and Folklore of Baseball*. New York: Freeman, 1990.

Watts, R., and E. Sawyer. "Aerodynamics of a Knuckleball." *American Journal of Physics* 43 (1975): 960.

Weyrich, S., et al. "Effects of Bat Composition, Grip Firmness, and Impact Location on Post-Impact Velocity." *Medicine and Science in Sports and Exercise* 21 (1989): 199.

Zarins, B, et al. (eds.) *Injuries to the Throwing Arm: Based on the Proceedings of the National Conference*. Sponsored by the United States Olympic Committee Sports Medicine Council. Philadelphia: Saunders, 1985.

Basketball

THE ORIGINS OF BASKETBALL can be traced to thousands of years ago, when humans first began the practice of throwing balls through hoops and rings. The ancient Toltec culture of the Valley of Mexico is believed to have originated a game—more a religious rite than a sport—that involved hurling balls through a series of rings vertically placed along a wall. Mysticism drove these games. The results were believed to determine the life of future generations, droughts, rains, and hurricanes. Participants feared performing in a way that would not please the gods, and some historians speculate that the game lasted for weeks or even months and involved human sacrifice, perhaps of the leader of the losing team.

Modern basketball may be considered the most indigenous major team sport in North America. All other major sports were largely adapted from other established sports. Basketball began quite humbly in 1891. As the story goes, Dr. James Naismith needed a game to attract more youngsters to the local YMCA in Springfield, Massachusetts, so he fastened a couple of wooden peach baskets at opposite ends of the gymnasium, divided players up into two teams, and gave them a large rubber ball. They were directed to dribble (bounce) and pass the ball up the court, and once near their peach basket, shoot the ball through the hoop. Thus "basket ball" was born.

Around this time, baseball assumed its title as the national pastime of the United States. But despite its wide popularity, it had a major drawback: play was limited to 6 or 7 months of the year. Cold weather, frozen ground, and snow restricted play the rest of the year. Basketball conveniently filled this off-season void.

Naismith devised a game that was easy to learn and quite portable—enjoyable indoors as well as outdoors. Because he wanted a game that did not emphasize a player's weight or strength, body contact was strictly forbidden. His game would be more dependent on adept eye-hand coordination, speed, and team play. Individual talent would be important, but success would require blending individual players' skills into an effective team strategy.

When Naismith fastened those first peach baskets, he could not have predicted that basketball would develop into the exciting, fast-paced game of the 1990s. Old films show just how much the game has evolved. The jump shot has replaced the set shot, the one-hander has replaced the two-hand shot, and the dunk has replaced the layup.

Strategy has changed dramatically as well. Whereas games of the past emphasized passing and ball control, the emphasis in the 1990s is more on dribbling and "fast-breaks." That is why a typical collegiate game in the 1930s might end with each team scoring about 30 points, not 80 points, which is the average for a 1990s game.

The quickening pace of the game has put an even bigger premium on athletic ability. Many believe that basketball, with its acrobatic dunks and nonstop action, requires more all-around athleticism than any other major sport. Players need cardiovascular fitness for endurance, eye-hand coordination and motor control to dribble and shoot effectively, strength and leaping ability to rebound, and individual and team rhythm to smoothly set a pace and flow for the game.

Shooting Mechanics

Unlike throwing a javelin or pitching a baseball, in which the attempt is to maximize release velocity, basketball shooting is a controlled-motion activity, in which eye alignment and controlled velocity at release are much more important than maximum velocity. By developing good mechanics, shooters can develop the controlled motion of a consistent shooter. Good mechanics account for much of the uncanny accuracy of great shooters and help to limit the poor shooting streaks that plague even the best of shooters (*see also FIELD ATHLETICS: THROWING*).

The most common explanation given by coaches for poor shooting is a lack of concentration or confidence. Actually, a lack of confidence is the effect, not the cause. When the ball fails to drop through the net, confidence and concentration naturally wane. Developing good mechanics and a consistent shooting style improves shooting accuracy, which in turn boosts a shooter's confidence and concentration.

In addition to the psychological factors, there are four key mechanical skills to fine-tune: positioning, sighting, generating force, and the follow-through. Shooting accuracy will improve with improvement in any one of these skills. But since they are interrelated, better accuracy depends upon improvement in all four.

Positioning

For throwing sports that involve maximizing release velocity, the forward foot is the one on the opposite side of the throwing hand. This is done to maximize deliverable acceleration through trunk and shoulder rotation and leg drive off the rear foot. But in basketball, where the need for accuracy far outweighs the need for power and acceleration, the forward foot is the one on the same side as the shooting hand. There is no need to develop large hip, trunk, and shoulder rotational momentum (mass × velocity about a pivot point; *see also ACROBATICS*).

Both feet should be pointed forward so that, whatever forces are imparted to the ball are all in the direction of the basket (no tangential forces to the left or right). The key concern for shooters is to "square up"—to point the eyes, shoulder, elbow, and wrist in a direct line to the basket. The less pronounced the limbs' actions are, the more accurate the shot, and the slower the velocity of the ball. (*The importance of a slower, controlled release is explained below, in "Physics of Shooting."*)

Two interesting aspects of physiology need to be considered with regard to shooting, especially free throws and wide-open shots. First, the ball should be rotated in the hands, not only to get a with-the-seams grip, but to stimulate touch pressure nerve receptors in the fingertips and joints. The fingertips have small, well-defined, receptive fields that provide precise information about the contours of the basketball indenting the skin. However, the joints have large receptive fields with obscure boundaries. Through fingertip and joint feedback, the ball's position in the hand is communicated to the shooter's brain for processing.

Second, there should not be too much delay before shooting. Basketball commentators will often attribute a missed wide-open shot to a player's "psyching" himself out because he hesitated—he took too long to think about the shot. Actually, this has more to do with mechanics than psychology. The biomechanist John Cooper reports that a pause longer than 1.7 seconds causes the body to lose some fluidity in its muscular coordination and efficiency of movement (Adrian, 1989). Pausing compromises efficient motor control.

Sighting

It might look as if good shooters aim, but what they really do is sight. Aiming involves the dividing of attention between pointer and target, a two-dimensional fix on a specific target (e.g., the back of rim, or a spot on the backboard). Sighting, on the other hand, involves locating, focusing on, and determining a target in three-dimensional space to correctly judge distance. In a matter of milliseconds, the brain controls motor movement during the shot. Shooters fix on the target in three-dimensional space, and the visual cortex of the brain computes an intercept trajectory.

Once sighting begins, the visual cortex continually updates a three-dimensional fix on the target. The smaller the target, the smaller the "fix point," and consequently, the greater the shooter's accuracy. The great difficulty during sighting is that there is no tangible target for the eyes to focus upon. Except for bank shots, a player shoots so that the ball goes through the hoop, rather than hits the hoop. Therefore, she must choose a part of the rim, usually just inside the back rim, or just over front rim. Comparing the sighting against experience, the visual cortex computes distance by focusing on texture, converging lines, and contrast.

This information is relayed by brain cells (neurons) to the motor cortex, which controls the muscle movements necessary to shoot. Neurons receive, analyze, and transmit information through communication channels called synapses. Practice enhances transmission across synapses, improving vestibular-ocular tracking (the ability to receive signals from the inner ear to track motion). Consequently, practice allows a player's shooting skills to improve dramatically as these synapses facilitate transmission of neural signals. The action is recorded and later fed back to the shooter. To take advantage of kinesthetic memory (memory of appropriate musculoskeletal movement), good shooters make a concerted effort to ensure the sighting point remains in constant focus from the moment they "square up" to shoot through the follow-through and release. The goal is to "feel" the ball through the hoop (*see also VISION; MOTOR CONTROL*).

Generating Force

From the light, 6-inch tip-in to the 30-foot "bomb," there is a great variety of shooting "touches" (proper thrust). For a typical shot, the shooter releases with a smooth wrist and finger motion, fully extending the elbow and shoulder through the follow-through. Alignment of the index and middle finger should be in a straight line pointing toward the targeted basket. The index finger should be the last finger that touches the ball, imparting backspin to the ball as it travels in the index finger's follow-through direction. The nonshooting hand should be placed on the side of the ball at about the nine o'clock position. As the shooter rises, the nonshooting hand, with fingers pointed up, drops away from the ball.

All forces imparted to the ball should pass through the fingertips. The fingertips control the ball by making fine-tuning adjustments in release trajectory and imparting backspin. Many experts believe fingertip feel and control become the ultimate determinant of shooting accuracy. Good shooters keep the ball on the fingertips and off the palm at all times.

Palm shooters are often poor shooters. If the ball remains in the palm instead of on the fingertips, the ball must be released more quickly and ends up being pushed, not shot. It is also difficult for palm shooters to impart backspin because the ball's center of gravity (mass concentration point) lies lower in the palm.

Players with extremely small or large hands have a hard time keeping the ball off their palms. This partly explains why Shaquille O'Neal, the 7-foot 1-inch Orlando Magic superstar, struggled to improve his free-throw shooting, which was only around 50 percent.

Accurate shooting also depends upon elbow extension, forearm follow-through, and wrist flex. Good shooters position themselves with a greater angle at the shoulder and a smaller angle at the elbow (*see Figure 1*). For set shots, in addition to the upper body motion, the legs also play an important role. As the shooter's legs thrust upward, she should rise to the balls of her feet as simultaneously as possible with the motion of her arm and wrist coming forward.

Musculoskeletal skills are slightly different for the airborne jump shooter because power cannot come from the legs and feet. Force (mass × acceleration) to elevate comes from the legs and feet, which means the arm, wrist, and fingers must provide most of the force for the shot. Because the lower body generates very little force

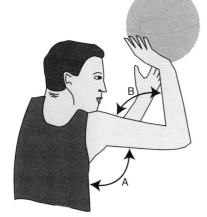

Figure 1. *One of the most identifiable features of a good shooter is his greater shoulder angle and smaller elbow angle. These angles not only are more efficient biomechanically, but also give good shooters a more advantageous higher release point.*

for the jump shot, shooting range is naturally less than that for a set shot.

Where a jump shooter's launch force comes from varies tremendously. Some players generate their launching force with just the wrist, some with the wrist and forearm, and others with the whole arm. There is no single correct combination. Instead shooters should remember one basic principle: keep the elbow under the ball—as perpendicular to the floor as possible—so that the ball does not carry left or right. Mechanically, it is very difficult to launch a straight trajectory with the elbow sticking out away from the body. The wrist and arm must generate force directly at the target and must also counter the tendency of the elbow to create a sideways force. Shooting with the elbow away from the body also tends to impart sidespin to the ball; thus, even if the shot is fairly accurate in direction, sidespin will cause a sideways carom on contact with the backboard or rim. This greatly reduces the probability of a "friendly" bounce.

Follow-Through: Balance and Timing

It is important that there is a constant sighting of the basket, from "squaring up" to follow-through. The buildup of the launching forces reaches a maximum on release, as the ball leaves the fingertips. To guide the ball onto its proper trajectory, these built-up forces need to diminish in a coordinated smooth motion, with the arm stretching out toward the basket. The shooter should finish with the wrist fully flexed (bent over with fingers pointing downward). After release, the shooter should freeze like a statue until the ball reaches the basket. This is not superstition. By remaining in place, a player develops consistent kinesthetic memory for touch at any given distance.

Balance, or body control, is an important aspect of shooting and varies tremendously depending on the shot. The running hook shot across the lane, the recovery required after a fast break one-hander, and a leaning and hanging jump shot where the ball is released well after the peak of the jump all require different body control skills. Only when a good shooter is properly balanced can he coordinate the efforts of each muscle to produce a net force in the direction of the basket. From the setup through the follow-through, there should be a smooth, continuous motion.

When one sees a "hot" shooter slightly sprain his ankle or knee, the importance of balance becomes obvious. His uninjured ankle or knee will provide more lifting force than the other. This results in an unbalanced vertical jump, which throws off his shot. However, with time and practice, the brain can adapt to the physiological change of the body. A good example of this is the National Basketball Association (NBA) legend Bernard King, one of the game's greatest jump shooters until a very severe knee injury sidelined him for over 2 years. Amazingly he turned in an all-star year upon his return for the 1991–1992 NBA season. Although his healthy leg provided more vertical lift than the rehabilitated leg, his kinesthetic memory adapted to

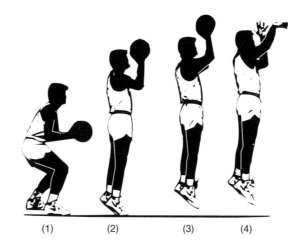

(1)   (2)   (3)   (4)

Figure 2. *A well-executed jump shot can be broken down into four stages. (1) The shooter sights the basket and crouches to begin the jump. (2) The legs extend, the wrists cocks, and the elbows align under the ball. (3) At peak height, the nonshooting hand drops away and the shooting arm straightens. (4) The wrist uncocks to release the ball, with the middle and index fingers following through toward the basket.*

the physiological change caused from the injury. He successfully developed a different balanced shooting position and consequently remained an excellent shooter.

In addition to balance, good shooters need to develop proper timing. For the set shot, good timing requires the development of one continuous fluid motion from the floor upward through the fingertip release. Although timing is important for successful set shots, it is critical for jump shots. There are two timing steps involved in the jump shot: the first when the lower body provides the force for the vertical jump, to elevate over the defender (the sum of ankle flex, knee extension, and hip extension); the second at the peak of the jump when the arm, wrist, and fingers provide the shooting force. Coordinating these motions takes a great deal of practice. When it is done well, it gives the illusion that the player is hanging in the air.

A jump shooter's balance is precarious. Any defect in this sequence of motion leads to a loss in accuracy, a lower release height, or improper release velocity. Even a minor head jerk can throw off a shooter's rhythm and adversely affect the trajectory of the ball.

Because many teams play at a "run-and-gun" frantic pace, it is imperative that their players learn to gather their balance and shoot quickly. The institution of the shot clock in college basketball has greatly accelerated the pace of games and has put a premium on getting the shot off quickly. No longer can teams just sit on the ball, waiting for the perfect shot. When the shot clock is ticking down, a player must release a shot quickly, often leaping in an off-balance position. He goes from a state of equilibrium, where any torque (rotational force around a fixed axis) exerted on the body is counteracted by an equal and opposite torque, to a state of disequilibrium.

Whether the player is airborne or not, the center of gravity of the body must be kept above the base of support. Great players will use the follow-through motion from the shot and other compensating limb actions to regain their equilibrium without falling. In comparison, a very young basketball player does not yet possess the ability to recover and finds himself in a state of extreme disequilibrium, usually resulting in a nasty fall.

In Search of "The Zone"

In game one of the 1991–1992 National Basketball Association finals between Chicago and Portland, Michael Jordan of the Chicago Bulls hit six 3-point shots in the first quarter. He sheepishly shrugged his shoulders in disbelief as one bomb after another fell through the net. Athletes credit shooting exploits like this to the player being in "the zone."

Scoring is a skill learned by imitation, trial and error, and constant practice. Good shooting is a marvel of human kinetics. It requires the shooter to consider the launch angle and correct launching speed for a variety of distances. In game situations, under pressure, the average professional player will hit slightly under 50 percent of his shots. If the player is left unguarded, his percentage increases to around 70 percent, and for free throws, the percentage is even higher.

It seems unbelievable that the human body can be trained to reproduce the required movements so accurately. The kinesthetic memory, or memory of movement, allows a shooter to recall and duplicate the shot. Although all experienced players possess the visual memory through both physical and mental practice, there is wide disparity among their shooting percentages. This disparity certainly can be traced to different skill levels, but a significant proportion can be attributed to lack of confidence: an inability to overcome self-doubt as a player prepares to shoot ("maybe I am aiming too long, or too short"). Thus, the zone may be nothing more than a relaxed state of concentration. While in the zone, athletes experience a heightened level of focused concentration in the brain, yet maintain a very relaxed muscle state in the body.

Since the early 1930s, scientists have known that the brain emits very faint electromagnetic emissions (about one-millionth of a volt) that can be detected by attaching several electrodes to the scalp. Simplifiers strengthen these signals and send them on to a computer for processing, enabling researchers to relate them to specific brain functions. Electroencephalography (EEG) measurements help doctors diagnose seizures, and a "flat" encephalogram is sometimes used as legal evidence of death. Sometimes an EEG pattern responds predictably to certain external stimuli, but often the brain-wave patterns become partly obscured by "noise," or interference, from other brain activities.

Some people can consciously control their brain emissions and, with training, can use this control in nearly superhuman ways. The U.S. Air Force has developed a computer that can detect and measure that part of the visually evoked response signal caused by a pilot's conscious sensory brain effort and translate it into instructions sent to motors that control a simulated airplane (Browne, 1995). The Air Force hopes that someday pilots will fly jets remotely by brain wave, eliminating some of the valuable milliseconds between visual processing in the brain (80 milliseconds) and motor action (115 milliseconds).

In a similar way, scientists at Syracuse University have questioned whether the zone can be identified and replicated (Waters, 1993). They have been monitoring the brains of shooters who are in the zone to identify distinguishable patterns in the flow and rhythm of their alpha wave patterns (the brain's electric wave activity). They theorize that the zone may be directly tied to alpha wave activity. If it becomes possible to specifically identify the alpha wave patterns responsible for the zone, it may be possible to train players to find the zone. If their efforts prove successful, brain wave monitoring equipment may someday be marketed to coaches as a cure for basketball shooting slumps and the poor putting streaks of golfers (*see also MOTOR CONTROL*).

John Zumerchik

The Physics of Shooting

There are several decisions shooters must make that involve physics. Players know that it is unwise to shoot with too high or too low an arc, with too little or too much backspin, or at too great a launch speed. However, even the best shooter seldom can offer a precise explanation. Good shooters develop their shooting style from hours of trial-and-error practice, developing a "feel" for an efficient range for speed, spin, and arc. Surprisingly, science concurs with much of the anecdotal explanations offered by players.

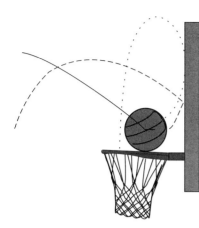

Figure 3. *Backspin increases the likelihood of a friendly bounce. Although two shots may be launched at the same angle and velocity, they may not bounce at the same angle and velocity. The ball with backspin (dotted line), the "softer" shot, is more likely to bounce off the rim and through the basket than the spinless shot (dashed line).*

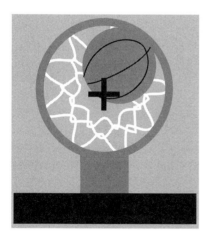

Figure 4. *The 29.5- to 30-inch circumference of the men's ball is slightly greater than half the diameter of the rim at its cross-section. Given that women's hands are smaller than men's and that the women's game is more of a finesse game than a power game, a smaller ball was adopted in the mid-1980s to improve ball handling and increase scoring. The women's basketball is 28.5 to 29 inches in circumference, about half the size of the hoop and 2 to 5 percent smaller than the men's ball.*

Value of Backspin

Announcers often use the term "friendly roll," or "lucky bounce," to describe shots that bounce on the rim several times before going in. Is there an explanation for the "friendly roll" phenomenon, or is it one of the great mysteries of the sport? One leading theory suggests that shooters who regularly get "friendly rolls" use greater than average fingertip action. Fingertip action helps in two major ways: it helps achieve better control because the ball will remain in the hand longer as the wrist flexes, and it helps the flexing wrist itself create more backspin.

Backspin is important because it creates a "softer" shot, the speed of which decreases from friction when contacting the rim. The ability to decrease ball speed upon contact with the rim results in what coaches call a soft shot. When a basketball with no spin bounces off a rim, it will bounce off with some forward spin and a negligible increase in speed. A ball with forward spin will bounce off with about the same forward spin and will speed up; a ball with backspin will bounce off with less backspin and a large decrease in forward speed. This large decrease in forward speed is what makes the ball more likely to bounce in than bounce away (*see Figure 3*).

Another great advantage of backspin is that it will slow the basketball in flight. Just as in baseball the spin of the curveball causes speed to decrease, and in tennis the backspin causes the ball to float and the speed to decrease, spin also affects a basketball's flight. Backspin decreases the air pressure above the ball and increases it below the ball, and as a result creates an aerodynamic lift force (the Magnus effect). This slows the forward speed of the ball even before it ever hits the rim and affects the trajectory, further exaggerating its parabolic flight path, so that the ball descends more vertically than a no-spin shot. If one is looking for a more "friendly" shooting style, she should consider learning how to increase the backspin on her shot (*see also VOLLEYBALL and GOLF*).

Shooting from the Field

The original objectives for the ball used by Dr. Naismith still hold today. He believed the basketball should be large and light, easy to handle, and difficult to conceal. While one is watching a game on television or in person, the ball is almost always in sight, and highly skilled players possess adept ball-handling skills—dribbling, passing, and shooting with uncanny ease.

Because the rim is 18 inches (45 cm) in diameter and the men's basketball must be 29.5 to 30 inches in circumference (the women's must be 28.5 to 29 in.), the ball is a little more than half the diameter of the rim (*see Figure 4*). This means that the ball does not have to travel in a perfect arc to fall through the basket. Thus shooters have a fairly generous margin for error and a range of different trajectories for scoring. Is there one launch angle and speed superior to all others? Probably not. The optimal arcs will vary with the height of the player (release point), shooting technique, and distance from

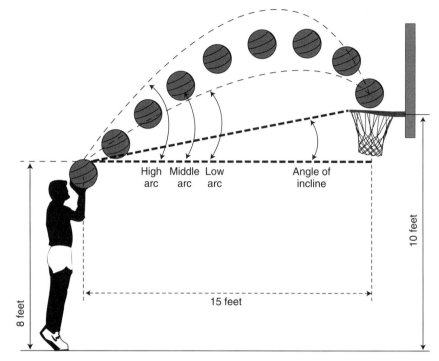

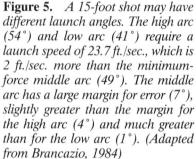

Figure 5. *A 15-foot shot may have different launch angles. The high arc (54°) and low arc (41°) require a launch speed of 23.7 ft./sec., which is 2 ft./sec. more than the minimum-force middle arc (49°). The middle arc has a large margin for error (7°), slightly greater than the margin for the high arc (4°) and much greater than for the low arc (1°). (Adapted from Brancazio, 1984)*

the basket. The interrelationship of these various factors makes the answer to this question far from simple.

Although a player must make a split-second determination about the type of shot to use and an appropriate launching force and angle, it is to the shooter's advantage to use as little force as possible. A smaller launching force means that the shot can be released quickly and with less effort. This is particularly important when a player is closely guarded and must attempt a quick jump shot over the out-stretched arm of a defender. Of course, it is also highly dependent on the shooter's distance from the basket. A layup from 2 feet away requires far less launching force than a 25-foot 3-point bomb.

If the launch point and the landing point are at the same elevation, the smallest launching speed to cover any set distance involves a 45-degree launch angle. But because no basketball player is tall enough to launch the ball from a height of 10 feet, a higher trajectory is necessary. Thus, the ball takes a parabolic flight path from, say, a 7- or 8-foot launch height to the 10-foot landing height of the rim, which means a launch angle greater than 45 degrees. The launching angle requiring the minimum force and maximum range is 45 degrees plus half the angle of incline (Brancazio, 1984; *see Figure 5*). Since incline is seldom more than 14 degrees, the optimal launch angle is between 45 degrees and 52 degrees. In short, shooters try to launch the ball high and let gravity take over in bringing the ball down through the hoop.

Another consideration is launch speed. The best shooters naturally develop a shot that uses the minimum-speed angle. In other words, for any launch angle, there is a range of launch speeds that will

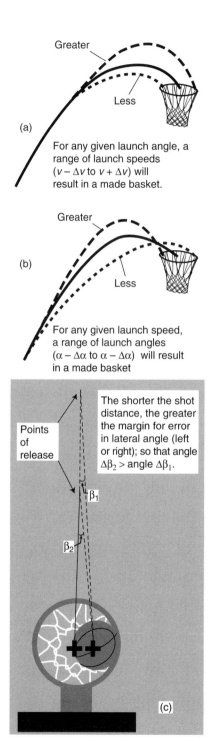

For any given launch angle, a range of launch speeds ($v - \Delta v$ to $v + \Delta v$) will result in a made basket.

For any given launch speed, a range of launch angles ($\alpha - \Delta \alpha$ to $\alpha - \Delta \alpha$) will result in a made basket

Points of release

The shorter the shot distance, the greater the margin for error in lateral angle (left or right); so that angle $\Delta \beta_2$ > angle $\Delta \beta_1$.

Figure 6. *Shot making requires the right combination of release velocity (a) and angle (b), while minimizing lateral error (c).*

result in a basket. Because the ball is smaller than the rim, a slightly higher speed shot will hit the back rim and drop through, and a slightly lower speed shot will graze the front rim and drop through (*see Figure 6*). The speed margin of error is greatest when the shot is launched at the highest possible angle. Thus, strictly from a speed perspective, a slower moving, high arcing shot is preferable to a line drive. Gravity does not discriminate: it exerts a force equally on a high arcing shot and on a line drive. Therefore, the line drive shot must be launched at a much greater velocity; if it were launched at the same velocity as the high arcing shot, it would fall well before the rim.

These results show the advantage of a minimum force shot, and, if one is to err, it is best to err with more arc rather than less. Historically, the best NBA shooters—for example, Larry Bird, George Gervin, and Alex English—have used a full range of arcing shots. They often resort to a very high arcing shot for longer range shooting. The high arcing shot has many advantages: it is difficult to block, it hits the rim with less forward speed (making it "softer" and more likely to bounce in), it has the largest margin for error, and biomechanically it is easier to release with greater backspin. Having the largest margin of error means the ball has a greater chance of going in if it is slightly off-center.

Since shooters have a larger margin for error the higher the arc, why not shoot with a high arc all the time? The answer is accuracy. Unfortunately, a higher arc usually results in a proportional loss of accuracy because the ball is taking a less direct path to the basket. The higher angle of entry that gives the greater margin for error requires much better release accuracy (*see Figure 7*). For example, during any type of target practice, such as darts, the impulse is to throw the object directly on a line toward the target. Throwing the ball on a line, instead of with an arc, significantly lowers the chances of missing the target high or low. However, because the basketball must rise and then drop through the basket, shooting at a basket is not really like target shooting. The lower the arc, the more likely it is that the shooter will hit the targeted rim; the higher the arc, the larger the margin of error. But the higher arc is also more likely to result in an error with regard to release speed or accuracy. For that reason, most players use a moderate arc, which gives them both accuracy and a fair margin for error.

Legendary shooters, such as Larry Bird, use many different arcs depending on the distance from the basket. Bird's strategy made sense. For shots close to the basket, a player is much more confident of his accuracy, so a lower trajectory is logical because a large margin of error is not needed. The farther away from the basket a player is, the more unsure he is about his accuracy. In this case, because the ball is less likely to be right on target, it is more useful to use a high-arcing shot, which gives the ball a greater margin for error. From years of practice, great NBA shooters acquire the refined "touch" to quickly measure distance; thus, their arc and shot repertoire is more varied than at the collegiate or high school level. In a fraction of a

Figure 7. *Shot making is not as easy as it may seem. The margin for error in shooting varies, depending on the angle of entry, the angle at which the ball approaches the rim. When the ball drops straight down (a), the shooter has a large margin for error. For a line-drive shot (d), there is little margin for error. The bottom of the ball must clear the front rim, but it must also clear at a slow enough velocity and a steep enough angle for the top of the ball to drop down and under the back rim.*

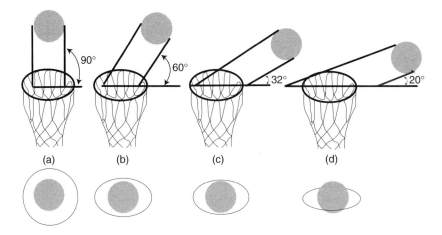

second, shooters decide between the accuracy of a lower trajectory and a less accurate high arc that has a greater margin of error.

Comparing Free-Throw Shooting Styles

Because of the comparatively mundane nature of free-throw shooting, it has been somewhat neglected compared with other game skills. Despite its vital importance (approximately 20% of all points are scored from the "charity stripe"), the free throw remains under-appreciated. Shooters have neither a hand in their face nor someone hurrying their shot, yet many players shoot a very poor percentage from the free-throw line.

Critics of the modern game claim a decline in the art of shooting. However, poor free-throw shooting is not a recent phenomenon. The average free-throw percentage of all NBA players has remained steady, near the 75 percent mark, since the late 1970s.

Coaches often can be heard stressing the importance of the free throw. No matter what the level of play—high school, college or professional—one of the most quoted lines from a losing coach is: "If we could only have hit a few more free throws . . . " A case in point was the tightly contested 1993 playoff series between the Chicago Bulls and New York Knicks: Were it not for the Knicks' poor free-throw shooting (around 60%), the Knicks, not the Bulls, might have advanced to the finals. According to several studies, the outcome of one-fourth to one-half of all games is decided at the free-throw line. The importance of the free throw has further increased in the NBA since the abolition of the bonus free throw (three chances to make two) in 1981.

Because of the one-plus-one rule—whereby a bonus is given for a make—used at the collegiate and high school level, good foul shooting is at an even greater premium. Total free throws taken and made varies tremendously between a 50 percent and a 90 percent shooter in the bonus situation. Assuming that each shooter takes 100 "front-end" free throws, the former player will make 50 of the 100 "front-end" attempts and 25 of the 50 "back-end" bonus attempts, for a mere 75 points. The latter will hit 90 of the first 100 "front-end" attempts, plus 81 of the 90 "back-end" bonus attempts, for a total of 171 points—a 96-point difference (*see also STATISTICS*).

Most coaches teach players to use the same form for the free throw as for the set shot. The rationale is that the player needs to learn and practice only one style of shooting for both the field goal and the free throw. Commonly called the overhand push shot, in which the ball is moved in a straight line from near the shoulder to the release point, this is primarily a one-handed shot, the other hand going into a supportive and directive role.

Despite the overwhelming use of the one-hander today, at one time two other free-throw styles competed with the overhand shot: the two-handed underhand and two-handed chest shot. In the two-handed chest shot, the ball is held symmetrically between two hands and moved from the chest to the release point. Except for a slightly lower release, the trajectory is basically the same as the one-hander.

In the underhand loop shot, the trajectory is entirely different from both the overhand and the chest shot. As in the two-handed chest shot, the ball is held symmetrically between two hands during the entire motion. What sets the underhand shot apart is its release point. The shooter starts his motion by slightly bending his knees, with the arms swinging the ball from just above the knees forward and upward in an arc. The knees straighten as the ball is released near the waist.

From a scientific perspective, the free throw occurs under controlled conditions (15 ft., abundant time, no defenders), making it ideal for studies comparing the different styles. Several studies conducted during the 1950s and 1960s indicated that the percentage of free throws made was the highest for the underhand shot, followed by the chest shot. This seems to suggest that the overhand shot is inferior. Ironically, these "better" methods were gradually abandoned in favor of the overhand style, first by the men's game (in the 1950s) and later by the women's game (in the 1970s and 1980s). The underhand shot is generally used only by small children, while the chest shot has virtually gone out of existence.

During the 1950s and the early 1960s Bill Sharman and Dolph Schayes were the dominant forces in NBA free-throw shooting. They collected 10 free-throw titles between them (Sharman 7; Schayes 3) using the chest shot. In the late 1960s and through the 1970s Rick Barry was practically the only player in the NBA and the ABA to use the underhand shot. Yet he set many free-throw records, including the most consecutive free throws made (60), the highest free-throw percentage in a season (94.7%), the highest career free-throw percentage in the NBA (90.0%) and seven free-throw titles in the NBA and the ABA. Among players active in the 1990s, the two-time free-throw champ Mark Price has used the overhand shot successfully in matching Barry's lifetime 90-percent average.

As prodigious as these shooters were and are, the greatest free-throw shooters historically have not been NBA players. Bunny Levitt, who played with the Harlem Globetrotters in the 1930s, was undoubtedly the greatest free-throw shooter of his time. He used the underhand style, but could also shoot behind his back, through his legs, and even blindfolded. He held the world record of 499 consecutive free throws for many years until a retired army officer, Ted St. Martin, broke his record. St. Martin, who never played college or professional basketball, repeatedly bettered his streak in reaching his world-record mark of 2,036 consecutive shots. As of 1996, he held the record for most shots made in a 24-hour period: 13,355. At first, St. Martin alternated between the overhand shot and the chest shot, but he eventually settled on the latter. He considered the chest shot the best style for him because it requires the least body movement. By minimizing body motion, he found it easier to consistently attain the best combination of launch speed and direction for accuracy.

Since the overhand and the underhand shots are so different from one another in style—both in biomechanics and in trajectory— several theoretical studies were undertaken to explore the underlying cause of the superior results obtained with the underhand shot (Tan and Miller, 1981; Brancazio, 1982; Tan and Taylor, 1982). Figure 8 shows the basic geometry of the two styles.

The most fundamental difference between the two shots lies in the locations of their release points. The release point of the underhand shot is considerably lower and farther away from the basket than that of the overhand shot. Consequently, the angle of incline from the release point to the center of the hoop is steeper for the underhand shot, and the range of the incline is also longer. The release points are of paramount importance because they determine most of the kinematic and trajectory (flight path) parameters of the

Free-Throw Woes

Although some of the tallest players in.the game, such as Wilt Chamberlain and Shaquille O'Neal, have been poor free-throw shooters, height is not necessarily a disadvantage. At a height of 7 feet, Jack Sikma turned in the leading NBA free-throw percentage in 1981, and many players like 6-foot-11-inch Bill Lambeer (83.7% career) have been among the NBA league leaders throughout their careers. Chamberlain attributed his poor free-throw shooting percentage (51% career) not to his height, but to focusing his strength training on developing only the areas of the body that appealed to him aesthetically. He blamed his unbalanced muscle development for adversely affecting his shooting (*see also STRENGTH TRAINING*).

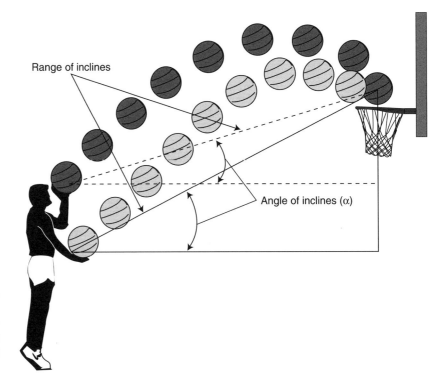

Range of inclines

Angle of inclines (α)

Figure 8. *Trajectories of the underhand and overhand free throw vary. The underhand shot has a steeper angle of incline and a longer incline range, and thus has to be launched at a greater velocity.*

shots. Once the release point is determined, the optimum flight-path characteristics of the two shots can be calculated from the laws of physics.

The trajectory of any shot is entirely determined by two physical quantities: the launch angle and the launch speed. First, the most accurate shot in basketball is a "clean shot," or "swish," in which the ball enters the basket without hitting the rim. There exists a minimum launch angle at which the ball will swish through the hoop. Any angle less than this minimum launch angle necessitates that the ball will hit the rim before falling through the net. Thus, for best results, the shot must be released at angles steeper than this angle. A *Sports Illustrated* study considered the optimum launch angle as the angle for which the launch speed is minimum (Durbin, 1977). However, a minimum launch speed requires the least muscular effort, so the assumption must be made that the shooter has a steady enough hand to maintain control while launching a slower shot. A minimum launch speed also provides the least air resistance because the ball is moving more slowly in relation to the air.

Among other criteria used for the optimum shot are the launch angles at which the allowable errors in the launch angle ($\Delta\alpha$), launch speed (Δv), and their product ($\Delta\alpha \, \Delta v$) are the greatest (Tan and Taylor, 1982; *see Table 1*). At these angles, the shooter has the luxury of making the greatest errors in launch speed, launch angle, or both, while still swishing the ball through the hoop. Apart from shooting the ball with proper launch speed and angle, the shooter also needs to aim properly in the forward direction. For any shot, there is a maximum allowable angle $\Delta\beta$ in the lateral direction that will still allow the ball to swish through the hoop. In three dimensions, the two mutually perpendicular angles $\Delta\alpha$ and $\Delta\beta$, respectively, define an error cone whose solid angle is $\pi\Delta\alpha \, \Delta\beta$.

The table summarizes the results of the above studies for an average NBA player who stands 6 feet 6 inches tall and wears size 13 shoes. For the overhand shot, the optimum launch angle according to all criteria is the same. The optimum launch angle for the underhand shot, on the other hand, is different for different criteria and an average value is entered. The smaller launch speed of the overhand shot, as explained earlier, makes it preferable to the underhand shot. The slower entry speed, on the other hand, favors the underhand shot, since it makes the shot "softer," which means it has a greater chance of falling in the hoop after bouncing on the rim.

Anecdotally, it is easy to understand that the shorter flight path and the shorter time of flight both will favor the overhand shot. The longer it takes a launched object to approach its destination, the greater air resistance it will encounter and the less accurate it will therefore be. The overhand shot allows a greater error $\Delta\alpha$ in the launch angle, whereas the underhand shot allows the greater error Δv in the launch speed. The overall edge (product $\Delta\alpha \, \Delta v$), however, goes to the overhand shot. Similarly, even though there is a slight advantage for the underhand shot in $\Delta\beta$, there is a huge advantage for the

OVERHAND AND UNDERHAND FREE-THROW SHOOTING:
A FLIGHT PATH COMPARISON

	Overhand	Underhand	Advantage
1. Angle of incline	11°	24°	
2. Inclined range	13.3 ft.	13.8 ft.	
3. Minimum launch angle for "swish"	46°	57°	
4. Launch angle for minimum launch speed	51°	58°	
5. Launch angle for maximum Δv	(*see* 15)	51° 58°	
6. Launch angle for maximum $\Delta \alpha$	(*see* 14)	51° 60°	
7. Launch angle for maximum $\Delta \alpha\ \Delta v$	51°	63°	
8. Optimum launch angle	51°	60°	
9. Entry angle	40°	47°	Underhand
10. Launch speed	22.6 ft./sec.	24.6 ft/sec	Overhand
11. Entry speed	18.6 ft./sec.	17.2 ft./sec.	Underhand
12. Length of trajectory (Flight path)	15.3 ft.	16.1 ft.	Overhand
13. Time of flight	0.91sec.	1.03 sec.	Overhand
14. Maximum error in launch angle ($\Delta \alpha$)	3.25°	1.30°	Overhand
15. Maximum error in launch speed (Δv)	0.11 ft./sec.	0.18 ft./sec.	Underhand
16. Product ($\Delta \alpha\ \Delta v$)	0.37° ft./sec.	0.24° ft./sec.	Overhand
17. Maximum error in lateral direction ($\Delta \beta$)	1.52°	1.56°	Underhand
18. Product ($\pi \Delta \alpha\ \Delta \beta$) (Solid angle of error cone)	0.0060	0.0024	Overhand

Key
Δ = change in
α = vertical angle
v = velocity
β = horizontal angle
In the language of mathematics, Δf signifies a small change in the value of f.

Table 1.

overhand shot in the product $\pi \Delta \alpha\ \Delta \beta$. Overall, the kinematic and trajectory advantages of the overhand shot outweigh those of the underhand shot.

The true strength of the underhand shot must be attributed to biomechanical factors, which more than compensate for its inferior kinematics and trajectory. First, it is easier to balance, control, and shoot the ball with two hands than with one. Second, in the underhand shot, the entire length of the arms goes into the swing, with the shoulder joint as the fulcrum. In contrast, only the forearm is rotated around the elbow joint in the overhand shot as the ball is pushed forward along a straight line. The error in the launch angle usually will be smaller when the hand moves in a larger circle, as in the underhand shot. Third, backspin is imparted more naturally with the underhand shot. This makes the underhand shot more likely to be the recipient of a "friendly" bounce off the rim. These subtle advantages of the underhand shot make it particularly suitable for children as their motor control develops.

As for the chest shot, it seems to have the best of both worlds: it has a flight path that closely follows the superior trajectory of the overhand shot, and the two-handed nature of the shot gives it many of the advantages of the underhand shot. Moreover, the chest shot requires the least body movement of all styles of delivery. According to Ted St. Martin (whose free-throw record was noted above) this minimizes errors in launch speed and direction.

Considering the advantages of the underhand and chest shots, it is perhaps surprising that these shots are almost exclusively playground shots. One explanation for the exclusive use of the overhand shot is that coaches want their players to improve all shooting—free throw, set shot, and jump shot—so they push players to use one form for all three. However, if the underhand and chest shots are superior, as studies indicate, and players do practice other specialty shots, like the hook shot, it might make sense to develop an additional shot for free throws as well.

Shots on the Move

Most basketball players remember with humor the first time they tried to shoot a running layup. They remember thinking that their shot was all lined up on the approach, and then watching as it ricocheted powerfully off the backboard with too much speed, completely missing the rim. The problem was that they failed to take the inertia of their body into account. Inertia is the tendency of a body in motion to stay in motion, so the proper way to shoot a layup is to release the ball vertically upward with respect to the body. This is accomplished either by calculating the forward speed of the body or by using the last step to gather balance and to decrease vertical inertia.

The same holds true in attempting a sweeping hook shot. If, for example, a shooter is moving from left to right across the middle of the lane, and if she does not take into account the left-to-right inertia, the ball will carom off the backboard too far to the right of center (too far in the same direction as the body). Of course, this advice is necessary only for beginners. Early on, skilled players develop a feel for what is happening as they shoot on the move and learn how to make appropriate adjustments.

Hang Time and Shot Blocking

Like magicians' levitation tricks, some players' jump shots and drives to the basket give the appearance of midair suspension. Referred to as "hang time," this is probably the most treasured of all skills among players, particularly around city playgrounds.

Because of good hang time, superstars can freeze a defense by double pumping jump shots, faking passes and then shooting, or switching from the right to the left hand and still scoring—all to the delight of their fans. Great leapers seem to hang in the air, but do they really defy gravity?

Actually, hang time is an illusion. As soon as the player's feet leave the ground, whatever upward velocity is attained immediately starts to decrease at 9.8 meters per second^2 (the acceleration of gravity). When upward velocity reaches zero, the player is at a maximum height. Once he begins to fall, he gains velocity at exactly the same rate. Time rising must equal time falling, with hang time being the sum of the two. If a player's center of gravity is the same at takeoff and landing, once he is airborne no amount of arm and leg flailing can change his hang time. Physicist and basketball fan Paul Hewitt calculated that even a prodigious flier like Michael Jordan, with a vertical jump of 1 meter, can stay airborne for only 0.9 second (Hewitt, 1994).

Good hang time is thus the result of a high-velocity takeoff, a combination of horizontal and vertical speeds, and airborne contortions that keep a player's center of gravity higher during descent—all of which fool fans into thinking he is hanging in the air for an unusually long period of time. He takes off with a high center of gravity and lands with a low center of gravity. Time rising will be less than time falling. Takeoff occurs in a fully extended position, and landing occurs with knees bent, which significantly increases the hang-time illusion.

The leaper's vertical speed is greatest when he first takes off and diminishes to zero as he reaches his peak. Shortly before and shortly after the peak, the vertical distance from the ground changes little, yet the leaper continues to move horizontally at a steady rate, creating the illusion of hanging in the air. In other words, the leaper is using his horizontal velocity, coupled with body contortions, to create an illusion. A high jumper in field athletics also creates such an illusion by raising her center of gravity. She contorts her body so that she clears the bar with her center of gravity at or below the height of the bar. To the observer, it seems that the high jumper is momentarily suspended directly over the bar (*see also FIELD ATHLETICS: JUMPING*).

When a player like Michael Jordan drives to the basket, with two or three defenders leaping vertically to block his shot, his hang time comes in handy. His hang time is greater because the vertical takeoff velocity is larger with a running jump than with a standing jump. Without a running start, gravity does not allow the vertical leaping defenders to stay airborne as long as Jordan, who arrives with vertical and horizontal velocity. Jordan's horizontal movement against the background of the defenders further enhances the illusion of hanging in the air (*see Figure 9*). It appears as if the defense will block the shot at point A or B, a point where most players must release the ball. However, Jordan's greater vertical takeoff velocity carries him past the defenders' extended arms to a point C, where he can release his shot. Michael Jordan seems to achieve extended hang time because of his rare motor skill ability to release the ball well after reaching his vertical peak (often raising his legs to delay touchdown), a point well beyond the defense. Jordan rarely gets his shot blocked because of his unique ability to release the ball at either points A, B, or C. Most players can only effectively shoot while rising (A), or at the peak of the vertical leap (B).

Coaches debate whether to teach young players to release the ball on the way up or at the peak of the jump. Many believe in releas-

Ball Movement and Hang Time

The ball's position plays a key role in the hang time illusion of stars like Michael Jordan. Jordan quickly raises the ball well overhead as he takes off toward the rim. As he rises to the peak of his airborne trajectory, Jordan slowly lowers the ball to near his waist (he goes up, the ball goes down). When he is descending, he again raises the ball. Although his center of gravity follows a parabolic path, he keeps the ball at about the same vertical height above the ground from the moment he takes off until he releases the ball.

Figure 9. *A combination of great hang time and superior motor skills is the reason a player like Michael Jordan rarely has his shot blocked. Most players release the ball either on the way up (A) or at the peak (B). Jordan can release the ball on the way up, at his peak, or on the way down (C). When he releases the ball on the way down, he does so about 0.6 second after leaving the ground. The vertically jumping defender, without horizontal velocity, can stay airborne for only about 0.5 second. Thus, good shot blockers must anticipate the shooter's release point and time their jumps appropriately. If a defender times his jump thinking Jordan will release at point B, he has no chance to block the shot if Jordan delays release until C.*

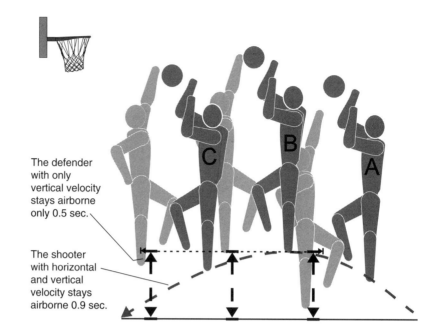

The defender with only vertical velocity stays airborne only 0.5 sec.

The shooter with horizontal and vertical velocity stays airborne 0.9 sec.

ing the ball at the peak of the jump because body movement is at a minimum. A steady state of zero vertical velocity is achieved—the upward vertical velocity and the downward force of gravity neutralize each other—which makes it easier to shoot accurately.

Although a release point at the vertical peak may be more accurate than any other release point, release on the rise has some strategic benefits. Many quick leapers like to release the ball on the way up, before the defender has a chance to react. For exceptional players like Michael Jordan, the debate does not apply. With equal effortlessness, he can release the ball on the way up, at the peak, or on the way down, and can make his decision based on which release point offers him the best "look" at the basket.

The best jump shooters are usually the ones that can feint, fake, and spin to create space between themselves and the defender. They need to negate some of the defender's inherent jumping advantages. Because the defender need raise only one hand, and does not have to raise a ball while jumping, he can jump much closer to his maximum height in attempting to block a shot. A defender who closes the distance between himself and the shooter—positioning himself closer to the point of release—greatly increases his chances of blocking the shot. In reality, shot blocking is as much about anticipation and good timing as it is about great leaping ability.

Raise the Basket to Twelve Feet?

Every year the average height of NBA and college players increases. As of 1996, the average height in the NBA has reached 6 feet 8 inches, and the jumping ability of most players allowed them to extend well

Figure 10. *The proposed raising of the basket to 12 feet would help the shorter players. There would be a five-fold increase in the taller woman's range (distance from release point to rim), but only a doubling for the shorter woman.*

above the rim. All but a few of the 324 players on the NBA roster could dunk the ball. When Dr. Naismith decided to set the baskets at 10 feet, he probably never imagined that someday top athletes would play the game "above the rim."

If the basket were raised to 12 feet, many wonder how the game would change. More specifically, who would benefit most, the shorter or taller players? There have been several attempts at experimenting with a raised basket. In 1932, Kansas coach Phog Allen and California coach Pete Newell experimented with 12-foot baskets. Though they reported that the higher baskets neutralized the taller players and made the game much faster, basketball in 1932 was quite different from the 1990s game and, more important, the average player was much shorter.

Regardless of the average height, some general conclusions can be made. First, raising the basket makes shot blocking less of a factor. The number of blocks would decrease because the optimal shooting trajectory for a 15-foot shot would increase from about 51 to 55 degrees or more. Taller players would no longer be able to block as many shots, or force the shorter players to adjust their shot trajectory as often. Conceivably, the upwardly adjusted shot to avoid a block for a 10-foot basket would be in the optimal trajectory range for a 12-foot basket. Shorter players could more often shoot at the optimal trajectory instead of having to shoot a higher arc to avoid having their shots blocked.

Second, the emphasis of the game would move farther away from the basket. The short-range shot would be far less automatic, especially for the taller players. It is a matter of scale (*see Figure 10*). A tall woman, who releases the ball 6 inches below a 10-foot-high rim, would be releasing the ball 30 inches below with a 12-foot rim, a five-fold range increase. Her shorter counterpart would not be penalized as much. If she released the ball 24 inches below the 10-foot rim, she would be releasing the ball 48 inches below a 12-foot rim, only twice the range.

Obviously, the short-range shooting percentage of both tall and short players would decline, with tall players experiencing a much greater drop. Strategy would also drastically change. No longer would coaches put such a premium on getting the ball inside to the tall player.

Passing

Passing is often called a lost art. Passing is about getting the ball to the right people at the right time. Much like shooting, it takes speed, spin, and touch. Passing is easy when the line of sight is direct, but it becomes an art when it is necessary to weave the ball past several defenders and into the arms of a teammate. Great passers—like John Stockton or the 1960s star Bob Cousy—are highly coveted, for a team's star center is worthless unless someone can pass him the ball. As great a center as Kareem Abdul-Jabbar was, his performance was twice as good when his teammates Oscar Robertson and Magic Johnson—two of the best passers of all time—were around to get him the ball.

Great passers use a variety of passes—the chest pass, the bounce pass, and the baseball pass—and are accurate with them all. The chest pass, or two-hander, is usually the first skill players are taught. As the name indicates, the ball is held close to the chest and is thrust forward. Young players sometimes have difficulty with this pass because they lack the wrist strength to quickly snap the pass out of their hands.

There are two primary reasons that a quick release is at a premium: it gets the ball to a cutting player while he is still open, and defenders have less time to adjust to the intended pass. Great passers, like Magic Johnson, rarely need to use the two-handed chest pass because they have very large hands, a distinct advantage in passing. In one swift motion, great passers take a high dribble and flip the ball over their opposite shoulder with pinpoint accuracy. In that split-second, thinking the passer will maintain his dribble, a defender does not even have enough time to put his hands up to block the pass. Although many players in the NBA predominantly rely on a one-handed pass because of the size of their hands, the same principles apply as for two-handed pass. A quick wrist snap with the index and middle finger maintains prolonged contact for control and velocity and the ball can be released well before the defender has a chance to react.

The bounce pass is a very effective pass in certain situations. Because the ball usually bounces near the feet of the defenders, the chance of a steal is greatly reduced. This pass also has a great advantage in that different combinations of spin imparted to the ball make "thread-the-needle" passes possible. Figure 11 shows the different rebound angles of two types of spins: forward and back. When the ball strikes the floor, friction causes a change in the ball's horizontal velocity and rotational motion. Regardless of the type of spin, there will be a loss in total energy. Backspin will cause greater loss than forward spin.

For the basketball bounced with no spin, friction will cause a

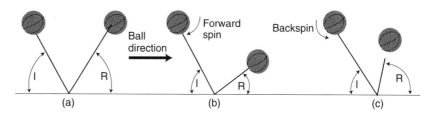

Figure 11. *For a ball with no spin contacting the floor (a), the angle of incidence (I) equals the angle of reflection (R). The angle of reflection is less than the angle of incidence with forward spin because there is less ball-floor friction (b). With backspin, the angle of reflection is greater owing to increased ball-floor friction.*

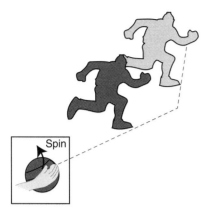

Figure 12. *On a fast break the "hook" bounce pass is often the pass of choice because it bounces near the feet of defenders and then bounces up near the intended recipient's waist. Passes received between the waist and shoulders are the easiest passes to catch.*

rotational force around the center of gravity, which means that there will be a decrease in forward velocity but an increase in rotational energy. Forward spin will cause an increase in the horizontal velocity, and the ball will bounce at a lower trajectory because the effects of gravity will be minimized. The ball will gain speed after bouncing and will rebound at a lower angle. Friction is greatest for the ball thrown with backspin (rotational energy directly counters horizontal velocity), so the backspin bounce pass will have the largest loss in horizontal velocity and rotational motion. It will usually reflect off the floor with a slight forward spin.

For a smooth ball bounced on a frictionless surface the angle of incidence equals the angle of reflection. That is, the ball will rebound upward at the same angle as it was thrown downward. However, basketballs have a rough leather grain, which increases friction with the floor, so that spin has a greater effect on rebound trajectory. Using backspin slows the ball and makes the rebound angle more pronounced than the delivery angle, while using topspin makes the ball accelerate and rebound at a lower angle. If the floor is well polished, it too will make a difference. With less friction at the point of contact, the ball will tend to skip more and stay lower (*see also BOWLING*).

"Hook" bounce passes are among the most exciting plays because they are almost exclusively used on fast breaks to bounce near the feet of the defender and reach a teammate without that teammate breaking stride. Players on the move take a high dribble, up near the shoulder, and push the ball forward and down with a combination of sidespin and topspin or backspin (*see Figure 12*).

In some ways hook bounce passes are analogous to trick shots in billiards. In billiards, spin is often imparted to curve the ball around another ball; in basketball, sidespin passes carry the ball around an opponent—the ball will kick left or right, long or short, depending on the spin imparted. For a left carry, the hand(s) are rotated counterclockwise at release so that the ball veers to the left after hitting the floor. For a right carry, the hand(s) are rotated clockwise.

Defense

If there is a secret to good defense, or at least one essential piece of advice, it would be to keep one's center of gravity low. Biomechanist John Cooper found that the center of gravity, measured from the floor, averages about 57 percent of a male's standing height and 54 percent of a woman's standing height (Cooper, 1987). When an offensive player uses the crossover dribble (left-to-right hand) to get the defensive player to shift her center of gravity too far left or right, the offensive player can dribble by the defender. It appears as if the defender is standing in cement shoes. That is why defenders fear having to guard someone with a lightning-quick crossover dribble. A good dribbler gets her defensive opponent leaning left with a quick

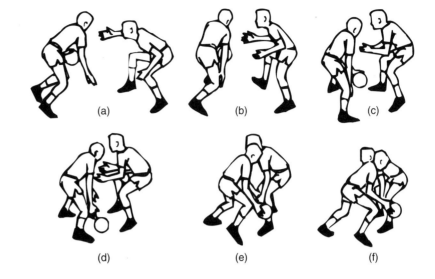

Figure 13. *A quick crossover dribble is one of the most difficult moves to which a defender can react. The dribbler starts moving to his left (a), which requires the defender to cut off, or intercept, the dribbler by matching his movement left (b). The crossover move (c and d) allows the dribbler to move past the defender caught off-balance, leaning too far to the left. The dribbler now has a clear path downcourt (e and f).*

first step. Then as the defender shifts her center of gravity, she uses a quick crossover dribble to blow by the other way before her opponent can readjust and recover (*see Figure 13*).

When a shooter receives a pass and prepares to shoot, the defensive player must raise his center of gravity to contest the shot as he straightens up. Now the body is too erect (the center of gravity is too high) and the feet are too close together to quickly recover. With a quick pump fake, the offensive player can dribble right by the defender. One of the offensive players most proficient at this move was Larry Bird. Because he was 6 feet 9 inches and an extremely accurate shooter, it was imperative that the defender raise his center of gravity, often having to rise off his toes, to contest the potential shot attempt. Bird's high field goal percentage made this necessary even when the defender knew it was highly probable that he would only fake the shot.

A higher center of gravity is also the reason centers have a hard time guarding smaller forwards and guards. The smaller man's lower center of gravity allows him to initiate movement more quickly. A taller player can compensate for this disadvantage by lowering his own center of gravity and spreading his feet farther apart to improve his lateral mobility and speed. This is easier for an athlete with proportionally longer legs, who can lower his center of gravity with a wider base of support, than for someone with shorter legs and a longer torso. One does not need long legs to play basketball, but it is a physical attribute that comes in handy while playing defense.

John Zumerchik and Arjun Tan

References

Adrian, M. and J. Cooper. *Biomechanics of Human Movement*. Indianapolis: Benchmark, 1989.

Braman, B. "Shooting the Three-Pointer." *Popular Mechanics*, June 1994.

Brancazio, P. "Physics of Basketball." *American Journal of Physics* 49, no. 4 (1981): 356–365.

Brancazio, P. *Sports Science*. New York: Simon and Schuster, 1984.

Browne, M. "How Brain Waves Can Fly a Plane." *New York Times*, 7 March 1995.

Cooper, J. *Basketball: Player Movement Skills*. Indianapolis: Benchmark, 1987.

Cousy, B. *Basketball: Concepts and Techniques*. Boston: Allyn and Bacon, 1983.

Durbin, E. J. "Free-Throw Styles." *Sports Illustrated*, vol. 47 (26 Dec 1977): 25 and 124.

Garwin, R. "Kinematics of an Ultraelastic Rough Ball." *American Journal of Physics* 37 (1969): 88.

Hewitt, P. *Conceptual Physics*. Needham Heights, Massachusetts: Allen and Bacon, 1994.

Miller, S., and R. Bartlett. "The Relationship between Basketball Shooting, Kinematics, Distance, and Playing Position." *Journal of Sports Science* 14, no.3 (1996): 243–253.

Northrip, J., G. Logan, and W. McKinney. *Biomechanic Analysis of Sport,* 2nd ed. Dubuque, Iowa: Brown, 1979.

Tan, A., and G. Miller. "Kinematics of the Free Throw in Basketball." *American Journal of Physics* 49, no. 6 (1981): 542–544; Brancazio, P. "Comments on Kinematics of the Free Throw in Basketball." vol. 50, no. 10 (1982): 944; reply, A. Tan and K. Taylor. "Reply to Comments on Kinematics of the Free Throw in Basketball." vol. 50, no. 10 (1982): 946.

Waters, M. "Brain Study Seeks 'The Zone.'" *Post-Standard*, 14 September 1993.

Williams, J. *Color Atlas of Injury in Sport*. Chicago: Yearbook Medical Publishers, 1980.

Bowling

AS A PARTICIPATORY SPORT, bowling has few equals in the United States. Though it may not possess the lure of a more glamorous sport such as golf or tennis, it has an avid following. Bowling has three advantages that are difficult to match: it can be enjoyed equally by young and old, it requires a minimum of space, and it is not dependent on the vagaries of the weather. According to the American Bowling Congress (ABC), approximately one out of three Americans has tried bowling, about 53 million bowl at least once a year, and in 1995 5 million Americans participated in league bowling.

There are many different forms and variations of bowling: lawn bowls, boccie, skittles, and ninepins, to name just a few. The principles of physics that affect a rolling ball on a uniform surface are the same for any of these games, but the collision with pins as in skittles or ninepins adds a certain randomness—a mixture of skill and chance. This element of chance may explain why bowlers might be tempted to try their luck against a more skilled opponent, and it may be a substantial reason for the popularity of bowling.

For thousands of years, games have existed that involve balls of stone and wood rolled at objects and at each other, although written records and artifacts that chronicle bowling as an important pastime of antiquity are sparse. In an Egyptian tomb dated approximately 5200 B.C.E., archeologists discovered, among other objects, close likenesses of today's bowling balls and pins. Early Germans commonly carried an all-purpose club, for fighting, for various contests, or for just hammering something. This club was called a *kegel*, and the person who used it was a *kegler*, a term sometimes applied to a present-day bowler. The kegel was also used for a religious purpose: it was considered to be proof of a chaste life. The kegler was required to place his club at the end of a long aisle in the cloister of the church, then to knock it over by rolling a round stone at it. If the kegler failed, he had to return for another test, since he was not yet considered pure enough to enter the church. This practice was eventually adapted into a recreation. Definite rules governed the games, though these rules varied from place to place. For example, only three pins were used in some parts of Germany, while other areas preferred as many as seventeen.

In England, there is evidence of significant interest in bowling among the nobility during the Elizabethan era. Apparently, women as well as men bowled, since in Shakespeare's *Richard II*, an attendant suggests to the queen that she engage in a game of bowls. She declines, though, making a perplexing statement: "'Twill make me think the world is full of rubs, and that my fortune runs against the bias." "Bias" probably refers to weighting or shaping the ball so that it would hook more. It seems, then, that the effects of asymmetrical balls were known at least a century before Isaac Newton, the father of mechanics, proposed his laws explaining how it all worked. Furthermore, this knowledge existed five centuries before computers would make such an application of Newton's laws feasible.

There is a wealth of fascinating folklore behind the number of pins used in bowling. Martin Luther (1483–1546), who led the Protestant Reformation in Germany and was evidently an avid bowler himself, lent a bit of theological reasoning to the choice of the number of pins. After some experimentation, he concluded that the ideal configuration was nine pins set up in a three-by-three square with one corner toward the bowler. Perhaps this square of three held some significance for him because he associated it with the Christian Trinity. Whatever the reason, bowling remained for the most part the game of ninepins in Europe and later in the United States until the mid-nineteenth century.

From about 1835 to 1840, bowling became very popular from New England southward to Washington, D.C. Gamblers wasted no time devising ways to cash in on this game of skill and chance. Matches were conducted for enormous side bets, and it did not take long before disgruntled bettors protested what they considered "sell-outs." Things reached such a rancorously hostile pitch in Hartford and New Haven that the Connecticut legislature in 1841 passed a law banning the game of "bowling at nine pins." The sport quickly lapsed until a few sportsmen, who apparently enjoyed the game for its own sake, worked out a plan for bowling at ten pins, subtly circumventing the law that was aimed specifically at "nine-pin bowling." The change was a lasting one, creating what most twentieth-century Americans call bowling.

The Basics

The objective of bowling is quite simple: roll a ball, 8.5 inches (about 21 cm) in diameter and weighing between 10 and 16 pounds (4.5 to 7.2 kg), down a 60-foot (18-m) lane to knock down all ten pins in a triangular array (*see Figure 1*).

Bowling strategy centers on the headpin, because it is nearly impossible to knock down all the pins without first hitting the headpin. When the massive ball thunders into the much lighter pins, it must drive the pins somewhere. Pins scatter sideward and backward toward the pit behind the pin deck. Once the ball passes the headpin, then, the probability of a chain reaction among the pins that would

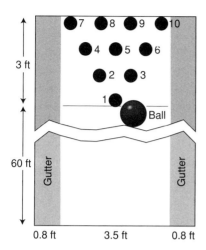

Figure 1. *The bowling lane is 60 feet long, from the foul line to the head pin, and only 3.5 feet wide. To knock down any pins at all, the ball must stay on the lane—an error of only 1.7 degrees to the right or to the left results in a "gutter ball." The ten pins are arranged in a triangular formation, with the headpin at the apex, toward the bowler, and with four pins forming the base of the array, along the tail of the pin deck. The pin deck adds 3 feet to the lane, and the approach to the foul line another 15 feet, for a total lane length of 78 feet.*

cause a pin to topple forward and knock down the headpin is slim indeed. Such a chain reaction is not impossible, however. It does not violate any known laws of physics, since the pins easily topple over from a standing position to the more stable state of lying down; it does require, though, a series of remarkably lucky pin collisions. Actually, more than a few people have claimed just such a feat.

Since each pin has a diameter of about 4.75 inches (slightly less than 12 cm), one-ninth the width of the lane, it seems logical that hitting the headpin should be more difficult than avoiding the gutters, which are almost 10 inches (25 cm) wide. On the other hand, the size of the ball greatly increases the effective size of the target, which equals the diameter of the ball (8.5 in.) plus the diameter of a pin (4.75 in.), a total of 13.25 inches (about 33 cm). To hit the headpin, the ball—as viewed by the bowler—must have a trajectory within 0.5 degrees of the center line. However, to knock down all ten pins, the bowler should not hit the headpin directly but should find the all-important "strike zone," the "1-3 pocket." This important area, approximately 4 inches (10 cm) wide, lies in the space between the pins numbered 1 and 3 (for left-handed bowlers, the strike zone is the 1-2 pocket). To hit this pocket requires high precision, for the ball's margin of error is less than 0.16 degrees.

According to professional bowlers, the probability of a strike—knocking down all ten pins with one throw—is maximized by rolling the ball into the 1-3 pocket and "hooking" the ball at an angle of about 6 degrees right to left. (For a left-handed bowler, the direction of hook and the position would be reversed. From here on, however, this article will assume a right-handed bowler.) It is not possible, even with the widest sweeping hook, for the ball to hit every pin. Therefore, good "pin action" is required to knock down the pins that the ball misses. Much of bowling folklore centers on ways to throw a hooking ball and the dynamics of good pin action. A majority of this folklore can be explained because it adheres to proven principles of physics, yet much does not, lying instead in the realm of pure fiction.

The most coveted achievement, and the one most steeped in folklore, is rolling a perfect game—a "300" game, consisting of twelve consecutive strikes. Even though only 120 pins are knocked down in such a game, bonuses result in a count of 300 pins. Perfect games are rare, of course; the probability of a perfect game is one in about every 20,000 sanctioned league matches.

Most matches involve a three-game series. A distant dream, even among the elite who compete in the Professional Bowlers Association (PBA) tour, is to throw a perfect series: three perfect games in a row, for a count of 900. This has been achieved a few times, but each one of these series has been disqualified by the American Bowling Congress (ABC) on controversial technicalities. The two most common grounds for disqualification are that the lane was not oiled uniformly enough and that the three games of a series were ruled to not be in the same tournament. Some people believe that the ABC unfairly guards this goal. Skeptics reason that without it, many play-

Bowling Ball Specifications

The bowling ball is specified by the ABC to have the following characteristics:

Circumference: Circumference may not exceed 27 in. (68.6 cm), or a radius of 4.3 in. (10.9 cm).

Weight: Total weight, or mass, may not exceed 16 lb. (7.26 kg).

Shape: The ball must have a constant diameter—it must be spherical in shape.

Imbalance: The ball can have an imbalance of not more than 10 lb. (3.73 kg), of not more than 3 oz. (93.3 g) along the finger-hole diameter, and of not more than 1 oz. (31.1 g) along any other two perpendicular axes. This would shift the center of gravity—the point at which all the weight can be considered to be concentrated—a maximum of 0.08 in. (0.2 cm) from the geometrical center for a 10-lb. (7.26-kg) ball, and proportionately less for a 16-lb. (7.26-kg) ball.

Dynamic imbalance: The radii of gyration—for a particular spin axis, the distance from the geometrical center at which the mass may be concentrated in a ring to determine the moment of inertia [the resistance to changes of spin about that axis] must be between 2.43 and 2.80 in. (6.17–7.11 cm). The radii of gyration can be adjusted by using various shapes and densities for the core of the ball. For a uniform ball, the radius of gyration is 2.72 inches.

ers would lose much of their motivation for the game and defect to other recreations.

Bowling can be broken down into three phases: (1) the throw of the ball, (2) the roll of the ball, and (3) the scattering of the pins. The following sections examine the underlying physics behind each of these aspects.

Throwing the Ball

The ball, despite being very massive, must be launched with high speed for good pin action. This may seem a formidable task to a beginner hurling a 16-pound ball for the first time. To throw with good speed and avoid undue muscle exertion, it is necessary to take advantage of the considerable force of gravity on the ball by using an underhand motion with a fully extended elbow.

At the start of the throw, the bowler gives energy to the ball by lifting it slowly, with both hands, up to about chin height while facing the pins and aiming the ball. The bowler then pushes the ball forward, extending the arm holding the ball and steping toward the foul line. In large part the ball falls by its own weight: first, swinging downward behind the bowler as the bowler's shoulder drops, and then swinging forward to the point of release.

The throwing motion is much like a pendulum attached to a forward-moving support. The pendulum (ball and arm swinging from the shoulder joint) efficiently converts the potential (positional) of the lifted ball into kinetic (motional) energy at the launch. The higher the ball is lifted, the faster it will go. These dynamics make it possible for even a bowler of only moderate strength to throw the ball with a speed of 30 feet per second (9.1 m/sec.).

Ball velocity is important, but its effectiveness reaches a point of diminishing returns. Greater speed produces more pin action, but a speed of 20 to 25 feet per second is more than adequate to produce effective pin action. "Power" rollers are unlikely to believe this, but increasing the ball's velocity by 5 to 10 feet per second, though visually impressive, is only marginally more effective at increasing pin action—and it is even less effective if one considers the resulting loss of precision and decrease in hook. The minuscule margin of error (0.16°) for hitting the pocket and the need for a good hook make precision much more important than speed, and professional bowlers wisely choose not to throw the ball as hard as they can.

Owing to the conservation of energy, an object that is lifted up to a certain height and then allowed to swing back down to floor level, from an extended arm in a pendulum motion, has the same speed as an object dropped from the same height. In either case, the object's gravitational potential energy is efficiently converted into kinetic energy. If the object is lifted to, for example, 5 feet, this energy conversion results in a velocity of 18 feet per second. Adding the speed of approach of the bowler toward the foul line (typically 5 ft./sec.) sends the ball down the lane at 23 feet per second, which is entirely adequate for excellent pin action. With good technique, taking advantage of the pendulum-like motion, the ball can be launched with very little strain.

Of course, styles of throwing are as varied as the number of bowlers. Some lift the ball to the chin; others lift it only to the waist. Some push the ball forward with their first step; others just let it drop. Almost all professional bowlers use four or five steps in their approach to the foul line. A beginner might use no steps, which results in a much slower ball. No matter how the ball is thrown, it takes practice to manage the footwork and to time the approach to correspond to the natural pendulum motion.

The period of a pendulum swinging in a 3-foot arc is about 2 seconds (*see Figure 2*). It is no coincidence that the throwing motion also takes place over about 2 seconds, since it involves the pushing motion plus three-quarters of a period of the pendulum (swinging front to back for half a period, and then down to the lowest position of release for another quarter of a period). This period depends neither on the mass of the ball nor on how high the ball is initially lifted, since the period of a pendulum depends only on the square root of its length. The bowler, in the 2 seconds of the throw, covers about 10 feet of approach at the typical speed of 5 feet per second while executing the throwing motion, then 2 or 3 feet more to stop and avoid stepping over the foul line. The minimum available approach of 15 feet, specified by the ABC, is thus consistent with the requirements for a smooth launch of the ball at an optimum speed. The four-step approach is the stepping pattern most likely to result in a smooth motion (*see Figure 3*).

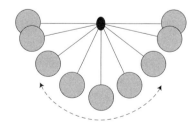

Figure 2. *A ball tied to a 3-foot-long string will take about 2 seconds to swing all the way back and forth. Therefore, a throwing motion that takes less than 2 seconds from start to finish will be rushed, not allowing the ball to swing from its own weight (inertia).*

Figure 3. *The four-step approach is the most popular approach because this step pattern best fits in the approximate 2-second time frame of the pendulum motion of the ball.*

The moving approach in bowling is used for the same reason that a javelin thrower uses a running launch: to get more speed (*see also FIELD ATHLETICS: THROWING*). However, the javelin thrower does not have to coordinate footwork with swinging a 16-pound pendulum. The pendulum-like motion of the typical throw of a bowling ball adds a constraint that limits the useful length of approach—how far the bowler can move while the ball makes one swing back and forth (2 seconds) while still stopping short of the foul line. That constraint is, for most bowlers, about 15 feet. A much shorter approach would greatly reduce the speed at which the ball could be thrown; a much longer approach would be of minimal benefit, as many bowlers do not use the full 15 feet available, simply because they do not or cannot move that far in 2 seconds.

The pendulum concept is helpful for achieving accuracy in throwing. Instructors recommend that instead of aiming at the pins, a bowler should line up the pendulum from a particular spot at the start of the approach and release the ball to pass over a particular target arrow. These target arrows, embedded as a pattern between 12 and 16 feet from the foul line, make it possible for a bowler to roll the ball without even glancing at the pins. In fact, a bowler has thrown a perfect game with a curtain dropped halfway down the lane, hiding the pins. The pendulum motion is effectively a free swing from 12 feet behind the foul line to 12 feet beyond the foul line. This 24-foot line is more than ample to ensure consistency from throw to throw. The bowler can make small adjustments in the initial position in relation to the target arrows to fine-tune the aim of the ball. Assuming an error of plus or minus 0.75 inch (2 cm), this target-arrow method has a precision of plus or minus 0.16 degrees, accurate enough to hit the pocket every time.

Whether an athlete uses an overhand or underhand throwing motion, it is virtually impossible to throw any type of ball without spin. Throwing a bowling ball is no exception. The natural pendulum motion described above results in a small amount of backspin on a horizontal axis parallel to the foul line. To produce certain desirable

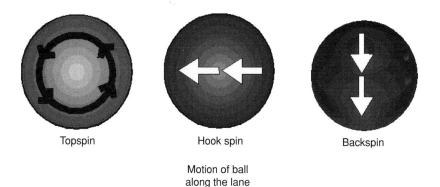

Topspin   Hook spin   Backspin

Motion of ball
along the lane

Figure 4. *The arrows depict the relative motion of the top surface of the ball for the three components of spin as viewed from above (looking down on the ball).*

effects, bowlers enhance this spin and also add spin around two other axes (*see Figure 4*). Increasing backspin, for example, increases the distance the ball slips on the lane before it starts rolling and can increase the total hook. Spin around the axis parallel to the lane, or hook spin, is the primary means of hooking the ball. Vertical-axis spin, or topspin, makes some difference in the way the pins scatter but has no effect on the hooking of a balanced ball. For a weighted ball, however, topspin can influence the hook of the ball by gyroscopic effects, which will be explained later.

Hook spin is most easily given to the ball by releasing the thumb first so that the fingers on the right side of the ball can create an off-center force, causing the ball to spin left. A ball thrown in any conventional manner will initially slip as it is released on the slick lane surface; it would require an extremely awkward motion to throw a ball with enough forward spin so that it begins rolling immediately. The natural motion of a right-handed bowler is to hook the ball to the left, at the same time imparting topspin and a little backspin. In launching the ball, the bowler does not think about three different spins, just as a baseball pitcher does not think three-dimensionally in throwing a curve ball. With one smooth swing of the arm, a twist of the hand and wrist, and perhaps a last-second flick of the fingers, the bowler releases the ball, sending it spinning down the lane. Only after the ball has been released can scientists begin to divide the ball's spin into three components (backspin, hook spin, and topspin) to evaluate the dynamics involved.

The Path of the Ball

As the ball travels down the lane, any deviation from a straight line or any change in speed is caused by the forces acting on it in accordance with Newton's laws of motion. The situation is two-dimensional (forward and backward, left and right), but not three-dimensional (up and down), because the upward contact force of the floor counters the downward force of gravity to keep the geometrical center of the ball at a constant height. Professional bowlers intentionally "loft" the ball a little in order to keep it from contacting the first 2 or 3 unoiled feet of the lane. This very common practice results in a few short bounces, but it produces behavior only minimally different from a smooth launch. For simplicity, this presentation assumes a smooth launch of the ball with little or no bouncing and with an average upward contact force equal to the weight of the ball.

The force that has the most significant effect on the path of the ball is friction at the sliding contact between the ball and the lane. The lane is dressed, or oiled, for the first 30 to 40 feet so that the ball slides easily at least halfway down the lane. When it reaches the undressed (unoiled) part of the lane, sometimes called the rug, the frictional force increases to the point that the ball usually stops slipping and starts rolling in a short distance. Scientists determine frictional forces between surfaces by measuring the coefficient of friction, the ratio of the frictional force to the normal force (upward in this case). A coefficient of 0 means that there is no frictional force at all; a coefficient of 1 means that the frictional force is the same as the normal force; for very rough surfaces, coefficients can be greater than 1. Typical coefficients of friction encountered by the ball are: oiled lane, 0.03–0.08; dry lane, 0.12–0.25; rolling without slipping, about 0.005.

Bowlers have considerable latitude to roughen the ball's surface to make the coefficient of friction greater or polish it to make the coefficient of friction smaller. The only restriction is that the coefficient must remain below 0.39 on the dry part of the lane. This upper limit is a large coefficient, but it represents no inherent advantage, because a coefficient of as little as 0.2 ordinarily ensures that the ball will be rolling, not sliding, when it reaches the pins. In fact, bowlers usually prefer a coefficient lower than 0.39 because a coefficient that high delays the hook. All bowlers, for the sake of precision, benefit from a late hook (*see section on Pin Collisions*). The rolling coefficient of friction (the frictional force that opposes rolling without slipping) for a bowling ball on a level surface is very small and can be ignored. With a typical rolling coefficient of only 0.005, a ball rolled at 20 feet per second would go 1/4 mile (400 m) before it came to a stop. Stringent ABC specifications—1 part in 1,000 for the tilt of the lane and levelness within 40/1,000 inch for the length—rule out any significant effects of rolling either across the lane or "downhill."

Wind resistance on a bowling ball traveling at 30 feet per second (about 20 miles per hour, MPH; or 32 KPH), is about 0.2 pound (0.09 kg). In comparison with surface friction, this is less than half the friction on a well-oiled lane and a little over twice the rolling friction. The wind resistance would slow a 16-pound ball traveling at 30 feet per second by only about 0.8 feet per second in 60 feet. Wind resistance varies as the square of the velocity, so its force decreases quickly as the speed of the ball decreases. A slightly lower velocity of 21 feet per second (14 MPH, or 22.4 KPH) results in a tremendous drop in wind resistance, to only 0.1 pound (0.045 kg). Wind resistance is not entirely negligible, but it plays a small role in the most interesting aspects of the path of the ball—where and in which direction the ball hits the pins. The wind resistance is directly opposite the motion of the ball, and thus does not significantly affect either the ball's hook or its spin.

Effects of Spin

Although the components of spin—backspin, hook spin and topspin—of the ball change as it makes its way toward the pins, the hooking of a uniform bowling ball occurs entirely from the spin imparted upon release. A variety of units can be used to measure spin. The most common are radians per second (rad/sec.) and revolutions per minute (RPM). Both radians and revolutions measure angles the ball has turned. In one revolution of turn, a rolling ball would advance by its circumference, whereas in one radian of turn, a rolling ball would advance by its radius. RPM is the more common measure, but in many cases radians per second is more enlightening; there is a simple relationship between the spin in radians per second and the speed of the surface of the ball (relative surface speed = radius × rad/sec.).

To get a better idea of the spin of a ball relative to its speed, it is also useful to express the rate of spin as the surface speed of the ball relative to its center (ignoring RPM or rad/sec. altogether). This is a much more direct way of expressing spin. For instance, to say that a ball rolling without slipping at 20 feet per second is spinning at 20 feet per second is easier to interpret than saying that the same ball is spinning at 55.9 radians per second or 351 revolutions per minute.

A ball released with backspin slides along on the well-oiled lane, rotates backward for awhile, then stops its backspin and begins to pick up forward spin, and finally ends up rolling without slipping. The rate at which the ball goes from backward to forward spin depends on the coefficient of friction. Consider a typical example: a ball thrown at 25 feet per second with a backspin of 5 feet per second on a standard oiled lane (coefficient of 0.05 for the first 40 ft. and 0.20 for the last 20 ft.). It will rotate backward for 30 feet, after which it will reverse and rotate forward. By the time it hits the dry area after 40 feet, its forward velocity will have dropped to 22.3 feet per second and its forward spin will have increased to about 2 feet per second. After about 18 feet of slipping on the dry area, it rolls (without slipping) into the pins at a speed reduced to 16.4 feet per second. Whenever any ball rolls without slipping, the rate of forward spin exactly matches the forward speed.

The dynamics of a ball slipping for such a long distance are important because of the very narrow lane and the necessity of causing the ball to arrive at the pins at a relatively sharp angle—about 6 degrees—to maximize the probability of knocking down all the pins. If the lane were two or three times as wide, bowlers would not have to worry about how far the ball slips or about hook angles. They could just step to either side of a wider lane and throw the ball

Three Ways to Measure Rotation (Spin) Rate

Rate of rotation of a bowling ball can be expressed as degrees per second, radians per second, or revolutions per second. Angular velocity can be measured in degrees or radians because:

$$2 \pi \text{ radians} = 360° \text{ (circle)}$$

Angular frequency is measured by revolutions per second or minute (RPM).

$$\text{Angular velocity } (w) = \text{angle traversed/time interval}$$

$$\text{Angular frequency } (f) = \text{number of revolutions/time interval}$$

Angular velocity measured in radians (w) is related to angular frequency measured in revolutions (f): $w = 2 \pi f$

at the desired angle, straight into the 1-3 pocket, without resorting to a hook.

Because slipping is a critical characteristic for a hooking ball, bowlers continually experiment. The distance of slipping can be increased by increasing either the amount of backspin or the speed of launch. Of course, the amount of slipping also can be decreased by decreasing either of these variables.

Another option bowlers can consider in controlling the slipping distance is the smoothness of the ball's surface. Virtually every bowling center has machines that smooth a ball's surface to lower its coefficient of friction, or abrade its surface to raise its coefficient of friction. Most professional bowlers have more than one ball, each with a different degree of roughness or smoothness. After a few practice throws, they select the one that best suits the lane on which they happen to be bowling. There is no rule against changing balls in the middle of a game, but it is thought wiser to make adjustments in the way a familiar ball is thrown than to switch from ball to ball.

The ball's moment of inertia also affects how far it will slip on the lane before it begins to roll without slipping. The moment of inertia determines the torque (twisting force about an axis) necessary to get a ball to spin (*see also FIELD ATHLETICS: THROWING*). The larger the moment of inertia, the more torque it takes to get a ball spinning in a given time, or, conversely, the more time it takes to get a ball spinning with a given torque. This is calculated by adding together the squares of the distance to the axis of rotation times the mass for every particle of mass in the ball. In other words, the farther away from the axis, the more a mass particle contributes to moment of inertia. The moment of inertia of a ball can be increased with a light core and a heavier outer shell; likewise, a heavy core and light shell will decrease a ball's moment of inertia.

If the radius of gyration is known, moment of inertia can be calculated or measured: moment of inertia = mass × (radius of gyration)². The radius of gyration of a uniform spherical bowling ball is 2.72 inches (6.8 cm). The radius of gyration of a ball with a light core and heavy outer shell will be greater, and that of a ball with a heavy core and light shell will be smaller. The ABC specifications require that the radii of gyration of bowling balls fall between 2.43 and 2.80 inches.

The time of slipping increases directly with the moment of inertia, while the moment of inertia itself increases with the square of the radius of gyration. Thus, any small percentage of change in the radius of gyration results in twice that percentage of change in the time of slipping. (For example, 1.01 squared is about 1.02, 1.02 squared is about 1.04, and so on. That is, small incremental changes are doubled when a square is involved.) The time of slipping for the smaller 2.43-inch radius of gyration (about 10% less than the 2.72-in. radius of gyration of a uniform sphere) would be decreased by about 20 percent. The larger 2.80-inch radius of gyration (about 3% more than for a uniform sphere) would increase slipping time by about 6 percent. The only consensus among bowlers is to use a ball that suits the individual's style.

To achieve the desired hook, a ball is thrown with a component of spin perpendicular to the lane (hook spin) so that it rubs against the surface in such a way that some of the frictional force will push perpendicular to the motion of the ball, thereby deviating it from a straight path. The rate of hook (changing of the angle) is directly proportional to the rate of hook spin relative to the speed of the ball. On a uniformly oiled lane, the acceleration of the ball is equal to the coefficient of friction times the acceleration of gravity (32 ft., or 9.8 m, per sec.²). The direction of this acceleration is directly opposite the relative velocity of slipping between the ball and the lane. As the ball reaches the dry part of the lane, the coefficient of friction increases significantly, creating more sideways frictional force as well as the much larger backward frictional force; as a result, the ball hooks and slows down even sooner.

Fortunately, the dynamics for a uniform ball cause this direction of acceleration to be constant, which makes the path easy to describe. The path of any constantly accelerated object is a parabola. The apparent sudden change in direction in the dry area near the pins is a result of the larger frictional force causing the ball to follow a segment of a more sharply curving parabola. The small sideways force minimally affects the ball's path on the well-oiled part of the lane but is more than adequate to "bite" and create the late hooking action on the dry part of the lane (*see Figure 5*).

In the ball's path from release to pin contact, most of the hook does in fact occur near the pins, which is to the advantage of the bowler. If the ball were to follow a wide sweeping arc from the point of release to pin contact, as it would on a uniformly oiled lane, the position where it hit the pins would be hard to control. The reason for

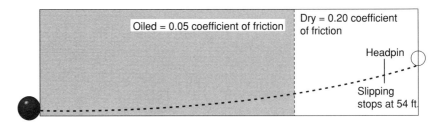

Figure 5. *The ball path for a typical hook leading to a strike is shown here. If a ball is launched at 25 feet per second with a hook spin of 4 feet per second, it will hook and slow to 18 feet per second as it slips for 54 feet. From there it rolls in a straight line at constant speed without further slipping, making contact with the pins at a 3.7-degree angle. An additional 3.5 feet per second of backspin makes the ball slip nearly 60 feet and roll into the pocket at 16 feet per second at an angle of 4.1 degrees. Topspin has no effect on the balanced ball shown here.*

this is that it is much easier to consistently line up the ball by using the target arrows than it is to give it a consistent amount of hook spin. If the ball hooks early, the total deviation by the time it gets to the pins will be larger than if it hooks late. If it hooks in the last few feet, then a slight variation in the hook spin will not cause the ball to miss the pocket, whereas a slight variation in hook spin for an early-hooking ball could cause it to miss the pocket entirely (*see Figure 6*).

According to the ABC specifications for dressing (oiling), the oil must be applied across the lane surface nonuniformly, with a gradual decrease from the center toward the sides. An extreme example shows why this rule is necessary. Suppose that a strip of the lane leading toward the pins is oiled very heavily and a strip just to the right is very dry. If a right-to-left hook spin ball is mistakenly released with too much angle to the right, once it moves onto the dry strip it experiences a strong force back toward the left, in effect correcting the error. The dry strip acts like an invisible wall or a force field to keep the ball from drifting too far to the right.

A bowler can use this invisible wall to guide the ball into the pocket every time. Undoubtedly, because inflated scores please cus-

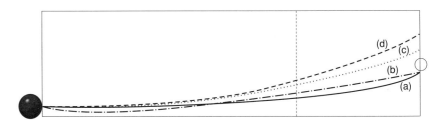

Figure 6. *The effect of early hooking is shown here. The two tracks (a and b) that hit the pocket are both thrown with a hook spin of 4 feet per second, but the one that starts at no angle has a late hook (a). The second one (b) hooks at a constant rate and must be launched at 0.7 degrees to the right to compensate for its increased deviation. The two tracks ending up on the far, or "Brooklyn," side of the headpin (c and d) have a hook spin of 6 feet per second. The one deviating the most is the one hooked at a constant rate.*

tomers, a great temptation exists for unscrupulous proprietors of bowling centers to put most or all of the oil on the center of the lane, leaving the edges relatively dry. As mentioned earlier, the nonuniformly oiled lane is one of the common technicalities by which the ABC has disqualified a perfect three-game series. Even though nonuniformity is part of the specifications, it was ruled that the lanes in question had overdone it.

The Weighted Ball

To grip and throw the ball with precision and speed, pioneer bowlers drilled finger holes into the ball. In a uniform bowling ball, these finger holes had a secondary, perhaps unexpected, consequence: they resulted in an out-of-balance ball that naturally hooked the wrong way. The ABC allows manufacturers to compensate (actually, to overcompensate) for this by adding weights to the interior of the ball. The ABC specifies that the ball can be out of balance by as much as 3 ounces (84 g) along the fingerhole axis and by as much as 1 ounce (28 g) along the perpendicular directions. This seems like a small amount—in fact, when the standard was first instituted, the ABC may have believed it to be inconsequential—but ball manufacturers and finger-hole drillers quickly learned how to take maximum advantage of this "loophole." If a modern bowling ball is sliced in two, it is possible to see a carefully designed core that shifts the center of gravity and adjusts the radii of gyration within ABC specifications. The inside of the ball looks like, and indeed is, a gyroscope. A 3-ounce imbalance shifts the center of gravity of a 16-pound ball by 1.2 percent, or about 0.05 inch (1.3 millimeters)—more than enough to profoundly affect the path of the ball.

A few general principles of gyroscopic motion are helpful in understanding the effects of weighting a ball. A spinning bowling ball can be considered a gyroscope with torques acting on it, much like a spinning toy gyroscope supported horizontally on the end of a finger. The gyroscope precesses (turns slowly) in a horizontal circle. The torque on the gyroscope lies about a horizontal axis at right angles to the angular momentum (moment of inertia times angular speed, with a direction along the spin axis). The result is that the angular momentum continually changes direction but not magnitude (precesses). A wheel rolling freely along a level surface also acts like a gyroscope and will precess if it is weighted or tilted to one side. The wheel rolls along the arc of a circle turning toward the direction of the weight or tilt. For the same reason, the bowling ball rolls along the arc of a circle (*see also FIELD ATHLETICS: THROWING, "Frisbee: The Most Popular Disk"*).

Using an ABC maximum imbalanced 16-pound ball as an example, we can see the significance of this gravity-induced hook. For a rolling speed of 20 feet (about 6 m) per second, the resulting radius of curvature is 1,480 feet (450 m)—about the same radius of curvature faced by drivers at high-speed motor racetracks. Over a distance of 60 feet (about 28 m), this results in a hook of 2.3 degrees. This

Figure 7. *These hypothetical paths of an unbalanced and a balanced ball assume a full roll and no slipping. The balanced ball rolls in a straight line; the unbalanced ball curves toward the weighted side (to the left of the right-handed bowler.*

EFFECTS OF TOPSPIN

Topspin (rad./sec.)	Hook Angle (degrees)	Spin-WT Angle (degrees)
0	0.00	90.0
1	0.46	76.8
2	0.89	64.0
3	1.24	51.9
4	1.52	40.8
5	1.68	31.0
6	1.79	22.5
7	1.82	15.6
8	1.80	10.9
9	1.76	8.8
10	1.71	8.5
11	1.71	7.4
12	1.65	4.9
13	1.62	2.1
14	1.55	3.2
15	1.55	4.7

Table 1. *This table shows the hook of a maximally weighted ball thrown at 25 feet per second with various amounts of topspin. There is a maximum hook for a spin of about 7 to 8 rad./sec. (about 80 RPM), a speed well within the range of a good bowler. The weighted axis ends nearly parallel to the spin axis, except in the case of very small initial spin. For zero initial spin the weighted axis just rolls end over end with no hook in either direction.*

amount of hook is due entirely to the weight distribution of the ball; the bowler need not make any extra effort. These maximally weighted balls are sometimes called "cheater" balls, but they are entirely within ABC specifications (*see Figure 7*).

The above analysis applies only when a ball is rolling without slipping, but there is a considerable hooking effect in any event. A simple case that highlights the effects of weighting is a ball released with topspin, weighted side up. As the ball slips along toward the pins, the frictional force produces a torque to the left. This torque causes the top of the ball to precess over to the left. Once the center of gravity begins to precess over to the left, the gravitational torque begins to turn the ball so that it develops a left hook spin. As the ball slips down the lane, its forward spin increases, owing to friction; and it slowly precesses and hooks toward the left, owing to the off-center weight.

The hook of the weighted ball with topspin is fairly stable. That is, a bowler can double the amount of topspin while the amount of hook changes only a little. An analysis similar to that of R. L. Huston, a scientist at the University of Cincinnati, shows the effects of different amounts of topspin on a 16-pound weighted ball thrown at 25 feet per second on a lane with a coefficient of friction of 0.05 for the first 40 feet, and 0.20 for the remaining 20 feet (*see Table 1*). Left-handed bowlers should note that if the topspin is negative as they would normally throw it, then the ball hooks right so that they also get an appropriate hook. A spinning ball, thrown like those in the table, starts out touching the lane at only one point. As it gains forward roll, the spin axis tilts away from vertical toward the left. As the forward spin builds up, the point of contact with the lane becomes an ever-increasing circle around the original spin axis and original contact point. This circle of contact is called the ball track. As the ball starts to roll without slipping, the ball track is at its maximum and stationary. Any other way of throwing the ball results in a similar pattern of contact between the ball and the floor.

The initial contact circle for other throws is, however, larger than the single point in this example. A ball thrown hundreds of times in a consistent manner forms wear marks along the stable ball track. An examination of this track reveals the axis around which the bowler initially spins the ball upon launch and also the amount of topspin relative to the speed. A so-called semiroller has the ball track 45 degrees around the ball from the axis. In this case, the topspin is so fast that the leftmost surface of the ball is at rest relative to the lane.

It is as if the ball were rolling along a side wall without slipping on either the floor or the wall. For a ball moving at 20 feet per second, it would take topspin of about 350 RPM to create a semiroller.

Debate about the relative advantages of full rollers (no topspin), semirollers (some topspin), and spinners (more topspin) continues among bowlers. Objectively, the effects of topspin are small. One of the effects of topspin is to scatter the pins differently. (The dynamics will be discussed in the next section.) As shown above, some topspin is required to produce a consistent hook in some circumstances, but topspin does not have a major effect on the path of the ball if it is accompanied by a significant component of hook spin. For a symmetric ball, topspin does not affect the path of the ball under any circumstances. The ball track depends on the topspin and determines the amount of oil the ball picks up as it moves in contact with the lane. If the weighting axis is not aligned with the spin axis, the ball will wobble, or precess, causing the ball track to flare, or become wider. This is said to have some advantage, in that a fresh ball surface is always in contact with the lane. Since less oil is carried down to the dry part of the lane, it results in more traction near the pins and subsequently more hook as long as the ball is still slipping on the lane. If a balanced ball does not slip, it just rolls in a straight line; if its weight is unbalanced, it continues along a slow gyroscopic turning path.

A greater moment of inertia around one axis over another axis has a small effect on the path of the ball. In general, the ball tends to orient itself so that it eventually rolls around the axis with the largest moment of inertia. This is always the case where kinetic energy can be dissipated by friction (here, between ball and floor). For instance, a cigar-shaped satellite will tend to tumble end over end if left to itself. However, the bowling lane, unlike space, is a confined area: it is not long enough for the bowling ball to completely orient itself. As the rolling ball orients itself, the amount of hook continues to change throughout each turn of the ball. For any given throw, it is possible to calculate the exact trajectory; however, the results depend so much on the nearest fractional turn of the ball as it reaches the pins that there are no general conclusions practical enough to benefit a bowler.

For instance, suppose that a ball with a radius of gyration 2.80 inches along one axis and 2.43 inches along the other two axes (the most extreme allowed by ABC specifications) is thrown at 25 feet per second with 20 radians per second of hook spin. Near the pins, its hook will vary from 5.5 to 6.5 degrees with each turn of the ball, approximately one cycle for each 2 feet traveled. By contrast, a uniform ball thrown the same way has a smooth trajectory ending with a hook of 6.5 degrees.

It is possible to make just such a nonuniform ball. These "wacky" balls, given names like "Rambo Recker," are not widely recommended by professionals, for one very good reason: they are difficult to control. Although different components of moment of inertia have an effect on the path of the ball, the effect is neither as much, nor as controllable, as those due to the off-center center of gravity.

Popular Spins

Bowlers use different combinations of backspin, hook spin, and topspin to launch the ball. However, once the ball stops slipping along the lane, the remaining roll may be one of the following.

1. *Semiroller*. The ball track is 45 degrees around the ball from the axis. The topspin is just fast enough that the leftmost surface of the ball is at rest relative to the lane.

2. *Full roller*. A full roller does not have any topspin. The ball track has the maximum diameter.

3. *Spinner*. A spinner has a small ball track and rotates more like a spinning top than a rolling ball. Advocates of this excessive topspin claim better spin scatter.

Pin Collisions

The goal of bowling is, obviously, to knock down all ten pins. The bowler hopes to accomplish this all with the first throw (a strike), but otherwise to finish off the remaining pins with an accurate second throw (a spare). (Actually, however, professional bowlers consider anything short of a strike a failure.) Through experience, bowlers come to realize that the best results are achieved by hitting between the 1 pin and the 3 pin. They also learn that the ball must hook at about a 6-degree angle and with enough speed (about 20 ft./sec.) to bounce pins off the kickback plate (a panel on each side of the gutter at the pin deck). This bounce is often necessary to knock over a few stubborn pins that did not fall from the direct scattering of the pins.

Various combinations of collisions between pins, and between pins and the kickback plate, create some interesting dynamics for spares as well as strikes. The primary difference between pin action for a strike and a spare ball is predictability. It is much easier to predict the outcome of collisions for the spare ball because fewer collisions take place—in all, fewer random outcomes occur.

In any collision, both linear and angular momentum (mass × velocity) are conserved (remain unchanged). Kinetic energy, however, decreases as energy is transformed into heat, sound, and damage to the pins and ball. Many physical parameters govern the collision: the masses of the objects, the coefficient of restitution (ratio of relative velocities after and before the collision), the coefficient of friction between the surfaces of the ball and the pins, the moments of inertia of the objects, and whether the collision is head-on or glancing. What makes bowling seem so random is that there are eleven objects (the ball plus ten pins) that can hit each other, and all the collisions happen in such a short time (about 0.2 seconds) that they appear chaotic. With so many objects and so many parameters involved, just how a change in one parameter might affect one or all of the others ends up in the realm of conjecture. In such a complex system, even a slight variation can have a significant effect; thus two seemingly identical throws may have entirely different results. However, this element of randomness (or luck), although substantial, need not be considered an uncontrollable factor. By keeping in mind certain basic principles governing collisions, bowlers can appreciably improve their odds.

At ball-pin contact, the ball strikes the pin about 1.5 inches (3.75 cm) below the pin's center of gravity (mass concentration) and about 0.25 inches (0.62 cm) below the maximum diameter. This natural undercutting causes the collision to lift the pin slightly, and in a direct on-center collision the top of the pin rotates down and sharply strikes the top of the ball. Thus the pin is propelled with an upward component of velocity as well as the expected straight backward velocity. In some cases, the struck pin actually flies over another pin, completely missing a pin it would otherwise have toppled if it had caromed straight backward without any upward trajectory.

When scientists discuss outcomes of collisions, they refer to something called the coefficient of restitution, which is a measure of the relative speed with which two colliding objects bounce apart, expressed as a number between 0 and 1. A coefficient of restitution of 1 is a perfectly elastic collision, that is, the relative speed of departure of the objects after the collision is the same as the relative speed of approach before the collision. In this case, the total kinetic energy is unchanged. At the other extreme, a coefficient of restitution of 0, the relative speed of departure of both objects after the collision is zero. The objects stick together, abosrbing all of each other's relative kinetic energy. (An example of a 0 coefficient of restitution might be two soft sponge balls.)

For a typical 16-pound plastic bowling ball colliding with an undamaged plastic-coated pin, the coefficient of restitution is approximately 0.7. The ABC specifies a coefficient of restitution between 0.65 to 0.78. But (as with a tennis ball that has lost its bounce), the coefficient of well-worn pins drops to around 0.5. The difference, 0.2, is substantial enough that any experienced bowler needs only a few throws to tell the difference between new pins and pins that are, say, 5 years old and well-worn.

The coefficient of restitution for a pin-on-pin collision between new pins is about 0.5, less than that of a ball-on-pin collision. When pins rebound off one another at a high speed, that is an obvious effect of a high coefficient of restitution. But another and perhaps more important effect is the subtle impact on direction of scatter. When pins have a very low coefficient of restitution, they tend to be carried along in the direction of the ball (at 0, they stick together); at a high coefficient, they scatter over a wider angle (*see Table 2*). The wider angle of scatter is thought to result in a more effective chain reaction among the pins—what bowlers refer to as better "pin action."

How the pins scatter is a matter of the transfer of momentum. When a ball strikes a pin, it transfers momentum to the pin, and the pin transfers an equal and opposite amount of momentum back to the

EFFECT OF COEFFICIENT OF RESTITUTION OF PINS ON SCATTERING

COR	Ball angle	Pin angle
0.5	7.20°	29.42°
0.7	8.59°	30.31°
0.9	0.04°	31.03°

Table 2. *Different coefficients of restitution (COR) between new and well-worn pins affect not only the speed but also the angle at which pins scatter. In this example, a 16-pound ball strikes the pin 4 inches off-center in each collision. A 1- or 2-degree difference in pin angle may seem insubstantial, yet such a change can determine whether some other pin farther down the line will be hit or missed in the subsequent chain reaction.*

ball. (Newton's third law about the equality of actions and reactions applies here.) Because a pin weighs 3.375 pounds (about 1.5 kg), the pins have more than enough mass to significantly alter the speed and direction of the ball during a collision. In a head-on collision between a pin and a 16-pound ball traveling at 20 feet per second, the ball slows to 14.1 feet per second. while the pin bounces away at 28.1 feet per second. This assumes a coefficient of restitution of 0.7. Note the change in relative speed from 20 ft./sec. to 14 ft./sec. (0.7×20 ft./ sec.). The total momentum is the same after the collision as before it, but the total kinetic energy is less (*see also FOOTBALL*).

How pins scatter also depends on the surface properties of the pins and the ball. The coefficient of friction between the surface of the ball and the surface of the pin is the factor that makes a semi-roller scatter the pins differently from a full roller. As mentioned previously, the left surface of a semiroller is not moving relative to the lane, but the right surface is moving twice as fast as the rest of the ball. Thus a pin struck with a glancing blow involving the nonmoving left hemisphere of the ball rebounds differently from a pin struck by the fast-moving right hemisphere. But this is true only if a frictional force exists between the ball and the pin so that the ball can "grab" the pin. If the coefficient of friction were 0, the spin of the ball would make no difference at all in how the pins scattered. However, the friction coefficient has been measured at about 0.2 between a dry (unoiled) plastic ball and a new plastic-coated pin. This is significant; it is about the same as the coefficient of friction between a similar ball and a dry lane.

Strikes

Many reasons have been given to explain how to throw strikes consistently and why pins are sometimes left stubbornly standing. Some of these reasons are quite logical, though others are laughable. Popular theories about how to throw a strike include the following: (1) Use the heaviest ball possible. (2) Do whatever possible to increase spin. (3) Do not throw the ball too fast, or the pins in front will fly right over the pins in the back row instead of knocking them down. (4) Do not throw too slowly, or the headpin will not be able to bounce off the kickback plate to knock down the solid 7 pin. (5) Buy a high-tech ball, which will grab the pin deck and drive through the pins.

With regard to theory 5, it should be noted that a ball has no way to "grab" the pin deck except by friction; and the dominant force on a ball while it is among the pins is not "grabbing" friction but the average force of the collisions with the pins, which is about 32 pounds (typically, in colliding with three pins the ball slows from 20 ft./sec. to 7 ft./sec. in 0.2 sec.). The frictional force of the pin deck on the ball is only about a tenth of this amount.

With regard to the other theories, to separate fact from fiction and identify some general effects, a two-dimensional model of pin scattering is provided here. This model examines several variables, including weight and speed of the ball, hook angle, spin, and coeffi-

FACTORS AFFECTING STRIKES

Variant (lb.)	Weight (ft./sec.)	Velocity (deg.)	Angle (ft./sec.)	Spin (in.)	Pocket (41 rolls)	Strikes	Pins Left
1. Reference throw	16	20	4	20	0.6–4.6	31	14
2. Speed	16	25	4	25	0.6–4.6	33	11
3. Speed	16	15	4	15	0.6–4.6	29	16
4. Weight	10	20	4	20	0.4–4.4	20	28
5. Hook	16	20	0	20	0.6–4.6	15	43
6. Hook	16	20	2	20	0.7–4.7	24	20
7. Hook	16	20	6	20	0.8–4.8	29	13
8. Hook	16	20	8	20	0.7–4.7	28	15
9. Hook	16	20	10	20	1.5–5.5	25	18
10. Spin	16	20	4	0	1.8–5.8	32	9
11. Spin	16	20	4	30	0.3–4.3	30	14
12. COR=0.5	16	20	4	20	0.5–4.5	29	13
13. COR=0.9	16	20	4	20	0.5–4.5	25	20

Table 3. *The next-to-last column shows the number of strikes resulting from a 16-pound bowling ball colliding with a set of 10 pins in 41 equally spaced throws across a 4-inch-wide pocket. The last column gives the total number of pins left standing for the 41 throws; this is an indicator of the effectiveness of various values. Line 1 is a reference semiroller throw (topspin and velocity are equal). In the other lines, one paramater at a time is varied to provide a comparison with this reference throw. Lines 2 and 3 vary only speed. Line 4 varies ball weight (10 lb. versus 16 lb.) Lines 5–9 vary hook angle. Lines 10 and 11 check the effects of topspin using a full roller (no topspin) and a spinner (topspin of 30 ft./sec. is greater than the ball velocity of 20 ft./sec.). Lines 12 and 13 vary coefficient of restitution (COR) of the ball-pin collision. Pin-pin coefficient is always assumed to be 0.5, as it is for new pins.*

cient of restitution. The results can be summarized for a ball entering somewhere along the 1-3 pocket (*see Table 3*). In the first example, a 16-pound ball traveling at 20 feet per second as a semiroller collides at 4 degrees into the pocket. The spin is given as the surface speed relative to the center of the ball. This standard roll is then changed, one variable (one factor) at a time, to observe the different results. The effectiveness of each scenario is measured in terms of how many strikes are made out of 41 rolls of the ball spaced 0.1 inch apart across the pocket. Calculations were made across a much wider area, but for purposes of comparison the best 4-inch continuous span was used as the definition of the pocket.

These results confirm most of the accepted wisdom of bowling. Faster is better, and a heavier ball is better than a lighter ball. The faster ball is better because it gives more pin action—a more lively rebound from the kickback plate. The angles of scatter and the details of chain reactions are the same in this model for any velocity of the ball. Thus the only reason speed makes a difference is that a minimum speed (assumed to be 2 ft./sec.) is required for a pin to clear the gutter on a rebound from the kickback plate and knock down more pins. A heavier ball is better for somewhat the same reason. The greater mass increases the linear momentum available to transfer to the pins for good pin action. Increased mass also changes the scattering angles, resulting in more effective chain reactions among the pins primarily because the heavier ball is deflected less by the collisions.

A hook in the 4- to 6-degree range is best. As the degree of hook drops below this range, there is a very marked drop in the probability of a strike. Moreover, a hookless ball greatly reduces the chance of a strike even when the ball slips perfectly into the pocket. Compared with a ball with optimum hook, a hookless ball results in only about half as many strikes in the 4-inch-wide pocket. The optimum 4-degree hook may leave the 8 pin or 10 pin standing for various spots in the pocket; but a straight throw tends to leave the 8 pin and 10 pin standing more often, as well as the 5 pin. Chain reactions differ only slightly, but the difference is greatly in favor of the 4-degree hook. Perhaps surprisingly, a hook larger than 4 degrees is of no advantage. A larger hook does, however, increase the probability of the 7-10 split if the pocket is missed slightly to the right.

Topspin makes very little difference. If anything, there is a slight preference for a full roller (no topspin). For the same position of the ball relative to the headpin, the greater the topspin, the farther to the left the headpin rebounds. This has the effect of shifting the strike pocket to the left (that is, it is necessary to strike the headpin more directly). For the full roller, the best 4-inch-wide pocket is between 1.8 and 5.8 inches to the right of the headpin. For the spinner, the range is between 0.3 and 4.3 inches to the right. After accounting for this shift, the difference is just a single extra pin left standing for some throws. There are no other general effects due to topspin.

The results for coefficient of restitution are surprising. As expected, a low coefficient of restitution is slightly worse, but a very high one is much worse. A high coefficient of restitution seems to result in faster pin reaction, but it does not cause more pins to be knocked down. There is apparently some advantage from "pin carry" because a ball with a lower coefficient of restitution tends to carry pins along in its direction. In fact, the highest scores are obtained with the ABC specifications for coefficient of restitution (the range).

Although the calculations here assume that the ball enters the 1-3 pocket, strikes are certainly possible outside this pocket in either direction. Strikes are even possible on the other side of the headpin (sometimes referred to as the "Brooklyn" side). For any ball, however, the best roll is into the 1-3 pocket. The one exception is the non-hooking full roller—the most common throw for beginners. Since its spin is symmetric and it follows a straight-line path, it gives the same results on either side of the headpin.

The first throw listed in the example indicates that a person throwing the ball consistently into the pocket will get about three strikes for every four throws. For this bowler, the chance of throwing a perfect game (12 strikes in a row) is about 32 in 1,000 (0.75^{12}). The probability of a perfect series (36 strikes in a row) is about 32 in 1 million. During the bowling season of 1990–1991 in the United States, there were 14,192 perfect games in sanctioned league matches, or one perfect game for every 20,595 games. From these figures it can be calculated that for a league bowler, the probability of throwing a strike is about 0.44. Each throw must therefore come very close to hitting the pocket, and even then a strike is by no means guaranteed.

Bowling is a game of luck as well as skill. The probability of a strike can be maximized by throwing the ball into the pocket, but a strike cannot be absolutely ensured unless a bowler can consistently hit the 1-inch-wide portions of the pocket to achieve the same pin action every time. This is one thing that makes bowling interesting—and sometimes frustrating. An apparently bad throw can result in a strike and a seemingly perfect throw in an 8-10 split. Within the pocket, which pins are hit by the ball and which ones are hit by other pins are details that will change with minuscule changes in the position of the ball as it enters the pocket.

Contrary to popular belief, a ball in the pocket usually hits only three pins: either 1, 3, and 5 or 1, 3, and 8. The other seven pins are hit by these and other pins in a chain reaction that sometimes involves a carom off the kickback plate. Generally, a series of closely spaced throws will all have the same pattern of pin action; however, a throw even 1/10 inch over can have a greatly different scatter pattern.

Bad splits occur when the pin action switches from one identifiable pattern to another. For instance, the entire line of four pins on the left of the triangle (the 1, 2, 4, and 7 pins) can be felled in a direct chain reaction by hitting the headpin for a range of impacts, but an error of 1/10 inch either way will leave the 7 pin standing. Even automatic pinsetters cannot consistently place pins on the pin deck at precisely the same spots from one frame to the next. This is noteworthy because a difference in placement as slight as 1/10 inch can change the pin action pattern and perhaps result in a pin left standing (*see also STATISTICS*).

Spares

Even apparently good rolls into the pocket can leave some pins standing. The most feared combinations of pins left standing are called splits because the wide spaces between the standing pins make it difficult to produce the pin action necessary to knock them all down. One of the most common bad splits, even when the ball hooks into the pocket, is 8-10. A ball hooking into the pocket can also leave the 5 pin standing alone. If the first ball is on the right edge of the pocket, it often leaves an 8-10 split, and just a few inches farther to the right might leave the rare 7-10 split if a ball has a large hook. The 4-6-7-10 split—a bowler's nightmare—occurs when the ball hits the headpin nearly head on (*see Figure 8*).

The two-dimensional model, discussed above for strikes, has been used to explore possible ways to pick up these and other spares. The difficulty of picking up particular spares can be expressed in terms of the target width, in inches (*see Table 4*). This is the total distance from side to side within which the ball can vary and still knock down all the remaining pins. To assess the difficulty of picking up

Splits, Splits, Splits!

Shirley Topflight of Las Vegas, Nevada, rolled a record 14 consecutive splits in 1968. If a professional bowler tried to duplicate her feat by, say, aiming directly at the headpin, the probability of success would be approximately 1 in 1 million.

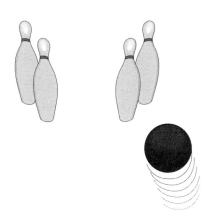

Figure 8. *The 4-6-7-10 split is very difficult to pick up. The bowler must slice the 6 pin so that it caroms across the lane to knock down the 4 and 7 pins.*

TARGET WIDTH FOR SPARES

Pins left	Target width (in.)	Comment	Rank (1=easiest)
Single	13.250		1
7 or 10	9.375	Diminished by the gutter	3
5 and 8	12.611		2
7 and 8	1.250		5
6, 9, and 10	11.972		4
6, 8, and 10	0.969		6
4, 6, 7, and 10	0.616		8
7, 9, 8, and 10	0.512	Increases to 0.693 for spinner	7
7 and 10	0.290	Spinner and 4° hook	9

Table 4. *Interestingly, a 7-10 split is twice as difficult to pick up as a 4-6-7-10 split, which itself is nearly 10 times as difficult as throwing a strike.*

these spares, remember that the width of the pocket for getting a strike is about 4 inches. It is assumed that the ball is thrown straight at 20 feet per second as a full roller unless specified otherwise.

Using target width, spares can be ranked by level of difficulty. The easiest spare to pick up is a single pin. Here, the width of the target is the diameter of the pin plus the diameter of the ball (4.75 + 8.5 = 13.25 in.). Naturally, it is far more difficult to "pick up" a single 7 or 10 pin because of the proximity to the gutter. The same off-center contact that "slices" a 4 pin drops into the gutter and misses the 7 pin altogether.

For two pins side by side, such as a 7-8 split, the ball can be thrown directly between them, and there will be 0.625 inch of ball hitting either side. Therefore, target size is twice 0.625 inch, or 1.25 inches.

To pick up the 6-9-10 split, a ball thrown straight at the 6 pin hits all three pins as the 6 pin is knocked between the 9 pin and the 10 pin. However, for a ball thrown slightly to the right of the 6 pin, the 6 pin still passes between the 9 and 10 pins, but the ball misses the 9 pin, leaving it standing. A bowler who wants to be absolutely sure will aim far enough to the right that the 6 pin hits the 9 pin and the ball takes care of the 10 pin. This is the pin action assumed here (*see Table 4*), giving a target width of 5.07 inches. Throwing the ball at an angle of 4 degrees as a semiroller increases the width of the target by about 0.2 inch, to 5.271 inches. If for a particular bowler a hooking semiroller is harder to control than a straight full roller, then the additional target width is of no benefit.

The 7-9, 8-10, and 7-10 splits cannot be picked up with a straight full roller; these absolutely require some hooking action. The 7-9 needs at least a semiroller with a hook, or the 9 pin will be carried with the ball into the pit no matter how lightly it is touched. This occurs because of the carrying effect of the ball on the pins with a coefficient of restitution around 0.7. The target for the 7-9 split is increased by 0.279 to 0.693 inch if a spinner (topspin of 30 ft./sec. surface speed) is used instead of a semiroller. A spinner is more effective than the semiroller, because the spinning ball will kick the 9 pin backward as it hits toward the left so that the 9 pin remains on the pin deck to hit the 7 pin.

To pick up the 7-10 split, the bowler needs to take advantage of the kickback plate at the sides of the pin deck. A hooking spinner needs to graze the right side of the 7 pin so that it is knocked at nearly a 90-degree angle to the left and back into the kickback plate. If it clears the gutter on the rebound, it will then slide across the pin deck and knock down the 10 pin. It is about ten times more difficult to pick up the 7-9 or 8-10 than it is to throw a strike in the first place, and the 7-10 split is even harder. Because a glancing blow is required to pick up these difficult splits, it is very easy to miss everything and knock down no pins. Professional bowlers, recognizing the high degree of luck involved, almost always forgo the fancy stuff, play it safe, and make sure they knock down at least one pin.

Don C. Hopkins

References

Adrian, M., and J. Cooper. *Biomechanics of Human Movement.* Dubuque, Iowa: Benchmark, 1989.

Aulby, M., and D. Ferraro, with D. Herbst. *Bowling 200+.* Chicago: Contemporary, 1989.

Herbst, D. *Bowling 300: Top Pros Share Their Secrets to Rolling the Perfect Game.* Chicago: Contemporary, 1993.

Hopkins, D., and J. Patterson. "Bowling Frames: Paths of a Bowling Ball." *American Journal of Physics* 45 (March 1977): 263–266.

Hopkins, D. "Physics of Bowling: Ball-Pin, Pin-Pin Collisions." Unpublished paper presented at the American Association of Physics Teachers Summer Meeting (1983).

Huston, R., et al. "On the Dynamics of a Weighted Bowling Ball." *Journal of Applied Mechanics* 46 (1979): 937–942.

Nash, B., and A. Zullo. *Gutter Humor: Amazing but True Bowling Stories.* Kansas City, Missouri: Andrews and McMeel, 1994.

Russell, D. *Bowling Now.* Cranbury, New Jersey: Barnes, 1980.

Boxing

MODERN BOXING has its origins in the ancient cultures of the eastern Mediterranean. In the archaeological record, Minoan frescos, which can be dated to approximately 1600 B.C.E., depict young boxers in training. While Greek mythology designates Apollo as originator of the art, the earliest hard literary reference to an organized competition may be the story of the match between Epios (creator of the Trojan horse) and Euryalos in Book 23 of the *Illiad*.

By the late nineteenth century, boxing had evolved into a modern sport. On 7 September 1892, an American boxer, James Corbett, claimed the title of world champion by knocking out John L. Sullivan in a fiercely contested 21-round battle. With a purse of $20,000 and a stake of $10,000, the contest ushered in a new era of popularity for prizefighting. In a rushed determination to outlaw these "brutal bare-knuckle battles," American legislators introduced the Marquis of Queensberry rules—use of gloves and three-minute rounds.

Nearly 4,000 years after the Minoans and more than 100 years after Corbett and Sullivan, prizefighting continues to enjoy popularity as a sport. Heavyweight-title fights often net each fighter more than $20 million for 36 minutes of work.

Critics continue to argue that boxing—with its frequent injuries and occasional deaths—is too brutal to be considered a sport; and given the considerable money involved in professional boxing, officials have shown some willingness to placate the critics with minor rule changes. Following the nationally televised knockout of Du Ku Kim by Ray ("Boom Boom") Mancini in 1982, which resulted in Kim's death shortly thereafter, protesters marched to Washington, D.C., demanding that boxing be banned in the United States. To pre-empt congressional action, prizefight promoters limited fights to 12 rounds (many championship fights had gone 15). Other than this one concession, however, boxing officials have done little to protect prize-fighters since the time of Sullivan and Corbett.

In the twentieth century, hundreds of fighters have died as a direct result of boxing (450 since 1918, when records were first kept). Thousands need to be hospitalized immediately following a bout—often suffering damage that permanently affects the quality of their life. Although statistical evidence is not available, it is probable that a great many boxers have suffered premature deaths as a result of

Activity	Kcal/hr. /lb. of body weight
Boxing, in ring	6.04
Running, 8-min. mile	5.68
Cross-country skiing	2.7–5.5
Swimming, freestyle	3.48
Cycling (10 MPH)	3.18
Aerobics	3.02
Golf, walking	2.32
Golf, power cart	0.9–1.4
Sitting	0.47

Table 1. *As an alternative to the monotony of aerobics, treadmills, and stair climbing, many men and women are turning to boxing for physical fitness. Boxing is increasingly popular among white-collar professionals, perhaps because it relieves frustrations and burns calories. Most participants engage in shadow-boxing—rather than actually pummeling an opponent—as part of a rigorous aerobic session. (Adapted from Lamb, 1984)*

boxing injuries. In addition to internal injuries, the severe beatings received by professional boxers cause disfiguring scars and other cosmetic damage that serve as lifelong reminders of their time in the ring.

Boxing represents a mixture of brutality and artistry that often draws an emotional response from its proponents as well as its critics. Proponents argue that boxing is a sport that requires strength, coordination, conditioning, endurance, strict discipline, and courage. Yet for every bout between equally matched fighters, there are ten or twenty ugly fights between mismatched, slow, or unskilled boxers. Such fights raise an outcry from people who ask how a civilized nation can condone, and even encourage, a sport in which the objective is to knock the opponent out by damaging—sometimes permanently—neural tissue in the vital centers of the brain. It is true that participants in football and other contact sports also face risks to their health and safety, but in these games injuries are a side effect rather than the objective. Nevertheless, the willingness of fans to spend enormous amounts of money to watch boxing matches ensures that the sport will continue unless it is outlawed.

Not all boxing is the same, however. Amateur bouts have little resemblance to professional prizefights. The equipment and rules used in amateur boxing stress skills and limit the chance of a knockout, making it a far safer sport than professional boxing.

In this article, the physics and biomechanics of amateur and professional boxing are explored. An understanding of how much force a boxer can generate, what happens when a fighter strikes a target, and the relative merits of protective equipment requires a wider knowledge of the underlying physics of boxing.

Punching Power

Punching power is a combination of linear and angular momentum. Linear momentum (mass × velocity) from the forward acceleration of a punch develops as the fist moves toward its target; angular momentum (rotation around a fixed axis) from the accelerating forces created from the body's twisting motion develops as the punch is delivered (*see also ACROBATICS and FIELD ATHLETICS: THROWING*). Some punches depend primarily on either linear or angular momentum, but big blows usually maximize both forces.

Because jabs, hooks, uppercuts, and straight punches draw on different linear and angular momentums from the body, a range of deliverable forces and damaging effects will result from each blow. For example, the left-hand jab of a right-handed boxer is delivered off the lead foot, with power coming from the linear momentum of stepping forward. In comparison, the hook, uppercut, and straight punch, delivered with the dominant right hand, can generate considerably more power, for two reasons. First, a punch gains force from

Why Do Men Fear a Low Blow?

As the champion pummeled the challenger, the crowd cheered with a deafening sound. The dazed and desperate challenger swung wildly in response, delivering a punishing low blow to the champion's groin. In almost complete unison, the wild cheering gave way to a pained sigh: "Ouuhhh."

Around the arena, hundreds of men grabbed their own groins as if the low blow had hit them, not the fighter. The previous blows, even those causing deep cuts and profuse bleeding, had drawn little or no empathy. Why do men look at a blow to the groin in a different light? A low blow is, of course, incapacitating—the pain leaves a man feeling totally helpless—but it may also reflect a man's primal fear of castration and impotence.

The rules governing low blows are extremely stringent: points are taken away from a fighter who delivers an illegal blow; and a 3-minute recovery time, and even one or more rounds, may be awarded to the receiver. At one time, the penalties were much worse: a fighter who received a low blow could be awarded the victory. However, it was possible for a fighter to feign receiving a low blow, and this feigning became so common and so successful that officials rethought the rule. Eventually, a "no foul" rule was established to ensure that a fighter could not win by feigning a low blow: every fighter had to wear a foul-proof cup, which prevents incapacitating blows to the groin.

The sensitivity and vulnerability of the groin area can make scrotal contusion particularly debilitating, causing excruciating pain and nausea. However, the damage is usually only temporary, even if a fighter is not wearing the cup. As with any contusion, the degree of bleeding, swelling, and muscle spasm depends on the intensity of the blow. The possibility has been suggested that blows to the testicles might cause testicular cancer later on; but to date, there is little evidence to support this theory. In fact, lifelong damage from sports-related injuries to the groin is very rare indeed. This is primarily because a projectile—whether a hockey puck, baseball, elbow, or fist—can rarely generate enough force to cause permanent damage to either the groin or the internal abdominal organs.

The groin and the abdominal organs are structured so that a significant amount of body fat and muscle acts as a buffer against external blows. The abdominal region consists primarily of hollow organs, such as the intestine and urinary bladder, but includes some solid organs, such as

angular momentum in addition to linear momentum as the shoulder and hip rotate forward toward the target. Second, the stronger, more practiced hand has more speed as well as power (work/time). Doubling the speed of the fist also doubles stopping time, and—more important—it quadruples stopping distance. However, the punch itself possesses four times the kinetic energy (energy of motion), which means that the blow penetrates four times as deep. Not surprisingly, much of a boxer's training focuses on increasing hand speed.

Although punching power is very important, the point at which the punch contacts the target is equally so. The effect felt by the recipient of the blow depends largely on location. The impact of a body blow is absorbed across a large surface area, mitigating its debilitating effect. But when a blow lands across the bridge of the nose—hitting a very small surface area—it becomes far more debilitating. A relatively weak blow across the bridge of the nose can be far more damaging than a maximum-force blow to the torso.

Heavyweights and Heavy Punching

Boxing fans devote much of their attention to heavyweights, large boxers who are not necessarily among those most skilled. In fact, the heavyweight division includes the greatest number of slow, plodding,

the liver and kidneys. When a hollow organ is not full, it absorbs impact force much better than a solid organ. A solid organ is less capable of dissipating energy from an impact, and this makes it more vulnerable to injury.

Of the solid abdominal organs, the kidneys are perhaps at greatest risk. The kidneys are two bean-shaped organs located near the skin surface just above the iliac crest (hips), one on each side of the spine. Although they are surrounded by a capsule and by a protective layer of fat—which is encased in a second layer of fat—the kidneys nonetheless make an inviting target for boxers, who often find themselves in a clinched position. While a fighter's arms are locked around the opponent, the kidneys are often the only target accessible for punching. Not only boxers but also football quarterbacks and receivers (who are sometimes "speared" from behind by an opponent's helmet) can receive blows that injure the kidneys.

A blow delivered to a kidney at a certain angle and with enough force can lead to flank pain, nausea, vomiting, and shock. In addition to pain that does not subside, the clearest indicator of kidney damage is the appearance of blood in the urine. Bleeding usually stops on its own, but surgery may occasionally be necessary to repair fractures to one or both kidneys. Repeated blows may result in a scarred, poorly functioning kidney; long-term effects may include hypertension (elevated blood pressure), insufficient kidney functioning, and even kidney failure. If both kidneys experience repeated trauma, or if an athlete has only one kidney (this can be a congenital defect), dialysis may become necessary. Dialysis is, in a sense, an "artifical kidney," but it is not an implant: it is a repeated process of artificially altering and regulating the concentration of toxic substances in the blood.

Top boxers, who keep their body fat extremely low in order to perform at high levels, are very susceptible to kidney contusions and fractures—their protective layer of fat may be only 1 centimeter (0.4 in.) thick. In contrast, in an obese or less-conditioned athlete, the fatty layer may be from 8 to 15 centimeters (3 to 6 in.) thick, providing far more protection.

Overall, however, the risk of injury from groin and abdominal blows is minimal. Thus it is ironic that boxing fans cheer as a fighter beats the opponent's head but consider a deliberate blow to the groin poor sportsmanship.

David L. Zumerchik, M.D.

clumsy, wildly swinging fighters. Perhaps the reason for the popularity of this division is that heavyweights have the ability to inflict the greatest damage and deliver more knockouts.

British engineers at the University of Manchester measured the punching force of boxers and found that well-trained boxers deliver an average punching force of 3,400 newtons (764 pounds). Deliverable punching force is determined by the effective mass and velocity of the fist, which in turn is determined by the fighter's skill, strength, weight, and arm length, and the distance at which the punch is thrown.

Although a bigger fighter and a smaller fighter may deliver comparable force, greater impulse (force × time; or the amount of linear momentum transferred) explains why a larger fighter inflicts more damage. For example, a 140-pound (63.6-kg) boxer, such as Julio Chavez, and a 220-pound (100-kg) boxer, such as Mike Tyson, may both generate a punching force of 3,400 newtons at impact. Even if the impact occurs at the same part of the opponent's body, the punch from the 220-pound fighter will be more effective because for any given force, a blow from a more massive fighter takes longer to stop. Thus, the distance of the head snap and the extent to which the brain is slammed against the skull depend on the size of the impulse. A force of 3,400 newtons delivered for 1 microsecond by a fly might

Figure 1. *The stance used in most sports—feet apart, knees bent, and crouching forward to lower the center of gravity—is completely different from that used by a boxer. If such a stance were used, the boxer would present the opponent with the largest possible target and could be toppled backward by even the lightest of punches. Instead, boxers position themselves with one foot forward and one back, nearly perpendicular to the opponent. When they are hit, this stance enables them to keep their center of gravity between their two feet and not fall backward. Often, when a fighter lands a powerful punch, the force of the blow sends the opponent stumbling backward until the back foot can be repositioned behind the center of gravity to regain balance.*

sting a little but would cause no harm at all. By contrast, the same force delivered to the chin for a few milliseconds by a heavyweight could jar the head abruptly enough to cause unconsciousness.

Heavyweight fighters also face a greater risk of permanent injury. All fighters learn to "punch through" the target, to concentrate on a fictitious target within the actual target, training to terminate a punch several inches within the opponent's body. To maximize the effect of a blow, a boxer applies the greatest possible force for as long as possible. Lengthening the period of contact makes the linear momentum of the blow more effective. When a punch is terminated "within" the target, instead of at the point of contact, mass is more important than velocity. This is due to inertia (a component of mass)—the tendency of something in motion to stay in motion and something at rest to stay at rest. When a fist collides with a body, two inertial forces are at work. The reaction force of the body being hit acts on the fist; this inertial force slows the fist's acceleration. At the same time, the reaction force applied to the contacted body is equal and opposite to the inertial force of the fist and therefore determines the direction and acceleration of the body. These accelerations must be moving in opposite directions. This explains why an extended follow-through of a heavyweight like Mike Tyson delivers a much more effective blow than that of a much smaller fighter like Julio Chavez, especially when hand speed is about equal.

Punching Power and Mistakes

A punch becomes even more effective when the opposing fighter makes a costly miscalculation, such as stepping into the punch. When a powerful fist collides with a skull, each possesses linear momentum in the direction of the other. The fighter receiving the blow quickly comes to a stop, and the acceleration of the head reverses, or snaps back. By stepping into the punch, fighters inflict additional damage on themselves because the force of the blow is sustained over a longer period of time. Thus good fighters try to "roll" with a punch, extending the time of impact and "riding" the punch by moving the head back (instead of forward and into the punch).

Head Movement and Concussions

When a part of the brain suffers trauma, the result is often a concussion, or a disturbance of neurological function. Concussions can be caused when a cyclist's head strikes a curb during a fall, when players' helmets collide in football, or when a boxer receives a blow to the head.

In boxing, a blow that produces an angular acceleration of the head causes more brain movement than a linear force that does not rotate the head. Blows of identical magnitude and force that occur tangentially—not through the head's center of gravity—produce a much higher acceleration. For example, a punch directed crosswise that catches the side of the chin would result in at least 3.5 times

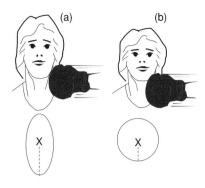

Figure 2. *The angular rotation of the head depends, in part, on the shape of the head. A tangential blow to an ellipsoid-shaped head and to a rounder head result in different rotational accelerations. When a football and a soccer ball are kicked below center, the ellipsoid football rotates more in flight than the round soccer ball. Likewise, a fighter with an ellipsoid-shaped head will experience more rotational acceleration when receiving a blow to the chin than a fighter with a rounder head, because the radius (dotted line) from the head's center of gravity is greater.*

greater acceleration of the head than a blow to the cheek, directly through the center of gravity. In practice, the acceleration is more than 3.5 times greater—the calculation for a solid sphere. Because the head is a nonsolid ellipsoid (oblong), the acceleration may be as much as 4.2 times greater (*see Figure 2*). Headgear may actually worsen this effect, as it provides an enlarged target that makes the head susceptible to even greater rotational acceleration.

The internal dynamic properties of the head are not as easily measured as the external blow's impact on the skull. Several complex biological factors play a role: (1) mass, (2) oscillation of the head (vibration), (3) damping (of vibration), and (4) the involuntary nervous-system reaction to the blow. Factors 2, 3, and 4 are, for the most part, heavily dependent on factor 1: mass. Because the head-neck system remains fairly stationary, change in the head's momentum decreases with greater head mass. Heavyweights not only have the advantage of greater punching power but are less likely to be affected by head blows because of the greater mass of their head-neck system, which includes a larger, more muscular neck.

The thickness of a fighter's skull is probably a minor factor in determining the probability of concussions. Numerous studies have shown that bone mass varies among individuals. The skull consists of soft, cancellous bone—interlocking plates and a porous bone structure. A thicker skull can significantly reduce the risk of hematoma (a blood clot at the point of impact) but probably has little or no effect on the conditions causing long-term brain damage: inertia of collision as the brain is forced backward and against the skull (*see also SKELETAL SYSTEM*).

Forces on the Brain

The central strategy of boxing is to launch a series of powerful blows so that fatigue, exhaustion, and injury collectively crush the opponent's will to continue fighting. To accomplish this, a skilled fighter focuses on pummeling the head, because the head houses the strategic command center—the brain. A fight is all but over when the brain loses some or all of its functions: balance, coordination, reflex, memory, instinct, and strategy. In many ways, a boxing match is much like a war: just as the first strategy in warfare is to disable an enemy's strategic command center, a boxer's primary target is the brain.

As noted above, boxers attempt to maximize their follow-through by accelerating "through" the target. The surface of a boxing glove, as opposed to a bare-knuckle blow, delivers the force over a wider area. A punch to the head is therefore not particularly damaging to the face itself; rather, it causes a rapid rearward acceleration of the head. The force of gravity is 9.8 meters per second squared (32 lb./ sec.^{2}); a well-executed, clean (nondeflected) blow to the head can cause an acceleration of the head 80 times this. A boxer's fist functions as a small projectile that is rapidly accelerated toward a small

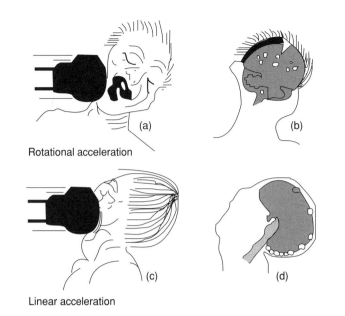

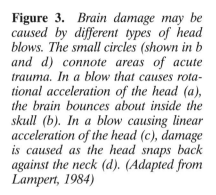

Figure 3. *Brain damage may be caused by different types of head blows. The small circles (shown in b and d) connote areas of acute trauma. In a blow that causes rotational acceleration of the head (a), the brain bounces about inside the skull (b). In a blow causing linear acceleration of the head (c), damage is caused as the head snaps back against the neck (d). (Adapted from Lampert, 1984)*

target, the head. After a blow to the head, the muscles of the neck prevent the head from snapping back and create a force countering the punch. Since the brain floats in the skull much as an egg yolk floats in the shell, it lags behind the accelerated head and ricochets around in the skull, straining brain tissue and stretching and tearing blood vessels.

Most knockouts are caused by a blow to the chin, and unconsciousness occurs almost immediately following the blow. Some doctors argue that a knockout takes place so suddenly because a nerve in the chin is damaged, sending the brain into shock. Others argue that the sudden head rotation disrupts the balance mechanism, the vestibular system, located in the inner ear (*see also ACROBATICS*). Although the complete physiological explanation for the abrupt chin knockout remains unclear, part of the reason is the chin's distance from the center of gravity (mass) of the head. As mentioned above, a blow to the tip of the chin creates greater peak acceleration of the skull than a blow landing elsewhere on the head.

The rotational acceleration caused by a blow to the chin represents the greatest possibility of stretching and twisting the brain stem (*see Figure 3*). Because all nerve signals to and from the body pass through the brain stem, its operation, or lack thereof, affects motor control throughout the body. The brain stem also controls the rhythm of breathing and the rate and force at which the heart pumps blood.

Any hard blow to the head can transiently affect the brain stem and cause a concussion, but continuous head blows damage the surface and interior of the brain, killing nerve cells and splitting blood vessels. Unlike the internal surface of an eggshell, the internal surface against which the brain ricochets is nonsymmetrical. The many protrusions of the skull concentrate the impact force over a smaller

The Value of Headgear

Headgear can reduce the acceleration of the head for blows at or near the head's center of gravity by 15 to 25 percent. Yet despite thick padding around the lower jaw and chin, there is no measurable reduction in head acceleration from blows to the chin. Because the chin is the point on the head farthest from the head's center of gravity and axis of rotation, the head experiences the greatest angular acceleration from a blow to the chin.

area of the brain, causing greater trauma to the small part of the brain hitting the protruding parts of the skull.

By rolling with punches, a fighter limits adverse effects on the brain. Maintaining a strong, stiff neck—an asset shared by many championship fighters—may, paradoxically, be a leading contributor to long-term damage to the brain. Recoiling, or "giving a little," lengthens the impact of an opponent's punching force. The boxer receiving a blow moves the head backward in unison with the impact to increase the distance of the stopping action. The effect is similar to that achieved in the picnic game of egg toss. A tossed egg is least likely to break if the catcher extends the arms as far forward and upward as possible. This position allows the catcher to move the hands backward at a speed slightly slower than that at which the egg is traveling and to lengthen the time of impact. To prevent the egg from breaking, the catcher utilizes a very long impact interval—gradually slowing the backward velocity of the egg by moving the hands from the front of the body to well behind it (*see also CATCHING SKILLS*).

In the same way, the strong, stiff neck muscles of an alert fighter may increase the impact of a head blow on the brain. Stiff neck muscles cause the brain to accelerate more quickly in relation to the skull and to ricochet around inside the skull with great force—the same dynamics that make an egg likely to break when caught by hands that are held in place. Although weak or loosely held neck muscles might also facilitate a knockout, the chance of permanent damage to the brain is decreased because the looser neck muscles absorb impact over a longer period and over a wider area.

The strategy of rolling with punches should not to be confused with grogginess, in which the neck is flaccid. A fighter who becomes groggy is not alert enough to slowly decelerate the skull when hit and thus usually suffers the worst damage. The head accelerates quickly upon collision, and then sharply snaps back as the boxer falls down and crashes on the surface of the mat.

Figure 4. *The diagonal line represents the theoretical 50 percent probability of concussion. The greater a primate's brain mass, the more likely that it will suffer a concussive blow from rotational acceleration. From any rotational accelerating force, a human being, with the massive human brain, is twice as likely to suffer a concussion as a chimpanzee and more than 10 times as likely as a squirrel monkey. (Adapted from Ghista, 1982)*

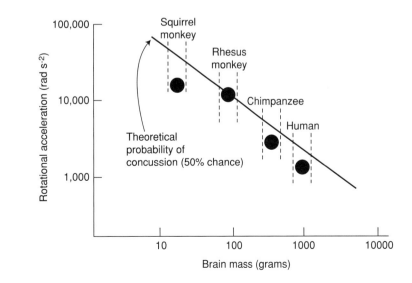

How Dangerous Is Boxing?

In boxing, unlike any other sport, the prime objective is to knock the opponent unconscious—temporarily shutting down all higher brain functions. Head blows may also shear the microscopic fibers known as axons. Like the wires in an old-fashioned telephone switchboard, axons provide the vital connections among brain cells. As a result of a knockout, many neurons are damaged, often irreversibly, including those necessary for higher intellectual functions.

If a blow to the head is sufficiently severe, it sends a jolt to the brain stem that disrupts the electrical signals that regulate breathing, heartbeat, and blood pressure. Depending on the severity of the blow, these symptoms subside in a few minutes, a few hours, a few days, or perhaps a few weeks.

Although an athlete who regains consciousness appears to return to normal, there is increasing evidence of long-term repercussions. Repeated fighting creates cumulative damage as more and more axons snap and degenerate. A few severed axons may not produce symptoms, but the number increases with each fight and each blow. The long-term implications of blows received over a multiyear career are not precisely known, but many doctors fear that boxers are likely to suffer a steady decline in memory and other cognitive abilities. Veteran fighters demonstrate a high frequency of chronic brain damage when given three different kinds of tests: electroencephalography (EEG), computed tomography (CT), and psycho- metric tests. Approximately 70 to 87 percent have showed evidence of chronic brain damage in at least two of these tests (Jordon, 1990).

Contrary to popular belief, it is not the single high-intensity blow that causes most chronic brain damage, but repeated low-intensity blows. Championship fighters usually suffer the most brain damage because they fight the toughest opponents over the longest careers. Ironically, the physical gifts that served them so well in the ring end up working against them. The superior skills that allowed them to prolong their careers means that although they receive far fewer blows per fight, they receive many more blows over the length of a career. They hold a top ranking for a long time and square off against the very best fighters—the ones most capable of inflicting severe damage.

Categorizing brain trauma that results from boxing is difficult because there are a wide range of anatomical differences among boxers, and the blows come from a variety of angles and velocities. Damage can occur anywhere in the brain. The following are some of the most prevalent boxing-related brain and eye injuries.

Detached retina.   Punches received in and around the eye can cause rips and holes in the retina (the back of the eye, which converts what is seen into useful information for the brain), which may lead to retinal detachment and blindness. Severe trauma can also cause cataracts, leading to blindness.

The early stages of retinal injury are usually unnoticed because the boxer maintains good eyesight. Only a thorough eye examination can detect rips in the back of the eye that may lead to retinal detachment. To ensure early diagnosis, many doctors recom-

mend that all boxers periodically have a thorough eye examination.

Although Sugar Ray Leonard—the dominant welterweight champion of the 1980s—returned to the ring after suffering a detached retina, he was taking a tremendous risk. Surgeons can reattach the retina, but the repaired eye is very vulnerable, and a traumatic blow can lead to blindness (*see also VISION*).

Hematomas   Most ring fatalities are caused by intercranial hemorrhages (ruptured blood vessels) and their resulting complications, such as hematomas (blood clots). Hematomas are a particularly troubling injury because they may be caused by just one punch. In a fight in 1995, the Venezuelan boxer Jimmy Garcia

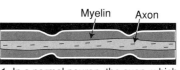

1. In a normal neuron, the axon, which is protected by a myelin sheath, is not broken or otherwise distorted.

2. After a consussive blow, an axon might twist or bend, interrupting communication between neurons.

3. If a concussion is severe enough, the axon swells and disintegrates. Less severely damaged axons return to normal.

Boxing Gloves

Boxing has come a long way from the bare-knuckle days of the nineteenth century. Although the earlier boxers took tremendous beat-

lapsed into coma; he died a few weeks later. Garcia's death was attributed to a hematoma on or near the surface of his brain. The hematoma was a result of the brain bouncing against the interior wall of the skull. Although the bleeding was not severe in terms of volume, it created enough pressure to compress and destroy the brain. A boxer also must worry about brain damage not from the knockout blow itself, but from the impact of the head against the canvas in the ensuing fall, with its rapid deceleration.

Concussions. Physicians consider a concussion a temporary impairment of brain activity, a traumatically induced disturbance of neurological functions. Severity of concussions ranges from mild (where the individual is dazed or disoriented) to moderate (where a loss of motor control occurs without loss of consciousness) to severe (where there is a prolonged loss of consciousness, loss of motor control, and amnesia). Although most doctors agree on the short-term and long-term dangers of severe concussions, there is debate concerning whether mild concussions cause gross or microscopic brain damage. This is because axons twisted by a concussive blow (*see the figure*) sometimes return to normal but are sometimes permanently damaged.

One factor in the mechanics of concussions has to do with the muscles in the neck and the magnitude of changes in the acceleration and deceleration when the head snaps backward as the neck muscles hold it in place (*see Figure 3*). A shearing stress (stress along a tangential plane) occurs near the foramen magnum, the hole at the base of the skull where the brain stem passes into the upper cervical cord, which in turn causes a dis-

ruption of the neural tissue, impairing bodily function. A minor disruption often makes the legs wobbly and weak as equilibrium is lost. In more severe cases, where the tangential head movement is greatest, knockouts occur (*see also MOTOR CONTROL*).

Dementia pugulistia Commonly known as "punch-drunk syndrome," this is the most severe form of boxing dementia. It shows up in about 17 percent of retired professional boxers (Rosenthal, 1990). The neurological damage often goes unnoticed during a boxer's career, but as the normal process of neuron attrition occurs with aging, the first symptoms, such as loss of coordination, begin to appear (*see also AGING*).

Cavum septum pellucidum. In this condition, fairly common among former boxers, a cavelike space emerges between the two membranes that divide the brain, causing symptoms that may include slurred speech, loss of coordination, muscular weakness, and a persistent feeling of fatigue. After retiring in the early 1980s from a boxing career that had spanned more than 30 years, Muhammad Ali showed symptoms of Parkinson's disease. He denied that he was suffering from dementia pugulistia but conceded, "There is a great possibility something could be wrong." Although Ali had been one of the quickest heavyweights of all time—moving in and out with his jab without getting hit himself, "floating like a butterfly, stinging like a bee"—it is unlikely that he could have remained dominant for 30 years without damaging his brain. Because he had so many fights, and because of his remarkable ability to take a punch, he received hundreds of thousands of blows over the years. Possibly the

cumulative effect of these blows was to increase the cave space between the two membranes of his brain (*see also MOTOR CONTROL*).

Part of the solution to the problem of boxing injuries lies with equipment materials and design. Professional fighters could begin wearing headgear; also, the old-fashioned foam headgear used in sparring and amateur boxing could be replaced with improved impact-absorbing materials. Some technology could be borrowed from advances in protective equipment in football. For example, football helmets contain an internal, inflatable sack designed to cushion blows. A newer device called the Pro-Cap adds a second layer of shock-absorbing polyurethane cushion, attached to the exterior of a helmet, which may further reduce the effects of head blows.

Injuries could also be reduced by wider use of thumbless gloves (in such a glove, the thumb is attached to the palm), which are already being worn by amateur boxers and in some professional bouts. Thumbless gloves help prevent eye gouging.

More frequent medical examinations could also help, as could better training of ringside physicians and referees, so that they would be more likely to recognize signs of serious injury.

Some efforts are under way. Referees and ringside physicians stop many fights earlier, and better CT scanning equipment and improved diagnoses allow doctors to pinpoint subtle changes in the brain. Perhaps when doctors are better able to predict problems, boxing officials will revoke a fighter's license before permanent neurological damage occurs.

John Zumerchik

ings, nothing then compared to today's gloved boxing—which is more like offensive warfare than the "manly art of self-defense." Because of the enormous risk of injury to the brain, it is often pointed out that boxing gloves could potentially be altered to prevent injuries (as with

Is There a Link between Sex, Testosterone, Aggression, and Performance?

In the movie *Raging Bull*, Robert DeNiro, playing the boxer Jake Lamotta, pours a pitcher of ice water down his shorts. He hopes that this drastic measure will quell his sexual desire when he is with his wife just before a major fight. Although the film puts a humorous spin on this incident, Lamotta, one of the meanest and most aggressive fighters of all time, was indeed afraid that sexual activity would affect his performance; and many professional trainers still try to persuade boxers to abstain from sex during the weeks preceding a major prizefight. Actually, this idea is not unique to boxing but is widespread among athletes and coaches. During the 1994 World Cup, for example, coaches for the Swiss and the German soccer teams strictly prohibited players from engaging in sex.

Although the reasons behind this practice remain unclear, it is probably attributable to an age-old notion that sexual relations impair physical performance and, particularly, that sex will make a fighter or a warrior less aggressive. This belief in turn may be based on the sense of gratification and peace that many people experience after sex—which is the exact opposite of the state of mind trainers want to instill in boxers. Boxers strive to be aggressive, ornery, and mean.

What trainers are worried about is not the act of intercourse as such, but orgasms, which are believed to drain fighters of aggression. An orgasm is the neurophysiological climax of sexual intercourse. Muscles throughout the body become tense, and then neuromuscular contractions discharge this accumulated sexual tension; an orgasm releases minute quantities of more than 30 elements (including fructose, ascorbic acid, cholesterol, creatine, citric acid, lactic acid, nitrogen, and salt).

It is true that an orgasm relaxes neuromuscular tension; in fact, this release of tension often results in falling asleep. However, nothing is lost in this process that could lower the body's level of energy. In a relatively short time, a healthy person recovers fully from the aftereffects of an orgasm. Protracted fatigue is usually a result of other activities that precede or accompany sex, such as drinking, taking drugs, or going without sleep. The baseball manager Casey Stengel summed up the problem: "It isn't sex that wrecks these guys; it's staying up all night looking for it."

Stengel was largely correct. No research has found that sex before an athletic performance hinders the athlete's abilities in any physiological way. Actually, many athletes believe the contrary—that sex helps them perform better. The American Medical Association's Committee on the Medical Aspects of Sports agrees that if sex is a regular part of an athlete's life, sexual relations on the night before a game will not impair performance.

Still, although sex before athletic competition seems to have no physiological effect, it may have a psychophysiological link—an emotional change that can impair performance. Does sex reduce aggressiveness by altering the levels of serum testosterone and other hormones? Does it therefore reduce the "killer instinct" necessary in many sports, and especially in boxing, hockey, and football?

Much higher levels of serum testosterone (that is, testosterone in the blood) are found in men than in women: 300–1,000 nanograms per deciliter are typical in men, but only 40–120 in women. Studies have found that a high level of serum testosterone is an accurate predictor of male dominance in animals. Can the same be said of humans? A study at Georgia State University involving 4,500 men concluded that white-collar professionals had low testosterone levels; blue-collar workers had higher levels; and unemployed men, football players, and violent criminals had the highest levels (Sharpe, 1993). This would seem to

headgear; *see the sidebar earlier in this article*). However, boxing gloves have changed very little over the years.

Many critics of boxing say that gloves came into use to protect the fighter's fists, not the opponent's brain. Before gloves came onto the scene, boxers resorted to head blows only selectively, and with restraint, for the simple reason that delivering head blows was more likely to break their own knuckles than to incapacitate their opponents. Fighters like John L. Sullivan and James Corbett,

suggest a link between testosterone and aggression in human males, similar to that found in some other aggressive male mammals, but this idea remains controversial.

Many endocrinologists argue that testosterone does not deserve its reputation as the hormone of aggression. Instead, they hold, testosterone deficiency may lead to aggressive behavior. In one study, angry, edgy, and irritable testosterone-deficient men were given testosterone replacement therapy and reported a general improvement in their sense of well-being. They became friendlier, more optimistic, less angry, and less agitated. Moreover, there is some evidence that testosterone therapy can give men and women more energy and improve concentration. On this theory, the cause of aggression might be hormonal imbalance, such as heightened levels of estrogen (Angier, 1995). While it is not likely that hormonal imbalance is responsible for all aggressive behavior, individuals predisposed to aggression may find that hormonal imbalance contributes to it.

Studies have been undertaken to measure levels of serum testosterone and estrogen after sexual activity, but it is not yet known whether an orgasm triggers a hormonal response that alters these levels. Hormone levels are not entirely dependent on physiological triggers but can also be affected by the environment. For example, stress affects hormone levels in ways that researchers are only beginning to understand. When tennis players lose matches and wrestlers lose competitions, their disappointment registers as a fall in blood levels of testosterone (Mazur, 1983). Thus if blood levels of testosterone and estrogen are in fact altered following sex, it may make sense for coaches and trainers to ask athletes to abstain from sex in order to remain aggressive.

However, another point may need to be considered in this regard. Even if sex does alter hormone levels in a way that reduces aggression, how important is that? In other words, is aggression an overrated factor in sports? The answer to this question may have more to do with coaches' and athletes' own attitudes than with physiology or psychology. Even if there is evidence to the contrary, most coaches will continue to encourage aggression. Some studies have even suggested that instilling aggression in players improves performance. In an 8-year study of aggression and its effects on hockey records, a team of Canadian psychologists found a significant relationship between aggressiveness and scoring (McCarthy, 1978). Players with high aggression—quantified in terms of penalty minutes and through psychological tests—consistently outscored players with low aggression. In addition to scoring more goals, they had more shots on goal.

Another aspect of this issue is that there seems to be a point at which athletes may cross a threshold between aggression and hostility—that is, they may begin to engage in uncontrolled aggression, severely harming their performance. Some athletes, such as the former tennis superstar John McEnroe, are able to channel aggression and hostility into productive energy, so that they actually play better. This is unusual, however; uncontrolled aggression usually impairs performance.

To ensure that athletes perform at an optimal degree of arousal—a level of aggression that is high but not too high—many coaches have turned to concentration training. Controlled aggression, they believe, is more productive than reduced aggression. However, coaches must be careful about this: they need to push athletes to the edge of aggression without pushing them over the edge into uncontrolled violence. Each year in many kinds of sports events, countless incidents occur that can be attributed to overblown aggression.

As a clearer scientific understanding of the link between aggression and violence begins to develop, sports officials can institute appropriate changes to better control violence. Possibly, though, aggression in sports will continue, if only because sports mirror trends in society at large. Many people believe that it is futile to hope to eradicate violent crime, and it may be equally futile to strive to eradicate violence in sports.

whose careers marked the transition from the bare-knuckle era to modern gloved boxing, soon realized that gloves allowed them to attack an opponent's head with impunity. Because gloves eliminated the risk of injuring the fists, the head quickly became the target of choice.

Another way gloves have changed boxing is a result of the asymmetrical position of the knuckles. When a fighter makes a fist, the knuckles do not line up in the same plane. The middle knuckle protrudes farthest forward, followed by the index, ring, and fourth knuckles. Many blows in boxing are not "clean," meaning that the four knuckles do not make uniform contact against the striking surface. Gloves help distribute the impact load more evenly among the knuckles, again greatly reducing the risk of injury to the hands. Thus gloves have allowed fighters to swing with much greater freedom, knowing that their hands are protected.

In amateur and intercollegiate boxing, unlike prizefighting, officials have gone to great lengths to protect the athletes. Amateur fighters wear gloves that are more heavily padded (and they must also wear headgear). Amateur boxers up to the 147-pound welterweight class wear 8-ounce (0.22-kg) gloves; all higher-weight classes wear 10-ounce (0.28-kg) gloves. For intercollegiate boxing, gloves are even more protective: they must be a minimum of 12 ounces (0.33 kg).

Professional fighters use gloves that are more lightly padded (and wear no headgear at all). In most professional bouts, the gloves are only 8 ounces—occasionally, only 6 ounces (0.17 kg) for championship bouts. Although it is the heavier, experienced, hard-hitting professional fighters who need more protection, they actually use less than their amateur counterparts.

It should be noted that glove padding does offer some protection for boxers receiving low-impact blows. Because the padding does not fully compress, its absorbing (cushioning) properties lessen the severity of the impact. But as the velocity of blows increases, the gloves quickly "bottom out": just as a bad spring sends a jolt through the occupants of a car, more of the force of a blow is transferred to the point of impact on the receiver's body. To make boxing somewhat safer and reduce the number of severe head and brain injuries, it would be necessary to increase the surface area of the glove or improve its cushioning properties.

John Zumerchik

References

Angier, N. "Is Testosterone Responsible for Aggression? Perhaps Not." *New York Times*, 20 June 1995, C1.

Brancazio, P. *Sports Science*. New York: Simon and Schuster, 1984.

Carlson, N. *Physiology of Behavior*. Needham Heights, Massachusetts: Allyn and Bacon, 1994.

Casson, I., et al. "Magnetic Resonance Imaging Comparisons in Boxers." *Journal of the American Medical Association* 263 (1990): 1670.

Hewitt, P. *Conceptual Physics*. Needham Heights, Massachusetts: Allyn and Bacon, 1984.

Jordon, Barry. *Medical Aspects of Boxing*. Orlando, Florida: CRC Press, 1992.

Katchadourian, H. *Fundamentals of Human Sexuality*. New York: Holt, Rinehart, and Winston, 1985.

Lamb, D. *Physiology of Exercise*. New York: Macmillan, 1984.

Martland, H. "Punch Drunk." *Journal of the American Medical Association* 91 (1928): 1103.

Mazur, A. "Hormones, Aggression, and Dominance in Humans." In B. Svare (ed.), *Hormones and Aggressive Behavior*. New York: Plenum, 1983.

McCarthy, J. "Aggression, Performance Variables, and Anger: Self-Report in Ice Hockey Players." *Journal of Psychology* 99 (1978): 97.

Rosenthal, E. "Rebel Neurologists Say Boxing Can Be Safe." *New York Times,* 22 May 1990, C1.

Sharpe, A. "Spit Testing May Be Hard to Swallow in the Workplace." *Wall Street Journal,* 29 November 1993, A4.

Vander, A., et al. *Human Physiology*. New York: McGraw-Hill, 1994.

Walker, J. "Physics of Karate Strikes." *American Journal of Physics* 43, no. 10 (1975): 845–849.

Wallace, R., and M. Schroeder. "Analysis of Billiard Collisions in Two Dimensions." *American Journal of Physics* 56, no. 9 (1988): 815–819; comment: 57, no. 5 (1989): 476.

Wilk, S., et al. "The Physics of Karate." *American Journal of Physics* 51, no. 9 (1983): 783–790.

Yamada, H. *Strength of Biological Materials*. Baltimore: Williams and Wilkens, 1970.

Catching Skills

CATCHING SKILLS are perhaps the most underrated of all athletic skills. Although an integral aspect of many major sports (like baseball, football, and basketball) and minor sports (such as lacrosse and jai alai), catching skills receive little attention. Making the catch is generally considered automatic, a simple feat that should be accomplished without any difficulty. When a football receiver drops a potentially winning touchdown pass, he is labeled the "goat" should his team lose, regardless of how poorly the rest of the team played. Dropping a pass ranks high on the list of unforgivable blunders, alongside pass interceptions and fumbles.

But catching is a complex art. When a baseball player tracks down and catches a fly ball, for example, a complex configuration of events occurs. Although most thrown or struck objects follow a parabolic flight path, wind, temperature, altitude, and the speed and type of spin may all affect the flight path and distance that a ball will travel. Lower air densities, higher temperatures, and higher altitudes are all optimal conditions that aid the distance that a ball will travel, and a ball thrown or hit with back spin will cover a greater airborne distance and drop more abruptly (*see THROWING*). A swirling, blustery wind, as well as the way the ball comes off the bat, has caused even the most experienced major league ball player to occasionally misjudge a fly ball.

This article explores some aspects of catching a ball. In addition to covering the basic mechanics of catching, it also explains the equally vital skill of judging the flight path of the ball. It concludes with a discussion of one catching sport: lacrosse.

Judging a Fly Ball

Few plays in baseball are as exciting as home-run-stealing catches. When a fleet-footed major league outfielder like Ken Griffey Jr. looks away and takes off at the crack of the bat, then jumps halfway over the wall to catch the ball, many fans are awestruck. They are amazed not only at his ability to sprint, scale the wall, and catch the ball, but also at his quick and accurate estimation of where the ball will come down.

Figure 1. *Because outfielders stand a great distance from the hitter, they often must sprint quite a distance to track down a fly ball. Their accuracy is attributable to much more than guesswork. They draw on memories of experiences with fly balls to estimate pitch speed, bat speed, and flushness of contact, which includes the spin of the ball off the bat. It usually takes years of experience before outfielders accurately and consistently judge fly balls.*

An outfielder makes this estimate of a fly ball's trajectory by judging the direction, range, and time of flight, based on its motion during the first split seconds of its flight. A player like Griffey has the uncanny ability to make the judgment with only a short look at the initial trajectory. A quick read serves him well, for the longer it takes to make his decision, the less time remains for him to arrive at the ball's landing point. And when someone like Griffey tries to scale the wall to pull off a home-run-saving catch, a delayed start significantly reduces the probability of arriving at the wall before the ball does. In developing this often overlooked skill, there is far more sensory feedback than one might think.

An athlete's catching skills may be exceptional, but they amount to little unless he quickly sees, reads, reacts, and runs to the right spot to catch the ball. Receivers and punt returners in football rely on their ability to judge the flight of the ball. In football, unlike round-ball sports, such as baseball or lacrosse, players receive a very early clue owing to the unique shape of the ball. From the determination of ball flight, tumbling end over end or spiraling, and the limited distance the ball travels, they can quickly judge where to position themselves to catch the ball.

A baseball outfielder, on the other hand, has a much more difficult task in judging the flight of the ball. He stands two or three times farther away and receives no early visual clues because the ball is round; no matter how acute an outfielder's vision, he simply is too far away to determine spin by picking up seam rotation. He must also estimate pitch speed, bat speed, and flushness of contact. Though it is not an easy task, surprisingly few baseball coaching books offer a step-by-step guide on how to judge a fly ball—suggesting, perhaps, that it is an unteachable skill. Like most athletic skills, tracking a fly ball is accomplished by practice: hours upon hours of drills to develop the necessary sensory reflex skills. From a wide range of sensory clues, auditory as well as visual, outfielders develop the ability to figure out precisely where the ball is going to land.

Seville Chapman, a physicist at the Cornell Aeronautical Laboratory, proposed that outfielders rely on simple principles of geometry when judging the flight of fly balls. In essence, the best outfielders track down fly balls as military radar tracks enemy planes. Outfielders

Figure 2. *Judging the flight path of a batted or thrown ball is in large part a matter of geometry: following the angle of elevation from angle e_1 to angle e_3.*

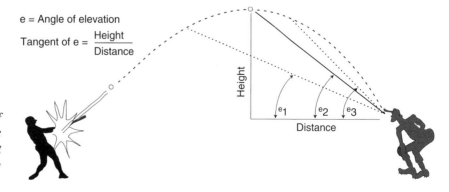

e = Angle of elevation

Tangent of e = $\dfrac{\text{Height}}{\text{Distance}}$

quickly decide on an interception course, as a military command center would plot an antiaircraft missile to intercept incoming planes.

Chapman's study examined what happens when a fly ball is hit directly at a fielder, who must run either backward or forward, but not sideways, to catch the ball (*see Figure 2*). He concluded that outfielders judge fly balls by calculating the changes that occur in the ball's angle of elevation. The term *angle of elevation* refers to the angle from the ground to the outfielder's sight line to the ball. Changes in the angle of elevation, occurring over time, allow outfielders to track fly balls. As the ball comes off the bat, the angle of elevation increases as it rises ever higher up into the air (angle e_1 to angle e_3). For balls hit in front of the fielder, such as infield pop-ups or "bloop" singles (pop-up flies that fall between the infielders and the outfielders), the angle of elevation increases at a decreasing rate. For home runs, the angle of elevation increases at an increasing rate. And in the case of balls hit directly to the outfielder, the angle of elevation appears to increase at a steady rate.

Chapman observed that an outfielder moves toward the ball by maintaining a course that is based upon the constant rate of increase of the tangent of elevation. In other words, if the rate of increase of the tangent of elevation continues to rise, the outfielder knows he had better start sprinting. The pattern of an outfielder's movement appears to back up Chapman's theory. Rarely does an outfielder sprint backward and wait for the ball; instead, he drifts back slowly, arriving at the same time as the ball. Or he might sprint for 5 or 10 yards, then start drifting back slowly as the angle of elevation reaches a steady rate.

Chapman's analysis looked only at fly balls hit on a line directly at the outfielder. Intuitively, it would seem that a ball hit in a direct line toward an outfielder would be the easiest ball to catch. Outfielders know from experience, however, that the ball hit directly at you is the most difficult to judge. In this situation, geometry is not as effective a judgment tool. Balls hit in a straight-line trajectory toward the outfielder can be judged in only two dimensions: horizontal and vertical. Without a three-dimensional view of the oncoming ball, it is more difficult for the outfielder to judge changes in the angle of elevation. Because center field is the position most likely to receive the most balls hit on a direct line to the outfielder, most managers wisely put their best outfielder in center field.

Note: Other factors in judging fly balls. Some baseball players have an uncanny ability to judge fly balls. Bobby Bonds, three times the major league's most valuable player, often would not even move, or look back, when a ball was "well-tagged." If he recognized the angle of elevation increasing at an increasing rate, he saw no need to make the mandatory jog back to the fence. Of course, he ran the slight risk of a tremendous embarrassment: if a gale force wind kicked up, it could pull the drive right back into the field of play.

When a gale-force wind does develop, air resistance makes it impossible to judge a ball simply by a calculation based on the geometry during the first seconds after bat-ball contact. Because the ball no longer follows a perfect parabolic path, the angle of elevation alone can no longer predict the path of the ball. Under windy conditions, even the best outfielders have trouble judging fly balls. Air resistance forces can make it very difficult to judge the ball's flight path. Nevertheless, more often than not, top outfielders still catch the ball. Some of this ability to make the catch comes from outstanding depth perception. Depth perception depends on binocular vision, in which comparisons occur between the two eyes' different views of the ball as it moves across the background. Although depth perception is primarily a phenomenon based on the difference between the visual perceptions of the two eyes, with practice a one-eyed individual can also develop depth perception, albeit not to the same degree (*see VISION*).

Peter Brancazio, a Brooklyn College physicist, observes that nonvisual sensory input also makes a significant contribution in judging a fly ball (Brancazio, 1985). The nervous system constantly monitors a variety of mechanical stimuli. The major mechanical sensory apparatus used by the nervous system, the vestibular system, is located in the inner ear. It helps to maintain balance, discerns between up and down, and ascertains changes in acceleration. Seasickness is a vivid example of the results of disorientation of the vestibular system, which in turn creates havoc throughout the body's nervous system. Being tossed around in a boat—moving up, down, and all around—sends a series of confusing signals that the vestibular system has difficulty interpreting (*see ACROBATICS*).

According to Brancazio, what starts an outfielder moving toward a fly ball—in addition to the visual signal and the auditory signal of bat meeting ball—is a mechanical process that occurs in the vestibular system. This occurs because the brain processes auditory signals at a faster rate than visual signals and mechanical signals faster than auditory signals (*see also MOTOR CONTROL*).

Triggering the vestibular system into action is the outfielder's head jerk—a movement upward as the eyes follow the ball coming off the bat. A simple eye-tracking experiment demonstrates how much faster the vestibular system reacts to movement than just a visual clue. When one tracks the movement of a pencil shaken quickly back and forth by eye movement alone, it is difficult to retain focus on the pencil at all times. But if one holds the pencil steady and shakes one's head back and forth, a much sharper focus on the pencil results. A ballplayer's rapid reaction to a fly ball develops through years of trial-and-error practice with the vestibular system. The mechanical signals generated by the movement of the head are transferred into electrical signals that are rapidly processed in the lower brain. As a result, an outfielder quickly arrives at the landing point of a fly ball.

Catching Technique

Catching with a Stick

Hurling, a very popular game in Ireland, entails catching and throwing a ball on the end of a flat stick. Because there is no energy-absorbing basket or webbing at the end of the stick to catch and cradle the ball, this is considered an extremely difficult skill to master. Nevertheless, skilled hurlers make catching the ball look routine. Folklore has it that one man repeatedly threw and caught a ball on his hurling stick as he walked a distance of nine miles, without once letting it hit the ground.

In its most basic form, catching is the act of reducing the momentum (mass × velocity) of a ball to zero or near-zero velocity and then retaining possession. A transfer of momentum takes place as the momentum of the ball is absorbed by the hands, body, or sports equipment. To prevent a ball from rebounding out of one's hands or catching apparatus (e.g., glove or lacrosse stick) a gradual loss of the kinetic energy (energy of motion) of the ball is necessary. This can be accomplished in three ways: (1) by using as much distance as possible to reduce velocity, (2) by increasing the time over which the force is absorbed, and (3) by increasing the area that receives the force of impact. Most athletes use some combination of all three methods.

Distance and time can be increased by pulling the hands in toward the body while transferring weight from the front foot to the back, or by taking a few steps backwards during the catch. Usually the catcher "gives a little" himself, or recoils with a catching implement to slowly reduce the momentum of a moving ball. The catcher moves his hands, or the catching equipment, backward in unison with impact to increase the distance and time of the stopping action, thereby softening the catch. It is also important to make use of all the natural shock absorbers in the body: muscles, tendons, and various joints.

An example of giving a little appears in the common game of egg toss. The egg is least likely to break if the catcher extends her arms as far forward and upward as possible (assuming it is a position that does not inhibit her from moving her hands backward at nearly the egg's speed at contact). To prevent the egg from breaking, the catcher uses a very long impact interval, gradually slowing the backward hand velocity, from far in front of her body to well behind it.

Increasing the area that receives the force of impact is possible in sports such as baseball and lacrosse by increasing the size of the pocket of, respectively, the glove and the head of the lacrosse stick. Although a larger webbed pocket makes it easier to catch a ball, it does have inherent disadvantages. Generally, it makes it more difficult for a lacrosse player to throw the ball as accurately, and often a baseball player waering a large glove might make a dazzling catch, but then be unable to get the ball out of his glove, enabling the runner to advance.

Another factor governing a catcher's ability to reduce the force of impact is the distance from the point where the ball is received to the catcher's center of gravity (the geometric center of mass distribution). If the ball is caught high over the head or well out to one side, the force of impact occurs at the end of a long lever arm, which gives the ball a rotational effect on the body and makes it more difficult to gradually absorb the ball's kinetic energy.

In football, good receivers catch the ball with their hands, gradually absorbing the kinetic energy of the ball, and they try to avoid trapping the ball against their bodies. If the ball is trapped against the

Soft Hands?

Sportscasters often say that good football receivers have soft hands. In reality, the receivers' hands are no "softer" than anyone else's. "Soft hands" is simply an expression that describes the very smooth way that they gradually bring the high-speed, spiraling ball to rest against their bodies, gradually decelerating its velocity by the skilled use of their hands.

body, the moment of impact is extremely short, so the hands and arms engulf the ball, preventing it from rebounding away. Because extending the impact interval is nearly impossible when trapping the ball, it is extremely difficult to catch a high-velocity pass.

To catch a football, receivers must anticipate and absorb the football's spin around the ball's vertical axis as well as its forward speed. A receiver positions his hands in a manner that will counter the spin and bring the ball to rest in his hands. Usually one hand gradually reduces the velocity of the ball while the other hand stops the spin of the ball. If the receiver is accustomed to the clockwise spin of a right-handed passer or a right-footed kicker, catching a ball with a counterclockwise spin (thrown or kicked by a left-handed player) necessitates a countering hand adjustment in the opposite direction. When receivers do not make this adjustment, the ball often seems to pop right out of their hands (*see Figure 3*). The superstar receiver Jerry Rice had to make such an adjustment when Steve Young replaced Joe Montana as the San Francisco 49ers quarterback. It took a subtle adjustment to enable Rice to catch left-handed passes. After catching Montana's passes for several years, he had become accustomed to a clockwise spin. His hand preparation had to change to account for Young's counterspin.

Sometimes a ball can be caught in a way that will assist the throw. In sports such as basketball and water polo, a great advantage is gained by gradually reducing the kinetic energy, catching the ball in a way that serves as the preparatory motion for throwing the ball. Water polo players receive additional benefit from this type of execution because of the dense medium of the water from which they must catch and throw. It is easier for the arm, moving backward during the catch, to stretch the shoulder and trunk muscles, because the lower body is anchored in the much denser water. This muscle stretching action, or coiling, during the catch contributes mightily to the throw's velocity, or uncoiling (*see also SHOULDER, ELBOW, AND WRIST*).

Basketball players make similar adjustments, albeit not as exaggerated as those of the partially submerged water polo players. Play often dictates catching the ball by allowing the kinetic energy of the ball, moving at a high velocity, to bring back the arm and rotate the body into a favorable throwing position. The player thus makes the transition from catching to throwing in one continuous motion, aided by the momentum of the ball.

Figure 3. *The position of the arm and hand changes to counter the rotation of a football. Catching a ball from a left-handed quarterback (c) requires a slight adjustment in arm and hand position.*

(a) No spin   (b) Right-hander's spin   (c) Left-hander's spin

Lacrosse: A Unique Catching Sport

Lacrosse is unique in that the same equipment is used for throwing and catching (*see Figure 4*). The lacrosse stick lengthens the lever arm so that players not only have tremendous reach for catching errant throws but also generate tremendous velocity throwing the ball. The extended arm lever throw means that the ball spends a considerable amount of time flying around at velocities greater than 100 MPH.

Lacrosse players have considerable latitude in selecting a stick: stick length, pocket size, and pocket depth all vary. The two major considerations in choosing a stick are the type of pocket and the length of the handle. Liberal rules allow sticks between 40 and 72 inches (100–180cm) in length—except for the goalie's stick, which may be any length. The pocket can vary between 6.5 and 10 inches (16–17.5 cm).Defense players usually use longer sticks (56 to 72 in.), and offense players normally use sticks with the smallest pockets (6.5 to 7 inches) for better ball control and dodging. The net of the pocket is triangular and may be composed of a variety of materials: gut, rawhide, nylon, or other synthetic material. A guard stop is located at the bottom of the throat so that the ball does not fall right out. The netting cannot be so loose that the top surface of the ball is below the bottom edge of the wall. This rule was instituted because defenders had great difficulty dislodging the ball from deep pockets.

There are two techniques used by lacrosse players when catching the ball: catching and cradling (*see Figure 5*). The catching technique requires the player to extend forward toward the ball and to move the stick in the ball's direction on impact. In the cradling technique, the ball is caught by rotating the stick, which requires the basket to dissipate more of the kinetic energy.

One trait necessary for consistently catching the ball is excellent eye-hand coordination ("soft hands"), enhanced by an adept recoiling or cradling motion. To minimize problems with eye-hand coordination, it is best to catch the ball by bringing it back along one's line of sight, a straight motion backward, ending near the ear. It is important that a player not fully extend his arms forward. Coaches recommend keeping the elbows slightly bent so that it is easier to time the recoil with ball impact.

Of course, wild throws give players few positioning options when catching the ball. A ball thrown directly at the body requires a quick choking up on the stick; high, far left, and far right passes force the catcher to slide his top hand down the stick in order to extend the arms and the stick as far as possible.

When the ball strikes the lacrosse basket, there is energy absorption as the ball and basket deform. Although considerable basket deformation can readily be seen, considerable ball deformation also takes place. The two in combination absorb most of the ball's energy, but do not dissipate all of it—the ball still possesses a sizable amount of kinetic energy and can rebound out of the basket. The ball's

Figure 4. *The lacrosse stick lengthens the throwing- and catching-arm lever. This longer lever allows players to throw at much higher velocities than those achieved by, for example, baseball pitchers, and extends the reach in catching. The lacrosse ball, and the pelota used in jai alai, have been recorded attaining speeds exceeding 150 MPH (240 KPH). This exceeds the top speeds reached in other high-speed throwing and striking sports: the tennis serve has been recorded at 130 MPH, the hockey slap shot at 115 MPH, and the baseball fastball at 100 MPH.*

Figure 5. *The lacrosse catching (a) and cradling (b) techniques absorb the kinetic energy of the ball. The catching technique requires the player to extend forward toward the ball and move the stick in the direction of the ball during the catch (about 2 ft.). In the cradle technique, the ball is caught by rotating the stick, which requires the basket to dissipate more of the kinetic energy.*

rebound energy (a coefficient of restitution of 0.55 meaning that it rebounds 5.5 feet up from the ground if dropped from a height of 10 feet) is slightly less than a tennis ball and about the same as that of a baseball or softball. Therefore, a lacrosse player must also move his hands, arms, and stick in the direction of the ball's flight to lengthen the distance. Usually this is a backward motion, which decelerates the ball over a longer period, absorbing the remaining kinetic energy.

It has been determined that when the ball is moving at 20 meters (66 ft.) per second before impact, about 90 percent of the kinetic energy of the ball can be absorbed by the deformation of the basket and ball. From observational data, it was determined that the basket needs to recoil approximately 0.6 meter (2 ft.) in order to absorb the remaining 10 percent of the kinetic energy and reduce the velocity of the ball to zero (Adrian, 1989).

Often lacrosse battles occur in very tight quarters, with opponents closing in from all directions. In these situations, recoiling 0.6 meter takes too much time and often places the ball and stick in a poor offensive position; players must then rely on the cradle technique. The cradle technique involves rotating the stick back and forth around its longitudinal axis. The ball comes to rest after rebounding against the sides of the stick head. Whereas the catch involves a linear motion of 0.6 meter to ensure that the ball remains in the basket, the rotational cradle method keeps stick and body movement to a minimum. This is very beneficial from an offensive point of view, as it more effectively prepares the player to quickly catch and throw the ball. Elite players are extremely proficient at catching and throwing the ball and apply the energy gained during the catch to start the throw.

In stopping the ball, the basket deforms, the stick bends, and the muscles stretch—all ways of storing energy. In a quick, well-timed reflex, this energy can then be transformed into kinetic energy as the ball is launched in a new direction. This makes lacrosse one of the few sports in which catching and throwing are not two distinct skills: the same motion used to catch the ball often is used again to throw it, only in reverse.

References

Adrian, M., and J. Cooper. *Biomechanics of Human Movement.* Dubuque, Iowa: Benchmark, 1989.

Brancazio, P. "Looking into Chapman's Homer: The Physics of Judging a Fly Ball." *American Journal of Physics* 53, no. 9 (1985): 849–855.

Brancazio, P. *Sport Science.* New York: Simon and Schuster, 1984.

Chapman, S. "Catching a Baseball." *American Journal of Physics* 36 (1968): 868.

Hudspeth, A., and V. Markin. "The Ear's Gears: Mechanoelectrical Transduction by Hair Cells." *Physics Today* 47, no. 2 (1994): 22–28.

Urick, D. *Sports Illustrated LaCrosse: Fundamentals for Winning.* New York: Sports Illustrated Winner's Circle Books, 1988.

Cycling

CYCLING is a popular international sport. For a few weeks every spring, European attention is focused on the Tour de France—a multifaceted race consisting of time trials, road races, and mountain climbs. It is a grueling test of endurance. At the other extreme are some very local cultural events. One example is the "Little 500," hosted every May by Indiana University. This 500-lap team relay race was dramatically portrayed in the movie *Breaking Away*.

Cycling also plays important socioeconomic roles in many parts of the world. For instance, in China and the Netherlands cycling is much more than a recreational sport; it is the primary means of commuting. In the Netherlands, flat terrain and very narrow streets often make the bicycle the fastest and easiest means of transportation. And in China, because of the density of the population, the minimal amount of mass transit, and the relatively small number of automobiles, the bicycle is the preferred means of commuting. In comparison with the United States, where there are 1.7 people per car, in China there are 680 people for every car (Ellis, 1994). Every day the streets of Shanghai are clogged not by cars, but by bicycle traffic, as approximately 4 million commuters pedal to work. If only half the hundreds of millions of Chinese who commute by bicycle started commuting by moped or car, the world would experience another energy crisis almost instantly.

After the development of the chain-drive bicycle in the 1880s, and before Henry Ford popularized the automobile in the 1910s, cycling became extremely popular in the United States as a means of transportation. It was over three times faster than walking and more convenient and cheaper than a horse-drawn carriage. Presently, because of the detrimental effects of the car on the environment, there is a growing movement to encourage greater use of the bicycle as a means of transportation. Its prospects for success appear to be remote, however; weaning people away from the convenience, luxury, and freedom of automobile travel would be a monumental task.

However, as a sport cycling has always remained popular. Some of the reasons for its fairly consistent popularity have been technological innovation and the continual evolution of new forms of the sport. In the 1930s and 1940s track (sprint and pursuit) racing around a steeply angled oval track was the rage. Probably because of the inaccessibility of oval tracks to the greater population, track racing waned and inter-

TRANSPORTATION ENERGY REQUIREMENTS

Mode	Vehicle mileage	Energy consumption
Bicycle	1,560	80
Walking	470	260
Car	30	1,030
Bus	5	550
747 Jet	0.1	3,440

Table 1. *The bicycle is a very efficient means of transportation. Energy consumption is given as British termal unit (BTU) consumption per passenger mile, and vehicle mileage as miles per gallon of gasoline or its equivalent in food or other fuel. (Source: Romer, 1976)*

Figure 1. *On 22 September 1992, the Dexter-Hysol Cheetah set a speed record for a human-powered vehicle at 68.73 MPH. In addition to employing lightweight materials, the Cheetah used aerospace bonding agents to distribute stress and load over a greater area than conventional fasteners, increasing strength and diminishing speed-reducing vibrations. (Photo courtesy of The Dexter Corporation)*

est in road racing and time trials grew. In the 1980s, the small-frame, high-clearance, dirt mogul track bike garnered significant interest. And in the 1990s, with the development of larger frames and nobbed tires, mountain bike racing joined road racing as a popular alternative.

Along with advances in bicycle technology, advances in cyclist training methods have pushed up speeds. As of 1996, speed records were at levels that could never have been imagined just a few years earlier. For a 1 hour period, single-rider aerodynamic bicycles have reached speeds of 51.30 kilometers per hour (KPH), or about 31.88 miles per hour (MPH). And at the edge of aerodynamic advances is the Dexter-Hysol Cheetah—a semirecumbant two-wheeled bike enclosed in an aerodynamic shield—which, on 22 September 1992, set a speed record for a human-powered vehicle: 110.62 KPH (68.73 MPH; *see Figure 1*).

Frame Geometry

The frame is the most important part of a bicycle. Other parts are secondary because they can be adjusted, but the frame has no adjustments. Although frames all look about the same, there are many differences—some of which are obvious, others quite subtle.

Four major parts directly affect speed, comfort, and efficiency: the seat tube, top tube, head tube, and down tube. These four tubes

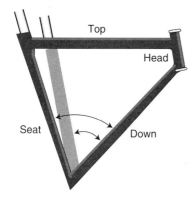

Figure 2. *A wider seat tube angle (black) and a tighter seat tube angle (gray). Frame geometry affects wheelbase length, weight, and pedal mechanics, which all affect performance.*

are configured in what is called the frame geometry. The angles of the seat and head tubes are of primary concern. Their angles determine the wheelbase, the distance between the front and rear wheels. Except for some of the newer mountain bikes, which have active suspension (spring and shock systems similar to motorcycles), the wheelbase of the frame geometry is the primary means of "cushioning" the ride. Much as a longer boat rides over the crests of several waves with less pitching, a longer wheelbase provides more cushioning and less pitching. This is true because the bike does not make as much of a pronounced dip when traversing rough roads. A longer wheelbase keeps the bicycle at a more consistent horizontal angle.

Bicycles with tighter frames (more upright angles) have a shorter wheelbase, give a stiffer ride, and are naturally lighter. In contrast, the wider (lower) angle frame has longer tubes, has more mass, and provides a ride with more cushion. Not only does a wider-angle frame have more mass, but the center of mass is well forward of the rear wheel, increasing its stability. Greg Le Mond has argued that frame builders have steepened the seat tube angle to make bikes look more aggressive and to give the impression that they are more responsive. Seat tube angles range from 68 degrees to 74 degrees. Le Mond uses a bike in the middle of this range, with about a 72.5-degree seat tube angle. At 74 degrees, he argues, the seat tube is too far forward for optimal pedaling.

Figure 2 compares a tight and a wide frame. With a steep seat tube, the rear wheel can be fitted very tightly behind the seat tube. If the head tube is also very steep, the wheelbase is shortened. Short - wheelbase bikes are less stable and are overly responsive on turns and corners. A tighter frame also fatigues a rider because it generates an excessive amount of vibration.

Frame Materials

There are three major types of tubing used for bike frames: straight-gauge, double-butted, and triple-butted. Straight-gauge tubing is the old standard, one step up from commonplace pipe tubing. The more recent double-butted frame uses a highly resilient steel alloy containing chromium and molybdenum. It is called double-butted because the tubes' walls are thicker near the end and thinner in the middle. Very expensive triple-butted frames are butted not only at the ends but in the middle as well. Manufacturers claim that an additional butt in the middle dampens vibrational energy more quickly. In theory, this should be true. It is analogous to the string dampeners that tennis players use. Placed on the strings near the racket throat, they dampen vibrations created in the strings before they can reach the frame (the hand at the grip).

Aluminum and graphite frames are increasingly used as an alternative to steel. Until they can be efficiently mass-produced, however,

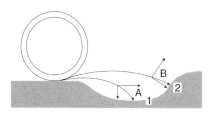

Figure 3. *The dynamics of wheel loss on rough surfaces for the path of a wheel at two speeds: slow (1) and fast (2). The component of kinetic energy perpendicular to the surface is lost. The relative kinetic energy loss of landing at point 2 will be greater than at point 1 because angle B is greater than angle A. (Adapted from Whitt, 1974)*

these frames will remain much more expensive. These materials offer the great benefit of weight reduction; this usually comes at the cost, however, of less dampening of vibrations. On rough roads, and for long-distance riding, most experienced riders opt for a heavier steel frame bike over the lighter, yet less dampening, aluminum frame. But in a mountain sprint (climb) race, where riders wage a battle with gravity, the benefits of a lighter-weight aluminum frame might outweigh the disadvantages of greater vibration.

The trade-off between light weight and strength (limited vibration) continues to make the development of bicycle frames a difficult challenge for manufacturers. This dilemma will probably continue until better composite materials become more readily available—when affordable composite frames will give riders both the strength and comfort of steel and the lightness of aluminum (*see also EQUIPMENT MATERIALS*).

Every time a rider hits a bump in the road, the center of gravity (geometric center of mass distribution) of both the bike and the rider comes forward, then quickly shifts back (*see also ACROBATICS*). Much of the kinetic (movement) energy is lost during this shift in the center of gravity (*see Figure 3*). This loss, along with the loss to vibrational energy, is responsible for limiting a significant amount of bicycle speed.

Ideally, the centers of gravity of rider and bike should be as close together as possible. Rough roads shift the center of gravity forward and require the rider to compensate by moving her center of gravity backward. Each time the rider adjusts her center of gravity, the result is a speed loss. It is comparable to what occurs during sailing: yacht racers try to keep their movements to a minimum and position themselves as near the boat's center of gravity as possible. Any movements vary the center of gravity, decreasing the boat speed because the energy wasted bobbing or pitching comes at the expense of forward motion (*see also SAILING*).

Stability

Stability is probably the part of bicycle design most taken for granted. There are a number of factors that affect stability, but of primary importance is sideward friction force. When the sideward friction force is missing—as happens on wet ice or slipping on loose gravel—no amount of steering will prevent a fall. The rider hits the road almost immediately.

Figure 4(a) shows a balanced, steady turn. The horizontal friction force (F) of the road on the tires provides the necessary acceleration for the cyclist to move in a circle. Without this force, she would move in a straight line. At the same time, the road exerts an upward normal force (N) that exactly balances the downward gravitational force (mg). The road force (F) is applied at the point of contact, but in this

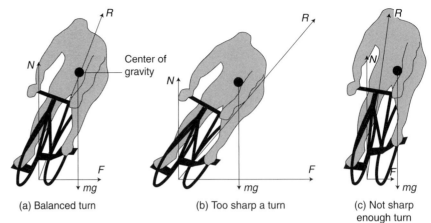

Figure 4. *A cyclist may turn in a position that is balanced (a), too sharp (b), or not sharp enough (c). Cyclists continually adjust the angle of tilt and the amount of turn to maintain balance. Experienced cyclists either turn into the tilt or tilt into the turn.*

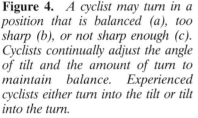

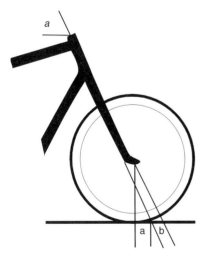

Figure 5. *The head tube angle (a) and the fork rake (b) produce the trail length (a + b). They create a sideways force on the front tire that produces a torque on the steering axis, lowering the bike's center of gravity. The longer the trail, the better the bike's ability to self-steer.*

case, the line of action is the sum of the two components (R), which passes through her center of gravity.

For purposes of determining the torques (rotational forces about an axis) acting on her, the gravitational force can be considered to act at the center of gravity. Because she is in a balanced position, the cyclist's angle of tilt does not change. The net road force and gravity both act through her center of gravity, exerting no torque about that point. The situation changes when turning too sharply, as in Figure 4(b), and not sharply enough, as in Figure 4(c). In (b) the horizontal friction force is larger than in a steady turn. It now takes more force to turn in a smaller circle at a given speed. The net road force, R, no longer passes through her center of gravity. It forms a couple with the gravitational force, tending to rotate the rider into a more upright position. The opposite occurs in (c). The horizontal frictional force is so small that R now passes to the left of her center of gravity. This creates a torque about her center of gravity that tends to rotate the rider down toward the ground.

Riding a bicycle requires a continuous adjustment of the angle of tilt and the amount of turn in order to maintain the balance point. It does not take long for most beginners to figure out how to achieve the dual goals: to avoid falling while moving in the desired direction. Experienced riders either "turn into the tilt" or "tilt into the turn." It is often impossible to tell which comes first.

Paradoxically, the faster one rides, the easier it is to steer. That is because a smaller steering adjustment is needed to make a centripetal (outward to inward force) correction to keep the bike from falling. This is attributable to gyroscopic action (an ability to maintain forward direction by virtue of the rapidly spinning wheels). Generally, gyroscopic action makes a very minor contribution to stability (*see also* FOOTBALL).

A secondary factor affecting stability is frame-related: the self-stabilizing geometry of the bike's front fork. A riderless bicycle will remain upright for about 20 seconds when pushed, but only about 2 seconds when stationary. Bicycles come with the front forks raked (curved) forward 1.25 to 2.75 inches (about 3–7 cm) in order to increase stability and lower the center of gravity as the front wheel produces a torque on the steering axis (*see Figure 5*). The rake creates a force pushing upward from the ground. This force is behind the steering axis, yet in line with it, so it stabilizes without creating a turning force. When the bicycle leans sideways to the left, the steering axis moves with it as well. The upward force moves to the right of the steering axis, causing the fork to turn left to self-correct and thus preventing the bicycle from continuing to fall to the left. A study by physicist David Jones showed that when the front fork is raked back instead of forward the bike is very unstable, almost unrideable (Jones, 1970). If a small rake increases the trail and the self-steering effect, it seems logical to presume that an even larger rake would result in more self-steering. Although a larger rake further lowers the center of gravity, it is not more stable. There is a point when a large trail becomes very dangerous because it is likely to oversteer—the front fork wants to turn too far. Therefore, bicycle manufacturers avoid designs that bring the front fork too far forward.

Larger-forked bikes can be steered through turns with no hands because they react when the rider shifts his balance. For wobbly riders, a large rake is not recommended. Instead, they will do better with an insensitive bike that travels straight no matter how much the rider wobbles. Rough-road riders also want an insensitive bike because a sensitive bike cannot tell the difference between the balance shift of a rider and the balance shift caused by a pothole.

Forces Acting on Bike and Rider

There are many forces acting on a rider trying to propel a bicycle along. These forces have large and small effects and vary with conditions. Figure 6 shows the propulsive and retarding forces acting on a bicycle and rider.

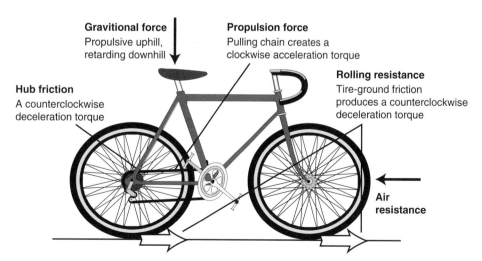

Figure 6. *Propulsive and resistance forces act on a bicycle and its rider.*

Rolling resistance and air resistance are the two forces that always act against the forward motion of the bicycle and its rider. Rolling resistance varies depending on wheel diameter, road surface, tire type, and inflation pressure; air resistance varies with speed and the frontal area projected by the bike and rider.

Inertia and Fighting Gravity

Although gravity is a constant force on the bicycle and rider, it becomes far more apparent, and a much bigger factor, in riding hilly terrain. To understand how gravity affects a cyclist, consider a ball set on a wobbly table. If the table is level, the ball remains stationary. Gravity is acting on the ball, but in only one direction: directly into the table. This changes when tilting the tabletop. The ball begins to roll, not from any change in the force of gravity, but because the ball now has a direction in which it can move: down the tilted table.

Figure 7 shows the gravitational forces that confront a cyclist on flat terrain and hilly terrain. Gravitational forces (*W*) on the rider are the same for all these examples. Gravity acts in the same direction, vertically downward, and is equal to the combined weight of the bicycle and rider. *R* represents the resulting force affecting the bicycle and rider. On level ground, much like the ball on a level table, *R* equals zero. But as the terrain becomes increasingly hillier, so does the resisting force. *R* acts against the rider for the uphill and acts in favor of the rider for the downhill.

Weight and resistance are inversely proportional. For every 1 percent increase in total weight (*W*), there will be a 1 percent reduction in the force component (*R*) (Faria, 1978). The actual force of resistance is minimal for slight inclines, yet it becomes very significant for steep hills. And at any given power output, rider speed and resisting force are inversely related; that is, cutting the resistance force (either air or mass) in half will double the speed. For example, a cyclist trav-

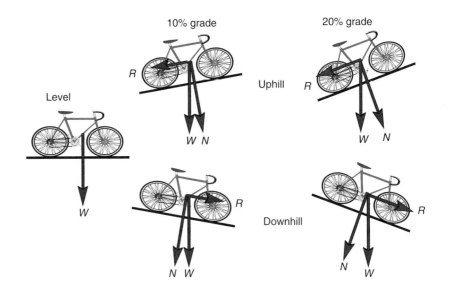

Figure 7. *The effect of gravity on bicycle and rider level and at two different uphill and downhill grades. In each case, gravity acts vertically downward (W) and is equal to the combined weight of the bike and rider. However, the resulting force (R) becomes greater on steeper terrain. (Adapted from Faria, 1978)*

eling at 10 MPH, using a very upright position and wearing a loose windbreaker, can increase her speed to 20 MPH by wearing tight clothing and assuming a more prone position.

Anything that can be done to cut rider and bicycle weight improves the ability of riders to climb hills. Gravitational forces do not discriminate between bike and rider mass. It becomes a matter of personal choice: whether to shed those additional "dead weight" pounds, or to spend, sometimes lavishly, on the latest high tech lightweight frame. Bicycles come in a tremendous range of sizes, shapes, and prices, with prices inversely related to frame weight. For example, a 15-pound (68-kg) lightweight carbon fiber racing bike can easily cost several thousand dollars, while a 40-pound (18-kg) steel tubular touring bike can be purchased for about $200.

Road races require constant acceleration and deceleration. To accelerate, the cyclist must either use more power or lower total mass. Assuming that a cyclist and bicycle with a combined weight of 190 pounds (86-kg) takes 9 seconds to accelerate from zero to 25 MPH, a 2-pound heavier bike (total of 192 lb.) will increase acceleration time to around 9.1 seconds. This does not make much difference for a quick acceleration sprint or for a constant pace during a long-distance race on flat terrain. But in road races, where riders are constantly accelerating and decelerating, inertia becomes a major factor. Inertia is the tendency to seek a steady state: if a body is moving, it tends to remain in motion; if a body is stationary, it tends to remain stationary. Because of inertia, an elite cyclist is always looking for ways to lower her bike's weight. The greater the bicycle's mass, the greater its inertia and the greater its resistance to changes in speed.

The mass of a wheel also possesses inertia that, like the rest of the bike, resists acceleration and deceleration. However, unlike the rest of the bike, a wheel not only has to be accelerated along the road but also must be set in spinning motion. The resistance to rotational acceleration is the moment of inertia. For a wheel with most of the mass on the rim, the effective inertia of the wheels can be nearly doubled owing to the effect of the moment of inertia. This results in a great disadvantage for races requiring quick acceleration, yet it can be of tremendous advantage on flat courses requiring a constant pace. For example, in the early 1980s Francesco Moser broke the world record for distance covered during a 1-hour period using heavier wheels. He outfitted his rims with rotating weights, which worked like ball bearings, to further increase the bike's inertia. Many riders who attempted the feat before him tried equipping their bikes with the lightest possible wheels. They thought that since a light bike is very advantageous for hills and has a lower moment of inertia for quick acceleration, it would serve them well trying to break the 1-hour record. However, because the 1-hour record is attempted on flat terrain and benefits most from a constant pace, the greater inertia of heavier wheels gives a rider a distinct advantage.

Rolling Resistance

Anyone who has ridden a bike with a flat tire realizes that tremendous rolling resistance is created by underinflated tires. Rolling resistance is almost directly proportional to the total weight on the tires. It is the sum of deformation of the wheel, tire, and road surface at the point of contact. Energy loss occurs when the three do not return all of the energy to the cycle. Even the best tires encounter some rolling resistance, but the rolling resistance a top-of-the-line racing tire encounters on smooth pavement is two or three times less than that of a heavily nobbed mountain bike tire.

Regardless of the bike's speed, rolling resistance remains fairly constant, which means that as speed increases, the rolling resistance factor becomes relatively less important (compared with wind resistance). Rolling resistance declines on smoother and harder road surfaces, or with the use of larger-diameter wheels, higher tire pressures, smoother and thinner treads, and narrower tires. In the case of rough, potholed roads, energy is lost in bounce. For soft surfaces like gravel or sand, energy is stolen and absorbed by the surface. Anyone who has ridden off the road and into mud can attest to the extreme loss of human energy that results from trying to pedal through the muck.

It is common knowledge that a cyclist with underinflated tires requires additional work to keep up with a cyclist riding on fully inflated tires. With the idea that more is better, manufacturers began experimenting with superinflated tires. If the standard tire with 80 pounds per square inch of pressure significantly decreased rolling resistance compared with a 40-pound-per-square-inch underinflated tire, perhaps a superinflated tire could provide more significant advantages. At ten times the cost, bike tires now can be purchased that can be inflated to 120 to 140 pounds per square inch.

Timothy Ryschon, an exercise physiologist at the University of Texas, tested seven cyclists riding a fixed distance on an indoor treadmill. They rode four times, with tires inflated to 80, 100, 120, and 140 pounds per square inch. On the basis of the rider's weight and the amount of oxygen burned, the work expended for each ride was calculated. Surprisingly, for every tire pressure tested, the metabolic energy expended was the same. It seems that superinflatable tires offer no noticeable advantage because they do not appreciably decrease rolling resistance (anonymous, in *Health*, 1993).

Wheel size can have as dramatic an effect on rolling resistance as underinflation. Smaller wheels, popularly used with most folding bikes, generate an unacceptable level of rolling resistance for many riders. They are slower over the whole range of speeds, and even more so over rougher roads. Rolling resistance is inversely proportional to the radius of the cylinder; that is, given the same conditions, smaller-wheeled bikes experience more resistance to motion than larger-wheeled bikes. Smaller wheels probably will remain a very popular choice for folding bikes, yet rolling resistance will limit their popularity for general touring bikes.

Air Resistance

As mentioned earlier, air resistance is a bigger drag factor than rolling resistance. In any sport, to overcome drag forces, additional power must be created. Drag forces are basically power-stealers. Physics tells us that the power developed by a force is the force times the velocity in the direction of the force. If the force is constant, as in lifting a weight against gravity, a weight lifter can lift 5 percent more weight at the same speed by generating 5 percent more power.

The cyclist is not so lucky, since the drag force increases with the square of the velocity. A 5 percent increase in velocity results in about a 10 percent increase in force. To find the power, this larger force is multiplied by the larger velocity, resulting in a total increase of a little over 15 percent. Doubling the velocity would result in an eightfold increase in the power to overcome air drag. At low speeds, without a headwind, air resistance is a minor factor. But at speeds greater than 25 KPH, air resistance becomes a major obstacle, and the muscle power required to overcome air resistance exceeds that required to overcome both rolling and mechanical resistance.

When speed is increased from 12 to 32 KPH, the relative power requirement for overcoming mechanical resistance increases by 225 percent, and that necessary to overcome rolling resistance 363 percent; however, over this same range of speeds, the increase in power required to overcome air resistance is nearly 1,800 percent (Adams, 1975).

It is important to remember that relative speed, and not bike speed, is of greater importance. Relative speed takes into account both bike and wind velocity. This means a rider traveling at 20 MPH into a 15-MPH wind encounters as much air resistance as a rider traveling at 35 MPH under windless conditions.

Figure 8 shows the effects of air resistance on a cyclist, a car, and a train. As the cyclist increases his speed, air resistance becomes more and more of a factor compared with the car or the train. This difference exists because of the much greater moment of inertia of a car or a train. However, because of the significant increase in drag that a rider encounters as speed is increased, far more possibilities exist for cyclists to adjust bike and body contours in order to alter energy expenditure than for the already streamlined car or train. Air resistance can be changed by alterations in all the following factors: clothing, frame design, handlebars, wheels (spokes), size of rider, and the race strategy of drafting.

Profile drag. Taking the rider and bike as a whole, the human body accounts for approximately 70 percent of the wind resistance encountered, while the bicycle accounts for only 30 percent. Of course, whatever a rider's size, crouching over the handlebars greatly affects just how much air resistance the rider encounters. Anything that can be done to improve the aerodynamic profile of the rider greatly reduces drag. For example, crouching to reduce the frontal area of the rider by 20 percent will reduce drag force by 20 percent.

Dangers In the Quest for Greater Speed

Realizing that greater speed is heavily dependent on assuming a very aerodynamic posture, cyclists are continually experimenting with ever more strange-looking positions. Graeme Obree, who set 1-hour record in 1994, and captured the 1995 world championship in the individual pursuit race, developed a position where his center of gravity was well forward with his head extending far in front of the handlebars. His arms, tightly tucked under his chest, rested with his chest atop the handlebars. Although Obree's unconventional style was highly effective, the International Cycling Union outlawed this position in 1996 because it considered the posture dangerously unstable.

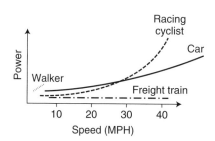

Figure 8. *A walker, a racing cyclist, a car, and a freight train have different propulsive requirements for maintaining a given speed. Propulsive requirements are greater for the cyclist than for the car or the train owing to his nonaerodynamic profile and his smaller mass (smaller inertia). (Adapted from Whitt, 1974)*

Unlike a sleek automobile, the bike and rider make up a very inefficient aerodynamic profile. Encircling a rider and bike fully or partially in a streamlined casing can reduce the drag coefficient by 0.25, resulting in speed increases from 30 to 36 MPH. However, this gain may be somewhat negated on hot days because of the body overheating or from the instability caused by gusty crosswinds.

Does the larger frontal area of heavier riders handicap them relative to their lighter counterparts? Of course, their larger frontal area creates more speed-robbing drag, but this can be countered by their greater muscle mass, which exerts more force on the pedals. Additionally, heavier riders' wind resistance does not increase in direct proportion to weight. Assuming that their added weight is predominantly muscle and not fat, the net result is that the heavier rider can accelerate slightly faster.

It is best to think of air resistance being proportionally related to the surface area of the rider. Although a large cyclist presents a larger frontal area, his oxygen consumption in relation to body weight is less than that of a smaller cyclist. One study found that a large cyclist (84.4 kg, or 186 lb.) had a 22 percent lower rate of oxygen consumption relative to body weight than his smaller counterpart (59.4 kg, or 131 lb.) at all speeds tested: 10, 15, 20 MPH (Swain, 1987). The larger cyclist had a distinct advantage on level roads owing to his 16 percent lower ratio of frontal area to body weight.

Hills are another matter. A cyclist traveling across level ground at about 18 MPH will slow down to 6 MPH for a 6 percent grade (6-ft. rise for every 100 horizontal ft.). Returning down the same hill, she would travel approximately 35 MPH. For the heavier cyclist, her additional weight would increase her downhill speed beyond 35 MPH yet would require more energy to maintain a 6-MPH pace on the uphill 6 percent grade.

Not only is rider size a factor, so is the clothing worn. The drag coefficient for a cyclist averages about 0.9 pound, but if the rider wears loose clothing, the drag coefficient increases by about 30 percent (Nonweiler, 1958). Racing cyclists therefore wear wrinkle-free clothing that perfectly fits the body's contour. Clothing that ripples and flutters in the wind creates a significant amount of skin friction drag (turbulence as the air flows around the body). A 0.2-pound drag increase from skin friction can handicap a racer's time by over 2 seconds in a 4,000-meter pursuit race.

Drafting. Because aerodynamic drag is the major impediment for high-speed cyclists, the benefits of drafting are enormous. A cyclist drafts by riding in the lead cyclist's wake. The higher the lead cyclist's speed, the more effective drafting becomes. Improved design for bicycles, with a smaller front wheel, a rear disk wheel, aerodynamic handlebars, and a sloping top tube, has been shown to reduce oxygen uptake (a measure of energy needed) by as much as 7 percent for a cyclist maintaining a 40-KPH pace while drafting. In addition to the 7 percent reduction in oxygen uptake from superior technology,

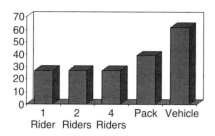

Figure 9. *To maintain a speed of 40 KPH, the drop in oxygen consumption (measure of energy needs) caused by drafting behind one rider, two riders, four riders, a pack, and a vehicle. Drafting behind one to four riders had a minor effect on oxygen consumption, but drafting behind a pack or a vehicle showed a sizable effect. (Adapted from McCole, 1990)*

drafting can reduce oxygen uptake anywhere from 18 to 39 percent for speeds of 32 to 40 KPH (McCole, 1990).

Figure 9 shows how, riding at 40 KPH, drafting one rider or a line of two or four riders all resulted in the same reduction in oxygen consumption. However, riding at the back of the pack formation (eight riders) at 40 KPH reduced oxygen uptake significantly more than riding behind one, two, or four riders in a line. And the greatest decrease in oxygen uptake occurred in drafting behind a vehicle. The ventilation and respiratory exchange ratio also decreased as a function of the reduction in oxygen consumption (*see also RESPIRATION*).

Drafting becomes increasingly effective the closer the drafter is behind the lead cyclist. When the drafter's front tire is within 0.2 meters behind the lead cyclist's rear tire, wind resistance can be reduced by 44 percent. At ten times that distance, or 2 meters, wind resistance is still reduced 27 percent. Drafting actually entails two drag-reducing phenomena: the obvious reduction in the frontal headwind force pushing a rider back, and the subtle pulling force from the greater air pressure behind the rider pulling him forward (*see also PADDLE SPORTS*).

To visualize the pulling force, consider a helium balloon in a car. Although helium is lighter than air, and the balloon is suspended, it does not fly from the front to the back of the car as the car accelerates. Instead, the air pressure behind the balloon allows it to remain suspended in place during acceleration or during turns.

The larger the "drafting train," the greater the trailing air pressure will be. For example, when a semitrailer passes a car, the semitrailer creates a tremendous push of air; once it is past, there is a pull of air that draws the car toward the rear of the semitrailer.

The importance of following dangerously close behind another high-speed cyclist is one of the major challenges of team racing. The risk is usually well worth the reward. Only the lead cyclist need work hard. The other team members save energy by traveling in his wake. In this way, the speed of the whole team increases as each rider takes a turn leading.

Aerodynamic Handlebars

It was the fifth stage of the 1989 Tour de France, a 45-mile (72-km) time trial through wet and windy Brittany, in what the French call "the race of truth." Greg Le Mond, who had recovered from an accidental gunshot wound to the chest suffered in 1987 while turkey hunting, was not even among the 50 favorites, though he had won in 1986. Almost the entire cycling community was surprised to see that he was a strong contender as he entered the fifth stage.

Le Mond liked his chances but decided to gamble on new technology. He clipped on the new aerodynamic handlebars developed by Boone Lennon, an American cyclist. Prior to the race, Le Mond had experimented with them only briefly, as he did not want to arouse the interest of his competitors.

It was a gamble that payed off. Le Mond's fifth stage proved the turning point in his quest for another Tour de France victory. He believed that the aerodynamic handlebars not only gave him a better aerodynamic position but allowed him to assume a more relaxed and rested position on his bike—resting his upper body and allowing him to push at a higher gear. In this time trial, he covered the rainy, wind-swept course in 1 hour, 38 minutes, and 12 seconds at an average speed of 28 MPH, capturing the yellow jersey (worn by the overall leader). More important, his margin of victory over three of the favorites was impressive: 24 seconds faster than Pedro Delgarno, 56 seconds faster than Laurent Fignon, and 1 minute and 51 seconds faster than Thierry Marie. Because it was his first win since his hunting accident 18 months earlier, he gained tremendous confidence.

Although he was again racing well, Le Mond still found himself trailing Fignon by 50 seconds as they entering the final stage. Almost everyone conceded the Tour to Fignon, as 50 seconds was considered an impossible time to make up in the 15-mile (24-km) Versailles-to-Paris final stage. With the aid of the aerodynamic handlebars, however, Le Mond won the final time trial, beating Fignon by 58 seconds, for an 8-second Tour de France victory.

Some consider Le Mond's effort in the final stage a "mutation performance," a feat comparable to American long-jumper Bob Beamon's record setting performance in the 1968 Mexico City Olympics—a record that stood for more than 20 years. While acknowledging the sheer determination shown by Le Mond, it is inaccurate to equate the two performances. Since air resistance comes mostly from body profile, one can safely assume that Le Mond never would have won without the innovative handlebars. Aerodynamic handlebars help riders create a streamlined profile, much as foils placed over the cabs of large truck trailers reduce drag. Aerodynamic handlebars have been reported capable of decreasing wind drag enough to increase speed from 25 to 26 MPH (Niles, 1992).

This greater speed can be obtained even with slightly less power output because aerodynamic handlebars require less power for any given velocity. They also bring the rider's center of gravity forward, closer to the bicycle's center of gravity, which is more efficient from a mechanical and biomechanical perspective. In the final 15-mile leg of the Tour de France, the aerodynamic handlebars alone could easily account for 45 seconds of Le Mond's 58-second margin of victory over Fignon.

Spokes

The aerodynamic design of the wheels can considerably reduce a bicycle's aerodynamic drag, owing to the wheels' large surface area and to the fact that they are in motion. Until around the early 1980s, manufacturers and racers directed their efforts toward experimenting on the number and pattern of a wheel's spokes. With the proliferation of new and improved materials on the market in the 1990s, however, the range of choices has expanded tremendously.

Two spoke styles are common: standard spokes, which come with

The Hazards of Aerodynamic Handlebars

Although aerodynamic handlebars can improve performance, a rider's ability and the riding conditions should be considered for several reasons: with the rider's center of gravity farther forward, the chance of tumbling on a rough road increases significantly; quick avoidance maneuvers and braking are more difficult; the head-down, outstretched posture means less visibility and thus less ability for the cyclist to protect her face with her hands and arms in the event of a fall.

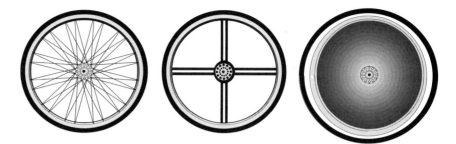

Figure 10. *Aerodynamic spokes, blade-like spokes, and solid-core wheels can influence aerodynamic drag from 1 to 4%. In windless conditions and on a very smooth road, the solid-core wheel may improve bike speed by 4%; on rough roads and in high crosswinds, it might pose a 4% disadvantage to the spoked wheel. For a cyclist, mere 1% additional drag can mean the difference between finishing a race first or last.*

a circular cross section; and aerodynamic spokes, which come with an elliptical cross section. They look very similar from the side, but when viewed from the front, aerodynamic spokes are thinner and thus more efficient. Aerodynamic efficiency is gained at the expense of the greater strength of standard spokes' circular cross design. Most bikes have 32 to 36 spokes, while some racing bikes may have as few as 28 or 24. The fewer the spokes—and thus the fewer the times that a spoke cuts through the wind—the less the wind resistance.

Solid-core carbon wheels have become popular among racers in the 1990s, as they further reduce air resistance. When confronted with a crosswind, however, the solid-core carbon wheels provide increased resistance and thus reduce speed. Another problem is that they are unable to absorb road shock as well as spokes. A promising wheel with a four-bladed design of carbon and Kevlar may give riders both the aerodynamic performance of a carbon wheel and the shock-absorbing qualities of spoked wheels (*see Figure 10*). Although the new wheel's four flexible, blade-like spokes are rather wide, their extreme thinness greatly reduces air resistance.

Biomechanics

In examining the biomechanics of cycling, one must consider both the goals of the rider and the bike-rider interface. Even a slight change in equipment can make a difference, as factors such as the distance of a race, the type of terrain, and the goal of the rider all affect the optimal pedal rate, trunk position, and saddle and handlebar height.

Saddle and Handlebar Adjustments

Adjustments in handlebar and saddle-post positions change the rider's aerodynamic profile and allow her to find the most effective position for pedal-force production. The ideal position often entails

Can Cycling Be Hazardous to a Male's Sex Life?

As the saying goes, be careful about getting too much of good thing—even exercise. It seems that logging many miles on ergonomically firm, sleek saddles has created considerable anxiety for male long-distance cyclists.

Erectile dysfunction (impotence), a well-kept secret among world-class cyclists, is far more common than reported. As many as 70 percent of male racing cyclists experience some degree of reduced sexual sensation (Legwold, 1993). But because of the stigma associated with impotence, cases of erectile impotence among long-distance cyclists are extremely underreported.

Cyclists often suffer from penile numbness and from impotence caused by pressure on the perineum (located between the rectum and penis). The perineum is the area of the body that has the most contact with the saddle, and in time it may bruise from the weight of the rider upon the saddle.

Although the prostate is located above the perineum and fairly deep beneath the skin, the pressure from the rider's weight on the saddle may cause injury to the prostate and to surrounding structures due to compression of the perineum. The up-and-down motion of the legs and the different amounts of pressure exerted on the pedals place the prostate under considerable pressure as it is squeezed between the weight of the rider (from above) and the saddle (from below).

The prostate has several important functions. Its smooth-muscle fibers contract to send about a teaspoon of semen out of the penis during ejaculation. Only about 10 percent of semen is sperm (containing 100–600 million individual sperm). Prostate glandular tissue secretion—consisting of sugars and nutrients—accounts for the remaining 90 percent. This secretion is as important to fertility as the sperm because it helps the sperm swim and neutralizes vaginal acidity.

A cyclist who logs a minimal number of miles is not likely to develop prostate problems. Prolonged riding, on the other hand, means prolonged pressure, heightening the probability of bruising the prostate. Bruising causes the prostate to swell, which in turn puts pressure on the nerves that lead into the penis—the perineal, dorsal, and pudendal nerves. In rare instances, the pressure of the saddle may directly injure these nerves and lead to penile numbness and impotence. Both conditions will usually disappear with rest, so physicians recommend abstaining from riding for at least 2 weeks. Anatomically, male cyclists are all a bit different. Some can develop this condition riding a few miles each day, while others might

Preventing Saddle Pressure

1. Raise the handlebars slightly and assume a more upright position.
2. Tilt the nose of the saddle down a few degrees to better distribute one's weight.
3. For men, use more standing intervals and shift one's weight while pedaling to reduce prolonged periods of pressure on the nerves that lead to the penis.
4. Switch to a bike with fatter tires to limit the shocks and jolts of riding, as fat tires better cushion rough road riding.
5. Avoid aerodynamic handlebars, as they require a more prone position, putting additional pressure on the perineum.

a trade-off, as the most efficient pedaling position might result in a poor aerodynamic position.

Assuming uniform aerodynamics across the range of different seat-tube heights, the optimal seat-tube angle will still vary with the physiological characteristics of the cyclist, particularly her leg length. For riders with a longer femur (thighbone), a wider-angle seat tube is preferable; for those with a shorter femur, a steeper seat-tube angle may be best. This makes sense biomechanically because it enables the femur and the tibia (shinbone) to work together at the optimal angle. The knee bends very little during any segment of the pedaling motion; when it bends at more than a 90-degree angle, the pedaler loses efficiency. In a similar way, deep-knee-bend squats are far more

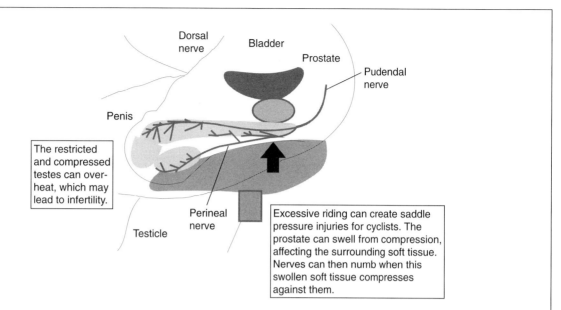

Dorsal nerve

Bladder

Prostate

Pudendal nerve

Penis

The restricted and compressed testes can overheat, which may lead to infertility.

Testicle

Perineal nerve

Excessive riding can create saddle pressure injuries for cyclists. The prostate can swell from compression, affecting the surrounding soft tissue. Nerves can then numb when this swollen soft tissue compresses against them.

never experience symptoms despite riding hundreds of miles a week. Several preventive steps can be taken. First, to minimize the compression on the prostate, one should include more standing intervals and shift the body's weight while pedaling. Second, one should adjust his equipment by raising the handlebars, tilting the nose of the saddle down slightly, and switching to a wider and softer saddle. These steps can help alleviate the pressure on the perineum and prostate. Moreover, riders should be cautious about using aerodynamic handlebars, which require more forward lean and thus put additional pressure on the perineum and prostate.

In addition to the risk of impotence, male cyclists may be concerned about the effect of bicycling on infertility. Testosterone, a hormone produced in the cells located between the seminiferous tubules (the coiled, thread-like tubules that make up the bulk of the tests), is responsible for sperm development. During strenuous or prolonged exercise, testosterone may drop by 20 to 30 percent. This problem may be particularly acute for a cyclist, because his testicles reside within the hot environment of tight-fitting shorts and are further compressed by the saddle. In this state, the scrotum cannot drop to keep the testicles cooler than the body, thereby reducing the body's

ability to produce sperm and, to a lesser extent, testosterone.

Much like penile numbness and impotence, decreases in sperm production and in hormone levels are only temporary. Only a very small percentage of male cyclists ride long enough and hard enough to suffer from penile numbness, impotence, or infertility. In fact, the rewards far outweigh the very minimal risks. Overwhelming evidence shows that moderate exercise in the form of cycling is extremely beneficial at increasing the male sex drive as well as for overall health.

John Zumerchik and David Zumerchik, M.D.

difficult than half-knee-bend squats (the greater knee bend angle is less efficient; *see also WEIGHT LIFTING*)

Perhaps surprisingly, many professional cyclists do not use bicycles that match their physiological profiles. Some experts believe that many still excel due to muscle memory—when muscles adapt to riding in an incorrect position they eventually provide optimal oxygen consumption. For example, if a rider's muscles become accustomed to pedaling in a crouched position, a sudden shift to a more anatomically efficient position usually results in a temporary drop in performance. When a world-class cyclist decides to increase his saddle height, he will do so very gradually, raising the saddle by only a fraction of an inch every two weeks until the goal is attained. Many cyclists and experts argue that this allows the rider's muscles to become slowly accustomed to the new saddle height.

There are many theories concerning how to determine the optimal saddle height. Experts generally agree that the leg should be extended at a range of 96 to 99 percent of its maximum length (measured from the heel to the bump of the hip). There is less agreement on saddle height because variations in the height of the saddle do not significantly change muscle activity. Experts who have measured oxygen uptake as a function of seat height have found that saddle height can vary considerably for a single rider without any metabolic or biomechanical effects. When seat height does harm performance, the effect is primarily in the recovery phase (6 to 12 o'clock), where riders lose the ability to effectively use their toe clips.

Saddle height and position also vary with the type of cycling. Sprinters prefer the saddle a bit higher and farther forward for greater power production from the weight of the upper body and for stronger pushing force from the quadriceps (thigh) muscles. Endurance racers, on the other hand, often position the saddle a bit lower and farther back to minimize energy expenditure and upper-body fatigue.

Gears

Gears were designed to enable cyclists to continue pedaling at a constant rate regardless of hills or terrain changes. Just as walkers and runners take shorter strides when traveling uphill and longer strides going downhill, the bicycle has gears that accomplish the same task. Gear systems are designed so that riders can maintain a constant, comfortable pace whether going uphill or downhill, with or against the wind. Most racing and mountain bikes have 15 to 21 gears, with two or three chain sprockets and 5 to 7 rear sprockets.

The larger the diameter of a chain sprocket, the greater the torque, or force, necessary to accelerate the pedal. For the rear sprockets, a larger size means that less torque is necessary to accelerate the pedal. With a big chain sprocket and a small rear sprocket—when the cycle is in a high gear, as for downhill grades—a rider travels farther for each pedal revolution. Lower gears—smaller chain sprocket, larger rear sprocket—require less effort to turn the pedal, but the cyclist must pedal more to maintain the same speed. In other words, to produce the same amount of torque, a smaller amount of force is needed in the lowest gears. Hill climbing is therefore much easier after shifting to a larger rear sprocket (*see Figure 11*).

There is, however, a trade-off between distance and force (pedal cadence efficiency and force efficiency). In lower gears, one exerts less force but must pedal faster to maintain speed. High gears, on the other hand, trade force for distance: one pedals less rapidly but must exert more force per pedal revolution. To cover the same distance, the twentieth gear increases the movement distance of pedaling twenty times that of the first gear. Provided the switch from first gear to twentieth gear happens on level terrain, the twenty-times increase

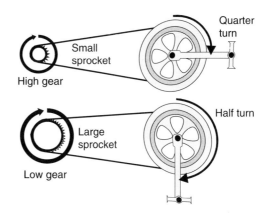

Figure 11. *The chain sprocket is shown with a large and a small rear sprocket. Traveling uphill, the cyclist selects a large rear sprocket (below). On level ground or when traveling downhill, a small rear sprocket (above) is used. Because there are twice as many teeth on the large rear sprocket as on the small rear sprocket (24 as compared with 12), the chain sprocket must turn twice as far for the rear sprocket to complete one full turn.*

in movement distance requires 20 times the pedal force. If a rider uses her gears properly, that permits her to maintain the same cadence and force efficiency over all grades.

Alternative Propulsion. The circular sprocket, or chainwheel, design of most bicycles is not very efficient. Regardless of a rider's ability, it is inefficient to pedal when nearing the very top of the circle (11 o'clock) and when nearing the very bottom (5 o'clock). Manufacturers continue to experiment with alternatives in hopes of eliminating these deficiencies. For example, an elliptical chainwheel was developed to reduce peak-force demands and to better match the rider's force potential with the mechanical resistance she is experiencing. As the crank arm reaches a horizontal position—where the body has the least ability to generate force—the gearing changes to a slightly lower value, so that pedaling is easier at a higher velocity. This sprocket should, at least theoretically, result in a reduction of peak force exerted at any given power level. But because a world-class cyclist develops a riding rhythm and a comfort pattern from years of experience, the noncircular chainwheel has failed to grow in popularity. Perhaps the elliptical chainwheel would best serve slower-pedaling, inexperienced riders. Novice riders have not yet developed the high-speed rhythm of the elite cyclists, who pedal at a much higher rate and thus minimize the inefficiencies of the circular sprocket design.

Lever propulsion—requiring an up and down, stair-climbing motion—is often proposed as an efficient replacement for the pedal and crank system. Experiments have shown, however, that the muscle efficiency for pedaling a chainwheel is not inferior to that associated with stepping and steep-grade walking (Whitt, 1974). The theory behind lever-propulsion systems is that the leg's muscles work most efficiently when pushing the whole stroke vertically; movements over the top and under the bottom waste energy. While there is certainly some efficiency loss during the backward and forward motion, it is minimal. Furthermore, the introduction of toe clips and of better variable-gear systems has eliminated concern about the "top-dead-center" problems associated with the circular sprocket design.

Stroke Rate

Most cycling experts agree that the most efficient pedaling cadence for elite cyclists is 75 to 130 revolutions per minute (RPM), with the 90- to 100-RPM range usually optimal (Hagberg, 1981). This is much faster than the 40- to 70-RPM average of the recreational cyclist. For elite and recreational cyclists alike, the optimal RPM range will vary from person to person.

Attempts to increase efficiency at rates above 100 RPM have not proved worthwhile. A spin rate of 130 to 140 RPM has even proved quite detrimental, as spin efficiency is determined by the optimal combination of speed and workload—more a matter of how force is applied to the pedals than spin rate. Muscles will tire whether producing tremendous power for an instant or exerting minimum power over an extended period (*see also WEIGHT LIFTING*). When pedaling at 130 to 140 RPM, even an elite cyclist's legs will reach a point where they fail to deliver enough power for the motion.

Although most racing cyclists pedal at 90 to 100 RPM, numerous studies suggest that a 40- to 60-RPM rate brings the lowest metabolic rate and the highest efficiency. The difference between the optimal-efficiency RPM rate and the average RPM rate of elite cyclists has been attributed to a racer's ability to estimate the workload according to the force used—a force that decreases with increasing speed at constant power (Bonning, 1984). In other words, the above-optimal metabolic rate of the fast pedaler is countered by a smaller oxygen cost.

Better efficiency requires that both legs apply force as equally as possible. Just as one is likely to be left- or right-handed, one is also likely to be left- or right-leg dominant. This fact is significant for cyclists. Some riders have shown a force asymmetry of over 70 percent. Such a cyclist uses his dominant leg to make a much greater contribution to propulsion than his nondominant leg (Daly, 1976). Though this type of imbalance is often unnoticed, it results in a quicker onset of fatigue and in poorer performance than when both legs apply equal force.

Muscle fatigue decreases the optimum pedaling rate because pedal forces will start increasing at a lower pedaling rate. Fatigue will begin to decrease at a pedaling rate that is higher than optimum but lowers the necessary crank force. Other factors contributing to the difference between inexperienced and elite riders include the inability of inexperienced riders to apply force perpendicular to the crank, and their use of excessive body motion.

Toe clips, which fasten the rider's shoes firmly to the pedals, may improve stroke rate for both beginning and advanced cyclists. Studies

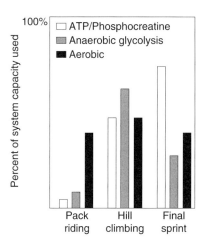

Figure 12. *Although cycling is primarily an aerobic activity, during a road race, the physiological demands vary. For hill climbing and the final sprint, the cyclist relies more heavily on either anaerobic energy or ATP (phosphocreatine) energy. In a multi-day road race like the Tour de France, many riders are well known as specialists. For example, some excel in the climbs and win a climbing stage of the race. They need to fare particularly well in the climbs because they usually do not perform well in the sprints, or in the stages involving pack riding over long stretches of flat terrain.*

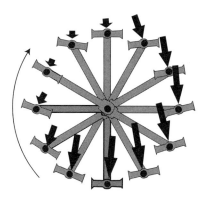

Figure 13. *Force exerted on the pedals peaks at the 3 o'clock position but remains effective between 6 o'clock and 9 o'clock. The downward force never disappears during the rear foot's upswing.*

have shown toe clips to benefit both aerobic exercise (a level of continuous exercise that can be sustained without causing exhaustion) and anaerobic exercise (short term exercise that demands more oxygen than the body can supply; *see also ENERGY AND METABOLISM).* Cleated shoes used in conjunction with toe clips also increase pedaling efficiency by allowing for improved flexor muscle utilization during the backstroke and by distributing the workload and peak demand on the quadriceps muscles (Davis, 1981). Because recreational cyclists use a slower, less rhythmic cadence, however, toe clips are not as essential for them.

Experts have argued that toe clips give elite riders a false sense of power production during the stroke recovery phase. Many elite riders believe that toe clips double the deliverable pedal power by exerting an upward force with the trailing leg in addition to the usual downward force of the forward leg—a coordinated push-pull effort. No matter how skilled the cyclist, he can only push downward because the pedaling cadence is too great to create a pulling-up force.

Although some world-class cyclists may unload much of their weight on the upstroke leg, they are often surprised to learn that they have not unloaded all of it. As illustrated in Figure 13, the downward force is minimized while the leg is engaged in the upstroke, but the force is not eliminated because there is still a negative force from the weight of the rearward leg. Perhaps the major reason world-class cyclists believe that they are actually pulling up is the inertia associated with a pedaling cadence of 100 or more RPM. Toe clips are important, however, in that they stabilize the foot and more effectively generate a pushing force during the recovery stage.

When an elite cyclist pedals at a slower cadence—initiating sprints or climbing out of the saddle—she can better control her pedaling dynamics and better unweight the recovery leg during the upstroke. She knows when to use recovery-leg muscle power to unweight for the upstroke and when to let the driving leg do more to lift the recovery leg. This may explain the greater power output for cyclists with better pedaling technique. To travel at the same speed, a cyclist with better technique need produce only 70 percent as much force as a less skilled cyclist.

Floating Pedals

To maximize speed, cyclists have long argued that the foot-pedal connection should be as rigid as possible. Cyclists have even used nail-on cleats and double toe straps to achieve this firm grip. But since many riders experience knee pain—the most common chronic affliction of cyclists—the rigid foot-pedal setup is losing favor to the "floating" pedal. Miguel Indurain, a four-time Tour de France champion, is among the many competitive cyclists who have converted to the floating pedal, which allows 20 degrees of rotation at the shoe-pedal connection. In a study of two groups of elite riders, one group experiencing no knee pain and the other with chronic knee pain, floating pedals were shown to reduce the torque on the knee without decreasing power output (Adrian, 1988).

Preventing Cycling Injuries

In an 8-year study in the United States, bicycling accounted for 905,752 head injuries and 2,985 deaths from head injuries (62% of all bicycling deaths; Sacks, 1991). Analyses suggest that universal use of helmets could have prevented at least 2,500 of these deaths and 757,000 of these head injuries.

Serious head injuries occur because the force of impact occurs at an acute point, a small area of the skull. Helmets reduce the force of impact by absorbing and distributing the force of impact throughout the skull and spine. Thus, the force required to cause damage to the skull is much greater when a helmet is worn, and the better the fit of the helmet, the better the distribution of the force at impact.

Helmet choice presents riders with a safety-speed trade-off. Wind-tunnel tests have shown that a smooth, aerodynamic, hard-shell helmet is superior for speed. These teardrop-shaped helmets can shave 30 seconds off the time of road racers for a 25-mile time trial.

Unfortunately, helmets designed for speed provide poorer protection of the skull. On impact they do not distribute the force well and result in greater rotational head motion (*see also BOXING*).

Although head injuries are the most traumatic of all cycling injuries, most injuries result from overuse and abuse. The symptoms of overuse (compressive- and inflammatory-type) injuries, when treated with rest, usually quickly subside. Finding sufficient time to rest is, however, nearly impossible for a world-class cyclist in the midst of training. To reduce the likelihood of these types of injuries, she selects an appropriately sized frame, properly adjusts the saddle height, develops the right riding position, and follows a training schedule designed

A standard helmet and an aerodynamic tear-shaped helmet. Although the tear-shaped helmet benefits riders by improving performance, it comes at the cost of less protection against impact.

to suit her age and general medical condition.

As with most endurance sports, fatigue contributes to cycling injuries for riders of all abilities. Fatigue sets in quickly when a rider climbs many hills and is exacerbated by improper gear selection, causing "torque overload"—pedaling in too high a gear. Most of the torque overload occurs at the knee. Of all overuse and abuse injuries, injuries to the knee are the most prevalent among cyclists. Since healthy muscles can exert a force of about 42 pounds per square inch, and since the quadriceps (which are highly involved in pedaling) are among the largest muscles in the body, tremendous stress occurs at the knee joint. Knee injuries to cartilage and ligaments are common. A major factor contributing to the onset of knee pain and injury occurs when the rider tries to generate additional force, usually by pedaling in too high a gear, and in excessive hill climbing. Recreational riders can reduce or avoid knee pain and injuries by using lower gears, pedaling consistently, and properly aligning the foot on the pedals. Studies also suggest that "floating" pedals may reduce knee injuries.

David H. Janda, M.D., and
John Zumerchik

Floating pedals use a centering feature, which applies a slight rotational pressure to maintain a toes-forward position. Most riders push their heels outward during the downward stroke and inward during the upward (recovery) stroke, thus creating a torque, or twisting force, at the knees. Riders with the chronic knee pain tend to experience the greatest twisting. Likewise, higher torque has been recorded when the rider increases her power output. As manufacturers identify the different pedaling mechanics of riders, they will probably offer a range of floating pedals, enabling each cyclist to select the pedal that best matches her body structure and her pedaling mechanics.

Crank Length

Studies suggest that optimal crank length varies with upper leg length. One study concluded that cranks with a length of 16.4 and 16.6 centimeters (6.5 and 6.6 in.) were optimal for mean- and peak-power output, respectively (Inbar, 1983). If these figures are correct, then the crank on most commercially available bicycles is probably too long for most riders. Whereas variations in seat height affect only the application angles of muscles, crank length affects many additional factors, such as attainable torque (from longer cranks), increased muscle fatigue (from decreased cranks), and the force-to-velocity ratio that maximizes power.

Maximizing Muscle Power

By moving forward on the bicycle—this is accomplished by using a lowered handlebar, a moveable seat, a bent seat post, or a position forward in the saddle—cyclists can generate more power and speed (*see Figure 14*). Each of these adjustments reduces the hip angle at flexion (bending) and allows the powerful gluteus maximus (buttock) muscle to better contribute to pedal-force production.

Researchers agree that the peak pedaling force is at a crank-arm angle of 90 degrees, the point at which the hip and knee levers together generate the most power. Although the hip generates peak power over a wider range, at 90 degrees the hip and knee are both at peak power (optimum force and speed). A useful analogy is two people trying to dislodge a car stuck in a snowbank by rocking it. When the two do not time their push, little progress is made. By timing their pushing action, they are much more likely to dislodge the car from the snowbank. Here, the timed cooperative effort yields a result greater than the sum of its parts.

The two muscles that generate pedaling power are the gluteus maximus and the quadriceps (thigh). Although the gluteus maximus is the primary source of power, it is the cooperation of the muscles that facilitates peak pedaling force. The powerful gluteus maximus is much slower during the top half of the stroke than during the bottom half. The quadriceps is slightly faster during the top half of the stroke, with peak power occurring near the bottom.

A study by the biomechanicist Rick Niles found that the peak power overlap for the standard seat adjustment occurs at the 100-degree position, whereas the peak power overlap with the seat 6 centimeters forward occurs over the entire 10 degrees of the peak power output of the quadriceps. The small (6-cm) movement forward lowers the peak power range of the quadriceps and raises the peak power range of the gluteus maximus so that the two muscles' peak power ranges overlap. The result is a more effective delivery of muscle power.

John Zumerchik*

*The author would like to thank Don C. Hopkins for his contribution to the section on stability.

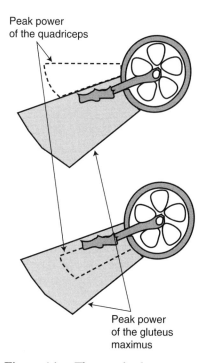

Peak power
of the quadriceps

Peak power
of the gluteus
maximus

Figure 14. *The standard seat position (above) varies from the optimal position, with the seat 6 cm forward (below). This 6-cm forward change repositions the hip and knee—opening more at the hip joint, bending more at the knee—which in turn increases peak leg muscle-power ranges. When using aerodynamic handlebars, cyclists move slightly forward in the saddle, presenting a more aerodynamic profile and improving muscle power. This is the peak power range of the gluteus maximus and the quadriceps. (Source: Niles, 1992)*

References

Adams, W. "Studies of Metabolic Energy Expenditure in Bicycling." Davis, California: University of California Department of Civil Engineering, Report 75–82 (1975).

Anonymous. "Hard Bike Tires Don't Cut Friction." *Health*, November/ December 1993.

Bonning, D., Y. Gonen, and N. Maassen. "The Relationship between Work Load, Pedal Frequency, and Physical Fitness." *International Journal of Sports Medicine* 1, no. 5 (1984): 92–97.

Daly, D., and P. Cavanaugh. "Asymmetry in Bicycling Pedaling." *Medical Science in Sports* 8, no. 3 (1976): 204–208.

Davis, R., and M. Hull. "Measurement of Pedal Loading in Bicycling." *Journal of Biomechanics* 14 (1981): 857–872.

Drake, G. "Circular Thinking." *Bicycling*, May 1993: 52–54.

Ellis, W. "Shanghai: Where China's Past and Future Meet." *National Geographic*, 185, no. 3 (March 1994): 2–35.

Faria, I. "Applied Physiology of Cycling." *Sports Medicine* 1 (1984): 187–204.

Faria, I. and P. Cavanaugh. *The Physiology and Biomechanics of Cycling*. New York: Wiley, 1978.

Hagberg, J., J. Mullin, M. Giese, and E. Spitznagel. "The Effect of Pedaling Rate on Submaximal Exercise Responses of Competitive Cyclists." *Journal of Applied Physiology* 51 (1981): 447–451.

Hunt, R. "Bicycles in the Physics Lab." *Physics Teacher* 27 (1989): 160–165.

Inbar, O., R. Dotan, T. Trousil, and Z. Dvir. "The Effect of Bicycle Crank-Length Variation upon Power Performance." *Ergonomics* 26, no. 10 (1983): 1139–1146.

Jones, D. "The Stability of the Bicycle," *Physics Today* 23, no. 4 (1970): 34–40.

Kyle, Chester. "Mechanical Factors Affecting Speed." In E. Burke (ed.), *Science of Cycling*. Champaign, Illinois: Leisure, 1986.

Legwold, G. "Psst, Hey Buddy . . . The Effects of Cycling on the Male Reproductive Organs." *Bicycling*, 34 (July 1993): 57–60.

Le Mond, G. *Complete Book of Bicycling*. New York: Putnam, 1987.

McCole, S., D. Claney, J. Conte, R. Anderson, and J. Hagberg. "Energy Expenditure during Bicycling." *Journal of Applied Physiology* 68 (1990): 748.

Nightingale, J. D. "Which Way Will the Bike Move?" *Physics Teacher* 31, no. 4 (1993): 244–245.

Niles, R. "Forward Is Faster." *Bicycling*, November 1992: 162–163.

Nonweiler, T. "The Work Production of Man: Studies on Racing Cyclists." *Proceedings of the Physiological Society* (11 January 1958).

Okijama, S. "Designing Chainwheels to Optimize the Human Engine." *Bike Technology* 2 (1977): 1 ff.

Resnick, M., and P. Yates. "Aerodynamic Handlebars." *Journal of the American Medical Association* 266 (1991): 515 ff.

Romer, R. *The Energy Fact Book*. Amherst, Massachusetts: Department of Physics, Amherst College, 1976.

Sacks, J., P. Holmgreen, P. Smith, and D. Sosin. "Bicycle-Associated Head Injuries and Deaths in the United States from 1981 to 1988: How Many Were Preventable?" *Journal of the American Medical Association* 266 (1991): 3032 ff.

Swain, D., J. Coast, P. Clifford, M. Milliken, and J. Stray-Gunderson. "Influence of Body Size on Oxygen Consumption during Bicycling," *Journal of Applied Physiology* 62 (1987): 688 ff.

Swift, E. M. "Le Grande Le Mond." *Sports Illustrated*, 25 December 1989, pp. 54–70.

Whitt, F., and D. Wilson. *Bicycle Science*. Cambridge, Massachusetts: MIT Press, 1974.

Equipment Materials

MATERIALS IN SPORTS can be divided into four basic groups: (1) metals, such as aluminum, steel, and titanium; (2) ceramics, such as glass, and concrete; (3) polymers, such as rubber, plastic, and synthetic fibers; and (4) composites, such as wood, graphite, and fiberglass. Until the 1960s, most sports equipment was made of just a few materials: steel, wood, and leather. By the mid-1990s, aluminum and fiber-reinforced composites (such as fiberglass and graphite) had replaced steel and wood as the materials of choice for sports equipment ranging from tennis rackets to yacht hulls, and even recreational joggers had benefited from technological advances—modern shoes constructed of synthetic materials were offering greater comfort and support than the canvas sneakers predominant in the 1970s.

Because athletes come in various sizes and shapes, and because they compete at a wide range of intensities, their needs vary tremendously with regard to equipment. Top Olympic and professional athletes seek equipment and materials that can maximize their performance. Amateurs of average or below-average skills, on the other hand, need equipment with stable performance and maximum "forgiveness."

The overall impact of new materials also varies considerably. The aluminum baseball bat, for example, has had no effect on major league competition. When aluminum baseball bats were introduced in the 1970s, they were warmly received by softball and amateur baseball players, because they improved performance, minimized painful vibrations, and reduced the costly problem of breakage (they also contribute to conservation of the diminishing supply of white ash—the wood used for wooden bats). But major league baseball officials prohibited aluminum bats, to prevent a change in the dynamics of the game: a ball hit off an aluminum bat tends to carry much farther, so adopting aluminum bats would have dramatically increased the number of home runs. In yachting, by contrast, composite hulls, aluminum and fiber-reinforced masts, and laminated sails have dramatically improved performance. Modern materials have also had a dramatic effect in pole vaulting, as the original wooden poles were replaced by tubular bamboo, aluminum, and then fiberglass (*see Figure 1*; *see also FIELD ATHLETICS: JUMPING*). In some sports, such as golf, the effects have been more subtle. The introduction of new

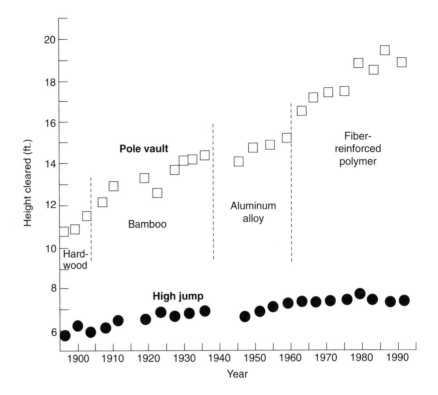

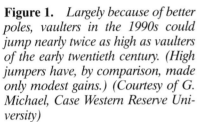

Figure 1. *Largely because of better poles, vaulters in the 1990s could jump nearly twice as high as vaulters of the early twentieth century. (High jumpers have, by comparison, made only modest gains.) (Courtesy of G. Michael, Case Western Reserve University)*

golf clubs and golf balls, starting in the 1960s, has not appreciably improved scores for professional golfers (Jorgenson, 1994). However, athough there are no useful statistics for amateur golfers, experts believe that the scores of beginners and intermediate players have been improved by the new clubs, because most innovations have made the clubs more forgiving of off-center hits. The reason for this difference is that a bigger "sweet spot" is less significant for professional golfers, who almost always hit the ball on center.

Indeed, the individual needs and the complexities of sports performance make it extremely difficult to predict the consequences of using a new material, and so the prospects for improvement may be uncertain. Regardless of perceived or real benefits, though, the pressures of marketing and competition continually drive manufacturers to introduce new materials for sports equipment.

This article begins by outlining some basic principles used by scientists and engineers in considering materials for sports applications. Next, it discusses in some detail the selection of materials for bicycles, golf equipment, and athletic shoes. These discussion are followed by a short synopsis of materials used in several other sports.

Selecting Materials

Manufacturers of sports equipment, and innovators, try to take advantage of the opportunities presented by new materials, to fulfill the athlete's hope of better performance and thereby to distinguish themselves and their products in a very competitive market. Unfortunately, however, the consumer's expectations about improved performance—or, by the same token, about greater comfort, greater durability, and so on—are seldom based on knowledge of scientific research or engineering analyses. In other words, consumers may not know much about how materials are selected, how equipment is developed, or how well that equipment works in actual use.

Background

One point to note is that after a material has been selected, considerable research and development are often necessary before a manufacturer can actually produce the equipment. For example, the evolution of tennis rackets from wood to aluminum and, shortly thereafter, to graphite (any of numerous variations of fiber-reinforced composite materials) required considerable retooling by manufacturers. Another point is that when new equipment is first introduced, it may provide only limited improvement; gradual refinements are often needed to adapt a material for use—although such refinement can eventually lead to a significant improvement in performance. One factor in the process of refinement is competition from other manufacturers, who usually make further variations in design and materials and then make claims about additional improvements in performance. However, claims regarding such "generational" refinement—even when genuine—are difficult to substantiate scientifically.

Since the mid-1980s, there has been increasing use of mathematical analyses and modeling of athletic performance and of sports equipment as a factor in performance. In time, these methods will undoubtedly have considerable effect on equipment design, materials selected, evaluation of performance, and further innovation; but it must be said that as of the mid-1990s, the methods were, scientifically speaking, rather unsophisticated. In fact, such analysis has been used primarily to confirm an exisiting direction of innovation or an improvement already claimed.

Most new equipment is tested by making a prototype—a preliminary version—which is then tried out by experts. Although this form of testing is sometimes effective, it cannot account for individual differences in athletic performance, which are complex, varied, and difficult to measure. For example, the tennis strokes of a tall male professional, like Pete Sampras, are as different from those of a short female professional, like Arantxa Sanchez Vicario, as they are from the strokes of an amateur player. Furthermore, what one professional seeks in equipment may not satisfy another professional and may be entirely inappropriate for an amateur.

How equipment performs depends on the properties of materials. In considering this rather complex subject, it will be helpful to use the vaulting pole as an illustration.

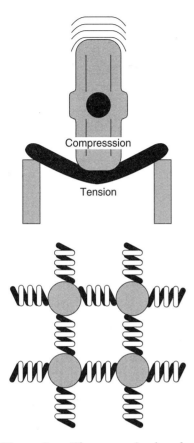

Compresssion

Tension

Figure 2. *The atoms (and molecules) of a material are held together as if by springs that allow for movement back and forth. For instance, when a sledgehammer strikes a plank suspended between two supports, the "springs" between the atoms are pushed together at the point of impact (compression) and pulled apart on the underside (tension). Different materials have different "spring" responses.*

Example: The Vaulting Pole and Properties of Materials

Elasticity, strength, and density.   A vaulting pole is a long, slender beam, loaded at one end by the weight of the vaulter. The vaulter must be concerned with three properties of the pole: (1) springiness (elasticity), to maximize the amount of energy returned to the vaulter as the bent pole gradually straightens; (2) strength, to minimize breakage (breakage was a reasonable fear in the days of the bamboo pole); and (3) lightness (low density), to maximize approach velocity.

For early poles, "manufacturing" was simple: an appropriate piece of wood or bamboo was chosen and cut to the desired length. Because these early poles were virtually in a raw, or unprocessed, state, it was extremely difficult to make them with a high degree of uniformity. When aluminum poles were developed, in the 1940s, manufacturers could achieve a high degree of control, through well established processes for manufacturing metals: the aluminum was melted to a liquid, then solidified in a mold (a process called casting), and then extruded and drawn into tubing.

Most solids become liquid when enough energy is applied to overcome the internal bonding forces. During this process, the ordered structure of the solid is converted to the random arrangement of a liquid. In a liquid, atoms (or molecules) move past one another fairly easily and constantly. In a solid, by contrast, the forces between the atoms are stronger and the atoms are therefore in a much more fixed position, though they are not necessarily stationary. When a moderate force is applied to a material, neighboring atoms act as if they were connected to each other by springs (*see Figure 2*). The applied force, or stress, on the material results in a proportional deformation, or strain. Then, when the force is released, the atoms spring back to their original positions, and the material returns to its original size and shape.

A *modulus* expresses the degree to which a substance possesses some property. The modulus of *elasticity*, also known as Young's modulus, is a measure of the stiffness of a material. For example, for equally sized bars of rubber, wood, and aluminum, it would take different loads, or amounts of force, to bend the bars a given distance (*see Figure 3*). The modulus of elasticity of aluminum is about five times that of most woods; therefore, if a load (force) of 10 kilograms (about 22 lb.) is required to bend the wooden bar 2.54 centimeters (1 in.), 50 kilograms (about 110 lb.) will be needed to bend the aluminum bar the same distance.

Any material is considered elastic to some degree, because its atoms usually return to their normal positions after a force pushes or pulls them apart. If a force is sufficient to push a material past its elastic limit, its atoms shift with respect to each other and it is considered permanently strained. Even greater stress may split a material in two or shatter it. This depends not only on elasticity but also on another property, *strength*.

As a vaulter bends a pole, there are two forces acting on the pole:

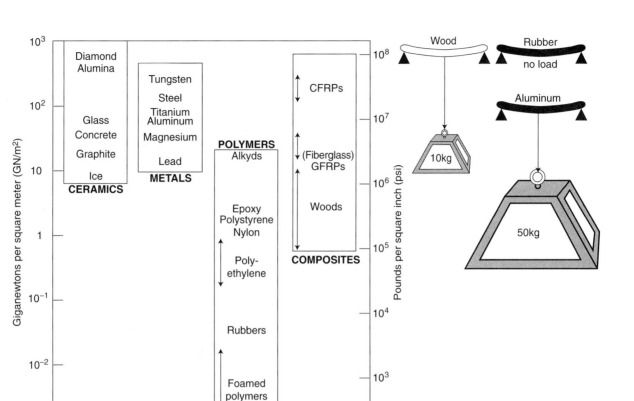

Figure 3. *Modulus of elasticity varies from material to material. For bars of equal size, it would take a different load to bend each material a given distance. The modulus of elasticity of steel, for example, is 50 times that of polyethylene.*

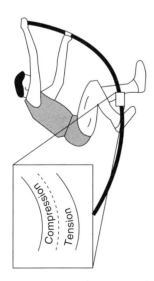

Figure 4. *A vault causes both compression and tension forces on the pole.*

compression (atoms squeezing together) on the side nearer the vaulter and tension (atoms stretching apart) on the side farther away from the vaulter (*see Figure 4*). Thus the stress of bending the pole creates strain—the elongation of material along the far side of the pole. When a bamboo vaulting pole broke in two, splitting started from the tension force on the far side of the pole.

Depending on the stiffness (elasticity) and strength of a pole, strain will have one of three results: first, the pole may bend and then return to its original form; second, the pole may bend but remain permanently strained; third, the pole may break. The yield strength of a material is the stress at which there is no longer linear proportionality between stress and strain—the point at which the material is first permanently deformed. Different materials have different yield strengths (*see Figure 5*). In the case of vaulting poles, the yield strength of the fiberglass-composite pole is comparable to that of the aluminum pole, which it replaced, but the fiberglass-composite pole is much lighter.

One of the advantages of a multimaterial composite, as opposed to a single material (such as aluminum), is that it allows equipment to be customized to meet particular stress requirements. Usually this entails strengthening the equipment to withstand both tension stress

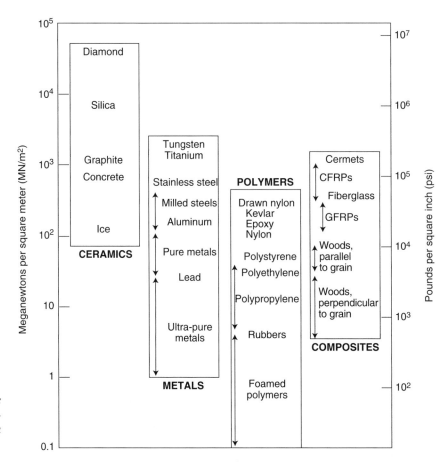

Figure 5. *Yield strengths of various materials are shown here. Many metals, polymers, and composites have a wide range of yield strengths.*

and compression stress. Designers must also consider other types of stress, including torsion (twisting) and shearing (sliding).

Differences in the elasticity and strength of materials are due to differences in the nature of atomic bonding. Metals—which include pure metallic elements, such as copper or iron; and alloys, such as bronze (a mix of copper and tin) or steel (a mix of iron and carbon, and often additional elements)—have a crystalline structure: their atoms are arranged in regular three-dimensional groups. Metals are typically the most ductile materials; that is, they can be shaped (by hammering, rolling, or pulling) without fracturing; and they can be fabricated by forging or by casting, depending on the specific metal or alloy.

Ceramics have a predominately crystalline structure consisting of a matrix of oxygen atoms, which enclose atoms of metals such as aluminum or magnesium. Ceramics are typically brittle and have higher melting temperatures than metals. Their major drawback is the difficulty encountered in fabrication, a process that often involves forming a solid from a powder.

Polymers, or plastics, consist of long-chain molecules and are usually based on bonding between hydrogen and chains of carbon atoms, and often other light elements as well. They may be natural in origin, such as cellulose and rubber; or synthetic, such as polyethylene, nylon, and acrylic (like Plexiglas). Polymers may contain crystalline or noncrystalline components. Generally, the crystalline structures are strong and tough, while the noncrystalline types are more brittle. Unlike ceramics, polymers are easily molded.

Composites are mixtures of two materials, usually fibers or powders of one material in a matrix of another. Common composites include glass fibers in a matrix of polyester or epoxy polymer (commonly called fiberglass); carbon fibers (also called graphite) or boron fibers in epoxy; tungsten carbide in cobalt (metal-matrix composites, or MMCs); and titanium fibers in aluminum oxide (ceramic-matrix composites, or CMCs). Composites are assembled in such a way that the finished product has mechanical properties superior to those of any individual component. For example, the addition of one (discrete) component material in the other (matrix) often reinforces the strength of the former. One such composite material is carbon fiber–reinforced polymers (CFRP); another is glass fiber–reinforced polymers (GFRP).

Composites are of great interest because, as noted above, their properties can be tailored to the needs of the equipment. For example, a vaulting pole or the mast of a sailboat can be made very strong by aligning most of the reinforcing fibers along its length. By contrast, a thin sheet of material—such as would be used for the hull of a boat—has fibers in many directions for uniform strength. In 1995, many of the sailing yachts in the America's Cup had a hull in which a sheet of CFRP was layered around aluminum honeycomb for lightness, stiffness, and strength (*see also SAILING*).

Many of the directionally averaged properties of a composite follow a simple rule of mixtures. An average property is related to the fraction of each component material in the composite, by volume. One such property is the density of a composite; density is an important consideration for applications where high strength and light weight are desired.

This brings us to a third important property of a material, in addition to elasticity and strength—its *density* (*see Figure 6*). The density of a material is its mass per unit volume. Lead is often referred to as a heavy metal and aluminum as a light metal because lead is more than four times as dense as aluminum—11.3 versus 2.7 megagrams per cubic meter (Mg/m^3). Aluminum, in turn, is almost four times as dense as oak (0.72 Mg/m^3), and oak is more than five times as dense as balsa wood (0.13 kg/m^3). Most woods float because they are lighter than water, which has a density of 1 megagram per cubic meter (*see also SWIMMING*).

Many design applications require trade-offs among properties, such as selecting strength or stiffness at minimum weight (*see Figure 7*). For example, designers try to find materials that are lighter but offer equal or better strength, stiffness, or both. The specific strength, or strength-to-weight ratio, of a material is obtained by dividing its yield strength by its density; the specific elasticity, or elasticity-to-density ratio, is obtained by dividing its elasticity by its density.

Trade-offs among properties of materials often represent a

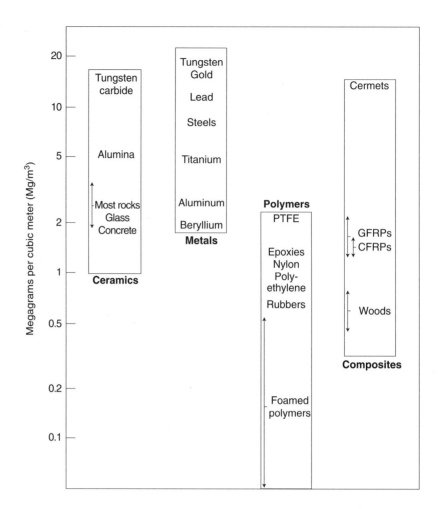

Figure 6. *The density of various materials.*

dilemma for designers of equipment. For the vaulting pole, a simple mathematical model helps clarify some of these trade-offs. The pole behaves like a spring, gradually returning the energy of the bent pole to the ascending vaulter. The goal of the designer is to obtain maximum energy per unit weight of the pole—the most spring from the lightest pole—without the pole's breaking. The mathematical model shows that the best pole has the highest value of the performance parameter for a spring (Ashby, 1992):

$$\frac{(\text{failure strength of the material})^2}{(\text{modulus of elasticity}) \times (\text{material density})}$$

Materials used for vaulting poles over the years have varied in this regard (*again, see Figure 7*). As of the 1990s, fiber-reinforced composites formed into tubes—an efficient shape for light beams—were the materials of choice. Composites are much stronger than wood, but they are somewhat higher in density. Polymers, such as nylon, have the desired low modulus of elasticity and low density, but they bend too much to be used for vaulting and are also weak. Fiberglass-reinforced composites (GFRPs) are preferred over carbon- or graphite-rein-

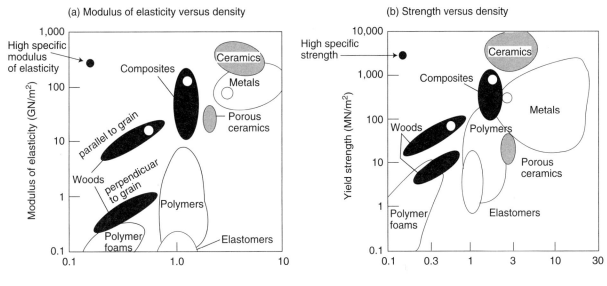

Figure 7. *Selecting materials involves trade-offs among elasticity (stiffness), strength, and density (weight). (a) Materials shown near the upper left-hand corner have a high specific modulus of elasticity; materials near the lower right-hand corner have a low specific modulus of elasticity. (b) Materials near the upper left-hand corner have higher specific strength, and materials near the lower right-hand corner have low specific strength. The dots shows the evolution in vaulting poles from wood to aluminum and then to a composite (fiber-reinforced polymer).*

forced composites (CFRPs) because their elasticity is lower (*refer back to Figure 3*), making them superior as springs. Note, however, that GFRPs are not necessarily preferable for all polelike structures. For example, CFRP is preferred for a sailboat mast because its higher modulus of elasticity reduces mast oscillations (sway).

It is helpful to contrast the vaulting pole with a rubbery bungee cord. In the bungee cord, like the vaulting pole, the goal is "spring" and energy recovery, but in the cord this is combined with extreme elongation. The same performance parameter applies, but now a very low modulus of elastcity is not only tolerable but desired. A rubber cord is an excellent spring, and also surprisingly strong. But because rubber weakens and becomes brittle with exposure to sunlight and oxygen in the air, it must be replaced regularly to ensure safety.

Whatever the application, the point to be noted is that there is a great deal of give-and-take involved in selecting any material when there are conflicting requirements. In fact, balancing conflicting requirements is at the heart of selecting materials. The vaulting poles being used in the 1990s apparently optimized the trade-offs among strength, elasticity, and density—they were well "tuned" to the needs of the vaulter. It might be predicted, then, that further advances would probably be incremental in nature and probably would not entail entirely different types of materials.

"Damping" versus elasticity. According to the law of conservation of energy, energy can be neither created nor destroyed, though it can be

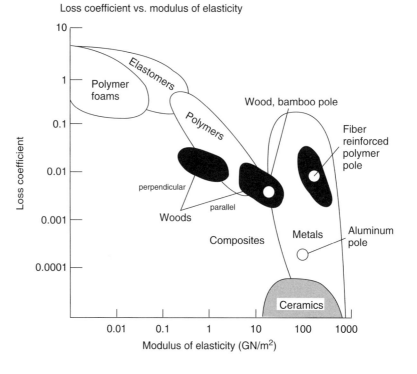

Loss coefficient vs. modulus of elasticity

Figure 8. *How well a material returns energy from a collision is an important factor in selection. Materials shown near the upper left-hand corner damp the majority of received energy; materials near the lower right-hand corner return the energy elastically. Dots indicate the evolution of the vaulting pole.*

transferred from one form to another. When a force is imparted to a material, either the impact energy is absorbed—"damped"—by the material, or the energy is returned elastically to the striking object.

For example, a bat hitting a baseball damps some of the impact energy, but it elastically returns most of the energy to the ball. That is, a portion of the energy will be lost, or damped, within the material, and the remainder will be returned to the ball (elastic energy). Although wood is much stronger when struck against the grain (perpendicular), its elastic energy is greater when it is struck parallel to the grain.

When a vaulting pole is loaded, or bent, to a certain level of stress, it stores a certain amount of elastic energy; when it is unloaded, it returns that elastic energy. The loss coefficient is a measure of the damping that takes place within the pole. Thus, plotting damping ability (loss coefficient) versus stiffness (modulus of elasticity) illustrates how efficiently a material transfers energy (*see Figure 8*). Materials with a high modulus of elasticity, like aluminum vaulting poles and composite poles, have low energy loss—they transfer energy efficiently. By contrast, ceramics, although they have a very high energy return (a low loss coefficient), are too brittle to be used in a vaulting pole.

Bicycles

The diamond-shaped bicycle frame was devloped in the 1880s and remained virtually unchanged until the 1980s. The main triangle in front and the smaller triangle supporting the rear wheel form a

Figure 9. *Advances in materials research in the 1990s made possible widespread experimentation with bicycle designs other than the conventional diamond frame, which dates from the 1880s. (Courtesy of Zipp Speed Weaponry)*

strong, light structural truss, similar to the truss structures in many bridges and buildings. In the early 1990s, the aggressive introduction of other frame materials as alternatives to steel tubing and the growing popularity of mountain bikes spurred significant experimentation with the geometry of the frame. Composite materials have made possible radical new designs for bicycle frames (*see Figure 9*).

Innovation also has affected wheel design. The early invention of the tension-spoke wheel and the pneumatic (inflatable) tire produced a light, strong, comfortable wheel that influenced many developments in airplanes and automobiles. Like the frame, the bicycle wheel remained virtually the same for a century, but then began to change with the appearance of versatile composite materials, which make possible aerodynamic wheels having just a few rigid spokes. Such wheels had first been conceived in the nineteenth century, but they were too heavy for optimum performance and too expensive for mass production. In fact, in the mid-1990s composite wheels continued to be very expensive, costing 10 to 20 times more than conventional tension-spoke wheels; but despite their cost, composite wheels were being used by competitive cyclists to improve performance.

Bicycle Frames

Light, high-quality bicycle frames were originally manufactured from wood and bamboo. Inexpensive steel tubing was introduced in the 1880s—a development motivated by the rapidly growing market for bicycles—and soon became the preferred material for the frame. A standard diameter and a standard wall thickness were quickly established for tubing. The frame then remained relatively unchanged until the 1930s, when steel alloy tubing was developed.

This new tubing was stronger but had thinner walls, with "butting"—thickening of the walls—at the ends of the tubes, that is, at the frame joints, where stresses were greatest. This became the standard for light, high-performance frames.

High-strength aluminum tubing first appeared in the 1970s, but it did not immediately replace steel, because aluminum has only one-third the modulus of elasticity of steel. When designers realized that larger-diameter aluminum tubing provided better rigidity, however, aluminum became an attractive alternative.

Experimentation with materials continues to bring new equipment to the marketplace. In the mid-1990s, bicycle designers were able to work with a wide range of materials suitable for frames; some of these materials are described below.

High-tensile steel. The term *high-tensile steel* is something of a misnomer, since this is actually the lowest-strength material used. It has a yield strength of about 240 meganewtons per square meter (MN/m^2; *again, see Figure 7*), or 35,000 pounds per square inch (psi). Tubing of high-tensile steel is usually 2.54 centimeters (1 in.) in diameter, with a wall thickness of about 2 millimeters (0.08 in.). The major advantages of high-tensile steel are that it is inexpensive, easy to weld, and durable. These are the reasons why it is still the most popular material for frames. Its only major drawback is its weight, which reduces speed.

Chrome-moly steel. This alloy steel contains about 1 percent chromium, 0.2 percent molybdenum, and 0.3 percent carbon (which is also the main strengthener in high-tensile steel). Alloying and "cold drawing"—pulling the tubing through a restricted die opening, as in the drawing of wire—produce a yield strength nearly three times that of high-tensile steel (690 MN/m^2, or 100,000 psi); even greater strength can be achieved with additional heat treatment. The tubing is often more than 2 inches in diameter, with a wall thickness of 0.6 to 1 millimeter (0.024–0.04 in.): the thinnest chrome-moly walls are only one-third the thickness of high-tensile steel. Chrome-moly is preferred by many bicyclists because it offers the same advantages as high-tensile steel but is much lighter; also, it is widely considered to provide a comfortable ride because it damps road shocks.

Aluminum. Cyclists often call aluminum simply "alloy." The most commonly used aluminum contains about 1 percent magnesium and 0.6 percent silicon for strengthening—this is designated alloy 6061-T6 by the aluminum industry. Its yield strength is more than 275 MN/m^2 (40,000 psi); thus its specific strength, or strength-to-weight ratio, is similar to that of chrome-moly steel. To provide the frame with sufficient rigidity, tubing is typically 3.2 to 3.8 centimeters (about 1.25–1.5 in.) in diameter, though it is sometimes as large as 5 centimeters (about 2 in.); wall thickness is at least 1.1 millimeters (0.043 in.). Joints are usually held together by welding, or sometimes by adhesive bonding, which avoids local softening in the heat-affected zone (HAZ)—

that is, the area affected by the heat of welding. Some higher-strength "7000 series" alloys are also used, but these present greater difficulty with welding. Some cyclists believe that aluminum frames give a rough ride, because of the rigidity of the large-diameter tubing.

Titanium. Titanium, generally alloyed with 3 percent aluminum and 2.5 percent vanadium, was originally developed into tubing for aircraft hydraulic systems. It works well for bicycle frames and is available in a range of diameters and wall thicknesses. Because the oxygen in air makes titanium become brittle, the welding of the frame joints must be done with great care. The major advantage of titanium is its combination of light weight and high strength—its yield strength is about 725 MN/m^2 (105,000 psi). Its major disadvantage is its high cost; but its cost is beginning to decrease because of wider use, improved manufacturing methods, and competition.

Carbon-fiber composites. Carbon-fiber composites like those used in the aerospace industry are light, stiff, and strong. Composite tubes can be made individually and then assembled into a diamond frame by adhesively bonding the tubes to lugs made of composites, aluminum, or titanium. Quite different monocoque—one-piece—designs can also be made from carbon-fiber composites. These frames have the advantage of being very strong, but under extreme stress they can fracture with little warning (as can composite tennis rackets, skis, and yacht hulls and masts). Another major drawback is that the molding process is very expensive, though improvements will probably bring the cost down. In 1994, only about 10 percent of road bikes and 4 percent of mountain bikes sold in the United States had carbon-fiber composite frames.

Other materials for frames. Numerous materials with properties comparable to those described above may offer technical or marketing advantages in bicycle frames as research and development continue. These newer materials include strong, tough steels, aluminum-lithium alloys, aluminum-beryllium alloys, aluminum metal-matrix composites (MMCs, with an aluminum alloy matrix reinforced by particulate silicon carbide, fibrous boron carbide, or silicon carbide), and fiber-reinforced composites with a thermoplastic polymer matrix. The last-named are particularly promising because they may eventually be easier to manufacture than the current composite frames and may be less susceptible to sudden fracture.

Bicycle Wheels

The conventional tension-spoke bicycle wheel is extraordinarily light and—as it must be—strong. The spokes themselves must be extremely strong because they are highly tensioned during wheel assembly and are subjected to increased and variable tension during riding; the wheel rim and the hub must be strong enough to support the spokes without deformation or collapse. The rim also serves an important function as the friction surface for braking. Wheel designs vary depending on intended use. For example, mountain-bike wheels

Steel

Aluminum

Figure 10. *These cross sections illustrate the evolution in bicycle rims from the original steel designs to three modern aluminum designs.*

have stronger rims, and often larger spokes, because they encounter more severe loading during off-road use.

Rims were originally handcrafted from wood, but steel has been the standard material since the late nineteenth century (*see Figure 10*). Rims are formed from either strip tubing or flattened tubing and are always plated, for appearance and to resist rusting. In the 1920s Mavic, in France, introduced the first strong aluminum-alloy rims, which gradually proved superior to steel and were also considerably lighter. Aluminum-alloy rims are expensive, however, and are generally supplied only on bicycles selling for more than $300. Aluminum rims are usually extruded as straight sections and then formed into circles. Most aluminum rims are made from the same 6061 alloy used in frames, because it is widely available, its cost is reasonable, it can be extruded, its strength is adequate, and it resists atmospheric corrosion.

Low-cost spokes are made from high-strength cold-drawn carbon steel wire and plated to resist corrosion. Drawn stainless steel spokes of similar strength are also common, but more expensive. The threaded end at the rim has rolled rather than cut threads, because rolled threads are more resistant to repetitive, or "fatigue," loading. Spokes made of titanium and fiber-reinforced composites are slightly lighter, but as of the mid-1990s they were prohibitively expensive.

Composite wheels are increasingly used on racing bicycles. Many are molded in one piece, with airfoil cross sections for rims and spokes to reduce aerodynamic drag and with aluminum rims and hubs molded in (*see Figure 11*). Other wheels have only an airfoil-shaped composite rim with stainless steel spokes that may be flat-

Figure 11. *Composite wheels are used increasingly on racing bicycles. Many are molded in one piece, with airfoil cross sections for rims and spokes to reduce aerodynamic drag, and with molded-in aluminum rims and hubs. Although these aerodynamic spoke designs had existed for years, only in the 1990s did designers develop composite materials sufficiently light and strong for wide use. (Courtesy of DuPont)*

tened, or bladed, to further reduce drag (*refer back to Figure 9*). While composite wheeels have been finding wider acceptance among very serious cyclists, their high cost (from $300 to $500 per wheel as of 1996) made them a dubious investment for recreational cyclists.

Numerous innovations have emerged since the early 1980s. These recent developments may even surpass those of the century that followed the introduction of the traditional bicycle. The diamond frame and the spoked wheel continue to dominate, however, because of their very good performance and their reasonable cost (*see also CYCLING*).

Golf

Interest in golf continues to grow: hundreds of new courses are built every year, and in 1995 the United States Sporting Goods Association estimated that in the United States more than $1.4 billion was being spent annually on golf equipment. This growing market has motivated, and supported, technological innovations in golf clubs and golf balls. As noted earlier, advanced-techology equipment is likely to improve the performance of golfers of modest ability, but it may make little difference for professionals or highly skilled recreational golfers. This is because many improvements minimize the consequences of hitting the ball poorly and thus are of little value to a golfer who seldom hooks, slices, or hits the ball off center.

Golf Balls

The maximum distance a golf ball can be driven is primarily a function of velocity and loft angle, although there are additional factors, including wind, the surface of the ball, and the spin, or rotation, of the ball.

Maximum velocity is achieved when the tranfer of energy between two nearly rigid bodies—the club head and the golf ball—is optimized. A rigid body has a high degree of "stiffness," or a high modulus of elasticity. Transfer of energy is perfect when all the energy is returned upon impact. For example, if a perfectly elastic ball with a given velocity hits a perfectly elastic rigid or stationary body, the ball bounces back in the opposite direction at the same velocity. If the ball is inelastic, it will "damp" some energy during the collision. Inelasticity can be expressed as a coefficient of restitution (COR)—the ratio of the velocity of the ball as it rebounds from a hard, immovable surface to the incident velocity. The COR is also equal to the square root of the proportion of the energy that was dissipated in the collision. The COR of a golf ball varies from about 0.8 at 32 kilometers per hour (KPH) (20 MPH) to 0.6 at 160 KPH (100 MPH); by comparison, the COR of a baseball is about 25 percent lower. Laboratory test conditions for a golf ball are typically 38 meters per second (125 ft./sec., or about 75 MPH). In a collision between a driver and a golf ball, a rather massive club head (450 g, or 15.75 oz.) strikes a much lighter ball (42 g, or 1.47 oz.) for about 0.0005 second. The short time span of the collision and the vast difference between the two masses are not ideal conditions for effective energy transfer to the ball.

The typical golf ball is 4.27 centimeters (1.68 in.) in diameter. It has a dimpled surface, which significantly affects spin and distance. Much design work has been focused on the dimpling pattern and on the construction materials (*see also GOLF*). Although the size, the depth, and the number of dimples on a ball may differ, all golf balls are produced from polymeric resin concoctions, including ultra-high-molecular-weight polybutadiene, carboxyl-rich ionomer resins, polyurethanes, and blends of copolyetherester or copolyetheramide.

Modern golf balls may be divided into two basic categories, according to their construction: two-piece or three-piece. A two-piece ball consists of a large core made of rubber compounds and a cover of durable Surlyn, a blended ionomer polymer resin developed by DuPont. In a high-performance two-piece ball, softer blends of thermoplastic materials are used. A three-piece ball is also known as a "wound" ball because its rubber core is surrounded by windings similar to thin rubber bands. One version of three-piece construction is the softer, balata-covered ball, which has a liquid-filled core. The manufacturing cost of a three-piece ball is considerably greater, so there is considerable incentive for manufacturers to move to the two-piece ball if golfers are not willing to pay more. A wound ball has better "feel" and control, but a two-piece ball is durable and hard and gives greater distance. In the mid-1990s, designers were working on developing a new type of two-piece ball, which would combine the feel and spin of a wound ball with the distance of the traditional two-piece ball (*see also GOLF*).

Golf Clubs

Golf clubs may be divided into woods, irons, and putters. As the terms imply, *driver* woods are used for long-distance drives from the tee and *fairway* woods on the fairway. Irons, also called wedges, are used for accuracy and placement rather than distance. Putters are used exclusively on the green.

The woods all have faces that are inclined by only about 10 to 15 degrees from the vertical; from the 1-wood (the driver) to the 4-wood, the face angle becomes more inclined. The greater loft angle of the 4-wood tends to produce drives that are higher and shorter than those produced by the 3-, 2-, or 1-wood. Irons, or wedges, range from the 1-iron, which has a face inclined at 20 degrees; to the 9-iron, whose face is inclined 45 degrees. As the angle increases, a hit with the same force will produce a trajectory that is successively higher and shorter. The difference between any two consecutively numbered clubs is about 9 to 13 meters (10–15 yd.).

Experts have devoted considerable effort to analyzing the physics, the mechanics, and the materials science of the perfect swing—the ideal conditions which lead to and include the ball-club collision and the subsequent drive. The problem is complex because the transfer of energy is not only a matter of the impact of club head and ball. Energy transfer is also related to the flexibility (stiffness) of the shaft; to torque (rotational force about an axis) between the ball and the club head, which is asymmetric with respect to the shaft; and to biomechanics—the complex interactions in the golfer's swing.

Some physicists have suggested an "inertia matrix" to measure the ability of a club head to resist rotation. (Inertia is a property of mass—the tendency of an object at rest to stay at rest, and an object in motion to stay in motion.) The inertia matrix describes resistance to rotation up and down as well as to rotation right and left (*see Figure 12*). In terms of their inertial matrix, club heads fall into three categories: (1) jumbo heads resist rotation equally around any axis; (2) midsize metal woods resist movement around one axis, but at the expense of movement around the other axes; (3) club heads with a thick soleplate offer resistance primarily to heel-toe errors—that is, to "topping" the ball.

Theoretically, the range of a drive is maximized when the initial angle is 45 degrees (*see also FIELD ATHLETICS: THROWING*). Any other takeoff angle, whether greater or smaller, will produce a shorter drive. Assuming no air resistance, the range of a ball hit at a 45-degree angle is exactly four times the maximum height the ball is driven. In reality, however—that is, for a golf ball subject to lift and linear drag—maximum distance occurs when the takeoff angle is about 12 to 13 degrees. For this reason, the usual loft angle for a driver club is 11 degrees. At this angle, the maximum distance is about six times the maximum height, so that a ball that reaches a height of about 37 meters (40 yd.) will travel a distance of about 220 meters (240 yd.).

Maximum energy transfer to the golf ball, the longest distance the ball can carry, requires the maximum stiffness (highest modulus of elasticity) for both the club and the golf ball. When the club head is made of a material with a lower modulus of elasticity (because of other design considerations, or to reduce costs), the manufacturer compensates for this by using face inserts made of a material with a higher modulus of elasticity. Experts agree that for maximum performance, the club head should be as large as possible (to provide a large "sweet spot" for a good hit), the head should be as stiff as possible (highest possible modulus of elasticity), and the shaft should also be as stiff as possible.

During impact with the ball, the shaft bends (flexes) about 3 degrees. Given the usual 10-degree angle of loft of the driving wood, this flexing of the shaft will increase the effective loft by a few additional degrees. Golfers used to believed that a "whippy" shaft, one with a flex of more than 3 degrees, would give some additional elastic energy to the impact between club head and ball. However, phys-

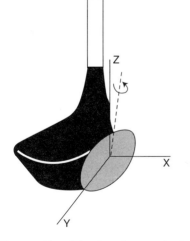

Figure 12. *The inertia matrix is one way that scientists can make measurements in three dimensions to determine what causes the club to rotate in a player's hands during an off-center impact.*

ical modeling has indicated that energy transfer is optimized by a stiff shaft and a stiff head (*see also ARCHERY*).

All club heads have approximately the same weight. The formula for momentum (mass × velocity) might seem to indicate that a heavier head (greater mass) would make the transfer of momentum more effective and thus would send the ball farther. In fact, though, a heavier club head offers little benefit, because it usually reduces the velocity of the swing; thus manufacturers have made the club head lighter over the years.

Manufacturers have used improved materials to increase the volume of the head or to build in extra local mechanical support for specific structural needs. A larger head, for example, will require a lower-density, or lighter, material with a higher modulus of elasticity. The market for jumbo-head drivers has boomed as a result of new technology making it possible to meet these criteria. One manufacturer eliminated the hossle, or stem, of the club head but had to compensate by building up the face to prevent it from caving in. The weight saved by using a lighter yet stronger material allowed this manufacturer to better weight the perimeter of the club and therefore to reduce torque, the rotational inertia caused by an off-center hit. Interestingly, golf rules do not specify the weight of a club head. If a golfer desires, lead tape can be added to the head to increase its weight.

The shafts of golf clubs are made with steel, aluminum, or titanium alloys and graphite or boron fiber-reinforced composites. These high-stiffness materials have allowed manufacturers to lengthen the shaft. Previously, shafts had not been lengthened, because steel shafts were too heavy to be made longer and early graphite shafts had too much torque—a longer graphite shaft would have flexed excessively. The longer shaft became feasible only when manufacturers of composite shafts were able to reduce torque by using graphite with an ultrahigh modulus of elasticity, in some instances incorporating boron to add strength. For example, a 133-centimeter (52-in.) graphite-shaft driver weighs less than a 109-centimeter (43-in.) steel-shaft driver. The longer shaft produces a significant increase in rotational momentum, translating into greater club-head speed at impact as well as a longer drive.

Machine forging of iron club heads began around the turn of the twentieth century. Since the 1960s, casting technology, originally devised for the aerospace industry, has increasingly replaced machine forging. The incorporation of "investment casting" technology, which is used for complex and high-precision shapes, gave manufacturers greater latitude in design—particularly in creating club heads with a larger "sweet spot." Investment casting, along with the availability of new materials, has made it possible to develop "metal woods"—clubs filled with a polymer foam that react like wooden clubs. (The term *metal woods* is an oxymoron; it is used because drivers have traditionally been referred to as woods.) Because the weight is concentrated around the perimeter—the face, the surrounding walls, the sole, and the crown—the designer is able to adjust the weight to increase the center of mass and hence the moment of inertia. The hollow-cast club head also allows a larger head, and thus a larger sweet spot, so that contact is less likely to twist the club (*see also TENNIS*).

In terms of materials, the head is the most challenging part of the golf club to design. The most important properties for the head of a driver, for example, are high modulus of elasticity, low specific damping capacity (loss coefficient), and low density. Strength, hardness, and toughness are also important considerations.

Perimeter-weighting has also been used to create cavity-back iron clubs. For these clubs, most of the weight is at the perimeter or at the heel and toe, rather than either evenly spread or concentrated directly behind the impact area, as in standard irons.

A Note on Inserts.   Until 1992, the USGA specified, in Rule 4-1(c), that "if the basic structural material of the head and face of a club, other than a putter, is metal, no insert or attachment is permitted." When this rule was dropped, manufacturers began experimenting with club design and insert materials. In the mid-1990s, club manufacturers could use one set of designs and manufacturing criteria for the body of the club head—perhaps for light weight and high modulus of elasticity—and use another material for the face, to achieve some other design function.

One of the ways in which clubs changed after 1992 (when the rule prohibiting inserts was dropped) is that face inserts were introduced. In driver and fairway woods, hard inserts with a high modulus of elasticity—made of materials such as zirconia ceramics, graphite, and Ti MMCs (SiC or TiN particulates in a Ti-6Al-4V alloy; *see Figure 7*)—are used to increase drive distance. These lightweight materials move the center of gravity toward the back of the club and allow for perimeter weighting. In wedges, insert materials such as WC-bronze MMCs are used to provide better control and backspin. "Soft" materials, such as thermoplastics and thermoplastic polymers, which have low modulus of elasticity and high loss, have been used as face inserts in putters. These materials appear to increase dwell time—that is, the time of contact between club face and ball—by a factor of about two. The putter face, in essence, hugs the ball for a moment longer, resulting in a better "feel," topspin, and an immediate rolling motion (rather than a skidding motion).

Ceramic inserts have also been used for the striking face of a club head. Because the grooves or holes for countersunk screws in the ceramic insert make it more prone to cracking, fracture-resistant, toughened zirconia, rather than alumina (Al_2O_3), is used. Because of the rule of mixtures, MMCs can improve modulus of elasticity—more so than by using different metal materials—while maintaining toughness. (Thirty percent SiC by volume in cast aluminum would have a large effect on stiffness.)

Athletic Shoes

Most sports require significant foot-to-ground interaction. This interaction may be necessary simply to support the body, as in shooting and bowling, or it may be of primary importance, as in running and high jumping. Whenever there is contact between the foot and the supporting surface, a force is applied to the foot to enable propulsion. The force may be light and incidental, or it may result in damage to the foot. Further complicating matters is the fact that people move differently and have different types of feet. For example, a high-arched foot tends not to pronate, or roll, enough, so an athlete with high arches needs a cushioned shoe with plenty of flexibility. A flat foot tends to overpronate, so the athlete needs a shoe with a firm midsole (*see also ANKLE, FOOT, AND LOWER LEG and VOLLEYBALL*). Thus a wide range of shoe styles are needed to meet the needs of each sport and of each individual athlete.

With growing interest in exercise for physical fitness in the second half of the twentieth century, footwear was adapted for athletic purposes for men, women, and children. Until the late 1960s, athletic shoes were mainly limited to sneakers—a multipurpose athletic shoe worn for a large number of sports. By the 1990s, manufacturers were marketing specialized footwear for every major and minor sport and for athletes of every size, age, gender, and skill level.

Athletic footwear is designed for some combination of protection, appearance, and improvement of performance. Many athletes are primarily concerned with performance, but protection is an important secondary consideration. Experts who have conducted biomechanical studies of movements in sports have identified the need for footgear designed for individual sports as well as for the variety of human sizes, foot structures, and motion patterns—all of which contribute to the process of the load development on the foot. Modern technology has provided a huge diversity of materials and manufacturing techniques for shoes, and each year brings dozens of new features and styles.

During the interaction between footwear and surface, a shoe's performance depends on its ability to provide support, to absorb impact, and to create friction. The relative importance of each of these factors depends on the sport. For basketball, football, tennis, and boxing, footwear must provide sufficient friction for quick go-and-stop action. Track and field, bicycling, and rowing, on the other hand, do not require go-and-stop action or quick lateral moves on the part of the athlete. For those sports, good support from the shoes is most essential. Although there are great differences between the amount of support and the amount of friction that sports-specific shoes provide, all are designed to minimize the impact forces that act on the foot during foot-ground contact. This is a complex problem because the shoe often has to perform a number of conflicting tasks. It should provide support, but still be comfortable; it should be stiff, but still provide a good degree of cushioning; it should be shock-absorbent, but still provide energy return. To meet these needs, shoe designers do a lot of experimenting to develop the right combination of materials that will result in a superior shoe.

The jolt a runner feels each time a foot touches the ground is called an impact wave. Good footwear is designed to protect the human musculoskeletal system from impact waves. The magnitude and shape of these waves depend on the type of activity, but the result is microdamage to bone and to cartilage, such as the meniscus in the knees (*see also KNEE*). This microdamage is a natural reaction of the body to external loads. A certain amount of dynamic loading on the bone stimulates a type of cellular activity that actually strengthens bone. Unfortunately, doctors do not yet know at what intensity and duration impact waves result in optimal bone strengthening and at what level irreversible damage results. Thus, the better a shoe absorbs, or cushions, impacts, the longer and harder an athlete can train.

The number of variables facing shoe designers is immense. Running shoes, for example, require firm support in the midfoot and shock protection at the heel; a heel-to-ball runner will want some of the impact energy returned from the heel strike in order to aid propulsion. Such demands can be satisfied by incorporating a large number of material components into the outsole, insole, and midsole of the shoe.

The Outsole

The outsole, or bottom, of a shoe is the site of contact between the shoe and the surface. Its main function is to provide adequate friction while withstanding the effects of the environment and contact with water and sharp particles. Outsoles can vary considerably depending on the sport and the athlete's level of ability.

Elastomer styrene-butadiene rubber is one of the most common materials used in outsoles, although a highly abrasion-resistant rubber filled with carbon fiber is becoming increasingly popular because of its added flexibility. Flexibility is desired, especially across the ball, to accommodate the natural twisting motion of the foot. Outsoles also incorporate treads in a variety of patterns intended to improve shock absorption and traction. While performance seems to depend, in part, on the outsole's tread pattern, manufacturers have been unable to develop a widely accepted laboratory methodology for testing tread designs.

The Insole

For most sports shoes, the insole is made of a molded flexible polymer material with a fabric cover. The main purpose of the insole is to provide good fit and comfort, and to contribute to shock absorption. To achieve these goals, manufacturers of sports shoes utilize a variety of materials. Polymer foam is popular because it is inexpensive and easily replaceable. Some designers incorporate several materials to maximize fit, comfort, and shock absorption, particularly at the heel area.

The Midsole

Sandwiched between the outsole and insole is the midsole—perhaps the most important part of the shoe, not only because of its function but also because of the sheer volume it occupies. Although shoes vary depending on foot type, the heel and ball region are generally designed to be more elastic for greater shock absorbance, while the arch is stiff to provide support (*see also ANKLE, FOOT, AND LOWER LEG*). The most popular midsole material is a polymer foam made of ethylene, vinyl, and acetate (EVA). Its tremendous range in strength, density, and stiffness (elasticity) allows it to be manufactured so that its composition and functionality differ along its length as well as its width (*refer back to Figures 3 and 5 through 8*). The result is a midsole with mechanical properties that vary from heel to toe in terms of hardness, density, elasticity, and resilience.

EVA has one drawback, however: it tends to break down over time and from heavy use. As the air bubbles that form the foam and provide stability break down, the shoe loses its shock-absorbing properties. Running shoes with EVA midsoles usually lose much of their cushioning after about 500 miles of roadwork. To counter this problem, some manufacturers try to redistribute the bubbles in an effort to delay and prevent breakdown; others incorporate parts made of different materials. One of the promising approaches incorporates pieces made of various rubber-like polyurethane elastomers. These materials provide excellent shock absorption without breaking up, and they can sustain their viscoelastic behavior for many years of extensive use. (*Viscoelastic* means having both viscosity—a property that restricts flow—and elasticity.) The only drawback of polyurethane elastomers is that their greater density makes them considerably heavier.

Some designers have incorporated multiple hollow or gas-filled chambers into the areas of the midsole that receive the most impact. Depending on the sport, these chambers may be at the heel, at the ball of the foot, or both. When these chambers were incorporated into shoe designs in 1979, tests showed that they provided superior shock absorption and elasticity; athletes, however, reported poorer stability (Frey, 1995). This problem was overcome with refinements in chamber positioning and design. Chambers were better tuned to the modulus of elasticity and the loss coefficient of the EVA material within which they were incorporated, resulting in comparable stability with better durability, shock absorption, and elasticity.

Heel Counters and Other Shoe Parts

Manufacturers use heel counters to provide stability and prevent excessive pronation—outward roll of the ankle. Immediately after a heel strike, the foot begins to sink into the shoe and tends to roll into a flat position. Very often this motion will continue to create exces-

Energy Return

Most tracks, the midsole of the shoe, and the human foot are all viscoelastic. Following shoe-ground impact, the viscoelastic components of the foot, the shoe, and the track all "damp" and store energy and return it to the athlete. Theoretically, shoes that return more elastic energy to the athlete should reduce the need for oxygen, and this in turn should improve performance. Few studies, however, have been able to substantiate this claim.

The Perfect Shoe?

The problem of conflicting requirements—that is, trade-offs—exists for nearly all parts of a shoe, and this makes it impossible to produce the "perfect" shoe. There is always a need for compromise, and this is the supreme challenge facing designers. Further complicating matters is the fact that people do not run or walk the same way and do not have identical feet. A high-arched foot tends not to pronate enough, so it requires cushioning with plenty of flexibility; a flat foot tends to overpronate, so it requires a firm midsole. Only "smart" combinations of modern materials, developed through extensive laboratory testing, will allow for advances in the direction of better sport shoes for everyone.

sive pronation, which can cause knee injuries. The heel counter must also support the foot: it should be flexible and stiff at the same time. It must prevent excessive sinking and twisting of the foot while maintaining appropriate shock absorption. The most common solution is the use of a variety of stiff, injection-molded plastics that have been incorporated into a light, compressible material.

The remaining parts of the shoe—the uppers, the heel collar, and the lacing—are mainly of cosmetic value. Style, ease of cleaning, weight, and breathability are achieved through the use of a variety of synthetic leathers, polyester and polypropylene fabrics, nylons, and tricots.

Other Sports

The range of materials used in other sports is as wide as the range of sports and recreational activities themselves. The following list illustrates some of the conventional materials as well as some of the materials that have been developed by new technologies.

Archery

Bows were originally carved from carefully selected and carefully shaped wood. By the 1990s, bows were being made of sophisticated combinations of fiber-reinforced composites, wood, and high-strength alloys. Crossbows are similar. Because traditional wooden arrow shafts are susceptible to warping, they have been largely replaced by aluminum alloys for high-performance archery. Aluminum itself is being enhanced by wrapping it with fiber composites to increase stiffness, to reduce vibrations, and hence to improve accuracy during flight.

Baseball and Softball

Professional baseball bats must be wood, usually northern white ash. Most players believe that lighter bats permit a faster swing and greater hitting distance, although some still argue that heavier bats are better. Most amateurs use bats made almost exclusively of high-strength aluminum alloys because they are lightweight, durable, and allow for flexibility in design. Bats of fiber-reinforced composite materials have received only limited use because of their high cost and their unproved performance.

Basketball

For competition, high-strength tempered-glass backboards have widely replaced wood, metal, and fiberglass boards. Breakaway, spring-loaded rims minimize shattering from forceful dunks. Clear or tinted acrylic polymers are also available and provide lighter, less expensive backboards that look and play just like glass.

Canoeing, Kayaking, and Shelling

More than 20 materials are used in the production of canoes, including the traditional wood planking with canvas overlay, aluminum alloy, polymers and polymer laminates, sandwich construction with solid skins over less dense plastic foam or wood core, and fiber-reinforced polymers, often hybrid composites with more than one type of fiber (glass, Kevlar, carbon, Spectra). Kayaks are primarily made of high-performance composites. Shells for competitive rowing are also made of the most advanced composites.

Fishing

Fiber-reinforced composite materials have largely replaced wood and bamboo in fishing rods because of their design flexibility, strength, and durability. Fishing rods are hollow tubes that differ in control of sensitivity and in touch, depending on need. Tube diameter and wall thickness are also tapered according to need, and the selection and directional placement of reinforcing fibers can vary. Hybrid construction is common, with less-stiff glass fibers combined with stiffer carbon fibers. Manufacturing methods are similar to those for other tubular products, such as boat masts and vaulting poles.

Football

Protective gear for this intensive contact sport has evolved from leather and fabric layers to advanced helmets and a variety of specialized pads. Hard shells and soft foam layers spread and absorb impacts to the body and the head. Face masks attached to helmets are made of grids of welded and coated steel wire or molded impact-resistant plastic. Shoes are designed to function on grass or artificial turf and in different weather conditions.

Hockey

Wood is traditionally used for hockey sticks, but many sticks are wrapped with fiber-reinforced composite materials. The shaft of an ice hockey stick is often made of rectangular aluminum tubing, adhesively bonded to a replaceable reinforced wooden blade. Field hockey sticks are made from fiber-reinforced composite materials.

Ice Skating

Blades of high-quality skates are made of high-carbon steel, with the highest hardness commensurate with toughness needed to prevent breakage. Hardened stainless steel prevents rusting but does not grind as satisfactorily as carbon steel.

Sailing

The hull of a racing boat has much the same requirements as those of any boat—stiffness and strength with light weight. For racing boats, however, these needs are more difficult to meet, because of such factors as the larger size of racing yachts and the willingness of racers to take extreme measures to obtain a small edge in performance. One risk is that strength will be insufficient in heavy seas, leading to catastrophic hull failure, as happened in 1995 in the America's Cup. Sails have advanced greatly with the use of high-strength fibers such as polyester, Kevlar, and Spectra, as well as with improved construction methods.

Street Hockey

The street hockey ball is a simple but instructive example of how performance can be controlled through material properties. Ball rebound is tailored for different temperatures by variations in polymer composition. A warm-weather ball is firm at about 70 degees F (21°C), giving the right combination of energy absorption and resilience when struck. When it is cold, however, this ball becomes hard—because polymers are sensitive to changes in temperature—and its rebound is too large. A cold-weather ball, on the other hand, is soft and has no rebound when it is warm, but hardens sufficiently below 30 degrees F (-1° C) to perform properly.

Tennis

The first racket frames were made of wood and, later, of laminated wood. In the 1960s, aluminum became widely used because of its strength, its light weight, its insensitivity to moisture, and the ease with which it could be formed into frames. Beginning in the 1970s, however, graphite became the material of choice; with its greater rigidity and lighter weight, it offered significant performance improvements over aluminum. In the 1990s, the most popular materials were fiber-reinforced composites with several grades of carbon fiber (graphite) and fiberglass. Aluminum survives in some inexpensive rackets.

Michael R. Notis, David A. Thomas, and Arkady Voloshin

References

Ashby, M. *Materials Selection in Mechanical Design.* New York: Pergamon, 1992.

Easterling, K. *Advanced Materials for Sports Equipment.* New York: Chapman and Hall, 1993.

Frey, C. "The Shoe in Sports." In D. Baxter (ed.), *The Foot and Ankle in Sport.* St. Louis: Mosby, 1995.

Fritz, S. "High(tech)tops." *Popular Science*, July 1994, 67–72.

Gaffney, A. "Running on Air." *Popular Mechanics*, May 1994, 35–37.

Jorgenson, T. *The Physics of Golf.* New York: American Institute of Physics, 1994.

Field Athletics: Jumping

IN THE EARLY DAYS OF HUMANITY, jumping was an important skill—though not in track and field competitions. Jumping was more a matter of survival: to escape from a predator or an enemy and to chase prey, early humans had to be good jumpers. Anyone hiking in the woods today can easily imagine early humans jumping across a narrow creek, or bounding from rock to rock to cross a wider stream, or leaping over a fallen tree. This skill, originally essential, eventually led to sports involving jumping.

The four competitive jumping events are the high jump, long jump, triple jump, and pole vault. These all share some basic principles and have a common objective: to maximize either distance (the horizontal dimension) or height (the vertical dimension). The high jump and long jump are rather straightforward events, with the goal of achieving the greatest possible height or distance, respectively; but the triple jump and pole vault involve additional factors. The triple jump puts a premium on maintaining momentum through each phase; in the pole vault, the vaulter must utilize the elastic potential energy of the pole.

World-class jumpers tend to be tall and long-legged, but speed, quickness, agility, timing, launch angle, and technique are just as important as these physical characteristics in clearing a height or propelling the body over a long distance. This article covers the basic physics and biomechanics involved in jumping. It starts with scientific concepts that apply to all types of jumping, and then goes on to discuss some of the specifics involved in the four field jumping events.

Takeoff Speed and Center of Gravity

Before analyzing jumping in field athletics, it is useful to look at the simplest type of jump: the standing vertical jump. To begin this jump, a person crouches down, knees bent, and then pushes downward on the floor as the legs straighten. The jumper accelerates upward and leaves the ground on tiptoe.

The jumping height that can be attained depends on the takeoff speed as the jumper becomes airborne, and this in turn depends on the average force exerted by the feet on the ground and also on the depth (or vertical distance) of the jumper's crouch. This vertical dis-

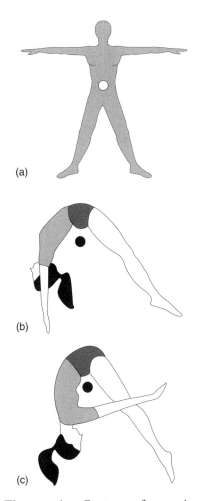

(a)

(b)

(c)

Figure 1. *Center of gravity depends on the position of the body. (a) Raising the arms raises the center of gravity. In (b) a back bend and (c) a closed pike position, the center of gravity actually lies outside the body.*

tance directly affects how long the force can act to propel the jumper upward—that is, how long the jumper's feet are in contact with the ground, exerting force. Increasing either force or crouch distance (force time) within reasonable limits increases takeoff speed. However, if the jumper crouches too low, the jumping muscles (for a standing vertical jump, these are primarily the quadriceps muscles along the front of the thighs) become overstretched, and the available force decreases. Hence, taking off from too deep a crouch will actually produce a smaller jump.

From a crouch distance of about 0.4 meter (16 in.)—corresponding to a position in which the jumper's thighs are parallel to the ground—a person can exert a force on the ground of about twice the body weight (Alexander, 1992), producing a takeoff speed of roughly 3 meters (slightly under 10 ft.) per second and a vertical jump of 0.4 meter. Peter Brancazio, a physicist at Brooklyn College, has reported that in 1976 an NBA basketball player, Darrell Griffith, achieved a standing vertical jump of 1.2 meters, three times as high as this (Brancazio, 1984). This means that Griffith was able to exert an average force on the ground of about 3,100 newtons (700 lb.), more than 3.5 times his body weight. But even Griffith's jump is quite small compared with a world-class high jump of 2.3 meters.

How do high jumpers manage to leap so high? The answer lies partly in the position of the jumper's center of gravity, or center of mass. Within the body is a point where all its mass can be assumed to be concentrated, at least for the purpose of calculating, for instance, how high or how far a person can jump.

When a person stands erect with arms hanging by the sides, the center of gravity is located about 5 centimeters (2 in.) above the hip joints. Because men tend to have broader shoulders and narrower hips than women, the center of gravity for a man is typically slightly higher than for a woman of the same height. The center of gravity usually changes when the body assumes different positions (*see Figure 1*). If the arms are extended upward, the center of gravity is raised. In a backward bend or a loose pike position, the center of gravity is actually outside the body. If this seems paradoxical, consider a wedding ring: its center of gravity is at its geometric center, although there is no actual mass there.

The distance of a standing vertical jump—for example, the figure mentioned above, 0.4 meter—is also the height reached by the center of gravity relative to its position at takeoff. Since the shape of the jumper stays essentially the same during the airborne portion of a standing vertical jump, the distance by which the center of gravity is raised is the same as the height of the feet above the ground (*see Figure 2*).

This is not the case for a high jumper, whose body changes continuously in shape and orientation throughout a jump. At takeoff the center of gravity is several centimeters above the hips; thus for a world-class high jumper, it might be 1.4 meters (about 4.5 ft.) above the ground (Hay, 1973). Although this may seem improbably high, it is explained by the fact that world-class high jumping is dominated by tall, long-legged athletes. In a study of the physiques of Olympic athletes,

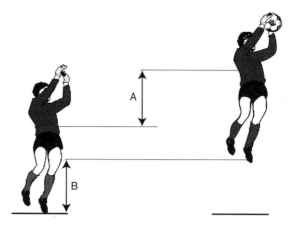

Figure 2. *In a standing vertical jump, the increase in height of the center of gravity (A) is the same as the increase in height of the feet (B). (Two common examples of the vertical jump in sports are a soccer goalkeeper making a save and a basketball player hauling down a rebound.) The dynamics of field jumping are different: the increase in height is much greater for the feet than for the center of gravity.*

James Tanner, a medical doctor, concluded that male high jumpers "are tall men;... they have the longest legs relative to the trunk of all the athletes (with the possible exception of the hammer throwers)" (Tanner, 1964; *see also FIELD ATHLETICS: THROWING*).

Although a tall, long-legged physique helps in high jumping, results also depend on takeoff speed. The vertical takeoff speed attained by a world-class high jumper can be as much as 4.2 meters (nearly 14 ft.) per second, resulting in a jump that increases the height of the center of gravity by 0.9 meter (about 3 ft.). To determine the center-of-gravity height at the top of the jump, this increase is added to center of gravity at the start, 1.4 meters above the ground: 1.4 + 0.9 = 2.3 meters, or about 7.5 feet.

This figure, 2.3 meters, is a useful benchmark in comparing dif-

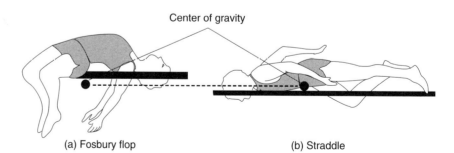

Figure 3. *The two major high-jumping styles are (a) Fosbury flop and (b) straddle. Although center of gravity is the same height above the ground in the two styles, the flop allows a higher bar to be cleared. In the straddle, the jumper's center of gravity passes about 0.1 meter above the bar. By contrast, in the flop the center of gravity can actually pass slightly under the bar; the jumper "snakes" over the bar, keeping the center of gravity lower, and this maximizes clearance height.*

ferent high-jumping styles. In the Fosbury flop technique (*see Figure 3a*), introduced by Dick Fosbury in 1968, the jumper faces upward and bends backward while passing over the bar. As a result, the center of gravity is just outside the jumper's arched back. The flexible spine and the back arching backward actually make it possible for the center of gravity to pass slightly under the bar; therefore, a trained jumper can just clear a bar 2.3 meters high. By contrast, in the straddle technique (*see Figure 3b*) the center of gravity typically passes about 0.1 meter (3.9 in.) above the bar, and so the height of a bar that can be jumped is reduced by this amount, to about 2.2 meters. This sizable difference between the two styles—0.1 meter—hastened the decline of the straddle technique and the dominance of the flop.

Note that with either technique, more than half the height results from the initial height of the center of gravity: 1.4 meters, to use the example above. The remaining height, in this case 0.9 meter, is still well above the increase in height of the center of gravity in the standing vertical jump, 0.4 meter. Because high jumpers are running during the approach to the bar, they can achieve much greater vertical takeoff speeds than standing jumpers and, therefore, higher jumps (*see also BASKETBALL*).

The center of gravity is also important in other jumping events. In the pole vault, the vaulter passes over the bar in essentially a loose pike position with arms and feet pointing downward; the center of gravity passes just under the bar. In the long jump, the trajectory of the center of gravity determines the path of the airborne jumper. To prolong the flight, a long jumper tries to make the center of gravity very high at takeoff and very low at landing.

Muscle Forces and Jumping Ability

To obtain an advantage in the "competition" between muscle force and body weight, coaches in sports that require jumping, such as volleyball and basketball, urge the athletes to keep their weight down. At the same time, though, they want the athletes to increase the size of the muscles in their jumping engines—their legs.

In all types of jumping, the body must exert force against the ground. The best performance results from a combination of the greatest impulse by the takeoff foot (force × time) and the optimal angle of takeoff. Force exerted is obviously important, but equally important is how long the takeoff foot is in contact with the ground. Too brief a contact means that the force does not act long enough to produce a high takeoff speed; too long a contact creates too much braking, rotating the body forward and negating some of the momentum gathered in the run-up.

Some interesting conclusions can be reached by considering the force exerted on the ground by the jumping muscles of animals of various sizes. This force must be greater than the force of gravity acting on the animal, that is, the animal's weight. There is a trade-off: a more muscular animal may be able to exert a greater force on the ground, but stronger muscles are usually bigger muscles, which can weigh the animal down.

Muscular force is proportional to the cross-sectional area of muscle, but body weight increases in proportion to the total volume of the animal. For a small animal, such as a flea, muscle area is relatively large and weight is small, giving a very large ratio of area to volume (A/V). Hence, a small animal tends to be able to jump to many times its own height because the force exerted by its muscles can be many times its weight.

However, in a small animal like a flea, surface area is also large relative to weight, producing considerable air resistance, which becomes an extremely important factor determining the height it can reach. A related phenomenon is that a relatively large surface area makes airborne navigation difficult or even impossible in a strong wind. That is why biting insects—such as flies—are much less bothersome on a windy day.

The A/V ratio decreases as an animal's size increases; in other words, for increasingly larger animals, weight increases more rapidly than muscular force available for jumping. To take an extreme example, an elephant has a much smaller A/V ratio than a flea. In fact, an elephant has virtually no ability to jump at all; its weight is so large in comparison with the strength of its muscles and bones that if it could jump even 50 centimeters (less than 2 ft.), its skeletal system might collapse on landing.

Animals of intermediate size, like humans, have an A/V ratio large enough to allow them to leap to modest heights (unlike an elephant), but small enough that air resistance is not the limiting factor (as it is for the flea). Using muscular energy and total body weight, it can be calculated that animals about the same size as humans—such as bears, kangaroos, and deer—should all be able to jump to roughly the same height (Hallett, 1992); and this is borne out by the actual data (*see Table 1*).

JUMPING ABILITY

Animal	Horizontal	Vertical
Human male	9 m (29.5 ft.)	2.5 m (8.2 ft.)
Deer	9 m (29.5 ft.)	2.5 m (8.2 ft.)
Horse	12 m (39 ft.)	2.6 m (8.5 ft.)
Kangaroo	8.2 m (27 ft.)	2.7 m (9 ft.)

Table 1. *Perhaps surprisingly, jumping heights and distances are quite similar for humans and animals of intermediate size. (Source: Adrian, 1989)*

High Jump

In most track and field events, athletes look for some small adjustment of style (such as a more pronounced arm swing) or some new technology (such as an innovative shoe or spike) that might give them a competitive edge. When an event is decided by a hundredth of a second or a tenth of an inch, even the slightest advantage becomes important.

Revolutionary changes in technique or equipment are rare, but one such radical innovation was developed in the late 1960s: Dick Fosbury's "no-look" technique, the Fosbury flop. Before then, in all

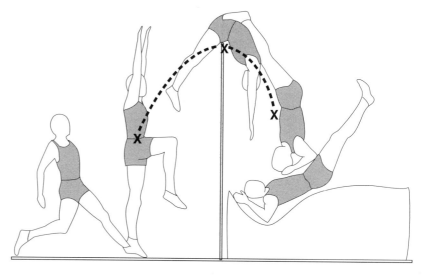

Figure 4. *A possible high-jumping style of the future has been suggested by James Hay. Though currently prohibited by the rules of competition, this style would have three advantages: (1) greater approach velocity; (2) greater vertical force at takeoff; (3) pike position to keep the center of gravity as low as possible under the body, and consequently as low as possible under the bar.*

the styles used by high jumpers the bar was always in full sight. The Fosbury flop was unprecedented: in this style, the jumper's back is to the bar at the top of the jump, and the bar is out of sight from shortly after takeoff until just before landing. At the end of the run-up, as the bar disappears from view, the jumper has to rely on other visual clues, and on a "feel" for timing that is partly intuitive and partly learned. As explained above, the flop has become the prevalent style primarily because it offers the best chance to keep the center of gravity low (relative to the body) while clearing the bar, though the straddle is a close second (*refer back to Figure 3*).

Although the flop dominates today, James Hay, a biomechanist at the University of Iowa, has suggested that there might be a better way (Hay, 1978). He believes that the eventual high-jumping style might be a high-speed frontal approach, a takeoff with both arms raised vertically to position the center of gravity as high as possible at takeoff, and a pike position over the bar (*see Figure 4*).

Actually, a high-speed approach and a takeoff with both arms raised vertically are features of some existing styles of high jumping; what sets Hay's proposed technique apart is the combination of frontal approach and pike position. The frontal approach has a

HIGH JUMP RECORDS

World

Men's: 2.45 m (8.04 ft.)—Javier Sotomayor, Cuba, 27 July 1993, Salamanca, Spain
Women's: 2.09 m (6.86 ft.)—Stefka Kostadinova, Bulgaria, 30 August 1987, Rome

Olympic

Men's: 2.39 m (7.84 ft.)—Charles Austin, United States, 28 July 1996, Atlanta
Women's: 2.05 m (6.73 ft.)—Stefka Kostadinova, Bulgaria, 3 August 1996, Atlanta

How Should High Jumps Be Measured?

Before ever leaving the ground, tall high jumpers possess an inherent advantage because of their higher center of gravity. If a more equitable high jump competition had been instituted—measuring the jump distance from an athlete's center of gravity to the bar height—perhaps the world record would have been held by Franklin Jacobs (5 ft. 8 in.) rather than by Javier Sotomayor (6 ft. 5.4 in.). In 1978 (in New York City), Jacobs was credited with a record for the highest jump above an athlete's own head: 59.1 cm (23.25 in.), for a jump of 2.32 m (7 ft. 7.25 in.). Since Jacobs's center of gravity was several inches lower than Sotomayor's, this jump probably bested Sotomayor's world record by 1 inch or so.

twofold advantage: greater velocity and the ability to exert more force at takeoff. The pike position is best for positioning the center of gravity under the bar and as low as possible under the body.

Technique in the High Jump

Anyone who has tried to dunk a basketball knows that a jump preceded by a run-up has a much better chance of success than a jump from a standing position. The reason is simply that someone who is running can exert much more vertical force against the ground and hence can achieve more takeoff speed, producing a higher vertical jump. However, the horizontal momentum (mass × velocity) of the run-up must be redirected into vertical momentum at takeoff; some sacrifice of one is necessary to optimize the other. One great advantage of the Fosbury flop is that it allows a smooth transfer of horizontal momentum generated in the run-up into vertical momentum as the jumper swings the arms upward and arches backward at takeoff.

It seems logical that keeping the takeoff foot on the ground longer would produce more height—the longer the foot is in contact with the ground, the longer the vertical force can act to produce upward takeoff speed. In fact, however, longer contact does not necessarily lead to a higher jump, and better jumpers actually keep the foot in contact with the ground for a shorter time than mediocre jumpers (Hay, 1985). The better jumpers more than compensate for the shorter time by exerting much greater forces during their foot-ground contact at takeoff. By reducing the time during which the jumping muscles contract, they greatly increase the power they exert, because power equals work done divided by time interval.

Most people would expect to find a difference in foot-ground contact time between mediocre and world-class high jumpers, but there is also a difference in contact time among world-class jumpers. High jumpers choose either a "speed" takeoff or a "power" takeoff. The speed takeoff uses a very fast run-up and a less pronounced "lean-back"; the jumper spends less time on takeoff and runs more on the front of the feet than on the heels. The power takeoff uses a slower run-up and a more pronounced lean-back; to achieve this exaggerated lean-back, the jumper must land heels first during the last few strides. In a speed takeoff, the run-up generates more horizontal momentum; the power takeoff generates more takeoff force. Everything considered, the two techniques give comparable results. The choice between them is essentially a matter of personal preference, based largely on a jumper's build and natural talent—both running ability and potential power at takeoff.

Technique is also important when a jumper is clearing the bar. After approaching the bar at high speed, the athlete appears to be levitating magically at the top of the jump, suspended gracefully in midair directly over the bar. There are two keys to this achievement: the jumper must first raise the center of gravity as high as possible and then contort the body to pass over the bar. In the Fosbury flop, a world-class jumper has such a pronounced back bend that the center of gravity remains below the bar as the body goes over it.

Long Jump

The long jump is one of the simplest and most natural events in track and field: the athletes run up and then jump as far as they can. Perhaps this explains why it is the oldest Olympic jumping event; it was the only jump in the ancient Olympic games (*see the box "Weight-Aided Jumping"*).

In the long jump, the runner tries to jump as far as possible from a wooden takeoff board 20 centimeters (8 in.) wide, set flush with the runway. Jumpers try to take off from the very front of the board, because a jump is measured from its forward edge to the nearest mark made in landing. If the takeoff foot falls, say, 5 centimeters short of the forward edge of the board, the jumper essentially imposes a 5-centimeter penalty on the jump.

There is evidence that ancient jumpers were required to hit a takeoff mark, but the modern takeoff board was introduced in 1866; before then, a long jump was measured from wherever the jumper happened to take off to the nearest heel mark at landing. A takeoff board is actually a physical and psychological impediment; and it has been speculated that if the takeoff board were abandoned and the jump distance measured from the takeoff point, long jumps would be increased by several centimeters.

In the long jump, no one style is superior to all others: techniques differ and will continue to differ as athletes experiment. However, many of the subtle differences have to do with individual strengths and weaknesses. One of the greatest long-jumping contests of all time took place at the Olympics of 1992, in Barcelona, between two athletes with radically different styles: Mike Powell (then the holder of a world record) and Carl Lewis (then a two-time Olympic champion). Lewis, who was believed by many to be the greatest sprinter of all time, used the full runway to attain high velocity and maintained a more horizontal flight path. Powell took a more deliberate, measured run-up, relying on late acceleration and a power takeoff—a more propulsive last step. Powell's technique depended more on precise timing and less on raw speed. At takeoff, Powell flexed the ankle, knee (*see also ANKLE, FOOT, AND LOWER LEG and KNEE*), and trunk more than Lewis; this greater flex generated more explosive muscular force with the final step. Also, because Powell was not running as fast as Lewis, the braking force created by the final step was not as detrimental to distance for Powell as for Lewis (*see Figure 5*).

The advantages and disadvantages of these two styles balanced

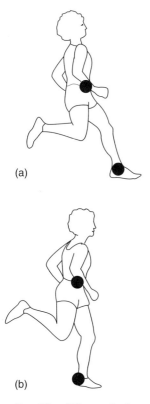

(a)

(b)

Figure 5. *The different body positions at takeoff for a power takeoff (a) and a speed takeoff (b).*

Weight-Aided Jumping

Long jump aided with halteres, *as practiced by the ancient Greeks.*

Ancient Greek long jumpers used an aid that would be illegal now: weights. Jumpers held weights, called *halteres*, in their hands to help them gain a little extra distance during the jump. This seems to contradict logic—why could anyone jump farther by holding a weight?

The answer has to do with the ingenious way *halteres* were used: they were swung up and ahead of the body at takeoff, and then thrust down and backward while the body was in the air. According to a law of physics known as conservation of momentum, as the weights were thrust backward and down, the body and legs moved a slight extra distance forward and up. Some modern jumpers apply the same principle by thrusting their arms powerfully backward; but because they are not holding weights, the effect they achieve is not as dramatic.

Museum specimens of *halteres* have masses of between 2 and 9 kilograms (about 4 1/2 to 20 lb.) per pair. A jumper of mass 70 kilograms (154 lb.) using a pair of *halteres* of total mass 7 kilograms (not quite 15 1/2 lb.) could add about 0.1 meter (4 in.) to

Haltteres

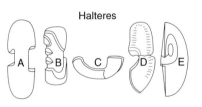

the length of the jump (Alexander, 1992). An even greater increase could be achieved if the jumper threw the *halteres* away, behind the body; but this technique does not seem to have been used by the ancient Greeks—perhaps it was against the rules.

Surviving *halteres* are of various shapes; evidently their shape depends on the era in which they were used. The earliest version was made of stone or metal and was shaped like a modern telephone receiver. The *halteres* shown here (*see the figure*) include one of that shape (C), as well as later versions, one of which was a cylindrical stone with finger grooves (B).

Ernie McFarland

out; each jumper had developed a technique that matched his own talents. In Barcelona, this made the duel between Lewis and Powell particularly exciting. As it happened, though, Powell's precision seemed a bit off, and Lewis won his third consecutive gold medal in the long jump. (In Atlanta in 1996, Lewis won a fourth gold medal; Powell was hampered by a leg injury.)

Technique in the Long Jump

First and foremost, long jumpers must be excellent or at least fair sprinters, because success depends to a large extent on the speed achieved during run-up. Long jumpers must be able to accelerate over a distance of 40 to 50 meters (130 to 160 ft.) and jump at nearly their top speed. At the same time, they must remain "on stride": that is, they try not to be between strides as they approach the takeoff

LONG JUMP RECORDS

World

Men's: 8.95 m (29.36 ft.)—Mike Powell, United States, 30 August 1991, Tokyo
Women's: 7.52 m (24.67 ft.)—Galina Chisyakova, Soviet Union, 11 June 1988, Leningrad

Olympic

Men's: 8.90 m (29.20 ft.)—Bob Beamon, United States, 18 October 1968, Mexico City
Women's:7.40 m (24.28 ft.)—Jackie Joyner Kersee, United States, 29 September 1988, Seoul

board. A jumper caught off stride will miss the takeoff board or will be able to hit it only by making an inefficient adjusment of stride.

Researchers have found that most top-class long jumpers have a run-up of 17 to 23 strides, and use the last three or four steps to make adjustments for the best placement of the final step. Just before the last step, a long jumper reaches a speed of up to 10.5 meters (nearly 35 ft.) per second; this is close to the peak speed of a world-class sprinter—12 to 12.5 meters (about 40 ft.) per second.

At takeoff, the jumper drives upward with full extension of the takeoff leg on the board, a high knee lift of the free leg, and an exaggerated arm-pumping action to raise the arms, shoulders, and chest (*see Figure 6*). All this helps raise the jumper's center of gravity as high as possible. As mentioned earlier, the higher the center of gravity at takeoff, the longer the jump.

Regardless of how skilled a long jumper is, horizontal velocity just after takeoff—typically slightly more than 9 meters (almost 30 ft.) per second—is less than it was at the end of the run-up, because of the braking force created when the final step hits the board hard in order to generate vertical velocity. Some braking force is always created by foot-ground contact (whether one is running or jumping); but if the braking force is too great, distance will be lost in the jump.

Figure 6. *Phases of the long jump.*

At takeoff, the jumper needs to strike a balance between increasing vertical velocity and decreasing horizontal velocity.

During the final step, the takeoff foot exerts a huge force on the ground: up to 12 times the jumper's body weight. This force has the effect of increasing the jumper's vertical velocity from essentially zero to approximately 3.5 meters (11 1/2 ft.) per second during the small fraction of a second that the foot is in contact with the ground.

One major factor determining distance is takeoff angle, the direction in which the jumper's center of gravity is moving relative to the ground. Lowering the takeoff angle permits an increase in takeoff speed, and today's lower angles account for much of the improvement in modern athletes' performance. The takeoff angle used by Jesse Owens, the Olympic champion in 1936, was measured at about 25 to 26 degrees above the horizontal; by contrast, the takeoff angle now used by world-class long jumpers is only about 17 degrees (Adrian, 1989). This lower trajectory makes sense because the human body produces velocity more efficiently by running in a horizontal plane than by jumping upward in a vertical plane.

Takeoff angle is, in principle, much like the angle of release in throwing. However, a 17-degree takeoff angle is very different from the optimal launch angle for most projectiles—about 45 degrees (*see FIELD ATHLETICS: THROWING*). At least three factors account for this difference. First, much of the difference can be attributed to the fact that for a long jumper, vertical momentum is increased at the expense of horizontal momentum. Second, air resistance must be taken into account. Third, the 45-degree angle is optimal for projectiles that land at the same height at which they took off, but a long jumper's center of gravity is lower at landing than at takeoff (by about 0.4 m, or 16 in.); thus a lower takeoff angle gives a longer jump.

Flight and Landing in the Long Jump

The flight distance of any projectile is determined by a combination of launch speed, launch angle, gravity, and air resistance. In a long jump, however, these factors are all essentially determined while the jumper is in contact with the ground. There is almost nothing an airborne jumper can do to influence the trajectory of the center of gravity, except to reduce air resistance by adjusting body position—and this has only a small effect. During flight, then, the jumper's most important objectives are to maintain balance and prepare for landing.

Three general techniques are used in this phase of the jump: the sail, the hang, and the hitch kick. In the sail, often used by jumpers who jump less than 6.5 meters (just under 21.5 ft.), the jumper assumes a landing position shortly after takeoff and spends much of the flight with arms and legs extended forward. In the hang, used by many jumpers in the 6- to 7-meter range (up to about 23 ft.), the jumper's body is nearly vertical for much of the flight, with the arms above the head. Many elite jumpers—those who can jump more than 7 meters—use the hitch kick, "running in the air": the jumper flails the arms and legs back and forth as if running. The hitch kick coun-

Barrel Jumping

A men's world record in the barrel jump was set by Yvon John of Quebec on 25 January 1981. John cleared a span of 29 feet 5 inches (9.0 m), 29 barrels. A women's world's record of 20 feet 4 1/4 inches (6.2 m), 21 barrels, was set by Janet Hainstock on 15 March 1980. It is interesting to note that these record distances were close to distances achieved in the long jump. Barrel jumpers, who glide on skates across nearly frictionless ice, have the advantage of reaching a higher velocity by takeoff, but this is offset because the propulsive force attainable at takeoff is so limited. (Barrel jumpers use a two-footed broad-jump takeoff.)

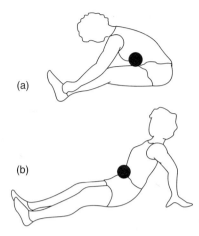

Figure 7. *Good landing technique involves a compromise. (a) Landing with thighs against chest would maximize flight time but result in a short distance between center of gravity (dot) and heels. (b) In the opposite type of landing, the distance between center of gravity and heels is large, but the center of gravity has not traveled as far during flight, and the jumper may sit back.*

ters the natural forward rotational momentum of the body and the decrease in horizontal velocity caused by the braking action of the takeoff foot.

The hitch kick also affects landing. To maximize distance, a long jumper wants to land with feet far out in front of the body—well ahead of the center of gravity, though of course not so far ahead that he or she sits back in the sand. When a jumper "runs in the air," the lower limbs move farther ahead of the center of gravity, so that the body is in a better position for landing.

Spectators are so enthralled by the long jumper's flight that they often consider the landing anticlimactic. Practically speaking, however, the landing is crucial: an improper landing technique can rob even the best jumper of 1 or 2 feet of distance. To land properly, long jumpers bend their legs at the knees to ensure that the hips follow forward. This prevents sitting back, which obviously subtracts significantly from distance. The jumper is trying not only to extend the flight path of the center of gravity as far as possible, but also to land with the heels as far forward as possible while still maintaining balance—it is the heels that make the crucial marks in the sand.

To some extent, achieving a long flight path and keeping the heels forward are mutually incompatible goals. To maximize flight time, a jumper would land with the thighs high against the chest (*see Figure 7a*); in such a landing, however, the distance between the center of gravity and the heels is not very large. To maximize the distance between the heels and the center of gravity, a different kind of landing is needed (*see Figure 7b*); but in this landing the center of gravity has not traveled as far along its path, and the probability of sitting back is higher. (Naturally, though, the greater the horizontal velocity during flight, the farther forward the legs can reach without the jumper's falling backward.) The best landing is necessarily a compromise between these two extremes.

Triple Jump

The term *triple jump* is something of a misnomer. The older name for this event was *hop, step, and jump*, and that is a far more accurate description, because the three phases are different from each other (*see Figure 8*). In the first phase, the "hop," the jumper takes off on one foot and lands on the same foot. In the second phase, the "step," the jumper essentially just takes a long step, landing on the opposite foot from that used on takeoff. The third phase, the "jump," finishes like a long jump, with a two-foot landing.

With its three phases, the triple jump is much more complex than the long jump. Whereas a long jumper makes one decision regarding takeoff angle and speed, a triple jumper must make three separate decisions—and so has three chances to err. In other words, the triple jumper must make three different judgments in order to find the best

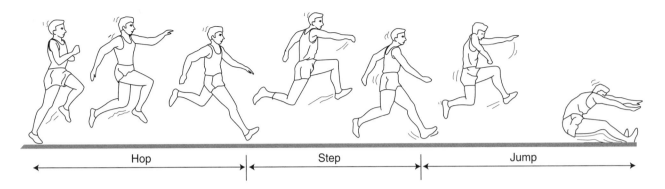

Hop | Step | Jump

Figure 8. *In the triple jump, the hop must land on the same foot used for takeoff (here, the right foot). In the step, support is transferred to the other leg (here, to the left leg). The finishing jump resembles a long jump in both takeoff and landing (here, left is used for both). Hop and finishing jump each account for about 35 percent of the distance; the step accounts for 30 percent.*

compromise between horizontal velocity and vertical lift. Triple jumpers are allowed an unlimited run-up. They therefore start with a great deal of velocity, but with each planting of a takeoff or landing foot, they lose considerable horizontal momentum. Admittedly, there is room for improvement even among world-class triple jumpers; still, the distance covered in this event will never approach three times that of the best long jump: far too much velocity is lost at each stage of the triple jump.

There is considerable disagreement over the best ratio of distances for the three phases of the triple jump; in fact, this is probably the foremost debate among coaches. A ratio of 10:7:10 (37%: 26%: 37%) is often recommended for beginners, and a ratio of 7:6:7 (35%: 30%: 35%) for elite performers. This latter ratio, applied to a total jump of 17 meters (56 ft.), gives distances of 5.95 meters (19.5 ft.) for the hop, 5.10 meters (16.8 ft.) for the step, and 5.95 meters for the jump. As an athlete's skill and understanding of the event improve, many coaches advocate a slight increase in the hop; this gives a ratio of 36:30:35 instead of 7:6:7.

For some years, Russian coaches believed that great gains could be made by improving the initial hop. They maintained that this phase is drastically underutilized; that it should actually be close to the best long jump; and that by holding back on the hop, athletes were not making every jump count. This emphasis on the hop seems unwarranted. An enormous hop robs Peter to pay Paul: it creates a huge braking force on landing and thus diminishes the distance of the step and jump. Nevertheless, the Soviet theorists were given credence for a long time because of the performance of their star pupil, Viktor Saneyev.

Saneyev excelled in the hop stage in part because he had begun as a long jumper; he turned to triple jumping after a knee injury in the early 1960s. That injury proved to be fortunate for him. Few athletes have left such a legacy as Saneyev did in the triple jump: he won three consecutive Olympic gold medals, in 1968, 1972, and 1976.

TRIPLE JUMP RECORDS

World

Men's: 18.29 m (60 ft.)—Jonathan Edwards, Great Britian, 7 August 1995, Gothenburg, Sweden
Women's: 15.50 m (50.85 ft.)—Inessa Kravets, Ukraine, 10 August 1995, Gothenburg

Olympic

Men's: 18.09 m (59.35 ft.)—Kenny Harrison, United States, 27 July 1996, Atlanta
Women's: 15.33 m (50.29 ft.)—Inessa Kravets, Ukraine, 27 July 1996, Atlanta

Saneyev's performance in Moscow in 1980, for which he won a silver medal, was perhaps even more noteworthy than his succession of gold medals. He competed magnificently and finished second despite the fact that he was recovering from a series of tendon operations, and despite his age—he was then 34.

Technique in the Triple Jump

To conserve as much horizontal momentum as possible through the three launches, the takeoff angle for each jump is between 8 and 12 degrees from the horizontal. This angle is, of course, significantly smaller than the 17-degree angle in the long jump. But if a triple jumper used a larger takeoff angle, the hop would be too high and the landing would be so forceful that it would be difficult to initiate a successful step and jump. Many triple jumpers use a double arm shift (driving both arms backward with each jump) to get extra force from the ground. Although this technique assists each takeoff, it is not a natural movement; it requires a motion very different from the normal arm-swing in running.

In the landing from the hop, the forward leg is ahead of the center of gravity and the jumper's body leans slightly backward. The trailing leg is carried considerably behind so that its forward swing can help maintain horizontal momentum for the takeoff of the step. The key to executing the step and jump is to conserve as much horizontal momentum as possible.

Good triple jumpers sometimes seem to float, but only in the hop and jump phases—the step is used more as a setup for the final jump. During the final jump, most jumpers use the "sail" or "hang" technique (*see "Long Jump," above*) instead of a hitch kick. A "hitch kick"—running in the air—usually requires more time and control than the triple jump allows.

Pole Vault

In earlier times, people in rural areas found it very useful to learn how to jump with the aid of a pole, so that they could cross creeks and ditches filled with water—in fact, poles were kept handy for this pur-

POLE VAULT RECORDS

World
Men's: 6.14 m (20.1 ft.)—Sergey Bubka, Ukraine, 31 July 1994, Sestriere, Italy

Olympic
Men's: 5.92 m (19.4 ft.)—shared Jean Galfione, France; Igor Trandenkov, Russia; Andrei Timonchik, Germany; 2 August 1996, Atlanta

(The pole vault is not yet a women's event at the international level.)

pose. Pole vaulting was introduced as a gymnasium sport in Germany during the early 1800s, but early pole-aided jumping competitions, unlike those of today, were designed for distance rather than height.

The pole vault is unique among track and field events in that the jumper uses a tool: the pole. The implements or objects involved in the other events are not tools: a discus or javelin, for example, is merely thrown, and a hurdle is merely an obstacle. In the pole vault, by contrast, the pole is used to increase the height of the jump. An unaided high jumper can reach roughly 2.5 meters (about 8 ft.); a pole vaulter can reach 6 meters (nearly 20 ft.)—two and a half times as high.

Still, the pole vault is a difficult event, because pole vaulters have more variables to deal with than any other track and field athletes. Moreover, most of the subtleties of technique come into play during the time a vaulter is in the air. Maneuvering while airborne, without the aid of a surface to push off from, takes considerable skill (*see also ACROBATICS*).

The Pole: Elastic Energy in Action

The pole contributes to the vault by providing elastic energy, much like a spring. A vaulter running toward the bar has kinetic energy—energy of motion. But while the jumper is clearing the bar, almost no kinetic energy remains; virtually all of it has been converted into gravitational potential energy—energy of height. Between these two phases, most of the original kinetic energy is stored temporarily in the pole itself, as it is bent into a curve. The pole stores energy as elastic potential energy—energy of deformation. Energy of deformation is the same type of energy that is stored in a stretched elastic band or a bungee cord. The bent pole releases this energy as it straightens out and helps push the vaulter over the bar.

In the 1800s, pole vaulters used a long, heavy wooden pole, usually made of ash or hickory. In the first decade of this century, bamboo became popular because of its light weight and flexibility. (Pole vaulters at that time were reaching only about 3.7 m, as compared with 6 m today.) After World War II, bamboo poles from Asia were difficult to obtain, so vaulters began using poles of lightweight metal, particularly aluminum. The greatest advantage of a metal pole over a bamboo pole was resilience: metal poles broke far less often. The importance of this feature should not be underestimated, because coaches agree that one of the biggest problems for pole vaulters is

Soft Landings

Fortunately for the athletes, new materials for the landing pit were introduced at about the same time as fiberglass poles. The former pit fillers—loam, sand, and sawdust—were replaced with more forgiving plastics, foams, and rubbers. These new materials are safer and softer and require less maintenance. They were developed just in time: jumpers were now falling onto their backs from heights of more than 5 meters (more than 16 ft.) above the ground.

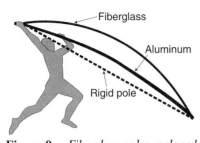

Figure 9. *Fiberglass poles replaced aluminum poles in 1961. A fiberglass pole effectively allows a higher handhold, and this dramatically increases the height a vaulter can reach. Before 1961, the grip was at about 4 to 4.2 meters (around 13.5 ft.)—about 1 meter lower than the grip used today.*

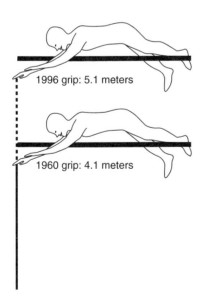

Figure 10. *Vaulters can raise themsleves about 1 meter (3.3 ft.) above the grip. The higher grip of present-day vaulters—made possible by the fiberglass pole—allows them to vault well over 1 meter higher than their counterparts of 1960.*

fear. Despite the limitations of the early metal poles, knowing that the pole was not going to shatter gave vaulters more confidence.

The year 1961 ushered in the era of the fiberglass pole. Some people had experimented with fiberglass as early as 1948, but the early fiberglass poles broke easily and were never widely used. Modern fiberglass, however, offers both the strength of metal and the flexibility of bamboo. A fiberglass pole consists of up to 12 layers of glass fiber wrapped around a thin metal cylinder. It is slightly thicker around the middle, where it bends most, and tapered toward the ends. Such a pole is very effective at transforming a large fraction (about 90%) of the vaulter's initial kinetic energy into gravitational potential energy, through the intermediary of elastic potential energy. With the metal pole, which was more rigid, energy was absorbed by the vaulter's arms instead of being transferred to the pole. The flexible fiberglass pole, by contrast, acts more like a spring; and it is better "tuned" to the speed and muscular force of the vaulter, efficiently storing and then releasing energy. As a result, a fiberglass pole allows a higher handhold—with dramatic effects on the height of the vault (*see Figures 9 and 10*). The mathematics of this effect is simple: vaulters can raise themselves about 1 meter above the grip; thus (other things being equal), the higher the grip, the higher the vault.

Once fiberglass poles became commonplace, a long series of record-breaking pole vaults were achieved: new world outdoor records were set nine times between May 1961 and June 1963, with the height increasing from 4.83 meters to 5.08 meters. Arjun Tan, a physicist at Alabama A & M University, has estimated the extra height a vaulter can gain by using a fiberglass pole (Tan, 1988–1989; *see Figure 11*). He plotted Olympic gold–medal vault heights by year, drawing two straight lines through the data points: one line for heights attained before the introduction of fiberglass and one line for heights after fiberglass was introduced. The height added by using a fiberglass pole is clear; Tan estimated it to be about 0.53 meter (21 in.).

World-class pole vaulters today have advanced beyond even fiberglass; they use a highly sophisticated hollow carbon-fiber composite pole designed for a specific stiffness, minimal twisting, and extreme lightness (*see also EQUIPMENT MATERIALS*).

Technique: Vaulter Meets Pole

A pole vault takes place in several stages (*see Figure 12*) and requires the athlete to be part sprinter and part gymnast.

The vaulter first runs as fast as possible for about 30 to 40 meters before planting the pole in the box, a shallow pit in the ground just in front of the bar. The vaulter's speed just before takeoff is a crucial factor in the ultimate height. Because kinetic energy is proportional to the square of speed, a 10–percent increase in speed results in about a 20 percent increase in vault height. For example, if a runner's speed increases from 10 meters per second to 11 meters per second—a 10 percent increase—the square of the speed increases from 100 to 121, a 21 percent increase. Thus many experts believe that the run-up is the key

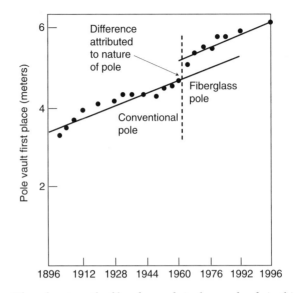

Figure 11. *The advantage the fiberglass pole is shown clearly in this graph. After fiberglass was introduced in 1961, there was a sharp increase in the height of Olympic gold medal vaults: about 0.53 meter (21 in.). (Source: Tan, 1988–1989)*

to pole vaulting. A vaulter who uses a tentative run-up, slowing down over the last few strides, reduces the kinetic energy available. This in turn will reduce the height possible during the arc of ascent—the airborne upward path that the vaulter's center of gravity follows as it is lifted from the ground toward the bar.

At the instant before takeoff, the vaulter must be prepared to decelerate quickly as the pole absorbs the kinetic energy of running and bends before the vaulter leaves the ground.

At takeoff, the position of the top hand on the pole is crucial. With a pole that bends readily, as opposed to a stiffer pole, a vaulter

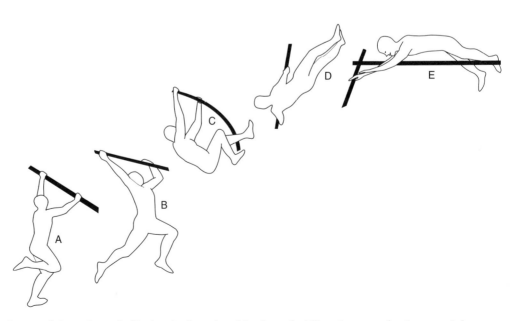

Figure 12. *Stages of the pole vault. Notice the huge bend in the pole (C) as it stores elastic potential energy.*

can place the hands higher along the pole and also farther apart. As a result, a huge bend is produced in the pole (*see C in Figure 12*), converting a great deal of the vaulter's kinetic energy into the elastic potential energy of the pole. By choosing a pole with just the right degree of elasticity, a vaulter can find a match for body weight, speed, and technique, so that the maximum energy is returned from the pole to the vaulter at the top of the vault.

Once a vaulter has left the ground, the vaulter and the pole form what is called a "double pendulum." The vaulter swings from the pole, much as a pendulum swings; and vaulter and pole are also swinging together as an inverted (upside-down) pendulum whose base is the point where the pole is planted.

As the pole straightens, it converts its elastic potential energy into gravitational potential energy of the vaulter, who gains height as a result. At the instant when the pole is completely straight, the vaulter has gained from it all the "catapulting" energy possible. But there still remains some potential for increasing height. The vaulter, now momentarily hanging from the pole high above the ground, shoots the feet and body upward by pulling up with the arms, and then pushes down on the near-vertical pole to raise the body even higher (*see D and E in Figure 12*). This is a matter of timing more than strength. The vaulter's legs then pass over the bar, with hips slightly above the bar.

The vaulter now assumes a loose pike position. At this stage, vaulters should have virtually no horizontal momentum left; the vaulter is traveling very slowly and hence is in danger of falling onto the bar. Then, in a very subtle motion, the vaulter must push the pole away quickly and skillfully, so that—in reaction to this push on the pole—the rest of the body follows the legs over the bar. It does a vaulter little good to catapult the center of gravity higher than a competitor if the body descends onto the bar.

Quantitative Considerations in the Pole Vault

The conversion of kinetic energy to gravitational potential energy places a limit on how high a person can vault for a given running speed. The calculations involved are based on a law of physics known as conservation of energy. For a running speed of 10 meters (33 ft.) per second (people can run faster, up to roughly 12.5 meters—about 41 feet—per second, but not carrying a pole), the maximum height is roughly 5 meters (16.5 ft.). From this figure, 10 percent must be subtracted for losses to heat in the pole and to energy lost when the pole hits the ground; this gives 4.5 meters (14.8 ft.). However, the world record as of 1996 was 6.14 meters (about 20 ft.); this is 1.64 meters (more than 5 ft.) higher than the theoretical maximum. Two factors account for this apparent discrepancy.

First, 4.5 meters is the increase in height of the center of gravity. Since the vaulter's center of gravity is initially about 1 meter above the ground and is at about bar height at the top of the vault, 1 meter should be added. This gives 5.5 meters (slightly over 18 ft.) as the height of the vault measured from the ground.

Second, as described earlier, at the top of the vault the athlete essentially does a handstand, first pulling up on the pole and then pushing down on it. In doing so, the vaulter gains approximately 0.5 meter (nearly 20 in.) of height; hence the total height from the ground is about 5.5 + 0.5 = 6 meters.

Thus the theoretical calculation of attainable height corresponds well with heights actually attained. Future increases in height must come either from a faster run-up, which would increase the initial kinetic energy; or from poles that convert kinetic energy to elastic energy and then to gravitational potential energy more efficiently than fiberglass or the newer materials now being used.

Another quantitative consideration is the height of the pole. Most vaulters use a 5-meter (16.5-ft.) pole (which, incidentally, has a mass of approximately 2.7 kg, just under 6 lb.); some use a pole as long as 5.3 meters. A longer pole, along with a grip farther up the shaft, gives a potential for increasing vault height. However, the choice is not simple: the greater the length of the pole, the greater the run-up speed needed to bend the pole optimally. If a vaulter cannot increase run-up speed, a longer pole will usually worsen performance.

Environmental Factors in Jumping

How high or how far a person can jump depends not only on factors such as takeoff speed and takeoff angle, but also on evironmental—that is, external—variables: conditions such as gravity and air resistance. The effect of gravity can vary slightly from location to location, and air resistance is highly dependent on altitude and weather conditions.

Gravity: The Variable Constant

Basically, jumping is a battle against gravity. To achieve height or distance, jumpers try to stay in the air, but gravity is always tugging them down.

Most people tend to think of gravity as a constant, but in fact it varies from place to place around the earth. Scientists measure gravity as gravitational acceleration, symbolized g, in units of meters per second per second (m/s^2). The average value of g at the earth's surface is 9.8 m/s^2; this means that—disregarding air resistance—the speed of an object dropped from rest increases by 9.8 meters (about 32 ft.) per second during every second of fall. Thus, after 1 second, the object is falling at 9.8 meters per second; after 2 seconds, it is falling at 9.8 + 9.8 = 19.6 meters per second, and so on.

The spinning earth and g.   One reason that gravitational acceleration varies from place to place is the shape of the earth. Because the earth rotates, it is not a perfect sphere: it bulges slightly at the equator and flattens somewhat at the poles. Thus, there is a difference of 29 kilometers (18 mi.) between its equatorial radius (6,378 km) and its polar radius (6,357 km). As a result, a person standing at the equator is farther away from the earth's dense core than a person standing at either pole, and this means that gravitational acceleration, g, is slightly less at the equator. The actual difference between the equatorial and polar values of g is 0.018 m/s^2, or 0.18 percent. The value of g generally increases with increasing latitude—that is, g is stronger as one moves away from the equator and toward either pole.

An additional effect due to the earth's rotation is a decrease in g due to what is known as centrifugal force: the outward-flinging effect on anything moving in a circle. Because the earth rotates once a day, any object on its surface describes a complete circle once per day and thus is subject to centrifugal force. Actually, centrifugal force is not a true force like gravity (*see FIELD ATHLETICS: THROWING*); it is referred to as a "fictitious" or inertial force. Nonetheless, it is very important in analyzing motion on the rotating earth.

Centrifugal force depends, in part, on the rate of rotation and the radius of the circle. Rotation rate is the same (one rotation per day) for all objects on earth, but the radius of the circle varies from 6,378 kilometers at the equator to zero at a pole; thus the centrifugal effect of the earth's rotation is greatest at the equator and nonexistent at the poles. As a result, g is decreased by the centrifugal effect most at the equator but is not decreased at all at the poles. Specifically, the equatorial value of g is 0.35 percent (0.34 m/s^2) less than its polar value. This centrifugal effect, combined with the effect of the earth's nonspherical shape, reduces g by 0.53 percent between the equator and a pole.

Altitude and local variations in g. Gravitational acceleration also depends on altitude. A person who is climbing a mountain is moving farther from the earth's dense core; thus gravity becomes weaker as the climber gains altitude. The decrease in g is roughly 0.002 m/s^2 for every kilometer of elevation on land. The decrease per kilometer of air altitude is 0.003 m/s^2. This difference is explained by the fact that if someone is gaining altitude on land—as in climbing a mountain—the earth beneath the person exerts a downward gravitational force, and thus g does not decrease as rapidly as it does during an air ascent (such as going up in an airplane).

In addition to variations in g with altitude, there are variations due to the local density of the earth. For example, high-density mineral deposits produce local increases in g. These increases, though small, are of great importance to geologists, who use them to find minerals, oil, and gas.

Air Resistance

Another environmental factor that affects a jumper's performance is air resistance. This factor is particularly important in events like the long jump and the triple jump, where the jumper must reach a high speed during the run-up. Air resistance is proportional to atmospheric (air) density, which decreases exponentially with height for elevations of interest in athletics (*see Figure 13*). At an elevation of only 1,600 meters (1 mi.) above sea level—as in Denver, Colorado—air density has dropped by 17 percent from its value at sea level.

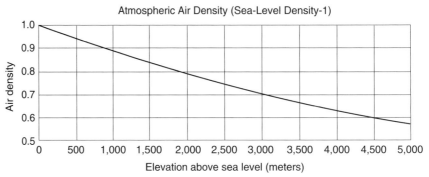

Atmospheric Air Density (Sea-Level Density-1)

Figure 13. *Air density versus elevation: the higher the altitude above sea-level, the less the air density. Lower air density is a factor in many records, but the affect of air density is not as dramatic as most people think.*

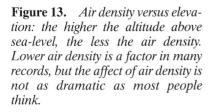

VALUES OF g
AT VARIOUS LOCATIONS

Location	Latitude	Altitude (m)	g (m/s²)
Mexico City	19.3°N	2,300	9.779
Los Angeles	34.0°N	50	9.796
Montreal	45.4°N	50	9.806
Moscow	55.5°N	150	9.816
North Pole	90.0°N	0	9.832

Table 2. *Gravitation (g) varies with latitude and altitude. Many people attribute the numerous records set at the Olympics in Mexico City in 1968 to its lower g value (along with its lower air density).*

Environmental Factors in Mexico City

Comparative values of latitude, altitude, and *g* in different places can be significant (*see Table 2*). For places close to sea level, *g* increases as latitude increases. Of all the places listed here, Mexico City—which is close to the equator and is also at a high altitude—has the lowest value of *g*. It therefore is not surprising that many world and Olympic track and field records have been set at Mexico City.

In the triple jump, for example, an Olympic record (17.39 m, 57.1 ft.) set in Mexico City in 1968 lasted until 1988, and a world record (17.89 m, more than 58 ft.) set in Mexico City in 1975 lasted until 1985. One of the longest-lasting and most famous records in the long jump was also set in Mexico City: Bob Beamon's 8.9-meter (29.2-ft.) jump in the 1968 Olympics (*see Figure 14*). As a world record, this remained unbroken for 23 years—a virtual eternity for track and field—until 1991, when Mike Powell jumped 8.95 meters during the World Championships in Tokyo. As of 1996, Beamon's jump still stood as the Olympic record.

Beamon's remarkable record motivated research using computer simulations to determine how much advantage a jumper actually has in Mexico City (McFarland, 1986). These simulations indicated that a world-class long jumper can jump about 5 centimeters (2 in.) farther in Mexico City than in Moscow. (In Moscow, the site of the 1980 summer Olympics, *g* is relatively large; *again, see Table 2.*) Actually, only about half of this 5-centimeter advantage in Mexico City is due to reduced gravity; the rest is due to decreased air resistance.

A triple jumper, who covers approximately twice the distance of a long jumper, can jump about 13 centimeters (nearly 5 in.) farther at Mexico City than at Moscow. Roughly one-third of this increase is due to reduced gravity; two-thirds is due to reduced air resistance. Air resistance is more imporant in the triple jump than the long jump because a triple jumper is upright during a large portion of the total jump—a position that creates high air resistance.

In these simulations it was assumed that takeoff velocity was constant; thus the advantage represented by Mexico City over Moscow in these events would be due only to reduced *g* and reduced air resistance. This assumption, however, leads to some interesting considerations with regard to Beamon's performance.

Subtracting 5 centimeters—the advantage in the long jump at

Figure 14. *Bob Beamon in Mexico City, setting a world record of 8.9 meters in the long jump—a record that stood from 1968 to 1991. (Source: Allsport Photography, Inc.)*

Mexico City—from Beamon's 8.90-meter jump gives 8.85 meters, which would still have been the Olympic record as late as 1996. Note also that in 1968 the silver medalist jumped only 8.19 meters: 71 centimeters (28 in.) less than Beamon. How did Beamon manage such a tremendous jump? Several factors were involved.

For one thing, Beamon's takeoff speed was higher than normal. He sprinted hard and hit the takeoff board well—one newspaper account referred specifically to his speed and his "height off the board." It is not clear whether this higher takeoff speed was the result of merely hitting the board well or whether increased sprinting speed was also a factor. Beamon was undoubtedly aided in his sprinting by reduced air resistance, but increased speed before hitting the board does not necessarily mean increased takeoff speed; an increase in approach speed means that the jumper's foot will be in contact with the board for a shorter time, thus making the development of a large vertical takeoff velocity more difficult. Since the board is only 20 centimeters (8 in.) wide, the timing, stride length, and rhythm of the approach are all extremely important.

An additional factor aiding Beamon was a high tailwind. Records in jumping and sprinting are approved only if any tailwind aiding the athlete is no more than 2 meters (6.6 ft.) per second. During Beamon's jump, the recorded wind velocity was 2 meters per second, the maximum allowable. Computer calculations show that this tailwind would have added 3 centimeters (more than 1 in.) to his jump. If these 3 centimeters are added to the 5-centimeter advantage calculated for Mexico City, environmental factors would have accounted for 8 centimeters of Beamon's jump. Subtracting 8 centimeters from 8.90 meters leaves 8.82 meters: as of 1996, this would still have been the Olympic record.

In sum, the explanation is that everything was right for Beamon. He turned in a once-in-a-lifetime performance under some extremely advantageous environmental conditions—low gravity, low air resistance, and a high tailwind.

It should be noted that the advantages at Mexico City are not as pronounced for high jumpers or pole vaulters as they are for triple and long jumpers. For a high jumper, in fact, the advantage is only 3 millimeters (0.12 in.); and because high jumps are measured only to the nearest centimeter, this advantage is negligible. For a pole vaulter, the increase in height is somewhat larger—2 centimeters (0.8 in.)—but this is still a relatively insignificant fraction of the total vault, which is roughly 6 meters (19.7 ft.).

Ernie McFarland

References

Adrian, M., and J. Cooper. *Biomechanics of Human Movement*. Dubuque, Iowa: Benchmark, 1989.

Alexander, R. M. *The Human Machine*. New York: Columbia University Press, 1992.

Anderson, I. "Pole Vaulting Goes Aquatic." *New Scientist*, 2 August 1984, 12.

Brancazio, P. J. *Sport Science*. New York: Simon and Schuster, 1984.

Easterling, K. *Advanced Materials for Sports Equipment*. New York: Chapman and Hall, 1993.

Hallett, F. R., et al. *Physics for the Biological Sciences*, 2nd ed. Toronto: Holt, Rinehart, and Winston, 1992.

Hay, J. G. *The Biomechanics of Sports Techniques*, 2nd ed. Englewood Cliffs, New Jersey: Prentice Hall, 1978.

Hay, J. G. *The Biomechanics of Sports Techniques*, 3rd ed. Englewood Cliffs, New Jersey: Prentice Hall, 1985.

Hay, J. G. "A Kinematic Analysis of the High Jump." *Track Technique* 53 (September 1973), 169ff.

McFarland, E. L. "How Olympic Records Depend on Location." *American Journal of Physics* 54, no. 6 (June 1986): 513–520.

Quercetani, R. L. *A World History of Track and Field Athletics, 1864–1964*. London: Oxford University Press, 1964.

Ryan, F. *Pole Vault*. New York: Viking, 1971.

Schmolinsky, G., ed. *Track and Field*. Berlin: Sportverlag, 1978.

Tan, A. "Athletic Performance Trends in Olympics." *Mathematical Spectrum* 21 (1988–1989): 78–84.

Tanner, J. M. *The Physique of the Olympic Athlete*. London: Allen and Unwin, 1964.

Tiupa, V., et al. "The Biomechanics of the Movement of the Body's Center of Mass during the Long Jump." In *Theory and Practice of Physical Culture* (1982): 11–14.

Field Athletics: Throwing

THROWING IS A VITAL SKILL in a wide array of sports, from baseball to water polo. For a special few—the field events of discus, javelin, shot put, and hammer throw—this skill is the sole basis of competition. While this article covers the physics and biomechanics of throwing in general, its focus is on the specific human and environmental factors involved in field throwing.

The origins of the shot put and hammer throw can be traced back to twelfth-century Scotland, England, and Ireland. The shot put began among Scottish and English soldiers as leisure-time test of strength; they used a round stone or a small cannonball and competed to see who could throw it farthest. This became an event in the old Scottish Caledonian games and eventually emigrated to become a part of track and field athletics throughout England and North America. Along with the discus (and a number of throwing events that are no longer in existence), the shot put was an event in the first modern Olympics in 1896.

Like the shot put, the hammer throw involves heaving a large, round, heavy weight. When the hammer throw began, in Ireland or Scotland, a heavy sledgehammer was launched for distance. The hammer later evolved into a small iron ball attached to a short wooden handle. Eventually, a steel chain and then a steel wire were added to connect the ball to the handle. The hammer of the 1990s weighs 16 pounds (7.27 kg)—including ball, wire, and grip—and is launched from within a confined ring by an athlete's whirlwind spinning motion. Originally, the rules for hammer throwing imposed virtually no restrictions: an unlimited run-up and unlimited rotation were permitted. The combination of a fast run-up and a dizzyingly fast rate of spin placed everyone in the stadium in peril, so throwers were later confined within a 7-foot (2.2-m) throwing ring. Even when confined to this 7-foot ring, a thrower can develop incredible hammer velocity before release, so much so that the world-record hammer throw is over three times as far as that for the shot put, which uses an object of exactly the same weight.

Of the four field throwing events, the discus throw seems to be the only one that did not originate as a skill of war or hunting. However, some historians believe that warriors crossing rivers were the first to experiment with the discus: to rid themselves of the weight of their round or oval shields before swimming across, they may have hurled the shields to the opposite bank. In ancient Greece, the discus throw was not only part of the Olympics, it was regarded as the sport of the gods. No sports heroes were celebrated and idolized more than discus champions. The Greek sculptor Myron, in his famous statue *Discobolos*, portrayed a discus thrower with a magficient physique, wielding a discus much larger than the one used in modern times, though considerably smaller than a typical shield would have been.

The javelin was also part of the ancient Olympics, but it certainly dates back much earlier, as a hunting instrument. The first spear throwers were using a skill that was essential for survival—to feed or defend their village or tribe. These hunters needed to throw a spear at the greatest speed possible in order to penetrate the flesh of the prey and bring it down. The present-day javelin is still slightly similar to an ancient spear, but there is an important difference in purpose: whereas a spear was thrown at a target, a javelin is thrown to maximize distance. Although javelin throwing involved accuracy in ancient Greece and throughout the Middle Ages, the modern event—like other modern field throwing events—is a distance competition.

Environmental Considerations: Forces

A study of the physics of throwing an object—whether it is small, light, and round (like a baseball) or large, moderately heavy, and flat (like a discus)—must be concerned with the forces that act on the object. Three principal forces act on any object thrown with the hand: (1) the force of gravity, (2) the force exerted by the hand, and (3) the force of the air (aerodynamic force). The force of gravity is constant, which is not the case for the forces of the hand or air. The force exerted by the hand varies in a complex manner to accelerate the object and release it at the highest possible speed. The aerodynamic forces depend on the properties of the object (its size, shape, etc.), on the velocity (speed and direction) and spin of the object, and on the density of the air and the velocity of the wind. Of course, the force of the hand acts only while the object is in the hand; after the object is released, only the forces of gravity and the air act on it—until it hits the ground or is otherwise intercepted.

Gravity

Isaac Newton's laws of motion describe the movement of objects that are acted on by forces. Newton's first law of motion is sometimes called the law of inertia. All objects have inertia, a property that resists changes in their motion. According to the law of inertia, in the absence of external forces a body at rest will remain at rest, and a body in motion will remain in motion at a constant velocity, provided the body is viewed from an "inertial frame of reference." The frame

Figure 1. *To calculate the acceleration of an object it is necessary to sum the external forces acting on it, taking into account both the magnitude and the direction of each force. If two men attempt to push a heavy box in opposite directions, one man pushing with a force of 600 newtons (135 lb.) to the right, and the second man pushing with a force of 500 newtons (122 lb.) to the left, the net force is 100 newtons (22 lb.) to the right.*

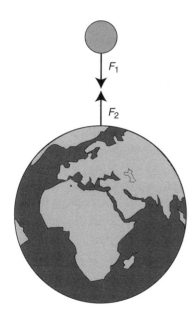

Figure 2. *According to Newton's third law, as the earth pulls a ball down, the ball pulls the earth up with an equal and opposite force. Of course, the earth's mass is so large that its acceleration upward is negligible.*

of reference of the fixed stars is an inertial frame, and all frames of reference which move at constant velocity with respect to the fixed stars are also inertial frames.

Newton's second law of motion states that, when observed from an inertial frame, the net external force F on a body equals its mass m times its acceleration a, that is, $F = ma$. Acceleration is the rate of change of velocity; an object accelerates if there is a change in its speed, a change in its direction, or both. The net external force is computed by adding up the individual forces, taking into account their directions as well as their magnitudes (*see Figure 1*). Newton's second law makes it possible to calculate the path of an object if the forces on it are known. A consequence of this law is that if a force is applied to any object, its acceleration is inversely proportional to its mass.

Newton's third law states that if one body exerts a force on a second, the second body exerts an equal and opposite force on the first (*see Figure 2*). It is this law that is responsible for the recoil of a fired gun. In a throwing event, the third law means that if the thrower exerts a large force on a projectile, the projectile exerts an equally large force on the thrower, subjecting the thrower's body to stress.

Because the earth continuously rotates, it is not an inertial frame. Consequently, although an object not acted on by external forces moves in a straight line at constant speed relative to the fixed stars, it accelerates when viewed by an observer on the rotating earth. This acceleration appears to violate Newton's second law, which says that an object will accelerate only if there is a force acting on it. However, Newton's second law can be made to hold for an object measured from the earth (or from any noninertial frame) if "fictitious" forces, sometimes called inertial forces, are added to the "real" forces (such as gravity) that act on the object. Although fictitious forces are absent from the point of view of a person making measurements from an

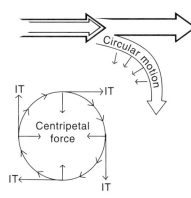

Figure 3. *The centrifugal force and the Coriolis force are the two inertial "fictitious" forces that apparently act on all earthbound bodies. A centripetal force, which is a force toward the center of the circle, must be exerted to maintain circular motion. It counters the outward centrifugal force. Because of inertia, without a centripetal force, the body would move in a straight line, tangential to its original path, and would leave the surface of the rotating earth. The Coriolis force causes a body traveling above the earth to move in an apparently curved path, as the earth rotates under it.*

inertial frame, they seem real from the point of view of somebody in a noninertial frame.

If the earth (or any rotating body) is chosen as the frame of reference, the fictitious forces acting on objects are called the centrifugal force and the Coriolis force (*see Figure 3*). Centrifugal force is a fictitious outward force that balances the inward (centripetal) force acting on an object that is at rest on earth. Any object traveling in a circle is subject to a centripetal force that pulls toward the center of the circle. An object at rest on earth is really moving in a circle and is thus subject to a centripetal force. Otherwise, the object would fly off the earth's surface tangentially in a straight line, in accordance with the law of inertia. The centrifugal force works in the earth's frame to counterbalance the centripetal force, because the object does not accelerate relative to the earth. The effect of the fictitious Coriolis force on a thrown object is very small and can be ignored here. In brief, fictitious forces are not really acting on objects, but are introduced so that earthlings can pretend that they are in an inertial frame.

The force of gravity on an object is called its weight. According to Newton's second law, the weight of an object is equal to its mass times its acceleration due to gravity. But we measure the weight of an object on the rotating earth, and this effective weight includes the centrifugal force on the body. The effective weight of an object measured on earth can be defined as its mass times its initial acceleration when dropped from rest (in the absence of wind). This acceleration, which is denoted g, includes both the acceleration due to gravity and the acceleration due to the centrifugal force. In symbols, the equation for effective weight is $w = mg$. This is actually a specific example of the general equation $F = ma$, the effective weight of an object of mass m being the force of gravity (and centrifugal force) on it and g being its acceleration in the absence of other forces. In ordinary language, the word *effective* is omitted, and simply the *weight* of an object is referred to. From measurements of the initial acceleration of objects, the value of g is determined to be about 9.8 meters per second per second (9.8 m/sec.²) or 32 feet per second per second (32 ft./sec.²).

Although g is fairly uniform on or near the surface of the earth, its value varies slightly from point to point. This depends on latitude—g is about 0.5 percent larger at the poles than at the equator—and for altitude: g decreases about 0.03 percent for each 1 kilometer (0.6 mile) above sea level (*see also FIELD ATHLETICS: JUMPING for a table of values of g*). There are also local variations in g that are independent of latitude or altitude, but these are small enough to be disregarded. Because g varies, the weight of an object is slightly different at different places on earth. To account for these differences, values of g have been tabulated as a function of latitude and altitude. Because centrifugal acceleration is included in the value of g, it is no longer necessary to take into account the fact that the earth is rotating. In other words, the earth can be treated as an inertial frame of reference, and Newton's second law can be safely applied.

The force of gravity acts on every bit of matter in an object. However, it is possible to simplify the action of gravity by assuming that it acts at only one point of the object. This point is called the center of mass or the center of gravity (*see also ACROBATICS*). If an object in free fall is not rotating, gravity will not cause it to rotate; if it is rotating, gravity will not change its speed of rotation. In order for a force to change the speed of rotation of an object in free flight, it has to act at a point other than the center of gravity. Such a force leads to torque on the object, causing it to change its speed of rotation. Torque is defined as the force times the perpendicular distance from its line of action to the axis of rotation of the object. If an object is subject to other forces besides gravity, such as aerodynamic forces, then the other forces can exert torque on the object. Just as mass is a measure of the inertia of an object (its resistance to being accelerated by a force), moment of inertia is a measure of the resistance of an object to being accelerated by torque. Moment of inertia depends not only on the mass of an object, but also on its size and shape.

The Force of the Hand

Other things being equal, a person throwing any object for distance wants to maximize both its height and its speed at release. If in developing an optimum technique for a distance throw, there must be some trade-off between height and speed at release, the thrower should choose speed at the expense of height. This is the better strategy because, for an object released at the optimal angle, the distance traveled is approximately proportional to the square of the speed, but an increase in height will increase the distance by only a comparable amount. For equal amounts of extra effort, as measured by additional energy expended, the thrower usually can get approximately twice the increase in range by putting the extra effort into the speed of the object, rather than into its height, at release. The word *energy*, which has just been introduced, should be defined, but before this can be done, the concept of *work* must also be introduced. In order to accelerate an object, the thrower must exert a force on it. A person who exerts a force on an object, moving it in the direction of the force, is said to be doing work on the object. If the force is constant, the amount of work W is the force F times the distance d the object travels while the force is acting: $W = Fd$. This is an oversimplification, however, because in fact both the magnitude and the direction of the force change during the time the object is in the thrower's hand. Under these circumstances, calculating the work done becomes far more complicated.

Energy is defined as the ability to do work. In order to do work on an object, the thrower must expend energy. Energy can be neither created nor destroyed, but it can be transferred from one object to another and from one form to another. Energy is stored in the thrower's body as chemical energy. When the thrower moves, some of this stored chemical energy is transformed into kinetic energy—energy of motion—which is proportional to the square of speed. The work done on an object may give it kinetic energy, potential energy, or both. Potential energy is energy of position; for an object acted on by gravity, potential energy is proportional to the height. If a car is parked on a steep hill and its brake is released, the potential energy of the car is converted into kinetic energy as the car rolls down the hill, losing height and gaining speed.

In throwing an object, the more energy the thrower uses, the more work can be done on the object while it is still in the hand, and the greater will be the height and speed of the object at release. However, not all the energy exerted by the thrower goes into useful work; some of this energy does work on parts of the thrower's body, and some of it is dissipated as heat. How the object gets released is of great importance as well. If the thrower spends energy giving the object too much spin or sending it off at the wrong angle, energy is wasted because the object does not travel as far as it would if an equal amount of energy had been expended with flawless execution.

A thrower's purpose is to do as much work as possible on the object in the short time it is in the hand, giving the object as much energy as possible. Here the concept of *power* becomes important. Power is equal to work W divided by time t, that is: $P = W/t$. Doing the same work in less time, then, means doing it with more power—the value of P will be larger (*see also WEIGHT LIFTING*). Consequently, the more power a thrower can achieve during the time the projectile is in the hand, the farther the thrown object will go, provided that the added power does not come at the expense of a loss of control over the height and angle of release.

In three of the four major throwing events (shot put, discus throw, and hammer throw), the participant is confined to a ring when launching the projectile. In order to maximize the velocity of the released object in these events, the thrower moves in a curved path while holding the projectile. To understand why, consider the thrown object while it is still in the thrower's hand, particularly in the hammer and discus throws, where motion is closer to circular.

For circular motion, another concept becomes significant—*angular velocity*, which is proportional to the number of rotations an object makes per second. The actual velocity of an object, sometimes called its linear velocity, is equal to angular velocity times the radius of the circle in which the object moves. A thrower who rotates the body with a certain angular velocity can maximize the projectile's linear velocity by holding the object as far from the center of the circle as possible. Rotating the body faster and faster while holding the projectile will increase its linear velocity more and more. If this goes on, though, the thrower will eventually lose balance; therefore, release occurs before that happens.

Two additional concepts are needed at this point: *linear* and *angular momentum*. The linear momentum of an object is defined as its mass multiplied by its velocity. The angular momentum of an object moving in a circle is defined as linear momentum multiplied by the radius of the circle.

Linear momentum is important because, in the absence of an

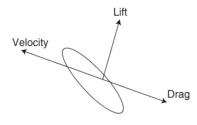

Figure 4. *Upon release, the discus modifies airflow as the air moves around it. Airflow along the surface of the discus slows, owing to contact with the surface. The speed and direction of the airflow change because the discus exerts forces on the air contacting it; the air reacts by exerting equal and opposite forces on the discus (lift and drag). There is a rippling effect whereby the layer of air in contact with the surface of the discus tends to slow down the adjacent boundary layer, and that layer slows down the next layer, and so on.*

Drag Factors

1. Fluid (air) speed relative to the object
2. Shape of the object
3. Texture of the surface

external force, it remains constant over time. Likewise, angular momentum is important because, in the absence of any external torque, it too remains constant. To illustrate the importance of linear momentum, consider the javelin throw. To acquire linear momentum, the thrower, holding the javelin, runs forward as fast as possible before turning sideways to hurl the javelin forward. During this turning maneuver, the thrower slows down, losing some momentum but transferring as much momentum as possible to the javelin. Because the javelin has a mass much smaller than the thrower, the velocity of the javelin after release must be much larger than before, in order to keep the linear momentum constant. Unavoidably, however, some of the thrower's momentum is transferred to the earth and is wasted. In the hammer throw, the thrower moves faster and faster in a circle, gaining angular momentum, and then transfers some of this angular momentum to the hammer when releasing it. The hammer flies off at a high velocity because its mass is much smaller than the mass of the thrower.

Aerodynamics

Aerodynamic forces modify the path of a thrown object, compared with the path it would take in the absence of air (in a vacuum). The forces exerted on an object by the air depend not only on the intrinsic properties and velocity of the object, but also on the local density of the air and on wind velocity. The density of air in turn depends on altitude, temperature, and other climatic conditions such as air (barometric) pressure. The density of air decreases as the altitude above sea level increases. At a given altitude, the lower the temperature and the higher the pressure, the greater the density of air.

The total force of air on a moving object is often divided into two components, drag and lift (*see Figure 4*). Drag is a retarding force, which occurs in the direction opposite to the velocity of the moving object with respect to the air. Lift occurs in a direction perpendicular to drag.

If the direction of lift is above the horizontal, the lift is said to be positive; if it is below the horizontal, the lift is negative. The drag on an object moving through air acts to shorten its flight path by slowing it down. Positive lift is desirable because it lengthens the flight path by opposing gravity, thereby keeping an object aloft for a longer time, while the object continues to move forward because of its inertia. Whether lift or drag is morc important depends on the size, shape, and orientation of the moving object. Both the lift and the drag on a thrown object are usually approximately proportional to the square of its speed relative to the air.

If an object is thrown with spin, then the air generally exerts an extra force on it that is absent when the object is not spinning. For a spherical object, the deflection arising because of this extra force is called the Magnus effect. If the spin axis of a spherical object is vertical, the air acts to give it a horizontal deflection. This effect is important in baseball, as it enables a pitcher to throw a curveball.

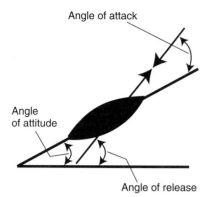

Figure 5. *Three angles of importance during discus or javelin flight are angle of release, angle of attitude, and angle of attack.*

Because there are substantial (though often subtle) differences among projectiles, two different kinds can curve in opposite directions even if they have the same spin. For example, a baseball, which has a rough surface, curves toward its slower-moving side, but a very smooth ball will curve in the opposite direction. Thus, the Magnus effect is very complicated (*see also BASEBALL, GOLF, SOCCER, and VOLLEYBALL*).

Although spin around a vertical axis may make a ball curve, it has little effect on the distance the ball will travel when thrown. However, if a ball has a spin around a horizontal axis perpendicular to the direction of the velocity, then the spin can give either a positive or a negative lift to the ball, substantially influencing the distance it travels. Usually, for a rough ball topspin decreases the distance it travels, while backspin increases the distance. In golf, for example, the driver club is designed to impart backspin to the ball: the ball gets lift from the air and travels farther than it would if it did not spin. A golf ball is dimpled to make it rougher, and so backspin significantly increases this lift, and the distance traveled. If the ball were smooth, the trajectory with backspin (relative to no spin) might actually drop instead of lifting.

A person who throws an object intending to maximize the distance it travels has control, within limits, over the velocity (speed and direction) of release, the height of release, and the spin at release. If the object is nonspherical, the thrower also controls its orientation with respect to its velocity at release. In general, three angles are required to specify the orientation of an object: angle of release, attitude, and attack (*see Figure 5*). Often, however, a simplified approach is taken in which the orientation is approximately described by a single angle, which may be either the angle of attack or the angle of attitude.

For a flat object, such as a discus, angle of attack is defined as the angle between a forward line in the plane of the object and the angle of its velocity (relative to the air). Angle of attitude is defined as the angle between a forward line in the plane and the horizontal. These angles describe the orientation of a flat object provided it does not tilt to one side. If it does tilt, the tilt angle is needed as well. (For an object like a javelin, which is not round, a third angle may be needed.) Because both lift and drag depend on the angle of attack (or, on the angle of attitude), the angle of attack can play a large role in determining the distance the thrown object travels. Angle of attack is more useful in theoretical analysis, but angle of attitude is easier for the thrower to estimate.

Dynamics of Field Throwing

In the principal field throwing events—shot put, discus, javelin, and hammer throw—the masses and sizes of the projectiles vary and are sometimes different in high school and college competitions. The standards for international competition differ for women and men (*see Table 1*).

The effect of gravity (as modified by centrifugal force) is calculable for all these events. If air resistance is not calculated, then the object is in free fall from the moment it leaves the hand of the thrower until the moment it hits the ground. It undergoes gravitational acceleration, which is independent of its size, shape, and mass. Unless an object is thrown straight up or straight down, it follows a curved path (trajectory), a parabola, when it is in free fall. Both the path and the range of a thrown object in free fall can be calculated from its height, speed, and angle of release, and from the local value of *g*. (The effect of the Coriolis force is neglected.) Because of aerodynamic forces, however (*see above*), the path of an object thrown in air will deviate from the curve of free fall. Aerodynamic forces are complicated: they depend on the shape, size, stiffness, orientation, velocity, and spin of the thrown object, as well as on the density of the air and velocity of the wind.

Technique: General Considerations

Whether an athlete is putting a shot or throwing a javelin, discus, or hammer, the same dynamic forces are present. When several forces act in the same direction upon the same point of an object, the result is the same as a single force equal to the sum of the several forces. However, if forces act at different points, torque may result. A discus thrower exert both force and torque on the discus in order to impart velocity and spin. In exerting this force and torque, if the fingers should accidentally pull up on the underside of the discus as it is being released, unwanted torque will result, which will send the

Optimal Discus Conditions with a Headwind

1. Higher air densities
2. Lower temperatures
3. Lower altitudes

Optimal Conditions for Shot, Hammer, and Discus with a Tailwind

1. Lower air densities
2. Higher temperatures
3. Higher altitudes

INTERNATIONAL STANDARDS IN FIELD ATHLETICS

Implement	Mass (lb.)	Mass (kg)	Diameter or length (cm)	Diameter or length (in.)
Men's shot	16.0	7.26	11.0–13.0	4.3–5.12
Women's shot	8.13	4.0	9.5–11.0	3.74–4.33
Men's discus	4.41	2.0	21.9	8.62
Women's discus	2.21	1.0	18.0	7.09
Men's javelin	1.76	0.8	260–270	102–106
Women's javelin	1.32	0.6	220–230	86.61–90.55
Men's hammer	16.0	7.26	13.0	5.12

Table 1. *The hammer has a wire attached (117.5 to 121.5 cm long) for men; there are no international standards in the hammer for women. Although the women's discus, shot, and javelin are all smaller than the men's, the 1994 world records in shot and javelin were greater for men, while the discus record was greater for women. In the discus throw, men's greater strength is offset by the lighter projectile used by women. The balance of three factors—(1) strength of athlete, and (2) mass and (3) size of discus—makes the distances comparable for women and men in this event.*

discus off on a wobbling flight path. To avoid this, motor control must be continually refined by practice, so that the forces can be coordinated optimally.

Release velocity. All field throwing events have the same objective: to maximize the distance the object is thrown. The distance the projectile travels is approximately proportional to the square of the release velocity; in other words, when the release velocity is doubled, the distance traveled increases approximately fourfold. (This proportionality is exact only if the object is released at ground level in a vacuum.) Thus, as mentioned earlier, release velocity is usually more critical in determining the distance traveled than other factors such as height and angle of release, or—in the case of the discus and javelin—angle of attack. In the shot put, for example, a put that is 10 percent less than the optimal release angle would reduce the distance by less than 1 foot (0.3 m), but a reduction of 10 percent in release speed could reduce the distance by 10 to 15 feet (3–4.5 m).

Release angle. For the discus throw, the optimal release angle is a little over 40 degrees. However, because the human body can throw much more efficiently in a horizontal direction than a vertical direction, it is best for the thrower to err more toward a flatter trajectory. This principle can be demonstrated by throwing two balls, one straight up and the other level with the ground. It will be apparent how much easier it is to launch a projectile horizontally.

Throwing time. Although many factors affect the distance an object can be thrown, the longer a force is applied to the projectile, the greater its velocity at the time of release. This can be derived from Newton's second law: average force F multiplied by time of application t and divided by mass of the projectile m is equal to release velocity v, that is: $Ft/m = v$. If the average force is the maximum the thrower can achieve, then release velocity—and consequently distance traveled—can be increased only by increasing the amount of time that the projectile remains in the hand. If, for example, a thrower exerts maximum force on a 16-pound shot for 2 seconds, the release velocity will be twice as great as if the same force was applied for only 1 second. That is why shot putters and discus throwers start out at the back of the ring, with the back turned and extended out beyond the edge of the circle, and end up at the front of the circle, with their center of gravity leaning out over the circle. By taking full advantage of the limited space, they increase the time over which they can apply force to the shot.

A discus or hammer thrower extends the arm straight out so that the distance from the projectile to the rotating body is as large as possible. The reason for doing this is that the velocity of the thrown object is equal to its angular velocity times its distance to the rotational axis in or near the body. Given the same angular velocity, if the thrower's arm is extended to hold the discus 3 feet from the axis of rotation, the velocity attained by the discus will be 20 percent greater than it would be if the discus were held only 2.5 feet from the rotation axis. However, a larger radius comes at some cost, especially for a hammer thrower. The center of the hammer thrower's body may be approximately 10 feet from the hammer, but a critical skill for the thrower is to maintain balance against the very significant centrifugal forces created by rotating the hammer at a such large radius.

Muscle power. A throwing event involves all the major muscle groups in the body. The muscle groups in different parts of the body work in series, one after the other. To get the most out of this sequence of motion, and to keep it fluid, it is essential for one muscle group to begin action at the moment that the previous muscle group applies maximum velocity to the object. Once the lower body is moving at its top speed (and thus is no longer picking up speed), the upper body springs into action and takes over. Next the shoulder takes over from the upper body, and then the elbow from the shoulder; finally, acceleration is transferred from the elbow to wrist and hand. To accelerate a shot, discus, hammer, or javelin, during the throwing cycle, each body part must move faster than the previous body segment, in the target direction. Much of the training for field throwing events is designed to improve motor control so as to train muscle groups to turn "on" and "off" with precise timing.

The stronger, slower muscles of the lower body start first; then, at the moment that the lower body has reached maximum velocity, the faster muscles of the shoulder, arm, and hand take over. The large-muscle groups contract swiftly to drive the body weight from one leg to another. Driving the pelvis ahead of the trunk allows a good thrower to exert an off-center force that creates torque, leading to rotation between the hips and shoulders. This in turn creates tension in the active trunk muscles, causing them to contract quickly (*see Figure 6*).

The importance of leg drive varies. In the javelin throw where a run-up is allowed and the thrower is not confined to a circle, final leg drive is a less important factor than it is in the shot put, hammer

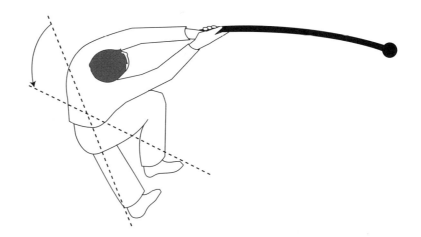

Figure 6. *Torque created between the hips and trunk in the hammer throw. There is a displacement angle between the axis of the hips and the following axis of the shoulders (arrow). The aligned hips lead the aligned shoulders. The arms remain fully extended, forming an isosceles triangle.*

throw, or discus. It is essential for acceleration created by the leg drive to be transmitted through the rest of the body and for wasteful absorption of energy by the body to be minimized. The arm must be fully extended and relaxed so that there is no absorption of the energy generated in the lower body by the partial contraction of the weaker, faster arm muscles.

The ground plays a critical part in determining speed of release. A thrower pushes backward on the ground, and, according to Newton's third law, the ground pushes forward on the thrower. This is called a frictional force. The ground exerts a beneficial frictional force that helps to power throwers' movements so that they can impart the greatest force on the projectile. Therefore, in all throwing events, participants do not leave their feet until the object is released. Throwers might leave their feet during the follow-through, but not while trying to maximize the force applied to the object.

It is sometimes asked whether there is an ideal physique for the field throwing events. It can be observed that, even at the high school level, throwing competitors are usually larger and heavier than average. Do compact, bulky competitors have an inherent advantage in throwing events? As long as the added mass is well-proportioned muscle mass, the answer appears to be yes. The force that a muscle can exert is approximately proportional to its cross-sectional area, which increases as the muscle mass increases. This means that the more mass individuals have, the greater the force they can exert. If this force were used to accelerate the entire body, there would be a net loss, as acceleration is inversely proportional to mass. But in fact, the force is applied to accelerate successively lighter parts of the body and finally the projectile itself, which has a given mass regardless of who is throwing it. Consequently, throwers with a large mass in the legs and trunk, who can transmit the forces to the arm, hand, and projectile, can acclerate a projectile more than throwers with less mass. Another important factor to consider in this regard is the size of the throwing ring. Since competitors must confine their movements to a ring in most of these events, they have very little space to develop acceleration; therefore, the thrower's mass plays an even more significant role.

Shot Put

Dynamics of shot putting. The shot put is easiest event to analyze in terms of physics. Because the shot is spherical and is thrown with little or no spin, the primary aerodynamic force is drag; and because the shot has a large mass (16 lb., or a little over 7 kg, for the men's event), drag does not affect it much. (The effect of drag acts in a direction opposite to the velocity with respect to the air, so it slows down the shot.) Furthermore, because the shot is normally in the air only about 2 seconds (the shortest time of all the major throwing events), drag does not have much time to act. For both reasons, the path of the shot deviates only slightly from the path of an object

SHOT PUT RECORDS

World:

Men: 23.12 meters (75 ft. 10 in.)—Eric (Randy) Barnes (United States), Los Angeles, 20 May 1990

Women: 22.63 meters (74 ft. 3 in.)—Natalya Lisovskaya (Soviet Union), Moscow, 7 June 1987

Olympic:

Men: 22.47 meters (73 ft. 8 in.)—Ulf Timmerman (East Germany), Seoul, 1988

Women: 22.41 meters (73 ft. 6 in.)—Ilona Slupianek (East Germany), Moscow, 1980

in free fall. Except for shortening the range of a good shot put by about 15 centimeters (6 in.), compared with the range it would have in a vacuum, air does not have any appreciable effect on the path of the shot.

In any given set of external conditions, the range of the shot depends on three factors over which the athlete has limited control: (1) height of release, (2) speed of release, and (3) angle of release, or launch angle (*see Figure 7*). The shot putter attempts to maximize the height and speed of release, and to launch the shot at the optimum angle—the angle that will give it the longest range for a given height and speed of release. Normally, the putter releases the shot with negligible spin; this is because extra energy is required to impart spin, and spin has only a marginal effect on a smooth, heavy shot.

Because of differences in latitude and altitude, a shot launched under conditions that would ordinarily allow it to travel about 20 meters will go about 6 centimeters (a little over 2 in.) farther in Mexico City than in New York. Of this extra distance, about 3 centimeters is attributable to the fact that gravity (g) is smaller in Mexico City than in New York. Two factors make g smaller in Mexico City: lower

Figure 7. *Height, angle, and speed of release all affect the distance a shot travels. Illustrated are two sample shot puts: The first (solid line) is released with a speed of 12.5 m/sec. at an optimal angle of a little over 41 degrees and travels a horizontal distance of 18.3 m from the point of release. The second (dashed line) is released with a speed of 10.0 m/sec. at an optimal angle of just over 40 degrees and travels 12.1 m from the release point. The optimal angle is the angle that leads to the longest put for a given speed and height of release.*

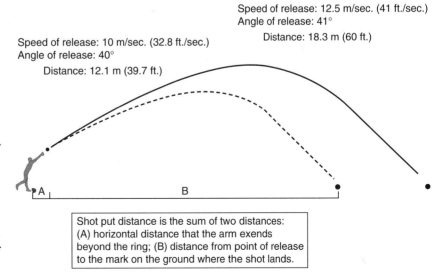

Speed of release: 12.5 m/sec. (41 ft./sec.)
Angle of release: 41°
Distance: 18.3 m (60 ft.)

Speed of release: 10 m/sec. (32.8 ft./sec.)
Angle of release: 40°
Distance: 12.1 m (39.7 ft.)

Shot put distance is the sum of two distances: (A) horizontal distance that the arm extends beyond the ring; (B) distance from point of release to the mark on the ground where the shot lands.

latitude and higher altitude. The lower latitude reduces *g* enough to account for 2 centimeters; the higher altitude accounts for 1 centimeter. The remaining 3 centimeters come from the fact that, because of Mexico City's higher altitude, the density of air there is lower than in New York, and so drag is reduced (assuming similar weather conditions). If there were a level surface on the top of Mount Kilimanjaro, which is almost 6,000 meters (19,800 ft.) high and near the equator, the shot would theoretically travel about 15 centimeters (6 in.) farther there than it would in New York. However, this is a hypothetical example; in reality, because the air on top of Kilimanjaro has so much less oxygen, the shot putter would probably be gasping for breath and would be unable to impart as much initial velocity as in New York; thus the distance traveled by the shot would probably be shorter, not longer (*see also RESPIRATION*).

If the shot were launched at ground level, it would achieve its maximum range if the angle of release were 45 degrees above the horizontal, independent of the speed of release. The air resistance (primarily drag) does not appreciably change this observation. But human beings cannot effectively throw from ground level, and as a consequence the best angle of release will always be less than 45 degrees. The actual optimum angle depends on both the height and the speed of release.

Air resistance has little to do with the best angle of release. The optimum angle of release depends almost entirely on the height and speed of release. A greater height at release decreases the optimal angle, and a greater speed at release increases this angle. A trigonometric formula derived with the help of Newton's second law gives the optimum angle for a given height and speed of release (Lichtenberg, 1978). This optimum angle is about 42 degrees above the horizontal for a shot released at a height of 7 feet (slightly more than 2 m) with a speed of about 14 meters (46 ft.) per second. (To get a sense of this speed, remember that a world-class athlete runs the 100-meter dash in about 10 seconds, at an average speed of 10 meters per second.) Under these circumstances, the shot travels about 22 meters (72 ft.).

Small errors in the optimum angle of release are not very important; for example, a 3-degree error reduces the range by only about 10 centimeters (4 in.). As the error in the angle gets larger, however, the effect on the range becomes more important; for example, a 10-degree error reduces the range by about 1 meter (3.3 ft.).

In summary, the effects of the air play only a minor role in the shot put. The putter strives to give the shot as much speed as possible at release and to launch it as high above the ground as possible. The putter also tries to release the shot at an angle near 42 degrees above the horizontal. However, because a small error in the angle of release does not shorten the range very much, aspiring shot putters should concentrate their training on increasing their power in order to increase the speed of the shot at release.

SHOT PUT RANGE (FT.) AS A FUNCTION OF RELEASE HEIGHT (RH, FT.), VELOCITY (v, FT./SEC.), AND ANGLE OF RELEASE(°)

Angle	Elite	College	High school
	RH = 8.5	RH = 8.5	RH = 8.0
	$v = 45$	$v = 40$	$v = 37$
45°	70.55	57.15	49.5
44°	70.75	57.35	49.65
43°	70.90	57.50	49.78
42°	70.95	57.60	49.88
41°	70.95	57.65	49.92
40°	70.90	57.60	49.92
39°	70.70	57.55	49.88
38°	70.50	57.40	49.80

Table 2. *This table shows the relative importance of release velocity. As a general rule, optimum angle of release decreases with a decrease in velocity (v) or an increase in release height (RH). Air resistance has been neglected. If it is included, these distances should be shortened about 0.5 feet. (Source: Northrip, 1979)*

Shot putting technique. Whereas the discus is thrown with a sidearm motion, the shot put requires an overarm, pushing motion. Although heaving the shot seems to be a very straightforward action, there are a few rules involved. The shot must be held close to the neck and not go behind the plane of the shoulders. The only permitted arm motion is the pushing action just noted. This rule in fact makes the shot put a push, not a true throw.

To maximize the linear velocity of the shot, the putter depends very much on linear and angular velocity created by hip and shoulder action. A shot putter begins facing the rear of the ring, extending the body outside the rear of the circle by using a pronounced knee flex (*see Figure 8*). This, in effect, gives a larger ring to operate from, and a larger ring allows the putter to generate greater linear and angular velocity. Almost all weight is placed on the rear foot.

Biomechanically, it makes sense to keep the elbow high behind the hand so that the put will have the intended trajectory. This also ensures that the thrower uses more of the stronger muscles of the upper arm and less of the elbow and lower arm.

Next comes a two- or three-hop movement across the circle, which should provide velocity to the body and shot and also blend smoothly into the delivery. In this way balance, body posture, and direction of movement can be properly delivered for the technique that follows. As the shot putter moves across the circle, body weight should remain over the back foot so that the leg and lower trunk muscles can be fully utilized during the release. The knee remains flexed so that extension generates additional force. After the hops, the right thigh comes forward so that the pelvis can rotate, adding crucial acceleration to the shot. Trunk rotation and shoulder action move the upper arm forward and upward as the hand flexes forward at the wrist. A putter uses a rapid "scissors" leg movement, a small jump from the left to the right leg, to keep from falling out of the front of the circle—a foul that would render the throw void.

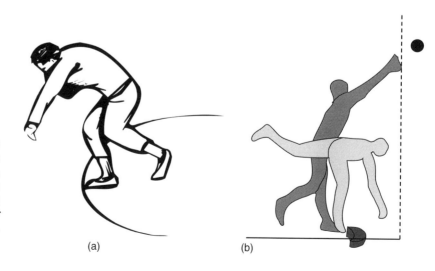

Figure 8. *(a) The starting position for shot putting—leaning outside the rear of the circle using a deep knee bend—in effect enlarges the ring. (b) The shot putter finishes leaning well out beyond the ring, with the point of release about 15 inches beyond the front of the ring.*

(a)   (b)

Debate continues over whether it is better to hop across the ring or use a spinning motion similar to that of a discus thrower. Proponents of spinning believe that it allows the thrower to impart additional angular velocity to the shot. On the other hand, because the sphere is positioned close to the neck, spinning does not give the projectile nearly as much speed as in the discus or hammer throw.

The relative heaviness of the shot, as well as its position close to the neck, makes strength training more important for shot putting than it is for throwing the discus (an intermediate-weight projectile) or the javelin (which is lighter still). This is because heavier objects require the thrower to have greater strength, to generate the body forces necessary for sufficient release velocity. In this regard, it is useful to compare the shot put and the baseball pitch.

The shot put, like the baseball pitch, is an overhand throw. Of course, the technique used in pitching is very different from shot putting: whereas a pitched baseball is released with a true throwing motion, a shot is released with a "put," which is a pushing motion. Thus a long, lanky baseball pitcher who can throw a 95-MPH fastball may do poorly in the shot put, and a champion shot putter could not pitch in the major leagues. Still, there are many parallels between putting and pitching that make the comparison enlightening.

Pitchers and shot putters both have to deal with inertia and gravity. Pitchers, though, depend on generating arm velocity to throw a very light ball, while shot putters must generate muscle power to overcome the force of gravity on, and the inertia of, the much heavier shot. Both apply the largest force possible, for as long as possible, to impart the maximum velocity to the thrown object; however, because the mass of the baseball is far less than that of the shot, a given applied force accelerates the baseball more than the shot. The shot putter generates more force for a longer time than the pitcher, but still achieves a far smaller release velocity. The heavy task of putting a shot requires the body's levers to act more simultaneously—by contrast, pitching requires each body lever to comes into action at the time that the prior one has reached maximum speed.

The shot putter expends much more energy to do much more work. The work done by a baseball pitcher in throwing a 90-MPH (40 m/sec.) fastball is 90 foot-pounds (about 120 joules). To launch a shot with enough velocity to go a world-class distance of 70 feet (about 21 m), a shot putter must do about 500 foot-pounds (about 680 joules) of work (Brancazio, 1984).

In addition to these strength requirements, the different methods of release used by shot putters and pitchers are also significant. Pitchers release the baseball in a parallel plane extended from the body, giving themselves a large axis of rotation to "whip" the ball forward. Shot putters extend the arm straight forward from the shoulder to release the shot in front of the body. If a shot putter tried to throw like a baseball pitcher, the elbow and wrist would be subjected to extreme torque and could be injured (*see also SHOULDER, ELBOW, and WRIST*).

Physique and the Shot Put

A putter's physique in large part determines the height of release and the horizontal distance that the arm extends beyond the ring. Other things being equal, a tall putter with long arms who reaches a release position with legs, hips, trunk, and throwing arm well extended will throw farther than a putter of smaller build, or one who does not extend as well.

World

86.74 meters (284 ft. 7 in.)—Yuriy Georgiyevich Sedykh (Soviet Union), Stuttgart, 30 August 1986

Olympic

84.79 meters (278 ft. 2 in.)—Sergei Litvinov (Soviet Union), Seoul, 1988

Note: The hammer throw is not an international or an Olympic event for women.

Hammer Throw

Dynamics of the hammer throw.   Like the shot, the hammer head is heavy and spherical. But unlike the shot, the hammer has a throwing apparatus attached to the head. The 7.26-kilogram (16-lb.) hammer is attached to a wire 117 to 121 centimeters (46–47 in.) long, which connects it to a handle, or grip. This, in effect, gives the hammer a greater surface area, and consequently it experiences greater drag in flight. Moreover, the hammer is released with almost twice the speed as the shot, and drag is approximately proportional to the square of the speed. Therefore, drag shortens the range of the hammer much more than the range of the shot. Typically, drag can shorten the range of a thrown hammer well over 100 centimeters (40 in.); the comparable figure for the shot is only 15 centimeters (less than 7 in.). But even so, the hammer travels more than three times the distance of the shot because of its greater initial speed. (*For the dynamics involved, see Figures 9 and 10.*)

The flight paths of the two objects also differ. The optimum angle of release of the hammer is about 44 degrees, about 2 degrees higher than the optimum angle for the shot. Furthermore, because of the increased drag, the path of the hammer deviates more from a parabola than the path of the shot.

Technique in the hammer throw.   Hammer throwers, more than any other field competitors, need to smoothly rotate and maximize angular momentum. The athlete grips the implement by the handle, rotates at increasing speed with the hammer extended outward, and releases after giving it a high velocity. To accomplish this, the thrower exerts a large centripetal force on the hammer; the wire is used to pull the hammer inward toward the body's rotating axis.

For any given rate of rotation, velocity increases proportionally to the radius. The length of the wire causes the spinning hammer to be farther from the thrower—it creates a larger radius—so that the thrower can release the hammer with greater speed for a given angular velocity. This is why the record distance for the hammer throw is greater than the record for the discus despite the hammer's greater mass. This longer lever, however, also demands more strength on the part of the thrower, because at a fixed angular velocity the centripetal force is proportional to both the mass of the hammer and its radius of rotation (*see above for a discussion of centripetal force and other*

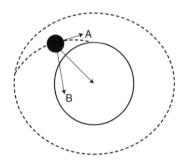

Figure 9.   *Force A increases velocity; force B changes the hammer's direction of motion. When the radius remains constant, the centripetal force of the wire is always at a right angle to the motion of the hammer. When the radius is shortened just before release, the force of the wire develops a component in the direction of the hammer's intended flight, which increases its velocity. This shortening of the radius can have a substantial effect. For example, if it were possible to shorten the length of the lever arm by half without sacrificing force, hammer velocity would double. These results follow from the conservation of angular momentum.*

Figure 10. *The hammer thrower exerts force on the handle that is transmitted through the wire to the hammer head. The thrower exerts both a centripetal force (toward the center) to keep the hammer going in a circle and a tangential force to increase the speed of the hammer. The hammer head rotates with the same angular velocity as the thrower, but the speed is proportional to the radius, and therefore is greater for the hammer head than for the hands of the thrower. The principal forces involved in increasing hammer velocity and changing the direction of motion are shown in (a) and (b).*

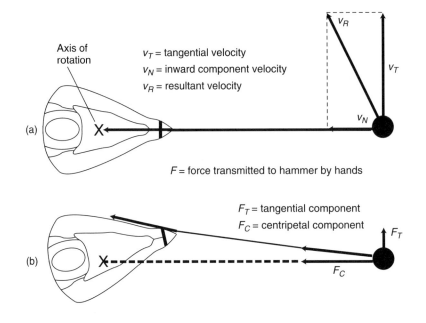

"*fictitious*" *forces*). As the speed of rotation increases, more centripetal force is required from the body to counteract the centrifugal pull on the hammer.

Because the hammer is 15 to 20 times lighter than the thrower, a thrower can generate ample centripetal force to launch the hammer with high velocity. The tricky part for the thrower is to maintain balance while increasing the time spent rotating. As the hammer accelerates, the thrower must spin faster and faster, rotating more quickly with each successive turn. During the three turns that most hammer throwers make in the ring, they accelerate so as to increase the angular velocity and thereby increase the speed of the throw. The thrower increases this acceleration gradually in order to maintain balance and control. If not for their fear of losing balance and control, hammer throwers might make even more rotations, which would let them exert torque over a longer period of time. Torque is created between the lower body, which tries to maintain a fixed rotation point on the ground, and the upper body, which is accelerating the hammer. The thrower rotates the hips ahead of the shoulders by anywhere from 45 to 90 degrees during turns, in order to increase the torque in the body.

Long arms are a definite advantage in the hammer throw because they increase the radius of the circular path of the rotating hammer. Experts believe that for every 2.5 centimeters (1 in.) added to the radius, the distance can increase by as much as 2 meters (about 6 ft.) (Doherty, 1976). Any time a thrower bends the elbows while exerting an inward force on the hammer, its radius decreases and its velocity is not maximized. Throwers can further lengthen their radius by "sitting and stretching" (squatting and extending the arms), by relaxing the shoulders, and by flexing at the knees. The "sitting," or squatting,

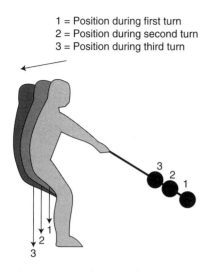

1 = Position during first turn
2 = Position during second turn
3 = Position during third turn

Figure 11. *The angular momentum of the hammer requires the thrower to continuously modify body position to maintain balance. In the sitting phase, the body moves from a upright position to one in which it begins to exert more and more centripetal force as the thrower squats and leans back. This effectively shortens the true radius of the hammer, increasing the hammer's velocity because of conservation of angular momentum. As the knees bend more and the trunk leans more, the hammer is brought into a smaller and smaller circle.*

Rotating Madness

Hammer throwers do not apply a smooth, consistent centripetal force while rotating. As force is incrementally increased, it undergoes a cyclical fluctuation, depending on the position of hammer and body. After the second turn, the hammer thrower is exerting a force of about 900 newtons (202 lb.), which declines to around 700 newtons (157 lb.) at the 2.5-turn mark and then approximately doubles to 1,400 newtons (315 lb.) at the point of release at the third turn (Adrian, 1988). The need to exert variable force makes mastering hammer throwing very difficult.

phase is necessary to keep the center of gravity over the feet. Flexing the knees aids throwers by lowering their center of gravity and making it easier for them to maintain their balance.

Most of the hammer's acceleration occurs during what is called the power phase: a period of intense "double support" during which there, is a strong push off the balls of the feet and the toes to create centripetal force. Thus, the time interval for double support should be maximized. For a right-handed thrower, the left heel is particularly important in accelerating the hammer in the power phase, and in controlling the release in the following single-support "glide phase." The left heel acts as the central axis of rotation, facilitating a smooth rotation (this can be compared to a smoothly spinning top versus a wobbly top). The tighter, or more stationary, the pivoting left heel, the more effectively angular momentum is transferred to the velocity of the hammer before release.

By leaning back before release, the thrower shortens the true radius of the hammer. Because of conservation of angular momentum, this maneuver causes the velocity of the hammer to increase (*see Figures 9 and 11*).

Discus Throw

Dynamics of discus throwing. The discus consists of a wooden core surrounded by metal. A good discus throw travels more than three times the distance of a good shot put. This is true partly because the discus has less mass than the shot, partly because a more efficient technique is used to impart force to the discus, and partly because of the aerodynamic shape of the discus. The smaller mass allows the same force to give more acceleration to the discus than to the shot. The discus thrower's technique allows the force to be applied for a longer time, leading to a longer period of acceleration and consequently to a much higher speed at release. This, of course, results in a much longer range. Because of the higher speed, lighter weight, and flattened shape of the discus, aerodynamic forces play a much greater role in its flight than in the flight of the shot.

For a discus thrown in still air (no wind), lift and drag have opposite and approximately equal effects on the range, so that the discus

DISCUS RECORDS

World

Men: 74.08 meters (243 ft.)—Jurgen Schult (East Germany), Neubrandenburg, Germany, 6 June 1986
Women: 76.8 meters (252 ft.)—Gabriele Reinsch (East Germany), Neubrandenburg, 9 July 1988

Olympic

Men: 69.4 meters (227 ft. 8 in.)—Lare Reidel (Germany), Atlanta, 31 July 1996
Women:72.29 meters (237 ft. 2 in.)—Martina Hellman (East Germany), Seoul, 1988

travels about as far as it would if launched in a vacuum (no air). This result does not occur because of a cancellation of lift and drag: for two forces to cancel, they must be equal in magnitude and opposite in direction, but lift and drag are perpendicular to each other and so can never cancel. What actually happens is that one effect (drag) decreases the range, and the other effect (lift) increases it. The discus must be launched at a lower angle in air than in a vacuum to achieve the same distance. In air, the discus follows a trajectory which is not a parabola.

A shot putter is best off if the density of air is low and the shot is thrown with the wind; both of these factors reduce drag and therefore allow the shot to travel a little farther. For the discus throw, the aerodynamic effect of the wind is opposite to the effect on the shot. If the discus is thrown against the wind (with the optimum angle of attack for the wind conditions), lift increases more than drag; thus the discus travels farther when thrown against a moderate wind than with it. (This is not true of the Frisbee, which—although it is shaped like a discus—is much lighter. The effect of even a moderate headwind usually shortens the range of a Frisbee; *see "The Frisbee: The Most Popular Disk."*) However, in a strong headwind, drag reduces the forward progress of the discus, even though the extra lift keeps it in the air longer.

The net effect of the density of the air is quite small if there is no wind. In a moderate headwind, increased air density acts cooperatively with the wind to increase the lift further, thus further increasing the range of the discus, by a small amount. In a tailwind, though, the discus thrower hopes for lower air density.

Like a shot putter, a discus thrower strives to maximize the speed and height of release, but favors speed if there must be a trade-off between speed and height. Also like the shot putter, the discus thrower tries to optimize the angle of release and the spin and orientation of the discus. A further complication is that the optimum orientation of the discus and the best angle of release both depend on wind velocity, which is assumed to be constant during flight. If the wind is horizontal, its speed and direction should be estimated. If it is not horizontal, its vertical component should also be estimated.

The following is a simplified discussion of the complexities of discus flight (Frohlich, 1981; *see also Figure 12*). First, it is assumed that the wind is constant and horizontal during flight and is either a head- or a tailwind. Second, it is assumed that at release the discus does not tilt either to the right or to the left. Under these circumstances, the orientation of the discus can be described by a single angle (either the angle of attack or the angle of attitude).

At release, the discus is normally given a spin of about 6 to 8 rotations per second. This rotational motion makes the discus act like a gyroscope, stabilizing the it against wobble and helping to keep its orientation from varying significantly during flight. The thrower wants to give the discus just enough spin so that it does not wobble in flight. Imparting any additional spin beyond 6 to 8 rotations per sec-

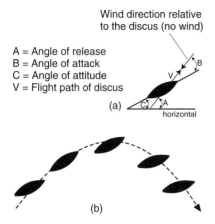

Wind direction relative
to the discus (no wind)

A = Angle of release
B = Angle of attack
C = Angle of attitude
V = Flight path of discus

(a)

horizontal

(b)

Figure 12. *Several quantitites are useful in describing the release and flight of a discus. The wind direction relative to the discus, shown in (a), is for a release with no wind relative to the ground. For a tailwind, the arrow would be more vertical; for a headwind, the arrow would be more horizontal. For a given release velocity, distance traveled is primarily affected by the tilt of the discus and by wind direction and velocity. A typical trajectory is shown in (b).*

ond does not appreciably improve the flight and therefore wastes the thrower's energy.

If the angle of the plane of the discus is less than the angle of its relative velocity (with respect to the air), the lift is negative. This corresponds to a negative angle of attack. (Note that angle of attack is sometimes defined with the opposite sign.) In still air or in a moderate wind, the optimum angle of attack is negative at release, leading to a negative initial lift. The reason for this is that the angle of the velocity decreases during flight, while the angle of the plane of the discus remains fairly stable because of its spin. In this way, lift becomes positive for most of the flight, while drag is minimized. If the angle of attack is positive at release, the initial lift is positive but the distance traveled is reduced by increased drag.

Drag is at a minimum if the angle of attack is 0 degrees. It remains rather small for small angles of either sign but rapidly increases as the angle of attack increases from about 20 to 90 degrees. On the other hand, there is no lift if the angle of attack is 0 degrees, and lift increases with increasing angle of attack up to about 25 degrees but then decreases as the angle increases further. The sign of the lift is, by this convention, the same as the sign of the angle of attack. The optimum discus throw is made at an angle of attack that imparts the largest possible lift-to-drag ratio during most of the flight. The height of release of the discus is not important, because it is much smaller than the distance traveled, around 70 meters (230 ft.). In still air, the optimum launch angle (angle of release) is a little under 40 degrees, and the discus travels approximately the same distance as it would if it were released without air at an angle of 44 degrees. With a tailwind of 10 meters per second (33 ft./sec.), the best launch angle is a little over 40 degrees; with a tailwind of 15 meters per second (49.5 ft./sec.), the optimum launch angle is about 50 degrees.

The reason for the variation of the launch angle with wind speed and direction is simple. With a headwind, the discus need not be launched at a high angle, because the air provides plenty of lift. In this case, to achieve maximum distance, it is best for the velocity to have a large horizontal component. With a tailwind, the air provides considerably less lift. In this case, a high launching angle increases the time the discus remains in flight, allowing the wind more time to push on it. When (very rarely) wind velocity exceeds about 20 to 25 meters per second, the discus will travel farther in a tailwind than in a headwind.

The optimal initial angle of attitude (the angle the plane of the discus makes with respect to the ground) also depends on wind speed and direction. This angle is about 30 degrees above the horizontal in still air, or about 10 degrees below the launch angle. In a tailwind of about 10 meters per second (33 ft./sec.), the best angles of release and attitude are both a little over 40 degrees; for stronger tailwinds, the best angle of attitude is larger than the release angle. Because the best launch angle and the best angle of attitude both depend on the wind, the discus thrower has to make a good estimate of the speed and direction of the wind in order to make an optimal throw.

Beneficial Winds

A headwind is rarely direct but usually at an angle to the direction of forward motion. For a right-handed discus thrower, a headwind coming from a 45-degree angle to the right—called a quartering wind—is even more advantagous than a direct headwind. A quartering wind, however, allows a longer throw only if the thrower orients the discus with a greater right tilt (toward the wind), which increases the lift and decreases the drag.

A discus throw that would travel about 65 meters (215 ft.) in still air will travel about 5 meters (16.5 ft.) farther in a headwind of about 10 meters per second (33 ft./sec.) and about 5 meters farther than that in a headwind of about 20 meters per second (66 ft./sec.). At greater headwind speeds, the distance traveled by the discus does not increase much; and when the headwind becomes too strong, the distance will decrease. In a tailwind of 5 to 10 meters per second, the discus will travel about 2 meters (6.6 ft.) less than in still air. However, with stronger tailwinds, the distance traveled increases again. With a tailwind of about 15 meters per second (49.5 ft./sec.), the discus travels as far as it would in still air. A wind speed of 15 meters per second is another marker, because at still greater tailwinds, the discus travels increasingly longer distances. These results, however, assume a world-class technique, because the angle of release and the angle of attack must be adjusted in an optimal way for wind conditions.

Technique in the discus throw.   From a biomechanical perspective, the discus throw is considered a sidearm throw. One significant advantage of a sidearm throw is that the thrower can increase angular velocity while rotating and thereby increase release velocity. Sidearm throwing allows the arm to be extended out away from the body, farther from the vertical axis, as the thrower increases rotational speed. The longer the lever (in this case, the arm), the longer the radius and the greater the velocity associated with a given angular velocity. Besides these biomechanical advantages, the sidearm throwing motion has one obvious aerodynamic advantage in comparison with an overhand or underhand throw: the plane of the discus is closer to horizontal on release, maximizing the amount of lift during flight.

The discus thrower holds the discus in a balanced way with the index and middle finger. To start, the thrower swings the arm back and forth several times before beginning an orbit of 1.5 to 2 rotations. This pivoting throwing motion must be controlled so that the athlete remains within the ring. In the 2.5-meter (8.25-ft.) ring, throwers can move from back to front and make as many rotations as they want. However, the tangential acceleration imparted to the discus diminishes substantially as the thrower rotates, and so the number of rotations is limited to reducc problems with orientation and balance. In the 1990s, many world-class discus throwers switched to the 2-rotation attack rather than the 1.5-rotation attack to increase the amount of angular velocity generated. It has yet to be proved, however, whether the advantages of the additional half rotation are worth the increased risk of a loss in orientation and balance, and thus the higher risk of a foul.

A world-class discus thrower tries to use as much of the ring as possible. Like a shot putter, a discus thrower starts by leaning out the back of the ring and finishes by leaning precariously over the front of the ring. Often, the thrower brings the follow-through to an end by bouncing on the left foot, exerting great toe pressure to stay within the confines of the ring.

Regardless of the number of rotations ultimately used, for a right-hander the first step is taken with the left foot toward the front of the ring. A right-handed thrower generates angular momentum with the left side of the body to be able to transfer angular momentum to the trailing right side of the body. As rotations are made, the knees remain slightly bent to keep the center of gravity as low as possible to aid in balance. The discus remains down and close to the body and slowly extends outward and upward during the rotations.

Also as the rotations are made, the opposite arm extends outward, acting as a counterweight to the axis of the shoulders. In short, the discus thrower moves slowly through the first rotation, moves faster during the step phase and second rotation, and explodes forward during the release phase, while accelerating in all phases. As the lead left foot points in the throwing direction at release, it thrusts the body in the throwing direction to enhance discus rotation and velocity. A good release is highly dependent on exploding forward off the lead foot—not spinning off it—and properly rolling the discus off the index finger and thumb to maximize linear velocity and to impart the spin required for a controlled flight.

The Javelin

Dynamics of javelin throwing.   Although the javelin has a different size, shape, and weight from the discus, the world-record distances for these two events are comparable. Also, in both events the outcome depends on the thrower's understanding of lift and drag. However, the javelin is not only lighter than the discus but is thrown in a different way and experiences different aerodynamic forces. A javelin thrower is allowed a run up to the "scratch line" and (unlike a shot putter, hammer thrower, or discus thrower) is not confined to a small ring. During the run-up, javelin throwers must stay within markers and behind the scratch line as they follow through. Another regulation is that the javelin must land tip first, but this is seldom a problem because of the "self-tipping" aerodynamic design of modern javelins.

The javelin consists of three parts: a metal head, a shaft, and a cord grip at the center of gravity. It is the lightest of all the field-event projectiles: the men's javelin has a mass of 800 grams (1.76 lb.) and

JAVELIN RECORDS

World
Men: 95.54 meters (313 ft. 5 in.)—Jan Zelezny (TCH) Petersburg, South Africa, 6 April 1993
Women: 80 meters (262 ft. 5 in.)—Petra Felke (East Germany), Potsdam, 9 September 1988

Olympic
Men: 89.66 meters (294 ft. 2 in.)—Jan Zelezny (TCH) Seoul, 1988
Women: 74.68 meters (245 ft.)—Petra Felke (East Germany), Seoul, 1988

The Frisbee: The Most Popular Disk

The ubiquitousness of flat circular disks—from pie tins and coffee lids found in the kitchen to the hubcaps found in the garage—makes pinpointing the origin of the Frisbee an uncertain endeavor. Nevertheless, Fred Morrison of California receives most of the credit. Morrison, a building inspector and garage tinkerer, developed the "Pluto Platter" in the early 1950s. In 1957, Wham-O, a struggling toy company in southern California, bought the rights to the Pluto Platter and staked its future on it. The company slightly altered the design of the Pluto Platter and renamed it the Frisbee. Before long, the Frisbee had a cult following, which emerged first among youngsters who threw the plastic saucer at beaches. This quickly spread to become a worldwide craze. People were irresistably drawn to these magical disks, which curved, soared, and hovered, seemingly defying gravity.

Despite its odd and faddish origins (Wham-O also marketed the Hula Hoop, one of the biggest fads of all time), Frisbee continues to remain a very popular sport, with numerous popular regional and national competitions. These competitions have posted some very impressive world records, such as 119 KPH (74 MPH) for the fastest throw, 15.5 seconds for the longest loft time, and 194 meters (637 ft.) for the longest throw. A more recent market entry, the halo-like Aerobie, by Superflight, Inc., boasts an even more impressive distance record: 383 meters, or 1,264 ft.—the length of over four football fields.

These records bode well for the future of the sport. No other thrown inert, wingless object can travel as far or stay aloft as long as these disks. Moreover, unlike competitors in the field throwing events, who typically have a massive physique, world-class Frisbee and Aerobie competitors are of average build—tall and short, heavy

and thin. No one needs a classic, chiseled body to become a champion Frisbee thrower.

Because the discus and the Frisbee have similar dimensions, people sometimes wonder how much alike they are. Although the Frisbee and discus look strikingly similar from the top, there are significant differences in the design, size, shape, and mass that make their flight characteristics very different. Whereas the flight path of a discus is close to a parabola, a Frisbee can fly along a nearly horizontal path over long distances. The reason for this is that the the Frisbee is lighter than the 2-kilogram (4.41-lb.) discus; thus the lifting force on the Frisbee is proportionally larger than the gravitational force, whereas for the discuss the most significant force is gravity. In other words, lift—which depends mostly on area—has less gravitational force to overcome with the Frisbee than with the discus.

Another major difference is release. A Frisbee is released with a sidearm motion, tilted at an angle slightly downward and away from the thrower's body. Upon release, the tilted Frisbee quickly encounters lifting forces that send it on an approximately straight and level flight path. A critical angle needs to be used so that the Frisbee can right itself, for a tilt either way results in either left- or right-banked curves.

Frisbees float along, covering great distances, much as a glider does. Despite their very different dimensions, the Frisbee and the wings of a glider both have a large surface-to-weight ratio, and each has a shape that enhances lift and minimizes drag. Aeronautical engineers tinker with lengths and shapes to create wing designs with excellent lift-to-drag ratios. Far less tinkering occurs with flying disks, though, because the circular shape limits the amount of lift.

The Frisbee and the discus are symmetrical in shape, and in the spin imparted; that is, in both the Frisbee and the discus the leading and trailing edges are the same. With a Frisbee or discus (like a wing), lift is generated by adjusting the angle of attack. The thrower uses subtle skill in tipping the front end of the Frisbee or discus up, at a slight angle of attack (positive) to deflect the airflow downward. According to Newton's third law of motion, the downward force the Frisbee exerts on the air is equal and opposite to the lifting force the air exerts on the Frisbee. For this reason, a Frisbee is still subjected to lifting forces even when thrown upside down, as long as it is thrown with a slight (positive) angle of attack.

Unlike the discus, the Frisbee has a distinct top and bottom. Besides the spin imparted by the thrower, its curved-edge rim makes the Frisbee a fairly stable flier, far more so than other everyday disklike objects, such as a hubcap or the lid of a coffee container. Some of these common objects are rimless, and that tends to generate a more destabilizing front-half lift.

A spinning object has angular momentum, which is proportional to its mass and angular velocity and also depends on its size and shape. The larger the angular momentum of an object, the less a given torque will change its orientation. The same dynamics maintain the stability of a gyroscope or toy top. Because the lift and drag on a Frisbee depend on orientation, a substantial change in orientation can lead to a large change in flight path. A slowly spinning Frisbee has little angular momentum, so airborne torque can easily affect its flight path. However, a fast-spinning Frisbee has a large angular momentum, so the same torque is inconsequential in altering its flight path.

A person throwing a disk imparts

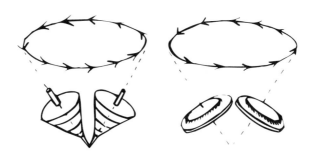

The Frisbee exhibits the same gyroscopic stability as a gyroscope or a spinning top. Upon release, the Frisbee nutates (the edges have a bobbing motion) for a brief moment until it gains gyroscopic stability around its fixed axis. A Frisbee's spin and uneven lift increase the torque on the Frisbee that causes it to dip and veer. As one side dips, the Frisbee veers or banks in that direction. A typical backhand throw that spins the disk clockwise (viewed from top) tends to dip left and roll left in flight (thrower's perspective).

spin for gyroscopic stability—an effect similar to a spinning top or a gyroscope (*see the figures*). Torque on a spinning Frisbee causes its axis of rotation to shift from one plane to another. This is called gyroscopic precession, and it results from aerodynamic forces. If the aerodynamic forces do not act at the center of mass of a Frisbee, torque can result that may cause horizontal precession. If the spin axis is nearly vertical, the precession is very slow and the Frisbee is very stable. But as the spin axis becomes more tilted (more horizontal), torque increases. At this point, more and more rapid precession continues until the Frisbee dips and veers right or left, perpendicular to the spin direction.

The lighter mass of the Frisbee makes gyroscopic stability much more important than it is for the discus. The greater mass of the discus implies a greater moment of inertia, which requires a larger torque to stop it from spinning around its axis. Therefore, the discus does not require as much orientational control as the Frisbee. Spinning creates gyroscopic stability around the center axis point, which maintains the initial launch angle. Without spin, the Frisbee and the discus would wobble in the air. When the discus "stalls," its greater weight allows it to maintain a trajectory that is close to a parabola. Under the same

conditions, a stalling Frisbee sails off course, since it lacks the weight necessary to maintain a trajectory close to a parabola. Moreover, the lighter Frisbee experiences greater orientation changes not only from torque exerted by calm air, but also from torque caused by wind gusts.

Although the optimal spin rate for the Frisbee is the same as for the discus—360 to 480 revolutions a minute—spin is much more important for the Frisbee because maintaining orientation depends on the object's moment of inertia, which, for a given size and shape, is proportional to its mass. For example, a light poke with the index finger on the underside of a Frisbee that is traveling at a moderate velocity can easily alter its orientation. With the much heavier lead discus, such a poke would make almost no change in orientation.

In resisting a change in orientation, not only mass and spin are important, but also the distribution of mass. A Frisbee compensates for its lightness by having much of its mass near the rim of the disk; the center is thin and light. This design results in a larger moment of inertia than a design with more mass at the center. With more mass toward the rim the Frisbee has a greater angular momentum at any given rate of spin.

Undoubtedly spin creates a great

deal of stability for both the discus and the Frisbee; however, the only purpose of a discus throw is distance, whereas Frisbee players like to launch a variety of throws, including slow "floaters," or "hover flights," which seem to slow to a stop in flight and drift gracefully down, like a helicopter coming in for a landing. A floater is a straight throw with an unusually large rate of spin (a Frisbee thrown with little rotation would lack the stability necessary for a floater). In a floater, as linear velocity declines, the large angular momentum from spinning prevents the Frisbee from banking during the closing phase of its flight. What makes the floater possible is the fact that the linear and rotational speed of a Frisbee—unlike a bicycle—can be "uncoupled." As a bicycle wheel (which, of course, is bound to the ground) spins more slowly, its linear speed decreases proportionally, so that it becomes difficult for the cyclist to remain balanced. In the less resistive airborne environment of a tossed Frisbee, that does not happen. Instead, drag slows the Frisbee's speed more quickly than its angular momentum, and the angular momentum allows the Frisbee to maintain its axis of rotation and float even after it has stopped flying forward.

This is the reason that a Frisbee can stay aloft for as long as 15 seconds.

(continued)

The Frisbee *(continued)*

When a projectile like a ball is launched at 119 KPH (74 MPH) with a 45-degree release angle, it travels about 113 meters (370 ft.) and remains in the air for about 5 seconds (assuming no drag, which shortens both distance and time). But because a Frisbee can float and catch updrafts, it can stay airborne much longer, especially if it maintains a near-vertical axis of rotation.

It should be noted that although throwing a floater seems easier when the Frisbee is launched into the wind, this is only apparent. Actually, a headwind simply slows the Frisbee's flight speed with respect to the ground. The Frisbee does not actually float better with respect to the air as it spins about a fixed vertical axis; but because its position relative to the ground is more stationary, to an earthbound observer it appears to float better.

When a Frisbee is thrown for distance, air hits its underside and creates the most lift during the last part of the flight. During this time, if the angle of attack is too steep, the Frisbee will stall in flight and rapidly lose linear velocity and altitude. Because it is much lighter than a discus, a Frisbee thrown with too steep an angle of attack is more easily affected by the vagaries of the wind, which carries it off in a downwind direction. However, unlike a discus thrower—who hopes for a moderate headwind—world-class Frisbee distance throwers favor a modest wind at their back. By throwing with the wind, they can use nose glide, a clever trick of the trade called "toejam power." What they attempt to do is use a high height of release and toss the Frisbee in such a way that the nose drops during the later floating period. When the speed starts to decline, a wind gust can push the Frisbee along, much as a billowing spinnaker sail catches a downwind gust to accelerate a yacht.

Although the discus event has many fans, and excellent discus throwing is enthralling to watch, the Frisbee is far and away the more popular participant sport. It seems to have become the "average person's" discus—a sophisticated and extremely appealing flying device that allows the thrower to experiment with lift and drag by making subtle adjustments in the release. In competiton and on a leisurely day at the beach, the Frisbee is a floating wonder.

John Zumerchik

Note: Frisbee is a registered trademark of Wham-O, Inc. Aerobie is a registered trademark of Superflight, Inc.

the women's 600 grams (1.32 lb.). The flight path of the javelin looks less like a parabola than the paths of many other thrown objects (*see Figure 13*), because it is light and aerodynamic. If the javelin is thrown properly, the air passing by it in flight exerts a substantial lift and not much drag; that is, it has a large lift-to-drag ratio.

Changing the design of any flying object (such as an airplane) changes its flight characteristics. In the case of the javelin, manufacturers experiment with different taper and weight distribution to improve the aerodynamics. Much as air acts on the wings of an airplane to create lift, the air acting on the large-diameter stabilizing tail of the javelin—called the planform—provides the lift that enables the javelin to remain in the air a long enough time to travel a long distance. A larger-diameter planform causes the rising air to provide more lift in the back than in the front, improving the flight path. In the javelin used between 1955 and 1986, which had such a planform, the lift acting on the planform had a much larger effect than drag, which slows the forward speed of the javelin. In designing a javelin, however, there is a trade-off between lift and flight characteristics. If a javelin is designed with excessive lift, it will not easily land in the required tip-first position—as was the case with the javelins of 1955–1986 (*see Figure 14*).

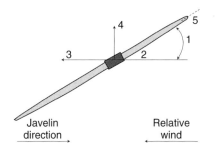

Javelin direction   Relative wind

Figure 13. *For a javelin, aerodynamic and inertial forces result in a trajectory that varies from the near-parabolic flight path of a ball. In addition to gravity, the major factors affecting the flight of a javelin include: (1) angle of attack, (2) center of gravity, (3) drag, and (4) lift. Because the moment of inertia around the longitudinal axis of the javelin (5) is small, there is very little angular momentum for stability. Scientists, coaches, and athletes have for years debated whether spin has a stabilizing effect; but because the increased stability is marginal, to spin or not to spin is mostly a question of biomechanical preference.*

To maximize lifting forces, javelin throwers are concerned with both the angle of release and the angle of attack. The angle of release is the initial angle of the velocity at the moment of launching; in still air, the initial angle of attack is the angle at which the javelin tilts upward from the angle of release. As the javelin begins the upward part of its trajectory, the angle of attack decreases, and the tilt of the javelin closely follows its trajectory. Then as the trajectory turns downward, the tilt of a well-designed and well-thrown javelin pitches, or tips, downward at about the same angle as the descending flight path.

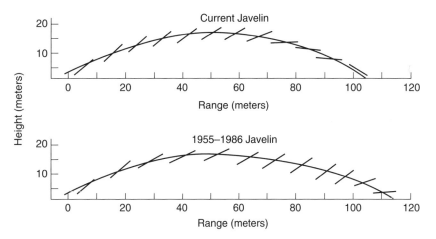

Figure 14. *The physicist Peter Brancazio estimated that changes in the design of javelins in 1955 (below) increased distance by an average of 11 meters (about 35 feet), solely because of better lift relative to drag. But that design made it more difficult to get the javelin to land tip first. The self-tipping javelin used since 1986 ensures that tilt will closely follow trajectory to produce a tip-first landing. World-class javelin throwers use a consistent angle of release (about 30 to 35 degreees) regardless of the wind conditions (Adrian, 1989), but they vary the angle of attack depending on wind direction and velocity. Angle of attack can vary from 0 to 10 degrees (Mont, 1988).*

When a javelin is thrown into the wind, the relative velocity of the air past it increases, improving lift. Because the wind speed creates more lift, the angle of attack is adjusted downward. The opposite holds in throwing downwind: the angle of attack is adjusted upward so that the planform tips more vertically into the oncoming air.

In 1986, responding to continual improvements in the design of the javelin and in the abilities of javelin throwers, track and field officials made a change in the rules, with the intention of curtailing the distances thrown. Another consideration they had taken into account was safety: with world-record throws exceeding 100 meters (330 ft.)— about the length of a football field, which is in fact the setting for most competitions—errant throws were occasionally flying into the stands. Under the new rules, the grip of the javelin (its center of gravity) was moved 2 inches (about 5 cm) forward and the size of the planform was reduced, significantly limiting the contribution of aerodynamic lift to the total distance of the throw. This change in design causes the javelin to tip down sooner and thus to fall to the ground sooner. The reason is that, since air imparts a different degree of lift to different parts of the javelin, torque is created, causing the javelin to rotate around its center of gravity during flight in such a way as to make it more consistently land tip first. Officials welcomed this change, which eliminated many close calls—"fair versus foul" judgments.

After the rule change, throwing distances were decreased by approximately 20 percent. Also, because the new javelin had a different optimum angle of release and attack, the athletes had to adjust their technique: on average, javelin throwers had to increase their angle of release about 5 degrees (Santos, 1991). However, as athletes developed an understanding of the aerodynamic characteristics of the post-1986 javelins, distance records soon began to increase again, and by 1994 distances were only 10 percent less than those recorded before the design change.

Angle of release and angle of attack are not the only factors javelin throwers must consider. They must also maximize release velocity—a combination of run-up velocity and throw velocity. For each individual athlete, release velocity is determined by the strength and direction of the forces applied to the throw and by the distance and time over which these forces are applied. Of course, for the javelin (as for the other field throwing events), attaining world-class release velocity is no easy task. It requires physical strength, years of practice, and tremendous will.

Javelin technique. Unlike the shot put, discus, or hammer throw, the javelin event does not limit the thrower's movements to a ring. Instead, a javelin thrower generates linear momentum in a horizontal direction by using a long run-up to the scratch line. A controlled 10- to 12-stride run-up creates significant linear momentum. Upon approaching the scratch line, a javelin thrower "sets up" in a wide throwing stance and follows through with the body, in the direction of the released javelin, with a powerful crossover step to impart as much linear momentum as possible to the javelin.

The plant, or braking foot, that initiates the crossover step is very important. When a right-handed thrower plants the left leg, linear momentum from the run-up is transferred to the arm and javelin. In the throwing motion, there is an extreme uncoiling of the arm muscles (*see Figure 15*). This throwing motion has much in common with that of a pitcher in baseball, and even more with that of a bowler in cricket.

Don B. Lichtenberg and John Zumerchik*

*Don B. Lichtenberg, who wrote the sections on physics, extends his thanks to John Wills and Phil DiLavore for helpful discussions. John Zumerchik wrote the sections on technique.

Figure 15. *A javelin is gripped with the thumb and middle finger just behind the cord. Top javelin throwers keep the nonthrowing arm straight in front of the body to counter the natural rotation of the trunk during release and follow-through. A straight arm pulling toward the body is much more effective at limiting rotation than a bent arm. Because javelin throwers are allowed a run-up, this is the one field event where size is not necessarily an advantage. Jan Zelezny, who set a world record in 1996, was rather long and lanky.*

References

Adrian, M., and J. Cooper. *Biomechanics of Human Movement.* Indianapolis, Indiana: Benchmark, 1989.

Black, I. "Hammer Throw." *Track and Field Quarterly Review* 80 (1980): 27ff.

Brancazio, P. *Sports Science.* New York: Simon and Schuster, 1984.

Brody, H. "An Experiment to Measure the Density of Air." *Physics Teacher* 27, no. 1 (1989): 46ff.

Dapena, J. "A Kinematic Study of Center of Mass Motions in the Hammer." *Journal of Biomechanics* 19 (1986): 147ff.

Doherty, J. K. *Track and Field Omnibus,* 2nd ed. Los Altos, California: Tofnews, 1976.

Erhlichson, H. "Maximizing Projectile Range with Drag and Lift, with Particular Application to Golf." *American Journal of Physics* 51, no. 4 (1983): 357–362.

Frohlich, C. "Aerodynamic Effects on Discus Flight." *American Journal of Physics* 49, no. 12 (1981): 1125–1132.

Gregor, R., et al. "Kinematic Analysis of Olympic Discus Throwers." *International Journal of Sports Biomechanics* 1, no. 2 (1985): 131–138.

Gold, M. "The Fairy Tale Physics of Frisbees." In *Newton at the Bat: The Science in Sports.* E. Schier and W. Allman, eds. New York: Scribner, 1984.

Hay, J. *Biomechanics of Sports Techniques,* 3rd ed. Englewood Cliffs, New Jersey: Prentice-Hall, 1985.

Hubbard, M. "The Throwing Events in Track and Field." In *Biomechanics of Sports.* Edited by C. Vaughan. Boca Raton, Florida: CRC Press, Inc., 1989.

Leary, W. "Lift, Drag, Spin, and Torque: Sending Toys Aloft." *New York Times,* sec. C, 1:3 (20 June 1995).

Lichtenberg, D., and J. Wills. "Maximizing the Range of the Shot Put." *American Journal of Physics* 46 (1978): 546ff.

Northrip, J., G. Logan, and W. McKinney. *Introduction to Biomechanic Analysis of Sport,* 2nd ed. Dubuque, Iowa: W. C. Brown, 1979.

Payne, H. *The Science of Track and Field Athletics.* London: Pelham Books, 1981.

Santos, J., and K. Shipman. *Track: The Field Events.* New York: Sports Illustrated Winner's Circle, 1991.

Schuurmans, M. "Flight of the Frisbee." *New Scientist,* 127 no. 1727 (28 July 1990): 37–40.

Shelton, J. "The Physics of Frisbee Flight." In S. Johnson (ed.), *Frisbee.* New York: Workman Publishing Co., 1975.

Terauds, J. *Biomechanics of the Javelin Throw.* Del Mar, California: Academic Publishers, 1985.

Football

SEVERAL AMERICAN UNIVERSITIES—Princeton, Rutgers, Columbia, Yale, and Harvard—can all claim the genesis of the hybrid sport called football. Most historians date the break of football from soccer and rugby to the nineteenth century. The first intercollegiate football game was played between Princeton and Rutgers in 1869, though that game more closely resembled soccer than football. In October 1873, football made a formal break from soccer and rugby when Princeton, Rutgers, Columbia, and Yale drew up standardized rules. Just 2 years later, Harvard and Yale began the United States' oldest college football rivalry—rivalry that continues to this day.

Football began to enjoy widespread popularity after World War II, when television brought the sport into homes across the United States. In the 1990s, it is one of the most popular team sports in America. Each year on New Year's Day, hundreds of thousands of Americans watch college football's many televised postseason bowl games. In January each year, millions watch the National Football League (NFL) season finale, the Super Bowl. Football is also a popular high school sport, particularly in rural America, where local football games provide both entertainment and a sense of community.

The rough physical contact among football players may be partly responsible for the game's devoted following. Yet as violent as the sport seems today, it was once even more so. In 1885, members of the Harvard faculty considered football so brutal that it was temporarily banned. Despite such concerns, football became even more physically intense. In 1888, for example, a major rule change allowed tackling below the waist, significantly increasing the risk of injury to players.

Around this time, coaches began to devise playing strategies that had tragic consequences for some players. One such maneuver was the locking interference play, which featured blockers running, arms linked, with the ball carrier following closely behind. In 1909, thirty-three deaths occurred in college football, most of which were attributed to locked-arm blocking, prompting President Theodore Roosevelt to call for major changes in the sport. In an attempt to reduce the number of injuries and deaths, college officials outlawed locked-arm blocking and introduced the forward pass, which facilitated progress downfield with somewhat less physical contact.

In football, perhaps more than in any other sport, well-conditioned athletes, improved equipment, and new playing strategies continuously challenge officials to improve safety without sacrificing excitement. Officials use caution in modifying rules, however, as the game's appeal may be largely due to its physical nature as a contact sport. (Vince Lombardi, a well-known professional football coach, disagreed with the characterization of football as a contact sport. "Dancing is a contact sport," Lombardi once said. "Football is a collision sport.")

Collision Dynamics

Momentum, a term common in the vernacular of football announcers and commentators, may be the most overused word in football. It is, however, a useful term for describing gridiron collisions. The formula for linear momentum (mass × velocity) states that as an object's weight or speed increases, its momentum also increases, in a straight line. Mass is a measure of inertia, the tendency of an object at rest to stay at rest and of an object in motion to maintain motion. Velocity is speed, or the rate of motion. Force is needed to change the momentum of an object. An accelerating force causes momentum to increase; a decelerating force causes momentum to decrease. No change in net force means that momentum remains constant.

When a running back is moving upfield, the job of the defense is to tackle or to stop him. To do so, the defensive player must apply enough countering force to reduce the momentum of the running back to zero. The greater the momentum of the running back, the more force is necessary to stop him; the faster or heavier he is, the greater his momentum.

Time is another consideration. A small force acting for an extended period is as effective as a large force acting for a shorter period. The longer the force acts, the greater the change in momentum. For instance, a running back often pushes against the backs of his linemen as they, in turn, push against the defensive linemen. The running back's contact may help move the "pile" forward, but as the defensive players counter by pushing back, the offensive linemen and running back may come to a standstill and then, like a wave, begin flowing backward.

According to the principle of conservation of momentum, when two players collide, the increase in one player's momentum is equal to the decrease of the other player's momentum. Since a player's mass is constant, a change in momentum means a change in velocity. A lighter player moving with greater velocity will push back a slower but heavier player. If two players collide at the same velocity, the lighter player will be driven back.

Although mass is important in predicting the outcome of a collision, velocity largely determines the amount of momentum created prior to a collision. To make the most of his mass, a player should keep his feet on the ground during impact. If he collides with another player while airborne, his deliverable mass is equal to his body weight alone. If he makes contact while driving forward with his feet planted, however, his deliverable mass is equal to his weight plus the force generated by his leg muscles pushing his body forward.

Thus, a 180-pound (81-kg) defensive back can in fact tackle a 260-pound (118-kg) tight end. If the tight end has good forward momentum—for example, is moving at 20 feet per second, about 13 miles per hour (MPH; 21 KPH)—the 180-pound defensive back moving at the same speed will pose no challenge. At the instant prior to collision, the tight end has 162 momentum units, while the defensive back has only 112. The tight end's 44 percent greater momentum means he will easily overpower the defensive back. However, if the 260-pound tight end is moving at only 10 feet per second (81 momentum units) while the defensive back's speed remains at 20 feet per second, the defensive back, though smaller, can overpower the running back by virtue of his 38 percent greater momentum.

These scenarios are based on the assumption that the collisions take place head-on and at each player's center of gravity (central point of body's mass concentration). In practice, action is so fast, and players' speed so great, that one player usually has a lower center of gravity. A relatively light (180-lb.) defensive back learns quickly that one way to neutralize his 80-pound mass deficit and bring down a 260-pound running back is to hit him low.

Most violent collisions in football occur in the open field, where linebackers and defensive backs generate tremendous momentum by increasing their velocity as they prepare to tackle running backs and receivers. In comparison, linemen, shoulder to shoulder with each other and nose to nose with opposing linemen, have little room to accelerate before a collision. Because their primary tasks are to push back opposing linemen and to defend the line of scrimmage, they spend little time in the open field and, thus, rarely experience the most violent collisions of the game. On the few occasions when a 300-pound offensive lineman travels downfield at a high speed, a 200-pound defensive back faces a much greater risk of injury if the two collide. As each generation of linebackers and defensive backs have become faster and heavier—and thus capable of generating greater momentum—open-field collisions have become increasingly violent.

Collisions can also be evaluated in terms of kinetic energy (energy of motion). When a 100-pound tackler running at 16 feet per second hits a 160-pound running back moving at 10 feet per second, he brings to the collision the same linear momentum as a 320-pound tackler moving at only 5 feet per second. Despite significant weight differences, each of these players has the same momentum (running back, 160 × 10; small tackler, 100 × 16; large tackler 320 × 5; *see Figure 1*). Because the small tackler's greater speed gives him more kinetic energy than that of the large tackler, he collides with the runner with greater force. When the speed is doubled, the necessary stopping time also doubles, although the distance required to stop increases fourfold. The small tackler's greater speed gives him four

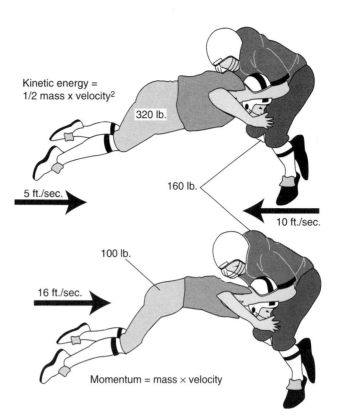

Kinetic energy =
1/2 mass x velocity^2

320 lb.

5 ft./sec.

160 lb.

10 ft./sec.

100 lb.

16 ft./sec.

Momentum = mass × velocity

Figure 1. *Through conservation of linear momentum, a small tackler (below) and a large tackler (above) may be equally effective at stopping a running back.*

times the kinetic energy of the large tackler, which means that he penetrates four times as far into the running back's body. A smaller tackler's bonier body also deforms less on contact with the running back, so less energy is absorbed by his own body and more is transferred to the running back.

The principle of conservation of momentum illustrates the importance of body size. Optimum performance for football players requires a balance among weight, ease of mobility, and speed. Neither size without mobility nor mobility without size is useful to a player. With strength, speed, and flexibility training, players of the 1990s have been able to increase their bulk (and strength) without compromising their speed or their flexibility. With the exception of running backs and receivers—whose weight and size approach the NFL average—the All Pro players are generally taller and heavier than average.

Despite this increase in player size, advances in conditioning and in protective equipment, along with rule modifications, will probably negate many of the effects of increasingly violent collisions.

A note on linemen and collision dynamics. The objective for linemen is penetration—to push the opponent off the ball. To fill these positions, coaches look for the biggest and quickest players.

**ESTIMATED VISUAL AND AUDITORY REACTION TIMES
(MILLISECONDS)**

	Offensive lineman	Defensive lineman
Minimum auditory process	50	50
Start motor action (ball snap)	25	25
Minimum visual process		80
Start motor action		35
Total	75	190

Table 1. *Offensive linemen are able to react more quickly than their defensive counterparts because they respond only to the auditory signal from the quarterback. Defensive linemen experience a double delay: they must wait until the offensive center receives the auditory signal and initiates the snap of the ball. The brain processes auditory signals (frequency, direction, and intensity) much faster than visual signals (movement, contours, textures, and colors). To offset this handicap, coaches guide quick, large players toward the defensive line. (Source: Griffing, 1987)*

Because a player can increase his blocking force (momentum) by increasing either his mass or his velocity, linemen are the heaviest players on the field. Lined up helmet to helmet and facing their opponents, they have little room to increase their momentum by greatly increasing their velocity—unlike players positioned well away from the line of scrimmage. Mass, therefore, is the most important factor for lineman.

Nevertheless, the lineman's ability to quickly increase his velocity (accelerate) is very important. If he can accelerate faster than his opponent, he will have greater momentum at the moment of contact. By traveling farther and by closing the distance between himself and the defender, he will make contact at a more advantageous location, and this will enable him either to knock his opponent off balance or to penetrate through a gap.

The positioning of linemen varies with different playing levels. Defensive players attempt to time their muscular action to coincide with the snap of the ball. Players' feet are positioned either squarely or staggered, and players line up in a 2-, 3-, or 4-point stance (these numbers refer to the number of hands and feet touching the ground). Studies show that the staggered position is superior to the square position because the force exerted by both legs increases as the distance between the feet increases to about 28 to 36 inches. The 4-point stance is best for the bull rush, or straight-line charge; the 3-point for quick accelerations of 7 or 8 yards; and the 2-point for maximum acceleration over 3.3 yards. Although the 4- and 3-point stances are recommended for many circumstances, the time necessary to travel one yard forward is lowest when only 5 percent body weight is applied to the hand or hands on the ground. (Paige, 1973)

Often, a quicker 250-pound defensive lineman will dominate a heavier 300-pound offensive lineman during the first half of a game but will lose his advantage as his muscles fatigue during the second half. At that time, his slower reflexes will make it difficult for him to continue accelerating more quickly than his opponent (*see also SKELETAL MUSCLE and SOCCER*).

Throwing

Football adopted a spheroidal, end-tapered ball instead of a round ball because of its better aerodynamics. Its shape allows it to be thrown so that it spirals along its long axis, maintaining an aerodynamic profile that allows it to travel a great distance. The amount of drag experienced by a spiraling football is only about two-thirds that of a round ball of similar cross-sectional width, such as a volleyball. In other words, as the football pushes its way through the air, it meets far less resistance than a round ball of the same volume.

The best quarterbacks in professional football take full advantage of the aerodynamic shape of the ball: some can throw it over 60 yards (55 m). A good spiral is essential for a good throw. Air resistance greatly affects a wobbling pass, slowing the ball and sending it off target. Because of different hand sizes and arm strengths, quarterbacks use different throwing motions, which result in slight spiral variations. However, arm power does not separate power passers, like John Elway, from wobbler throwers, like Jim McMahon and Fran Tarkenton. Although arm strength is essential for distance throwing, it has little to do with throwing perfect spirals, which depend instead on wrist action (*see Figure 2*).

Most experts agree that a quick release of the thrown ball is just

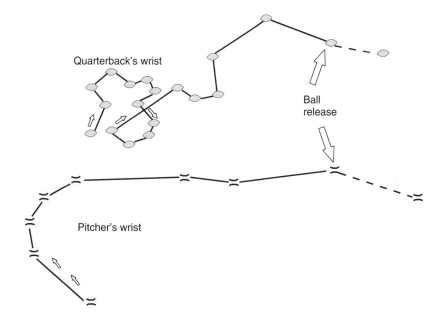

Figure 2. *The arm motion used by a quarterback to throw a football differs from the wrist action that a baseball pitcher employs. Whereas the baseball pitcher releases the ball at the greatest height of the wrist, the quarterback releases the ball as the hand is moving downward and underneath the ball. (Adapted from Adrian and Cooper, 1989)*

as important as a strong arm or good foot speed for enabling a quarterback to elude the defense long enough to throw an accurate pass. For example, at the time of this writing the Hall of Fame player Dan Marino had the slowest feet of any NFL quarterback. But with his extremely quick release, he rarely got sacked (tackled behind the line of scrimmage before having released the ball). By waiting until the last possible moment to release the ball, he could "freeze" the defense and deliver the ball to late-opening receivers. Additionally, Marino's quick release minimized the chance that he would telegraph his passes. (Telegraphing occurs when a quarterback signals where he will throw the ball; it is based on his body movement and direction of sight.) As a result, he had relatively few pass interceptions.

Upon release, the football goes into a flight with gyroscopic motion—the motion of a spinning top. When a top is set on a flat surface, it falls, but when it spins it is able to stand upright and seems to defy gravity. The top rotates around a horizontal axis, and the spinning creates a force that allows it to continue rotating around its axis. As it spins around its long axis, a spiraling football exhibits properties similar to a top. Any change in the orientation of its spin occurs from aerodynamic lifting and drag forces created by wind conditions (*see also FIELD ATHLETICS: THROWING*). When the external forces are minor, the spin axis remains fixed. However, a throw is affected by high winds much as a spinning top is affected when it bumps into another object: its path is altered and it may wobble, but as long as it spins rapidly enough it will return to its spinning pattern. Likewise, though a gust of wind may alter a football's flight path, the football will generally recover and maintain its spiral, albeit following a slightly different flight path. Quarterbacks generally try to throw good spirals on windy days, though their accuracy may be greatly curtailed. Some try to compensate for blustery conditions by throwing harder, or "tighter," spirals, which react less to wind.

Although a perfect spiral should not wobble at all, most quarterbacks throw with a slight, yet patterned, wobble. Figure 3 compares

Figure 3. *The football in flight exhibits the same gyroscopic action as a spinning top or a bicycle wheel—around a vertical axis. Unlike the top or the wheel, however, the ball does not revolve around a fixed point. The shape of the ball also creates a slight wobble because of the aerodynamic torque. In the illustration, the point F_1 intersects the long axis at a distance (D) from the center of the football. If the aerodynamic torque occurs to the left (F_2), the ball assumes a tighter spiral. If it occurs to the right (F_3), the ball exhibits an excessive wobble. Note: mg = mass × gravity, or effective weight.*

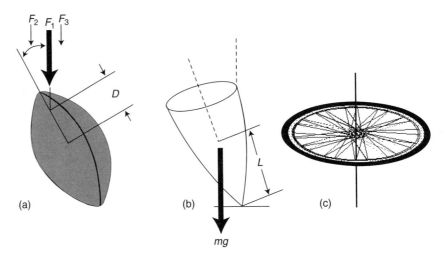

the gyroscopic motion of a bicycle wheel around a vertical axis and the gyroscopic motion of football around a vertical axis. When set in motion, the bicycle wheel exhibits an initial bobbing motion around the vertical axis, called a nutation. Bicycle-wheel nutations gradually dampen due to friction at the pivot point (a fixed anchor). A football, on the other hand, is a projectile in motion and therefore has no fixed pivot point to diminish nutations. Therefore, most spirals spin among two or three axes, alternating in a fairly uniform pattern. The slight wobbly motion is the result of nutations.

Pass spirals are classified into three categories: tight, semitight, and wobbly. For a tight (nonwobbling) spiral, release occurs with the ball rotating only along its long axis. Good throwing technique requires that the wrist remain locked. As the arm extends forward and the ball spins off the fingers, wrist motion imparts an angular velocity along another axis. Semitight spirals are released with substantial rotation around the long axis and an additional, slight rotation along another axis. Wobbly passes, sometimes called "wounded ducks," occur when a quarterback is rushed or when the ball slips out of his hands, causing a large rotation along an axis other than the long axis. Peter Brancazio has calculated a wobble-to-spin ratio of three wobbles for every five spins for all but the worst ducks. This ratio is independent of the rate of spin, linear speed, and trajectory of the football (Brancazio, 1987).

Punting

A punter enters the field when an offensive drive has failed and the ball must be returned to the other team. Punting usually takes place only a few times during the game, so punters are under considerable pressure to maximize those opportunities. The aim is to kick the ball as far downfield as possible and to keep the ball in the air as long as possible, enabling the punter's team members to run upfield and tackle the receiver soon after he catches the ball.

The punter drops the ball and kicks it as it falls, aiming for a combination of height and distance. From the point of contact, speed and launch angle determine the distance the ball travels as well as its hang time, or airborne time. The dual goals of maximizing distance and maximizing hang time counter each other. To achieve greater hang time, one must sacrifice distance; to achieve greater distance, one must sacrifice hang time. For any projectile, including a football, maximum range is achieved by launching it at an angle of 45 degrees; maximum hang time is achieved by launching it straight up (an angle of 90 degrees). Good punters aim for a distance of 55 to 60 yards (45–50 yd. from the line of scrimmage) and a hang time of 4.5 seconds. Strategy and field and wind conditions often dictate a wide range of takeoff angles—from line drives to extra-high punts. Figure 4 shows contact points for a typical punt and a high-trajectory punt.

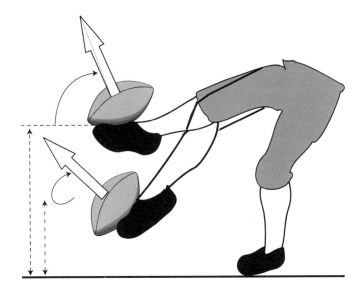

Figure 4. *A good punt requires excellent timing: the punter must coordinate the drop of the ball with the motion of his swinging leg. When the kicking goal requires different trajectories, the optimal angle of the ball and height of contact change. The typical punt (above) varies from a high-trajectory punt (below). If the kicker wants to launch a line-drive punt, the ball is dropped along its long axis and the point of contact is closer to the ground. The angle of the kicking foot in relation to the ball is as responsible for determining the ball's trajectory as is the height of contact. (Adapted from Hay, 1985)*

A punter was judged by only his punt-yard average until the late 1970s, when the measure was proved an unfair barometer of performance. A line-drive punt can easily travel over 70 yards, but it may be caught by the other team well before the punter's teammates can position themselves for a tackle. Therefore, long line-drive punts—which boosted the punter's average—often resulted in an outstanding return and good field position for the opposing team. To ensure that punting statistics would account for good hang time, the NFL began tracking net punt yards—the difference between the line of scrimmage at the time of the punt and after the punt return.

Punting is a challenging skill to master because the spheroidal, end-tapered shape of the football makes contact more difficult than for a round ball. Regardless of its shape or of the manner in which it is kicked, a ball in flight is subject to the effects of gravity and of air resistance. Gravity is constant, but air resistance—ball speed relative to the ground combined with the speed and direction of the wind—varies considerably. No matter how a round ball is kicked, it will encounter nearly uniform air resistance across the surface (with slight variations caused by the ball's seams). A football, on the other hand, must travel nose first to ensure distance and accuracy. A ball punted broadside (a sideways trajectory) is an aerodynamic nightmare for a punter wishing to maximize punt distance, as its air resistance is three or four times that of a nose-first kick. The sideways trajectory creates a large frontal area, which causes the ball to drop abruptly when kicked into a strong wind. For a stable, nose-first flight, the ball must be kicked to spiral around its long axis. This gyroscopic action keeps the football from falling and makes it considerably more resistant to changes caused by gusts of wind.

Throwing a spiral is easy because the ball can be gripped with the hand. Kicking the ball so that it spirals is much more difficult. For a right-footed kicker, a spiral flight requires a kick in which the top of the leg accelerates the foot from right to left across the bottom of the ball, giving it a clockwise spin. To transfer the greatest amount of energy to the ball, the punter should kick the ball at its most resilient point; thus, punters position the ball's laces upward and away from the impact point.

The coordination of the timing of the drop with the foot upswing is crucial to a good punt. If the timing is off or if the ball is dropped off-center, the punter must adjust his stride, his footwork, or his leg and foot speed; and the launch angle, spiral direction, and speed of the kick will all be affected. Good punters can make adjustments for poor drops, but these adjustments come at some expense to the launch angle, hang time, spiral, and speed.

Gusting wind is one of the major causes of poor punts. The punts are bad not because of the wind's effect on the kicked ball, but because the dropped ball's trajectory changes as the punter prepares to kick. If he cannot adjust, he "shanks" the punt—he either kicks the ball with the wrong part of his foot or misses it entirely. Punters must learn to master the wind, but even the very best have trouble. In a January 1986 play-off game against the Chicago Bears, an unexpected gale-strength gust caused the New York Giants's punter Sean Landetta to miss the ball completely. The Bears recovered the ball and scored shortly thereafter, winning the game by a score of 20 to 0.

Like a discus thrower, a punter would rather kick into a slight breeze than with a strong tailwind. A tailwind creates a negative lift on the upper part of the ball, pushing it downward; the ball drops quickly and does not travel as far. However, punters kicking into a stiff breeze try to punt lower to maximize lift and reduce backward force. Crosswinds present the most difficulties. When the wind is blowing from a right-footed punter's left to his right, the drop angle of the nose of the ball must be to the left in order for the wind to carry the ball back to the intended line of flight. When wind is blowing from right to left, he cannot drop the nose of the ball at an angle because it will not spiral.

Placekicking Dynamics

A placekicker is used in two situations: for kickoffs, when the ball is first put into play, and for field goals, as a means of scoring. When the score of a game is close—as is often the case in football—the final

Funny Air Punting?

○ Helium-filled ball

● Air-filled ball

In a 1993 game, the Mississippi State coach Jackie Sherrill accused the Auburn punter Terry Daniels of punting with a helium-filled ball, which Sherrill believed would outsail an air-filled football. The physicist Thomas Braid found that although the lighter helium-filled ball is a bit faster as it leaves the kicker's foot, it slows because of the air resistance along its flight path. The helium-filled ball has the same hang time as the air-filled ball but does not travel as far because of a greater drag effect. Results: Sports Illustrated experiment, 25-inch difference; Braid's calculations, 7-inch difference.

(BEFORE) $M_{body} \times V_{body} + M_{ball} \times V_{ball} = M_{body} \times V_{body} + M_{ball} \times V_{ball}$ (AFTER)

During a 1993 Auburn-Mississippi State game, Terry Daniels, the Auburn punter, kicked 55- and 71-yard punts. Jackie Sherrill, coach of Mississippi State's Bulldogs, called foul, claiming that Daniels's punting—a nation-leading 48.3-yard average—seemed too good to be true.

Sherrill thought Daniels was slipping "doctored" helium-filled balls into the game just prior to punting. Like many people, he believed that a ball filled with helium—a gas lighter than air—would travel farther when punted. *Sports Illustrated* tested the hypothesis by filling two balls each to 13 pounds per square inch, one with helium and one with air (Reed, 1993). The mass of a helium-filled ball was 7.9 grams less than the mass of the air-filled ball (408.4 g compared with 416.3 g). In a double-blind test (neither the kicker nor his feeder knew which ball was filled with helium until afterwards), *Sports Illustrated* had each ball punted ten times.

The conditions for the experiment were near perfect at 71 degrees F with no wind. The air-filled ball's average distance was 59.8 yards, with an average hang time of 4.93 seconds. The helium-filled ball averaged a shorter 57.7 yards and had a shorter average hang time (4.66 sec.).

A comparable experiment, to confirm the *Sports Illustrated* results, would be very difficult to carry out. First, the test must be "double-blind," with the punter noticing no difference between the air- and helium-filled balls. Second, the number of trials should be large enough to allow conclusions to be drawn. According to the law of large numbers, ten punts is too small a sample to generalize from (*see*

outcome may be determined by a last-second field goal attempt. Although a placekicker may have only one opportunity to score during a game, his kick often determines whether his team wins or loses.

Tee kickoffs and kicks from a holder's set are much different from punts because the ball is teed or held against the ground rather than dropped. Instead of kicking the ball into a spiral, the placekicker strives to launch the ball so that it tumbles end over end. By contacting the ball below its center of gravity, he sends it spinning around a

STATISTICS). With so few tries, one or two kicks could have a major effect on the average. In light of the limitations on physical experimental trials, a mathematical or computer model offered a better alternative for testing the results of the *Sports Illustrated* experiment (Braid, 1995).

Although the lighter ball will travel a little faster as it leaves the kicker's foot, it slows more quickly because of the increased air resistance encountered along its flight path. To determine which of these competing effects predominates, one must first determine the momentum at foot-ball impact. According to the conservation of momentum principle, the ball velocity at impact depends on how much foot momentum (leg mass and foot velocity) is transferred to the ball (*see equation with figure*).

The initial velocity of the ball is inversely proportional to its mass. A helium-filled ball is slightly lighter than the air-filled ball because helium has one-eighth the density of air. Therefore, the mathematical model found that a helium-filled ball has a slightly greater initial velocity as it leaves the kicker's foot. If both the air-filled ball and the helium-filled ball were kicked in a vacuum (no air resistance), the helium-filled ball would undoubtedly travel a tiny bit farther. But when a body is moving through air, a drag force slows it down and reduces its range. Is the earth-bound drag force the same for the two balls? If the answer were yes, the helium-filled ball should definitely travel farther.

The details of the drag force affecting the two balls are quite complicated, yet the general principle is fairly simple. The force that air exerts on a moving object depends on the object's shape and area. The drag force is inversely related to the object's mass and directly related to its area. In other words, a heavy object with a small cross-sectional area (e.g., a cannonball) experiences far less drag than a light object with a large cross-sectional area (e.g., a beach ball). If two objects have the same cross-sectional area but vastly different masses, the difference will be substantial. For example, you can throw a heavier golf ball (0.1 lb.) much farther than a Ping-Pong ball (0.006 lb.) although the two have about the same cross-sectional area (diameters of 1.68 in. and 1.47 in., respectively). More specifically, though both leave the hand at approximately the same velocity, the more pronounced drag force on the lighter Ping-Pong ball causes it to decelerate much more quickly. In the case of the two footballs, the area is the same for the helium- and air-filled balls, but because the mass is slightly different, the drag force on the lighter helium-filled ball is slightly greater.

Of course, wind would have an additional effect on the amount of drag. In a tailwind the velocity of the air passing the ball slows, diminishing the distance difference between the two balls. The opposite occurs for a headwind: air speed passing the ball increases, favoring the heavier air-filled ball even more than when no breeze is blowing.

The air-filled ball encounters a lesser drag force that is significant enough to counter the helium-filled ball's higher initial velocity. After factoring in the very small additional drag effect on the helium-filled ball's greater initial velocity, it becomes clear that the helium-filled ball indeed travels a shorter distance. For the average 60-yard punt, the air-filled ball lands 7 inches beyond the helium-filled ball. The mathematical and computer models agreed with the *Sports Illustrated* experiment, though the difference in distance was much less dramatic than the 25 inches reported by the magazine. (Unlike the *Sports Illustrated* study, the mathematical and computer models found that the two balls had the same hang time.)

Contrary to popular belief, a helium-filled football does not, in fact, travel as far as an air-filled football. Had Coach Sherrill checked his beliefs against simple physics, he might have refrained from making his "juiced ball" claim, which both calculation and experimentation disprove.

Thomas H. Braid

transverse (central, rather than long) axis. A quickly tumbling, end-over-end kicked ball is remarkably stable because its spin axis remains fairly constant through its entire flight trajectory.

Unlike punters, placekickers prefer to kick with the wind rather than against it. Because the tumbling ball does not create an efficient aerodynamic profile—it has much more drag than lift—kicking against the wind greatly impedes its progress. Nevertheless, tumbling about a transverse axis, just like spinning about its longitudinal axis, does give a football enough stability to minimize its drifting either to the left or to the right in a strong crossbreeze.

In recent years the proficiency of placekickers has dramatically improved, and more NFL and collegiate kickers are able to kick the ball deep into, or well out of, the endzone. Because a ball kicked into the endzone is a touchback (the receiving team starts the play from the 20-yard line), the kick return—one of the most exciting plays in football—is increasingly uncommon. In the mid-1970s, to encourage more kick returns, the NFL moved the line of scrimmage for kickoffs back from the 40-yard line to the 35-yard line. For the first few years following the rule change, few kickers could send the ball through the endzone. Prior to the 1994 season, as the number of touchbacks had again increased, the NFL moved back the line of scrimmage for kick-offs another 5 yards, to the 30-yard line.

Placekicking technique has improved for field goals as well. Statistics show that field goal–kicking percentages (makes compared with misses) have steadily increased since the early 1980s. The average field goal percentage in the 1990s is higher than the career mark of Kansas City's Hall of Fame kicker Jan Stenerud (66.85%, 1967–1985). If Stenerud had been a rookie in the NFL of the 1990s, some fans claim, he might not even have made the roster for most teams. Perhaps the fact that kickers have more power, better coordination, and fewer mishaps with players on specialized kicking teams explains their higher kicking percentages. In the early 1980s, in an effort to counter a growing trend among teams to keep tall, high-jumping players on their roster for the sole purpose of blocking field goals, the NFL added the rule that players must line up on the line of scrimmage if they wish to block a field goal attempt. These players had previously approached from 5 or 10 yards back from the line of scrimmage and jumped to block kicks. The run-up allowed them to raise their hands to about 11 feet to block a kick—a distinct advantage over down line-men, who can often reach only as high as 9 feet. Since the kicker kicks from 7 yards (21 ft.) behind the line of scrimmage, the new rule improved the geometry for the kicker (*see Figure 5*): a kicker must launch the ball at a steeper angle when trying to clear a 10- to 11-foot-

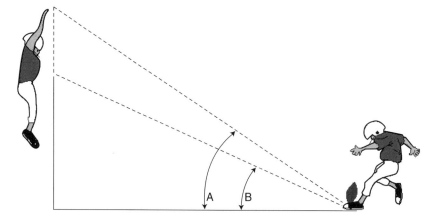

Figure 5. *The rule change that prohibits players from using a run-up to block a field goal attempt has improved the chances of success for kickers. Having to kick the ball over an 11-foot-high wall of players requires a much steeper angle kick (A) than trying clear a 9-foot-high wall (B).*

high wall of players than when trying to clear a 9- to 10-foot-high wall of players. In short, the rule change gave kickers a greater margin for error. It also allowed for a lower launch trajectory, closer to the optimal angle of 45 degrees, which maximizes range and thereby increases the chances of successful long-distance field goals (*see also FIELD ATHLETICS: JUMPING*).

Placekickers may maximize height, distance, or both. For extra points and "chip-shot" (short) field goals, kickers emphasize height; for long-distance field goals, they strive for distance. For the ball to tumble around its horizontal axis, it must be struck below the midpoint of its length. For maximum distance, the optimal launch angle of most projectiles is approximately 45 degrees. When the football is placed on the ground, rather than on a tee, a launch at 45 degrees or more is very difficult. The nature of the football is such that it must be kicked at a 45-degree launch angle to be contacted well below the horizontal axis (a spot on the ball with a lower coefficient of restitution, or rebound ability), which severely restricts the distance that the ball can travel.

Sprinters as Receivers?

Although speed has always been an important asset for a football player, since the 1980s it has become even more so. Coaches and general managers often argue that "speed kills"—weakens the defense—because fast receivers may force the defense to play back from the line of scrimmage. When a defensive back is confident that a receiver cannot run past him, he may creep closer to the line of scrimmage in order to limit the offense's ability to execute short passes and running plays. With a fast-running receiver, on the other hand, the defense backs usually must position themselves back from the line, giving the receiver an advantage.

Since the 1980s, Al Davis, owner of the Los Angeles Raiders, has often gambled on recruiting elite track sprinters as well as drafting the swiftest of standout collegiate receivers. Of the ten or so NFL players with the greatest speed in 1993, five played for Davis during the 1993 season: James Jett, Tim Brown, Alexander Wright, Willie Gault, and Rocket Ismail. Jett, Brown, Gault, and Ismail were standout track stars as well as outstanding collegiate football players. Wright, the fastest of them all, was a big gamble for Davis because he came to the NFL with only track experience.

The strategy of recruiting track stars has brought mixed results. The Dallas Cowboys' Charlie Hayes, the 1964 Olympic 100-meter sprint champion, had a stellar career in the late 1960s, as did Cliff Branch of the Oakland Raiders in the 1970s. Other former track stars, such as Renaldo Nehamiah and Sam Grady, failed to make the transition from track to gridiron. A receiver needs not only speed but "soft," sure hands to catch passes (*see CATCHING SKILLS*), and an understanding of the nuances of the game. However, there are additional reasons for the failure of track athletes in the NFL.

One mistaken belief is that all running is the same. While there are certain similarities, sprinters and receivers do not run in the same manner. While a sprinter emphasizes speed and power in his stride, a receiver must also possess maneuverability. Sprinters and hurdlers rely on long strides and all-out bursts of energy. A receiver, on the other hand, must be able to quickly alter his speed and direction, often making adjustments midstride in order to deceive defensive backs. This requires a rapid change in his accelerating force against the ground in a split-second, coordinated manner. In addition to using a shorter stride length and a higher stride frequency than a sprinter, a receiver needs a more erect stance, positioned directly over his center of gravity.

If a receiver uses long strides, a defensive back is able to more easily knock him over with a "chuck," or slowing push, at the line of scrimmage. Very few pass patterns are "fly patterns," (top speed and straight downfield) where a long-stride sprinting technique is most useful. If a sprinter does not adjust his stride length and frequency, he allows defensive backs to easily anticipate and read his "fly" pattern intentions. Thus speed alone does not make a good receiver, as a defensive back with as little as 1 second's forewarning can position himself deep to beat even the swiftest of receivers to the oncoming ball.

Sprinters as Receivers

Although speed is a receiver's main asset, many track sprinters have been unable to take their speed to the gridiron. They must virtually relearn how to run using shorter strides at a higher frequency in order to "sell fakes" and quickly change direction.

The Dynamics of Collision Injuries

Although the risk of injury in football is high relative to other sports, it is perhaps overstated. One study found that the risk of death for a teenager is nearly twenty times greater driving to and from a football game than playing in the game (Clark, 1979). When a player takes proper precautions, his risk of injury can be minimized.

Helmets: Head and Neck Injuries

Because football is a collision sport that requires a player to keep a low center of gravity, his head is usually extended in front of his body. Players and coaches have long understood the vulnerability of the head and neck to injury and the vital need for headgear. The first headgear was the lightweight leather skullcap developed in 1896. Like the headgear used in boxing today, skull caps provided only modest head protection. Consequently, a player avoided using his head to tackle unless absolutely necessary.

Because the advanced, hard-shell helmets of the 1990s give players a sense of security (perhaps false), some players may risk leading their tackles with the head. Unfortunately, many also neglect to take the precautions necessary to reduce the chances of injury.

To prevent head injuries, a player should take several steps. First and most important, he should make sure to use a properly fitting helmet—one without stress points (that is, without any tightness). An ill-fitting helmet can cause its wearer serious injury through constriction, restriction, friction, or pressure. In addition, it may lose much of its ability to absorb impact forces. (Manufactures are working to improve the helmet's suspension system and inner padding in an attempt to better distribute impact forces.)

Second, a player can reduce his risk of injury by training during his off-season to strengthen his neck muscles, improving both strength and flexibility. Though some athletes are naturally more able to take a blow (*see also BOXING*), flexibility training allows free movement away from the point of collision, while strength training enables the neck to counter and absorb impact forces. Both external and internal physiological differences among people account for variations in the risks to players. An athlete with a long, skinny neck, for example, has a greater than average risk of neck injury in football. Because the neck acts as a lever, a longer neck translates into greater angular accelerations of the brain—and a disproportionate amount of the most severe head and neck injuries.

Third, a player must practice proper technique, such as not lowering his head at the moment of contact. The New York Jets' defensive lineman Dennis Byrd made this mistake during his 1992 season and suffered a severe spinal injury (see *SKELETAL MUSCLE*). Because the neck is designed to bend backward but not much forward, the bones in the neck will break when an impact pushes the head downward at great velocity. A player should attempt a tackle with his shoulders elevated, with his head slightly raised, and with his neck muscles contracted. When the head is down, the neck loses most of its power and is more susceptible to severe spinal injury.

A helmet's face mask protects a player by shielding his eyes and preventing disfiguring injuries. But a mask may also act like a lever, delivering additional torque (force about an axis) to the neck region, measured from the face mask to the base of the neck. To reduce neck injuries, the NFL has outlawed "facemasking" (tackling by grabbing a runner's face mask) and head slaps. However, the practice of spearing (using the helmet itself as a weapon) has proven more difficult to control. In football's early days, when leather skullcap helmets were worn, a player using his head in such a manner risked causing himself more harm than his opponent. The hard-shell helmet, which was developed in 1939, does a better job of protecting the head but also allows a player to use his helmet as a weapon. However, in addition to the punishment that he can now inflict on an opponent, spearing causes more trauma to a player's own brain. This problem is compounded by the many helmet-on-helmet collisions.

No helmet can totally prevent brain trauma. A small amount of fluid and a thin membrane separate the brain and the skull. Helmet collisions exert two forces on the brain. The initial impact force occurs when the brain slams forward against the skull, toward the collision point, and a whiplash effect follows as the brain ricochets to the

What Are "Stingers?"

Stingers, or burners, are injuries that result from impact to the neck and collarbone area. They are marked by a numbness, followed by a searing pain in the shoulder, upper back, or arm—often traveling as far down as the fingers. The large nerves in the neck and collarbone area and the ligaments and the small joints of the upper spine are most often affected. Fortunately, stingers are usually temporary, and a player can quickly return to competition.

opposite side of the skull, slamming against the skull's ridges and bone boundaries. While the helmet absorbs impact blows, it can do little to prevent the brain from accelerating within the skull. A player must therefore be sure that the inflatable sack within his helmet is properly inflated and positioned to cushion blows. However, many players do not inflate the sack because, they argue, it makes the helmet fit too tightly.

The acceleration of the brain inside the skull can cause extremely dangerous concussions. In the middle of the 1992 season, Al Toon, an All Pro New York Jets receiver, retired after suffering his ninth and most severe concussion. Each new concussion came from a lesser blow than the previous one, and recovery time successively increased. Likewise, each new trauma was more debilitating than the last. A tackle imposes tremendous g forces on the brain. One g is equal to the force imposed by the earth's gravitational field (9.8 m/s^2). One can feel forces of multiple g's when accelerating very quickly. When a commercial jet accelerates for takeoff, for example, a passenger feels the force of 2 or 3 g as she is pressed back into her seat. Military fighter pilots, who undergo g-force training, can withstand higher g forces than the average person. Even a trained pilot, however, will fall unconscious if she accelerates at 8 to 10 g. A football player takes hits that accelerate his brain at speeds of up to 100 to 200 g, but he remains conscious because the forces last only a fraction of a second.

Doctors argue that concussions and other forms of brain injury occur from impacts averaging 110 g and lasting less than 70 to 400 milliseconds. During some of the most severe collisions, the brain accelerates at hundreds of miles per hour in just one-thousandth of a second. Helmets manufacturers design helmets to lengthen the time of acceleration by absorbing the blows through the compression and deformation of the helmet's material (*see also BOXING*).

One innovation that may reduce brain trauma is the ProCap—a shock-absorbing polyurethane cushion that attaches to the exterior of a helmet. The cushion absorbs about 30 percent of the g forces to the skull, so that the head bounces much less. This provides protection to the brain, much as foam encasing a baseball would limit the force of the bat on the ball and the distance a hit ball would travel. The ProCap provides additional protection to the brain by dampening the accelerating force of blows. Most players, however, find the cap too bulky and fear they may lose maneuverability and speed.

Flak Jackets

When a quarterback drifts back from the line of scrimmage to execute a pass, he lifts his arms out and away from his body, leaving his torso and ribs exposed to the 300-pound defensive linemen who are trying to sack him. In 1978, the Houston Oilers quarterback Dan Pastorini began wearing a flak jacket to protect his broken ribs, a practice continued in the 1990s by professional quarterbacks as well as many college quarterbacks. The lightweight flak jacket has layers

Rugby Danger?

Doctors have concluded that rugby injuries are no more numerous or more severe than soccer injuries, suggesting that rugby may be a safer sport than football (Stokes, 1994). Whereas leg injuries predominate in soccer, head and facial injuries predominate in rugby. For the 1992 season, the most common injuries for two Australian rugby leagues (Rugby League and Rugby Union) were lacerations to the head and face (11% and 20%, respectively) and concussions (8% and 5%; Seward, 1993). This study supports the view that helmet use is essential to reducing head injuries in football.

NFL TURF BATTLES

Year	Grass	AT
1964	22	0
1974	13	13
1984	11	17
1994	14	14

Table 2. *The NFL grass to artificial turf (AT) balance (since the latter's introduction in the Houston Astrodome in 1966) shows that many teams have returned to grass fields.*

of urethane-coated nylon filled with air. Several cylindrical air pockets, interconnected with fabric valves, remain open during normal movement to allow the jacket to conform the player's midsection. When a quarterback receives a hit to his ribs, the sudden increase in pressure closes the valves so that the air pockets absorb the blow. Tests have shown that flak jackets have the ability to deflect an impact of 587 pounds per square inch. One might expect that running backs and receivers would also wear the lightweight jackets to prevent rib injuries, but this is not the case because the jackets slightly restrict movement.

Artificial Turf versus Grass

At the start of the 1994 season half of the NFL home stadiums had artificial turf, as did many football fields (*see Table 2*). As the popularity of artificial surfaces increased during the 1970s, so did the debate over their merits as compared with grass. Critics of artificial turf contend that it is harder and faster, resulting in more injuries. Statistics, however, have yet to support this conclusion, as it has proved nearly impossible to design a statistically relevant study. A study cannot, for example, control for preexisting injuries, for weather-related field conditions, for differences among grass and artificial fields, and for differences in cleat design and length.

Critics and proponents of artificial turf do agree that players tend to be sorer after playing on artificial turf than on grass. The Chicago Bears' Dan Hampton, for example, retired after undergoing six operations on each knee. In 1992, the final season of his 12-year career, he was unable to recover as well or as quickly after a game on artificial turf than after a game on grass. Hampton could begin practicing within 3 days after a game played on grass; for artificial turf, he needed to rest for as long as a week, sometimes even missing the following Sunday's game. The NFL argues that there is no difference in the number of injuries sustained on grass and on artificial turf. However, even teams with artificial turf stadiums practice on grass fields.

Artificial turf originally cost less to install and less to maintain than grass, but by the 1990s this was no longer the case. When the Chicago Bears switched from artificial turf to grass in 1988, the cost of installation was slightly more than $1 million. The cost of putting in grass was around $700,000. Factoring in the additional cost of $25,000 to $40,000 per year to maintain a grass field, and the life span of an artificial turf field (8–10 years), the total 1990s cost is about the same. (Of course grass fields that experience heavy use and bad weather require more maintenance.)

Given similar costs, most future decisions about surface will likely be made in terms of other criteria, such as players' preferences and the merits of each field type. Artificial turf does have an advantage over natural grass, in that it is "tuneable" to players. As with indoor tracks that have been "tuned" for runners, artificial turf fields may be designed to complement the athletes' muscle elasticity (*see also RUNNING AND HURDLING*).

Artificial turf fields contain a cushion to more closely replicate the playing conditions of a grass field. Critics contend, however, that a ½-inch-thick layer of foam neither protects a player from injury from a fall nor lessens the chronic joint pain that results from running on a hard surface. By increasing the thickness of the foam and by continuing to set minimum surface standards, as was done in the Georgia Dome (a stadium used only for football), player injuries could be greatly reduced. Unfortunately, this is often impossible. For multipurpose fields designed for use by both baseball and football teams, such as the Minneapolis Metrodome, the field cannot be as cushioning because baseball must be played on a harder surface.

A softer surface helps prevent injuries, but the popular belief that grass is a much softer and more cushioning surface is unfounded. In fact, artificial turf is a softer surface on which players can accelerate more quickly. Softness can be categorized in two ways: a material's ability to absorb and then return energy to an object, in much the same way as a trampoline responds to an acrobat; and its ability to cushion an impact—decelerating an object over time, like the landing mats used by high jumpers. Both absorb energy over time, with the former returning energy to the object and the latter dissipating it (*see also EQUIPMENT MATERIALS*). In his study of the softness of athletic surfaces, Howard Brody, a physicist at the University of Pennsylvania, used a baseball bat–drop test and discovered that artificial turf provided a softer, more shock-absorbent surface than concrete, asphalt, clay, or even grass (Brody, 1992; *see Figure 6*).

Brody also found that surface deformation, which allows surer footing, was the greatest for artificial turf, and may perhaps be the

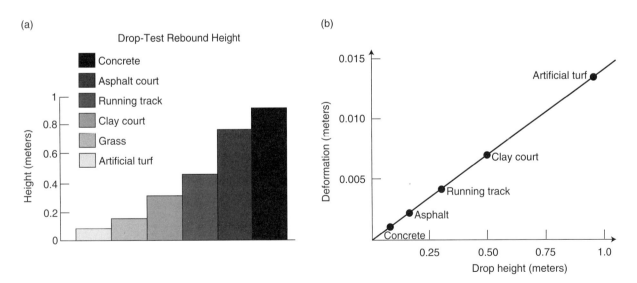

Figure 6.   *The "playability" of any surface is a function of its rebounding and deforming (cushioning) ability. (a) This bar graph shows the rebound height from a baseball bat-drop test for a variety of different court and field surfaces. (b) This line graph shows the surface deformation and interaction time for a baseball drop test. Grass varies the most with changing weather conditions. (Adapted from Brody, 1992)*

real cause of many artificial-turf injuries. The softness that absorbs shock also anchors the feet more because of the greater surface deformation. This friction prevents an athlete's feet from sliding. Some sliding is essential, however, as it increases the deceleration distance, thereby reducing the peak force acting between the athlete and the ground. Some scientists have argued that injuries could be greatly reduced by establishing a surface-shoe friction coefficient for sports. The shoe sole would work much like a ski binding that releases the ski upon an impact of high force. Once a certain coefficient of friction is reached, the sole would give way and allow the athlete's foot to slide.

The body also twists when an athlete's feet are well planted, further increasing his chance of injury. Sure footing allows players to stop and start and to accelerate and decelerate more quickly. In stopping, angular momentum (momentum about an axis of rotation) keeps a player's upper body in motion. When the feet are planted firmly, the body's joints must absorb more force to decelerate the body. This additional strain on the joints contributes to need for greater recovery time, as was the case with Dan Hampton.

Brody also found that an artificial surface, such as artificial turf, tends to lose its shock absorbency over time, particularly in more heavily trampled areas. Ultraviolet radiation, smog, dust, snow, ice, and traffic all cause artificial turf to deteriorate, contributing more and more to impact-related injuries, such as tendinitis and shin

NCAA INJURY STATISTICS FOR FOOTBALL, SOCCER, AND FIELD HOCKEY FOR THE 1984–91 SEASONS

Sport	Gender	Activity	Surface	% Injuries
Football	Male	Practice	Grass	11
			Artificial turf	11
		Game	Grass	7
			Artificial turf	12
Soccer	Male	Practice	Grass	27
			Artificial turf	32
		Game	Grass	26
			Artificial turf	31
	Female	Practice	Grass	26
			Artificial turf	28
		Game	Grass	22
			Artificial turf	28
Field hockey	Female	Practice	Grass	26
			Artificial turf	33
		Game	Grass	21
			Artificial turf	24

Table 3.

splints. The deteriorating artificial turf in Philadelphia's Veterans Stadium, for example, contributed to a number of severe injuries during the 1993 season. Several athletes, including Seth Joyner, Randall Cunningham, Scott Mitchell, and Wendell Davis, directly attributed their injuries to the field's hard surface. Regardless of whether artificial turf actually causes more injuries, the large number of indoor stadiums will probably ensure its continued use.

Cleats

Because a player may wear different shoes depending on the playing surface—longer cleats when playing on grass and short or spikeless shoes on artificial turf—it is virtually impossible to statistically determine the extent to which any particular type of playing surface contributes to injuries. But would the number of injuries be lower on natural grass than on artificial turf if players used the same type of cleat on both surfaces? Would regulations concerning cleat length for either surface cut down on injuries?

Players face a difficult choice. Although cleats allow for less slippage, greater traction translates into a greater probability of injury when a player makes a sudden stop or changes directions. Too much traction creates tremendous torques on the ankle and knee joints when a player's feet remain firmly planted. These torques are often compounded by the mass and momentum of two or three additional players. So, while a player might prefer to use shorter cleats to reduce his risk of injury, he will not often choose to use them when his opponent is wearing long cleats, as he will lose a traction advantage.

The NFL Championship game of 1934 between the New York Giants and Chicago Bears—dubbed the "Sneakers Game"—illustrates the importance of footing. On an extremely cold and icy day at the Polo Grounds in New York, the Giants trailed the Bears 13 to 3 midway through the third quarter and decided to discard their cleats for sneakers. The strategy proved successful, as the Giants were able to run past the Bears—whose players continued slipping on the frozen field—for a 30-to-13 victory. The hard, iced-over field allowed far greater sneaker-field friction than cleat-field friction. Any team making a voluntary unilateral decision to use safer cleats that are at the same time less effective (less cleat-field friction) places itself at a distinct disadvantage, albeit not as dramatic as the one the Giants imposed on the Bears.

Many experts argue that improvements in shoe and cleat technology, rather than changes in surface type, hold the most promise for reducing the number of injuries. In the 1990s, many players carry three or four types of shoes just for artificial turf. Some use a soccer-type shoe with eight half-inch plastic cleats; others prefer a basketball-style shoe with fifty or more smaller cleats; still others wear standard tennis shoes.

The heel cleat is another point of controversy. Anyone who understands the mechanics of the human body understands how slight an advantage the heel cleat provides. It provides only marginally better traction, yet it locks the heel in place, potentially resulting in major strains on the knee during cutting, turning, and player-to-player contact. The benefit of marginally bettering traction comes nowhere near counterbalancing the greater risk of injury.

Some experts have advocated a swivel-heel cleat to reduce this strain, but the style has not become popular. Unless mandated, it is highly unlikely that a swivel heel cleat design will become widely adopted. Although the heel cleat only offers a marginal advantage, it still gives some advantage, an advantage that most athletes would not be willing to forgo regardless of the associated increased injury risk.

John Zumerchik

References

Adrian, M., and J. Cooper. *Biomechanics*. Indianapolis: Benchmark Press, 1989.

Braid, T. "Computer-Model of a Punted Air-Filled and Helium-Filled Football." Argonne National Laboratory, 1995.

Brancazio, P. J. "Getting a Kick Out of Physics." *Discover* 64 (November 1984).

Brancazio, P. J. "Rigid-Body Dynamics of a Football." *American Journal of Physics* 55 (1987): 415ff.

Brancazio, P. J. *Sports Science*. New York: Simon and Schuster, 1984.

Brody, H. "Measuring the Softness of an Athletic Surface." *Physics Teacher* 30 (1992): 28–32.

Cerney, J. *The Prevent-System for Football Injuries*. Englewood Cliffs, New Jersey: Prentice-Hall, 1976.

Clark, K., and A. Braslow. "Football Fatalities in Actuarial Perspective." *Medicine Science Sports* 10 (1979): 94ff.

Farber, M. "The Worst Case: Doctors Warn That Repeated Concussions Can Lead to Permanent Brain Dysfunction." *Sports Illustrated*,19 December 1994, 38–46.

Northrip, J., et al. *Introduction to Biomechanic Analysis of Sport*. Dubuque, Iowa: Brown, 1979.

Paige, R. "What Research Tells the Coach about Football." Washington, D.C.: American Association for Health, Physical Education, and Recreation, 1973. Microfiche.

Reed, W. "Inside College Football." parts 1 and 2, *Sports Illustrated,* 1 November 1993, 72; 8 November 1993, 143–144.

Seward, H., et al. "Football Injuries in Australia at the Elite Level." *Medical Journal of Australia* 159 (1993): 298ff.

Stokes, M., et al. "A Season of Football Injuries." *International Journal of Medical Science* 163 (1994): 290ff.

Tietz, C. *Scientific Foundation of Sports Medicine*. Toronto: Decker, 1989.

Torrey, L. *Stretching the Limits*. New York: Dodd and Mead, 1985.

Gliding and Hang Gliding

SINCE ANCIENT TIMES, people have been fascinated with the idea of flying. Greek myth describes the flight of Daedalus and his unlucky son, Icarus. Leonardo da Vinci, the celebrated fifteenth-century artist and scientist, drew sketches of flying machines and made some attempts to explore the differences between powered and gliding flight. Although hot-air balloons carried humans into the air in France in the eighteenth century and kites that could carry a person appeared soon thereafter, it was not until the late nineteenth century that true flight was finally achieved. The first controlled flights were made not in powered aircraft but in gliders. Near the end of the nineteenth century, Otto Lilienthal designed and built a series of gliders; by 1896, he had made nearly 2,000 flights. He died that year in a crash of the last glider he had designed.

Many people considered the earliest gliders as merely a step toward achieving powered flight. The most famous early fliers, the Wright brothers, first built a series of gliders before they added an engine; but after the Wright brothers demonstrated that powered flight was possible, most of the early pioneers concentrated on improving powered aircraft. A few, however, remained dedicated to gliding for its own sake.

One such enthusiast was Oscar Ursinus, who organized several annual excursions of gliding enthusiasts to a site named the Wasserkuppe in Germany just after World War I. There they flew, talked about, designed, and even built gliders. Some of these early designs were oddly shaped, but by about 1922 the basic configuration of the modern sailplane took shape. As knowledge gained at the Wasserkuppe spread to other countries, new enthusiasts formed clubs and experimented with designs.

By the late 1930s, pilots from several countries, many of whom belonged to these gliding clubs, were regularly making flights over distances that had been unthinkable just a decade earlier. Worldwide interest prompted the scheduling of gliding as an event for the 1940 Olympics using a single design, named the Olympia. However, the onset of World War II canceled the 1940 Olympics and temporarily halted most recreational gliding in the western world. After the war, gliding resumed almost immediately in Europe and North America. Since then, there has been a continuing evolution of the sport through advances in aerodynamics, the availability of ever better materials, and increased knowledge of the physics underlying gliding. Pilots flying modern high-performance gliders can soar for hours and cover incredible distances.

In the 1990s, the typical glider flight begins with the pilot stepping into a modern fiberglass sailplane, fastening the seatbelts, and going through a preflight checklist. The actual flight begins with the launch, which can be either a leisurely tow to altitude by a powered aircraft or a quick kite-like climb at the end of a long cable being reeled in by a powerful winch on the ground. After the launch, the pilot and sailplane glide downward, losing altitude at a rate of a few feet per second until they encounter a thermal—a mass of air rising fast enough to carry them upward. After circling in the thermal and gaining a few thousand feet of altitude, the pilot may head off in the direction of a distant destination. Along the way, the glider will lose altitude between thermals but will enter thermals occasionally to regain altitude. After a flight of several hours, the pilot may land several hundred miles from takeoff site, having used no energy other than that which was extracted from thermals. The average speed and the distance traveled depend on the pilot's skill, the characteristics of the glider, and the weather. Of these, the pilot's skill is the most important.

The world records for unpowered soaring flight are truly remarkable. As of 1996, the record gain of height after release was 12,902 meters (42,303 ft., more than 8 mi.); the highest absolute altitude reached was 14,948 meters (49,009 ft., nearly 9.3 mi.); the greatest total distance flown was 1,647 kilometers (1,023 mi.); and the fastest average speed around a 100-kilometer (62-mi.) triangular circuit was about 195 kilometers per hour (121 MPH).

The high-performance gliders capable of achieving such records are costly. In the years just following World War II, gliders were made almost exclusively from wood and fabric; but modern gliders use materials such as carbon fiber and fiberglass and are made to precise specifications, with wing cross sections shaped to tolerances of a few thousandths of an inch. In the mid-1990s, a typical two-seat club

Figure 1. *The Glaser–Dirks DG 303 Elan. (Courtesy of Glaser–Dirks USA)*

GLIDER RECORDS

Tapping into airborne sources of energy allows glider flying to be much more than a gentle descent to earth. Some gliding records as of 1996 were:

1. Fastest average speed:

195 KPH (121 MPH) around a 100-kilometer (62-mi.) triangular circuit—Ingo Renner, 14 December 1982, Tocumwall, Australia

2. Greatest climb after release:

12,902 meters (42,303 ft., more than 8 mi.)—Paul Bikle, 25 February 1961, Mohave Lancaster, California

3. Highest absolute altitude reached:

14,948 meters (49,009 ft.)—Robert Harris, 17 February 1986, California City, California

4. Farthest distance flown (out-and-return):

1,647 kilometers (1,023 mi.)—Thomas Knauff, 25 April 1983, Ridge Soaring, Pennsylvania

5. Farthest distance flown (straight line):

1460 kilometers (907 mi.)—Hans Warner Gross, 25 April 1972, West Germany

trainer cost at least $40,000, and this was a modest sum compared with the price of a high-performance single-seater that would be competitive in a world-class gliding competition: more than $100,000. In the 1960s, when metal and fiberglass started to replace wood and costs started to increase, a number of gliding enthusiasts began to experiment with simpler, low-cost machines designed to be launched from foot, much like the early gliders designed by Lilienthal. These were called hang gliders. The first designs were based on the Rogallo wing, an improvement on parachute fabric originally developed as part of the United States' space program. The hang glider of the 1990s was much more refined—and much more expensive—than those designed in the 1960s; still, it offered a lower-cost alternative to the mainstream soaring movement.

The Physics of Flight

Flying was an extremely controversial idea until the ability to fly was actually proved. Before the Wright brothers demonstrated powered flight in the early 1900s, many other experimenters had tried and failed. Skeptics questioned whether powered flight would ever be possible, and some even believed they had proved that powered flight was impossible. The Wright brothers succeeded, in part, because they first sought to develop some understanding of the principles of flight. Their initial experiments took place on the ground with a wind tunnel that they had designed and built themselves. They were trying to understand the basic forces underlying flight—the forces of lift and drag.

Figure 2 shows a cross-section of an aircraft wing, as if the wing were stationary with the air moving toward it. Air flowing across the wing gives rise to a single net force, or a resultant force, on the wing; this force is conventionally considered as having two components, lift and drag. These two force components are perpendicular to one another: lift is the component of the force perpendicular to the oncoming airflow, and drag is the force parallel to it.

The cross-sectional shape of the wing is called the airfoil, and many textbooks explain lift in terms of Bernoulli's principle and airflow over the airfoil. Bernoulli's principle is a statement of the conservation of energy for fluids (*for an explanation, see BASKETBALL and VOLLEYBALL*). The usual textbook description is that the lift of an airfoil is due to lower pressure on the top surface of the wing and higher pressure on the bottom surface: the air has to go farther over the top than it does over the bottom and hence goes faster over the top. This is an unfortunate oversimplification which suggests that the most important factor producing lift is the shape of the airfoil. It is true that shape plays a role in determining lift, but shape is nowhere near as important as the orientation of the wing with respect to the airflow across it.

The airfoil deflects the oncoming air downward, thereby adding to it a downward component of momentum (*for a discussion of momentum, see also ACROBATICS or FOOTBALL*). This requires that the wing exert some downward force on the air and, by Newton's third law, that the air exert some upward force on the wing. Similarly, when one puts a hand out the window of a moving car and tilts the hand with respect to the airflow, one can experience a force that has an upward or downward direction, depending on how the hand is oriented with respect to the air. The hand can be curved or cupped to approximate the shape of an airfoil, but this will have much less effect on the lift than does changing the tilt of the hand with respect to the airflow.

The manner in which the wing provides lift is fairly straightforward. The total force of the air on the wing is equal and opposite to the force of the wing on the air, and this latter force is equal to the change of momentum, per unit time, of the air. The change of the momentum of the air (momentum has units of mass × velocity) depends both on the mass of air per unit time with which the wing interacts—the speed of the air going past the wing—and on the amount by which its speed is changed (which also depends on the speed at which it is going with respect to the wing):

Figure 2. *The angle of attack between the direction of oncoming airflow and the chord line of an airfoil is shown. The chord line is defined as a straight line joining the most forward point on the airfoil with the most rearward point.*

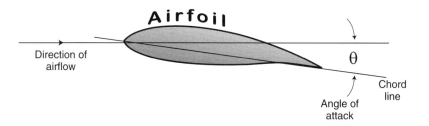

force = [mass of air per unit time] × [change in velocity of air]

The speed of the air appears in both the first term and the second term, so it is multiplied by itself. In other words, the total resultant force of the air on the wing is proportional to the square of the speed of the air past the wing. Both the lift and the drag are related to this force, so both of them are proportional to the square of the speed. Other factors that affect the two terms in this equation are the density of the air, the area of the wing, and, most important, the angle of attack. The angle of attack is the angle between the direction of airflow and the orientation of the wing (*see Figure 2; see also endnote for a more detailed description of how lift is related to airspeed or velocity*). An aircraft consists of more than just the wing. Other parts, such as the body, tail, wheels, and so on, add components of force to both the lift and the drag as the aircraft moves through the air. A powered aircraft, in level flight, will be in equilibrium—it will fly at a constant speed—when the forward force of the engine is equal to the total drag force and when the total lift force is equal to the weight of the aircraft (*see Figure 3a*).

In the case of a glider, there is no forward force from an engine, and the glider will be in equilibrium—it will fly at a constant velocity, but slightly downward instead of horizontally—only if the weight is equal and opposite to the total force (the vector sum of lift and drag; *see Figure 3b*). Since the drag force is along the direction of flight, the slope of the flight path of the glider is equal to the lift-to-drag ratio L/D. The ratio of horizontal forward speed, (which is approximately equal to airspeed) to vertically downward speed (which is called the sinking speed, or sink rate) is also given by this ratio. The slope of the flight path determines how far a glider will go from a given height in calm air. Some modern competition gliders have an L/D ratio of about 60 to 1 (60/1). This means that from a height of 5,280 feet (1 mi., or 1.609 km), these gliders can fly about 60 miles (97 km) before landing. By comparison, a space shuttle, with its short, stubby wings, has a much poorer L/D of about 3 to 1 (3/1); from a height of 1 mile, it can fly only 3 miles (4.8 km). Speed also affects L/D. A glider pilot changes speed by changing the attitude of the glider. Attitude is the

Figure 3. *The vector components of the forces on powered aircraft and gliders are shown for constant, nonaccelerated flight. (a) Force from the engine P is equal and opposite to drag D, while lift L is equal and opposite to weight W. (b) Lift and drag together are equal and opposite to weight.*

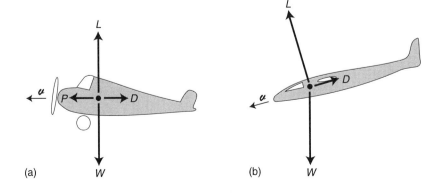

angle between the line of flight and the horizontal; by changing it, the pilot changes the angle of attack. To decrease speed, the control stick is pulled back, which raises the nose; the pilot can also decrease speed by shifting his or her own weight backward. In both cases, attitude will change and airspeed will decrease until equilibrium is regained. Both lift and drag forces will be different from what they were before the change in attitude, but the vector sum of the two forces will again be equal to the weight.

If the glide slopes are small, the magnitude of the lift will hardly change at all. In Figure 4, the glider on the right is flying down a slightly steeper glide slope than the glider on the left. The magnitude of the lift in each case, L_1 and L_2 respectively, is nearly the same and is approximately equal to the weight. Drag, however, varies significantly with attitude. The glider with the steeper glide slope has a significantly larger drag (D_2 is much greater than D_1) and will fly faster.

Drag has two components: profile drag and induced drag. Profile drag results because every part of the aircraft, including the wing, pushes through the air and therefore exerts a force on the air along the direction of flight. Profile drag is proportional to the square of the speed (*see endnote, equation 4*) and occurs whether or not the wing supplies lift.

Induced drag results because as the wing deflects air downward, there is a component of the change of momentum along the line of flight, in the direction of the drag. At slower speeds, the angle of attack of the wing must be greater in order to produce a lift equal to the weight (*see Figure 2*). One can experiment with induced drag when riding in a car by holding a hand out the window. The upward force (lift) and the backward force (total drag) on the hand are greater at higher speeds even though the hand is held at the same angle. In order to get the same upward force at a lower speed as at a high speed, one must increase the angle of the hand (the angle of attack) from what it was at the higher speed. Because the hand is flatter with respect to the air moving past it, the backward component of the force (drag) on the hand will be greater. This is induced drag.

At low speeds the angle of attack needed to produce enough lift to support the glider's weight must be large in order that induced drag is relatively large. At high speeds the necessary angle of attack

Figure 4. *At constant speed, the glider flying at a higher speed (left) has a steeper gliding angle than the slower glider (right). The resultant of the lift and drag force is always equal and opposite to weight W.*

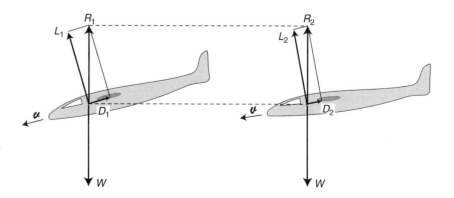

is lower, so induced drag is also lower. The magnitude of induced drag is proportional to 1 divided by airspeed (1/airspeed; in other words, it is inversely proportional to airspeed) for aircraft flying in equilibrium (at a constant airspeed).

For constant-speed flight, profile drag is proportional to the square of the speed; induced drag is inversely proportional to speed. Because L/D is equal to the ratio of horizontal speed to sinking speed, and horizontal speed is approximately equal to airspeed, a plot of sinking speed versus airspeed looks like a plot of drag versus airspeed (*see Figure 5a*).

Such a graph, showing sinking speed versus airspeed, called the polar of the glider, is the most informative piece of data about a glider's performance. The leftmost edge of the plot shows the slowest speed at which the glider can fly, called the stalling speed. The rightmost edge shows the maximum speed at which the glider was designed to fly without structural damage, called the redline speed, or the never-exceed speed. Redline speed is so called because this maximum speed appears on the airspeed indicator of the glider as a prominent red line, as a warning to the pilot.

A line drawn through the origin and tangential to the polar has a slope that is the reciprocal, or inverse, of the best L/D for the glide (*see Figure 5b*). The speed indicated by the point at which this line contacts the polar is called the "best speed to fly," as it indicates the flattest glide-path slope.

Flying at the airspeed corresponding to the bottom of the polar

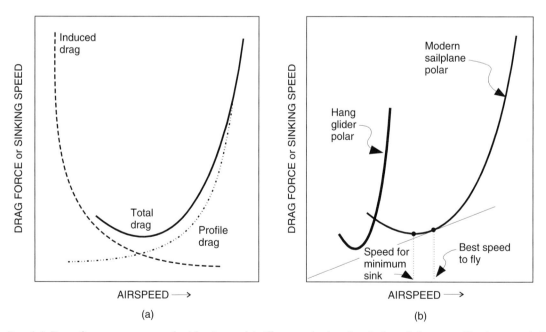

Figure 5. *(a) Drag force as compared with airspeed is illustrated, showing induced drag, profile drag, and their sum. (b) Because sinking speed is directly related to drag, the ordinate axis can also be shown as sinking speed. The polars of a modern sailplane and a hang glider are compared.*

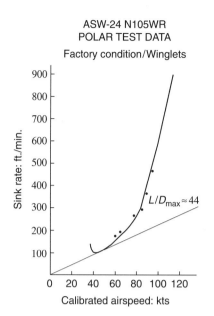

**ASW-24 N105WR
POLAR TEST DATA**

Factory condition/Winglets

$L/D_{max} \approx 44$

Sink rate: ft./min.

Calibrated airspeed: kts

Figure 6. *The polar for the ASW-24 sailplane is shown. The best lift-to-drag ratio L/D for this glider is about 44/1 at a best speed of about 79 KPM (49 MPH). (Data courtesy of Soaring Society of America.)*

gives the lowest possible sink rate. This speed is somewhat slower than the speed at which the glider has the flattest possible glide-path slope. Modern sailplanes have very broad polars and a minimum sink rate of about 0.6 meters per second (2 ft./sec.). This value depends partly on the glider's wing loading—the total weight of the glider divided by the area of the wing. Because hang gliders usually have lower wing loadings than sailplanes, they have lower sink rates and the speed at which this minimum sink rate occurs is less than that of a sailplane. However, hang gliders are not as streamlined as a sailplane, so they have greater profile drag and their polars are more steeply curved (*see Figure 5b*).

Figure 6 shows the measured polar of a glider that was still in production in 1996. Its best *L/D* is about 44 to 1 (44/1) at its optimal speed of about 49 knots (90 KPH or 55 MPH). The minimum sink rate for this glider is about 30.5 meters per minute (100 ft./ min.) at an airspeed of about 45 knots. The polar also allows the value of *L/D* at any speed to be calculated. For example, the glider has a sinking speed of about 274 meters per minute (900 ft./min.) at 110 knots, which corresponds to an *L/D* of about 12 to 1. Every glider pilot is well aware of the glider's polar. If the glider is flying at 110 knots at an altitude of only 610 meters (2,000 ft.) above the ground, the pilot will know, from the altitude-loss rate of 274 meters per minute (900 ft./min.), that there are only a few minutes left to either find another thermal or prepare for landing.

Glider competitions are basically races in which competitive gliders must have a good *L/D* at high speeds. Profile drag should be small because it is the most important component of drag at high speeds. Modern competitive gliders have narrow, streamlined bodies designed to reduce profile drag, and the small cross-section means that the pilot's position is reclined, rather than upright. Racing gliders also have smooth, rounded contours and joints that have been carefully sealed to reduce turbulence, as turbulence increases profile drag.

At the low-speed end of the polar, the most significant component of drag is induced drag. For a given wing area, induced drag can be reduced by designing the wing to be long and thin rather than short and wide. This ratio of wingspan (length) to wing chord (width) is called the aspect ratio. All modern gliders have wings with a very high aspect ratio—the wings are very long and narrow—in order to reduce induced drag.

These principles all apply to hang gliders as well. A hang glider has a large profile drag because rigging, bracing wires, and the pilot are all in the airstream. For this reason the polars of hang gliders are very steep, and the range of speeds for good performance is relatively small. Compared with regular gliders, hang gliders have a relatively low wing loading and, therefore, lower minimum sinking speeds. These minimum sinking speeds also occur at lower airspeeds than for regular gliders.

Sources of Energy

Gliding might have few enthusiasts if it consisted simply of a tow to some altitude and a glide straight back to the ground. For many people, the fun and the challenge of gliding lie in finding natural sources of energy that allow the glider to climb and to maintain height. Three sources of energy are widely used by gliders: (1) ridge, or slope, lift; (2) thermal lift; and (3) lee-wave lift. The first two have been known since antiquity from the study of birds that make use of both.

Slope Lift and Slope Soaring

The first human exploitation of slope lift was by the Wright brothers at Kill Devil Hill in 1902, when one of their early gliders maintained or perhaps even gained height briefly from slope lift. Otto Lilienthal, despite his numerous flights a decade earlier, had apparently neither observed nor experienced slope lift.

The basic principle behind slope soaring is very simple. Air flowing up a slope (*see Figure 7a*) has an upward vertical component of velocity. If a glider moving through this air has a rate of sink that is equal to this upward air velocity, it will maintain height. If the rate of sink is less than the upward air velocity, the glider will gain height. For a glider to maintain or gain height, the upward component of the wind velocity must be equal to or greater than the sinking speed of the glider. Because typical glider sink rates are about 0.6 meters per second (2 ft./sec.), a pilot need only find a place where there is a slope facing into the prevailing wind and where the upward component of the air velocity is often greater than 0.6 meters. The pioneers of the gliding movement in the 1920s and 1930s chose sites that fulfilled these requirements, such as the Wasserkuppe in Germany, Long Mynd and Camphill in England, and Elmira in New York.

The best sites for slope soaring have a long ridge facing into the wind. The glider is aimed partially into the wind in order to fly on a path over the ground that is parallel to the slope. It flies back and

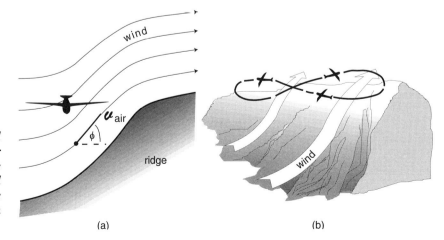

Figure 7. *(a) A cross-sectional view of a ridge is shown with a glider flying in front of it; φ is the angle between the wind and the horizontal at the location of the glider. (b) These flight paths are normally used in slope soaring.*

(a)   (b)

forth along the slope (*see Figure 7b*). There is some etiquette involved in flying these slopes, since there may be several gliders in the air at one time, flying in either direction. Rules of the "road" enable pilots to determine, for example, who flies closest to the slope when gliders are on opposing courses and how to turn on a slope to avoid collisions (always away from the slope).

Hang gliders are particularly suitable for slope soaring, since their low sinking speed allows them to soar on days when the wind is too slow to sustain regular gliders. Their slower flying speeds and smaller turning radii also allow them to use ridges that are too short for regular gliders. Many sites suitable for hang glider slope soaring are found along ridges facing the ocean or a large lake. When the weather provides a steady, moderate onshore breeze, such places become popular spots for hang gliding enthusiasts.

Slope soaring is usually confined to areas only a mile or two in diameter. The long ridge of the Allegheny Mountains, however, runs along the eastern United States from north to south. In the winter, strong winds often blow nearly perpendicular to this ridge, making it one of the best sites in the world for slope soaring. It has been exploited by glider pilots for some long-distance flights. The "out-and-return" world record as of 1996 had been flown along this ridge, for a distance of 1,646 kilometers (1,023 mi.)—more than 822 kilometers (511 mi.) out and back.

Thermal Lift

Whereas slope lift is caused by the motion of air along the contours of the ground, thermal lift is caused by convection—the transfer of heat by the physical motion of material—in the atmosphere. Many commercial airline passengers have experienced this same process as an updraft, or turbulence.

Convection can be demonstrated by a pot of water set on a stove's heating element. As the water at the bottom is heated by the element, it rises upward and is replaced by colder water from the top, which moves down to occupy the space: heat is being transferred by actual motion of the water. In principally the same way, heat is transferred from the ground to the air in the atmosphere.

If the atmosphere had a constant temperature at all heights above the ground, air that was slightly warmed would become less dense than its surrounding air and, therefore, would start to slowly rise. As the air reached a higher altitude, the surrounding pressure would be less and the air would expand and become cooler. If the air were cooler than its surroundings, it would also be denser than its surroundings and thus would sink. In other words, if the atmosphere were all at the same temperature, any air that was momentarily displaced upward would soon return downward to its original position. Such an atmosphere would be stable, and no convection would occur. If the atmosphere were actually like this, gliding would consist only of a tow to altitude followed by a downhill slide to the ground.

Gliding is exciting precisely because the atmosphere is rarely stable and because the earth's atmosphere is one in which the temperature is not the same at all altitudes. Temperatures decrease with altitude, at least up to the bottom of the stratosphere; the rate of decrease is called the atmospheric lapse rate. In the lower atmosphere, the value of this lapse rate depends on the altitude, local weather conditions, and the time of day. The rate at which air cools by itself as it rises is called the adiabatic lapse rate. When the actual atmospheric lapse rate is greater than the adiabatic lapse rate, any parcel of warmer air displaced upward will cool but will still be warmer than the surrounding outside air and so will keep on rising. When this happens, the atmosphere is said to be unstable, although the process is simply convection. In short, convection occurs when the temperature of the atmosphere decreases with height at a rate greater than the adiabatic lapse rate.

During a typical summertime daily cycle, the ground cools during the night because it radiates heat; the atmosphere as a whole does not. With sunrise, the ground temperature and the temperature of the air near the ground remain cool. The atmosphere is very stable near the ground and the temperature increases with height until, at some altitude, the gradient returns to its normal, decreasing atmospheric lapse rate. Meteorologists call this an inversion. As the day progresses, local solar heating causes the air near the ground to warm, eventually restoring the atmospheric lapse rate to near normal.

If the atmospheric lapse rate becomes greater than the adiabatic lapse rate, air that is warmer than the surrounding air will continue to rise, and convection will start. This may happen because, for many reasons, the sun warms the earth's surface much faster than it warms the air. One important reason is that air is transparent and does not absorb much solar energy. Another reason is that the earth does not have a smooth, uniform surface. Darker areas, such as freshly plowed fields, absorb more sunlight and cause the air above them to become warmer than air above neighboring lighter lands. If there is a wind, sheltered areas will be warmer than unsheltered areas. In fact, there are hundreds of reasons why some areas of the earth may be warmer or colder than adjacent regions (*see Figure 8*). Once air becomes a certain degree warmer than the surrounding air, a "bubble," or pocket, perhaps several hundred feet in size, breaks loose from the surface of the earth and begins ascending, creating a thermal. The shape and size of these thermals vary, and they often have an upward, swirling motion, similar to the way a smoke ring rises.

A person standing on the ground might detect a thermal breaking loose as a sudden change in direction of the breeze, a sudden gust of wind, or perhaps a circular motion of tall grass in a large field. When the atmospheric lapse rate increases as the ground becomes hotter, the instabilities become stronger, causing the air to rise more rapidly. Sometimes air rises with such strength and speed that it carries bits of grass and loose dirt upward, causing small whirlwinds, or dust devils.

The thermal continues rising and cooling until the moisture it

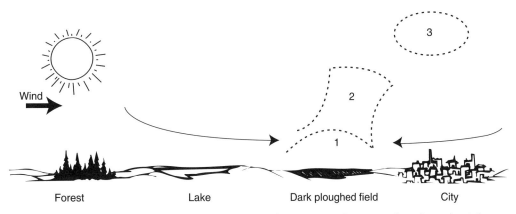

Figure 8. *Any part of the earth's surface that heats up more than surrounding areas has the potential to generate thermals—the principal source of energy for gliders. Here, (1) an air bubble forms because the air directly over the plowed field is warmer than surrounding ground-level air. (2) As the warm air begins to rise, forming a column, the surrounding cooler, denser air flows in under the column. (3) The warm air mass breaks away, heading upward and downwind. The thermal keeps rising until the moisture in it starts to condense, forming a cumulous cloud. Glider pilots "hop" from cloud to cloud because they know that a cumulous cloud will persist as long as the thermal keeps feeding it. (Adapted from Whittall, 1984)*

carries begins to condense and form a fair-weather cumulus cloud, which will exist as long as the thermal keeps feeding it. As the bottom of the thermal reaches the cloud base, no further convection occurs and the cloud begins to dissipate. A cumulus may last only tens of minutes, depending on the strength and size of the thermals.

Because the overall appearance of the sky may be unchanged, cumulus clouds often appear to last a whole summer day. This is caused by an ongoing process of convection taking place in the atmosphere, but an individual cumulus cloud does not last very long. By carefully watching a single puffy, white cumulus cloud, one can see it become ragged and eventually disappear within just a few tens of minutes.

Since thermals are confined in area and drift with the wind, a glider pilot must circle continuously to stay in a thermal. Cross-country flights are accomplished by climbing in a thermal, circling continuously until the glider is at cloud base or until the pilot decides that the glider is high enough, and then setting out on a course toward the distant goal. Altitude is lost when flying straight, but if thermals are numerous the pilot will climb by circling in each one. A cross-country flight, therefore, consists of a series of circling climbs followed by straight glides between thermals.

The secret of gliding for long distances—such as cross-country—is to make the best time possible. Because there are only a limited number of hours of good solar heating in any single day, distance gliding requires a high average speed, which depends on the time spent circling in thermals and the rate of climb. When the rate of climb in thermals is high, less time is needed to gain sufficient height to set off on the straight, or traveling, portions of the flight. On days when thermals are weak, time spent in thermals is necessarily longer, so the average cross-country speed may be much lower. Average speed also depends on the ability of the pilot to find thermals and exploit them. Thermal flying takes a keen eye and superior judgment. Even for pilots with years of experience, efficient thermal flying is very demanding and requires skill and concentration.

Most contest flights are races around a fixed course of a few hundred kilometers using thermals. Although a cumulus cloud is an obvious sign of a thermal, the glider pilot must continually make assessments. Is the cloud still forming because the thermal is still flowing upward from underneath? Is the cloud dissolving because the thermal underneath it has stopped? On really good days, the clouds may form in long rows, called "cloud streets," along the wind direction. At such times, one can often fly in roughly a straight line along these cloud streets, slowing down under the individual cumulus clouds to gain height from the thermals under them, and then flying quickly between them. Because the flight path is more or less in a straight line, but has a lot of motions upward (in the thermals) and downward (between the thermals), flying along cloud streets is called "dolphining." Dolphining from thermal to thermal usually results in high average speeds because no time is lost in circling.

Lee-Wave Lift

Lee waves are the least common form of lift used by glider pilots. They occur when the atmosphere is very stable with strong surface winds blowing perpendicular to ridges or mountain chains (*see Figure 9*). Lee waves form over and downwind of the ridge, whereas normal slope lift is found upwind of the slope. Because the atmosphere is most stable in the winter, lee waves tend to be more common at that time of year. Gliders can exploit these waves by flying into the headwind and staying at approximately the same relative position over the ground in an upgoing part of the wave. When conditions are right, these waves, which are downwind of the peaks, often allow pilots to reach extreme heights. A world altitude record of over 14,021 meters (46,000 ft.) was set by a glider flying in a lee wave generated over the Tehachapi Mountains in California, where the cliff causing the wave was itself only about 1,067 meters (3,500 ft.) high.

Lee waves occur in mountainous locations and are often indicated by the presence of lenticular clouds—very thin, lens-shaped clouds, which are often seen just downwind of a mountain range. Residents of Denver, Colorado, often see lenticular clouds over the mountains to the west because the prevailing wind comes from the west. In England, where strong, cold winds frequently blow in from the Atlantic Ocean, glider pilots routinely reach lee waves by climbing in slope lifts over one of the many mountain ranges until they reach an altitude where the waves exist.

In New Zealand, a glider was launched at a very low altitude and the pilot was able to slope soar and gain altitude over a mountain range near the southern tip of the South Island, where he contacted a lee wave after crossing the peak of the range and gained consider-

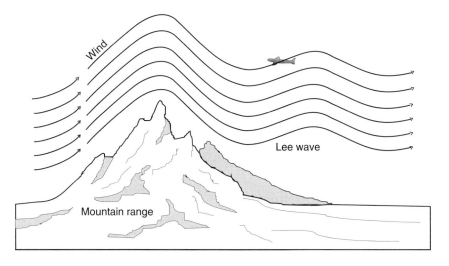

Figure 9. *Shown here are lee waves formed behind the crest of a mountain range.*

able altitude. He then flew in this lee wave to the northern tip of the South Island. His considerable height enabled him to glide downward across the ocean between the islands, to contact a lee wave over the mountains in the North Island, and then to fly onward to the northern tip of the North Island, where he landed. The unusual flight was made possible by the convergence of a number of factors: highly favorable weather, a very skilled pilot, and a high-performance glider.

Gliding as a Sport

Gliding is enjoyed by thousands of people worldwide. The sport's popularity varies from country to country, as does the way in which it is organized. Most noncompetitive gliding is organized through clubs, each of which may collectively own only a few two-seated training gliders and a small number of single-seaters. Regular gliders are fairly expensive, and the sport requires many individuals and some expensive equipment for the process of launch and recovery. In the United States and in a few other countries, commercial gliding sites offer individual training and glider rentals. Because hang gliders are far less expensive and more portable, they are typically owned by individuals, who may band together in loose informal clubs but usually fly as individual owners.

Gliding is regulated by the Federation Aeronautique International (FAI), which sets standards and oversees records. There are a number of FAI awards, which are based on proficiency. In the early days of gliding, when it was largely self-taught, tasks as simple as turning were rewarded with FAI badges. In the 1990s, the first badge was the C badge, which required some soaring flight. Next were the silver C and gold C badges. The gold C required a soaring flight of more than 5 hours' duration, a distance flight of more than 300 kilometers (186 mi.), and a postlaunch altitude gain of more than 3 kilometers

(1.86 mi.). The gold C badge could be augmented by three diamonds, awarded for a flight of more than 300 kilometers to a predetermined goal, a flight of more than 500 kilometers (310 mi.), and a gain in height of 5 kilometers (3.1 mi.). As of 1996, only a few thousand people worldwide had completed a gold badge with three diamonds.

In early competitions, goals included tasks such as staying up longest and traveling farthest. At sites where the wind blows steadily up a slope, the duration of a flight was a matter of personal endurance—how long the pilot could stay awake. Shortly after World War II, duration was dropped as a competition task. By the 1960s, distance was also dropped, as the distances flown were becoming so extreme that it often took more than a day for the retrieve crew to reach and bring back the glider and its pilot.

In the 1990s, most competitions were races around a fixed course, announced at the beginning of each day, and thermals were the principal form of lift. At some places along the flight path, the pilots might be able to use slope lift as well. A course might be 100 to 500 kilometers (62–310 mi.) around a triangle or a simple "out and return." The choice and length of a path would depend on the skill of the contestants and on probable weather conditions. To win a gliding race requires good knowledge of meteorology and of the physics of gliding. For a particular glider and a given rate of climb, there is a between-thermal flight speed to maximize the average cross-country speed. The presence of a headwind or tailwind, however, modifies the optimum speed, and the pilot must be continually aware of the wind speed and direction at the current altitude.

Technology has assisted the pilots of the 1990s, who usually carry small nomographs, computers that help them determine the optimum between-thermal flight speed on the basis of wind speed, wind direction, and estimated rate of climb in thermals. Even with this high technology, often only considerable experience and keen judgment help a pilot decide whether to take or bypass any particular thermal and when to leave a thermal.

In a race, launch order is normally determined by random draw, and launched pilots may loiter by soaring locally without going through the starting "gate" until they judge that the time is right to start the race. Knowing when to start a race is very tricky, because arranging for a flight to pass through the gate at the optimum time and with the maximum allowed height is complicated by the random time of launch. For pilots launched late, there may be no time to wait for the best conditions; for pilots launched early, starting too soon can be a problem. Choosing the right time to begin the course requires a running evaluation of what the weather is likely to be over the course. In general, flight conditions are poor in the early morning, when convection is just beginning and when cumulus clouds are just starting to appear. Conditions peak later in the day and diminish toward evening. The performance of the glider is just one factor in winning a race; the pilot's overall skill—particularly judging and reading thermals—is often much more significant.

Competition

Typical glider competitions are set up around a triangular course of 100 to 500 kilometers (62–310 mi.). The course will vary depending on expected weather conditions, and on the skill of the contestants.

In any competition, there are usually several classes of gliders. The most common classes are standard and open. "Standard class" is an FAI definition in which, for example, wingspan is limited to 15 meters (49.2 ft.). "Open class" is unrestricted and generally includes the highest-performance gliders. On the day of any given contest, the tasks for the standard and open classes are usually quite different, with the open class having much more difficult tasks. However, the sophistication of gliders in both standard and open class has increased—as has their cost—and as a result, the sport of competitive gliding has become more and more exclusive.

In an attempt to reverse this trend, the FAI created a "world class" in late 1994, in which all pilots would compete using a single glider design. This design is very similar in principle (although vastly superior) to what was proposed for the 1940 Olympics. The "world class" design was itself chosen through a competion, in which—in an effort to keep costs reasonable—it was specified that the glider was to cost no more than 50 percent of a "standard class" glider. The winning design, the PW-5—submitted by a group of faculty members and students from Warsaw Technical University—was a conventional modern construction of molded fiberglass with a very respectable best L/D of about 32 to 5 (32/5). It was certified in 1994 and was to be offered for manufacture in other countries. Worldwide competition was expected to begin when the FAI determined that a sufficient number of PW-5s existed to make competition worthwhile.

James A. Koehler

Endnote

The magnitude of the net force on a wing is equal to change of momentum per unit time of the air passing by the wing:

$$F = \frac{dp}{dt}$$

Change in momentum dp will depend on the mass of air moving past the airfoil per unit time, on the magnitude of its velocity, and on the change of direction. A measure of change of direction is angle of attack θ. Because change of momentum depends on mass per unit time interacting with the wing, it will depend on the density of the air ρ, on the area A of the wing, and on the velocity v of the air with respect to the wing. Change in momentum also depends on the magnitude of velocity v, so the velocity is squared. The way the change of momentum varies with the angle of attack is designated by a function, $G(\theta)$, producing the equation:

$$F \propto \rho v^2 A G(\theta)$$

where $\propto$ means "proportional to."

Lift and drag both depend on this force, so the equations for lift and drag are similar. By adding constants of proportionality that take into account the angle of attack, the equations for both the lift component L and the drag component D are (as usually written):

$$L = \frac{1}{2} C_L \rho A v^2$$

$$D = \frac{1}{2} C_D \rho A v^2$$

where C_L and C_D are the coefficients of lift and drag, respectively, and both contain the angle of attack dependence. In other words, each coefficient is a function of angle of attack. For a given airfoil shape, the coefficients may be evaluated by building a model of the airfoil and actually measuring lift and drag as a function of angle of attack in a wind tunnel, or by numerical calculation by computer, using suitable modern theories.

References

Hunter, Lloyd. "The Art and Physics of Soaring." *Physics Today* 37 (1984): 34–40.

Whittall, N. *The Complete Hang Gliding Guide*. London: Adams Charles Black, 1984.

Golf

GOLF HAS A UNIQUE OBJECTIVE: to propel a ball from a resting position through the air, around obstacles, and across the ground until it drops into a small hole or cup. The earliest roots of golf may go back to ball-and-club sports of ancient times, but the origins of the modern sport have long been a subject of controversy: although many historians believe that golf was first developed in Scotland in the fifteenth century, some argue that it can be traced to Holland.

There is rich documentary evidence of early golf in Scotland, and it can be seen from these records that some of the oldest Scottish courses, still in use in the 1990s, have remained virtually unchanged for centuries. St. Andrews, on the east coast of Scotland, was an important site in the early development of the game; in fact, golf became so widely popular there that James II contemplated banning it in 1457. Scotland was then at war with England, and the king feared that his subjects were spending too much time playing golf and too little time practicing archery—a skill crucial to the defense of the kingdom. However, concerned that a total ban would set off a rebellion, he instead lengthened the hours required for archery practice. In 1491, James IV did ban the game, though he himself would later became an avid player.

By the eighteenth century, golf had spread to North America, and by the nineteenth century it was widely played in India and other British colonies east of Europe. The twentieth century saw the sport gain a worldwide popularity that continues to grow. As of 1996, golf was played by more than 30 million people in eighty countries, with the number of players and courses increasing annually—Japan, for example, had more than 8 million golfers. In Japan, many golfers use multilevel driving ranges where hundreds of people can practice at the same time. These multilevel ranges are actually as close as some Japanese players may ever come to playing a real round of golf. Because land is scarce in Japan, golf is an expensive luxury—it can cost as much as $400,000 to join a club and the same amount for annual membership fees—and even club members must often reserve tee time months or sometimes years in advance.

This article will explore some of the physics of the game of golf, including swing power, putting, golf clubs, and the aerodynamics of golf balls.

Swing Power

One of the most difficult challenges in golf is to transmit as much power as possible from the club head to the ball without sacrificing precision and control. A professional golfer can accelerate the club head to a velocity of 129 to 161 KPH (80–120 MPH), while squarely striking a ball with a 4.27-centimeter (1.68-in.) diameter in a time frame of about 1 millisecond. If the ball is struck as little as 2 degrees off-square, a 229-meter (250-yd.) drive can be as much as 18 to 27 meters (20–30 yd.) off target. If the impact is farther off-center, and the club twists during contact, the ball can diverge even more from its target

Many people find it puzzling that golfers of small stature are able to hit the ball for great distances. For example, the professional golfer Ian Woosman, 5 feet 4 inches (128 cm) tall, could drive the ball 274 meters (300 yd.); by way of comparison, a recreational player who stands 6 feet 5 inches (192.5 cm) and weighs 250 pounds (114 kg) may be pleased with a drive of 229 meters (250 yd.). Since a player with considerable mass clearly has the potential to generate much more momentum (mass × velocity) than a smaller player like Woosman, why does Woosman's ball travel farther?

Part of the reason is that a player of Woosman's caliber is able to generate greater power—that is, work (force × distance) divided by time interval (*see also WEIGHT LIFTING*). Through many hours of practice, players at Woosman's level have learned how to move the club head very far very fast—in just a few milliseconds. A professional player constantly evaluates and fine-tunes the swing, and develops motor memory so that the perfected swing can be repeated consistently. Motor memory, in essence, is a "feel" for what Newton's laws of motion explain theoretically: how to transfer momentum to the ball so that the collision of club head and ball is optimized.

It should be noted that good golfers do not all develop the same swing. In fact, even among touring professionals the range of different swings seems almost infinite, and each golfer has what is known as a "swing signature": an individaul pattern of three-dimensional angles in relation to the club—at the shoulders, at the elbow, and at the wrist. It is by studying films of such "signatures" that scientists are able to measure the movements of the golf club over time to determine rate of acceleration, torque (rotational force about a pivot point), and total power delivered.

Nevertheless, despite differences in swing signatures, all swings abide by the same basic principles. A golfer attempts to transfer as much muscle power from the slower, more powerful legs, thighs, and back to the left arm (for a right-handed golfer) as it pulls the club through the swing. To achieve this transfer of power, a golfer needs to recruit as many fast-twitch (explosive) muscles as possible (*for an explanation of slow- and fast-twitch muscles, see SKELETAL MUSCLE*). About 50 to 60 percent of the body's muscle mass is located in

Figure 1. *The forward movement of the hips that initiates the downswing—a shift forward in the center of gravity—significantly increases the momentum of the club head and has the potential to significantly increase the transfer of momentum to the ball. The hip and leg muscles contribute 60 to 80 percent of the total power generated during a good driving swing.*

Swing Power

Club-head velocity can reach from 129 to 161 KPH (80–100 MPH) for irons and from 161 to 201 KPH (100–125 MPH) for the drivers. After an efficient transfer of momentum, the ball comes off the club head at speeds in excess of 241 KPH (150 MPH), with a backspin of over 8,000 RPM. During the 1 millisecond of contact, the club head exerts a force of about 600 inch-pounds on the ball. (Shorupa, 1992)

the lower body—that is, away from the actual swing action—and the golfer must recruit these muscles to deliver most of the power of the swing. Two professional golfers who demonstrate the importance of lower-body power are Jack Nicklaus and John Daly, who both have a proportionately large lower body that can generate tremendous drives. In *Golf My Way*, Nicklaus emphasized the importance of lower-body muscularity and "hitting the ball with your legs."

Although generating enough power to hit long drives is not everything, it certainly helps improve a golfer's overall game. A long drive allows a chipping wedge to be used for a second shot to the green, and this gives a tremendous advantage over an opponent whose shorter drive makes a long iron necessary for the second shot. Thus a good drive is the equivalent of being first out of the blocks in a sprint: it does not guarantee winning the race, but it definitely improves the odds.

A golf stroke can be analyzed as what physicists call a "two-rod model" (*see Figure 5 and the related discussion below*): the two rods—the arm and the club—are joined at the wrists. As the golfer comes forward through the swing, the center of gravity (geometric center of mass distribution) shifts, significantly increasing the momentum of the club head and thus, potentially, the momentum of the ball (*see Figure 1*). A well-timed swing can markedly increase the ball's velocity. Alistair Cochran, a Scottish physicist (and golfer), calculated that the forward movement of the hips and the forces generated by the hip and leg muscles during the downswing account for 2.5 horsepower (1,864 watts) of the total 3 to 4 horsepower (2,337–2,983 watts) generated during a good drive swing (Cochran, 1968). The large muscles of the lower body, therefore, make a huge contribution to the power of the swing.

Thus the tremendous drives generated by professionals, such as Ian Woosman, can be attributed to partly to power—including lower-body power. Other factors, of course, are excellent execution and timing, and precise club rotation.

Stance and Weight Distribution

Balance is essential to a good swing. This depends considerably on stance and distribution of body weight.

For a driver, professionals advise that the ball should "lie" (be positioned) in line with the inside of the left foot (for a right-handed golfer); for other clubs, the advice varies considerably. Some professionals argue that as clubs become progressively shorter—from the 2-iron through the 9-iron—the ball should be positioned increasingly back, toward the right foot. Another approach is to place the ball in line with the inside of the left foot for all shots. This second approach probably makes more sense in terms of consistency, as the ball will be addressed the same way for every swing. If the ball is postioned more and more toward the rear foot depending on which club is being used, the ball is hit earlier in the swing with some shots than with others, and thus the golfer may have difficulty developing consistency; accordingly, most coaches recommend that beginners line up with the

Optimum Ball Position?

Some professionals advise that the ball should be positioned in line with the inside of the left foot; others recommend that the shorter the iron, the farther back toward the right foot the ball should lie. For most golfers, it is best to try to address the ball the same way for all clubs to ensure consistency in the swing.

ball the same way all the time. However, this consideration is less important for professional golfers, who spend many hours each day practicing, than it is for recreational golfers.

In the most typical stance, the feet are positioned toes out (duck-like) and no farther part than shoulder width. A stance that is too wide restricts hip rotation during both the backswing and the downswing. The knees should be bent slightly to enable the hips to rotate freely, but excessive knee bend should be avoided—as with many apsects of life, too much of a good thing can prove detrimental. The tremendous rotational force away from the body created during the downswing pulls the shoulders down with about 100 pounds of force during the impact of club head and ball, and during the follow-through. If the knees are bent too much while all this force is pulling the body, the path of the club head can become too high, producing a weak "topped" shot.

For the golfer's center of gravity to be in a well-balanced position, body weight should be fairly evenly distributed between the two feet. However, weight distribution can vary depending on the club being used. For woods and long irons, 60 percent of body weight should be positioned over the right foot and 40 percent over the left foot; for midirons and short clubs, 40 percent of body weight is over the right foot and 60 percent over the left. (This is for a right-handed golfer; for a left-handed golfer, the proportions are reversed.) To execute a well-balanced backswing and downswing, weight should be slightly over the balls of the feet. If the toes cannot be wiggled easily, body weight is too far forward.

With regard to the position of the hands, calculations by the physicist Ted Jorgensen concur with the advice of professional golfers: at the impact between club head and ball, the optimal position for the hands is ahead of the ball (Jorgensen, 1994). Thus, it makes sense to keep the hands ahead of the ball before beginning the backswing, keeping the club face square, or perpendicular, to the intended target. The swing should be as pendulum-like as possible, so that the two arms can work in concert; to accomplish this, the elbows should be separated by about the width of a fist and should remain so throughout the swing.

Backswing

The backswing may be the most unappreciated aspect of the golf stroke, because it is often regarded as simply a preparatory movement. Actually, a number of subtle aspects of the backswing are vital to reaching an optimal position from which to start the downswing.

Before beginning a backswing, a professional golfer often goes through a "wobble" or "shake" maneuver. This movement is often taken as a sign of nervousness, but it serves the same purpose as analogous movements in other sports: to activate muscle memory. (Basketball shooters, similarly, bend their knees, dribble, and rotate the ball in their hands before a free throw; baseball players take practice swings.) "Muscle memory" is a process whereby the muscles move in a familiar manner, conditioned by training and by past experience.

The backswing used by professional golfers varies considerably with regard to tilt: some players use an underarm motion, while others prefer a roundhouse motion. In a study of elite professionals, the biomechanist David Williams found that although the path of the hands varied very little from player to player, the path of the club head varied considerably (Williams, 1969). Some golfers use an upright, vertical swing, while others use a flatter, more level swing.

Much of the difference between backswings may be attributed to equipment or to individual physiology. Clubs with a shorter shaft are usually swung on a more vertical plane. Physiologically, the relative rotation of the hips and shoulders greatly determines the plane of the swing. Hip rotation alone results in a very flat swing; shoulder rotation with little hip rotation results in a very upright swing. Neither style is intrinsically superior. Although most professionals recommend an underarm swing over a roundhouse swing, the choice is primarily a matter of personal style and personal preferences regarding equipment.

The club head begins its backward movement with a combination of hip and shoulder turning and an opening toward the golfer's backside. This pulling force should be applied by the entire right side of the body (for a right-handed golfer), not just by the arms and the hands. This, in essence, is a cocking motion, similar in principle to the coiling or "loading" of a spring. A golfer who brings back only the arms and hands is coiling or loading only the fast-moving muscles, not the more powerful slow-moving muscles of the lower body. Loading on the backswing creates a source of rotational power as the hips and shoulders rotate around the axis located on the right side of the body. The golfer should feel coiled tension, or stretching, throughout much of left side of the body as weight shifts to the right heel.

The effective shift of body weight during the backswing (*see Figure 2*) is crucial for maintaining balance and transferring maximum momentum during the downswing. For a right-handed golfer, body weight moves forward onto the left toes and backward onto the right heel. Shifting weight in this manner keeps the body's center of gravity stationary as the hips are turned, countering the shift caused by bringing the arms back during the backswing. Many golfers believe, mistakenly, that weight shifts from the left foot to the right foot during the backswing, but the major transfer is actually from toe to heel for the right foot and, to a lesser degree, from heel to toe for the left foot. There is very little, if any, backward and forward motion.

Seen from above, the backswing looks as though the golfer is coiling like a spring around a vertical axis. To assist in this twisting, the left arm remains straight while the right arm folds toward the body with the elbow pointing down and back, not out and up. This subtle motion creates a rotational effect around the vertical axis that leads the wrists to cock; it continues until the backswing is finished. How readily the wrists cock is mainly determined by the flexibility of the golfer's wrists and by the speed of the backswing.

When the backswing is overly deliberate (too slow), little momentum is generated and the angle of the wrist cock immediately before

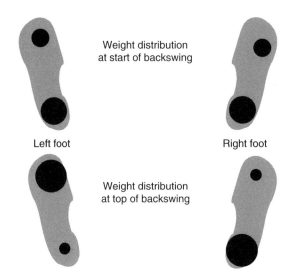

Figure 2. *In the backswing, optimal weight distribution changes from the start to the top of the swing. At the top of the backswing, weight distribution should be primarily over the ball of the left foot and the heel of the right foot. The view here is from above. (Adapted from Jorgensen, 1994)*

the downswing will be insufficient. This is called a "late hit." Cochran found that to increase coiling power, the forward motion of the hips should begin approximately 0.1 second before the club head reaches the top of the backswing (Cochran, 1968). That is, the hips begin to move forward while the club is still moving back and up. When this is done properly, there is no need for hesitation at the the top of the backswing—the "takeaway point"—and so additional velocity can be attained from the rebounding elasticity of the musculoskeletal system (*see also SKELETAL SYSTEM*).

Films of professional golfers during the backswing show that while the motions of the legs, hips, and shoulders are remarkably similar, there is considerable variation in the position of hand and club at the finishing point. Many casual golfers believe that the higher and the farther back the club is taken during the backswing, the greater the velocity of the club head at impact with the ball. While this may be true about swinging a sledgehammer, it does not apply to a golf swing. Jorgensen found that a golfer exerts the same force with an exaggerated backswing as with a reduced backswing and that the difference in speed of the club head at impact is minimal—the speed with a reduced backswing is only 2.5 percent less (Jorgensen, 1994). Also, exaggerated backswing increases the risk of not hitting the ball cleanly, and this risk outweighs the marginal increase in distance.

Wrist-cock angle is a far more important factor than the amount of backswing: an increase in wrist-cock angle at the takeaway point does significantly increase the speed of the club head at impact. Jorgensen looked at swings with wrist-cock angles of 90 degrees, 110 degrees, and 130 degrees (*see Figure 3*). He found that the larger the angle during backswing, and the longer the golfer could delay

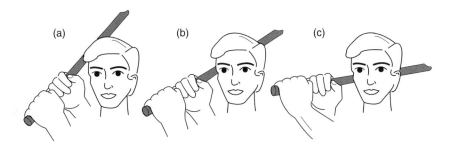

(a)   (b)   (c)

Figure 3. *Wrist cock during the backswing significantly affects power attainable in the downswing. Jorgensen found that the larger the wrist-cock angle during the backswing, and the longer uncocking was delayed before impact, the greater the distance of the drive (Jorgensen, 1994). In golf (unlike tennis or badminton), uncocking the wrists does not provide a major source of power, and it is detrimental to try to boost power by uncocking just before impact. It is more beneficial to practice increasing the wrist cock than to practice extending the backswing.*

uncocking before impact, the greater the distance of the drive. He also found that any attempt to boost power by uncocking the wrist just before impact was detrimental.

Delaying the uncocking of the wrists seems counterintuitive to many professional golfers and even to many scientists, who believe that extra power—a "boost"—can be imparted to the ball by uncocking the wrists and pushing down with the back wrist immediately before contact. It is true that uncocking the wrists provides a major source of power in sports like tennis and badminton, but Jorgensen found that it does not have the same effect in golf, because a golfer's arms act through a larger angle before the impact between clulb head and ball. The long arc of the golf swing makes it more effective to have the hands well in front of the ball at the point of contact. Although the length of backswing varies considerably among professionals, all use a large wrist-cock angle to generate high velocity with a high degree of directional precision. An exaggerated backswing, as noted above, provides only minimal additional velocity at a potential cost in directional precision.

At the peak of the backswing, golfers tend to make two common errors: bending the left arm and loosening the grip of one of the hands. These errors adversely affect the swing because the wrists begin to uncock, and the smaller wrist-cock angle reduces the radius of the swing. Both errors severely affect the angular velocity—the rotational momentum—of the club head during the downswing, which in turn affects the transfer of momentum from club head to ball.

Downswing

The downswing, which follows the backswing, is difficult to master because it requires coordinating the separate actions of the club and the arms to generate maximum club-head velocity. The body and the stroke of the downswing work together like a double pendulum, or a two-lever system (*see Figure 4*). One lever, formed by the shoul-

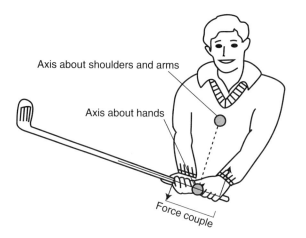

Figure 4. *The golf swing involves a double pendulum action (the two circles indicate the axes of this double pendulum). The lever consisting of the shoulder, arms, and wrists rotates around an axis in the upper chest; the club rotates around an axis formed by the hands. The "force couple" between the left and right hand during the downswing can significantly increase the velocity of the club head.*

der, arms, and wrists, rotates around an axis through the upper body; the second lever is the club rotating around an axis through the hands. This complex swing demands excellent timing to synchronize the movement of the body and the club.

In some ways, the downswing closely resembles the action of nunchaku sticks, a martial-arts weapon, the common principle being the fact that much more energy or momentum can be transferred by the swing of connected rods than by the swing of a single rod. A typical 20- to 24-inch (50- to 60-cm) riot club can certainly deliver a lethal blow, but its kinetic energy (energy of motion) is far exceeded by nunchaku—which are an instance of the "two-rod model" in physics. Nunchaku consist of two pieces of hardwood, each 10 to 15 inches (25–30 cm) long, held together by rope, a piece of leather, or a chain (*see Figure 5*). Extended, these two pieces are approximately the same length as the riot club, but nunchaku develop a far greater impulse (force × time interval) and far more transfer of momentum. (In fact, nunchaku can inflict such severe injuries that they are illegal in much of the United States.)

A similar principle applies to a bullwhip, which works like a series of short connected rods. If one swings first an 8-foot fishing pole and then an 8-foot bullwhip, one can quickly see how much easier it is to bring the tip of the whip to a high velocity than the tip of the fishing pole. In fact, acoustics researchers have demonstrated that a bullwhip's cracking sound—"cavitation"—is caused by a shock wave, as when a jet airplane breaks the sound barrier (Bernstein, 1958).

A bullwhip is typically wielded with an overhand or a sidearm motion; for the purposes of this discussion, an underhand or (backhand) motion can be considered much like a golf stroke (right-handed golfer, left-handed backhand). If a bullwhip is lying on the

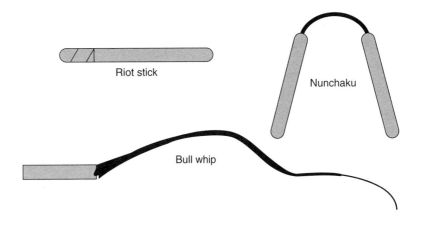

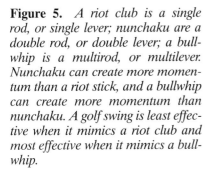

Figure 5. *A riot club is a single rod, or single lever; nunchaku are a double rod, or double lever; a bullwhip is a multirod, or multilever. Nunchaku can create more momentum than a riot stick, and a bullwhip can create more momentum than nunchaku. A golf swing is least effective when it mimics a riot club and most effective when it mimics a bullwhip.*

ground in a straight line, parallel with and behind one's body, one can move the arm holding the whip forward to put the bullwhip into motion in a straight line. As the whip is pulled, the straight-line motion begins at the handle and proceeds downward toward the tip. The hand creates a force on the bullwhip that increases its momentum, which in turn generates the whip's kinetic energy. At the forward position, the hand holding the handle will stop, while the rest of the bullwhip will continue to extend along its straight-line course. When the hand stops, it exerts a force on the handle that decreases the momentum of the whip, and that momentum is absorbed by the body. In sequence, additional segments of the whip come to rest, and the crack occurs when only the tip is still moving. At that point, there is tremendous velocity at the tip. Because the amount of kinetic energy will remain the same from the beginning to the end of the stroke, the final crack represents a concentration of the total energy of the swing. At the start of the whip stroke, the total mass of the whip moves at a moderate velocity; by the end of the stroke, a much smaller mass—just the tip—has absorbed the remaining momentum and therefore moves at a much higher velocity. In other words, all the momentum generated by the body, arm, and hand and imparted to the whip moves quickly to the tip as each successive segment of the body and whip comes to a rest. To repeat: the total kinetic energy remains the same but makes its way toward the tip during the whipping motion.

The downswing in golf works in a similar way. During the early part of a downswing, before reaching horizontal, the large muscles in the shoulder and back act in unison to begin releasing the coiled tension developed in the backswing. The positions of the shoulders, arms, hands, and club relative to one another remain unchanged early in the downswing as the hips drive forward. Once the swing begins moving horizontally, how the front arm pulls the club is just as important as the rotational acceleration (angular momentum) achieved relative to the shoulder joint. In wielding a bullwhip, the goal is to snap the whip forward with an underhand left-handed motion. To achieve maximum power, the upper end of the bullwhip must experience the starting and stopping action of the left shoulder over a very limited time and distance—a 38- to 51-centimeter (15- to 20-in.) path.

As the front arm pulls the body and the golf club toward the ball, the hip and the legs push the body and the club in the same direction. It is this combination of two actions, a "force couple," that maximizes the angular momentum in the downswing. Both actions should be completed before the contact between club head and ball, but the larger muscles pushing the hip and the legs into the stroke are vital.

Like baseball and tennis players, golfers learn that "stepping into" a shot makes the ball travel farther. Although the golfer's feet remain stationary, a good golfer shifts body weight forward during the swing. Jorgensen (1994) calculated velocities at the impact of club head and ball and found that for swings involving a weight shift, the velocity was about 52 meters (170.5 ft.) per second; without the shift, the impact speed was only 45 meters (149 ft.) per second—approximately 14.4 percent less. Given the same stroke motion, then, and assuming that the golfer can coordinate the more complex two-lever motion of the swing with the movement of the body, a drive that would travel 183 meters (200 yd.) without a weight shift will travel 209 meters (229 yd.) with a weight shift. But coordination is necessary here: if the stroke is not done effectively, the energy produced during the downswing will actually be reduced during its horizontal segment and at the moment of contact with the ball.

During the downswing, golfers must also resist the natural tendency to rush the club and force themselves to delay wrist action (since, as noted above, this delay seems "unnatural" or counterintuitive). The tendency to rush the club stems from the torque generated at the wrist. At the beginning of the downswing, there is only about 20 pounds of pull, or torque, from the club; near the release phase, torque quickly increases to 70 to 90 pounds. Uncocking the wrist during the release phase throws off the timing of the stroke and actually decreases the velocity of the club.

Filmed sequences of a professional swing show that when wrist action is delayed through the release phase, the large muscles of the body actually slow toward the bottom of the downswing. Jorgensen argues that the body slows in order to give the arm and the club a chance to catch up. This improves the transfer of momentum from club to ball because additional positive angular momentum is generated after the club head passes the horizontal position of the downswing. A golfer who uncocks early cannot generate this additional positive angular momentum. Ironically, this subtle movement runs counter to the typical definition of "good timing": a constantly increasing angular acceleration from beginning to end. Instructional books often try to convey this difficult concept by desribing the phenomenon as "hitting into a firm left side."

Follow-Through

Much as in other sports, the follow-through in golf involves a gradual slowing of the body and the club. The hands should pass through the lowest arc and maintain that low-arc path as long as possible. The club head should follow the optimal path of the swing and end in the position required for precision. A quick check of the final stance is a good indication of how well balance was maintained through the swing.

Sidehill Lies

If they were given the option, many golfers would like to hit every ball off a tee. But most shots are not hit off the tee. In fact, many have to be hit from bunkers, in deep rough, and from difficult sidehill lies.

Sidehill lies are particularly perplexing because the hill shifts the golfer's plane in relation to the ball. Professionals often instruct golfers to aim for a slice (a deviation of the ball's flight in the direction of the player's dominant hand) when the ball lies downhill from the golfer's feet; and to aim for a hook (a deviation in the direction opposite to the dominant hand) when the ball lies uphill. This makes sense because when the ball lies uphill from the golfer's feet, the intended plane of the shot will be tilted to the left. Another option is to slightly rotate the grip to present a toe-out club head, changing the dynamics of the shot (*see "Golf Clubs," below*). When the club head is toe-out, the hook is effectively eliminated and the ball will travel along a more horizontal axis. However, this method must be used carefully, because a toe-out 7-iron will react like a 6-iron hit with a regular grip. Also, if the club head is swung slightly toe out, an off-center hit that is too close to the toe of the club will turn the club head further to the right (for a right-handed player), and the ball will fade even more to the right.

Putting

In any given round of golf, half the strokes are putts. A drive off the tee might soar more than 320 meters (350 yd.), and an iron shot, with its exaggerated backspin, may send the ball onto the green like an arrow. But to ensure a good score, a golfer must also putt well. Many champion golfers—including Tom Watson, Jack Nicklaus, and Arnold Palmer—attribute numerous victories to their putting.

Much like a basketball shooter, who also needs to develop a "feel," a golfer "sights" a putt, determining the distance and path the ball should take. Many factors affect the decisions a golfer makes concerning the strength and the direction of a putt—an uphill or downhill slope, a hard (fast) or soft (slow) green, a dry or wet surface, and the length of the grass.

Golfers often have similar form off the tee, but no two golfers putt exactly alike. Variations in putting form include stance (open, square, closed), bend of the trunk, hunching of the shoulder, and placement of the hands on the grip.

Before the 1990s, most golfers positioned their hands similarly, but many top professionals then adopted "cross-handed" putting. Most right-handed golfers hold the putter with the right hand below the left, just as one would hold a driver or a baseball bat. In the cross-handed putt, the left hand is below the right; players who use this method argue that it gives greater stability and a better "feel." One reason that cross-handed putting is becoming popular is that it helps achieve the same goal as lengthening the shaft of the putter: making the putting motion more of a single-pendulum swing, rather than a double-pendulum swing as with irons or woods. Although a double-pendulum swing gives maximum momentum, a single-pendulum swing is superior for accuracy—and accuracy is of greatest importance in putting. The cross-hand grip enables the golfer to more closely match intention with execution because it forces the left arm and the putter to more nearly align in the same plane and therefore to move as one. The grip also makes it easier to eliminate left-handed wrist torque (for a right-handed putter) during contact and follow-through.

In the mid-1990s, Nick Faldo, Fred Couples, Tom Kite, and Payne Stewart were among thirty or forty famous golfers who used the cross-handed style. Perhaps more would have switched if not for motor memory, which makes switching difficult and may even preclude it. Some experts predict that in subsequent generations, all golfers will use the cross-handed method, which is increasingly being taught to beginners.

Golf Clubs

This section looks at two aspects of the design of golf clubs: perimeter weighting and the flexible shaft. (*See also EQUIPMENT MATERIALS.*)

Perimeter Weighting

Manufacturers of golf equipment have focused on designing what they call "game-improving" clubs for intermediate-level players. One design that became popular very quickly was the perimeter-weighted club. Because of advanced casting techniques, the mass of the club can be distributed around the outside edges of woods and irons, instead of uniformly throughout the club head. The main purpose of perimeter weights is improving performance on off-center shots. When the ball contacts the club face off-center, the club head turns from the large force created by the unbalanced area of the club head. As in modern tennis rackets, perimeter weighting enlarges the "sweet spot" of the club face to prevent and or at least reduce rotation of the club head around its center of gravity when a shot is hit off-center (*see also TENNIS*).

Taking Out Frustration

In a study of business executives conducted by Hyatt Hotels, 98 percent said that playing golf was a healthful way to relieve stress. More than half, however, admitted throwing or breaking a club after hitting a slice or hook. While some relieve stress by playing, others seem to take out their frustrations on their equipment.

Material Advances

As of the mid-1990s, at the forefront of golf club design was the wide-bodied carbon-graphite "wood" with a boron-reinforced shaft. Although carbon-fiber clubs and graphite clubs continued to gain market share, other composite materials were also becoming accepted. New materials are primarily incorporated in shaft design, since a lighter shaft allows more mass in the club head without an increase in overall weight. But such improvements have mostly helped hackers—the players whose swing is not fluid enough for consistent on-center contact. These are the players who need help to control slicing and hooking and who are looking for miracles. Modern "miracle" equipment can certainly help some of them. Still, the USGA emphasizes that even the best equipment cannot make up for all the deficiencies of a poorly executed swing.

However, experts have found that, compared with standard clubs, perimeter-weighted clubs improve performance only minimally (Cochran, 1990). Given the same off-center contact, a shot that would be 3 degrees off-target with a standard club will still be 2 degrees off-target with a perimeter-weighted club. Moreover, perimeter weighting has little to offer professional players, who seldom have problems hitting the ball cleanly on center.

Flexible Shafts

The physiological contribution of the shoulder and wrist to the generation of power is known with some precision. The contribution of the flexibility of the shaft, however, seems quite variable, owing to the different properties of the various materials from which shafts are constructed. The first shafts were made of wood (hickory. These were superseded in the early twentieth century by tapered tubular-steel shafts. Because steel was lighter, it not only allowed for greater swing velocity, but also gave a more flexible shaft.

The flex of a club can be demonstrated by holding it at the grip and wiggling it back and forth very quickly. Each time the shaft bends, it is said to "load"—to store additional energy before impact with the ball. Throughout the phases of the swing, the shaft loads, unloads, and then reloads. Although it may seem that the shaft bends backward and forward, or oscillates, just once before contact, it actually oscillates 1.5 times. At the top of the backswing, the club head loads by recoiling and by following behind the forward path of the wrists. As the downswing follows, the shaft begins to catch up to the wrists—unloading. Ted Jorgensen found that the shaft straightens in only about 0.29 second and then loads in the opposite direction and ahead of the swing (Jorgensen, 1994). While still in the downswing, the shaft straightens and then reloads behind the forward path of the wrists. At contact between club head and ball, the shaft of the club again straightens, or unloads. This final forward oscillation of the shaft creates a snapping effect, immediately before contact, that increases the velocity of the ball. Jorgensen found that a forward shaft flex of about 3.3 degrees can add 8.7 percent to the velocity of the club head.

Flex not only affects the velocity of the club, but also increases the loft angle. For the same swing, a highly flexible driver will usually give the ball a higher trajectory and more spin than a less flexible driver.

The Golf Ball

The golf ball has evolved considerably, from the earliest wooden balls of the fifteenth century to the featheries of the seventeenth century to the gutta-percha balls of the nineteenth century to the high-tech balls of the 1990s. In fact, the invention of the resilient rubber-core ball in 1898 contributed to the explosive growth of the game. Before

The Evolution of the Golf Ball

Featheries. In the seventeenth century, the first wooden golf balls were replaced by a new version called featheries. Featheries were made of boiled goose feathers stuffed tightly within a stitched cowhide casing; as the feathers dried, the ball became very hard. It was then pounded into shape, oiled, and whitened. Featheries were difficult to make and very expensive: a ball maker could produce only four or five in a day. Featheries could be driven about 137 to 160 meters (150–175 yd.) but were useless when wet.

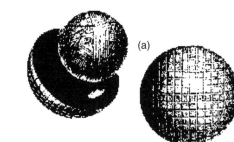

Gutta-percha rubber-core. *(a)* Gutta-percha balls began replacing featheries around 1848. Dried gum (balata) of the Malaysian sapodilla tree was heated to a putty-like consistency and rolled into a ball. This ball was cheaper to manufacture but would often break into pieces on impact (as could still happen with the one-piece, solid-core ball used on driving ranges in the 1990s). Its flight resembled that of featheries. In 1898, Coburn Haskell developed a three-piece rubber-core variation to overcome these deficiencies. It consisted of lengths of rubber yarn (or elastic band) stretched around a rubber core and surrounded by a gutta-percha cover. The rubber core made the ball livelier and gave the golfer greater control over flight and spin. This was the first three-piece ball.

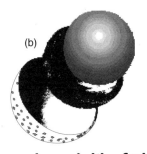

Three-piece (with Surlyn™ Cover). *(b)* This modern ball has a solid rubber core wound with rubber yarn. The cover is made from Surlyn™, a patented thermoplastic resin. Surlyn™ is more durable than balata and is virtually uncuttable. Cores have been made of metal, wood, and liquid-filled materials.

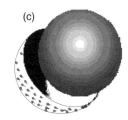

Two-piece. *(c)* This ball has a highly compressible acrylate or resin core and a durable Surlyn™ cover, which gives it the greatest carry. It is popular not only because of its distance but also because its cover is nearly indestructible. It is more difficult to control, however, because it has a lower backspin rate in flight.

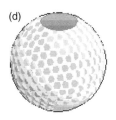

One-piece. *(d)* This is the ball of choice at most practice tees and driving ranges. It is injection-molded with dimples to form a solid cover of Surlyn™. With a lower coefficient of restitution, it travels less distance. It feels soft on contact because impact energy is absorbed by the club head without being returned to the ball.

Three-piece (Balata cover). *(e)* In the 1990s, the three-piece balata-covered ball was the newest and most costly innovation. Manufacturers claimed that it gave better distance and control because of its higher backspin rate. It consists of a liquid center, a polyurethane interlayer, and a synthetic balata cover. Balata makes contact between club head and ball more certain but may not be best for golfers who routinely hit and spin the ball off center. Unlike the tough Surlyn™ cover, which easily withstands off-center hits, balata covers are often cut.

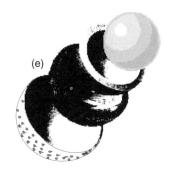

then, a player could make only a few "mis-swings" before the ball tore apart. Golfers still carry extra balls because some are likely to be lost during play; but early golfers carried even more of them, because a certain number would also be destroyed. The rubber-core golf ball was just one of many improvements in design and manufacturing. Further advances in materials made the ball of the 1990s far different even from that of the 1960s.

Coefficient of Restitution

The extent to which new materials have affected performance is not certain. Unlike major league baseball, which closely monitors the "liveliness" of the ball by measuring the coefficient of restitution (COR) for samples, the United States Golf Association (USGA) tests liveliness by measuring the distance a ball travels when launched from a driving machine. But the coefficient of restitution, measured through a rebound-bounce test, is a much better measure because testing can control for aerodynamic factors.

The COR for a golf ball is about 0.6. This means that when dropped from a height of 10 feet, a ball will rebound to a height of 6 feet. This is significantly lower than the COR of a tennis ball (0.7) or a handball (0.8). However, when each of these balls is dropped from a much greater height—reaching a velocity of 88.5 KPH (55 MPH)—the COR of the golf ball drops only about 3 percent, to 0.58; by contrast, the COR of the tennis ball drops 29 percent, to 0.5, and that of the handball drops 37 percent, to 0.5. Thus if the velocity of the collision between club head and ball is increased, the golf ball loses very little additional energy in rebounding. It follows that any improvements in the swing should be very evident, because a golf ball "steals" (absorbs) very little additional energy with a greater impact force.

The Collision between Club Head and Ball

In less than a thousandth of a second and in the space of less than an inch, the club head hits the ball at a very high velocity—a collision involving 3,000 pounds of force. Although it is too fast for the human eye to observe, the moment of impact can be captured by high-speed photography. When the club head strikes the ball, there is considerable deformation of the ball: that is, the ball takes on a oblong, flattened shape. Some golfers believe that the ball resumes its original shape almost immediately after impact, but it can actually remain somewhat deformed for weeks; and if the deformation is great enough, its flight path may be erratic.

According to the law of conservation of momentum, the horizontal momentum of the club head (generated during the rotational acceleration of the downswing) just before the collision must equal the sum of the horizontal momenta of the club head and the ball after the collision. That is why the ball leaves the tee with considerable velocity after impact with the club head, and why the club head slows during the transfer of momentum.

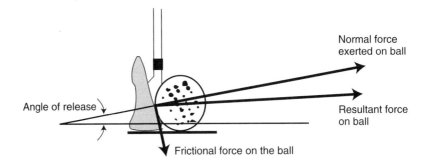

Figure 6. *Two forces act on the ball at impact with the club head: normal and frictional. A frictional force is created when the surface of the club face strikes the dimpled surface of the ball; this means that the ball's trajectory will be lower than it would be in the absence of friction. For example, a collision between a smooth iron and a smooth, polished ball would more closely follow the normal force exerted on the ball, which is determined by the loft of the club. (Adapted from Hay, 1985)*

Collision Theory

Collision theory states that a perfectly elastic ball (COR = 1) will leave the club head at nearly twice the velocity of the club head's velocity just before impact. But because collisions are not perfectly elastic and because all clubs have an angle of loft, the factor is actually considerably less—about 1.46 for a driver, 1.30 for a 5 iron, and 1.12 for a 9 iron.

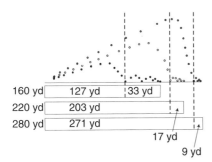

Figure 7. *Carry (flight) and run (bounce and roll) make a contribution to the distance of a drive. Here, in the 280-yard drive 97 percent of the total distance comes from the carry, but in the 160-yard drive only 79 percent of the total comes from the carry. (Data adapted from Hay, 1985)*

Although the result of the impact is determined largely by what has happened during the stroke (the backswing and downswing), several interesting phenomena take place during the moment of contact (*see Figure 6*). When the club head contacts the ball, the ball begins sliding up the angled profile of the club face; concurrently, there is an increasing horizontal force on the ball from the club head. Manufacturers of clubs cut parallel groves into the face to prevent excessive sliding and give more rotational "bite." These grooves increase the frictional qualities of the club face and increase the collision time between club face and ball. Increasing the frictional qualities of the collision ensures that the ball will rotate, rather than slide, up the club face. This rolling action gives the ball greater backspin. Greater club-head velocity at impact will not only send the ball farther but will also put more backspin on the ball. Backspin creates a greater lift force, keeps the ball airborne longer, and helps it fall more slowly. In the end, the ball carries much farther before hitting the ground (*see Figure 7*).

Sometimes environmental factors diminish the friction of the collision between club head and ball. For example, a golfer cannot generate the same amount of backspin when using an iron to hit a ball out of a deep, rain-soaked rough as on a well-groomed, dry fairway. When the ball is wet, there is less friction between it and the club face. Professional golfers anticipate this loss of friction and make the appropriate adjustments. They may, for instance, aim a wet ball short of the intended target to allow for its greater roll.

Aerodynamic Forces

Since a golf ball can be hit at velocities in excess of 137 KPH (150 MPH), in-flight forces of air resistance, or drag, are very significant. The size and weight of the ball, and its high velocity, can result in tremendous variability in trajectory. Anyone who has hit a ball with a slice or hook knows firsthand how variable its flight can be.

Surface characteristics are a primary factor determining trajectory. The aerodynamic dimpled ball (which by the 1990s had been in use for decades) came into existence almost by accident. When the first hard-surface "guttie" ball was used in 1901, golfers noticed that the longer they played with a particular ball, and the more nicked and roughened it became, the longer and farther it flew. This observation led to a series of experimental designs that brought over 200 different covers to the market between 1900 and 1920. The first experiment with the surface was the raspberry-like brambled ball, sometimes called the pimple ball, which was indeed more effective than the smooth ball. When the dimpled ball appeared in 1908, the brambled ball quickly became extinct, but this was primarily because dirt did not cling as much to the dimpled ball—not for aerodynamic reasons.

The airborne characteristics of a golf ball can be explained in terms of the boundary layer of air that is near the surface of a ball as it moves. Since air moves relative to an object, a ball that moves through the air restricts air movement forward and to the side. Before coming into contact with the ball, air is in an undisturbed state, and is said to be streamlined. Once air comes within a few inches of the ball, it begins to break into a disturbed pattern, called turbulent flow. If a ball has a smooth surface and is moving slowly, the airflow around it will remain streamlined (*see Figure 8a*). If the same ball is moving at a high velocity, the dynamics change drastically: the smooth surface creates separation of the boundary layer,

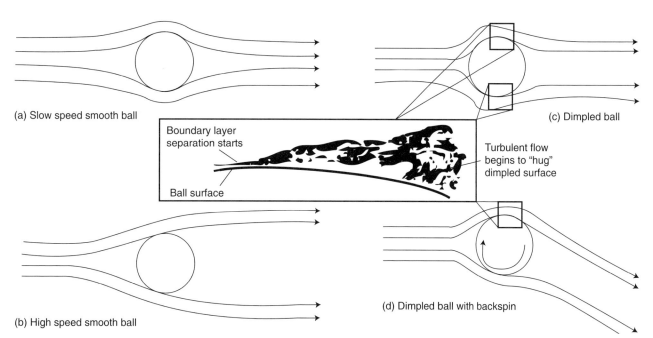

(a) Slow speed smooth ball

(c) Dimpled ball

Boundary layer separation starts

Turbulent flow begins to "hug" dimpled surface

Ball surface

(d) Dimpled ball with backspin

(b) High speed smooth ball

Figure 8. *(a) Air moves in a streamlined path around a smooth ball at low speeds. (b) At higher speeds, air experiences boundary-layer separation. (c) At high speeds the dimpled ball creates less boundary-layer separation and a more turbulent wake than a smooth ball. Airflow "hugs" its surface more closely. (d) When the dimpled ball is rotating with underspin, it creates lift (shifts the wake downward) by speeding up the airflow over the top of the ball relative to airflow around the bottom of the ball (the Magnus effect).*

Polara: The Ball That Set the "Too Good" Standard

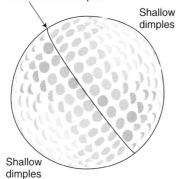

Around equator
conventional dimples

Shallow
dimples

Shallow
dimples

Polara: The Happy Non-Hooker.

Imagine the toughest golf course, with very thin fairways, superthick roughs, trees squeezing in on all sides, and numerous sand traps. Narrower courses of this nature—a hacker's nightmare—may become the norm, not the exception, if real estate costs continue to skyrocket. Imagine playing for money on this course against a player of equal ability. Now, imagine that you have an advantage over your opponent: you are using a golf ball that eliminates 75 percent of your slice.

This scenario may actually have occurred on a few occasions between 1976 and 1978, when the Polara golf ball was briefly on the market. The Polara was the brainchild of a physicist,

Fred Holmstrom, and a chemist, Daniel Nepela, neither of whom was a golfer. One summer, while Holmstrom was consulting for IBM, he came across an article on golf balls by John Davies in the *Journal of Applied Physics*. Though he may have wondered what an article about the aerodynamics of a golf ball was doing in that journal, he gave it little thought and went about his own research. But as he was leaving the library, his curiosity got the better of him, and he returned to the stacks to find and copy the article. A few days later, at lunch, Holmstrom showed the article to Nepela. At first they joked about it; then they began to give it serious thought.

Davies's article showed how increasing the backspin (RPMs) of a dimpled ball could dramatically improve the lift-to-drag ratio, why there is a negative lift with a smooth-surfaced ball, and what laminar versus turbulent flow does to a ball in flight. The article presented some very interesting results, and Holmstrom felt that there were still more conclusions to be drawn from Davies's insights. The article helped Holmstrom and Nepela understand why the surface of the golf ball had evolved as it did. Perhaps more important, it set them off on a quest to design a superior dimpled surface.

Since mathematical solutions of flight-path characteristics—the numerous factors involved and their complexity—were impossible at that time, they decided to let their intuition guide their experimentation. They believed that one key to a better design would be an asymmetrical dimple pattern that would limit the hook and slice for the majority of shots that come off the club with sidespin.

One of their major breakthroughs came when they devised an inexpensive way of modifying the dimple patterns themselves. Holmstrom lightly sanded fifty standard golf balls and coated them with an off-the-shelf silicone-based filler (RTV). Saran wrap was then pulled tightly over the surface to smooth out any irregularities. Next came the pressing and rolling of the material to form the balls with dimples of the desired shapes, patterns, and depths. In this way they reshaped fifty spheres without having to commission fifty expensive molds.

The Polara design—which, from a distance of 1 foot, looked only slightly different from a standard golf ball— proved to be a raging success. In fact, the working models suggested a wide range of possibilities. To begin with, the two "best" designs could cut a slice by 50 percent and 75 percent respectively. But one test model actually

and this in turn creates a large wake behind the ball (*Figure 8b*). This low-pressure zone behind the ball means that there is a net force directed toward the rear of the ball. The ball thus experiences drag— resistance directed opposite to its path.

As long as the ball's speed is low, airflow remains laminar, or streamlined; and as long as the airflow is laminar, Bernoulli's effect is relevant: as airflow speeds up, air pressure is reduced. (Bernoulli's effect can be demonstrated by blowing a stream of air between two helium balloons: because the air pressure between them is reduced,

overcorrected. Given a poor swing, another test model could change a hook into a slice and a slice into a hook without losing range, as if it could make airborne corrections in order to fly along an intended path. Another test model flew completely unpredictably: it could slice, hook, or fly straight without any real loss of range. Because these designs seemed too gimmicky, though—they changed the true nature of the shot—Holmstrom and Nepela decided to market only the designs that limited the slice and the hook.

The principle of the Polara ball, the so-called "Happy Non-Hooker," was quite simple. Conventional dimples were retained on only about 50 percent of the surface and were concentrated in bands around the ball's equator, or seam. The surfaces at the polar regions had shallower dimples. In flight, the band of conventional dimples created the Magnus deflection of a rough ball—plenty of turbulence to create the lifting force to maximize carry. Meanwhile, at the poles, the smoother surface and shallower dimples created the Magnus deflection of a smooth ball—opposite the direction of the ball's spin. This design was based on the paradoxical nature of the Magnus effect, which works simultaneously to create a negative lift (deflection) to keep the ball moving in a straight line (horizontal stability) and a positive lift (deflection) from backspin to allow the ball to carry. Holmstrom and Nepela were elated with their design: it was more

accurate and gave better distance than any other golf ball on the market at that time.

Manfacturers of golf balls, who had devoted considerable resources to develop balls that would carry farther, were caught by surprise by the Polara. They had never considered the possibility that a better dimple design would not only could improve distance but stay on the fairway more often.

Before Holmstrom or Nepela took the Polara ball to market, they sent manufacturing versions to the USGA for approval. At the time, the rules for a legal golf ball were simple and straightforward: "A ball must not weigh more than 1.62 ounces and must not have a diameter less than 1.68 inches." Although the Polara met this standard, the USGA withheld approval. Perhaps out of fear that such improvements would "reduce the skill required to play golf and threaten the integrity of the game," an amendment against a nonuniform distribution of dimples was soon proposed. However, almost all balls on the market already had a nonuniform distribution of dimples, so technically all of them would also have been illegal. The USGA withdrew the proposed admendment, and then devised a new rule: "A golf ball must be spherical in shape and be designed to have equal aerodynamic properties and equal moments of inertia about any axis through its center." To test this, a ball was struck at two extremes (both vertical and horizontal to its equator, or seam) with a club-holding driving machine.

Since the Polara had an intended asymmetrical pattern of dimples (in terms of shapes and sizes), it would show slight differences in launch angle and maximum height for the two orientations. Thus the test established a standard value that eliminated the Polara—but just barely. Most balls on the market were asymmetrical for various reasons and showed differences in performance; however, their differences lay within the new standard. The Polara design became the "too good" standard that is still in effect in the 1990s.

The USGA claimed that it "wanted to preserve the integrity of the game." Holmstrom and Nepela were disappointed and perplexed by the USGA ruling, however; they believed that the Polara would help achieve one prime objective of the USGA: to make golf more accessible to more people. Their ball significantly helped the worst golfers, only modestly affected a professional's game, and speeded up overall play because far less time was spent searching for lost balls. A typical golfer, therefore, could play a better game, a game that offered far less frustration and a lot more fun. But golf with the "too good to be true" ball was not to be.

The Polara patent ran out June 1991. It will be interesting to see if manufacturers eventually try to incorporate the basic asymmetrical design of these two nongolfing scientists.

John Zumerchik

the balloons will move toward each other. Sailors apply this principle by using a foresail to speed airflow past the leeward side of the main sail; *see also SAILING and VOLLEYBALL*.) When the airflow becomes turbulent, or chaotic, however, Bernoulli's effect is negligible or nonexistent.

The dimpled surface of a golf ball is effective because it makes the air passing around the ball turbulent, trapping a layer of air that spins along with the ball—a beneficial turbulence (*Figure 8c*). In other words, the dimples carry the turbulent layer of air farther along the surface of the ball. Dimples do not reduce the frontal drag that pushes the ball back, because the cross-sectional area of the ball is the same; they do, however, decrease the size of the low-pressure wake behind the ball, lowering the pressure difference between the front and back of the ball.

In conjunction with backspin, dimples keep the ball in the air longer by producing lift (*Figure 8d*). The turbulent boundary layer moves along with the ball as it spins from bottom to top, entraping air and confining it. As a result, the air at the top of the ball, in the direction of the spinning motion, moves more rapidly than the air at the bottom of the ball. The air along the bottom of the ball is, in effect, traveling against the wind, while the air layer at the top of the ball is moving with the wind. Because the air layer at the top of the ball is moving faster than the air level at the bottom of the ball, a downward momentum of air is created as it shifts the low-pressure wake behind the ball downward. This effect is called a lifting force. It makes the trajectory of the ball move upward; thus, the greater the spin rate, the greater the lifting force.

Although the relative motion of the air at the top and at the bottom of the ball can be interpreted in terms of Bernoulli's effect, this kind of turbulent flow is more correctly attributed to the Magnus effect. Whenever a ball spins, an extra force acts on it—the Magnus effect. For a dimpled golf ball, the spinning ball results in a deflection upward that creates greater air pressure on the top of the ball. The air pressure on the top of the ball, which is traveling relatively faster through the air on the bottom, creates greater pressure on the ball to deflect, or lift, it. As the physicist John Davies discovered, however, the Magnus effect can also generate negative lift (Davies, 1949). Given the same number of revolutions per minute (RPM) that creates upward deflection for a dimpled ball, a perfectly smooth golf ball will actually be deflected downward.

Because the golf ball is dimpled, backspin is crucial for distance. The upward motion of the golf swing and the angled face of the club head help impart backspin on the ball, so that a properly struck golf ball leaves the club with tremendous backspin. As would be expected, the greater the pitch of the club head, the greater the backspin: a 9-iron, for example, generates far more backspin than a 3-iron. Yet even with a driver, which has a face that is only slightly pitched, the ball can spin at up to 8,000 RPM. By comparison, this is three or four times the RPM of the fastest curveballs in major league baseball. In fact, the aerodynamic lift caused by the Magnus effect is probably greater in golf than in any other sport. The Magnus effect deflects a well-pitched curveball about 0.3 meter (1 ft.) and carries a long fly ball about 3 to 6 meters (10–20 ft.) farther. For a golf ball, the effect of backspin (that is, the Magnus effect) is dramatically greater. If two golf balls are hit with the same velocity, a ball hit with backspin will remain airborne as much as 2 or 3 seconds longer and end up traveling 18 to 30 meters (60–100 ft.) farther than a ball hit without backspin.

Dimples Everywhere?

Applying the aerodynamic benefits of the dimpled golf ball, bobsled drivers now tack a small round piece of sandpaper to the front of their helmets. In 1994, Jeffrey Di-Tullo, a professor of aeronautics at MIT, patented a dimpled baseball bat, which hitters can swing 3 to 5 percent faster—a difference sizable enough to add 10 to 30 feet to a long drive. Unless the rules are changed to forbid this kind of bat, the 340-foot fly balls of the early 1990s may be replaced by 360-foot bleacher shots.

Effects of Wind

Because it is small and light, a golf ball experiences substantial wind effects when airborne: for instance, a sudden gust of wind from 16 to 48 KPH (10–30 MPH) can alter where the ball lands by 9 meters (30 ft.) or more. A professional golfer must, therefore, become adept at reading the wind. Professionals are often seen tossing a few blades of grass into the wind in an attempt to ascertain the strength and the direction of the wind. When the wind is gusting and swirling in ever-changing directions, however, even the most experienced golfer will have difficulty predicting how the flight of the ball will be affected.

Whenever a golf ball is airborne, it is subjected to lift and drag (resistance) forces; changes in wind direction and wind velocity alter the magnitude of these forces. If a ball is hit directly into the wind, the velocity of the air moving past it will, of course, be greater than if there were no wind. The velocity of the air moving past the ball is equal to the velocity of the ball plus the velocity of the wind. Lift and drag forces are determined by this total velocity—not just by the velocity of the ball, and not just by the velocity of the wind relative to the ground. A ball hit into the wind will have greater lift, because it backspins through air that is moving more quickly past the ball than the ball is moving forward. It will also experience more drag, because its effective frontal area is creating greater resistance. When a ball is hit with the wind, the opposite effect occurs: less lift and less drag. Consequently, a professional golfer will drive a ball into the wind at a lower trajectory and with less spin, but will want a higher trajectory and more spin when hitting with the wind. When a ball is hit into the wind, both hooks and slices are exaggerated because air resistance is greater.

In practice, deciding on a trajectory is not simple, because golfers rarely encounter direct headwinds or direct tailwinds. A crosswind adds an additional component of drag, because a ball will carry, or drift, in the direction of the crosswind. In a crosswind, a ball is still subjected to drag along its own path, but it is also subjected to crosswind drag, which causes it to carry in the direction of the wind (*see Figure 9*). With high-speed winds, the ball will always carry much farther in the direction of the crosswind. In such situations, a golfer must take into account both frontal drag and drag that causes the ball to drift.

Slices and Hooks

Hitting a ball with a slice or with a hook will considerably reduce distance. For a right-handed golfer, a slice deflects at an angle of 10 or 11 o'clock, and a hook at an angle of 1 or 2 o'clock. Whereas a well-executed drive with backspin creates lift that can add 24 to 30 meters (80–100 ft.) to a shot, a ball that is hooked or sliced leaves the club face with sidespin, which is detrimental. Like a curveball in baseball, sidespin shifts the low-pressure wake behind the ball to the left or to the right, causing the ball to break, or pull, in the opposite direc-

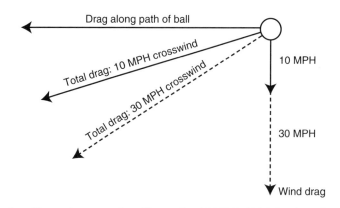

Figure 9. *Shown here are the effects of a 16-KPH (10-MPH) and a 48-KPH (30-MPH) crosswind on the direction an airborne ball will carry. The ball experiences drag along its path plus crosswind drag.*

tion. Not only will the ball lose some of the beneficial lifting forces of backspin, but it will also shift to the left or to the right of the intended impact point with the ground—as much as 30 meters (100 ft.) short and 9 meters (30 ft.) wide of the intended target.

Only exceptional golfers can routinely hit the ball squarely to the line of flight so that it spins solely around a horizontal axis, or with backspin. Generally, the degree of a hook or a slice is determined by the degree of tilt of the horizontal axis of spin as the ball leaves the club head. Hooking and slicing may result from an improper club-face angle at contact, from swinging the club head from outside to inside of the ball (slice), or from inside to outside (hook). This is called sliding the club across the ball.

If the hook or slice is small, it is referred to as a pull or a push, created when the ball has too much vertical spin. The pull or push of a hook or a slice is far less when higher-number irons are used than when drivers or low-number irons are used, owing to the backspin-to-sidespin ratio. If a ball hit with a 3-iron leaves the club face back-spinning at 6,000 RPM and sidespinning at 2,000 RPM, deflection resulting from the Magnus effect while the ball is airborne may cause it to land 18 meters (60 ft.) farther than and 12 meters (40 ft.) to the right of a spinless iron shot. Because a golfer will use the same swing with the 9-iron, the ball will still sidespin at around 2,000 RPM, but the steeper-pitched iron will increase the backspin to 12,000 RPM. Here, the Magnus effect might cause the ball to carry 12 meters (40 ft.) farther, but only 1.5 meters (5 ft.) to the right.

John Zumerchik and Fred Holmstrom

References

Bernstein, B., et al. "On the Dynamics of a Bull Whip," *Journal of Acoustic Society of America* 30 (1958): 1112ff.

Campbell, Malcolm. *The Random House International Encyclopedia of Golf.* New York: Random House, 1991.

Carlson, S. "A Kinetic Analysis of the Golf Swing." *Journal of Sports Medicine and Physical Fitness* 7 (1967): 76–80.

Cochran, A. (ed.) *Science and Golf*. New York: Chapman and Hall, 1990.

Cochran, A., and J. Stobbs. *The Search for a Perfect Swing*. New York: Lippincott, 1968.

Daish, C. *The Physics of Ball Games*. London: English University Press, 1972.

Davies, J. "The Aerodynamics of Golf Balls." *Journal of Applied Physics* 20 (1949): 821–828.

Edge, R. "The Spin on Baseballs and Golf balls." *The Physics Teacher* 19 (April 1980): 308–309.

Gambordella, T. *The Complete Book of Karate Weapons*. Boulder, Colorado: Paladin, 1981.

Hay, J. *Biomechanics of Sports*. Englewood Cliffs, New Jersey: Prentice Hall, 1985.

Holmstrom, F. E., and D. A. Nepala. *Patent No. 3,819,190: Golf Ball*, issued June 1974.

Jorgensen, T. *The Physics of Golf*. New York: AIP, 1994.

Martin, J. *The Curious History of the Golf Ball*. New York: Horizon, 1968.

Millburn, P. "Summation of Segmental Velocities in the Golf Swing." *Medicine and Science in Sports and Exercise* 14 (1982): 60ff.

Nicklaus, J. *Golf My Way*. New York: Simon and Schuster, 1974.

Richards, J., et al. "Weight Transfer Patterns during the Golf Swing." *Research Quarterly for Exercise and Sport* 56, no. 4 (1985): 361–365.

Shorupa, J. "The Mechanics of the Perfect Golf Swing." *Popular Mechanics*, June 1992.

Vaughan, C. "A Three-Dimensional Analysis of the Forces and Torques Applied by a Golfer during the Downswing." In A. Morecki (ed.), *Biomechanics VII-B*. Baltimore, Maryland: University Park Press, 1981.

Williams, D. *The Science of the Golf Swing*. London: Pelham, 1969.

Hockey

THE TERM *HOCKEY* is used to refer to both field hockey and ice hockey. In many parts of the world—in nations as disparate as India, New Zealand, Russia, Zimbabwe, England, Argentina, Germany, Pakistan, and the United States—field hockey is widely played by adults and children of both sexes, though the participation of women and girls is considerably less. Ice hockey naturally enjoys the greatest popularity in areas with cooler climates. In a few northern countries, such as Canada and many of the former Soviet states, the passion for ice hockey is so great that the sport is considered the national pastime.

Field and ice hockey are not the only forms of hockey, however. Another form, originally played primarily in urban areas where open fields were rare, is roller hockey, also called street hockey; this has been played at least since the 1930s. With the dramatic rise in the popularity of in-line skating since the 1980s, roller hockey—increasingly called in-line hockey—has gained a wide following in urban and rural areas alike. Roller hockey is played with the same rules as ice hockey, but players wear wheels and play on a concrete or wooden surface rather than on ice. It was originally played on roller skates, but since the 1980s it been played almost exclusively on in-line skates. In-line skates are much more similar to ice blades than are roller skates, making roller hockey more like ice hockey than ever. Avid ice hockey players, looking for off-season conditioning, have been increasingly drawn to roller hockey as a cross-training sport. Many other professional athletes, such as the baseball pitcher John Wetteland of the New York Yankees, have likewise turned to roller hockey for cardiovascular and strength training.

Although modern hockey has taken many forms, the game has ancient origins. Many historians believe that hockey was the first stick-and-ball game. Archaeological evidence dates field hockey to around 2000 B.C.E. in Persia. These early Persians, who also invented the game of polo, began playing "hockey on foot" well before experimenting with "hockey on horseback." Another early site of hockey was Greece, where a bas-relief on a wall, dating from the fifth or sixth century B.C.E., shows hockey players in a face-off. Additional historical evidence shows that versions of hockey were played by the Aztecs and by native North Americans, including the Makah, Wichita, and Sioux.

The exact origins of ice hockey, however, remain unclear. The hybrid nature of the game—a combination of field hockey and skating, with rules adopted from football and soccer—makes it difficult to pinpoint an exact time and place of origin. Some historians claim

Figure 1. *In the nineteenth century, when players seldom raised the puck off the ice, goalies required no protective padding. But as shooting skills improved, goalies looked to other sports for protective gear. With glove and chest protectors from baseball and shin pads from cricket, goalies felt adequately prepared to handle the flying puck. It was not until the 1950s and 1960s, however, that goalies began wearing face masks.*

that native North Americans were the first to play hockey on ice, but little evidence has been found to support the claim. Other historians date the origins of the game to the early nineteenth century, when the English, Irish, and Scottish versions of field hockey—known, respectively, as bandy, hurley, and shinty (or shinny)—were often played on iced surfaces during the winter months. As early as 1813, records show that members of the village of Bury Fen in England were playing a game called ice bandy. However, these early versions of ice hockey are not given credit for originating the sport, because the participants did not wear skates.

It is often argued that the first game of ice hockey was improvised by English soldiers on a frozen harbor in Kingston, Ontario, during the winter of 1855. Borrowing from the local sport of skating, which was then popular in Canada, the soldiers tied runners to their boots, found sticks, and began hitting around an old lacrosse ball. The first recorded use of a puck, rather than a ball, dates to 1860, also in Kingston.

In Montreal, which also claims credit as the birthplace of ice hockey, two thirty-member teams played a game at McGill University in 1879. Shortly thereafter, two students wrote the first known rules for ice hockey, which vary considerably from the rules of the National Hockey League (NHL) in the 1990s. Under the first rules, each side played nine (not six) players at a time, only forward passing was permitted, body checking was not allowed, and offensive players had to remain behind the puck at all times. Few would disagree, however, that the adaptation of the game of field hockey to ice play using skates radically changed the sport by making it considerably faster.

Ice hockey has since grown into a major worldwide sport. It is an extremely fast-paced game in which a slippery playing surface, aggressive collisions, and the ability of players to reach speeds in excess of 40 KPH (25 MPH) add to the excitement.

Ice hockey is one of the more violent amateur and professional sports, although stricter rules and harsher penalties have partly diminished the level and incidence of injuries during games. Some violence is likely to remain, however, if only because the players are skating at high speeds within a very confined area while carrying a sturdy stick—a weapon of sorts. Moreover, certain legal moves, particularly checks and collisions, can become violent; and players are sometimes admittedly motivated by vengeance. Still, a player does not necessarily come onto the ice planning to commit violent acts—such acts usually result in heavy fines and suspensions and also entail a risk of disfigurement. It is probably often the case that players simply fall victim to human nature, a natural result of what is a very physical game.

The Hockey Puck

When the soldiers in Kingston took the game of hockey to the ice, they must have quickly realized that moving a rubber ball along slippery ice was impractical: a ball was difficult to control, it bounced over the sticks. In 1860 the rubber ball was replaced by a puck, a flat rubber disk said to be cut from an original ball. The disk-shaped puck moved along the ice far more predictably than the old lacrosse ball.

Dynamics: Puck versus Ball

Any object moving along a surface must do so by rolling, sliding, or bouncing. When two objects slide across each other—as when a ball or a puck slides across a surface—a frictional force retards movement. The coefficient of friction—the friction force for a level surface relative to the weight—depends on the nature of the surfaces in contact. For example, a rubber tire on dry concrete has a coefficient of friction of about 0.8; sandpaper on sandpaper can have a coefficient of 1 or more. Smooth or lubricated surfaces generally have coefficients of less than 0.1. A hockey puck sliding on ice is in this lower range, around 0.08. A puck launched at 33 KPH (22 MPH) will slide the entire 61-meter (200-ft.) length of a hockey arena before coming to rest. If the puck were standing still, the coefficient would be larger. In hockey, however, the puck rarely stands still.

A ball is far preferable for sports like field hockey, in which considerable friction exists between the playing object and the surface. Friction impedes the progress of any object, but is also the reason a ball rolls: without friction, a ball could only slide. Friction creates a braking force at the point at which the ball meets the surface. This braking force creates torque, or rotational motion, which causes the top of the ball to move faster than the bottom. At the instant at which the top of the ball is moving twice as fast as the center of the ball, the bottom of the ball stops sliding on the surface and the ball begins to roll. A rolling ball is hindered much less by friction than is a sliding object. This same principle makes a ball-bearing wheel more effective than a standard wheel. In fact, the invention of ball bearings is largely responsible for making the sports of skateboarding and roller skating both possible and popular. Once a ball begins to roll, surface-ball fric-

The field hockey ball was originally a cricket ball (slightly larger than baseball), but now the sport has its own approved rubber ball that weighs 5.5 to 5.75 ounces and is 8 13/16 to 9 1/4 inches in circumference.

The puck is a disk of vulcanized rubber 3 inches in diameter and 1 inch thick, and about 5.5 to 6 ounces in weight.

Roller hockey uses an implement that is a "hybrid" ball: part disk and part ball. It has the same size and shape as an ice hockey puck, but it has a number of ball-like casters that protrude out from both sides of the disk. It slides more easily across the typical "high-friction" asphalt surface, yet is easier to control because it does not bound like a ball. Polymer balls are also used. They come in three temperature models—warm, cool, and cold—to bounce consistently at different outdoor temperatures.

Figure 2. *The field-hockey ball, the ice-hockey puck, and the roller-hockey puck are quite different. Roller hockey is sometimes played with a ball matched to the weather conditions.*

tion is no longer a factor because of the ball's small rolling coefficient of friction—about 0.01—which is much less than the sliding friction of either a puck or a ball on ice.

Instead of a ball, ice hockey uses a 170-gram (6-oz.) disk of vulcanized rubber, called a puck. Although some similarities exist between the motion of a ball and that of a puck on ice, major differences in dynamics considerably change the game and affect strategy. The similarity between a ball and a puck is that their coefficients of friction are nearly identical. If a puck and a ball of about the same size and weight are launched together along smooth, freshly frozen (or freshly resurfaced) ice, the two will slide side by side until the ball begins to roll. At that point, the ball will quickly move away from the puck and continue across the ice while the puck comes to a rest.

The sports of curling and shuffleboard are based on the predictable manner in which disklike objects slide. In curling, rock disks are slid across an ice surface; in shuffleboard, clay disks glide across a heavily waxed surface. Players in these sports must develop motor-control memory in order to slide the disk so that it stops in a scoring zone, neither short nor long of it.

The stopping point of a ball that has been rolled across ice is much less predictable than it is for a disk because the ball's small rolling coefficient of friction means that minor imperfections in the ice or ball will affect the outcome. Small chips of ice or ridges in the surface can divert the slowly rolling ball in almost any direction before it stops. Billiards and golf are played on felt and on short grass, respectively, to increase the rolling coefficient of friction in a controlled fashion, so that a rolling ball will stop predictably. The fact that the puck slows down predictably makes it easier for the ice hockey player to take a strong shot at the puck as it slows or momentarily stops moving.

Low surface friction makes wind resistance the dominant factor affecting the dynamics of the hockey puck at moderate to high speeds. Wind resistance, like friction, is a force that opposes the motion of the puck, depending on the orientation and the speed of the puck. Face-on, the puck has a larger area than it has edge-on, and thus a larger drag coefficient—resistance that impedes progress—so the wind resistance face-on is about four times the resistance edge-on.

In this respect, a puck is similar to a Frisbee (*see also FIELD ATHLETICS: THROWING*). A Frisbee can be thrown 100 meters (about 90 yd.) edge-on, but only about 1 meter (3.3 ft.) face-on. Wind resistance also increases as the square of the speed. For example, if speed is doubled, wind resistance increases four times. At 160 KPH (100 MPH) the wind resistances on a puck face-on and edge-on are about 20 ounces and 5 ounces, respectively. At 80 KPH (50 MPH) these forces are 5 ounces and 1.25 ounces. For a ball with the same volume and weight as a puck, the wind resistance would be about the same as for the edge-on puck. By comparison, the sliding frictional force on a puck or on a ball is a mere 0.5 ounce, about 10 percent of the wind resistance at 160 KPH (100 MPH) edge-on. At 48 KPH (30

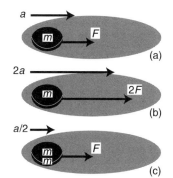

Figure 3. *The puck travels across ice in a much more predictable pattern than a ball. (a) F = force; a = acceleration; m = mass. (b) According to Newton's second law of motion, if the force F used to propel the puck is doubled, the puck's acceleration (a) also doubles. (c) With the same force, if mass (m) is doubled, acceleration (a) is halved. This is a directly proportional effect. The predictable manner in which disklike objects glide is the basis of curling and shuffleboard, in which disks are slid across a smooth surface so that they stop in a scoring zone. The same precision cannot be accomplished with a ball.*

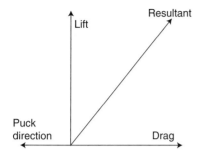

Figure 4. *Lift and drag are two forces that act on a puck as it travels through the air.*

MPH) the edge-on wind resistance and the sliding friction are about equal.

In considering the effects of wind resistance, one need not be concerned with the orientation of a ball in order to get minimum wind resistance. A puck, on the other hand, will quickly die in flight if it faces the wind or tumbles at random. However, the complete aerodynamics are a bit more complex. Aerodynamic effects at high velocities can change the trajectory of a puck much to the advantage of the hockey player. A puck that is hit with a spin about its axis will move with a stable orientation. If it is properly oriented, it will experience lift as well as drag and will virtually fly across the arena (*see Figure 4*). While a puck can glide airborne in a nearly horizontal trajectory at high speed, a ball struck similarly will follow a downward curve and bounce off the ice. The puck may skip across the arena in a few brief touches to the ice, but the ball will make many short bounces.

To most hockey fans, an unpredictably bounding ball would be far less aesthetically pleasing than the predictable skidding and skipping of a puck. Moreover, skilled hockey players can control a puck solely by feel, freeing their eyes to concentrate on the action going on around them. If ice hockey used a ball instead of the predictable puck, players trying to handle it with the hockey stick would probably often lose it while changing directions and speed to feint and fake their way past defenders; and they would need to take their eyes off their teammates and opponents much more often to sneak a peek at the ball. The aerodynamics of a flat disk and the controlled slide of a puck on nearly frictionless ice explain why the disklike puck was adopted in favor of the field hockey ball in the mid-1800s, early in the history of ice hockey.

Puck Trajectories

Many hockey experts agree that the most desirable shots in hockey are shots that stay close to the ice, around 5 to 10 centimeters (2–4 in.) from the surface. Low shots offer teammates the best opportunities to deflect the puck past the goalie, and are much more difficult for the goalie to stop with the knock-down glove or catching mitt. For even the best players, keeping the puck low when shooting a slap shot is not easy. Because the puck is usually struck so that it comes off the blade at a slight angle of attack, tilted upward, it has a natural tendency to rise. This angle of attack creates a lifting force on the bottom part of the puck that causes its trajectory to take an upward, drifting flight path (*see Figure 4*).

When a puck is struck so that the angle of attack alternates from positive to negative, it flutters up and down on its way toward its target. To see how this works, one can stick one's hand out of the window of a car traveling at about 97 KPH (60 MPH)—the speed and air resistance will be similar to that experienced by a puck. A tilt of the palm upward, with the index finger as the leading edge, creates a lifting force, which causes the arm to rise; a tilt of the hand downward creates a downward force, and the arm will be pushed down. In each case, as well as for an intermediate, or horizontal, position, it is drag that forces the arm backward.

In addition to variations in angle of attack, a puck's flight is affected by any spin at an angle to its axis. This type of wobble can be seen by tossing a coin into the air with various directions of spin. Wobble also makes the puck's flight path vary up and down as the amounts of lift and of drag vary. Just as with throwing a Frisbee, the rotation of the puck is important to maintaining a stable flight path. The same aerodynamic principles that hold for a Frisbee hold for the disk-shaped hockey puck (*see also "The Frisbee: The Most Popular Disk," in FIELD ATHLETICS: THROWING*).

With no spin at all, a puck tumbles through the air, orienting itself to suffer the largest possible wind resistance. It will act much the same way as a piece of paper dropped to the floor or as a leaf falling from a tree, swooping back and forth with the large surface area facing the air impeding the fall. A spinless puck will quickly lose its forward momentum because the wind resistance face-on is many times the weight of the puck traveling at a high speed. As the orientation to the wind shifts, the puck will also begin to move back and forth and take unexpected dives, just as the leaf and the paper dip back and forth during fall. Like a spinless pitch in baseball or a spinless serve in volleyball—both of which are called knuckleballs—a spinless puck will veer unexpectedly. Such a shot is difficult for a goalie to stop because the puck will move in and out of the direct line of sight (*see also VISION*).

Sticks and Shooting

A puck's speed, spin, and axis of rotation—which completely determine its flight path—are all controlled by the way in which the stick contacts the puck. A hockey stick consists of several parts: the blade toe, the blade heel, the shaft, and the butt end. Players attempt to hit the puck at the sweet spot of the blade, a spot closer to the heel than to the toe (*for a longer discussion of sweet spots, see TENNIS*). When the puck is contacted at the sweet spot, maximum energy is transferred from the stick to the puck. If the puck is contacted away from the sweet spot, toward the toe of the blade, the stick has the tendency to rotate in the player's hands. In that case, some energy is wasted because the stick absorbs more of it, rather than delivering it to the puck. Top players sometimes try to get the puck to roll from the heel to the toe of the blade so that the tailing spin makes the puck fade, or curve, toward the corner of the net and away from the goaltender.

Top scorers learn to deliver the optimal combination of velocity and accuracy needed to score. They become top scorers precisely because they are able to decide in a split second whether to blast a slap shot or to go for the corner with a quick wrist shot. No one type of shot—wrist, slap, or backhand—is superior to all others or in all circumstances. Each shot has certain advantages, so shot selection should be made with these advantages in mind.

Slap Shot

Although slap shots are seldom right on target, they are nevertheless often the shot of preference. This is because in a slap shot, the puck comes off the stick like a bullet out of a rifle. Despite control problems, the slap shot may still score if it beats the goaltender with pure speed or if it is deflected into the goal by a well-positioned teammate.

Accuracy is important, however, because the goalie—wearing large pads and gloves and holding a stick—occupies most of the goal opening, which is only 1.2 meters (4 ft.) high and 1.8 meters (6 ft.) wide. A 170-gram (6-oz.) puck will not push a 91-kilogram (200-lb.) goalie back into the goal, even if it hits him at 160 KPH (100 MPH). Scoring with a slap shot takes a bit of luck. Not only must the shot be on goal; it must also miss the goalie. Often the slap shot is used to set up an easier shot as the puck rebounds off the goalie or another defender. Other shots can be controlled more effectively and shot on net with greater frequency, but shooters like to terrorize goaltenders with a slap shot working its way through a maze of players in front of the net. In the slap shot, there is a trade-off. Accuracy is reduced for the sake of the key advantage of this shot: surprise. A 160-KPH slap shot taken from a distance of 9 meters (30 ft.) will reach the goal in about 0.2 seconds, the outer limits of the best reaction time theoretically possible for the goalkeeper (*see also MOTOR CONTROL*).

When shooting a slap shot, the player holds the hockey stick with one hand at the butt end as the other slides down near the shaft's midpoint. A baseball swing and a golf swing, with hands held close together, are both double-pendulum swings—with axes both at the midbody and at the hands. With one hand midshaft, the slap shot becomes a single-pendulum swing (*see Figure 5*). This lowers the moment of inertia—less torque is necessary to start the stick moving—and allows a quicker swing. Like a long-handled wrench, it also increases the amount of torque for any given force; a hockey player need not bring the stick as far back behind the head during the backswing as a golfer. This is important because the shorter the backswing, the greater the shooting accuracy (there is a better chance of contacting the sweet spot). And with one hand positioned at the flexing point—the point where the shaft bends the most—the shooter can monitor just how much the stick is flexing and make appropriate adjustments in the angle of the blade.

To transfer the maximum amount of power to the shot, the body should fully uncoil at the point at which the stick blade, the ice, and the puck meet. Weight should be transferred on the downswing from the back skate to the front skate. At contact, the weight transfer necessitates that the back leg and foot swing off the ice and behind the other foot. This acts to counter the force of the hands and arms snapping forward toward the target (*see Figure 6*).

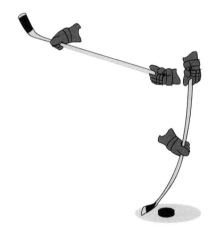

Figure 5. *For the slap shot, the shaft hand (the right hand here) begins in a position far down the shaft and slides upward through the swing, ending near midshaft at the moment of impact with the puck. The flexing wooden stick is an example of an elastic storage of energy: the shooter can send the puck flying at a greater velocity by striking the ice first—thereby flexing the stick—than by striking only the puck.*

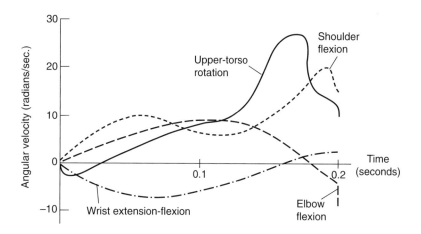

Figure 6. *In the slap shot, the upper-torso rotation and the dominant shoulder, elbow, and wrist joints during flexion (bending) and extension (straightening) have different velocity curves. (Typical curves are shown.) Upper torso rotation and shoulder flexion are vital factors in maximizing power.*

Conservation of the skater's angular momentum (mass × velocity about a fixed axis) is an inescapable factor during the slap shot. Just as a spinning figure skater uses this conservation law to slow down spin by extending the leg (*see also ACROBATICS and SKATING*), a hockey player uses the same principle to keep from spinning out of control while shooting. As the upper body rotates, swinging the stick toward the puck, the back leg swings around in the other direction to balance the angular momentum. Without the leg extended, the body would spin much faster in the direction opposite the swing of the stick, the shot would be very weak, and the player would probably fall clumsily to the ice.

The fact that a skater can maintain enough balance to develop tremendous stick-puck impact does not of itself ensure a high-velocity slap shot. This is because the impact force of the blade against the puck is not the sole determinant of puck velocity. The physicist René Doré of Ecole Polytechnique discovered an interesting phenomenon. One hockey player generated 22 foot-pounds of force on the blade and produced a shot moving at 26 meters per second (85 ft./sec.). Another player generated far less force (11 ft.-lb.) on the blade, yet produced a higher puck velocity, 29 meters per second (95 ft./sec.) (Doré, 1976). The additional variable that accounts for such a disparity is that early stick-ice contact increases stick velocity by the time the puck actually leaves the stick.

A slap shot with a hockey stick is an example of elastic storage of energy. Unlike an inelastic collision—for example, a collision between a steel pipe and an iron cannonball—blade-puck collision imparts additional velocity to the puck by nature of the elastic properties of the wooden stick itself. As the blade flexes backward at the initial ice contact, the elasticity of the wooden material springs the stick forward at a faster velocity than if the swing had taken place along a completely airborne trajectory. The flexible stick deforms on ice contact and then springs back to its original shape. In addition to elastic energy, two other factors contribute to the total energy imparted to the puck: inertia and the clamped grip of the player's moving hands. The stick vibrates, probably in many different modes, when given an impulse (force × time), such as when struck against the ice.

For simplicity, one may assume that as a result of the stick-ice impact, the blade of the stick oscillates only in simple harmonic motion relative to the player's moving hands, which do not slow down at all. The oscillation of the blade is then added to the overall motion of the player's hands, with the result that the blade velocity decreases just after the impact with the ice. When something opposes the motion of an object, the object slows down. In this case, however, the blade recovers its initial velocity within only one-fourth of a period of oscillation; by two-fourths of a period, the blade is moving faster than it was before it hit the ice. If blade-puck contact takes place at this moment, the puck will be propelled faster than if the stick had never hit the ice. All of this takes place in less than a few milliseconds, so timing is extremely critical. The velocity of a slap shot, therefore, depends on technique—the ability of the shooter to optimize the elastic energy of the stick—and not necessarily on the amount of force applied to the blade (*see Figure 7*).

As the stick bends during stick-puck dwell time, the blade often reaches a point at which it can no longer keep up with the shaft. A failure of the shaft to recoil rapidly enough means that the puck will leave the stick well before the elastic energy in the stick can be returned to it. This results in wasted energy—energy that remains with the stick and player, rather than being transferred from the stick to the puck. The blade and shaft of the stick need to be stiff enough to withstand the force of the blade striking the ice. Players strive to hit the blade on the ice just before hitting the puck, so that the stick can flex to a greater degree and therefore transfer more elastic energy to the puck.

When the blade makes contact with only the puck, less elastic

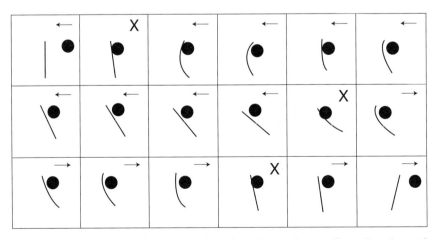

Figure 7. *During a well-executed slap shot, the puck actually strikes the stick three times. At first contact, the blade curves around the puck as it springs back and loses contact. For about the next 9 milliseconds, the puck and blade move backward together without actually touching. A second impact then occurs when the blade springs forward again, which leads to a second phase of separation. A final impact occurs when the blade again catches up to the puck and propels it away. (Source: Alexander, 1963)*

energy is imparted to the puck. Avoiding ice contact is not as effective because the puck's mass is only about 170 grams (6 oz.). Regardless of the velocity of the stick during the downswing, a 170-gram mass contacted over only a few milliseconds is not nearly enough force to flex the wooden stick enough to add appreciably to the velocity of the stick before the puck leaves the blade.

Of the many types of slap shots, a shot taken while moving toward the target will generate the greatest puck velocity. This is due simply to the added velocity of the player, who may be traveling toward the puck at 32 KPH (20 MPH) or faster. Skating in the shooting direction is an example of the same principle that is applied in baseball when a center fielder runs toward the infield to make a catch in order to move toward the throwing target: this results in a higher-velocity throw than would be possible if the player caught and threw the ball while standing still. For the hockey player, the tremendous angular momentum of the stick—created by the wrists, the forearms, and the upper body as they uncoil behind the shot—is transferred to the relatively light puck at the end of the stick, much as when a small bullet is fired from a large gun.

Wrist Shot

Bobby Hull, known to fans of the Chicago Blackhawks in the 1960s and early 1970s as the "golden jet," launched slap shots at 185 to 193 KPH (115–120 MPH), about 32 KPH (20 MPH) faster than the average NHL player. When the occasional puck flew out of play and into the crowd at Chicago Stadium, spectators would duck as it as it ricocheted off the back wall with a booming sound. Hull attributed his powerful slap shot to strength training, including farmwork in his youth. But just as Hull's career was nearing its end in the mid-1970s, Wayne Gretzky, a "finesse" player with a small frame, began a career that would result in a major revisions in NHL record books and would disprove the notion that a hockey player needs to be strong to be great.

Although in strength testing Gretzky was often found to be one of the weakest players on his teams, as of 1996 he still held more NHL season and career scoring records than any other player in the history of the league. In fact, his quickness, grace, and ability to make his feats look easy have led many people to consider him the greatest hockey player of all time. While Bobby Hull's slap shot was powerful because he could generate the massive acceleration of the upper torso and shoulder joint necessary to create power, Gretzky is known particularly for his wrist shot, which he released with speed, finesse, and incredible accuracy.

The wrist shot is very different from the slap shot. The slap shot involves an impact much like hitting a baseball with a bat, in which the stick velocity is much higher than with a wrist shot. In a slap shot, because of the long swing arc and the better collision dynamics, the puck is propelled even faster than the speed at which the blade hits it. In a wrist shot, by contrast, the puck is in continuous contact with the blade throughout the shooting motion and is propelled at approximately the same speed as the blade. The wrist shot thus generates less puck velocity than the slap shot, but it is much easier to control.

The execution of a wrist shot is actually quite simple. In a front-to-back straddled stance, the player places the majority of the body's weight over the forward leg, opposite the blade side. As the body shifts forward, the stick is lowered and the blade cups the puck. Next the arms come forward and the wrists snap forward, while the knee of the forward leg bends. At this point the stick shaft flexes, owing to the sudden application of torque. The knee of the forward leg bends so that more force can be exerted on the puck. A knee bend extends the length of puck-blade contact, making it possible to prolong the time over which force can be applied. At the same time, the rear leg moves up and behind the front leg to maintain balance in a similar way to the slap shot.

Many players try to use a quick snap of the wrist with a low follow-through to keep the puck from rising more than a few inches off the ice. A longer, more accentuated wrist snap and a higher follow-through toward the net will send the puck much higher. But because of the extended period of blade-puck contact, it is much easier to control the puck's angle of attack and amount of lift for the wrist shot than for the slap shot. To score, the threat of a high shot should always be present. A goalie who knew with certainty that a shot would be on the ice could easily block the entire 6-foot-wide goal with pads, stick, and body.

Although quick wrists are important for all great shooters, factors other than quickness must also be considered. In relation to the position of the puck, when and how the wrists are flicked is vital. A player needs timing, strength, hand velocity, and an understanding of stick-puck dynamics in order to execute wrist shots effectively and consistently. Although both hands move relatively parallel to each other throughout the shot, there are nonetheless some differences (*see Figure 8*). In his study of wrist positions for low and high shots, W. R. Halliwell discovered that for a high wrist shot, the lower hand—the hand positioned at the middle of the stick—was 13.51 centimeters (5.3 in.) ahead of the puck during blade-puck contact; for a low wrist shot, the lower hand was 8.30 centimeters (3.2 in.) behind the puck. In all, the total difference in wrist positions between the two shots is 21.81 centimeters (8.5 in.) (Halliwell, 1978).

Some of this lower-hand movement is a response to upper-hand action. During the shot, the upper hand moves toward the puck much like the lower hand, then suddenly changes direction and moves away from the target and toward the body. For a high wrist shot, this reversal occurs 0.03 second before impact; for a low wrist shot, 0.05 second before impact. The upper hand reverses and moves in the opposite direction of the lower hand, creating a countering pivotal force that generates more power. What determines shot velocity is the ability of a player's hands to reach high velocities while moving in opposite directions at impact. Because a high wrist shot requires more of a scooping motion to lift the puck into the air, the hand posi-

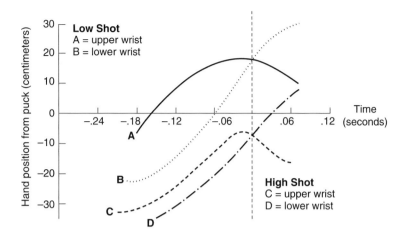

Figure 8. *Because the wrist snaps during the execution of a wrist shot, the positions of the lower and upper wrist differ before and after contacting the puck. The wrists work as a force couple at the time of puck release; as the lower wrist moves forward, the upper wrist moves back. (Source: Halliwell, 1978)*

tion at impact is different. The upper hand moves behind the lower hand by about 6.43 centimeters (2.5 in.) for a high wrist shot, and by about 1.84 centimeters (0.7 in.) for a low wrist shot.

The wrist shot also allows more spin to be imparted to the puck than is possible with the slap shot, and spin is very important for accuracy. Less tumbling through the air or along the ice results in a more controlled trajectory. A spin about the vertical axis stabilizes the puck and keeps it gliding smoothly in its path, much like a thrown Frisbee (*see also FIELD ATHLETICS: THROWING*). If it has no spin, it either tumbles through the air, encountering much more wind resistance, or bounces unpredictably off the ice. The rifling inside the barrel of a rifle adds spin to a bullet for the same purpose; spin keeps the bullet oriented in the direction of motion. A secondary advantage of a spinning puck is that it maintains a flat profile. A tumbling puck is more visible to the goalie and thus is more easily stopped.

Tight versus Loose Grip

In sports such as tennis and baseball, there is considerable debate over whether the racket or bat should be gripped tightly or loosely. In baseball, the main objective is power. Although grip firmness does not significantly affect the rebound velocity of the ball off a wooden bat, it is a large factor for the aluminum bat. For the wooden bat, vibrational waves created on bat-ball contact move slowly relative to the hands and do not allow the hands an opportunity to "damp" the energy. The hollow aluminum bat, by contrast, allows vibrational waves to travel quickly to the hands, which in turn play a part in damping wasteful vibrational energy. Limiting vibrational energy means that more energy can be delivered to the ball. In the case of tennis rackets, researchers found that grip firmness mattered only for off-center contact (that is, contact not in the sweet spot). Off-center contact causes the racket to twist in the player's hand, an adverse effect that severely reduces the accuracy of the shot.

Both of these examples are germane to shooting in hockey, because hockey players must try to maximize velocity as well as accuracy. In a study of grip firmness, John Alexander, a kinesiologist at the University of Alberta, found that for all shots there is a low correlation between accuracy and grip firmness and that the skating wrist shot is the most accurate (Alexander, 1963). It is unlikely that grip firmness is important for wrist shots, especially for skating wrist shots, because there is no impact velocity—the puck and blade slide together across the ice before the shot is made. On the other hand, for big-impact slap shots and for shots requiring the player to alter the puck's direction, a firm midshaft grip matters for two reasons. First, the chance of contacting the puck at the sweet spot of the blade is far from certain. The usual result of an off-center contact, even with a tight grip, is that the stick twists in the player's hands, so that the puck comes off the stick weakly and on an unintended course. With a weak grip, the effect is magnified. Second, a strong midshaft grip is necessary for power, as it maximizes the flex of the blade on contact with the ice and the puck.

The Hockey Stick

Choosing a stick.   Although players choose their sticks by feel, they want to find a stick that is most appropriate for their own particular swing. If a stick is too flexible, the force of blade-puck contact will be absorbed by the blade when the stick fails to return to its normal, preflex position before the puck leaves the blade. The puck does not spring off the blade and therefore will not follow the path of the follow-through. Instead, it will usually spin weakly off the toe of the blade, much in the way a slice comes of the end off a golf club head with much of the momentum generated in the downswing wasted (*see also GOLF*).

What should a stick be made of?   The NHL places no restrictions on the length of the hockey stick or on the materials of which it is made—the only restriction is on the amount of bend of the curve. Given the rapid advances in materials science, is wood still the optimal material for hockey sticks? Materials such as aluminum, graphite, and composites might improve performance, although any change in the flexibility, size, or weight of the puck or of the stick would require adjustments from the user (*for a discussion of technological advances in material science, see EQUIPMENT MATERIALS*). One advantage of a graphite or composite stick would be lightness: these materials weigh only about half as much as wood. A graphite or composite stick is less fatiguing to carry than the heavier wooden stick and can be swung at a greater velocity. Much as with swinging a baseball bat, the stick's velocity is far more important than its mass in generating puck speed (*see also BASEBALL*).

Another advantage of a graphite or composite stick would be flexibility. Like the graphite and composite tennis rackets common in the 1990s, a graphite or composite hockey stick could generate more elastic energy to the puck, particularly during slap shots, when there is considerable stick flex. As a wooden stick flexes, it does not return all the elastic energy to the puck—much of that energy is damped

Exceptional Traits of Hockey Players

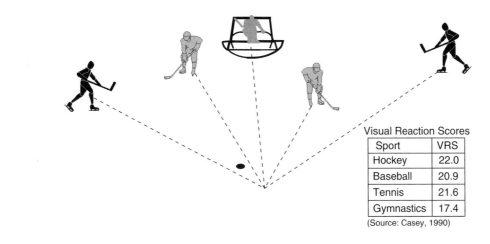

Visual Reaction Scores	
Sport	VRS
Hockey	22.0
Baseball	20.9
Tennis	21.6
Gymnastics	17.4

(Source: Casey, 1990)

Particularly for power plays and in the waning moments of a tight game, controlling the face-off—in which the puck is dropped between two players, one from each team—is crucial. Coaches often try to outmaneuver each other, shuffling players back and forth in an attempt to obtain the most favorable matchup for the face-off. When the puck is dropped, the opposing players drop their sticks to the ice and attempt to direct the puck to a teammate. Lightning-quick reflexes and the ability to see and react to the drop are vital, because the first player to reach the puck usually controls the face-off.

Quick reflexes are among the many attributes of hockey skaters, but for goalies they are paramount. A professional goalie's spot in the roster depends almost entirely on lightning-quick reflexes. Almost every year in the NHL playoffs, a stellar performance is turned in by a "hot" goalie.

Here, the word *hot* means that the goalie's reflexes and hand-eye coordination are exceptional. Hot goalies

confound, confuse, and eventually break the confidence of opposing players because they seem capable of stopping everything. A hot goalie can make a mediocre team good and a good team great; a "cold" goalie can make an otherwise great team no better than good, and a good team mediocre. For that reason, playoffs in the NHL result in far more upsets than playoffs in other professional sports.

In terms of reaction times and vision, hockey players compare very favorably with athletes in other sports. High-speed hand-eye coordination is necessary for a player to win a face-off or a goalie to stop a 160-KPH (100-MPH) shot. Jeffrey Minkoff, a physician, conducted a test of the exceptional visiual traits of hockey players (Minkoff, 1980). Of twenty-one NHL players tested, six received the maximum score (6) in tests of either eye speed or eye span (peripheral vision). Of these six, three had the maximum score in both tests: two of them were goalies and the third was the team's leading goal- and

point-scorer for the season. The eye test also proved a valid predictor of performance: the player coaches considered to have the least accurate shots received the lowest scores.

Because a hockey player must focus simultaneously on many things in the field of vision, eye speed and eye span are critical. A shooter must focus on the goalie, the net, the player to whom the puck will be passed, and the moving puck itself—all at the same time. In a face-off, a player must vigilantly watch the referee's hand; the opponent's position and stick movements; and the positions of the other players—teammates and opponents. Of the twenty-three professional baseball players tested, none scored higher than 5 in either eye speed or eye span. Baseball hitters do need excellent vision, but perhaps because they need to focus only on the ball, their play does not suffer from poorer eye speed or eye span (*see also VISION and MOTOR CONTROL*).

John Zumerchik

within the material itself. An ideal stick should be elastic but also nondamping. Manufacturers may eventually custom-design sticks to match each player's needs, much as with golf clubs. Perhaps wooden sticks will become obsolete; wooden tennis rackets disappeared in the late 1970s, and wooden-shaft golf clubs even earlier.

Curved blades and taping.   NHL fans will not soon forget the turning point of the 1993 Stanley Cup finals between the Montreal Canadians and the Los Angeles Kings. The Canadians had lost game one and were losing game two by a score of 2 to 1, with only 1:45 seconds remaining in the third period. Their coach, Jacques Demers, was puzzled as to why his team had scored only two goals in 118 minutes against Kelley Hrudey, the Kings' goalie. Perhaps in desperation, he asked to check the legality of the stick of the Kings' defenseman Marty McSorley.

According to NHL rules, the hook can be curved only 0.5 inch (0.2 cm). Demers's hunch turned out to be right: when McSorley's stick was measured, it was found to curve 0.75 inch (more than 0.8 cm)—a substantial deviation (0.25 in., or 0.62 cm) from the legal maximum. McSorley's stick was taken away, and he was sent to the penalty box for 2 minutes. Thanks to this penalty, the Candians had an advantage that enabled them to go on the attack and tie the game, which they they won in overtime; they would also win the next three games and the Stanley Cup. The impact of this penalty was so great that many fans wondered if an illegally curved stick offered enough advantage to warrant McSorley's gamble. (It should be noted, incidentally, that Demers's request was also a gamble: if he had been wrong—if the stick had been found legal—the Canadians would have themselves been penalized 2 minutes for delay of game.)

Many etymologists believe that the word *hockey* is a diminutive form of *hook*, and the game may indeed have originally been played with a hooked stick. But the NHL had good reason to limit the amount of hook, or curve, of the hockey stick. In the hands of a talented player, a curved stick gives two advantages: greater velocity and greater accuracy.

Increased velocity is possible because the curve lengthens the time of actual stick-puck contact: a shooter's force is applied for a longer period, and more of the elastic energy of the stick is imparted to the puck. Whereas the puck will come off the toe of a straight blade quickly, it will tend to remain on a curved blade slightly longer (longer dwell time), coming off with more speed and more spin. Puck velocity is greater with the curved blade because the shooter is doing more work (force × distance). For a given force, the longer dwell time with a curved stick means that the force is applied over a greater distance, thereby imparting greater energy to the puck. This increased dwell time also improves shooting accuracy. The longer the puck stays on the stick, the more likely it is that the puck will leave the stick at the intended angle of incline, or height, and in the desired direction. In McSorley's case, of course, since he was caught violating NHL regulations, his gamble did not pay off; but if his 0.25-inch advantage gave McSorley's shots even 10 percent greater velocity and accuracy, the temptation behind it is certainly understandable.

One legal option that improves stick-puck dynamics is stick taping, although the NHL does restrict the amount of tape that can be used, to prevent players from increasing the blade of the curve through extensive taping. All professional hockey players—and virtually all amateur players—tape their sticks to create a tackier blade surface that increases frictional properties between stick and puck. Taping makes it easier to control the puck by damping the impact of, or absorbing energy from, a passed puck. Once the pass is taken, the tape helps the player maintain the puck on the stick by creating greater friction. A secondary benefit of taping is that, along with blade curvature, it facilitates puck rotation and thus improves accuracy.

Skating Power and Power Skating

Physiologists classify hockey as a sport that is equally anaerobic and aerobic. The term *anaerobic* means that it requires explosive muscle power; *aerobic* means that it requires endurance. Hockey is somewhat unusual because skaters move at or near full speed while on the ice for shifts of about 3 minutes and then may sit on the bench for 10 minutes while other players replace them. (The goalie is an exception, although goalies may also be relieved as necessary.) Total playing time is 60 minutes, divided into three 20-minute periods with two 12-minute intermissions. However, a game usually lasts slightly over 2 hours, depending on the number of penalties and interruptions. To perform well under these circumstances, players need some of the endurance of a cross-country runner and some of the the power of a sprinter or a long jumper. Anaerobic capacity is necessary for the sporadic rapid bursts of energy that are interspersed with periods of rest; aerobic capacity is needed for times when players must give as much as possible for as long as possible.

Speed skating is rhythmic, fluid, and fast; figure skating is rhythmic, graceful, and slow. Hockey skating is not rhythmic at all. Hockey demands power skating, including rapid changes of direction and numerous stops and starts. Whereas a track sprinter may reach full speed at 25 to 30 meters (27–33 yd.), a hockey player, using power skating, takes more time and a longer distance to reach top speed. Due in part to the confines of the standard 91.4-meter (100-yd.) rink, skaters cannot reach full speed by skating from end to end: they are just starting to approach full speed when they must slow down to stop or to turn around.

In addition to power, a hockey player must possess incredible maneuverability. The slippery, near-frictionless nature of the ice surface gives skaters only a small margin of error as they continually stop, start, and maneuver around other players in pursuit of the puck. For this reason, inertia is a much more important factor for hockey skaters than for athletes who play on surfaces with a higher coefficient of friction. The same principle of inertia and the same proper-

Goaltenders: Students of Geometry

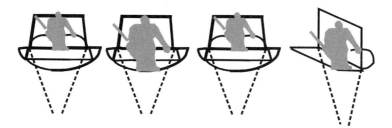

Great goaltending may not guarantee a team's success, but no team will win consistently without it. Carrying 16 kilograms (35 lb.) of equipment, a goalie must rely on flexibility, agility, and lightning-fast reflexes to stop shots. By playing high-percentage angles, he improves his chances of stopping 160-KPH (100-MPH) shots and screen shots. He continually adjusts his position to remain centered between the shooter and the goal, aiming for a stance that presents the largest possible physical and visual barrier.

Coming out. By coming out toward the shooter, the goalie blocks more of the net and makes scoring more difficult. At the same time, he becomes more vulnerable to side passes and stick-handling moves. In addition, he has less time to react to the shot.

Front versus side shots. Shots from directly in front of the goal offer the largest scoring area. As he moves deeper in, away from the net and closer to the boards, the shooting angle narrows and greatly favors the goalie, because more of the goalie's body can cover the net.

ties of ice that make possible a full-speed glide with little effort also make for very labored starts—the short, choppy strides players make to accelerate from a stop.

Aggressive turns and stop-and-go maneuvers, perhaps more than anything else, distinguish hockey skating from both figure skating and speed skating. In figure skating, for example, fluid strides are combined with athletic and artistic movement, as the skater displays skilled footwork and graceful jumps and spins. The power-skating hockey player, on the other hand, strives for power and maneuverability rather than fluidity or rhythm.

Physicists define power as work done over a given time interval. An athlete may expend power with explosive energy over a short period or with less energy over a longer period. Both methods, however, require the same power output. A hockey player's explosive acceleration, followed by stopping and "turning on a dime" maneuvers, requires the generation of explosive forces by the lower body.

A hockey skater's power depends on the strength of the push-off. Good skaters accomplish a powerful push-off by driving the blade of the toe-out rear skate into the ice and then outwardly pushing off. Charles Dillman, a biomechanist and a consultant for the United States Olympic hockey team, found that a drive technique that uses more knee flex can increase a player's range of movement during the first 2 seconds of acceleration by about 1 meter (3.3 ft.) (Dillman, 1984).

Many recreational hockey players skate with insufficient knee bend. Knee bend helps absorb more of the impact energy each time the blade touches down on the ice. Upright skaters, therefore, lose significant linear, or forward, momentum to the vertical plane. The less time the blade is in contact with the ice, the less force there is over less time. For this reason, one sometimes sees a skater bounce up and down. This bouncing motion is a natural temptation because it mimics running, which is the first way most people learn how to propel themselves at high speeds. The runner accomplishes this task by a downward leg drive against the surface, and the bouncing of a skater mimics this movement.

Bouncing does not really benefit the skater, as the mechanics of power skating are very different from those of running. A power skater does not use a straight-downward leg drive, nor do the skates leave the surface for 50 percent of the stride. Instead, the power skater uses a horizontal push-off, straight outward and away from the body. Even with good technique, though, there is a tendency to bounce, because natural elasticity within the muscles and joints gives the body some of the qualities of a spring. In addition to limiting bounce, a deeper knee bend helps increase the length of each stroke and allows for a greater push-off across the full length of the blade (*see also SKELETAL SYSTEM and RUNNING AND HURDLING*).

A hockey skater must master a technique that depends on smoothly shifting pressure from the outside to the inside of the skate blade. The best skaters learn how to maximize leg power while minimizing work and extraneous body motion. Perhaps the most important aspect of maximizing power is the speed at which the leg uncoils in reaching full extension. A skater must generate short explosive bursts of energy to reach peak power during the push-off, because the propulsion phase comprises only 10 to 15 percent of the full stroke cycle. That is, since the length of time to create propulsion is very short, a concentrated, short burst is essential. This is true more of a hockey player than, for example, of a cyclist. A hockey player's peak power output comes in short, quick bursts and is about three times larger than that of a cyclist, who has the luxury of exerting force over 70 to 80 percent of the stroke-cycle time.

Whereas speed skaters try to maximize extension with each stride, hockey skaters use short, powerful strides to ensure that they will maintain excellent balance in order to handle the stick, pass, and shoot with great precision. Shorter, choppier strides also make it easier to change direction and—equally important—to fake changes of direction. If hockey players used the same long-leg extension as a speed skater with each stride, they could travel up and down the ice quickly; however, even a slight bump could put them off balance and send them sprawling.

One commonality between a professional hockey player and a

world-class speed skater is body position: both use a relatively horizontal torso position and relatively sharp knee bend. This allows a skater to maximize ice-skate reaction force for each skate thrust and to execute longer, more explosive strides. Studies have found that the short explosive strides used by a hockey player make the abductor muscles surrounding the hip larger and stronger than those found on most other athletes. These muscles are vital for balance during the gliding phase because they permit the feet to maintain a narrow base under the body. The abductors provide little power, but they do provide stability to the gliding leg—the leg opposite the driving leg. These muscles grow in strength by continually providing stability and support (*see also SKATING*).

Don C. Hopkins and John Zumerchik

References

Alexander, J. "Comparison of the Ice Hockey Wrist and Slap Shots for Speed and Accuracy." *Research Quarterly* 34 (1963): 259–263.

Brasch, R. *How Did Sports Begin?* New York: David McKay, 1970.

Casey, M., C. Foster, and E. Hixson, eds. *Winter Sports Medicine*. Philadelphia: F. A. Davis, 1990.

Dillman, C. "Speed Capabilities of Ice Hockey Players." Unpublished U. S. Olympic Committee research paper, 1984.

Doré, R. "Dynamometric Analysis of Different Hockey Shots." In P.V. Komi (ed.), *Biomechanics V-B*. Baltimore: University Park Press, 1976.

Halliwell, W. R., et al. "A Kinematic Analysis of the Slap Shot in Ice Hockey as Executed by Professional Hockey Players." In F. Landry and W. Orbin. (ed.), *Ice Hockey*. Miami: Symposia Specialist, 1978.

Hull, Bobby. *Bobby Hull's Hockey Made Easy*. Toronto: Methuen, 1982.

Minkoff, J. "Evaluating Parameters of a Professional Hockey Team." *American Journal of Sports Medicine* 10 (1982): 285–292.

Roy, B. "Kinematics of the Slap Shot in Ice Hockey as Executed by Players." In P. V. Komi (ed.), *Biomechanics V-B*. Baltimore: University Park, 1976.

Volyenli, K., and E. Eriksen. "On the Motion of an Ice Hockey Puck." *American Journal of Physics* 53 (1985): 1149–1152.

Wild, J. *Power Skating: The Key to Better Hockey*. Scarborough, Ontario: Prentice-Hall, 1971.

Karate

KARATE WAS APPARENTLY developed for survival long before it became a devastating combative sport, and thus its exact origins are unknown. Those who consider karate a hybrid sport, a combination of wrestling and boxing, claim that its origins are ancient: around 4000 B.C.E. Egyptian military men regularly engaged in such a hybrid activity as a training exercise. Others dispute an Egyptian origin, maintaining that karate drew on fighting techniques developed and refined by several different cultures.

The first truly identifiable techniques probably came from India. Although no written records exist, statues from the first century B.C.E. depict temple guardians in karate-like positions. Whatever its origins, karate was nurtured in China. The Buddhist Shaolin monastery on Mount Shao-shih, deep in the Sung Mountains of China, was one of the legendary sites of its development. The Shaolin monastery provided sanctuary to fugitives, many of whom had a dual identity—they were monks, but also skilled warriors. Legend has it that karate was introduced by an obscure man, Bodhidharma, who arrived there from India around 500 C.E. He taught a series of exercises, designed to unite mind, spirit, and body, that was adopted as a practice by the monks at Shaolin.

Much later, around the fifteenth century, karate began to assume its present form on the island of Okinawa. Strategically located between China and Japan, Okinawa was at the center of many military conflicts. In 1470, the proliferation of karate was an unplanned consequence of an edict by the Okinawan king Hashi that restricted private ownership of weapons. Weapons were permitted but had to be stored in government warehouses under royal supervision. To defend themselves and their strategic island, the Okinawans refined karate—the art of "empty-hand" fighting.

Karate is best described as an art of hand and foot fighting—punching and kicking being the two most common attack methods. Karate is part art, part sport, and part mental exercise, and its appeal stems from its multifaceted nature. It is an activity that may be pursued for physical fitness, self-defense, self-discipline, or as a challenging game. At the elite level, the practitioner of karate, called a *karateka*, develops formidable offensive and defensive skills.

Although the focus of this article is karate, it should be noted that karate is just one of many martial arts—among them tae kwon do and kung fu—that evolved in Asia. There are literally thousands of different moves associated with these sports. Thus, individual moves will not be explained here. Instead, the emphasis is on the physical principles involved—a close look at the capacity of the human body to develop and exert tremendous physical force.

Balance and Base of Support

The evaluation of any stance in karate entails looking at three different components: balance, power, and mobility. These components are highly interrelated. For example, maximum balance occurs when the low crouching position is taken. If the position is too low, however, it restricts the ability of the inside muscles of the thigh to move the body, thereby reducing both power (work/time) and mobility.

It is essential that a practitioner of karate be aware of his base of support. To do this, a practitioner needs an intuitive understanding of some basic principles of the center of gravity (COG). When scientists refer to the COG of an object or of an individual, they are referring to an imaginary reference point around which the object, or the weight of the body, is equally distributed. The COG varies not only from person to person, because of differences in body structure, but also in relation to an athlete's body position. Even the slightest movement, such as lifting an arm, alters the COG. Sometimes—for instance when one reaches far forward or leans far back—the COG actually lies somewhere outside the body (see also ACROBATICS and FIELD ATHLETICS: JUMPING).

The stability of a karate stance is heavily dependent on the location of the COG. Because COG changes must occur at will and almost instantaneously, the stability of the position will change just as quickly. This is an extremely important consideration in delivering a blow. It allows the forces and torques (two or more forces acting in opposite directions at each end of a human body lever) to move the body, hands, and feet with great acceleration. Movement by the torso, with its large, slow muscles, is immediately followed by the turning of the smaller, faster muscles of the arms and legs. It is also important that the striker assume a stable foot-ground position so that the feet can contribute to the force of the blow. Without a strong base of support, the body cannot generate the power necessary to strike with such devastating force. Jumping up into the air to deliver a blow limits the amount of force.

With lightning-fast reflexes, a *karateka* can change from a stable base of support to an unstable base. This gives him the mobility to avoid a blow from an opponent. The two most popular karate stances are named for and based on animal stances: the horse stance and the cat stance (see Figure 1). The horse stance—a wide lateral position

Figure 1. *The two most popular stances in karate are the horse and cat stance. The horse stance on the left is primarily defensive, while the cat stance on the right is primarily offensive.*

with feet spread apart at shoulder width—provides a great deal of stability. The one-footed cat stance provides very little stability, but excellent mobility. The horse stance is primarily defensive, while the cat stance is primarily offensive.

Whether assuming an attacking or defending position, the *karateka* requires a continually changing base of support from a one-foot to a two-foot base. The body is most stable when directly over the base of support, yet considerable movement outside the base of support is necessary to accomplish many punches and kicks. For example, a whirlwind motion is often necessary to execute a punch or a kick. Despite being well away from the base of support after the execution of a move, a karate expert moves very quickly to reestablish it. In this way, he is less vulnerable and is ready to execute any countering defensive moves.

The most effective forward punches are those in which the COG stays in the same horizontal plane. With extraneous horizontal movement eliminated, the *karateka* can take the straightest line to the target. This allows him to get to the target quickly and deliver a blow with the most devastating force.

A telltale sign of the efficiency of a movement is the body position at start and completion. The starting stance initiates the large accelerations necessary to execute the technique; the completion stance attempts to deliver as much body mass as possible. Sometimes the starting and completion stances are very similar (the body hardly moves), but at other times a large shift of body weight takes place, so the stances at the start and completion of a move are very different. An accomplished *karateka* shifts from one stance to another: from a stance that stresses acceleration (change in velocity/time), as in a quick punch, to one that stresses momentum (mass $\times$ velocity), as in the whirlwind kick.

Generation of Force

Scientists consider a force to be any push or pull that accelerates an object or a person. Much like skilled performers in most other sports, practitioners of karate depend on a summation of forces when executing most of their moves. In other words, muscles contract in a sequential order so that the force of each muscle group is added to the force of the succeeding muscle group. If achieved in a well-timed manner, the total force at impact can be much greater than any individual muscle force.

The timing required to strike at maximum velocity occurs when the "firing on" of a succeeding muscle group takes place at the precise moment that the preceding muscle group "fires off." In executing a punch, the *karateka* depends on generating force starting with the slower and stronger muscle groups of the lower body, followed by the action of the faster, smaller muscle groups of the shoulder and arm. Kicks require a summation of forces, too, beginning with the muscles in the lower body and proceeding through the lower leg muscles surrounding the knee and ankle.

A primary objective of karate is to deliver tremendous impact force to a target. The only way to make this physically possible is for the striker to generate momentum, a product of the mass of the weapon and its velocity. Assuming an equal ability to create velocity, a more massive person generates greater momentum. According to the laws of physics, momentum is conserved. Momentum does not just go away; it is absorbed by the target. A large amount of momentum, generated by a coordinated motion of the whole body and absorbed in a short amount of time, is a very powerful blow.

Generating great momentum is not easily accomplished because the body parts of greatest mass, like the torso, also are the slowest to accelerate. On the other hand, the body parts capable of greatest velocity, the arms and legs, lack the mass to strike with great force. Therefore, to deliver the most mass at the highest velocity (the greatest momentum) requires efficient movement of the body's lever system.

The human lever system consists of bones and joints, which activate when force is applied by the muscles. Structurally, the speed of the levers, in both humans and animals, is a function of their length: the longer the lever, the slower its possible speed. For example, the small-winged hummingbird flaps its wings at 200 beats per second, while the large-winged stork flaps its wings at only two beats per second. If somehow the stork could flap its wings at 200 beats per second, the tremendous stress created at its shoulder joint would probably rip its wings off its body. Karate experts, like most top athletes, have an intuitive feel for the way to generate the greatest impact when considering the functions of the levers called upon to deliver that impact. For example, during the execution of a punch, the hand (located at the end of a multilever system) moves much faster than does the forearm, upper arm, or torso (located closer to the origin of the multilever system).

As best delivered, karate strikes should be made with more rigid levers than collapsible levers. That is, the striker should try to minimize the amount of muscle and tendon deformation, or flattening, on contact with the target. To attain the objective of delivering the maximum force possible, the *karateka* strikes with the smallest area possible, using the greatest amount of force possible. Punches are delivered with two knuckles of the fist making contact, rather than three or four; kicks employ the outside edge of the foot, rather than the sole; and hand strikes make use of the side of the hand, not the palm.

Sometimes, however, it is better to strike with the greatest area possible. Although this results in surface contact deformation of the striking hand or foot, thereby lessening the force of the blow, it also provides a great benefit: by better distributing the force of impact throughout the body, it significantly reduces the chance of injury to the *karateka*.

In addition to maximizing momentum and minimizing the contact

Figure 2. *A punch to the body is usually rigidly braced, much like a board used to brace or support a wall. The striker tries to "lock out" his joints (circles) to minimize the amount of muscle and tendon deformation on contact with the target. The locked arm and rear leg braces limit the amount of energy-stealing recoil.*

area of the striking part, karate experts also try to strike the smallest area of the target. Strikes to the smallest parts of a target, say, the nose and the knee, have the potential to be far more damaging than body blows. Such strikes concentrate the force, putting intense pressure on the target area. The pressure acting on any surface is the ratio between the force and the area, or the force per unit area.

Whenever a target is struck, a certain amount of energy is lost as the hand or foot recoils. In this case, the backward impulse of energy imparted on the target is not strong enough to move it rearward fast enough. By taking steps to minimize recoil, more of the kinetic energy, or energy of motion, generated by the striker gets delivered to the target. Two options exist to minimize recoil: a more firmly anchored stance by the striker, or a blow made "heavier" by increasing the effective mass hitting the target.

Strikes should be executed with full extension and with the joints locked out in place. Full extension of the wrist or ankle—in alignment with the striking limb—forms a rigid bar on impact. For example, a punch to the body is usually rigidly braced, much as bracing is used to support a wall. The rear foot and leg are extended back to help form a brace to counteract the recoil from impact. By bracing the blow, more of the momentum of the striking hand is delivered to the target, and less gets dampened or rebounds. If there is no bracing, recoil can cause the knee or elbow to bend, which dampens much of the kinetic energy of the punch. It is important that the upper body lean forward into the punch. With more weight moving forward over the front foot, the punch is much more likely to drive the target forward than to recoil the puncher's body backward.

Karate students are instructed to visualize punching and kicking right through the target. This is important because it maintains velocity and prevents premature deceleration of the striking hand or foot. Another benefit is that muscles remain tense on contact, resulting in less hand or foot deformation and less recoil at the joints. In all, more of the force will be imparted on the target, because less will be absorbed by the dampening rebound effect within the striking hand or foot. It is useful to compare a boxer and a *karateka* striking a target. A boxer attempts to impart a large amount of momentum to the entire mass of his opponent, knocking him off balance and back. Although the *karateka* also wants to impart a large amount of momentum, he wants to concentrate it on a small area of the target. When the target is an opponent's body, his blow provides more than sufficient power to break tissue and bone; it can also break wood, or even concrete.

Punching

Karate experts start a punch from a peculiar stance (*see Figure 3*). The nonpunching hand is extended well forward. As the nonpunching hand is pulled back, it helps initiate a whipping shoulder rotation about the rotating hips. This is analogous to the move-countermove of a hurdler who throws her arm back forcefully to counter the rota-

Figure 3. *To punch effectively, the forward step should be executed without raising the center of gravity. The body also should move forward as directly as possible. As the nonpunching hand gets pulled back (a), it helps initiate a whipping shoulder rotation about the rotating hips.*

tion of her body as her trailing leg swings around to clear the hurdle (*see RUNNING AND HURDLING*). The momentum of the *karateka* is quickly transferred from the back to the front leg as the striking fist darts forward. He tries to limit the amount of recoil by "locking out" his joints and closing and rotating the striking hand into a fist, so that the palm faces downward at the point of contact with the intended target. He also tries to step toward the target to add as much momentum to the punch as possible.

Kicking

Generating force during kicking is a bit more difficult—balancing on one foot is obviously much more difficult than standing on two. But as in punching, a kick becomes much more effective when the weight of the body firmly follows the kick. As the leg thrusts powerfully toward the target, more momentum can be developed by swiveling the hips for a roundhouse kick, or thrusting them forward for a straightforward kick. Once the leg is accelerated by the swiveling of the hips, the motion should not be cut short, for a well-executed follow-through motion gives the foot more momentum in striking the target.

Increasing kicking power when rotation is involved requires a whiplike motion, starting from the shoulders, that twists and accelerates the leg and foot forward. The back remains arched through the delivery so that the kicker can remain balanced, ready to counter the recoil from contact with the target. An arched back can help a roundhouse kicker withstand considerable recoil, but it is insufficient for maintaining balance. An alternative method to increase kicking momentum is to hop forward on the supporting leg just prior to impact. With the supporting foot directed at the target, it is easier to rock or bounce forward and back to maintain balance.

Breaking a Board: How Do They Do It?

When a *karateka* uses his bare hands or feet to break a stack of wooden boards, or sometimes even a concrete slab, it is quite a spectacle—a superhuman display of prowess that lends a mystical aura to the sport. Moreover, these feats seem even more impressive because they are accomplished by men of normal physiques. A typical reaction is, "He did it, and he's no bigger than I am. How?" Actually, though breaking a board is physically possible for many, few are willing to engage in the necessary training. It requires great precision entailing tremendous physical and mental discipline. Karate exhibitions showcase the amazing ability of the typical human to exert colossal and perfectly targeted physical force.

Most observers realize that massive force is needed to break boards or concrete slabs. They do not realize, however, that strength is not paramount; instead, a combination of training, hand speed, concentration, and self-discipline is vital. Figure 4 shows a typical karate demonstration, where the board is supported at the ends and the blow is directed at the middle. At hand impact, the force bends the board, causing it to split in two. The karate blow is directed as close to the middle as possible, because an off-center impact limits the amount of board deformation (bending) which reduces the effectiveness of the blow.

To understand the dynamics of the hand-board collision, it is necessary to consider the forces involved. As the hand comes down on the board, it creates a compression, or squeezing, force in the hand bones. The board receives both a compression force on the contact side and a tension, or stretching, force on the underside, which lengthens the wood. A karate expert does not break his hand because the board gives way before his hand does. In other words, human bone is better able to withstand compression than wood, or even concrete, can withstand it (*see also EQUIPMENT MATERIALS; ARCHERY; and SKELETAL SYSTEM*).

The board actually breaks from the bottom up, not from the top down. The wood begins to crack on the underside at a point directly beneath the impact point, and the crack proceeds upward until the board completely splits. The amount of force needed to break the board depends on both the thickness of the board and the span across which it is supported. For example, a board 1.9 centimeters (3/4 in.) thick, supported across a span of about 25 centimeters (10 in.), typically splits in two when bent about 1.5 centimeters (1/2 in.) at its midpoint. To accomplish this, the karate expert needs to generate a force of about 68 kilograms (150 lb.). Of course, a thicker board or a longer span requires a proportionally larger breaking force.

The elongation along the bottom surface, which breaks the board, is a result of the force delivered in a perpendicular plane to the board from the fist's impact. It is the stress caused by the fist that creates the strain—the elongation along the bottom surface of the block. Depending on the stiffness or elasticity of the material involved, the strain results in the block's either bending or breaking. Every material possesses a critical value, called the modulus of rupture, which identifies the elasticity point at which a material can no longer bend from the stress, and thereafter breaks.

Usually, karate experts break boards along the grain of the wood.

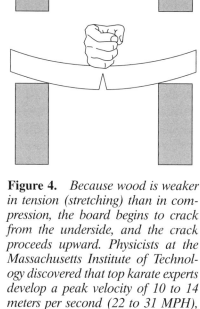

Figure 4. *Because wood is weaker in tension (stretching) than in compression, the board begins to crack from the underside, and the crack proceeds upward. Physicists at the Massachusetts Institute of Technology discovered that top karate experts develop a peak velocity of 10 to 14 meters per second (22 to 31 MPH), exerting a force as great as 675 pounds (Feld, 1979). A well-placed strike exerts more than enough force to break blocks of wood or concrete.*

The properties of wood are such that the ability to withstand a tension force along the grain is far less than the ability to withstand a tension force against the grain. Splitting concrete slabs is an entirely different matter. Concrete differs from wood in that it is far stronger, but much less elastic; stiffer and more brittle. Nevertheless, concrete breaks in the same manner as wood: from a tension force that works from the bottom up.

Of course, a great deal more force is needed to create the impact force necessary to break a concrete block than to break a wooden board, but this is, in part, counterbalanced by the fact that far less deformation, or bending, is required for the block to break. Only 1 millimeter (1/40 in.) of deformation is required for concrete, compared with 1.5 centimeters (1/2 in.) for wood (Feld, 1979). The lower elastic modulus (the ability to bend before breaking) of concrete block means less stress force is necessary to break the block because less energy is wasted in bending, straining, the material. Wood's greater elasticity—16 times greater than that of concrete—requires a greater energy input (*see also EQUIPMENT MATERIALS*).

Anyone who has tried to break both concrete and wood knows that concrete is more difficult to break than wood. But breaking wood does require a relatively greater energy output because not all the energy of the strike can be exerted on the target. Much of the energy of the hand striking the wood is wasted; it does not get efficiently transmitted to the target. Instead, it gets transmitted throughout the wood and back through the person as vibrational energy.

How kinetic energy, or the energy of motion, gets transmitted also depends on the masses of the colliding objects. For example, if a car collides with a haystack, the hay absorbs the car's energy and moves along in the same direction as the car. But if a car collides with a brick wall, the nearly immovable wall does not absorb the impact. According to the principle of conservation of energy, the energy must go somewhere. It must manifest itself either in the deformation of the car's body or in the speed at which it rebounds off the wall. The same principle holds when a karate expert breaks wood and concrete. When the target, such as a wooden block, is less massive than the hand, it accepts a great majority of the energy. The kinetic energy of the hand becomes the kinetic energy of the combined hand and wood. But when the target is more massive, such as concrete, a much smaller fraction of the energy is accepted, and much more gets absorbed from the deformation of the hand and concrete against one another. Therefore, despite the fact that it requires five times more force to break concrete than wood, it requires only three times more energy.

Breaking multiple boards. Often a karate demonstration builds drama by proceeding from very simple displays of prowess to daunting feats. A karate expert might begin by breaking one board with a simple downward strike, and then proceed to using a whirlwind of body contortions and different hand and foot strikes, to break boards from a variety of positions and angles. The grand finale might be a

BREAKING DYNAMICS

	Wood	Concrete
Hand speed (meters/sec.)	6.1	10.6
Force (newtons)	670 (150 lb.)	3,100 (696 lb.)
Energy (joules)	12.3 (2.93 cal.)	37.1 (8.86 cal.)

Table 1. *Although it takes nearly five times as much force to break concrete as wood, it takes only three times as much energy. The reason is wood's greater elasticity. It takes relatively more energy to break wood because energy is wasted in the bending of the wood before it breaks (Feld, 1979).*

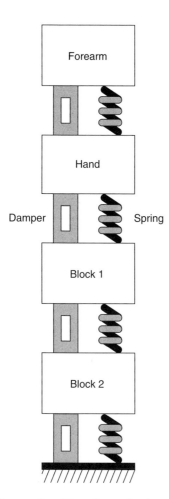

Figure 5. *The dynamic impact process of hand against a stack of boards, illustrating the dampening component and rebound component. Whereas the spring effect and dampening effect are nearly equal between the surface hand tissue and hand and lower forearm, the spring effect is relatively greater than the dampening effect between the blocks. (Adapted from Feld, 1979)*

demonstration of breaking multiple boards or concrete blocks. Audiences look on incredulously. One might wonder: if it takes 150 pounds of force to break one board, does it take ten times that much force (approximately 1,500 lb. of force) to break ten boards?

As might be expected, it does not take ten times as much force to break a stack of ten boards. High-speed photography shows that the karate striker makes contact only with the first one or two boards of the stack, not all eight or ten boards. As each successive board splits, it delivers sufficient momentum (from the mass and velocity of the hand) to split the board beneath it, which in turn can split the next board, and so on down the line. Because of momentum, a stack of ten boards will break with only a few hundred pounds of pressure; it does not require a cumulative 1,500 pounds. And, for that reason, karate experts often choose to break several thinner boards rather than a single board of the same total thickness.

Although it is always important to strike the block or board near the center, it is particularly important when trying to break an entire stack. When an off-center strike occurs, each successive board breaks closer and closer to its center. This means that some of the energy of the hand is wasted owing to the horizontal motion of the fracture wave. The greater the horizontal motion of the fracture wave, the less likely it becomes that the bottom blocks or boards will be broken (*see Figure 5*).

Limb speed in breaking boards. Karate experts usually begin a demonstration with the well-founded warning that the feats they perform should not be tried by the untrained. A well-founded warning indeed, for the untrained run a high risk of fracturing their hands. Considering the amount of force generated and the size of the stacks karate experts attempt to break, one would think hand injuries would be commonplace. However, injuries do not occur in large numbers, in part because the hand-board impact transfers energy from the hand to the board. A karate expert tries to maximize his hand speed in order to maximize the potential transfer of kinetic energy, because the kinetic energy of a moving object is proportional to the square of its speed. The speed of the hand is much more important than its mass. To equal the deliverable force created by doubling the hand speed, the mass of the hand would have to be increased fourfold.

On average, the total elapsed time for a board-breaking punch is 20 times longer than the contact time. This suggests that the force accelerating the striking fist is 20 times less than the force at impact. Acceleration forces, developed throughout the body to accelerate the striking hand, create the significant force that allows boards and concrete to be broken. Because of the potential to create such large forces by rotational acceleration alone, the *karateka* does not necessarily need to be in contact with the ground to deliver powerful and devastating blows. Foot-ground contact certainly helps generate powerful blows, but it is not essential. Table 2 shows that the *karateka* can generate large forces by pure rotational acceleration in an airborne

PEAK VELOCITIES REACHED BY ELITE ATHLETES

Maneuver	Peak Velocity (meters/ second)
Front forward kick	5.7–9.8
Downward hammer–fist strike	10–14
Downward knife–hand strike	10–14
Roundhouse kick	9.5–11
Wheel kick	7.3–10
Front kick	9.9–14.4
Side kick	9.9–14.4

Table 2. *(Source: Feld, 1979)*

state. Through high-speed photography, the downward speeds of experts' karate strikes have been measured to reach about 30 MPH. An effective force of approximately 650 pounds is delivered to the target when the striker's hand is moving at 30 MPH—plenty of force to break a stack of boards or concrete blocks.

The 650-pound impact blow does not break bones in the hand because the impact is both transferred to the board and distributed and absorbed throughout the hand and wrist. The bone, skin, muscles, and tendons of the hand and wrist effectively distribute and absorb the impact so that the hand is not damaged. Moreover, energy is rapidly transmitted to the forearm, the upper arm, and the rest of the body. This ability to distribute the impact makes the rupture modulus of the hand bone more than 40 times greater than that of concrete (Feld, 1979).

When an unfortunate striker does not generate enough hand speed at impact, or misses the midpoint, the force often is not large enough to split the boards. Excruciating pain usually results because the boards then rebound back against the hand. Energy is no longer transferred to and absorbed by the boards, so the hand ends up absorbing close to all of the 650 pounds of pressure rebounding back.

There is nothing magical or mystical about karate experts' breaking boards; yet it does take talent, considerable training, concentration, and self-discipline to deliver blows with sufficient force and precision.

John Zumerchik

References

Adrian, M., and J. Cooper. *Biomechanics of Human Movement*. Dubuque, Iowa: Benchmark, 1989.

Blum, H. "Physics and the Art of Kicking and Punching." *American Journal of Physics* 45 (1977): 61ff.

Feld, M., et al. "The Physics of Karate." *Scientific American*, 240, no. 4 (1979): 150ff.

Ingber, Lester. *Karate Kinematics and Dynamics*. Hollywood, California: Unique Publications, 1981.

Parulski, George. *Karate's Modern Masters: The Philosophies and Techniques of the Art's Living Legends*. Chicago: Contemporary, 1985.

Shroeder, C., and B. Wallace. *Karate: Basic Concepts and Skills*. Reading, Massachusetts: Addison Wesley, 1982.

Walker, J. "Karate Strikes." *American Journal of Physics* 43 (1975): 845ff.

Wilk, S., et al. "The Physics of Karate." *American Journal of Physics* 51 (1983): 783ff.

Paddle Sports

THE ORIGINS OF PADDLE SPORTS are obscure. Watercraft probably began simply as rafts for floating downstream: two logs tied together to carry a person, or several logs to carry cargo. Canoes may have been developed as early as the stone age; the "dugout" canoe, which reduces water resistance, would have made upstream transportation possible.

A dramatic picture of paddle technology has come down to us from the ancient world—the multi-oared slave galleys. These cargo craft were rowed from port to port by half-starved slaves who were shackled to their benches and were whipped if they faltered. Among the earliest rowers were the Athenians and Persians, who rowed to exhaustion in what may have been the world's first naval battles. The Athenians already understood the physics of levers, and this gave them a considerable technological advantage. Paintings on ancient pottery show that Athenian rowers used sliding seats—predecessors of the 75-centimeter (2.5-ft.) track rowers use in the 1990s. A movable seat not only allows the rower's legs to contribute significantly to powering the oar but also means that each stroke pull is lengthened.

Eventually, of course, paddle propulsion for utilitarian purposes was displaced by sails, which in turn were displaced by motors. But paddling, historically relegated to slaves and serfs, reemerged among sportsmen in the mid-nineteenth century for recreation and racing.

The Harvard-Yale rowing competition, the oldest intercollegiate sports event in America, began in the early 1850s. Surprisingly, however, it took until 1872 for the sliding seat to be rediscovered. The story is that Harvard's oarsmen achieved the effect of a moving seat by greasing their leather pants and sliding back and forth along their wooden block seats. They won by a large margin, but their trick had not gone unnoticed by Yale, and the next year the Yale rowers returned with a trick of their own: they lubricated their trousers and block seats with oatmeal. Within a few years, Harvard and Yale had both advanced beyond oatmeal and had begun using seats with wooden rollers, much like the seats used in the 1990s.

Paddle sports have been part of the modern Olympics since the first modern games, in 1896. In the 1990s, there are several forms of paddle sports: sweep rowing, sculling (*see Figure 1*), kayaking (*see Figure 2*), and canoeing (*see Figure 3*).

Sweep rowing and sculling are closely related sports. In sweep

321

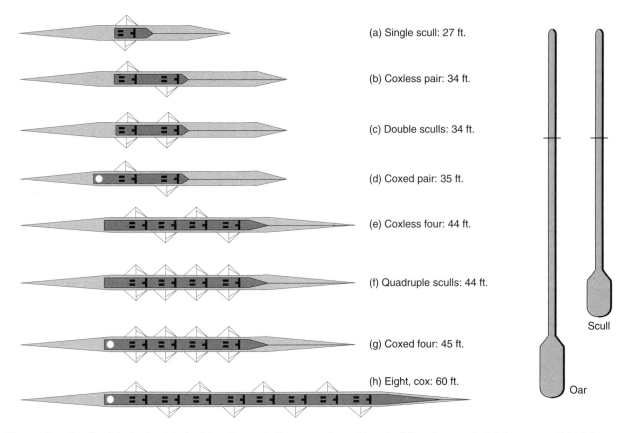

Figure 1. *Sculls: (a) single, (c) double, (f) quad. Sweep rowing: (b) pair, (d) pair, coxed, (g) four, cox, (h) eight, cox. Lengths are approximate.*

rowing, each paddler handles one long oar (360–380 cm; 12 ft.–12 ft. 8 in.). In sculling, each paddler wields two shorter oars (290–300 cm; 9 ft. 8 in.–10 ft.). The athletes compete solo or in teams of as many as eight members. Early sculling and sweep rowing had little resemblance to versions used in the 1990s. In the 1800s, a shell weighed more than 272 kilograms (600 lb.), was wide and bulky, and had stationary seats, like a rowboat. Modern materials have changed shell design almost miraculously (*see also EQUIPMENT MATERIALS*). It is possible to construct a shell with a hull only 0.15 centimeter (0.0625 in.) thick. These lighter shells, of course, sit higher in the water; this means that they create less resistance and thus can achieve higher speeds.

At the other extreme from sculling and sweep-rowing shells are kayaks and canoes—small craft generally designed for one or two paddlers. A kayaker wields a double-bladed paddle from a sitting position; a canoeist handles a single-bladed paddle from a kneeling position. The canoe originated with Native Americans, who used birch-bark canoes for transportation and cargo on inland waters, whereas the kayak originated with the Inuit, who used it for hunting seals on the open sea. For classification purposes, there are three distinct categories of these small craft: open canoes, flat-water kayaks, and white-water kayaks. But in reality, there is an almost endless range of hybrid craft—boats that overlap any definition.

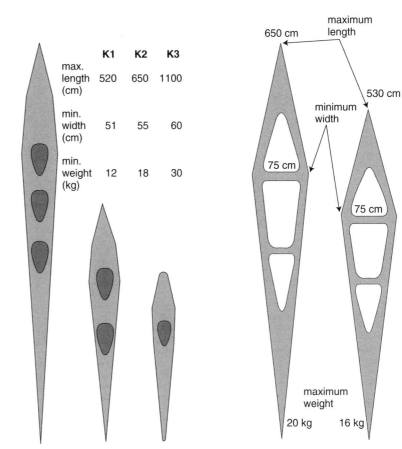

Figure 2. *Kayaking: Shown (from left to right) are K-3, K-2, and K-1.*

Figure 3. *Canoeing: Shown here are C-2 (left) and C-1 (right).*

Basics of Watercraft

In all competitive paddle sports—rowing, sculling, canoeing, and kayaking—the objective is the same, and very simple: to cross the finish line before the opponent. To accomplish this straightforward task, the paddler must maximize power output (work/time; *see also WEIGHT LIFTING*).

Generally, the greater the force produced by the paddle, the faster the boat will travel. However, there are two important qualifications to this generalization. First, power must be directed efficiently toward forward propulsion. An incorrect sweep of the paddle requires just as much energy as a correct sweep but may deliver far less power to propel the boat forward. In other words, most of the energy expended by the paddler is wasted: some of it is exerted in the wrong direction, some works against optimum motion, and some dissipates as body heat. Therefore, a paddler not only must apply force but also must translate the oar's total power smoothly to the propulsion of the boat.

Second, minimal power should be used to accelerate to top speed and then to maintain that speed. The reason for this is inertia. Inertia is an intrinsic property of the mass of an object or body: the steady state of that system. Because of inertia, a boat (or any object) at rest tends to stay at rest, and a boat in motion tends to stay in motion. When a paddler minimizes the power needed to accelerate, and then maintains a steady velocity, less energy is expended to cover a given distance. Thus paddle sports require minimizing friction forces on the boat and maximizing friction forces of the paddle—but both of these are easier said than done.

Water Flow and Resistance

The way water flows can be categorized as laminar or turbulent (*see Figure 4*). Under normal conditions, flow is laminar—that is, smooth and uniform. The water molecules flow in unbroken streams, either straight lines or curves. These streams may vary in velocity, but the variation from one flowing area to another will be smooth.

A laminar flow becomes turbulent when it encounters solid objects. For example, a river will turn white with turbulence if a fast-flowing current causes water to crash against rocks. The rocks impede the downstream course of the water, which is pushed up, down, and all around as it tries to make its way around them.

The same principle applies to boats; but whereas water moves in relation to stationary objects (such as rocks), a boat moves in relation to (nearly stationary) water. Turbulence—wild movement of water molecules—significantly increases resistance for watercraft.

Shells and kayaks are designed primarily for speed. The general principle, therefore, is to minimize resistance for a given volume. This is accomplished by minimizing surface area for that volume: hence the elongated, tapered shapes of these boats. If minimizing resistance were the only design consideration, they would all look like needles; and although there are other important factors to consider—such as stability, the size and shape of the passenger or passengers, and practical aspects of construction—a shell or kayak still needs to be as needle-like as possible. In fact, crew shells and kayaks are all inherently unstable because of the requirements of speed.

A boat (or any other object) traveling through water experiences resistance, commonly called drag. The term *drag* refers to a force in the direction opposite to velocity; here, drag is opposite to the pad-

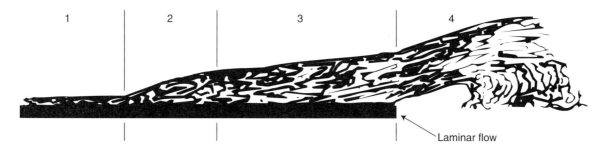

Laminar flow

Figure 4. *Four distinct regions of water flow can be identified: (1) completely laminar; (2) transitional, a mixture of laminar and turbulent; (3) turbulent; (4) point of breaking away or separation. A laminar flow underlies regions 1, 2, and 3.*

dler's thrust. Frontal drag and turbulent drag are caused by the weight of the boat, its size, and its shape (particularly the shape of the bow).

Frontal drag, as the term implies, occurs at the front of the boat—the bow. A boat pushes water molecules forward and sideward, and this impedes its progress; thus boats are designed with a tapered bow so that water molecules will be efficiently directed around the contour of the boat, with as few molecules as possible getting pushed forward.

Turbulent drag occurs at the back of the boat—the stern. Turbulence develops as water makes its way around the contour of the boat and then quickly fills in behind the boat. (This same filling-in can be seen when water in a fast-moving stream makes its way around a protruding rock.) The vacuous region behind the boat creates a force that actually "pulls" the boat slightly backward.

To remain competitive, paddlers must replace their boats periodically (as is also true for sailors), not only to take advantage of new technology, but because a hull loses some of its stiffness with age and use. This latter factor is important because if two boats of equal weight are paddled with equal proficiency, the boat with the stiffer hull will outperform the boat with the more flexible hull. The reason for this is that every time a boat flexes, some horizontal velocity is translated to vertical velocity, robbing the boat of some speed. Thus, the better a boat maintains its structural rigidity, or shape—this is known as its line—the faster it will be. A stiffer hull, obviously, maintains its line better when it encounters resistance (such as waves), and moves and flexes less in any direction other than forward, which means that more of the propulsive paddling force drives the boat forward.

Because of recent advances in materials, boat designers are able to build shells that are both lightweight and rigid. As noted above, a lighter boat sits higher in the water and thus has less surface area to create drag. Lightweight materials used for crew shells include composite plastic laminates, aluminum honeycomb, and carbon fiber. Wooden shells that weighed about 125 kilograms (270–280 lb.) have been replaced by shells made of these newer materials, which are often about 16 kilograms (30–40 lb.) lighter (*see also EQUIPMENT MATERIALS*).

Surface Resistance

The shape of a boat is the primary factor affecting resistance, but surface friction is second in importance. Surface friction (as the term suggests) depends on the quality of the hull's surface.

Fluid flows around a kayak or shell in what is called a boundary layer. The term *boundary layer* refers to all layers of flowing water disturbed by a boat as it passes through; and for a shell or a kayak in deep water, the boundary layer of water flowing around its contour is about 0.3 meter (1 ft.) thick. A boundary layer develops when water that was at rest is set in motion by an oncoming boat. Molecules of water are then slowed down by contact with the boat, and some of them lodge in its surface crevices and get dragged along. Water molecules also tend to bounce away from the hull, disturbing what were smooth laminar-flowing molecules farther away. These newly disturbed water molecules disturb other laminar-flowing molecules in an ever-widening path of turbulence.

To lessen this surface-friction drag, competitors treat the surface of a boat by light sanding or with chemicals—in effect, they form a blanket around the hull. Such a blanket will reduce surface-friction drag by as much as 40 percent. Other treatments are also possible. NASA has devoted much research to surface drag; and although it was found that waxing had little effect on surface friction, it was also discovered that microscopic grooves along the length of a hull did reduce drag moderately. The winner of the 1988 America's Cup, the yacht *Stars and Stripes* (Dennis Conner, captain), had a poly-mer-coated aluminum hull with such grooves—a treatment that increased its speed by 2 percent (Easterling, 1993). Over the course of a race, this is equivalent to a margin of victory of three or four boat lengths.

Surface friction is also affected by water temperature. This is because water is subject to effects of viscosity (stickiness or thickness)—that is, it exhibits fluid flow resistance—and its viscosity is in large part a function of its temperature. As the temperature of water drops, its viscosity increases rapidly.

Stability of Boats

Designing boats that are increasingly needle-shaped comes at a perilous cost: instability. Although hull design remains basically the same, there is a tremendous range of designs within each class of watercraft. What mainly differs is the width of the hull. Narrower boats are of course faster, but they are also less stable and more difficult to sit in. A narrow-beam (midpoint) kayak, for instance, can be handled easily and gracefully by a world-class paddler but can easily be capsized by someone who is less practiced. Thus all experienced paddlers develop a feel for balance.

In maintaining balance, scullers, rowers, and canoers are helped by the fact that most of their paddling takes place on flat inland waters: lakes and rivers. Sea kayakers, by contrast, must contend with the open sea, which can bring huge waves, high winds, and fluctuating tides. In this hostile environment, the sea kayak, despite its narrowness, is amazingly stable and has figured in some impressive voyages. The kayaker Valerie Fons, for instance, was the first woman to paddle around the Baja Peninsula, set a speed record for paddling the length of the Mississippi, and as of 1996 was the only woman to have paddled the 33,800 kilometers (21,000 mi.) from the Arctic to Cape Horn.

Because of differences in kayakers' abilities and needs, and in the waters on which kayaks are used (ranging from tranquil rivers to roaring seas), kayaks vary far more than shells in design. A wide, flat hull tends to give more upright stability and maneuverability on flat water; and a kayak with such a hull is usually designed with a fair amount of "rocker" (curvature of bow and stern upward from the center), to increase its upright maneuverability even more. However, these wider, flatter kayaks are mainly for beginners. Rough seas and high winds completely change a kayak's performance; and although the wide, flat design performs well as a recreational craft on flat water, it loses directional stability in adverse water and wind conditions; also, the large rocker deepens the boat's draft, increasing resistance and thus reducing speed.

Experienced kayakers prefer a craft that is narrower and more rounded, with little or no rocker. Such a design is directionally more stable, is faster, and requires less effort to paddle. However, its upright stability in flat water is relatively poor: upright stability has been sacrificed to improve secondary stability. These narrower, more rounded kayaks are more seaworthy; they handle better in swells because the center of gravity of paddler and boat and the center of buoyancy are aligned more closely with the centerline of the kayak. By contrast, a paddler in a flatter, wider kayak must expend considerably more energy leaning into swells (*see Figure 5*).

Another concern of sea kayakers is the volume of the bow. A low-volume bow is less buoyant; it ploughs into waves and plunges into troughs, but it encounters less wind resistance. A high-volume bow is more buoyant and it rides better over waves, with less plunging; but it does encounter greater wind resistance because of its high profile.

Ironically, the easiest way to make a kayak more maneuverable is to compromise its stability by tilting it to one side—the farther it tilts, the more maneuverable it becomes. The reason for this effect is that a kayak is curved more on the sides than the bottom. Tilting it therefore reduces the length of the surface in contact with the water: the wider middle drops deeper into the water, and the ends lift up. For most kayaks, this shortens the waterline or at least decreases the volume submerged at each end. A shorter, more curved sea kayak is more maneuverable for the same reason that turns and spins are much easier to execute with rocker-bladed hockey skates or figure skates than with long straight-bladed speed skates (*see also HOCKEY; SKATING;* and *SAILING*).

Gravity and Wave Dynamics

How far below the surface a floating boat sits is called its draft. Draft is determined by the hydrostatic pressure of water, which is a function of gravity. The effect of gravity on airborne objects is fairly simple: it brings them down to earth. (Throwing a ball up into the air and watching it come down is a basic demonstration of this effect.) However, the effect of gravity in water is more complex. Each layer of water, from the surface down, becomes progressively denser than the layer above it, because each layer of water must support the layer or layers above it. When a boat is dropped into water, it will displace water—that is, it will continue to sink—until it reaches a point of

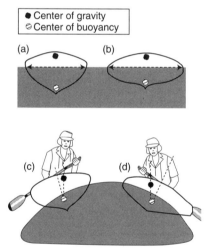

Figure 5. *(a and c) The sea kayak used by experienced paddlers is relatively narrow and rounded and has little or no rocker. It sacrifices "primary" stability and performance in flat water for "secondary" stability and performance in rough water. The center of gravity of boat and kayaker always lies directly over the center of buoyancy. (b and d) A kayak with a wider water line is more stable in flat water, but the paddler must expend considerable effort leaning into swells; otherwise, the center of gravity will no longer lie directly above the center of buoyancy, and the kayak will capsize.*

Left in a Wake

Modern lane dividers minimize the waves of a lead swimmer, which detract significantly from speed. Because shells compete without lane dividers, the wave resistance created by a lead shell on trailing shells can be substantial. A rowing shell has no keel and is therefore very unstable and easily rocked by the lead boat's waves. Rocking wastes much of the propulsive energy created by the rowers: it is diverted into other directions besides forward. Waves can also disrupt the timing of rowers in trailing boats. A team may start to fall out of sync and lose even more time trying to recoordinate. This is why a shell that starts poorly and falls behind by a full boat length can rarely recover and win.

equilibrium. Equilibrium is reached where the force of gravity pulling the boat down equals the density of the water: the force from below holding the boat up (*see also SWIMMING*).

When a boat begins to move, the hull cuts through the water to overcome the gravitational force that creates the draft. In this process, energy is converted or transferred from the moving boat to the water in the form of creation of waves. Although this creation of waves by the hull is fairly complicated, it can be modeled simply. Waves can be thought of as being generated from two pressure points: one located slightly behind the bow, the other slightly ahead of the stern.

Along each side of the hull, a series of fairly evenly spaced, diverging "trains" of waves develop; these can be pictured as a series of "humps" and "hollows" (*see Figure 6*). At certain speeds, wave crests from the bow will be added to wave crests from the stern, creating a large wave train (enhanced energy) behind the hull: this is a hump. But at other speeds, wave crests from the bow can converge with wave troughs from the stern, reducing the wave train: this is a hollow. By virtue of the additional energy it carries, a hump indicates greater resistance against the hull. The reduced energy of a hollow indicates less resistance against the hull.

What this means is that, for example, a short (4.5-m; 14.8-ft.), fast kayak hull, moving at a world-class speed of 4.5 meters per second (10 MPH), will transfer a lot of energy into making waves; a sculling hull, with its much longer surface (greater surface drag), will be subjected to less resistance from making waves. Resistance from wave making is also a function of the width of the hull: a wider hull displaces more water. For a given length and speed, a hull that displaces twice as much water will experience a fourfold increase in wave resistance.

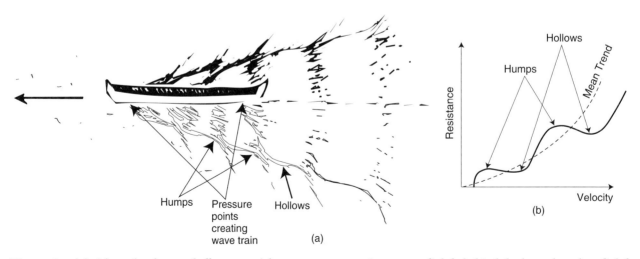

Figure 6. *(a) A boat (such as a shell or canoe) has two pressure points—one slightly behind the bow, the other slightly in front of the stern—from which wave "trains" develop. (b) A wave consists of a "hump" and a "hollow"; humps create considerably more resistance than hollows.*

Effects of Shallow Water

All watercraft, and particularly long shells, must contend with what are commonly called shallow-water effects. This is actually something of a misnomer, because for some very long shells, "shallow-water" effects occur in water as deep as 11 meters (36 ft.).

Shallow water slows a boat down by changing the dynamics of wave making—the "humps" and "hollows." As water becomes shallower, resistance from wave making increases rapidly. In the case of a shell, this resistance increases several times as a shell moves from deep water to shallow water; but eventually the shell reaches a point where resistance quickly *decreases* to half the deepwater resistance—because the now slower waves cannot keep pace with the hull and consequently fade altogether (*see Figure 7*).

Most people are familiar with wave dynamics and shallow- water effects from watching ocean surf crash onto the beach. The height and power of a wave depend on the wind blowing on it and the expanse of sea over which the wind has blown. Interestingly, although a wave moves forward, the molecules of water that make up the wave do not move forward: they just rotate in a circle. Even when the sea is flat, waves still come crashing onto the beach because the water molecules above speed up relative to the water molecules below. As a wave comes up a slope toward the shore, the "front" of the wave steepens until its crest spills over the top.

A similar yet less obvious scenario occurs if water moves from a deep to a shallow area, as when it crashes over large submerged rocks, reefs, and sandbars. When waves move into a shallow area, the deepwater relationship between wavelength and wave speed changes. Shallow water causes waves to slow down, so that they become longer and steeper. Instead of the three or four divergent waves (*refer back to Figure 6*), there may be as many as six or seven. As noted above, once these longer, steeper waves slow down, they cannot speed up again to maintain pace with a boat, and they quickly die. A very siz-

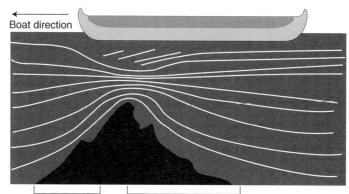

Figure 7. *Going from deep water to shallow water, the canoe slows as a result of shallow-water effects. The viscous drag on the canoe is larger because the boundary layer is thinner.*

Boat direction

Compared with deep water:

Half (waves no longer can keep up with pace of hull)

Wave making resistance increases several-fold.

able deceleration occurs from the effect of hull waves when a boat leaves deep water to traverse a series of very shallow (less than 1-ft-deep) submerged sandbars (*again, see Figure 7*). Anyone who has paddled across a body of water filled with such sandbars has experienced this effect. Crossing the sandbars affects the boundary layer (laminar streams) of water flowing around the boat. The thinner the boundary layer, the larger the viscous drag (the thickness, or "stickiness," of water) on a boat such as a canoe. In deep water, as mentioned earlier, the boundary layer is about 0.3 meter (1 ft.) deep; but in shallow water it is much less, and this increases drag significantly. When the bottom of a canoe clears a sandbar by only a few inches, the boundary layer can be no thicker than that; as a result, drag increases to several times its value in deep water. Actually, surface resistance increases fairly quickly whenever water is less than 1 meter (3.3 ft.) deep, even for small-draft craft like kayaks.

Shallow-water effects cast doubt on the value of "short-cuts." When there is a choice between a longer deepwater course and a shallow-water short-cut, the decision may not be clear. If there is a significant difference in depth, the greater drag of the shallow water may make it impossible to save time or energy by taking the short-cut.

Dynamics of Oars and Paddles

Walking along a shoreline in shallow water is very difficult, because to take a step, the water in front of the foot needs to be pushed out of the way, forward and sideways. Therefore, an adjustment of step is needed, so that recovery—the movement of the foot from back to front—can take place in the air. This adjustment is made without thinking; but if one did think about it, it would obviously make sense: air resistance (0.075 lb./ft.^{3}) is much less than water resistance (62.4 lb./ft.^{3}). Adjusting step in this way is very similar to using paddles and oars: the broadside of the paddle or oar pushes against the high-resistance water to create propulsion, and then the nonpropulsive recovery phase occurs through the relatively low-resistance air.

In any paddle sport, the length and power of the stroke and the paddler's timing are crucial. Oars and paddles, because of their large surface area, have a large coefficient of drag; thus the paddler's effort is maximized. At the same time, the boat has a small coefficient of drag because of its long, narrow shape. For this reason, when crew rowers plant and then pull their oars through the water, the oar does not actually move very far forward. The oar grabs and pulls, remaining quite stationary in the water, and most of the force generated goes into propelling the boat forward. The blade acts as a fulcrum, a point from which the shell pivots forward.

Behind the paddle, eddy currents (air cavities) form, following the contours of the blade tip, especially its lower edge. During the stroke, these eddy currents and the vortex system (whirlpools and other rotary

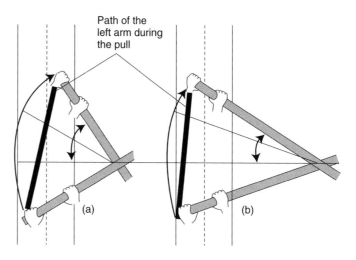

Figure 8. *Long- versus short-arc strokes. (a) An oar with a short inboard length requires the rower to swing much farther forward than one with a long inboard length (b). The position of the hands and arms moves more straight backwards in (b) than (a), allowing the inner arm and hand (here, right side) to make a greater power contribution. Although there is a wide range of distances the oar can be brought forward, the distance backwards is limited: the oar is stopped by the body and not mechanics.*

motion) grow and change shape and position relative to the moving blade. The force of the oar drops off toward the end of the stroke, because the water being moved by the paddle picks up velocity, so that it is moving at a velocity closer to that of the paddle. Any vortex system close to the tip of the oar results in a considerable generation of force along the edges of the blade; this is detrimental, because the total force acting on the blade will not be at right angles to the surface.

Selecting Paddles

When all canoe paddles were made of wood, there was not much to choose among them. The range of paddle designs available in the 1990s has been increased significantly by advances in materials research (developing lightweight plastics and composites to produce ultralight paddles) and biomechanical research (testing different lengths and shapes). Because of individual differences in watercraft and athletes—performance potential, size, and other characteristics—it is impossible to select paddles on the basis of any simple formula that would fit everyone's needs. Nevertheless, selecting a paddle is important because any individual's body can operate most efficiently, without tiring, at a certain stroke rate. A paddle should be selected that will, at the maximum sustainable cruising speed, allow the athlete to paddle at his or her most efficient cadence.

Length. Generally, the larger the surface area of a paddle and the longer its shaft, the greater the force needed to propel it through the water. Choosing length of shaft and size of blade depends on the length, width, and mass of the watercraft and one's own height and reach. For example, most sea kayak paddles are about 205 to 215 centimeters (82–86 in.) long; shorter kayakers usually select paddles a few inches shorter than 205 cm, and taller kayakers choose paddles a few inches longer than 215 cm.

A short paddle has less "swing weight" than a longer paddle, other things being equal. The moment of inertia of a paddle—that is, the force necessary to move it around an axis—is the product of its mass times the square of the distance from axis of rotation to center of swinging mass. Thus, doubling the mass in this equation doubles the swing weight. But doubling the distance in the equation has a more dramatic effect. Consider the paddle as two halves: if the distance from the center of gravity and the axis of rotation doubles, swing weight quadruples. For a paddle of any given mass, then, it takes more energy to generate force if the paddle is longer than if it is shorter. In other words, the lower swing weight means that a shorter paddle can be moved substantially faster than a longer one.

Whitewater river paddlers, kayak surfers, and slalom racers generally use shorter paddles: 190 to 205 centimeters (76–82 in.). These athletes want quick acceleration from a resting position, and they choose a shorter paddle because it has a "low gear ratio"—it is analogous to a low gear on a bicycle, which also allows quicker acceleration. A shorter paddle also lets the paddler keep the blade closer to the boat; this is particularly important for boats like whitewater kayaks that are not designed to track straight. "Self-tracking" sea kayakers, on the other hand, are more concerned with developing a cruising cadence, and do not rely as much on paddle technique to keep on track. Thus they use a longer paddle, which lets them develop a more relaxed pace for covering greater distances.

Blade. Selecting a blade of the appropriate size and shape is somewhat more complicated than deciding on the length of the paddle because there is more variability in size and shape of blades.

A typical kayak blade, for instance, is 45 centimeters (18 in.) long and 20 centimeters (8 in.) wide. The size chosen depends on what the paddler feels more comfortable emphasizing: power and length of stroke, or frequency of stroke. A smaller blade is less fatiguing for muscles and tendons, and (like a shorter blade) it allows quicker acceleration, but it requires greater stroke frequency.

The most appropriate shape for the blade depends on the paddler's style and strength. Paddlers with less physical strength tend to prefer a paddle with a smaller blade area; they offset the loss of power by increasing the frequency of strokes. Stronger paddlers, on the other hand, prefer a larger blade, which generates more force per stroke because it encounters greater water resistance per stroke. Recreational paddlers must also consider the load they are carrying: passengers or gear. With a fully loaded kayak or canoe, for instance, a longer paddle makes it increasingly more difficult to accelerate quickly and hastens the onset of muscle fatigue.

Most kayakers prefer curved and feathered blades (*see Figure 9*).

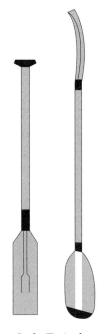

Figure 9. *Left: Typical canoe paddle. Right: Kayak paddle. The kayak paddle is popular because of its curved, feather-bladed profile (the two blades are at an angle to each other).*

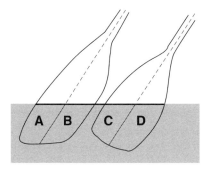

Figure 10. *The advantage of an asymmetrical blade (left) is that the center of resistance stays more in line with the centerline of the shaft. The submerged paddle areas (A and B) remain equal. This is particularly important when the blade first enters the water because a symmetrical paddle (right) is subject to a much greater twisting force: much of C is making its way through the air while D makes its way through the (denser) water. With a symmetrical blade, the paddler must postpone exerting force until the blade is well immersed.*

Criteria for Paddles

1. Lightweight.
2. Tapered rather than square.
3. Curved rather than flat.
4. Asymmetrical rather than symmetrical.
5. Long, narrow blade versus short, square blade: inconclusive.

Technically, the term *feathered* means that the two blades are at a 90-degree angle to each other. Blades are feathered so that as the submerged blade propels the kayak forward, the other blade moves forward with minimal air resistance. However, because a blade moves forward slowly, air resistance is minimal anyway—unless, of course, there is a gale-force headwind. In practice, therefore, blades are usually feathered at only 65 to 85 degrees, to prevent wrist injuries.

Curving the kayak blades has made a much greater contribution to propulsive power than feathering them. The bottom of a curved blade takes a more vertical position at the beginning of the stroke (90° relative to the surface of the water), as the shaft enters the water at about a 45-degree angle. More force is exerted in the horizontal direction and less is wasted in the vertical direction. The curved paddle might cause slightly less force to be generated at the end of the stroke, but because most propulsion occurs forward of the kayaker, the overall propulsive power of the curved paddle is still greater than that of a flat paddle.

Another choice regarding the kayak blade is between an asymmetrical and a symmetrical tip (*see Figure 10*). Symmetrical blades are square-tipped, whereas asymmetrical blades are tapered at the tip. Most experienced kayakers prefer the asymmetrical shape because it keeps the blade's center of resistance in line with the shaft as the paddle moves through the water. With the symmetrical blade, the paddler must apply torque (force around an axis) to prevent the paddle from twisting in the hand. The blade twists to the outside, especially when power is applied during entry, because water resistance is far greater on one side of the center of buoyancy than the other (*respectively D and C in Figure 10*).

Multiple Rowers and Speed

For multiple paddlers, an additional factor must be taken into account: a synchronized crew. A well-synchronized stroke rate and rhythm will determine, to a great extent, the rate at which a crew or kayak team will be able to accelerate to top speed and—equally important—maintain top speed.

It is important to realize that adding rowers does not increase speed proportionally: that is, a two-person kayak is not twice as fast as a solo kayak, and a shell with a crew of eight is not twice as fast as a shell with a crew of four. In 1992, a Norwegian four-man sculling crew had a 250-meter (about 275-yd.) split time of 42.08 seconds between 500 and 750 meters (550–825 yd.), a speed of 21.2 KPH (13.29 MPH). This is very close to the fastest recorded speed for a crew of eight: 22.4 KPH (14.03 MPH). Why is there so little difference?

Thomas McMahon, a researcher at Harvard University, developed a mathematical model that predicted a pattern for speeds of multiple-person crews (McMahon, 1971). Given shells of similar shape and equal draft, he calculated that speed should increase by $-\frac{1}{9}$ power with each additional rower. This model closely matches actual outcomes (*see Figure 11*). For a 2,000-meter (2,188-yd.) race, the

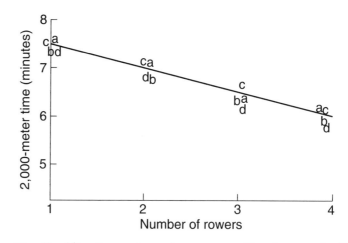

Figure 11. *Doubling the numbers of rowers or scullers does not double speed. Each added rower or sculler does increase speed, but the increment diminishes steadily. McMahon quantified this diminishing return (finding a figure of –⅑ power), and his model agrees closely with times recorded at (a) the 1964 Olympics, (b) the 1968 Olympics, (c) the 1970 World Rowing Championships, and (d) the 1970 International Championships.*

model predicts a time of 6.33 minutes for a shell with four rowers and 5.89 minutes for a shell with eight.

The reason why each additional paddler increases speed by only –⅑ power, rather than doubling it, is that each additional oar put into the water encounters less resistance. This is similar to the reason that a sprinter accelerates much more quickly from 0 to 24 KPH (0–15 MPH) than from 24 to 40 KPH (15–25 MPH): a sprinter who accelerates to greater and greater speed exerts a braking force and generates greater foot-ground friction for the next stride (*see also RUNNING AND HURDLING*). One paddler moves a boat at a certain speed; therefore, it is impossible for a second paddler to double that speed, because water is moving faster around the boat. A second paddler can add only incrementally to the speed.

To understand this point, remember that water is a fluid—not a solid—medium. This explains why, as water flows by a boat, it offers a less resistant medium from which a paddler can generate power. Consider, for instance, what would happen if someone tried to increase the speed of a motorboat by paddling: dropping a paddle into the water would create more resistance than propulsion—the paddle would fly backward the moment it penetrated into the water.

Canoers are aware of this (whether consciously or unconsciously): they always try to find slow-moving water, since that enables them to create the most propulsive power. In fact, they use a more vertical paddling motion that lets them "seek out" slower-moving water. Of course, a canoer's paddle blade will itself accelerate the water around it, making the water less resistant and thus reducing propulsive force; therefore, canoers often do not pull the paddle straight back but instead use a somewhat serpentine (S-shaped) motion.

Physique and Paddle Sports

In a sport like cycling, the advantage of being larger (greater muscle mass) is negated by greater rolling (tire) and air resistance (*see CYCLING*). Rowing is different, however. It is not coincidental that leading competitive rowers are much heavier than the norm: the average weight of male rowers is 94 kilograms (207 pounds), and the average weight of female rowers is 79 kilograms (174 pounds). Water is a denser medium than air, and the buoyancy of water is more "forgiving" with regard to supporting additional mass. In other words, at a given speed far less additional energy is required of 91-kilogram (200-lb.) paddler as compared with a 45-kilogram (100-lb.) paddler than would be the case with a 91-kilogram cyclist and a 45-kilogram cyclist. In fact, larger, more powerful paddlers have such a distinct advantage that rowing officials have created a lightweight category for events: a maximum body mass of 72.5 kilograms (about 160 lb.) for men and 59 kilograms (about 130 lb.) for women.

The need for two weight categories has been confirmed by studies in exercise physiology (Secher, 1992). In most sports, relative aerobic power (that is, aerobic power as a percentage of body mass) is the better predictor of performance. In rowing, by contrast, heavyweight paddlers are penalized only minimally by increased wind and water resistance, and so absolute (total) aerobic power is the better predictor (*see sidebar: "Rowers' Breathing Capacity"*). However, although rowing attracts more heavy, powerful athletes, the same is not true of kayaking. A kayak does not have a sliding seat, and so the leg muscles cannot be used for propulsion; also, a kayak is much lighter than a shell. As a result, top kayakers are typically much lighter, weighing about 80 kilograms (about 175 lb.). Also, a smaller paddler is able to fit into a kayak with a narrower beam (midboat width). The narrower-beam kayak encounters less resistance, and this more than compensates for any muscular shortcomings when a lighter paddler competes with a larger paddler in a wider-beam kayak.

Rowers' Breathing Capacity

The largest athletes usually have the largest respiratory capacity, because that capacity is directly related to body size. The British Olympic Medical Center, which tests most Olympic athletes, found that a male heavyweight rower had a respiratory capacity of 245 liters per minute and consumed 8 liters of oxygen per minute (Harries, 1994). This was well above normal capacity (180 L/min.) and oxygen consumption (5 L/min.); in fact, the figures were the highest recorded among all the athletes tested.

Paddle Sport Technique

The most efficient stroke rate and rhythm depend in large part on the distance to be covered. Paddlers must decide what internal "gear" to use: that is, what ratio they need between power and speed. Specifically, they must decide how deep they should be sinking the oar, and how hard and fast to pull. Should they use a deeper, slower, more powerful stroke or a shallower, faster stroke? There is no single correct answer to such questions; the decisions involved will be based on the length of the race and thus on the endurance of the paddler.

Paddlers try to increase the momentum of the surrounding water. There are two choices here: the paddler can impart a high velocity to a small amount of water, or impart a lower velocity over a longer period to a large amount of water. Practically speaking, the paddler can lower the oar (position it deep) and pull slowly, or put the oar in a shallower position and pull faster. This also means that (as discussed above) the larger the surface area of the paddle, the greater the pulling force needed; and the more pulling force is needed, the greater the surface area should be.

Sculling and Rowing Technique

In terms of biomechanics, sculling and rowing are among the few sports in which a blind athlete can compete effectively: vision is a negligible factor. In a crew, all the rowers paddle backward, pulling in rhythm as cued by the coxswain. In fact, a blind rower might have an advantage: there would be no temptation to look over the shoulder to gauge the competitors' progress; and a rower who could not see his or her position relative to the other boats might make a better, more consistent effort.

Rowers and scullers take what appears to be a very uncomfortable position: the knees are up under the chin, and the arms are stretched out to their full reach. From this position, the rowers engage in a unified pull; to a spectator, they resemble a series of uncoiling springs.

The rowers' pull accelerates the shell quickly. After about 10 strokes, the shell reaches its top speed—about 6 or 7 meters per second (13–14 MPH). The shell moves forward, pivoting from the tips of the oar blades, as the rowers straighten their legs and pull the oar back into the chest with considerable force. By extending their arms back as far as possible, and by sliding their movable seats back as far as possible, they increase the rotational inertia of the oar (lengthen the stroke).

On completing a stroke, the rowers lift their oars immediately (while the oar is still stationary in relation to the water). Without this quick lift, the oar is likely to continue its rearward motion, slamming into the rower's midsection with a gut-wrenching impact. For reentry, the blade is slowed down in relation to the boat by bringing the oar far forward, toward the bow, and beginning its backward motion in the air so that the blade enters the water with zero horizontal momentum (mass × velocity).

Speed is determined primarily by how efficiently the rowers direct their energy toward propulsion and by whether they can minimize wasted energy. Every movement by a rower either contributes to or detracts from speed. Synchronization—teamwork—is critical, because if a pair of rowers are not perfectly matched, a rotational (nonforward) component comes into play. The weaker of two rowers cannot create enough force to cancel out the pull of the stronger. Unequal strength between the left and right side of the body creates the same effect for scullers. Just as a chain is only as strong as its weakest link, the speed of a scull is limited by the weakest teammate. The coach has a particularly difficult task: to improve not only the

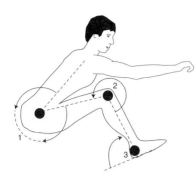

Figure 12. *Shown here are sequential motions in extension (straightening) by a rower. (1) The sequence starts at the hip joint; (2) this is followed by knee action; (3) the sequence finishes with ankle extension. This is what kinesiologist call a ballistic (full-power) motion in an open kinetic chain. Movement of the lever system begins at the pelvis, proceeds sequentially in a smooth action from one internal lever to another, and finishes at the interface of feet and floor.*

Injuries in Paddle Sports

Because water provides consistent resistance and a single, fairly repetitive motion is involved, injuries in paddle sports are rare. Most competitive paddlers are actually more likely to suffer injuries off the water (lifting weights or climbing up and down steps).

performance of each individual but also the collective performance of the crew. If one person improves while the rest of the crew does not, that can actually adversely affect performance.

As with most movements in sports, rowers must exert force in a smooth, sequential motion from hip to knee to ankle to foot to toes (*see Figure 12*). Rowers rely on the well-developed, thicker, more powerful muscles of the thighs, lower back, and shoulder to generate most of their power. However, these powerful muscles of the lower body also fatigue comparatively quickly. In longer races, individual rowers begin to experience different levels—or different intensities—of muscle fatigue. As fatigue worsens, it becomes very difficult to maintain cadence, and speed often drops. World-class rowers develop a feel for the right combination of power and finesse. They need to have enough strength to generate great force, and enough endurance to sustain it.

Kayaking Technique

Kayaking is completely different from sculling or rowing, for several reasons: the kayak is lighter; the paddle is lighter and shorter and has twin blades; and the paddle does not pivot about a pin. The shorter shaft of the paddle shortens the lever, greatly lessening the moment of inertia. Whereas rowers rely on a long, powerful stroke generated with the large-muscle groups of the lower body and the shoulders, kayakers find it far more efficient to use short, quick, propulsive strokes.

In kayaking, balance can be very precarious. The motion is asymmetrical—one side pulls while the other side pushes—and thus a leaning action is needed to counter the significant resistance force at the hand when one of the blades enters the (dense) water. To maintain balance and minimize "zigzagging," it is necessary to position and move the paddle effectively relative to the kayak and the water. To prevent zigzagging, kayakers must also develop symmetry of motion between the left and right sides of the body. This is a challenge, because in most people either the right side or the left side is dominant: one side of the body naturally wants to pull a little harder. World-class kayakers spend considerable time reviewing films of themselves to ensure that the cycles of body motion and paddle shaft motion on both sides match.

Because competitive kayaking requires muscular endurance, kayakers try to save energy by minimizing joint movements. Much of their muscle power comes not just from the arms but from the trunk, shoulder, back, and legs. The paddle should be held well ahead of the body so that the arms do not bend excessively. Halfway through a stroke, the arms extend completely, so that most of the power comes from the back, abdomen, and legs. In kayaking (unlike rowing or sculling), the paddle enters and leaves the water close to the hull of the boat; thus torso rotation is very important in aiding propulsion. A common error of novice kayakers is holding the hands too close together; this reduces power because it creates too short a span for

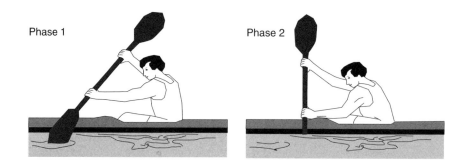

Figure 13. *In phases 1 and 2, hand and forearm remain aligned throughout the stroke. Because the arm muscles must work more as the forearm angle increases, the forearm should remain fairly straight until the paddle reaches a vertical position; it is bent slightly for the pull (left arm), and a bit more for the push (right arm). A conscious effort to keep the pushing elbow high helps keep it nearer the straightened horizontal position. During the pull, the upper arm (left arm) should be at a 20-degree angle at entrance; during the catch, its angle should reach 50 to 60 degrees. The pushing hand moves farther and generates more power than the pulling hand at entrance; the opposite occurs during the catch.*

the arm levers, and too long a span from the tip of the paddle blade to the hands. An efficient arm position can be found by laying the paddle across the top of the head and moving the arms out till the elbows are bent at a 90-degree angle.

The blade is pulled cleanly up and out of the water as it reaches a position perpendicular to the hips. To extend the paddle stroke beyond this point wastes energy by lifting water and pulling the stern of the kayak downward. Many kayakers make the mistake of not extending the paddle far enough forward as it enters the water, and then finishing each stroke too far behind them. The body should lean forward during the forward stroke, with back straight. The more balanced the kayaker's position is, parallel to the keel line (centerline) of the boat, the more closely the gravitational force exerted on body

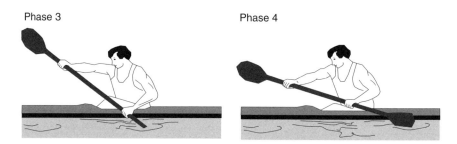

Figure 14. *In phases 3 and 4, the trunk bends and straightens very little, but from the catch to the pull the shoulders and trunk rotate significantly. The way the paddle enters and leaves the water is important. It should leave at the same place it enters: that is, the boat moves forward as the paddle stays in place. A poor finish, such as leaving the water too slowly, creates drag as the kayak moves the paddle forward relative to the water. In phases 1 through 4, the paddle is in the water about 70 percent of the time and is airborne 30 percent of the time.*

and boat will align with the direction of travel. More energy will go into propelling the boat, and less will be wasted keeping the kayak on course.

John Zumerchik

References

Armenti, A, "Why Is It Harder to Paddle a Canoe in Shallow Water?" *Physics Teacher* 23 (1985): 310–313.

Asami, A., et al. "Some Biomechanical Factors of Rowing Performance." In D. A. Winter (ed.), *Biomechanics IX-B*. Champaign, Illinois: Human Kinetics, 1985.

Broze, M. "A Quest for the Perfect Paddle." *Sea Kayaker* (Spring 1992).

DalMonte, A., et al. "Analysis of the Inertial Forces in Rowing Using a Force Platform." In D. A. Winter (ed.), *Biomechanics IX-B*. Champaign, Illinois: Human Kinetics, 1985.

Easterling, K. *Advanced Materials for Sports Equipment*. New York: Chapman and Hall, 1993.

Foster, Nigel. *Sea Kayaking*. Brighton, England: Fernhurst, 1991.

Harries, Mark. "Performance in Sport." *British Medical Journal* 309 (9 July 1994).

Kumamoto, M., et al. "Paddle and Paddling Style of Canadian Canoe." *Bulletin of Medical and Scientific Research of Sports* 4 (1980): 67ff.

Lezotte, S. *Rowing: Power and Endurance*. Chicago, Illinois: Contemporary, 1987.

Logan, S., and L. Holt. "The Flat-Water Kayak Stroke." *National Strength and Conditioning Journal* 7, no. 5 (1986): 4ff.

McMahon, T. "Rowing: A Similarity Analysis," *Science* 173 (1971): 349–350.

Noland, G., et al. "A Biomechanical Analysis of the Effects of Two Paddle Types on Performance in North American Canoe Racing." *Research Quarterly for Exercise and Sport* 53 (1982): 50ff.

Plagenhoef, S. *Patterns of Human Motion*. Englewood Cliffs, New Jersey: Prentice-Hall, 1971.

Schrier, E., and W. Allman. *Newton at the Bat: The Science in Sports*. New York: Scribner, 1987.

Secher, N. "Rowing." In R. Shephard and P. Astrand (eds.), *Endurance in Sport*. Boston, Massachusetts: Blackwell Scientific, 1992.

Senator, M. "Why Sliding Seats and Short Stroke Intervals Are Used for Racing Shells." *Journal of Biomechical Engineering* 103 (1981): 151ff.

Yoshio, H., et al. "The Electromyographic Study of Kayak Paddling in the Paddling Tank." *Research Journal of Physical Education* 18 (1974): 191ff.

Running and Hurdling

WHEN THE FIRST OLYMPIC GAMES were held in Olympia, Greece, in 776 B.C., spectators had to be sure to arrive on time: the one and only athletic event was a foot race called the *stadion*, lasting only a few seconds. In this race—held in honor of Zeus, the king of the Greek gods—runners sprinted along a sandy track about 192 meters (630 ft.) long. Tradition has it that Coroebus, a cook from the city of Elis, was the first winner and thus became the first Olympic champion. To honor his victory, that Olympiad was named for him.

Thereafter, athletic competitions were held in Olympia every four years. They became the most important ceremony honoring Zeus, and drew the fastest sprinters from the ancient western world to compete for fame, though not for fortune: until a symbolic wild-olive wreath was presented to the winner of the *stadion* at the seventh Olympiad, the only prize continued to be the honor of having the festival bear the victor's name.

After the Roman Emperor Theodosius abolished the ancient Olympics in A.D. 393, running ceased to exist as a high-profile athletic event until the early nineteenth century, when it reemerged as a sport called pedestrianism. The first major North American pedestrian event took place in Hoboken, New Jersey, on 5 July 1824. A $100 prize was offered for a half-mile race (about 1 km), and a $50 prize for a 200-yard sprint (about 180 m). In 1835, John Cox Stevens offered $1,000 to anyone who could run 10 miles (6 km) in less than 1 hour. This prize—enormous by the standards of the time—was intended to spur interest, and it did: there were 20,000 spectators. Of the 10 men who ran, only three finished at all; and only one, Henry Stannard, qualified for the prize: his time was 59 minutes 48 seconds. (Runners have obviously improved since then; if Stevens were making his offer today, he might have to give the $1,000 prize to more than 100,000 of them.) In addition to the prizes offered, immense sums were bet in some of these early pedestrian events.

Running is one of the simplest and most fundamental of all skills. As children grow, responding to stimulation from the environment and using and experimenting with their motor skills, these skills develop quickly and naturally. Self-propulsion develops as a child learns increasingly efficient ways to move from one place to another: first crawling, then toddling, then walking, and eventually running.

TOP RUNNING SPEEDS OF MAMMALS

Species	MPH	KPH
Cheetah	63	101
Gazelle	55	88
Red deer	42	68
Horse	40	64
Giraffe	32	51
Human	25	40
Elephant	12	20

Table 1. *The cheetah is the fastest mammal because of its extended stride, made possible by a very large rotation at the hip and shoulder joints; and by its extremely flexible skeleton, which permits the spine to curve up and down. As bipeds, human runners—even the best—do not perform well against most quadrupeds.*

Running is also an instinctive skill. For our early ancestors, it was necessary for survival, since it was a means of evading predators and tracking down game. In today's civilized world, running is seldom needed for survival, yet it remains a basic requirement for many sports. Although running is a simple, natural skill, sprinting at high speeds or running long distances efficiently calls for excellent technical form that usually requires considerable coaching.

Because of individual differences in anatomy, strength, and flexibility, each human being has a unique running stride, or gait. In addition, humans have different aerobic and anaerobic capacities. As a result, speed and endurance vary over a wide range. Running is also affected by other internal factors, and by certain external—that is, environmental—factors. Internal forces determine how the muscles react to ground forces, overcoming resistance caused by muscular viscosity (restricted flow of fluid chemicals in the muscles); and how the fascia, tendons, and ligaments of the skeletal system react to tension. External, or environmental, forces include gravity, air resistance, and ground forces affecting a runner's feet (or shoes). Becoming a world-class runner requires some understanding of all these factors, though among runners that understanding is often more anecdotal than scientific.

Basics of Running

Human locomotion in general, and running in particular, is extremely inefficient—that is, wasteful. For example, running requires approximately three times as much energy per mile as bicycling (*see also CYCLING and ENERGY AND METABOLISM*). Still, some people, such as world-class runners, are naturally more efficient than others.

In all humans, of course, the muscles work similarly—in concert—and the joints are connected similarly. What differs among individuals is the interaction of parts. World-class runners are efficient because their balance is excellent, their ability to relax is well developed, and their timing is precise: all this allows them to conserve energy and transfer it from one part of the body to another with relatively little waste. In other words, through training they have developed a running style that minimizes tension and unnecessary movements and thus minimizes wasted energy. World-class runners continually fine-tune their technique, but they do so without compromising their relaxed, rhythmic style.

Running is a series of takeoffs, flights, and landings in which each stride must blend easily with the next. However, not all running is alike; thus, it is often impossible to make generalizations about the mechanics of running, because different goals are involved. In fact, runners are distinguished both by the individual physical characteristics needed for running different distances and by the different techniques involved (*see Figure 1*).

Figure 1. *Because different distances require different running styles, world-class sprinters and long-distance runners differ significantly in physical characteristcs and running styles.*

Figure 2. *Sprint versus long-distance running. Sprinters (above) must swing their legs forward quickly, so they keep the swing radius as small as possible by pulling the heel up toward the buttocks when a foot leaves the ground. Very strong hamstrings are needed to keep the leg's center of gravity close to the hip. Long-distance runners (below) do not need great leg speed, so they do not bend much at the knee. This allows gravity to help them move the legs downward and forward.*

Physically, for example, sprinters need to be endowed with a high percentage of fast-twitch muscles, while distance runners need a high percentage of slow-twitch muscles. Although training can improve endurance and strength (often dramatically, and at any age), it is highly unusual for speed to increase by more than 10 percent, even over an extended period of training. The reason is that training cannot convert slow-twitch muscles to fast-twitch muscles; in other words, training can increase running speed only within a genetically predetermined range (*see also SKELETAL MUSCLE*).

In terms of technique, sprinting requires proper mechanics, exact motor control, and speed; distance running requires physiological endurance, efficiency, and optimization of pace. Joint action also is quite different in different types of running. For distance runners, joint action is moderate; but for sprinters, joint actions are extreme—as can be seen in the sprinter's high knee kick and the strong follow-through that brings the foot up close to the buttock (*see Figure 2*).

Because of anatomical factors and technique, then, the probability that the same athlete could win a world-class 100-meter sprint and a world-class marathon is almost nil; and it would be almost as unlikely for a sprinter to win a moderate-distance race, such as the 1,500-meter or mile.

One of the major differences between sprinting and distance running is foot-ground contact (*see Figure 3*). It is primarily distance that determines whether a runner's foot should roll from ball to heel or from heel to toe. In heel-to-toe running, which is typcial in moderate to long distances, the heel lands gently, allowing the forefoot to "roll over" quickly; the runner then pushes off from the ball of the foot. In ball-to-heel running, the outside edge of the ball of the foot touches down, the foot rolls inward from the impact, and the knee bends slightly to absorb the shock. Then, the heel touches the ground softly so that the entire sole is momentarily in contact with the ground. After that, the runner quickly pops up with a final thrust coming from

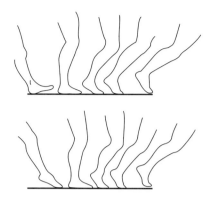

Figure 3. *Two primary styles of running: heel-to-toe roll (above) and ball-to-heel roll (below). Ball to heel is virtually required for a pace of less than 6 minutes per mile.*

the big toe as the foot leaves the ground. A short stride (as in jogging) makes ball-to-heel running difficult; thus ball-to-heel running is very natural for sprinting, difficult for medium and long distances, and nearly impossible at a slow pace. Typically, the speed at which ball-to-heel running becomes necessary is about 6 minutes per mile. This fast a pace can hardly ever be sustained running heel to toe.

Unless an athlete is well trained, ball-to-heel running requires more energy, because the muscles and tendons of the lower leg must absorb most of the impact from each touchdown and then create propulsion. By contrast, in the heel-to-toe roll the entire musculo-skeletal system of the leg and foot absorbs the impact of each stride. With either style, proper use of the body's elastic mechanisms (e.g., the achilles tendon and the ligaments of the foot) can reduce the metabolic energy needed for ball-to-heel running by about 50 percent (*see Figure 4*).

It is important not to confuse ball-to-heel running with "ball-of-foot" running. Even the best sprinters do not stay on the ball of the foot all the time. Sprinters momentarily have the full sole in contact with the ground to enlarge the landing surface area. The greater the contact area, the more evenly the landing load is distributed and the more effectively the forward propulsive force is generated. Without this "rocking back" to the heel, it would be impossible for the hips to move quickly ahead of the support leg before the push-off.

As noted above, ball-to-heel running is difficult with a short stride. To express this more positively, ball-to-heel running allows a longer stride. The typical heel-to-toe roll causes much more deceleration than a ball-to-heel landing (that is, more potential for stored elastic energy). Therefore, when performed properly, ball-to-heel running allows greater use of elasticity from the muscles and tendons in the legs and feet.

Structure	Energy storage (work done in stretching)
Achilles tendon	35 joules
Ligaments of foot	17 joules
Total	52 joules

1 joule = 0.737 foot-pound = 0.239 calorie

Mode	Joules
Total energy from footfall	100
Energy stored and returned	52
Energy dissipated	48

Figure 4. *A runner's foot has springlike characteristics. Total energy (potential + kinetic) lost and regained at each footfall is about 100 joules for a 70-kilogram (154-lb.) man running at 4.5 meters per second (10 MPH). About 50 percent of the energy is stored briefly as strain (spring) energy and then returned in elastic recoil. The greater the energy saved in strain, the less work the muscles need to do. (Source: Alexander, 1994)*

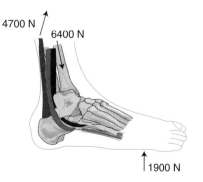

4700 N

6400 N

1900 N

Peak forces	Newtons
Downward	6,400
Upward (Achilles tendon)	4,700
Upward (foot ligaments)	1,900

1 newton = 0.225 pound

Aerodynamics of Running

"May the wind be at your back" is an ancient blessing, implying, of course, that with a tailwind one encounters less resistance and thus that life will be easier. Whether or not this is true of life in general, a tailwind certainly helps competitive runners.

A runner, no matter how fast or how slow, must expend energy to overcome air resistance, or aerodynamic drag. In other words, in order to get anywhere the runner must displace air. The air may be pushed to the sides or pushed farther out in front of the runner, but it must be moved somewhere, and this requires work. Work (force over distance) reduces the runner's kinetic energy (energy of movement) and thus reduces his or her speed.

Effects of Air Resistance

The effect of air resistance varies as the square of the runner's speed; for example, if the runner's speed doubles, air resistance increases fourfold. It follows that air resistance is greatest during sprinting and smallest during jogging. Another factor in air resistance is the frontal area—the contours—of the runner's body. A person of average size encounters approximately 0.45 square meter (about 4.84 sq. ft.) of air resistance.

Of the total force exerted by a runner, then, a certain percentage must be used simply to overcome air resistance. Mathematicians at Pennsylvania State University have calculated, for example, that at sea level, where air density is about 1.19 kilograms (2.6 lb.) per cubic meter (slightly more than 1 cu. yd.), about 3 percent of a sprinter's energy is expended on overcoming air resistance (Pritchard, 1994). (The majority of energy is lost as heat generated as a by-product of the metabolic reactions that control muscles, frictional effects in the joints, and overcoming gravity.) This figure (3 percent) obtained for sprinters is highly variable, however; it depends on wind velocity and direction relative to the runner. That is, the faster a runner's speed, the greater the relative wind speed opposing the runner's progress. Logically, running with a tailwind decreases aerodynamic drag whereas running against a headwind increases drag. A headwind of 1 meter per second (2.25 MPH), for instance, can reduce a sprinter's time in a 100-meter race by 0.12 second (*see Table 2*). Because many meets produce winning sprint times well within 0.12 of the world record, wind direction and speed are a major factor in setting world records.

To make record-setting fairer, international rules disallow a record in the 100-meter or 200-meter sprint if there is a tailwind of more than 2 meters per second (4.5 MPH). Accordingly, most competitors and coaches do some type of conversion in order to evaluate performance, since a track athlete competes not only against others, but also against his or her own best time. Also, this consideration helps runners to be realistic. For example, a sprinter in the starting

EFFECT OF WIND RESISTANCE ON RECORDED TIMES IN THE 100-METER

	Wind Resistance Factor	Adjusted Time	Wind Effect
Headwind	$13^2/10^2 = 1.69$	10.22	+ 0.22
Tailwind	$7^2/10^2 = 0.49$	9.85	− 0.15

Table 2. *This table indicates the effect of a tailwind of 3 meters per second for a pace of 10 meters per second in covering 100 meters (a "no wind" time of 10.00). Air resistance is proportional to the square of the runner's speed minus relative wind speed; thus, a headwind reduces sprint time more than a tailwind aids it. Running on a treadmill is effectively like running with a strong tailwind; this explains why many individuals record their best times on a treadmill. (Source: Pritchard, 1994)*

blocks facing a headwind of 1 meter per second (2.25 MPH) knows that there is little chance of breaking the world record if the existing record was set recently with a tailwind of 1 meter per second.

Because air resistance varies as the square of the runner's speed relative to the wind, a headwind reduces a runner's speed more than a tailwind aids it. As Table 2 shows, if 0.15 second is gained in a 400-meter sprint with a tailwind in the first straight, 0.22 second will be lost because of the headwind coming back in the second straight, for a net loss of 0.07 second. This in part explains why in races like the 400, 800, and 1,500 meters, records are rarely set on very windy days, regardless of wind direction: the advantage gained with a tailwind on one side of the track is not great enough to counteract the headwind on the other side of the track.

Considering the importance of wind, the question arises: why isn't a formula used to adjust for wind drag, so that every race would be a potential world-record race? This seems reasonable, but at least three problems arise. First, a wind rarely comes as a direct head- or tailwind. Second, a wind rarely blows at a steady rate. If, say, it gusts at 25 MPH at the gun but settles down to 10 MPH at the finish, which speed would be used to adjust for drag? Third, each sprinter has a different shape and size, and thus a different frontal drag. Would one body size be used as an "average," and if so, whose? Or would each competitor have his or her frontal area measured? Developing a formula to adjust for air resistance is plausible in theory, but the complexity of the real world makes it unmanageable in practice.

Drafting and Air Resistance

In cycling, a road race typically comes down to the wire; it is rare to see a single cyclist break from the pack and hold a big lead. The reason for this is drafting: the individuals in the pack take turns closely following—or drafting off—one another, taking turns as leader until they catch the leader. By contrast, a long road race such as a marathon is seldom tightly contested at the finish. This brings up the question of drafting in running. A cyclist averages 30 to 35 MPH; the average pace of a marathon runner, of course, is much slower: approximately 12 MPH for 26.2 miles (41.3 km). At 30 to 35 MPH, drafting is essential, but it is still useful at 12 MPH?

A runner cannot save as much energy as a cyclist by drafting, but the energy saved by a runner can still be substantial: less work is required, and this means less oxygen uptake and therefore less expenditure of energy. In one study, it was found that in running a 1,500-meter race at 7 meters per second (15.7 MPH), following 2 meters behind another runner saves enough energy to cut 1.7 seconds per lap (Kyle, 1979).

Drafting aids the runner in all wind conditions, but most significantly in a headwind. For example, a 13-MPH pace into a headwind of 5 MPH creates air resistance comparable to the effect of an 18-MPH pace with no wind. Under these conditions, a runner drafting behind the leader will encounter air resistance less than that with the

18-MPH pace, though still greater than that at 13 MPH with no headwind. This gives the "drafter" a sizable advantage over the "draftee" in a race like the mile or the 1,500-meter. These races are not usually won by someone who leads from start to finish. Rather, the winner has used a drafting strategy through most the race and then—using the energy saved while drafting—has exploded past the leader down the home stretch.

Sprinting

Perhaps no Olympic event is as eagerly anticipated as the men's 100-meter (330-ft.) sprint. The winner is acclaimed as the "fastest man on earth"—probably justifiably, for 100-meter sprinters attain amazing speeds. Instantaneous speeds have been recorded at over 12 meters per second (28.8 MPH) for men and close to 11 meters per second (24.6 MPH) for women.

A sprinter springs out of the blocks with the trunk leaning far out over the feet, and then slowly draws back to a slight lean while accelerating. This makes sense in terms of physics: the center of gravity is well out over the runner's driving feet. It also makes sense in terms of physiology: the large, powerful muscles of the buttocks can work most forcefully when the body is bent forward at the hips, because the distance between origin and insertion of the buttocks and hamstring muscles lengthens, thereby lengthening the effective muscular levers.

Sprinting is defined as running at or near maximum speed. To reach maximum speed, the runner accelerates one foot off of the ground as the trailing leg swings forward, launching the runner's body into the air. The swung leg, now stretching out in front of the body, then strikes the ground to complete the stride. In theory this suggests that to increase speed, sprinters need to take long strides as rapidly as possible. In practice, however, this is very difficult to accomplish. The reason is that—unlike automobile tires, which are in constant

WORLD RECORDS IN SPRINTS

Men

100 meters: 9.84 seconds—Donovan Bailey (Canada), Atlanta, 27 July 1996

200 meters: 19.32 seconds—Michael Johnson (United States), Atlanta, 1 August 1996

400 meters: 43.29 seconds—Butch Reynolds (United States), Zurich, Switzerland, 17 August 1988

Women

100 meters: 10.49 seconds—Delorez Florence Griffith Joyner (United States), Indianapolis, 16 July 1988

200 meters: 21.34 seconds—Delorez Florence Griffith Joyner, Seoul, 29 September 1988

400 meters: 47.60 seconds—Marita Koch (East Germany), Canberra, Australia, 6 October 1985

contact with the ground, allowing for uniform acceleration—runners spend the majority of their time airborne.

While airborne, sprinters have two problems: they cannot accelerate, because there is nothing to push off against; and they decelerate because of air resistance. With feet firmly placed in the starting blocks, it is easy for the sprinter to accelerate at the start of a race. But as the sprinter gains speed, it becomes more and more difficult to run faster, to continue to accelerate, because the feet have less and less time in contact with the ground.

Being airborne also presents a third problem—landing. Any landing creates a braking force; an obvious example is the braking force created when a jetliner lands: as the landing wheels are set in motion, the friction between tires and pavement actually sends up a cloud of smoke. In landing and continuing their forward motion, sprinters experience a similar, though less dramatic, phenomenon. Runners try to minimize this braking effect by rocking forward on contact, from ball of foot to heel to toe. First, the sprinter must exert a downward force with the foot to support the body weight in such a way that forward velocity is slowed as little as possible. Second, this brief contact time must be used to push the foot against the ground, creating forward acceleration. Sprinters try to achieve a tricky balance: to land without creating too great a braking force, they need to minimize contact; to accelerate, though, they need enough contact to generate a powerful forward force.

For these reasons, training for a sprinter includes a considerable effort to minimize the proportion of time spent airborne (*see the sidebar "Airborne Time"*). Excellent motor control is required to accelerate the legs forward; but in additon, excellent technique is needed to optimize foot-ground contact.

Many fans believe that sprinters are born and not made. Considering that no single physique dominates in sprinting, this conclusion seems overstated; in fact, most coaches agree that champion sprinters come in a variety of shapes and sizes. The Russian sprinter Valery Borzov, to take one example, was of modest height and build, yet he won a gold medal in both the 100-meter and the 200-meter sprint in the Olympics of 1972. Michael Johnson, who won the gold medal in both the 100 meters and the 200 meters in the Olympics of 1996, had been ignored by many collegiate recruiters because of his relatively short legs, but he more than made up for this by increasing his stride rate and keeping his trunk more erect (most sprinters lean forward 5 to 7 degrees).

Still, there is some genetic component in sprinting. In terms of biomechanics, world-class sprinters use two general techniques. Lighter, thinner sprinters seems to float gently over the track, like gazelles; compact, heavily muscled types power themselves toward the finish like tigers. The compact, muscular sprinters often do well at the beginning of the race, but as the race proceeds, neuromuscular organization becomes more important. How efficiently muscles "turn off" and "turn on" determines speed, which requires intense muscle

Airborne Time

A runner's center of gravity is always in a state of flux, moving up and down. At foot-ground contact, energy must be expended to stop the downward movement of the center of gravity and give it an upward movement. Although the running speeds and styles of sprinters and marathoners vary tremendously, the average air time (in between strides) of world-class competitors is surprisingly similar: 52 percent for sprinters and 50 percent for marathoners.

arousal—rapid and forceful contractions on cue. The nervous system has to produce a high level of arousal in the muscles and time the "on" and "off" switches optimally to generate maximum muscle forces on cue. The goal is to obtain maximum motion efficiently in the shortest time. The rapid arousal, activation, and relaxation of muscles explain why, as noted earlier, sprinters need a high percentage of fast-twitch muscles—which is primarily an endowed trait (*see also MOTOR CONTROL*).

Stride Length versus Stride Frequency in Sprinting

Both length of stride and frequency (rate or cadence) of stride are significant components of world-class sprinting. These two aspects of stride can be understood in terms of the dynamics of running.

Acceleration depends on the runner's ability to drive the legs backward faster than they are moving relative to the ground. At the point when the sprinter can no longer do this, maximum velocity has been reached. This aspect of sprinting must be combined with a second aspect: the impact force (800–1,440 lb.; 3,560–6,400 newtons, N) when a foot hits the ground. Before foot-ground contact, then, the runner must be prepared to take full advantage of the contact time to minimize braking and maximize propulsion. Braking is a frictional force; in takeoff, the frictional force is forward, but in landing it is backward. To avoid accelerating and decelerating with each stride (a characteristic of poor runners), world-class sprinters need to reduce horizontal friction, or braking, by taking off and landing smoothly and efficiently. To improve their preparation for foot-ground contact, sprinters use speed drills. Nevertheless, this skill is by no means easy to improve on. Times taken at different stages of a race show that most sprinters hit full speed at around the 60-meter mark (198 ft.), and it is very difficult for them to maintain this speed from there to the finish. The problem, as we have seen, is that the sprinter must accelerate body mass and apply significant force to the ground during a brief foot-ground contact.

With these dynamics in mind, coaches attempt to increase a sprinter's speed by increasing both stride frequency (rate) and stride length. Usually, when a sprinter increases stride length, it is at the expense of stride frequency, and vice versa. During training, most coaches stress stride length rather than stride rate. They believe that a longer stride allows more efficiency (that is, less waste of energy) in driving the sprinter forward; also, they hope that the excitement of competition will enhance leg speed without reducing the longer stride developed through much practice.

In addition to the obvious advantage of having long legs, an ability to generate considerable push-off with the feet—to propel the body forward through the air—is important in lengthening stride. If this push-off increases braking force, of course, there will be no increase in speed. But if there is no increase in braking force, and if the same frequency can be maintained, in any given time a longer stride will naturally cover more ground than a shorter stride. There-

Two Record Sprints

The 1988 Olympics produced the two fastest times ever for the 100-meter sprint. In the eagerly awaited showdown pitting Carl Lewis against Ben Johnson, they both fired out of the blocks quickly (1.36 and 1.32 seconds respectively), but Johnson pulled away with a super-human performance of 9.79 (versus 9.92 for Lewis). Later Johnson had to be disqualified because of banned substances found in his urine. His time of 9.79 was better than the Olympic and world record of 9.84 set by Donovan Bailey on July 27, 1996, at the Atlanta Summer Olympics. Because of better detection of banned substances, it may take another decade before the 9.80 mark is broken (*see also STATISTICS*).

fore, it is critical to find the right stride length. Overstriding creates too much braking; understriding creates too little push-off.

Every sprinter has to find the right balance between his or her own stride length and stride frequency. On average, men cover the 100-meter sprint in 44 to 53 strides and at a rate of 4.4 to 5.02 strides per second. Between the 50- and 60-meter marks, where instantaneous speed is highest, stride lengths typically range from 2.17 meters (7 ft. 1.5 in.) to 2.4 meters (7 ft. 10.5 in.), though some great sprinters have strides as long as 2.74 meters (9 ft.). In terms of body proportions, the average stride length of world-class sprinters, measured from foot takeoff to foot strike, has been found to be 1.14 times the runner's height and 2.11 times leg length. Coaches recommend that sprinters should not try to alter their own stride to match these proportions; instead they should use these figures as benchmarks in developing appropriate individual ranges.

Stride length depends in great part on the flexibility of the hip and ankle joint, the strength of the legs and ankles, and the length of the levers formed by bone and muscle; but it also depends on sprinting form. Stride can be lengthened only by increasing the power of the leg drive or the foot push-off; it cannot be lengthened by reaching the legs too far in front of the runner's center of gravity (*see also ACROBATICS and FIELD ATHLETICS: JUMPING*). In fact, the foot strike should be directly under the runner's center of gravity. If the center of gravity is too far forward, a significant braking force will be created: the body must "catch up" with the foot before generating a propulsive force. If the center of gravity is too far back, the propulsion generated by the driving leg is reduced, because the landing foot is partially "unweighted." To achieve optimal stride length and prepare for the next leg drive, it is important for the driving leg to have the greatest possible rearward extension.

Because any change in length of stride will affect the runner's output of energy, stride length also varies with the distance of the sprint. Thus in the 400-meter sprint, the stride is slightly shorter in order to save energy. Regardless of anaerobic training (explosive muscle power), at about the 300-meter mark the runner must start to draw on aerobic (that is, oxygen-based) energy; but shortening the stride slightly slows the depletion of anaerobic capacity. For this reason, not surprisingly, stride length is also a concern of long-distance runners.

Block Starts and Top Speeds in Sprinting

With the introduction of starting blocks in 1929, it became advantageous to use a crouched, coiled starting position, with the center of gravity well forward of the feet. If the footing is good, this the best position for accelerating forward rapidly.

To a great extent, blocks have relieved sprinters' fear that their feet will slip out from under them. In fact, the footing may actually be too good with blocks. Although blocks allow for rapid acceleration, sprinters often stumble and fall out of the blocks because they are

Attributes of World-Class Sprinters

1. Stride is long.
2. Knee action is high.
3. Foreleg reach is long.
4. Runner is high on toes.
5. Runner bounds forward rather than upward.
6. Trunk leans forward 5 to 7 degrees.
7. Back is straight.
8. Heels move high and close to buttocks during back kickup.
9. Knees stay bent during recovery (*see Figure 3*).
10. Front arm reach is low.

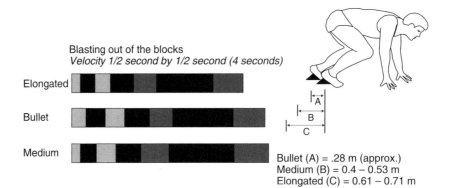

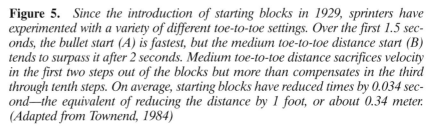

Bullet (A) = .28 m (approx.)
Medium (B) = 0.4 – 0.53 m
Elongated (C) = 0.61 – 0.71 m

Figure 5. *Since the introduction of starting blocks in 1929, sprinters have experimented with a variety of different toe-to-toe settings. Over the first 1.5 seconds, the bullet start (A) is fastest, but the medium toe-to-toe distance start (B) tends to surpass it after 2 seconds. Medium toe-to-toe distance sacrifices velocity in the first two steps out of the blocks but more than compensates in the third through tenth steps. On average, starting blocks have reduced times by 0.034 second—the equivalent of reducing the distance by 1 foot, or about 0.34 meter. (Adapted from Townend, 1984)*

unable to keep their feet under the trunk, which is leaning too far forward. Because the center of gravity is so far forward of the feet, the first five or six steps out of the blocks are critical—and atypical. Each of these first steps is short, and taken quickly, with the trunk gradually rising. As the trunk rises, the center of gravity moves more directly under the feet; this makes it possible for the sprinters to reach full speed quickly and smoothly.

Outstanding sprinters have excellent acceleration, a high maximum speed, and an ability to maintain that maximum speed through to the finish line. Still, every sprinter has a top speed. A sprinter begins to reach top speed in about 3 seconds (*see Figure 6*). At the start of the race the sprinter is stationary (velocity = 0). After 0.1 second (average time to react to the firing of the gun), speed increases rapidly for the first 3 seconds but then begins to level off, toward a constant pace of 25 MPH. The shape of the curve indicates the obvious fact that a sprinter cannot increase speed indefinitely. As the sprinter reaches higher and higher speeds, it becomes more and more difficult to continue to increase speed; therefore, the rate of acceleration decreases.

Of course, no two sprinters get exactly the same jump out of the blocks, nor do any two sprinters accelerate at the same rate. Peter Brancazio, a physicist at Brooklyn College, constructed a model comparing the velocity of two hypothetical sprinters (Brancazio, 1984; *see also Figure 6*). According to this model, sprinter A has greater acceleration and thus reaches top speed sooner; but B has a higher maximum speed. Although A is at an advantage in shorter sprints, B can overtake sprinter A in longer sprints. However, this model assumes that the sprinter can maintain maximum speed once it is reached; and that assumption seems unrealistic: fatigue and problems with motor

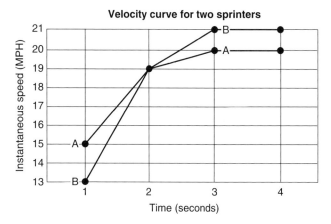

Velocity curve for two sprinters

Figure 6. *Sprinter A accelerates faster out of the blocks and reaches top speed more quickly, but sprinter B can achieve a higher maximum speed. In a short race A is at an advantage, but B can catch up and pass in the later stages of a sprint. In the 1988 Olympics, Carl Lewis (an example of type B, and renowned as a strong finisher), won the 100-meter sprint with a time of 9.92 seconds (26.95 MPH), the fastest instantaneous speed then measured. Not surprisingly, Lewis reached this speed between the 80- and 90-meter marks. Florence Griffith Joyner, the women's champion in 1988, reached the fastest instantaneous speed then measured for a women: 24.58 MPH, between the 60- and 70-meter marks.*

control make it difficult for runners to maintain maximum speed (*see also MOTOR CONTROL*).

Choice of Lanes in Sprinting

Running on a straightaway is quite simple: runners push downward and backward on the track to create a reaction force, propelling themselves forward. On a curved track, by contrast, the runners change direction as they round the turns, and so some of their acceleration force must be diverted from pushing forward to pushing outward. As a result, sprinters cannot increase their speed as much around a curve as they can on a straightaway. This basic condition has implications for running within lanes.

In the 200-meter and 400-meter sprint, runners must contend with the curve or bend in the oval track. Furthermore, because tracks are located in multipurpose stadiums and indoor arenas, sprinters must adjust to tracks with different radii (*see Figures 7 and 8*). When a sprint involves running around one or more curves, regardless of the curve radius, starting positions are staggered to compensate for the fact that the outer lanes have a larger circumference and thus involve running a longer distance.

Lanes are assigned by lottery: that is, at random. Nearly all sprinters dread drawing lane 1, the inside lane; they consider it—correctly—a disadvantage because the turn is "too tight" and adversely affects their stride. When starting into a curve, or turn, a runner experiences a horizontal force exerted by the ground against the feet, inward toward the center of the arc of the bend. This feeling is similar to the centripetal force—an impetus from outside to inside—

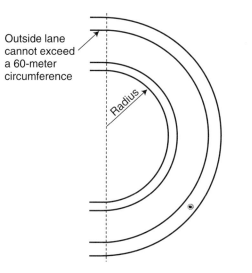

Figure 7. *Track curves are designed with a single center, with a radius varying between 36.6 and 40 meters (120.8 to 132 ft.) measured from a perpendicular line drawn through the ends of the straights to the curb. The width of each lane is 1.27 meters (4.12 ft.), with lane one starting 30 centimeters out from the curb (which is 5 cm high). Starting positions are staggered so that each competitor travels the same distance. For a record to be sanctioned, the distance along the curve (circumference) of the outside lane cannot exceed 60 meters. Over 60 meters, the curve is considered to be too straight, giving the outside-lane runner an unfair advantage. However, this regulation does not address "tight cornering" of the inside lanes, a disadvantage resulting from the smaller radius of the curve in those lanes.*

required to keep from falling off a merry-go-round. During the actual turn, there is an inertial tendency: a tendency to keep moving in a straight line. The runner must compensate for this intertia by leaning into the curve and pushing outward on the track surface with the legs and feet to generate a countering inward reaction, a centripetal force. In effect, runners adjust their center of gravity to exert this centripetal force, countering the inertial tendency to continue moving in a straight line. The greater the runner's velocity, the more lean is necessary (*see also FIELD ATHLETICS: THROWING*). Likewise, the sharper the curve, the more lean is necessary. Runners must expend more energy creating a centripetal force in lane 1, where the turn is "tightest," than in the middle or outside lanes.

Interestingly, sprinters not only want to avoid lane 1, which represents a real handicap, but also want to avoid lane 8—which involves no physical disadvantage. Not wanting to run in lane 8 is a purely psychological reaction: it arises because most sprinters like to keep their competitors in sight instead of having to listen for oncoming footsteps and never feeling quite confident about maintaining the lead.

Physicists at the University of Utah studied runners generating centripetal force in the 200-meter sprint, and developed a mathematical model for the adverse effect on their times (Alexandrov, 1981). According to their model, a time of 19.72 seconds in (inner)

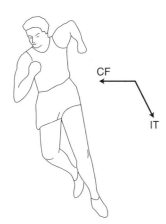

Figure 8. *A banked track turn eliminates much of the inward lean—the centripetal force (CF) needed to counter the inertial tendency (IT)—and the greater friction between track and foot that are necessary in unbanked turns.*

lane 1 corresponds to 19.6 seconds in (outer) lane 8. The difference is significant enough to result in a margin of victory of about 0.12 second, or 1 meter (3.3 ft.).

P. C. Jain constructed a similar mathematical model and came up with similar results (Jain, 1980). Jain felt that the disparity in times could be remedied in one of two ways: either by shortening the inside lane or by starting a sprint before the curve rather than on it (the present practice). Jain's second solution requires some explanation. If all competitors started before the curve, the sprinter in the outside lane would run the entire curve just like the sprinter in the inside lane. This is because the outside lane, while it has a gentler curve, also has a greater circumference as compared with the inside lane. Thus runners in the outside lane would need to create the same centripetal force as before, but for a longer distance and accordingly for a longer time—an effect that would tend to neutralize much of the advantage of the outside lane.

Jain's suggestions are logical; but shortening the inside track would hardly be acceptable to purists, and his second suggestion, though it holds promise, would probably not be much more palatable. Track officials and fans feel more comfortable with the current simple rule: for a record to be sanctioned, the curve of the outside lane cannot exceed 60 meters (198 ft.).

Whenever running speed is very high, or the radius of the curve is short (as in indoor tracks and inside lanes), sprinters must make a choice: slow down or adjust their stride. To help compensate for a short radius and the pronounced turns it creates, indoor tracks are built with banked curves. The purpose of banking is the same on a running track as on an automobile racetrack: the slope of the curve changes the vertical plane of the sprinter or the racing car, and thus gravity can be used to reduce the need to create a centripetal force. When runners must create a centripetal force, it is as if they were wearing handicapping weights or running in a stronger gravitational field. When a track is banked at the optimal angle, however, runners can maintain their pace and stride because they do not have to lean inward as much to adjust their center of gravity (*see also* CYCLING).

Distance Running

The strategy for distance racing is very different from the strategy for sprints. Sprinters accelerate rapidly and go all-out from start to finish. By contrast, distance runners maintain a fairly constant pace throughout the race, with the exception of a brief period of acceleration at the beginning and possibly a "kick" at the end. Successful distance running relies heavily on the long-term aerobic power of the muscles, not on anaerobic power.

The Physics and Physiology of Optimizing Pace

Every runner enters a race with a pace strategy. Runners must decide whether to start slow and finish fast, start fast and taper off, or maintain a consistent pace throughout.

At the start of a race, the body has a fixed amount of energy. One component of this energy supply fuels "anaerobic" activity, that is, activity that does not depend on oxygen. A 100-meter sprinter can rely solely on anaerobic processes: theoretically, these sprinters could hold their breath for the entire race without impairing their performance. The anaerobic pathway, however, is a limited source of energy; therefore, greater distances require the aerobic engine to kick in.

Aerobic energy involves an alternative chemical pathway, which uses oxygen and does not produce lactic acid, a waste by-product. The aerobic pathway (in contrast to the anaerobic path) is unlimited. However, if the body cannot supply enough oxygen to the muscles—if the muscles are using oxygen faster than the lungs, heart, and circulatory system are providing it—an "oxygen debt" is created. When this happens, the muscles will start to break down glycogen (the major form in which the body stores carbohydrates) anaerobically, that is, without oxygen. This breakdown does produce lactic acid. As a result, the runner experiences labored breathing, an accelerated heartbeat, and burning muscles and begins to slow down.

Fred Keller, a mathematician at New York University, developed a model of running (Keller, 1973) based on the initial energy in a runner's body at the start of a race, the maximum force the runner can exert, the resistive force opposing the runner, and the rate at which energy is supplied by

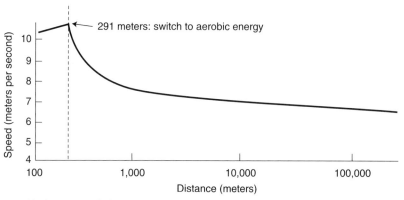

Maximum speed of a runner as a function of distance, according to Keller. The data points indicate actual maximum speeds. At 291 meters, the peak of the graph, a runner can no longer depend on the anaerobic pathway and must begin to rely on an aerobic pathway for energy.

oxygen metabolism. In this model—according to actual track records at various distances—the best strategy in a race of less than 291 meters (960 ft.) is to run at maximum speed for the entire race. The body's anaerobic fuel tank can supply enough energy to allow runners to go all-out for 20 to 30 seconds, and that will take them 291 meters. Beyond this distance, lactic acid starts to build up; this inhibits the ability of muscles to contract and eventually causes the runner to slow down.

The wide differences in speeds of middle- and long-distance runners coming down the "home stretch" are directly attributable to how much energy they have left. Measurements of velocity show that the exciting "come from behind" finish—in which a trailing runner seems to close in suddenly on the leader—is actually an illusion. Usually, what happens is not that the trailing runner accelerates but that the lead runner "runs out of gas" and slows down. Therefore, the real art of middle- and long-distance running is to be continuously aware of your energy supply—and particularly

of your relative utilization of the aerobic and anaerobic pathways.

For longer races, Keller's model suggests that the runner should accelerate for the first 1 or 2 seconds, then maintain a constant pace throughout the race, and finally slow down slightly during the last few seconds. This supports the coaching strategy of training runners to maintain as constant a pace as possible. The reasoning is that a runner burns fuel much as an automobile burns gasoline, so to maximize miles per gallon, it is essential to maintain a constant pace.

Some physiologists would disagree with this, however. They believe that the second half of a longer race should be run faster than the first half; that is, the runner should keep an anaerobic reserve (oxygen debt) for the later stages of the race. On the basis of this theory, the runner should minimize anaerobic effort to conserve energy, but once the end is in sight, the runner "throws the coal on" and finishes with nothing left in the furnace. In other words, a runner wants to finish a race by pushing the aerobic system to its

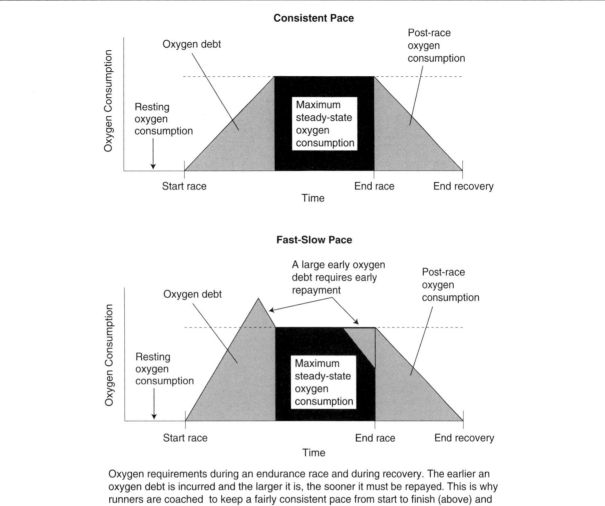

Consistent Pace

Oxygen Consumption

Oxygen debt

Post-race oxygen consumption

Resting oxygen consumption

Maximum steady-state oxygen consumption

Start race · End race · End recovery

Time

Fast-Slow Pace

Oxygen Consumption

A large early oxygen debt requires early repayment

Oxygen debt

Post-race oxygen consumption

Resting oxygen consumption

Maximum steady-state oxygen consumption

Start race · End race · End recovery

Time

Oxygen requirements during an endurance race and during recovery. The earlier an oxygen debt is incurred and the larger it is, the sooner it must be repaid. This is why runners are coached to keep a fairly consistent pace from start to finish (above) and not start too fast: they will accumulate an oxygen debt that starts to be repaid before the end of the race (below). A fast-slow pace is inferior to a constant pace because it consumes signigificantly more oxygen; but whether a slow-fast pace is superior is still unknown.

limit and exhausting the anaerobic energy supply. This does seem to be the pattern in middle-distance races like the 1,500 meters or the mile, but it may not result from a conscious effort; the explanation may be simply that in shorter events, experienced runners are better able to gauge their oxygen debt precisely.

In races over 1,500 meters, the pattern is just the opposite: times are faster for the first half of the race than the second. In a 5,000-meter race (5 km, about 3 mi.), the first half is usually run 2 to 5 seconds faster than the second half. This tendency is even more pronounced in a 10,000-meter race (10 km, or 6 mi.): the first half is run 10 to 20 seconds faster than the second. This may be because once an oxygen debt accumulates, the body begins to repay it even before the exercise finishes. For example, a 5,000-meter runner with a maximum oxygen uptake of 4 liters (1.06 gal.) per minute begins to pay back this debt at 0.5 liter per minute during the race, and thus will have only 3.5 liters of reserve aerobic capacity per minute to draw on. It seems, then, that using energy evenly throughout a longer race results in a slightly decreased pace in the second half, as the oxygen debt begins to be paid. Here, the key

to setting records is maximizing pace without ever fully depleting reserve aerobic capacity. In other words, push your aerobic capacity to full throttle, but stop short of "stealing" from your anaerobic capacity. Save as much of that as possible for the finish.

Perhaps no athletes are more concerned with pace than those in "iron man" events. How do these athletes pace themselves to swim 2 miles, cycle 110 miles, and then run 26 miles, without hitting the "wall"—the point of depletion, the point where the muscles ache and the mind can no longer get the body to respond to instructions? In an interview in *Runner's World*, Dave

(continued)

The Physics and Physiology of Optimizing Pace *(continued)*

Scott, a six-time "iron man," said, "I don't believe there's a wall out there. It's a bunch of baloney. You can control your glycogen stores (major carbohydrate storage form in the body) so that you never hit the wall." Evidently, Scott is able to gauge how much energy he has left and develop a race strategy that avoids fatigue.

Still, for longer races, what makes the mathematical and physiological theories untenable and produces an uneven pace is the difficulty of gauging how much is left of the body's energy supply—how much or how little remains in the fuel tank. One factor making this difficult is that everyone has good and bad days, and most runners are unsure beforehand whether a given day will be good or bad. Another factor is "psychological warfare." The strategy of running away early from the pack is designed to break the opponent's will, and this strategy contributes mightily to the faster pace seen during the first half of longer races.

Thus although physics and physiology both indicate that the optimal strategy is to maintain a consistent pace from start to finish, this strategy may be virtually impossible, given your own inability to assess your fuel supply beforehand, and the psychological tactics of your opponents. In reality, most runners set their pace by "feel"; and perhaps it is beyond the scope of physics or physiology to come up with a single theory of optimizing pace that would encompass all runners under all conditions (*see also HEART AND CIRCULATORY SYSTEM*).

John Zumerchik

Tactical considerations are a major component of distance racing. Some distance runners like to hold back, let someone else take the lead, and then finish with a big kick. Others like to set a fast pace and create a sizable lead; their rationale is to prevent "big kickers" from catching up with them, or to take the steam out of strong kickers by forcing them to expend extra energy early on, to keep pace with the pack.

Different distances require different balances between speed and

WORLD RECORDS IN DISTANCE RUNNING

Men

800 meters: 1:41.73—Sebastian Coe (Great Britian), Florence, Italy, 10 June 1981

1,000 meters: 2:12.18—Sebastian Coe, Oslo, Norway 11 July 1981

1,500 meters: 3:28.86—Noureddine Morceli (Algeria), Rieti, Italy, 6 September 1992

5,000 meters: 12:55.30—Moses Kiptanui (Kenya), Rome, 8 June 1995

10,000 meters: 26:43.53—Haile Gebrselassie (Ethiopia), Hangelo, Netherlands, 5 June 1995

20,000 meters: 56:55.6—Arturo Barrios (Mexico), La Flèche, France, 30 March 1991

Women

800 meters: 1:53.28—Jarmila Kratochvilová (Czechoslovakia), Munich, 26 July 1983

1,000 meters: 2:30.67—Christine Wachtel (East Germany), Berlin, 17 August 1990

1,500 meters: 3:50.46—Qu Yunxia (China), Beijing, 11 September 1993

5,000 meters: 14:37.33—Ingrid Kristiansen (Norway), Stockholm, 5 August 1986

10,000 meters: 29:31.78—Wang Junxia (China), Beijing, 8 September 1993

Improving Performance for Middle Distances

To improve performance, most runners first try to make some physiological change, but a biomechanical change can often be more effective. Here are six suggestions for biomechanical changes:

1. Reduce the braking force on the foot at contact by learning to run "springingly."

2. At touchdown, increase the backward angular velocity of the lower leg.

3. Also at touchdown, increase the backward angular velocity of the lower leg and foot relative to the forward velocity of the body's center of gravity.

4. Immediately after the leading part of the foot leaves the ground, bend the leg naturally toward the thigh.

5. Lengthen stride and increase stride rate by increasing the angular velocity of the thigh during support, and by decreasing leg extension (straightening) at toe-off.

6. Keep the upper body as relaxed as possible.

endurance. Because distance runners rarely run at top speed, their foremost concern is to improve endurance. By improving endurance, they can comfortably increase their speed over all distances.

Running on Hills

In most long-distance races, runners must contend with hills. Any cross-country runner, for example, knows that the majority of races are won by the runners who adjust most efficiently to uphill and downhill terrain. Unfortunately, adjusting to hills is not easy. Because humans have legs—not wheels—it is impossible to develop downhill inertia that could be conserved and utilized for an ascent. The frictional (braking) force created by foot-ground contact makes running far less efficient than any wheeled transportation.

Given this constraint, and assuming a steady stride pattern, the stride naturally will be longer going downhill (when the surface is farther away), and shorter going uphill (when the surface is closer). It is appropriate to lengthen the stride even more for the downhill. Moreover, the stride should not just be longer but should also "bound" more, to increase the flight phase between strides. Bounding saves energy because it synchronizes the acceleration and deceleration of the limbs: this has the effect of reducing the work required of the body's muscles. The lead leg should be unlocked—that is, not fully extended but slightly bent—as it comes forward: this lessens the jolting impact forces to the knee joint and thus helps prevent runner's knee.

Running downhill is mechanically more difficult than running uphill because the leg muscles need to do more eccentric (stabilizing) work. The leg muscles are asked to function more as shock absorbers because greater kinetic energy is created by the gravitational force encountered with a longer stride. This added stress is especially hard on runners with knee and back problems. By running ball to heel (rather than rolling heel to ball), however, many runners are able to diminish the jarring impact of downhill running.

When running uphill—as compared with running downhill or on the flat—world-class runners are more apt to run ball to heel. They lean slightly into the hill, and they shorten each stride. These adjustments may slow a runner's pace somewhat; but they help the runner avoid the onset of fatigue from excessive oxygen debt that results if the same stride length is maintained.

Form and Fatigue in Distance Running

Every distance runner must fight off fatigue; in fact, some people—including some top runners themselves—believe that the best distance runner is not necessarily the one who is most genetically gifted, but the one who is best able to cope with the painful effects of fatigue. Thus, whereas successful sprinters all depend on biomechanical efficiency, distance runners depend primarily on using energy efficiently; in other words, a distance runner's strategy centers on how to conserve energy. This means that distance runners must consume and use oxygen efficiently. By supplying more aerobic energy, in the form of oxygen, they are less likely to avoid the bane of all distance runners: oxygen debt.

To conserve energy, distance runners maintain a relatively constant pace throughout a race and try not to vary stride length or frequency. In addition, runners' "energy cost" is affected by wind, hills, and the weight and composition of their shoes: these external factors have been clearly shown to be factors in oxygen consumption, and therefore major contributors in the onset of fatigue. There is considerable debate about the importance of internal biomechanical fac-

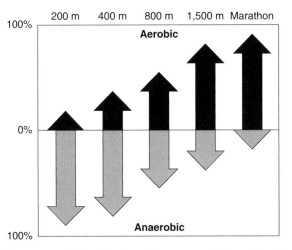

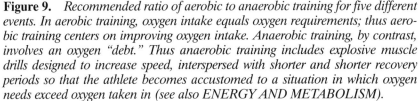

Figure 9. *Recommended ratio of aerobic to anaerobic training for five different events. In aerobic training, oxygen intake equals oxygen requirements; thus aerobic training centers on improving oxygen intake. Anaerobic training, by contrast, involves an oxygen "debt." Thus anaerobic training includes explosive muscle drills designed to increase speed, interspersed with shorter and shorter recovery periods so that the athlete becomes accustomed to a situation in which oxygen needs exceed oxygen taken in (see also ENERGY AND METABOLISM).*

Runner's High: Fact or Fiction?

The much coveted "runner's high" is often described as an overwhelming feeling of euphoria: a calm, even trancelike state in which some runners say that they feel as if they can run forever.

Explanations for this phenomenon began to emerge in the early 1970s, after scientists discovered opiate receptors on the brain cells of mammals. This finding implied the existence of naturally occurring opiates, pain-reducing chemical produced in the brain; and researchers did come across such a family of chemicals—the endorphins. Endorphins are produced in the region of the hypothalamus and are released by the pituitary gland (located behind and above the nose). There are several types of endorphins, but the beta-endorphins draw the most interest with regard to runner's high. Physiologists propose this theory: The physical stress of strenuous running brings about a flooding of beta-endorphins throughout the body. Beta-endorphins hook onto nerve receptors, cutting down the transmission of pain messages to the brain; this results in the characteristic euphoria.

Some researchers have discovered elevated endorphin levels in runners. However, these researchers note that not everyone experiences a runner's high, because endorphins are not produced immediately, or from easy jogging, but are proportional to the stress the runner experiences (Anderson, 1994). In general, a very strenuous workout, approximately 75 percent of

maximum heart rate, is required to stimulate the release of endorphins. Moreover—as with most phsyiological functions—the amount released is highly dependent on heredity. In this regard, runners form a continuum. For those at one extreme, endorphin levels start rising after only 30 minutes of running at 75 percent of maximum heart rate. Runners nearer the middle have a hard time getting the flow of endorphins started; they may have to run for 2 hours or more at 75 percent of maximum heart rate. At the opposite extreme are runners who never produce this flow of endorphins— these may be the people who seem to despise running and who scoff at the idea of a runner's high.

The term *high* is appropriate for the euphoria some athletes experience, and some athletes who seek this high evidently show the same addictive behavior patterns as drug abusers. Edward Pierce, a medical doctor who wanted to understand the obsession with running—and specifically the longing for the high—gave a written test to 150 runners whose training distances varied widely and scored their answers on an "exercise dependency" scale (Pierce, 1993). The scores indicated that many of them were addicted to running: they had an obsession with exercise that often led them to forsake their families and friends and to disregard their own health: many of them admitted that they had completed races regardless of the onset of serious injuries.

The degree of obsession and obsessive behaviors was found to be directly related to the distances run. Casual runners who competed in races of 3 miles or less scored low on Pierce's "exercise dependency" scale. Those who said they regularly ran between 3 and 26 miles proved much more exercise-dependent: their scores were on average 31 percent higher. And those who ran ultramarathons (50 miles) showed the most obsessive behavior, scoring 21 percent higher than the marathoners.

It seems, then, that runners can become habituated to the psychological and physiolgical pleasures of running. Like drug addicts, they eventually develop a tolerance: they need to run longer and longer to reach the same "high." And, again like drug addicts, they experience withdrawal symptoms when the high wears off: they become agitated and need another dose. However, the evidence for or against a physiological or psychological runner's high is not yet conclusive. A runner's high might be just psychological: the satisfaction of being active and in good condition; an experience of relief or release from everyday tensions; or a rewarding sense of mastery, an awareness of meeting a challenge and reaching a goal in an increasingly goal-driven society. There is, though, a good chance that the high might prove to be biologically triggered as the floodgate of endorphins opens—a true physiological high.

John Zumerchik

tors, such as angle of the trunk, bend of the knees, and vertical oscillation (up-and-down movement). Because of the wide range of body types among runners, there is no single style that fits all of them; however, distance runners do use less energy-consuming knee lifts and arm actions than sprinters.

Maintaining an effective mechanical position that requires less energy, such as a low knee lift and an upright trunk, can significantly

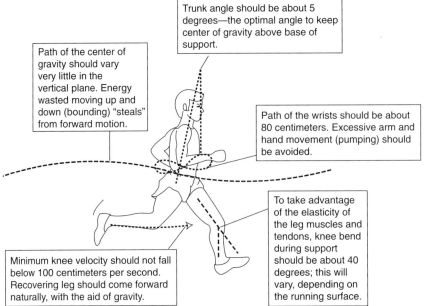

Trunk angle should be about 5 degrees—the optimal angle to keep center of gravity above base of support.

Path of the center of gravity should vary very little in the vertical plane. Energy wasted moving up and down (bounding) "steals" from forward motion.

Path of the wrists should be about 80 centimeters. Excessive arm and hand movement (pumping) should be avoided.

To take advantage of the elasticity of the leg muscles and tendons, knee bend during support should be about 40 degrees; this will vary, depending on the running surface.

Minimum knee velocity should not fall below 100 centimeters per second. Recovering leg should come forward naturally, with the aid of gravity.

Figure 10. *Energy-saving technique for long-distance runners, in terms of oxygen uptake. Other common factors known to contribute to the onset of fatigue include: (1) more ground time and less air time; (2) arms extended laterally from the body; (3) less leg lift; (4) too long a stride; (5) decreased stride frequency; and (6) legs farther apart, "waddling" from a wider base of support. (Adapted from Williams, 1987)*

Sweating

Although sweating can be uncomfortable, it is essential for cooling the body. Performance in long-distance races is determined in large part by the body's ability to cool itself. Smaller people have a better balance between internally generated heat and radiative surface area: their ratio of surface area to mass is higher, giving them more ability to dissipate heat. This is one reason that world-class long-distance runners are on average relatively small. The average for men distance runners is 5 ft. 10 in., 132 lb. (172 cm, 60 kg), and for sprinters 6 ft. 1 in., 163 lb. (181 cm, 74 kg).

delay the onset of fatigue (*see Figure 10*). An attempt also should be made to maintain the airborne interval. Distance runners have been found to divide airborne time and ground time about evenly until fatigue sets in. Then they begin to spend more time on the ground. This is inefficient from a biomechanical perspective because the longer the ground time, the greater the braking force. Instead, at the onset of fatigue, the runner should increase stride frequency and shorten the stride, because overstriding increases the demand on the cardiorespiratory system. Also, fatigue can be reduced—without greatly compromising speed—by maintaining a lower center of gravity and decreasing knee lift.

Identifying the underlying cause of fatigue in an individual case can be problematic: does poor form lead to fatigue, or does fatigue lead to poor form? Fatigue creates a curious physiological and biomechanical reciprocity between cause and effect. Poor biomechanical form results in an earlier onset of physiological fatigue. On the other hand, physiological fatigue often creates or compounds poor biomechanical form, resulting in even worse fatigue. Probably the main factor is the pain associated with fatigue. Pain seems to distract the mind and blur mental processes, making it difficult for the runner to become aware of a deterioration in mechanics.

Tuned Tracks

By developing a better understanding of how the muscles and reflexes work, scientists have shown that it is possible to design a faster running track—a track "tuned" to the body. If bones, muscles, and joints are considered in combination, they have some of the same mechanical properties as a spring. The idea, then, is to design a running surface whose stiffness is matched to that of the leg muscles. Such a surface increases running speed by decreasing foot-ground contact time and increasing stride length.

When a runner's foot strikes a surface, muscles in the leg decelerate the downward motion of the body and simultaneously transfer energy to the track surface as elastic energy. If the track surface has elasticity—that is, if it "gives"—it can return this energy to the runner while the foot is in contact with it. If the springiness or elasticity of a surface is "tuned" appropriately, the maximum energy will be returned to the runner. But if the surface is very hard, like concrete, it has little or no elasticity and will return little or no energy to the runner; and if it is soft or spongy (like the landing cushions used by high and long jumpers), the runner will sink into it and will be slowed by a shortening of stride and an excessive lengthening of foot-ground contact. The well-tuned track, then, lies somewhere between these two extremes.

"Tuned" tracks are designed to return elastic energy that minimizes contact time and maximizes stride length. Scientists at Harvard, studying the university's new "tuned" indoor track, observed a sizable increase in the recorded speeds of the track team during the first year—an average advantage of 2.91 percent (McMahon and Greene, 1978). Although 2.91 percent may not seem like much, it represents a substantial improvement for middle- to long-distance events: it is the equivalent of improving the best time in the 1,500 meters by 5 to 6 seconds. Gradually, "tuned track" technology has moved to outdoor as well as indoor arenas.

Tuned tracks can help runners break records, and this is an important consideration, because the chance of seeing a record-breaking performance is a primary attraction for many track fans. Gideon Ariel of Ariel Research Center in Trabuco Canyon, California, has estimated that a "tuned" modern synthetic-rubber track—in conjunction with modern lightweight track shoes and starting blocks—would have reduced Jesse Owens's time in the 100-meter sprint at the Olympics of 1936 by 0.4 second: from 10.3 seconds to 9.9 seconds (Allman, 1988). A time of 9.9 seconds would have been good enough to win the gold medal as recently as 1968.

Tuned tracks are not only faster but usually more comfortable to run on. Therefore, as more and better tuned tracks are installed, there should be a decrease in joint injuries.

Efficiency of Movement

Even the subtlest gait adjustment changes metabolic rate. Tribal Kenyan women can carry up to 20 percent of their body weight (balanced on head) without a metabolism increase. These women, who mastered carrying heavy loads on their heads as young children, benefit from their efficiency: the 20 percent gait energy saving offsets the 20 percent extra muscular energy (e.g., neck muscles) required to support the heavy load. Carrying extra weight on their backs and heads, adult Europeans subjects were unsuccessful in attempting to match efficiency of the well-trained Kenyan women.

Hurdling

Hurdling is much more than just jumping over a barrier. Timing and fluidity are needed to clear hurdles while maximizing sprinting efficiency and minimizing airborne time. The center of gravity should

Preventing Overuse Injuries in Running

There is widespread debate over whether competitive distance running does more "building up" or more "tearing down." Some experts believe that in competitive distance running—unlike fitness running—many runners cross a threshold beyond which the "pluses" for the cardiovascular system are outweighed by the "minuses" for the musculoskeletal system.

Competitive distance runners, who must undergo very demanding training, are much more susceptible to overuse injuries such as stress fractures and runner's knee than athletes in other sports. Each of a runner's feet strikes the ground over 1,000 times per mile, and each time a foot strikes the ground, the force of impact is three to four times the runner's body weight (Glover and Schuder, 1988). This adds up to a lot of impact.

Still, although continual impact plays a significant role, most running injuries result primarily from physical weakness and improper training. Also, although the pain associated with running injuries usually subsides with rest, it can recur if the resting period is insufficient.

The following should be taken into account in setting up and evaluating a training program:

Strain It is detrimental to be subjected to "fatigue on fatigue." To avoid cumulative fatigue, skip a day or two, cut mileage in half, or wait until energy has returned to its normal level before resuming normal running. It is all right to run with discomfort, but not with progressively worsening pain. When discomfort worsens and becomes pain, stop—the body is sending a message. Always be aware of warning signs, and quickly address the cause of the problem.

Efficient running Average runners should not try to imitate world-class runners, let alone superstars. Everyone is put together differently, and therefore everyone has a different optimal technique (e.g., stride length, foot contact). That said, however, all distance runners should attempt to develop a natural, smooth, relaxed style. It is important for heel-to-ball runners to touch down lightly, roll forward fluidly, and push off with the toes. Slow-paced long-distance ball-to-heel running (resembling sprinting) can eventually lead to problems with the achilles tendon.

Body weight. For obvious reasons, competitive runners are rarely overweight. Overweight is "dead weight," something useless that just has to be lugged around; it places an added burden on the cardiovascular and musculoskeletal systems; and it impairs the body's ability to dissipate heat. It also has a paradoxical aspect with regard to fitness and safety: people exercise to lose weight, but extra weight can cause injuries that necessitate inactivity—periods of rehabilitation—that

be no higher than is needed to clear the hurdle safely (raising it any more squanders time and energy); and as little time as possible should be spent in the air, because the more time is spent airborne, the less propulsive force can be imparted from foot-ground contact.

Because the hurdles are staggered, it takes dedicated practice to

WORLD RECORDS IN HURDLING

Men
110 meters (3 ft. 6 in.): 12.91 seconds—Colin Jackson (Great Britain), Stuttgart, Germany, 20 August 1993
400 meters (3 ft.): 46.78 seconds—Kevin Young (United States), Barcelona, 6 August 1992

Women
100 meters (2 ft. 9 in.): 12.21 seconds—Yordanka Donkova (Bulgaria), Stara Zagora, Bulgaria, 20 August 1988
400 meters (2 ft. 6 in.): 52.74 seconds—Sally Jane Janet Gunnell (Great Britian), Stuttgart, 19 August 1993

lead to more weight gain. However, overweight runners can circumvent this paradox by cross-training: a combination of running and low-impact cardiovascular activities like skating, swimming, and cycling.

Stretching and warming up Flexibility exercises before running are important to prevent muscle shortening and to improve range of motion of the joints. Stretching relieves muscle tension and increases flexibility. It increases the blood supply to muscles, ligaments, and tendons, making them more supple and helping them move more efficiently. "Cool-down" stretching after running is also important because muscles tend to tighten up with exercise. Stretching the hamstring muscles (back of the thigh) is particularly important because this makes it easier to run more fluidly and efficiently.

Strength training. Weight training should be designed to increase the propulsive force of ankles, feet, legs, and shoulders, and to ensure that opposing muscles (agonist and antagonist) are properly balanced. Moreover, strengthening and conditioning the tendons, muscles, and fascia of the foot and leg will make them more effective at damping impact force. Strong quadriceps help in the finishing sprint. The muscles of the upper body are equally important: strengthening them helps maintain posture during lengthy runs when fatigue becomes a factor (*see also STRENGTH TRAINING*).

Shoes and orthotics Runners must wear good shoes and take care of their feet. A good shoe must provide flexibility, cushioning, and support; a shoe that fails in any of these regards should be replaced. It is important to be aware that newer, "better" shoes, designed to prevent injuries, can actually cause injury. For example, a more flexible shoe with a more rigid heel counter may help prevent overuse injuries for some runners, but it can increase injuries for others. The same is true of greater cushioning: because the foot sinks farther into the shoe, it can increase the risk of achilles tendinitis and shin splints. On the other hand, a properly selected shoe, and orthotics such as heel pads and arch supports, can go a long way toward reducing the risk of overuse injury (*see also EQUIPMENT MATERIALS and ANKLE, FOOT, AND LOWER LEG*).

Aging Adjustments in intensity and frequency are warranted as a runner ages. With age, bones become more brittle; cartilage, ligaments, and joints become less flexible; and muscles gradually lose strength. The ability to regulate body temperature also declines, and this increases susceptibility to heatstroke and frostbite (*see also AGING AND PERFORMANCE*).

Rehabilitation After an injury, the return to training should be slow and progressive. For most compotitive runners, the lungs and heart will adapt to training more quickly than the musculoskeletal system; this means that it is important not to log too many miles too quickly just because your cardiovascular engine may allow it (*see also REHABILITATION*).

**David H. Janda and
John Zumerchik**

develop the stride patterns necessary for hurdling. In the 110-meter hurdles, for example, the first hurdle is 13.72 meters from the start; thereafter the hurdles are 9.14 meters apart, with the last (the tenth) hurdle 14.02 meters from the finish. The key is to clear each hurdle while maintaining running stride length and stride frequency as much as possible.

Because the lead leg is brought forward to clear the barrier and descends as the barrier is cleared, the distance from takeoff point to the front of a hurdle is about twice as long as the distance from hurdle to touchdown. Thus the approximate distance for takeoff is 2.2 meters (7.26 ft.) before the hurdle, and touchdown is about 1.1 meters (3.6 ft.) past the hurdle. However, takeoff distance varies considerably, depending on approach speed, the athlete's height (the height of the center of gravity), the length of his or her legs, the speed with which the lead leg can be raised, the stride length, and the athlete's skill at clearing barriers. Speed is particularly important: the greater the speed, the farther back the takeoff point. Likewise, as a hurdler's speed varies throughout a race, so his or her takeoff points will vary. When hurdlers do not move the takeoff point back as they increase speed, they will clip the hurdle as the lead leg rises.

Hurdlers do their utmost to minimize clearance. Leaving a large margin for error unnecessarily raises the center of gravity, and this impairs performance for at least two reasons. First, a high center of gravity means a delayed landing, less foot-ground contact time, and therefore less speed. Second, a higher jump further reduces horizontal velocity because with each stepping-over stride, more force is used for the vertical component than for the horizontal component. In clearing each hurdle, therefore, the trunk is leaned forward to lower the center of gravity. In effect, hurdlers reduce the height of the center of gravity necessary to clear the hurdle (*see Figure 11*). Willie Davenport, who won the 100-meter hurdle at the Olympics of 1968, explained it as follows: "You don't go up and over the hurdle; you come down over the hurdle. You are high on your toes like a ballet dancer, and you step down over the hurdle."

Most hurdlers are long-legged and thus have a high center of gravity. This type of physique means that the peak of the center of gravity as each hurdle is cleared is very close to its height between hurdles. Even so, however, it takes considerable training for world-class hurdlers to keep their center of gravity as constant as possible throughout a race.

Originally, the hurdles were firmly fixed to the ground. Because hitting a fixed hurdle at high speed would be extremely dangerous, earlier hurdlers resorted to a clumsy technique to give themselves a large margin for clearance. To relieve the athletes' anxiety and prevent injuries, the fixed barriers were eventually replaced with light, movable hurdles. These, of course, can be knocked over by a hurdler. At one time, a hurdler who knocked over three of the ten hurdles would be disqualified; but today there is no such penalty, because the officials have concluded that running through hurdles is not advantageous.

Many track fans still wonder, however, why hurdlers don't run right through the hurdles instead of clearing them. They reason that running through a hurdle would require raising the lead foot just high enough to topple it; this would mean that the hurdler's center of gravity would not have to be raised an extra 4 to 6 inches, and this would

Figure 11. *An athlete approaching a hurdle tries to step down over it—not so much jumping as continuing the running action. Because the lead leg rises forward of the body, 110-meter hurdlers leave the ground approximately 2.20 meters (87 in.) before the hurdle and land about 1.10 meters (43 in.) behind it. If the trunk is bent forward, the center of gravity does not rise by much (dashed line); if the hurdler remains more erect, the center of gravity is higher (dotted line).*

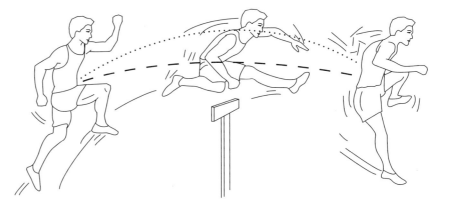

achieve longer foot-ground contact time and thus greater propulsion throughout the race.

The reasoning of the track officials is based on the weight of the hurdles. Since a hurdle must weigh at least 10 kilograms (26.81 lb.), a horizontal force of between 3.6 to 4.0 kilograms (9.65 to 10.72 lb.) is needed to overturn it. The officials feel that the force required is large enough to offset any advantage gained through lowering the center of gravity by knocking the hurdle down.

Experience also indicates that knocking the hurdles down would not be a superior technique: no world-class hurdler uses this strategy. The minimum force (3.6 kg) needed at the center of the horizontal bar may simply be too great, as the officials reason. Furthermore, even though hurdlers do have to raise their legs considerably to clear each barrier, most world-class hurdlers actually raise their center of gravity very little. Thus even for the more bulky competitors, the loss in linear momentum (mass × velocity) from foot-hurdle contact is greater than the gain from not rising as high.

Even if knocking down the hurdles were a theoretically superior strategy, it would require consistency: the hurdler would have to hit each hurdle with the same force and at the same height. Any variation in velocity would undoubtedly impair timing, probably throwing the hurdler "off stride." This principle can be seen in conventional hurdling: a hurdler who hits or even grazes the first hurdle is much more likely to hit or graze the next hurdle than a competitor who clears it cleanly.

Technique in Hurdling

Hurdling requires precise rhythm and fluidity, since it involves moving quickly from sprinting to rising or jumping. Much like sprinters and long jumpers, hurdlers need speed; in fact, hurdlers use much the same technique as sprinters. However, hurdlers accelerate with their hips raised (more perpendicular) to be in better position to attack the hurdle. They also lean the trunk forward more than a sprinter does at the moment of attack (takeoff) and in clearing the hurdle.

Because hurdling interrupts the sprinting motion, good hurdling technique requires a form that at first feels very unnatural. It is vital for the step-over movement of the lead leg, followed by the sideways swing of the rear leg, to be carried out efficiently. The lead leg always begins its upward motion with the thigh and knee—never the lower leg and foot. This is because the thigh is closer to the axis of rotation at the hip, and thus the moment of inertia (the necessary turning force) for raising the thigh first is far less than for raising the foot first. The greater force needed to raise the foot also might have the secondary effect of causing the body to rise too high.

The airborne acrobatics of hurdling are amazing. According to the laws of physics, for every force there must be a counterforce. In running, for example, the propulsive force of the driving leg and foot requires the counterforce of the ground. Such foot-ground contact is

Figure 12. *To keep their hips and shoulders square to the barriers at all times, hurdlers use a force-counterforce action. As the trailing leg and foot cross a hurdle, the arm on the same side must be flung back and the arm on the opposite side extended as a countering force. The arm motions prevent overrotation by "canceling out" the leg and foot motion.*

very simple and straightforward; but airborne movements are far more complicated—they require movement of one body segment to be countered by another segment.

Hurdlers first delay or interrupt a forward motion of the rear leg to assist the leading leg as it pivots upward and forward. Then the rear leg is brought around at an angle level with the lead knee. To accomplish this movement, the hurdler has to swing back the arm on the same side as a counterforce to the outwardly rotated trailing leg and foot. Leaning the trunk well forward and swinging the arm help the trailing leg to clear the hurdle, with only a slight elevation of the center of gravity (*see Figure 12*).

A hurdler leans into the barrier, exaggeratedly bending the trunk forward, because—among other things—leaning compensates for the angular momentum (momentum about an axis of rotation) created when the lead leg swings up to clear the hurdle. The swing of the lead leg transfers to the whole body in flight, tending to rotate the body backward. This means that on contact with the ground, when hurdlers once again become sprinters, they are no longer in the optimal sprinting position: a slight forward lean. It is important for the lead leg to remain in one vertical plane throughout, to minimize twisting forces that create inefficient angular momentum (*see also ACROBATICS*).

Hip mobility is also extremely important. The trailing leg needs to swing out from the body at an angle of nearly 70 to 80 degrees. If a hurdler does not have a enough mobility at the hip joint, the trailing leg will swing out only partially, remaining more under the body. This will be obvious in the awkward style and exaggerated clearance (further raising of the center of gravity) needed for the rear leg to clear the hurdle.

Physique and Hurdling

Many people believe that because taller hurdlers do not have to jump as high—they can, after all, step right over the barrier—they must have an inherent advantage. Surprisingly, this is not necessarily the case. Many factors determine the optimal physique for hurdling.

Obviously, a taller athlete does have one inherent advantage: a higher center of gravity. This means that less time must be spent airborne, and that the center of gravity does not need to be raised nearly as far as it does with a shorter hurdler. However, a taller athlete also has an inherent disadvantage: a longer, heavier lead leg. A longer, heavier leg has higher rotational inertia—that is, more force is necessary to move it; and thus more energy is required to lift it and swing it over the hurdle. Longer legs also require beginning the takeoff farther back from the hurdle.

Stride patterns are another critical factor. Because the hurdles are spaced uniformly, the competitors' stride lengths are nearly identical. Unlike a sprinter, hurdlers cannot use the stride length that would be optimal for speed; they must use whatever stride will be most efficient for the given spacing of the hurdles. An athlete who is very tall and long-legged may find the spacing of the 100-meter hurdles too close; and a short hurdler may need to overstride. This may also lead to a divergence in style: the tall, long-legged hurdler may need to use a slightly bent knee to clear the hurdles, while the shorter hurdler may have to fully stretch out the lead leg.

Edwin Moses, one of the greatest hurdlers of all time, took a a novel and aggressive approach to this problem of shortening and lengthening stride. He had a longer stride than most hurdlers—14 steps between vaults in the 400-meter hurdles—and he felt that it would be a real hindrance to shorten it. Therefore, he worked on lengthening it even more, so that it would be possible for him to drop a step. This "saved" step helped him win the gold medal in the summer Olympics of 1976 and dominate the event internationally for over a decade.

On the whole, neither the tall nor the short hurdler has a clear-cut advantage. The advantage goes to the hurdler with speed, strength, and technique who also has certain genetic gifts: length of legs and natural stride matching the height and spacing of the hurdles.

References

Alexander, R. "Human Elasticity." *Physics Education* 29, no. 6 (1994): 358–362.

Alexandrov, I., et al. "Physics of Sprinting." *American Journal of Physics* 49, no. 3 (1981): 254–257.

Allman, G. "Testing the Limits." *US News and World Report* (September 19, 1988): 50–58.

Anderson, Owen. "The Inside Dope on Runner's High." *Runner's World* 29, no. 8 (August 1994): 60–66.

Bellemans, A. "Power Demand in Walking and Pace Optimization," *American Journal of Physics* 49, no. 1 (1981): 25–27.

Brancazio, P. *Sport Science*. New York: Simon and Schuster, 1984.

Cohen, B. "Body Weight as an Application of Energy Conservation." *American Journal of Physics* 45 (1977): 867–869.

Fixx, J. *The Complete Book of Running*. New York: Random House, 1977.

Frohlich, C. "Effect of Wind and Altitude on Record Performance in Foot Races, Pole Vault, and Long Jump." *American Journal of Physics* 53 (1985): 726–730.

Glover, B., and P. Schuder. *The New Competitive Runner's Handbook*. New York: Penguin, 1988.

Jain, P. "On a Discrepancy in Track Races." *Research Quarterly for Exercise and Sports* 51, no. 2 (1980): 432–436.

Keller, J. "A Theory of Competitive Running." *Physics Today* 26, 9 (1973): 42–47.

Kyle, C. "Reduction of Wind Resistance and Power Output of Racing Cyclists and Runners Traveling in Groups," *Ergonomics* 22, no. 4 (1979): 387–397.

Levin, D. "The Runner's High: Fact or Fiction?" *Journal of the American Medical Association* 248 (1982): 24.

Linn, H. "Newtonian Mechanics and the Human Body: Some Estimates of Performance." *American Journal of Physysics* 46, no. 1 (1978): 15-17.

McAlpine, K. "Digging Deep." *Runner's World* (December 1993): 40.

McMahon, T., and P. Greene. "Fast Running Tracks." *Scientific American* 239, no. 6 (1978): 148–163.

Memory, J. D. "Kinematic Strategy of Self-Preservation for the Jogger." *American Journal of Physics* 47, no. 8 (1979): 749–750.

Noakes, T. *Lore of Running*, 3rd ed. Champaign, Illinois: Human Kinetics, 1991.

Pierce, E. F., et al. "Exercise Dependence in Relation to Competitive Orientation in Runners." *Journal of Sports Medicine and Physical Fitness* (June 1993).

Pritchard, W., and J. Pritchard. "Mathematical Models of Running," *American Scientist* 82, no. 6 (1994): 546–553.

Pugh, L, "Oxygen Intake in Track and Treadmill Running with Observations on the Effect of Air Resistance" *Journal of Physiology* 207 (1970): 823.

Radford, P. "The Nature and Nurture of a Sprinter." *New Scientist* (2 August 1984).

Reilly, T., et al. (eds.). *Physiology of Sports*. London: Chapman and Hall, 1990.

Riegel, P. S. "Athletic Records and Human Endurance." *American Scientist* 69, no. 3 (1981): 285–290.

Ryder, H., H. J. Carr, and P. Herget. "Future Performance in Foot Racing." *Scientific American* 234 (1976): 6.

Schmidt-Nielson, K. "Locomotion: Energy Cost of Swimming, Flying, and Running." *Science* 177, no. 4045 (1972): 202–227.

"Slight Change in Gait Makes Burden Lighter," *New York Times* (30 May 1995).

Strand, J. "Physics of Long-Distance Running." *American Journal of Physics* 53, no. 4 (1985): 371–373.

Townend, M. S. *Mathematics in Sport*. New York: Halsted, 1984.

Ward-Smith, A, "A Mathematical Theory of Running Based on the First Law of Thermodynamics and Its Application to the Performance of World Class Athletes." *Journal of Biomechanics* 18 (1985): 337.

Williams, K., and P. Cavanagh, "Relationship between Distance Running Mechanics, Running Economy, and Performance." *Journal of Applied Physiology* 63 (1987): 1242.

Wilmore, J., and D. Costill. *Physiology of Sport and Exercise*. Champaign, Illinois: Human Kinetics, 1994.

Wirhed, R. *Athletic Ability and the Anatomy of Motion*. New York: Wolf Medical Publishing, 1984.

Sailing

THE EARLIEST INDISPUTABLE EVIDENCE of sail power is an ancient clay model of a Mesopotamian boat dating back some 5,000 years. Some historians argue that sail-powered transportation had emerged at least 2,000 or 3,000 earlier, but determining the actual date of origin depends not only on evidence but on the definition of sailing. The very first wind-powered sailing vessels, perhaps designed to traverse small bodies of water, probably consisted of little more than a flat sheet of woven fabric attached to a horizontal pole inserted into a raft.

Square-sailed Egyptian and Roman vessels emerged a few centuries after the Mesopotamian boat. When positioned at a right angle to the wind, these baggy-shaped sails increased the air pressure on the windward side of the sail, pushing the sail forward, and along with it the boat. However, this early type of ship had a serious limitation: if the wind shifted against it, it would have to be rowed by slaves, or simply archored.

Through the experience, observation, and intuition of early sailors, better designs eventually evolved. The Vikings are widely credited as the first to successfully sail at an angle to the wind. Their ships had square sails that were rigged to pivot, with the sail shape altered to assume a flatter profile. Both innovations expanded the directions in which a vessel could sail. However, it was actually the Arabs living along the Persian Gulf coast around the seventh century, and not the Vikings, who can claim credit for designing the first boat that could sail across the wind (at 90° or better toward the wind). This boat, called a dhow, used a lateen rigging—a tilted triangular sail—which allowed it to sail closer than 90 degrees into the wind (*see Figure 1*). The design was so efficient that thousands of years after its first appearance, it still enjoyed wide popularity. The lateen Sunfish, which can sail within 45 degrees of the wind, was the largest class of sailboats in use in the 1990s.

But despite its ingenious sail aerodynamics, the dhow still had one major shortcoming: its hull lacked the necessary shape to resist the leeward push—a push sideward and away—of the wind. Its efficient sail surface was not enough, for sailboat performance depends on the dynamics of fluid flow in two mediums: water and air. The two must work in harmony for a boat to travel at a 40- to 45-degree angle into the wind.

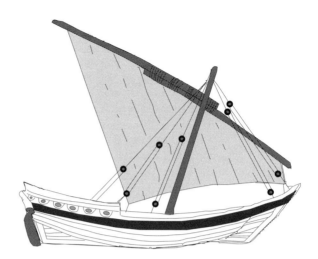

Figure 1. *The dhow, an early lateen rig vessel of Arabs along the Persian Gulf, is widely credited as the first boat to sail across wind (at an angle of 90° or less into the wind).*

The first successful attempt to travel windward probably relied on the crew's placing paddles on the downwind side of the boat, employing muscle power to exert a force against the water to prevent the boat from drifting sideward. When the lug rig appeared in the 1800s, windward aids, such as the paddle, became unnecessary. The lug rig was the first that coupled efficient aerodynamic sails with a sleekly tapered hull. Its hull design prevented leeward drift, resulting in efficient reach sailing (90° to the wind).

Advances in sailing know-how have had a tremendous, and underappreciated, bearing on history. Sailing vessels contributed mightily to major facets of life: transport, commerce, and war. Until late in the nineteenth century, when the development of the steam and internal combustion engines hastened the demise of sailing craft, the fate of many an empire rose and fell on whether military and commercial sailing vessels were used wisely or unwisely.

In the 1990s, few people depend on sail power for transport, commerce, or war. Instead, most sailing falls within the domain of leisure and sport—the quest to harness ever more speed from the wind. This article focuses on how the forces of nature affect sailboats as they operate in the dual mediums of air and water. The primary questions concern how to minimize speed-robbing water resistance and maximize wind power in ever-changing environmental conditions.

Air Forces on the Sail

If asked how a sailboat moves, many might say that the sail catches or blocks the wind, which pushes the boat forward. However, this is not the case. *Sailing*—the term for wind-driven propulsion—relies on the same forces as those employed in flying: lift and drag. Each occurs perpendicular to the other, with lift providing a force perpendicular to

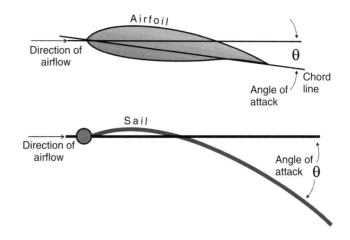

Figure 2. *Airflow around an airplane wing (above) differs from airflow around a sail (below). Because of the slower speed of the sailboat relative to the wind, the optimal angle of attack is much greater for the sail than for the airfoil.*

the airflow and drag providing a force parallel to the airflow (*see Figure 2*). The amount of lift is determined by the speed of the wind traveling past, rather than catching in, the sail. If a 40-kilometer-per-hour (25-MPH) wind blows against a stationary sail or wing, it creates the same magnitude of lift as if the sailboat moved along at 40 KPH in no breeze. This is the sole difference in the lift between a boat's sail and a plane's wing: the wind past the airplane wing occurs mostly because of a plane's high speed, while the wind past the sail occurs largely because of wind speed itself. Since the wind exerts a sideward force on the sail above the center of gravity of the boat, it will cause the boat to tilt, or heel. The ballast in the bottom of the boat provides a turning force, or torque, in the opposite direction to help keep the boat from capsizing. The crew can also move to windward to provide a counterweight to bring the boat to a more upright position (*see Figure 15*). A properly designed boat is ballasted to prevent capsizing. It helps the crew keep the boat in a more upright position, especially in the face of strong gusty winds.

The effect of a gusty wind depends on the sail area and on the angle of attack, or orientation, of the sail. A properly trimmed, or oriented, sail maintains a smoothly curved surface from the leading to the trailing edge. This allows a streamlined airflow over the outer surface of the sail. Streamlined flow means that the air flows smoothly, with no turbulence or swirling. Should the wind suddenly shift so that it comes more directly straight over the bow—the front of the boat — the sail will flutter and lose its curved contour, and it will no longer deflect the air in a perpendicular direction.

An equal number of air molecules exist on either side of the sail in windless conditions or when air is moving directly parallel to the sail. In these cases, the force exerted on each side of the sail is the same. As shown in Figure 3(a), the sail exerts no lift, but considerable drag. These dynamics change when the sail is positioned directly perpendicular to the wind. The number of air molecules colliding against the windward side increases, with few bumping up against the leeward side. In essence, no lift takes place, and the sail exerts a tremendous drag force to the wind. In both cases, the boat, sail, and on-deck equipment exert a drag force to the wind that pushes the sailboat

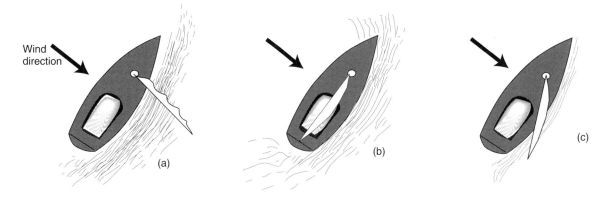

Figure 3. *(a) When the wind blows equally on both sides of a sail, the sail flaps in the breeze, providing no lift. The boat, sail, and even deck equipment create a drag force to the wind, pushing it along sideways. (b) When the wind blows against a perpendicularly positioned sail, the sail creates a tremendous drag force to the wind, pushing it along in the downwind direction, without any lift (c) When the sail is positioned between these extremes, or splitting the wind, it can maximize lift and minimize drag.*

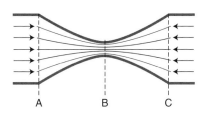

Figure 4. *Streamlines of air flowing through a tapered pipe constrict as they pass through B. Because the mass of airflow per second is the same at A, B, and C, the speed of airflow through B must be considerably greater than at A and C. Streamlines coming together increase the speed of airflow; streamlines moving apart decrease the speed of airflow.*

sideways, away from the wind, as shown in Figure 3(b). The sail needs to be angled between these two extremes to split the wind, as shown in Figure 3(c). For maximum lift and minimum drag—the greatest driving force—the sail is adjusted to trap just enough wind to maintain its shape. Trimming the sail more toward perpendicular detrimentally changes the dynamics so that lift decreases and drag increases. Letting the sail out too far, to a point where it loses its smooth-contoured shape, decreases lift.

A properly trimmed sail changes the air density on each of its sides: increasing it on the windward side and decreasing it on the leeward side, the side opposite the wind. And of course, the greater the wind speed, the greater the air pressure against the sail. The pressure of the wind increases as a square of the wind speed. This means that when a wind gust doubles from its former velocity, it exerts a fourfold increase in heeling, or tipping, effect. Small-dinghy sailors learn this quickly and scoot their bodies higher, toward windward, to counter the heeling effect. To do otherwise may leave the crew waterbound, as the boat could easily capsize.

In addition to the macroscopic change-in-momentum approach to explaining lift on the sail, Bernoulli's principle, a more microscopic theory, offers another acceptable explanation for lift. In 1738, Daniel Bernoulli discovered that whenever the speed of airflow increased, its pressure decreased. This curious phenomenon may be illustrated by considering airflow through a tapered pipe. Streamlines of airflow constrict and flow closer together as they reach the most tapered part of the pipe, as illustrated by point B in Figure 4. Because the same mass of airflow per second exists at points A, B, and C, the airflow must be greater at B than at either A or C. If all the smooth-flowing streamlines of air are to pass through B at the same time, the flow rate must increase at point B. Therefore, when streamlines come together, the speed of airflow increases; when they move apart, airflow decreases.

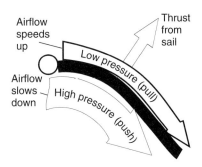

Figure 5. *The accelerating air on the leeward side of the sail creates a low-pressure region—a suction, or pulling, force on the sail. The air to the windward side slows, creating a low-pressure region—a pushing force. In combination, the two effects create the thrust responsible for propelling the sailboat. When the sail is trimmed in too tightly, much pulling force is lost.*

When a sail is trimmed properly, streamlines of air move around the sail surface. Figure 5 shows airflow around a sail. On the leeward side of the sail, airflow is constricted—sucked along hugging the sail's contour—much as it is through point B of the tapered pipe in Figure 4. On the windward side, the opposite occurs: streamlines expand from a small area to a larger area. Overall, the amount of air directed toward the windward side is less than the amount directed to the leeward side. This pressure differential from one side of the sail to the other creates an outward, lifting force, propelling the sailboat forward. A similar pressure differential occurs when one blows a stream of air between two helium balloons. The balloons do not move apart but instead come together (*see also VOLLEYBALL*).

Because of this effect, many boats come with a foresail as well as a mainsail. The primary benefit of a foresail, or jib, is to increase the total sail area and thereby the amount of lift possible. A secondary purpose of the jib is to speed up the airflow over the outer side of the mainsail by creating a slot effect with the jib. This slot forces streamlines of airflow to speed up, much as they would if they were passing through a tapered pipe. Moreover, whenever streamlines of air come together, as with the two-sail slot effect, this speed reduces the leeward pressure on the mainsail.

The slot effect is achieved neither by trimming the foresail parallel with the main, nor by making it overly baggy; instead, it is achieved by creating a parallel slot—a window of air between the windward side of the jib and the leeward side of the mainsail. As air compresses against the jib sail and thus decreases its pressure on the mainsail, it increases in speed as it passes through the parallel slot. This faster-moving air, with its lower pressure, rushes directly past the leeward side of the mainsail, greatly enhancing pulling power. The parallel slot's contribution to boat speed is mainly a result of creating the greatest jib sail lift without too detrimental an effect on the mainsail (*see Figure 6*).

Figure 6. *A foresail changes the lift dynamics of a craft. The upwash from the mainsail increases air circulation and accelerates airflow past the trailing edge of the foresail, which shifts the resultant lifting force more windward (L_1). With the slot effect, on the other hand, as the stream of airflow moves past the windward trailing edge of the foresail and along the leeward side of the mainsail, the faster-moving air reduces leeward pressure. This positively shifts the resultant lifting force on the mainsail aft (L_2).*

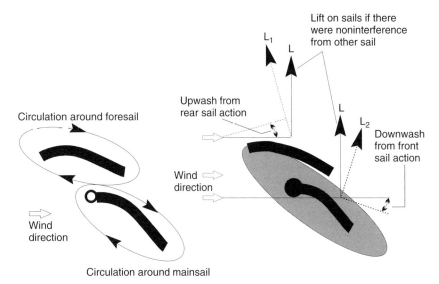

The jib can be trimmed tighter, more parallel, to the main to create greater lift, but the gain would be more than offset by the detrimental effect on the mainsail. The redirected airflow creates air pressure on the leeward side of the mainsail, altering the streamlined flow of air along the windward side of the sail. The jib needs to be positioned to create the greatest lift without negatively impacting the lift of the mainsail.

Directional Sailing

Through much trial and error, boatbuilders long ago mastered the principles necessary to design vessels that can sail in many directions. But compared with modern yachts, these early craft were ploddingly slow. Whereas Christopher Columbus made his transatlantic crossing in about 3 months, a modern sailing vessel can travel the same course in less than 3 weeks. A better understanding of fluid flow—in the mediums of both air and water—has led to yacht and sail designs that achieve high speeds downwind as well as upwind.

To prevent sideward drift, the large yachts of the 1990s are routinely equipped with massive lead keels, and small boats come with centerboards. Keels and centerboards create hydrodynamic lift, allowing the boat to travel in its intended direction without sideward drift. A boat equipped with a centerboard has the added ability to alter the amount of lift depending on travel direction and on weather conditions. Sailors can raise or lower the centerboard to either decrease or increase, respectively, the amount of resistance to the lateral force of the wind.

Sail design is a bit more complex. A sail must be trimmed at a proper angle to the wind, about 30 degrees, and it must have the proper camber, or shape, and draft. Camber is measured by the ratio between the depth of the sail's curve and the width of the sail from end to end. As a general rule, the baggier the sail, the more it bends to leeward and the greater its power. Beyond a certain bagginess, however, the streamlines of air cannot maintain an efficient curvilinear path as they travel around the sail.

The position of the draft matters as well. Figure 7 shows two inefficient sail designs: one with the draft too far forward (a), the other with it too far back (b). The draft needs to be positioned between these two extremes so that the pressure from the wind is fairly equal throughout the sail. If a sail is properly drafted, the onus falls on the sailor to adjust the sail camber for any given condition. Figure 8 shows how sailors use rigging to adjust the sail's camber: baggier in a light breeze, flatter in a heavy gale. Flattening the shape of the sail weakens its interaction with the wind, reducing the amount of heel, or tilting. This means that along with a significant decrease in drag, a drop in the lifting force also occurs. The overall power of these driving forces on the sailboat therefore falls.

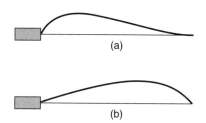

Figure 7. *To be efficient, a sail must be shaped to create a proper draft. An inefficient sail shape—with the draft too far forward (a) or too far back (b)—creates less lift and more drag.*

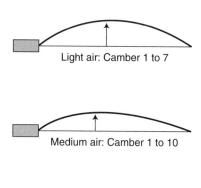

Figure 8. *To optimize lift, different cambers are needed because the ability of an airstream to cling to a curve decreases as airstream speed increases. Most mainsails are cut to provide a camber best suited for a 5- to 10-knot wind (at a reach). Total lift on the sail is the sum of lift due to camber plus the angle of attack to the wind. The two components make about an equal contribution to the total lift. Although most match racers buy sets of light-, medium-, and heavy-wind sails, most boats already possess the rigging necessary to adjust the camber of the sail for the conditions.*

Sail shape is also adjusted depending on the direction of travel. When sailing upwind, at an angle as great as 40 to 45 degrees, the sail or sails are altered to a more flattened profile. But when sailing downwind, the three sail corners are brought closer together, so that the sail is baggier and will catch more wind.

In addition to the intensity of the wind, sailing speeds and equipment adjustments are highly dependent on the direction in which the boat is traveling in relation to the wind. Figure 9 shows the various yacht tacks, or directions, and sail trims for traveling in all directions for a sailboat equipped with main, jib, and spinnaker sails. (A spinnaker sail is a large billowing sail positioned forward and over the bow.)

Downwind Sailing

When a yacht sails downwind, with the wind blowing over the stern, or rear, the sail acts as an aerodynamic drag to the wind. The wind, trying to move past the boat, encounters the sail. The wind pushes the sail (and the boat) along as it works its way around the sail. It then slowly bends its flow back in the direction of the wind.

Since the sail is an aerodynamic drag to the wind, the yacht's speed cannot exceed the wind speed. The boat moves only by drag and with no lift, so regardless of the amount of sail area rigged, it cannot travel downwind faster than at a reach or to windward. Nevertheless, many yachts are also equipped with spinnakers that are raised for downwind sailing. These big, billowing parachute-like sails are designed to catch even more wind. Despite their greater sail area, their drag-only speed cannot match that at a reach or into the wind because lift cannot aid boat speed.

Despite the lower speed limitation, the downwind run is usually the best leg on which to pass in match racing. In downwind runs, unlike windward and reach tacks, the wind reaches the trailing boat first. Thus, one very effective strategy for slowing the lead boat and facilitating passing is to move one's own boat between the oppoent's boat and the wind.

Reach Sailing

Early sailors found little difficulty in traveling downwind. However, it took centuries for the early design pioneers to discover how to travel at a right angle or greater into the wind. One particular problem was to prevent the boat from leeway sliding—sliding sideways, in the direction of the wind—as it moves forward. This required minimizing resistance to the forward motion of the boat while simultaneously maximizing resistance to leeway motion.

When a sailboat attempts to travel at a right angle to the direction of the wind, it is called reaching. Reaching is much faster than running with the wind because when the wind blows directly into the sail from stern to bow, the wind travels in the same direction as the boat; little, if any, lift needs to be provided by the centerboard or the keel to keep the boat moving in its intended direction. The boat is simply pushed along by the wind.

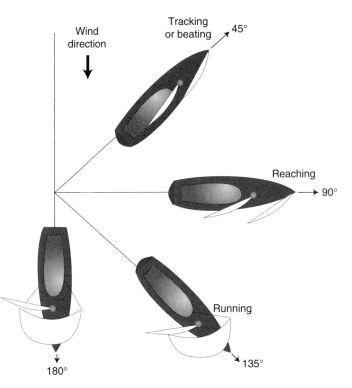

Figure 9. *Sail configurations vary in relation to the direction of the wind. Most sailboats can efficiently travel only as far windward as a 40- to 45-degree angle. The spinnaker sail is the big baggy sail used for downwind sailing (180°)—the slowest direction of travel because the wind acting on the sail is the least (the boat is running away from the wind). If the wind speed is 10 knots and the boat is traveling downwind at 180 degrees at 5 knots, the wind acting on the sail is only 5 knots. A typical keelboat does best on a reach (90°) and worst on a beat (45°).*

For maximum reach speed, the sail is positioned outward to the leeward side, splitting the wind. The force on the sail pushes the boat toward windward, yet, unlike what happens in downwind sailing, the boat does not travel toward the direction in which it is pushed. The resulting forward direction results because water forces are added to the wind forces. For a moving sailboat, the water forces and the air forces are exactly equal and opposite.

It is the lifting, or resultant, force which drives the sailboat forward. Figure 10 shows that the lifting force consists of two components: one lateral, or perpendicular, to the length of the boat, and the other forward, or parallel. The parallel component (F_R) acts to drive the boat toward its intended course, while the lateral one (F_H) drives it downwind, at a right angle to its intended course. The arrow (F_S) indicates the sum of all forces over the whole sail, or the resultant force. It acts at an imaginary center of effort on the sail, providing the driving component (F_R) and powering the boat forward, directly opposite the hull drag force (D_h). A driving force is possible only if the right-angle heeling force (F_H) created by the sail is canceled by an

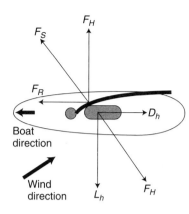

F_H = heeling force
F_R = sail driving force
F_S = total sail force
L_h = hull lifting force
D_h = hull drag force
F_S = total hull force

According to Newton's second law:
F_R must be equal and opposite D_h
F_H must be equal and opposite L_h
F_S must be equal and opposite F_H

Figure 10. *Various forces on a sailing vessel make reaching and upwind sailing possible. When a sailboat moves at a steady rate, the total sail force (F_s) is exactly equal and opposite the hull force (F_h). The larger the difference between the lifting force on the sail (F_s) and the drag force of the hull (D_h), the greater the boat speed. (Adapted from Garrett, 1987)*

High-Speed Sailing

As of 1996, the fastest sail-powered speed had been recorded in 1938. On a frozen lake in Wisconsin, John Buckstaff reached a speed of 230 KPH (143 MPH) in an ice yacht, with the wind blowing at 116 KPH (72 MPH).

equal and opposite lifting force from the keel and the windward side of the hull (L_h). The ability of the sail to create lift, in effect, is what enables the craft to be driven in a forward direction.

At slower speeds, the water resistance encountered by the submerged hull prevents the boat from being pushed sideways, or straight downwind. Because water is about 832 times denser than air, the relatively small area of underwater resistance by the submerged hull is enough to provide the necessary equal and opposite force to the air pressure against the very large surface area of the sail or sails. At moderate to high wind speeds, however, the submerged surface of the hull is not adequate to prevent the boat from drifting sideways. Hence, large yachts are equipped with a keel, and small craft are equipped with a centerboard. Both counterbalance the airborne lateral force of the wind on the sail. The keel and the centerboard reduce the wind's ability to push a boat sideways—a leeward, or lateral, drift—and at the same time enhance the lift that moves the boat forward. Keel designers seek a balance between reduced leeway drift and the smallest possible increase in resistance. There is much experimentation in keel design because the keel must provide ballast to prevent capsizing and also must serve the hydrodynamic functions of minimizing leeward drift and drag. Enlarging, or deepening, the underwater surface area to provide safety and prevent leeway is not always preferable because it comes at the expense of reduced boat speed.

Maximum speed can be obtained by sailing at a right angle to the wind. Greater reach speed is more closely related to the ability of the keel to transfer the wind's sideways force to the forward direction than is optimum sail aerodynamics. For a given constant wind, the sail should be positioned to split the wind in the same manner, regardless of the direction of travel. When the wind blows at a right angle to the sailboat's intended path, the component of motion in the wind direction is equal to the wind velocity; the direction of motion, however, is determined by the direction of the keel or of the centerboard. If the wind is to move any distance in a direction perpendicular to the reaching sailboat, the sail must move a greater distance along the track. This is analogous to squeezing a slippery watermelon seed out from between one's fingers. The fingers apply a perpendicular force to the direction the seed, which results in the seed shooting out along its path at a much faster speed than that of the fingers coming together. Another reason why maximum speed is achieved at a reach is that the speed of the sail and of the boat cannot catch up to the wind speed. Even when the boat reaches the point at which it is traveling as fast as the wind, there remains a significant impact force against the sail. Thus, only sailboats at near reach position have been clocked traveling faster than the wind.

For simplicity, one may consider a hull's hydrodynamic properties separate from the sail's aerodynamic properties; in reality, however, the two are very much interrelated. The amount of drag and lift of the sail must be considered in conjunction with the hull's ability to convert the lateral force from the wind into a forward direction. For example, a certain sail shape or size that is optimal for one boat may be totally inappropriate for another. To draw an extreme comparison for illustrative purposes, one may consider the dynamics of an iceboat and of a sailboat. The iceboat, with its maximum speed three or four times that of a sailboat, exerts a high sideways force through its runner blades—two back and one forward—with virtually no drag as a result of the near-frictionless nature of ice (*see also SKATING*). Therefore, iceboats are able to use flat sails with a minimal angle of attack, or more parallel to the wind direction. Although this provides only a very small driving, or lifting, force, it is sufficient because such boats possess a very high lift-to-drag ratio. In comparison, a 15.24-meter (50-ft.) ocean racing yacht experiences considerable hydrodynamic drag, which impedes forward motion. If an iceboat's flat sail were rigged to this large yacht, it would create very little forward motion. To achieve full thrust potential, such a yacht must possess a more cambered, or baggy, sail, set at a larger angle of attack, or closer to right angle to the wind.

Sailing into the Wind

Because it is physically impossible to sail directly into the wind, sailboats take an indirect route to windward. Each degree greater than a right angle (90°) to the wind direction means there will be a corresponding decrease in the amount of available lift. A sailboat can tack windward only as far as the lifting force from the wind on the sails continues to be greater than the wind-drag forces on the sails, the crew, and the equipment, and greater than the water-drag forces on the hull, particularly from waves. To locate sufficient lift to travel windward, sailors zigzag back and forth at 10 and 2 o'clock to the wind—a maneuver called tacking, or beating.

The best windward tack is approximately 40 to 45 degrees to the wind. Although most boats point windward in this range, precisely how much better a sailboat points windward varies tremendously depending on design. The better the windward design, the fewer tacks necessary. Tacks can be limited by sailing as close to windward as possible in one direction—for example, with the wind crossing the right side of boat—and then quickly turning across the wind so that it crosses the boat from the other side—from the left.

In sailing windward (unlike sailing downwind or at a reach), there is, theoretically, no limit to a boat's speed, because the relative wind speed against the sail always increases with the boat's own speed. In other words, the faster the boat sails windward, the greater the wind velocity against the sail. There are actually two winds involved: true and apparent. A boat's sails are trimmed, or oriented, to the apparent wind, not to the true wind (*see Figure 11*). Apparent wind is a combination of true wind and the wind effect created on an object as it moves through the air. For example, when wind blows a flag on a

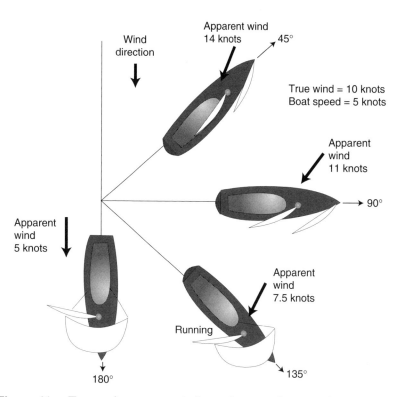

Wind direction

Apparent wind
14 knots   45°

True wind = 10 knots
Boat speed = 5 knots

Apparent wind
11 knots

90°

Apparent wind
5 knots

Apparent wind
7.5 knots

Running

180°   135°

Figure 11. *True and apparent wind speeds vary when traveling at different angles to the wind.*

stationary pole, the direction in which the flag blows indicates the direction of the true wind. If the flagpole was on a boat moving through the water, the flag would blow even if there was no true wind. The direction of the wind experienced by a traveling boat—the combination of true wind and the wind caused by the boat's motion—is the direction of the apparent wind. Thus, a vehicle moving at 16 KPH (10 MPH) into a 16-KPH wind experiences an apparent wind of 32 KPH (20 MPH). If it were to turn around and travel with the wind, the apparent wind experienced would be 0 KPH. The faster a sailboat travels, the greater the distortion of the apparent wind and, consequently, the more important it becomes.

In sailing windward, a portion of a boat's speed is added to the true wind to give the apparent wind. As with sticking a hand out a car window, the wind seems to be stronger and coming from a more forward direction. A sailboat traveling at 6.5 KPH (4 MPH) and on a 45-degree tack into the wind experiences about an 11-degree shift due to the apparent wind. In this way, apparent wind has huge consequences for the beating strategy into the true wind. A high-speed sailing vessel—such as a catamaran, a windsurfer, or an iceboat—must sheet in its sails much farther to compensate for the apparent wind. As a boat slows, the dynamics change completely because of the resulting wind lull. The apparent wind shifts aft because the boat speed, relative to

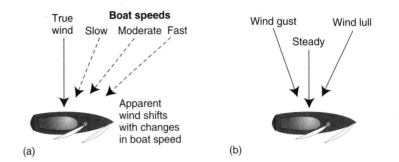

Figure 12. *(a) An increase in boat speed shifts the apparent wind more forward. (b) An increase in wind speed relative to the boat, such as from a gust, shifts the apparent wind in the opposite direction, or aft of the true wind. During a lull, boat speed is high relative to the wind as it dies, so it requires a sheeting in of the sails (setting them as tight and flat as possible). During a gust, the wind speed is high relative to the boat, so the sails should be eased out and slowly trimmed in as the boat picks up speed. Sailors must also trim their sails with a slight twist to account for the vertical variation in apparent wind. Twist is so named because the lower portion of the sail is trimmed in at a tighter angle to the wind than that of the upper sail. This vertical variation is necessary because of the slowing of the true wind caused by wind-water surface friction. Wind near the water surface blows a few knots slower than at a height of 9 meters (about 30 ft.). The vertical twist of the sail is in adjustment to this difference in apparent wind.*

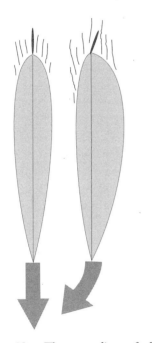

Figure 13. *The waterline of the boat is shown from underneath. Weather helm is caused by a distortion in the underwater contour of a sailboat as it heels. A few degrees weather helm is natural, but anything larger takes a greater corrective rudder action that significantly increases drag.*

the wind speed, decreases (*see Figure 12*). Sailors must anticipate gusts and lulls: a course closer to windward, a reduced angle, can be taken during a gust; a less aggressive tacking angle must be taken when wind lulls.

Greater wind velocity is accompanied by less lifting force against the sail. The sideward force on the sail is great, so the boat heels, or tilts, along its length. A certain amount of heeling is advantageous, but beyond a given point, it becomes detrimental to boat speed.

Optimal heeling angles vary depending on boat design. Generally, small centerboard craft sail best when they heel less than 15 degrees, while larger ballast boats can heel at up to 20 degrees without any significant decline in performance. When a boat heels as it tacks windward, it moves with a slight angle of attack farther to windward because the boat's underwater shape becomes asymmetrical along its centerline, creating greater drag and making it harder to steer. As Figure 13 shows, the normal-shaped hull (a), symmetrical along the centerline, takes on a distorted shape when it heals (b). This uneven underwater contour creates more drag for the half that is submerged farther, thereby creating a force that turns the boat to windward.

This natural tendency to turn toward a windward angle usually results in a 3-degree or smaller angle of attack for the boat. Sailors commonly refer to this phenomenon as weather helm, because it worsens with stronger winds and bigger waves. To compensate for weather helm, a corrective rudder action is necessary. A weather helm that turns the boat windward 3-degree requires a counterbalancing 3-degree adjustment leeward with the rudder. This 3-degree

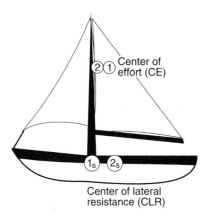

Figure 14. *When the center of effort of the wind is positioned slightly aft of the center of lateral resistance (1s), a boat is considered in balance and weather helm is limited. When the center of effort is forward of the center of lateral resistance (2s), the boat is likely to experience significant weather helm.*

rudder adjustment does not create appreciably more drag, but greater angles do. And excessive weather helm, 40 degrees or more, significantly slows forward progress.

Although slight weather helm is useful, sailors strive to tune their boats by monitoring the two factors responsible for a properly balanced boat: center of lateral resistance (CLR) and center of effort (CE). By pushing sideways on a boat, one may locate its CLR—the imaginary pivot point below the waterline about which the boat rotates. The CE refers to the sail rigging and is the centralized focus of the wind's pressure on the sail or sails. To limit weather helm to less than 3 degrees, the CE needs to be only slightly aft of the CLR; if it is too far aft, excessive weather helm will result. When the CE is forward of the CLE, the opposite occurs—lee helm, when the boat veers away from the wind (*see Figure 14*). A properly tuned sailboat improves performance because it will head into a gust, controlling the magnitude of the boat's heel. It will also fall off in a lull, assuming a better position to catch any forthcoming breeze. The tendency for a sailboat to turn directly into the wind when left alone has a secondary advantage: a dinghy skipper who slips overboard can usually swim to catch the boat as its sails flap in the wind.

Hull Design: Stability and Resistance

Boat designers want to minimizing water resistance without compromising stability. Stability must come either from the force of gravity pushing down on the boat or from buoyancy pushing up on it. These two forces together determine the boat's stability and its speed. In large part, stability hinges on the ability of the boat to withstand the wind's pressure, preventing capsizing.

Because of the tremendous variability of wind and waves, there are tremendous variations in the way boat designers achieve stability. Two factors affect a boat's stability: the center of gravity and center of buoyancy. The center of gravity is the point at which all the downward forces of gravity are concentrated. If a hanging rope was attached to the boat at the point of the center of gravity, the boat would remain suspended in a plane level to the horizon. The center of buoyancy is the point where all the concentrated forces of buoyancy push the boat upward, keeping it afloat.

An ocean-cruising yacht is equipped with a keel that significantly lowers its center of gravity. In fact, more than a third of the total mass of the average cruising yacht is concentrated in its lead keel. The heavy keel counterbalances the wind's pressure by acting as a lever that prevents capsizing. In this lever action, the fulcrum, or heeling point, is located at the center of gravity. The keel beneath the center of gravity counters the wind pressure on the sail and prevents the boat from capsizing (*see Figure 15*). Although a lightweight centerboard boat also uses lever action, its stability comes primarily from

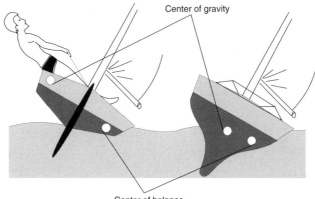

Figure 15. *The difference between a large, ocean-cruising keelboat and a dinghy sailboat has to do primarily with their methods for achieving stability. Each uses a different first class lever: lead ballast beneath the keelboat, and shifts in crew positions within the dingy. The keelboat's center of gravity and center of balance both lie beneath the water line, while the center of gravity must shift well windward and above the water line for the keelless dingy.*

crew members shifting the weight of their bodies to windward. In that case, the boat's fulcrum, or heeling point about the center of gravity, is shifted upward and outward, well above the waterline. The necessary ballast is created from the weight of the crew members as they lean outward over the windward side.

A flat-bottomed inland sailboat, such as a scow, can plane over waves—skim over the surface—because its center of gravity rises as its crew members shift their body weight to counterbalance windspeed increases. This is especially true for windsurfers. Because there is less boat-wetted surface, there is also less resistance. *Wetted surface area* refers to the amount of hull in contact with the water. The larger the wetted surface, the slower the boat speed. By raising the center of buoyancy, the boat presents a shallower, shorter waterline, so that the boat skims the surface in a higher plane of the water.

Maximum speed is a function of the boat's waterline and the waves it creates. The longer and deeper the waterline, the faster a boat moves and the more power is lost as the hull moves through the water, making waves. Energy is lost to wave-making as the bow and stern each create waves. Boat speed, therefore, is a function of wave-making, notated as the speed-to-length ratio. Figure 16 shows that for a speed-to-length ratio greater than 0.64 (indicated by the dot on the line of friction marking the point where wave-making resistance begins to radically affect friction), any increase in a nonplaning boat's speed is met by an exponential increase in resistance from wave-making. For example, a 6.7-meter (22-ft.) nonplaning boat that has 15 pounds of resistance at 3 knots will have 70 pounds of resistance at 5 knots and 450 pounds at 7 knots (1 knot = 1 nautical mi./hr. = 1.85 KPH = 1.15 MPH; Seidman, 1994).

The only boats able to overcome this wave-making resistance are the wide and flat lightweight craft that are able to plane over waves. When hit by a gust, such a boat will leave its stern wave behind, climb atop its bow wave, and surge forward. For this reason, windsurfers and flat-bottom inland-water racing craft can, with good planing, skim across the water at very high speeds (*see also* PADDLE SPORTS).

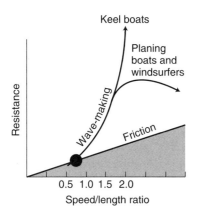

Figure 16. *The maximum speed that a sailboat can reach is a function of its water resistance. A moving sailboat creates speed-robbing resistance as it pushes water forward, sideways, and downward; it also encounters a pulling force sucking it back as water fills in behind it. The faster a boat's speed, the greater this force. The only sailboats able to overcome this wave-making resistance and to travel faster than the waves are boats that are able to plane. Sailboards, perhaps the quickest planing craft, have reached speeds greater than 80 KPH (50 MPH).*

Importance of Weight Distribution

Along with hull design, minimizing the weight of boat, crew, and equipment is a key factor in determining boat speed. Together they determine the boat's draft—how deep it sits in the water—which in turn influences boat speed, especially in stormier seas.

Given two identical, small racing boats, one with its weight equally distributed fore to aft and the other heavy in the center and very light in the bow and in the stern, the latter will usually outperform the former. This is due to pitching motion—when the bow and the stern rock up and down. Because of a difference in weight distribution, the two boats will experience entirely different pitching motions. The speed and the magnitude of the pitching motion determine how the bow plows into waves. This is important for two reasons: it affects the resistance to forward motion, and energy wasted in pitching means less energy is transferred into forward motion.

All objects pitch about an axis. Usually, pitch occurs about the center of gravity. The speed and the amount of pitch are determined by the amount of mass, by the length of the boat—distance from the center of gravity—and by the boat's distribution of mass. The dynamics of pitching can be demonstrated by considering a barbell with equal weights at each end. With the barbell held overhead, it is relatively more difficult to twist one's body vertically—about an axis perpendicular to the ground—with a longer barbell than it is with a shorter one. This is because for the longer pole, a great percentage of the barbell mass is positioned farther from the axis of rotation. With a shorter barbell, the weight is positioned closer to the axis of rotation, and it is therefore much easier to twist. For the same reason, a tightrope walker will use a long, thin pole for balance, rather than a shorter pole with weighted ends. Likewise, a figure skater spins at high speeds by tucking his arms tightly against the body and slows by extending the arms (*see also ACROBATICS*).

The ability to twist about an axis is affected not only by total mass, but also by distribution. For example, it is easier for someone holding a barbell to twist the body about a vertical axis if the ends of the barbell are equally weighted. Although the total mass would be the same, it would be easier to twist holding a pole with a 10-kilogram weight at each end than it would be with 5 kilograms at one end and 15 kilograms at the other.

Inertia—the tendency of an object at rest to stay at rest and one in motion to stay in motion—is a property of mass. The moment of inertia—a measure of the force necessary for rotation or for pitching—is determined not only by mass but also by mass distribution—the distance from the axis of rotation. Compared with a neutrally balanced boat, a boat heavily weighted at its bow and stern would require significantly more effort to start and to stop it from pitching when suspended on land. However, the same is not true for wave

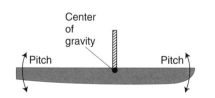

Figure 17. *By suspending a boat from a rope, one can determine its center of gravity as well as its centerline of buoyancy. When boat weight is distributed more forward and aft, rather than concentrated near the center of buoyancy, waves tend to pitch the boat more. Therefore, a crew strives to keep as close to the boat's center of buoyancy as possible.*

America's Cup: A Technological War on the Water

Spurred on by nationalistic pride, many countries spend millions of dollars in an effort to bring home the biggest prize in yachting: the America's Cup. Following the 1987 Cup, new rules were established to make the competition more interesting. Unfortunately, the rules significantly increased the cost of competing. The wide parameters encouraged experimenting with boat designs, and to cut down on the associated risk of experimentation, many syndicates built several boats.

In an effort to defend the Cup in 1992, Bill Koch, a multimillionaire trained as an engineer at MIT, spent $68 million building four boats, known as *America³*. The sum was modest, however, compared with the $120 million spent by Italy's Raul Gardini to build five boats and mount a challenge with *Il Moro di Venezia*.

In an effort to restrain such excessive spending by these zealous rich men, the 1995 campaign instituted spending limits. Koch and others, tired of trying to outspend each other, welcomed the measures. In order to

level the playing field and to encourage new competitors, the International America's Cup Class (IACC) allowed each new syndicate to build two boats (at a cost of about $5 million each); the experienced syndicates were limited to just one new boat.

The new rule that had triggered the explosive spending following the 1987 Cup was a formula that widened the parameters for experimentation. The formula gave designers wide latitude to experiment in striking a balance between, on the one hand, sail area and length along the waterline and, on the other, boat mass. Any change in one variable alters the performance of one or more of the other variables. Greater sail area and longer waterline increase speed but also require an increase in mass, which slows a yacht down. Likewise, a large reduction in sail area allows for significant reduction in mass. The overall trend, as of the mid-1990s, seems to be toward greater sail area, longer waterline, and more weight at the keel. Overall lengths averaged about 23 meters (75 ft.; waterline 17 m, or 57 ft.) for the 1992

Cup, with many creeping closer to 24 meters (80 ft.) in 1995.

In addition to the give-and-take decisions on sail area, boat weight, and hull length along the waterline as dictated by the formula, syndicates also consider hull, rudder, and keel designs, depending on expected wind and wave conditions. Again, changing one design element usually requires adjustments in all the others. Since improvements are incremental in nature, there can be no perfect design: every designer would concur that there is always room for improvement, particularly in keel design.

Most of the increased mass required—about 75 percent of a 22,700-kilogram (50,000-lb.) yacht—is added to the lead keel. At the bottom of the keel, which is limited to a depth of 4 meters (13 ft.), rests a torpedo-like bulb with winglets that reduce vacuous swirling water behind the tip. Every syndicate closely guards its keel design, because this is the variable with which designers have the greatest latitude and which often determines the outcome. The performance of the

action in water. The dynamics of the bow slamming into waves easily starts the boat rocking, overcoming the greater inertia of the heavier-ended boat. There is no appreciable difference in overcoming inertia (to start rocking) between a neutrally balanced boat and a heavier-ended boat in stormy seas. The heavier-ended boat will begin pitching almost as quickly as the lighter boat; once it begins pitching, however, its greater moment of inertia makes it more difficult to stop.

A sailor strives to bring the center of gravity of the boat, the equipment, and the crew as close together as possible to lower the boat's moment of inertia (*see also ACROBATICS*). For the Flying Dutchman, an Olympic-class boat, this is accomplished by positioning the helmsman and the crew as far forward as possible and the boat's center of gravity as far aft as possible. Paul Hinrichsen, a physi-

PACT 95 syndicate's *Young America*, which proved to be the fastest U.S. boat, has been attributed to its superior keel design—long, thinner, and torpedo-like, with small, straight, perpendicular winglets toward the rear. Most of the other keels were shorter and plumper, with downward-angled winglets.

MATERIALS AND BOAT DESIGN

Adding to the task of designers is the onus of staying current with constantly improving materials, particularly composites. Decisions are tricky because materials are interdependent, that is, they possess their own effect as well as affect other factors (see also EQUIP-MENT MATERIALS).

With so many design options to pursue, all the syndicates turned to computers in order to remain within the $20 million budget limit. Traditionally, boat designers built hundreds of scale models and tested them in tanks. Bill Koch and *America³*, for example, built 40 different 6-meter (20-ft.) hull models for testing in 1992. By 1995, all the syndicates relied more heavily on computer simulation. Thanks to advances in hardware and software, it was possible to do much of the complex modeling with workstations and desktop computers.

To validate the computational results, the keel models were subjected to wind-tunnel tests and hull models were tank-tested. Tank conditions were adjusted for a variety of different boat speeds, heel angles, and wave amplitudes (degrees of choppiness). Once the computations were validated, integration began: the most promising work of the sail, hull, and keel design teams produced several full-boat designs. PACT 95 then set up a series of computer-simulated match races—simulating a number of different wind speeds and wave conditions—to pit design against design. After completing these computerized races, they arrived at a final design that, according to the simulations, was superior to the others. Of all the Defender Series challengers, PACT 95 had indeed developed the superior boat. However, PACT 95's equipment problems, and perhaps some uncanny luck, helped Dennis Conner's *Stars and Stripes* team win the right to defend the America's Cup.

In a surprising and controversial move, Conner decided to switch boats in the final, choosing to sail PACT 95's *Young America*—instead of his own *Stars and Stripes*—against New Zealand's *Black Magic*. After defeating all comers in the Challenger Series, *Black Magic* entered the finals with an impressive record of 39 to 1.

In the years prior to the use of computer modeling, comparing the speeds of two boats was an imprecise project. New software, however, gave competitors the tools with which to judge the performance of any boat over a variety of conditions, and with great accuracy. Boat speed, for example, could be measured as accurately as within one hundredth of a mile per hour. Conner opted to sail *Young America* because computer modeling showed it would be far more competitive with the sleek *Black Magic* than would *Stars and Stripes*.

Despite the switch, however, Conner simply could not muster enough boat speed, crew skill, and luck to match *Black Magic*, and New Zealand swept the final (5–0). Conner's worries about his computer-predicted speed deficit proved true. Undoubtedly, the experiences of the 1995 campaign ensure that all syndicates in America's Cup events will make increasingly wider use of computer models and simulations.

John Zumerchik

cist working in the province of Quebec, calculated the moment of inertia of different boats competing in the 1976 Summer Olympics. As expected, he found that hull variations contributed to a 17 percent difference in the boats' moments of inertia. Mast, equipment, and crew can change the moment of inertia by as much as 11 percent. And position of the crew alone produced a 5 percent difference in moment of inertia. In all, adjustments that the crew can make to optimizing mast, equipment, and crew position are nearly as important as the pitch control designed into the boat (Hinrichsen, 1978).

Because centralizing mass is so important, many yachtsmen fear that boat designers and manufactures may be tempted to concentrate boat weight so close to the center of gravity that they produce inherently unseaworthy boats, with lighter bows and sterns. This concern is not unfounded, as many oceanic races have ended disastrously when very thin-bowed boats cracked up in heavy seas.

Match Racing: Wind and Weather

Although a boat's materials and fluid dynamics explain sail power, maximizing performance requires an understanding of wind and weather. Weather conditions affect both the wind and the waves that a boat encounters. Consulting forecasts from the National Weather Service helps a match racer devise a match-day strategy, but it is also vital to continually cast a watchful eye to the surrounding clouds to predict short-term wind and weather conditions.

Clouds are excellent weather predictors. High clouds are usually associated with distant weather conditions or with weather several hours away; low clouds relate to current conditions, portending that which is soon to come. The colors and movement of clouds offer additional clues. Dense and dark low clouds usually suggest an imminent weather change for the worse. If such clouds are lowering, rain is usually imminent; if they are rising, the weather is probably improving. Cloud shape is another factor. Flat clouds usually suggest stable air, whereas big, billowing cumulus clouds usually suggest unstable air. The ability to spot unstable air masses is particularly critical for match racers, for unstable air masses forebode a change in the strength and direction of the wind.

What makes "reading" the wind tricky is that no breeze is perfectly consistent. Wind blows first from one direction and then gusts from a slightly different direction. Marine weather forecasts usually include information about both direction and gust. For example, a typical wind warning might be, "winds are out of the south at 20 knots, gusting from the southwest at 30 to 35 knots." Unstable airstreams create wind gusts. Day-to-day variations in wind gusts can be attributed to convection—the transfer of heat by the movement of air masses—enhanced by the formation and dispersion of cumulus clouds (*see also GLIDING*). Convection creates gusts along the surface of the earth because it brings stronger winds downward.

Convection is strongest in mid- to late afternoon, as the sun heats up the surface of the earth. The cool, fast-moving air from above slows due to friction with other cells of air. The wind near the surface, meanwhile, is slowed and warmed by contact with the warmer water. The result is the creation of wind gusts that move in a circulation pattern, rolling like a tumbleweed over a prairie. Although wind gusts occur well out to sea as well as on inland bodies of water, gusts on inland lakes are usually far stronger because greater heat-generated convection occurs over land than over a large body of water.

When wind gusts or lulls, it changes direction either by veering or by backing. A veering wind in the Northern Hemisphere changes direction to the right as one faces it, in a clockwise direction; a back-

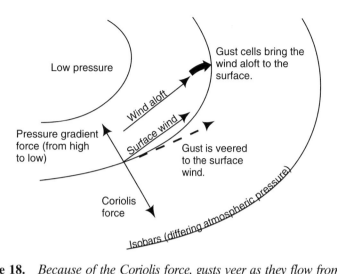

Figure 18. *Because of the Coriolis force, gusts veer as they flow from high to low pressure. The earth's rotation gives rise to the Coriolis force on the wind. The magnitude of the force depends on wind speed and is opposite the pressure gradient force.*

ing wind changes direction to the left as one faces it, in a counter-clockwise direction. The wind veers as it gusts because of the Coriolis force. This force does not act on objects at rest on the earth, but only on airborne objects that move with respect to the rotating earth, such as the wind. What actually occurs is that the spherical earth rotates under the blowing wind. The earth's spherical shape means that the strength of the Coriolis force depends on the velocity of the wind as well as its location—increasing closer to the poles, and decreasing closer to the equator. It is much like riding on a merry-go-round. If one throws a ball to a person riding on the horse directly ahead, it will appear to veer away from the center of rotation.

The Coriolis force is what makes the wind spiral inward, toward the low-pressure center, instead of moving straight at it. Satellite pictures of hurricanes and tropical cyclones show this spiral pattern. (This normal circulation is shown in Figure 18.) An additional gust in the direction of the wind veers like the ball thrown on the merry-go-round. It moves toward the right, away from the low pressure, and its magnitude depends on the wind speed.

The ability to predict gusts is important in match racing, particularly during the windward leg, when significant beating takes place. In the Northern Hemisphere, the Coriolis force causes the wind to veer to the starboard tack (wind over right side of boat) as it gusts; as it lulls, it backs, making port (left side) the preferred tack. In the Southern Hemisphere, the opposite is true: gusts veer to favor the port tack and lull to favor the starboard tack (*see Figure 19*).

By staying on starboard for gusts and on port for lulls, an alert sailor can shorten the total distance covered to the next mark. The quickest way for a sailboat to travel between two points during a windward leg is not a straight line; however, reading clouds and understanding the dynamics of wind gusts enables one to select a

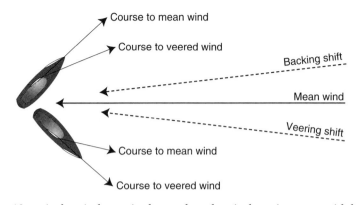

Figure 19. *As the wind gusts in the northern hemisphere, it veers to aid the starboard tack; as it lulls, it backs to aid the port tack. This is important for match racers because it reduce the time it takes to reach the end of the first leg. (Adapted from Watts, 1987)*

shorter course. By keeping a watchful eye on cloud formation, match racers can gain a head start to maximize gusts and lulls. As a general rule, the deeper the convection currents, the stronger the gusts. While small cumulus clouds signal limited changes in wind direction, speed, and frequency, large, lumpy, well-rounded cumulus clouds signal strong gusts. In extremely gusty conditions, short tacks are usually the best strategy.

The life of a gust lasts at least 213 to 305 meters (700–1,000 ft.) downwind and can continue on for much longer. With this in mind, trailing match racers can make up time during the windward leg by watching the lead boat to better time their own tacks. If a gust affects a lead boat 91 meters (100 yd.) windward in a 20 knot breeze, a trailing boat will have a 10-second warning to switch to a starboard tack to gain the greatest advantage from the wind veer that usually accompanies the gust (Watts, 1987).

Despite the difficulties of overcoming "bad air"—being caught in the lead boat's turbulent air—during a windward leg, alert and experienced sailors who are trailing have ample opportunity to begin to catch up. If they pay close attention to the leading boat or boats, they can take advantage of the advance warning of forthcoming gusts.

John Zumerchik

References

Beiser, A. *The Proper Yacht.* Camden, Maine: International Marine, 1964.

Bethwaite, F. *High-Performance Sailing.* Blue Ridge Summit, Pennsylvania: TAB, 1993.

Constable, G., B. Walker, and P. Payne. *Racing.* New York: Time-Life, 1976.

Ellsworth, J. "Understanding Apparent Wind." *Sail* 22 (October 1989): 55ff.

Garrett, R. *The Symmetry of Sailing.* London: Adlard Coles, 1987.

Hinrichsen, P. "Weight Distribution." *Yachts and Yachting* (3 February 1978): 347–351.

Marchaj, C. *Aero-Hydrodynamics of Sailing*. New York: Dodd Mead, 1987.

Norwood, J. *High-Speed Sailing*. New York: Granada, 1979.

Robinson, B. "America's Cup: Sailing's New Tacks." In E. Schier and W. Allman (eds.) *Newton at the Bat*. New York: Scribner, 1984.

Ross, W. *Sail Power: The Complete Guide to Sails and Sail Handling*. New York: Knopf, 1975.

Seidman, D. *On the Wind: Mastering the Art of Sailing*. Camden, Maine: International Marine, 1994.

Stetson, B. "Understanding Apparent Wind." *Sail* 24 (September 1993): 22ff.

Van Dorn, W. *Oceanography and Seamanship*. New York: Dodd Mead, 1974.

Watts, A. *Wind and Sailing Boats: The Structure and Behaviour of the Wind as It Affects Sailing Craft*. North Pomfret, Vermont: Newton Abbot, 1987.

Skating

AT THE 1994 WINTER OLYMPICS in Lillehammer, Norway, many spectators from abroad were surprised that the Norewegians seemed to have so little interest in figure skating, which is usually one of the most popular events. The Norwegians' lukewarm reception of figure skating was not a matter of failing to appreciate its pageantry, style, and grace; it was simply a consequence of their obsession with another type of skating: speed skating. In countries like Norway—and the Netherlands, to take another example—speed skating is the paramount winter sport. Fans are transfixed by the seemingly effortless yet impressively long and powerful glides of the top speed skaters. One reason why speed (and distance) skating has predominated in Scandinavia is that the setting is perfect: the climate is suitable, and there are numerous wetlands, canals, and lakes that are frozen for a good part of the year. Moreover, this kind of skating has traditionally been an integral part of the culture—for one thing, because frozen waterways could be used to visit friends and relatives who would otherwise have been difficult to reach in winter.

The origins of skating date to at least 1,000 B.C.E. Skating and skiing probably developed first in the Scandinavian countries, where people foraged for food by moving across ice and snow with pieces of wood strapped to their feet. Originally, skaters propelled themselves less with their legs and generated forward motion more by poling with a small staff or stick, much like skiers. The two sports diverged when these ancient peoples realized that skates—blades fashioned from polished bone—were superior for sliding over ice.

A revolutionary change in skating came during the ninth century, when the iron blade replaced polished bone. On the basis of archeological discoveries, some historians argue that this development marked a move beyond simple sliding to true skating. The squared-off, flattened bottom of the iron blade (as opposed to a knife-edge blade) allowed skaters to grip the ice with either edge of the runner and thus to move with less effort by increasing the amount of propulsive force generated in the sideward push-off. In addition, the flatter blade, which was also longer, extended the distance of the glide.

Initially, speed skaters used a blade similar in length to the blades used for hockey and figure skating, which are only slightly longer than the boot. Early speed skaters quickly learned, however, that speed could be vastly increased by using longer blades. A greater surface

Speed Skating for Fitness

Speed skating lends itself well to a lifelong program of exercise and conditioning. Gliding on near-frictionless ice makes the sport preferable to high-impact activities, such as jogging and running. Given that speed skating is also an aerobic exercise that burns many calories with low impact, it is an attractive option for those who want to exercise yet dislike running.

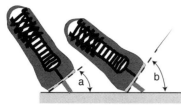

angle a < angle b

Figure 1. *As compared with the center-set blade (a), the offset speed-skating blade (b) allows the skater to lean farther inward before the edge of the boot scrapes the ice. Angle (b) is greater than angle (a). Speed skaters can use offset blades because they skate in only one direction around a track.*

length minimizes friction and increases the efficiency of the stroke: less effort is needed to restore the skater's momentum, that is, mass × velocity. (This gives rise to a natural question: If a long blade increases speed, why not use a blade as long as a ski? The answer is that there is a trade-off between speed and control. Blades are proportional to shoe size to enable the skater to maximize speed without losing control.)

As the longer iron blades came into use, competitions emerged for skaters to test the limits of speed. Some of the first races were held in the Netherlands in the sixteenth century. Local competitions were organized by the nobility, who offered prizes. Most of these early contests involved short distances, until the seventeenth and eighteenth centuries, when long-distance races grew in popularity.

Speed skating was firmly established in North America during the nineteenth century. Canada held its first speed-skating championship for men in 1887, and the United States followed a few years later.

The modern speed skating of the 1990s takes two forms: the traditional long-track, or metric, style; and the short-track, or pack, style. In the long-track style, competitors skate against the clock; in the short-track style, they compete against each other. The 111-meter (120-yd.) short-track events, which became a Winter Olympic sport in 1992, take place on a standard hockey rink. Because racers compete against one another, rather than against the clock, there is plenty of inadvertent contact among skaters as they aggressively approach turns. These tight turns require a greater inward, or centripetal, force to counter the natural tendency to move outward. Thus the skaters lean more and often wear reinforced skates. Since they skate in only one direction, most of them use offset blades, which allow them to lean even further inward (*see Figure 1*). Both long-track and short-track speed skating (even though the latter uses a hockey rink) are relatively inaccessible to the general public because facilities are limited; as a result, participation in these sports has also been limited.

Figure skating, on the other hand, has become very popular worldwide. The term *figure skating* was originally apt but is now something of a misnomer: the compulsory exercise of carving traced patterns ("figures") on the ice is now only part of any national or international competition. Free skating has become the most visible and emphasized aspect of competitions, and skaters may perform singly or in pairs. In the 1990s, freestyle figure skating and ice dancing are extremely popular spectator sports. Expanded television coverage of innovative professional competitions, designed to please the audience and unconfined by the rigid restrictions imposed on official events, has also played a major role in the sport's popularity.

Figure skating is of much more recent origin than speed skating. The person often considered the founder of this sport is Jackson Haines, a Chicagoan of the 1850s. Haines was an accomplished dancer who was able to transpose his art to ice; he was also an early innovator in skate design. He developed a "rockered," or curved, blade that was distanced from the boot and fixed to a toe and heel plate; this made changing directions smoother and more effortless (*see also the box "The Evolution of Figure Skates"*). In 1864, toward the end of the

Endurance in Figure Skating

To finish a 4-minute skating routine strongly, figure skaters undergo intense conditioning and stamina training: a mixture of anaerobic and aerobic training much like that used by a middle-distance runner or a basketball player. Because figure skating incorporates artistry into every movement and is coordinated with music—and often involves a partner—it requires many years of practice, on and off the ice, for a skater to reach the Olympic and world-class level.

Civil War, Haines took his workshop and technical innovations on a tour across North America and Europe, capturing the imagination of audiences and revolutionizing skating. He also mounted a touring show, with ornate costumes and a large variety of well-choreographed routines set to music. Haines's showmanship endeared him to many; and Vienna, then known as the city of music, was so impressed by his new art form that it named an ice rink after him.

After Haines, though, interest in figure skating gradually waned—until the swanlike Norwegian skater Sonja Henie arrived on the scene in the 1920s. Henie, a ballerina with the typical slight build (she was 5 ft. 2 in. tall and weighed only 79 lb.), incorporated many ballet movements into her routines. People packed into arenas from coast to coast to watch her, and she won ten consecutive women's world figure skating championships (1927–1936) and three Olympic gold medals (1928, 1932, and 1936) before turning professional in 1936. As a professional, she became by far the richest athlete, male or female, of her time.

The innovative, acrobatic routines of the early pioneers of figure skating were expanded on by later generations. Single and double acrobatic spins were replaced by triple and quadruple spins. In the 1990s, few exhibitions featured slow, measured movements; instead, skaters performed a series of high-speed movements, because speed makes even simple moves seem more daring and spectacular. There is considerable speculation about what direction figure skating will take in the future, and some observers predict that athleticism will come to dominate over the earlier emphasis on grace.

The Ice

This section will take up some significant aspects of the ice skater's medium: the ice itself.

Ice and Friction: A Mystery

As skaters glide across a frozen pond or rink, they experience the unique properties of ice that make near-frictionless movement possible. Friction is the force that resists the motion of an object in contact with another object: for example, as a box slides down a ramp, friction works against the force of gravity to slow the box's movement. The friction from contact between blade and ice in skating is best categorized as kinetic friction—an inhibition that results because two objects are sliding over each other.

As a skater slides over the ice, friction impedes progress. Two concepts are relevant here: (1) "reaction" force, which is the combination of vertical and horizontal forces applied to the skater from the ice; and (2) "normal" force, which is a component of the reaction force—the component that is perpendicular to the surface. Assuming no lean, reaction force and normal force would be the same: perpen-

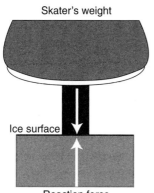

Skater's weight

Ice surface

Reaction force

Figure 2. *The coefficient of friction is the relationship between the normal force and the amount of friction as the skate blade passes over the ice.*

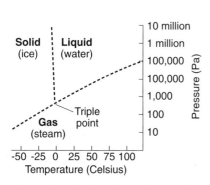

Figure 3. *In the phase diagram for water, the negative slope of the line dividing the solid state (ice) from the liquid state (water) indicates that as pressure is increased, the melting point (temperature) of ice slightly decreases. However, the fact that the slope is nearly vertical suggests that pressure-induced melting is a minor factor in the formation of the thin liquid film responsible for the low friction between blade and ice. Even at temperatures below freezing, a thin layer of liquid exists on the surface of solid ice.*

dicular to the surface and equivalent to the force applied downward on the ice, that is, the skater's weight. In reality, however, a skater is always leaning (*see the section below on the physics of skating*). The amount of friction, for a given skater's lean and given ice conditions, is proportional to the normal force that the ice applies upward on the skater.

The relationship between normal force and amount of friction experienced is expressed as a ratio, called the coefficient of friction (*see Figure 2*); that is, coefficient of friction equals friction divided by normal force, or, as it is more commonly stated, friction equals normal force times coefficient of friction. This coefficient is a way that scientists and engineers quantify friction. The lower the coefficient of friction, the less friction there is between two objects as they slide over each other. In skating, then, the product of normal force times coefficient of friction determines how much friction will resist the glide of the skates.

In one sense, friction is detrimental because it reduces the skater's speed. However, if there were no friction, skaters would not be able to propel themselves at all, so in that sense friction is essential. In other words, as a skater glides over the ice, velocity is lost because of friction; propulsion is therefore needed to restore velocity; and propulsion cannot take place without friction. *Stroking* is the term for the propulsive, or push-off, phase in which velocity lost to friction during the glide is recovered. The blade of the skate impresses shallow grooves, called "tracings," in the ice. Provided that the blade does not slip out of the groove, there will be enough friction for propulsion, or stroking.

There is a mystery with regard to friction on ice. The major determinants of the coefficient of friction are the properties of the materials that are in contact with each other—roughness, lubrication, and so on. In the case of skating, a thin liquid film develops between the solid ice and the skate blade as the blade passes over the ice. This liquid film acts as a lubricant, minimizing the contact between the steel blade and the solid ice. While most skaters realize that this liquid is responsible for the low coefficient of friction, scientists are still struggling to understand the mechanism involved.

The common explanation has to do with "pressure melting" and regelation: the melting and refreezing of ice through the application and release of pressure. This process depends on the unique "phase diagram" of water (*see Figure 3*). A phase diagram is a way of describing the transitions between different states of a substance: in the case of water, between solid, liquid, and gas. Although the curve that separates the area representing liquid from the area representing solid (ice) appears to be essentially vertical, it does have a slightly negative slope for pressure versus temperature. This means that as pressure is increased, the melting point of ice is slightly decreased: ice will melt at a lower temperature if sufficient pressure is applied to it.

Simple calculations show that the weight of a single ice skater on blades does not create enough pressure to produce all this melting

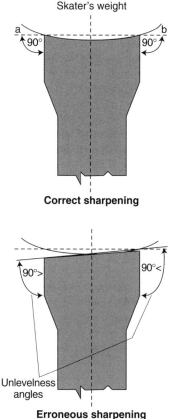

Correct sharpening

Erroneous sharpening

Figure 4. *An improperly sharpened blade impairs the skater's confidence because the two edges have different bites. A sharpening error of only 0.25 degree in the angle of levelness, or squareness, can significantly affect performance. The problem is that on an improperly sharpened blade, the edge-bite angles are different. Neither angle is ideal, because there is inadequate bite on the low edge and excessive bite on the high edge. This adversely affects both gliding and propulsion. (Adapted from Broadbent, 1993)*

(White, 1992). A more sophisticated approach to the calculation—taking into account the compressibility of ice and the irregularities of the interface of skate and ice—shows that pressure-induced melting is indeed an extremely important mechanism in ice skating. Still, by itself it does not account for all of the low-friction effects seen in skating.

If pressure cannot be the sole cause, why does a liquid layer form on the surface of the ice, enhancing the effects of pressure-induced melting? Much evidence points to frictional heating. Physicists have shown that in many instances, rubbing an object on ice can produce enough heat to contribute significantly to surface melting. In the case of skis on snow—a situation in which there is much greater friction than with skates on ice—frictional heating is the main mechanism of surface melting and thus of reduced friction (Bowden, 1953). However, this effect is due to the microscopically irregular surface of snow, whereas ice in a skating rink consists of macroscopically large crystals and thus has far fewer irregularities. Therefore, frictional heating must play a relatively small role in the glide of a sharp skate on, say, ice freshly resurfaced by the Zamboni machine; other factors must account for the layer of liquid.

In 1842, the physicist Michael Faraday proposed a hypothesis that apparently provides the key to this problem. Faraday theorized that a thin layer of liquid—so thin that it is not apparent to the naked eye—exists on the surface of a solid, even at temperatures below the bulk melting point of that solid. According to his model, a layer of liquid water already exists on top of (for instance) a frozen pond, independent of any pressure from skate blades. Faraday's hypothesis was all but ignored by his contemporaries and continues to be ignored by many today. Nonetheless, he has been vindicated; recent advances in experimental techniques have enabled scientists to confirm, and to refine, Faraday's concept of this surface liquid.

Interestingly, there is a mystery within a mystery here: Faraday could not possibly have known what actually happens at a microscopic level on the surface of a solid. Even the meanings of terms such as "thin liquid layer" have changed by orders of magnitude since his time, as a result of better understanding of atomic theory. In the 1840s, for example, a film was considered "thin" if it was on the order of many micrometers (millionths of a meter); in the 1990s, "thin" can mean thousandths of a micrometer—something on the order of tenths of a nanometer (which is a billionth of a meter). This magnitude, 1 ten-billionth of a meter, is called an angstrom.

Over years of study and debate, scientists have developed a general understanding of surface melting. Surface melting is a consequence of the fact that the free energy of the surface of a material is reduced when a thin surface layer is in the liquid phase (rather than the solid phase). In other words, a surface covered by a thin layer of liquid is in a lower-energy—and therefore a more "natural"—state than a surface without such a layer. A surface liquid is a disordered phase of the material: that is, its atoms are not lined up in the regular crystalline pattern characteristic of a solid but are positioned somewhat randomly. However, it has been found to have some slight order, dictated by the order of the crystal structure of the nearby bulk material. For this reason, some technical writers call this layer a "quasi-liquid." A less technical terms is simply "surface melt." The thickness of the surface-melt layer increases as the temperature approaches the bulk melting point of the solid (for ice, 0° C, or 32° F).

Through a variety of specialized surface-measurement techniques, the thickness of the water surface film for ice has been found to range from a high of 40 nanometers near 0 degrees C (32° F) to a low of 0.5 nanometers at –35 degrees C (–33° F) (Gilpin, 1980; Dash, 1989). (The film of water between skate blade and ice is greater than 40 nanometers, but it has not yet been accurately quantified.) As the temperature drops, the amount of liquid on the surface decreases. In skating, this reduces the lubrication between skate and ice, which in turn increases the friction experienced by the skater. On bone-chilling days, when the temperature is below –30 degrees C (–22° F), skating becomes very laborious: the blades stick to the ice rather than gliding over it.

What Makes Ice Conditions Ideal?

Experienced speed skaters claim that "good" ice has a certain sound: the blade makes less noise at the completion of each stroke. Ice that "sounds good" usually gives skaters confidence because it affords a sure, solid grip and allows them to extend every glide. What makes ice ideal or less than ideal? Two aspects of this question will be considered here: first, temperature; second, the creation of indoor ice.

Temperature and ice conditions.   The temperature of the ice is the most variable factor affecting conditions for skating. Even slight changes in surface temperature can result in dramatic changes in conditions. As has just been described, if the ice is too cold, the lack of a liquid surface film will result in a dramatic increase in the coefficient of friction. Under such conditions, the length and speed of the skater's glide will suffer. When the ice is too warm, on the other hand, the liquid film thickens, making the surface soft and slushy. At warmer temperatures, therefore, the blades dig deeper into the ice, and this too increases the coefficient of friction and greatly reduces the effectiveness of the glide. For "ideal" ice conditions, then, the temperature must be warm enough to create a sufficient liquid film, yet not so warm that the gliding blade sinks deep into the surface of soft ice.

Given these considerations, it is not surprising that temperature can have a dramatic effect on the outcomes of speed-skating competitions. An example occured at the Winter Olympics of 1992, in Albertville, France. Dan Jansen of the United States had been expected to win either a gold or a silver medal in the 500-meter, but unusually foggy, warm weather had softened the ice, and this worked against Jansen's long "power stride"—though it helped skaters with a short, quick stride. Jansen did not earn a medal at all: he placed fourth, behind two relatively unknown Japanese skaters, Junichi Inoue (36.26 sec.) and Toshiyuki Kuroiwa (36.18 sec.). Inoue and Kuroiwa had two advantages over Jansen: they had a quicker, shorter stride, and they weighed considerably less, so that they did not sink as much into the soft ice. (The gold medal was won by Uwe Jens Mey of Germany, with a time of 36.14 sec.)

Ice on indoor rinks. The development of indoor ice rinks has had at least three important effects on the sport of ice skating. First, it has helped to reduce competitive skaters' anxiety about the weather. As recently as the 1950s, skaters had to adjust constantly to the weather, because air temperature and the intensity of the sun on ice greatly affected speed and strategy. (For example, how aggressive a speed skater can be in turns is largely determined by weather conditions.) Second, it has enabled skaters from lower-latitude countries, like the United States, to train year-round. As a result, much of the advantage once enjoyed by skaters from colder climates—the Russians, Scandinavians, and Canadians—no longer exists. Third, and most relevant to our discussion here, indoor ice rinks have given scientists more opportunity to study the nature of ice and to examine how variations in its properties affect skaters' performance.

Doug Moore, an ice consultant for the 1988 Winter Olympics in Calgary, for the National Hockey League, and for local Canadian curling clubs (curling is a sport similar to shuffleboard but played on ice), maintains that for indoor arenas—with controlled temperatures and without sunshine—the ideal base, or subsurface, temperature for ice is around –5 degrees C (24° F), which results in a surface temperature of –3 to –1 degrees C (26–28° F). Base temperatures vary tremendously from arena to arena because the architecture, the ice-making equipment, and the water quality differ in every building. Also, the surroundings have an influence: for instance, a row of trees shading one side of the building can significantly affect the indoor air and ice temperatures.

Aside from regulating the temperature of the air and the ice, operators of indoor rinks have found various ways to optimize ice conditions. These strategies are based on the chemistry and physics of water and ice.

One such strategy has to do with the purity of the ice. Water molecules are bound together by a network of hydrogen bonds. When water changes from a liquid to a solid, its molecules organize into a periodic, crystalline structure, increasing the number of hydrogen bonds between the molecules. The network of hydrogen bonds in the crystalline structure holds the molecules farther apart than they are in the liquid phase. This increased distance between the water molecules results in a solid that is less dense than liquid water. Mineral impurities in ice, such as sodium, disrupt the regularity of the hydrogen bonds and the crystalline structure, weakening the ice. For this reason, ice made from demineralized water is harder than ice with mineral impurities. Harder ice not only lowers the coefficient of friction—thus improving skating conditions—but also reduces the

Oxygen in water causes air bubbles to form. As water freezes, these air bubbles become trapped beneath the surface.

Because indoor rinks freeze water from the bottom, air bubbles and minerals gradually work their way toward the surface, adversely affecting surface conditions by lowering ice density and thus increasing the coefficient of friction.

Figure 5. *Poor indoor ice conditions can be overcome, in part, by minimizing air bubbles in the water before freezing.*

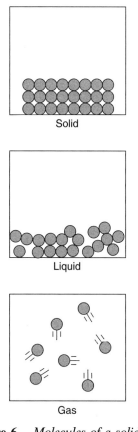

Figure 6. *Molecules of a solid are "attached" to one another; molecules of a liquid move about, but stay close together; molecules of a gas move about freely. The more a liquid or a gas is heated, the greater the movement of the molecules.*

required thickness of the ice. In addition, because minerals in water lower its freezing point, using demineralized water saves energy: not only is less ice needed (that is, the ice can be thinner), but the water freezes at a higher temperature than tap water, which contains many minerals.

Another strategy has to do with the problem of air bubbles in the ice, which are detrimental because they lower the freezing point of water and decrease the density and the hardness of the ice. Air bubbles in ice at a rink result mainly from frost. Surface frost tends to form on the top of the ice as it is being made. As additional ice layers form on top of the frost, air bubbles become sandwiched between layers of ice. The surface tension of the water as it is laid down on the ice traps the air, preventing it from escaping.

Rink operators prevent air from becoming trapped in the ice by outgassing—the release of air that was dissolved in the water. Liquids release gas bubbles (mostly oxygen) when they are heated or when the pressure of the atmosphere around them drops. For example, a soft drink releases carbon-dioxide bubbles when the container is opened and the air pressure inside the bottle drops; likewise, water releases air bubbles as it comes out of a faucet. Heating a liquid or gas increases the speed at which molecules move (*see Figure 6*); thus using hot water to make ice maximizes outgassing because of evaporational cooling. When a liquid evaporates, or changes from a liquid to a gas, it absorbs energy in the form of heat. (This is why the body cools as sweat evaporates.) Hot water evaporates more quickly than cold water, and the departing gas molecules remove heat from the water molecules left behind. Jet Ice, Inc., a consultant for many National Hockey League rinks, has found that the most efficient temperature for outgassing water is 70 degrees C (160° F). At that temperature, about 63 percent of the oxygen is dissolved. Heating the water any further is only marginally more effective: at 83 degrees C (180° F), only 3 percent more oxygen is released. Using warm water also reduces the formation of bubbles by melting surface frost. Many rinks add an air-release agent to the water as it is pumped onto the rink in order to speed up outgassing and prevent air from remaining as the water freezes.

Still another strategy involves humidity. Jet Ice has found that for ideal ice conditions, the relative humidity within an arena should be maintained at somewhere between 55 to 60 percent. When the relative humidity is too high, a layer of frost forms on the surface, raising the coefficient of friction. When the relative humidity is too low, air steals moisture from the ice sheet. Sublimation is the transition of a substance from a solid directly to a gas, without the intermediate formation of a liquid. (An example of sublimation can be seen on a cold morning, when the thin layer of frost that has formed on a car's windshield disappears as the car is driven.)

In a study conducted before the 1972 Winter Olympics in Tokyo, Japanese scientists found that higher air temperatures and increased humidity can raise the coefficient of friction between ice and skate blades very rapidly (Kobayashi, 1973). Conditions can be so variable that even if the first race takes place with an ideal coefficient of friction of 0.0003 (for a puck over ice; the coefficient of friction for a blade over ice can be 100 times greater), the condition of the ice might deteriorate significantly, to a coefficient of friction as high as 0.0005, by the time the last race takes place. Changes in indoor air conditions, along with the formation of frost on the ice between treatments, can cause the coefficient of friction to vary by as much as 0.0002. Although 0.0002 may seem to be an insubstantial difference, it is actually more than enough to affect the outcome of, for example, shorter speed-skating events, which are often decided by hundredths of a second.

Figure, Hockey, and Speed Skating: A Comparison

In comparing different types of skating, and in comparing skating with other ice sports, the concept of the "ice-edge interface" is important. A skater is always leaning on one or the other edge of the blade—left or right—and thus relies on a thin line of contact with the ice: about one-quarter of the width of the blade.

Edge-ice interface is the main distinction between skating and other sports that take place on ice, such as luge and bobsledding, but not, of course, the only difference. A luge or a bobsled has steerable runners, which are part of a vehicle and are not directly attached to the person; also, the vehicle is confined to a downhill serpentine track, as opposed to a level skating surface. Lugeing and bobsledding depend entirely on gravity for propulsion, and both sports involve speeds far greater than those possible in skating. Clearly, skating has much more in common with skiing. In fact, although skating and skiing diverged in the ninth century (as noted above), they are in some ways becoming increasingly similar. Cross-country skiing, for example, is becoming more like skating. Instead of poling and staying in grooved tracks—as in traditional, diagonal-stride skiing—cross-country skiers have been wearing shorter skis and using a skating technique that relies on the "edge-snow" interface (see also SKIING).

Although all types of skating have similarities, there are important distinctions between the three major modes of skating: figure, racing, and hockey.

Figure skating comprises the widest range of skating skills. Precision, more than power, is paramount in figure skating, which involves a variety of poses, turns, and lifts. The physical abilities of each skater, or each pair of skaters, necessitate subtle differences in style and in technique. Partner figure skating may take one of two forms: pair skating and ice dancing. Both partner events entail many skills, which world-class pairs must hone and coordinate through years of practice. Pair skating involves acrobatic skills, and aesthetics are often sacri-

The Evolution of Figure Skates

The wooden-body skate was typical of the early 1800s. Unhardened iron blades were attached to the wooden body, which in turn was strapped to an ordinary walking boot.

The one-piece iron skate also dates from the early 1800s and was also usually strapped to an ordinary boot. Steel eventually replaced iron, but the walking boot was still the norm.

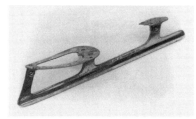

This skate—also from around 1900—had the sole and heel plate drilled for permanent mounting on the boot.

The high-carbon steel blade was developed around 1900. Steel-blade skates were constructed with rivets and were clipped to the boot.

Toe picks and skating boots arrived around 1910. The skate and boot were quite similar to those of the 1990s. With the blade edges resting squarely on the ice, the lowest tooth of the pick was about 3/8 inch above the surface—high enough not to interfere with gliding and stroking, yet low enough to be easily planted in the ice in order to execute a toe jump. Although it was of brazed construction, this skate still had mounting plates that conformed to the walking boot.

Co-Planer™. As of 1996, the latest blade technology used nonpeeling chrome-plated carbon steel heat-treated to 58/60 Rc hardness. The blade geometry was said to improve stroke efficiency by preserving momentum with less expenditure of energy. Manufacturers also claimed to have improved comfort and control, because the configuration of the sole- and heel-plate allowed the toes to lie more naturally within the boot, thereby eliminating the disadvantages of the earlier walking-boot versions.

ficed for athletic considerations. Ice dancing, by contrast, stresses aesthetics more than acrobatics and involves "flowing" maneuvers that (as the term *ice dancing* implies) are akin to dance. Overhead lifts and throws of the female skater are not allowed in ice dancing.

Hockey, like pair skating, involves teamwork, but otherwise these two types of skating contrast sharply. For a hockey player, skating is merely a means to an end, a way to move into position to convert the energy of the stick into the velocity of the puck. Hockey players must handle the puck with the stick and keep a watchful eye on their teammates as well as their opponents, all the time controlling their own energy at the edge-ice interface. They must continually select and alter skating maneuvers, remaining prepared for high-impact collisions. The action is faced-paced and characterized by a degree of unpredictability that figure and speed skaters never encounter.

Hockey requires continual stop-and-go and change-of-speed maneuvering. These essential skills are accomplished, respectively, with the hockey stop and the controlled stop, or skid stop. The very quick hockey stop requires the skater to lean into the ice with blades at a right angle to the skating direction (*see also HOCKEY*). Of equal importance is the controlled skid—a gradual decrease of speed and change of direction. The controlled skid is accomplished by skidding with one blade at slightly less than a right angle to the ice, allowing the skater to slow down and to change direction at the same time. Both skills are used extensively throughout a hockey game but are seldom used in figure skating and never used in speed skating.

Of the two methods of stopping, the skid stop is preferred, as a way to save energy. Unlike running, in which there is a significant frictional force at touchdown before the propulsive force is delivered at takeoff, skating is a gliding sport in which there is little frictional force to slow forward progress. Skaters, much like cyclists, try to take full advantage of their inertia—the tendency of an object in motion to stay in motion and of an object at rest to stay at rest. Because of inertia, it requires far less energy and creates far less fatigue for an athlete to skate at a constant pace of 32 kilometers per hour (20 MPH) for 2 minutes than to accelerate from 0 to 16 KPH (0–10 MPH) six times during the same period. The physiologically demanding nature of hockey forces players to devise ways to limit energy

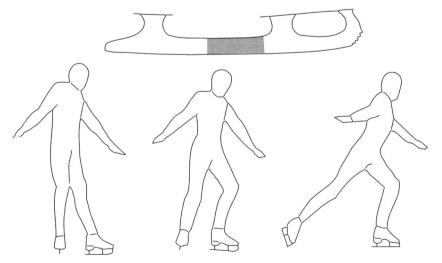

Figure 7. *The blades of figure and hockey skates are curved, or rockered, along the full length to assist in turning. Hockey skates have an additional curvature at both ends for safety (that is, to minimize injuries). The skater's weight should be primarily balanced over the center of the blade (shaded). In gliding forward, the skater's weight shifts slightly rearward on the blade; in skating backward, the weight shifts slightly forward.*

expenditure—for example, with the simultaneous slowing and change of direction in the controlled skid.

Speed skating, in comparision with figure and hockey skating, is perhaps the purest and simplest form. It is classified as power skating; and it has none of the intricate maneuvers of figure skating and is unencumbered by the equipment involved in hockey (sticks, pucks, and helmets, to name just a few items). Speed skaters skate only forward; thus only two modes of propulsion are required: the open stroke for straightaways, and the cross stroke for turns. Speed skating is the fastest means of nonmechanized, non-gravity-driven transportation available to humans: the top speed skaters of the 1990s were reaching speeds close to 56 kilometers per hour (35 MPH).

The Physics of Skating

Even though skaters do not rely on gravity for propulsion, they are still very dependent on gravitational forces. As they maintain their balance and change directions, accomplished skaters make dynamic, subtle body movements with gravitational effects under control, or countered.

Center of Gravity

Gravity "sees" the human body as a collection of molecules of random density and acts on each molecule proportionally. There is a point within this accumulation of molecules where gravitational effects can be assumed to be concentrated. This point is called the center of gravity (COG). For a skater, the terms *path, course, heading*, and *orbit* refer specifically to COG.

The path, it should be noted, is arcuate—an arc or a curve—and is rarely circular. The imprint left by the run of the blade, called the tracing, is likewise seldom circular. This explains, in part, the difficulty of tracing school figures (also called "compulsory figures"): an exercise in which the skater steers a very difficult circular path, leaving perfectly symmetrical tracings. School figures are so difficult not because the process is tedious but because they require the skater to perform an awkward task in a way that appears natural and graceful.

Equilibrium, Balance, and Passive Steering

The two edges of a skate blade make it possible to skate in a curved path. Many beginners do not realize this and encounter trouble when they try to navigate their first curved path: they try to skate on the flat of the blade—balanced on both edges at the same time—and so they can only waddle clumsily through large-radius turns. This problem is similar to trying to navigate a sharp turn on a bicycle with training wheels. Thus a skater must realize that there is no "straight line" in skating: a skilled skater is poised in equilibrium either on the outside or on the inside edge of one skate. With this realization, the

Types of Skating

FIGURE SKATING
Aesthetic skating in which each maneuver flows gracefully into the next. Maneuvers range from simple spins to acrobatic jumps that create the greatest "boot load" forces found in any type of skating.

Blade: Rockered, with a toe pick.

Boot: Triple-thickness leather for stiffness and good fit. The leather upper extends over the ankle. The heel is prominent.

HOCKEY SKATING
Power skating involving quick turns, accelerations, and stops.

Blade: Rockered, with additional curvature at the ends for safety.

Boot: Heavy lateral reinforcements provided by a variety of synthetic materials.

SPEED SKATING
High-speed fluid motion with no stopping and with only gradual turning motions.

Blade: Longer, nonrockered blade extending beyond the front of the boot by several inches; may be offset.

Boot: Softer leather; does not extend as far up the leg.

Balance and Arm Position

The farther the arms are extended outward, the greater one's balance (the more the moment of inertia is increased). In executing an arcuate, or curved, path, the inner arm drops as the outer arm rises. In walking or running, the arms and the legs swing forward in opposition; in skating, by contrast, they often move forward and backward together.

skater can begin to develop a more fluid style. The skill necessary to achieve this single-edge equilibrium and to travel in a curved path is, simply, balance, which requires a centripetal, or inward, force to counter the inertial tendency, or centrifugal force, that would otherwise keep one traveling in a straight line.

It is useful in this regard to consider a car taking a corner at a high speed: the seat belt applies the centripetal force necessary to keep an occupant in place. Another useful consideration is a bicycle, whose narrow base of support makes it possible to apply a centripetal force by leaning into a turn, much as a skater leans into a turn. For a cyclist, as for a skater, motion in a truly straight line is impractical and often virtually impossible. But a cyclist, out of necessity, needs to approximate a straight path most of the time (though a skater is not under the same constraint). To travel in a straight line, the cyclist, whether consciously or unconsciously, must wobble—create a curvilinear motion involving a small amount of lean, first to one side and then to the other.

Similarly, to travel in a straight line a skater must shift from side to side. At high speeds, the frequency and wavelength of a skater's wobble are so minuscule that the effect is difficult for even a trained eye to detect. Wobble is most noticeable during the very low-speed "school figures"—the symmetrical tracings described above—when the oscillations take place over a relatively short distance, that is, a distance measurable in centimeters or feet and inches (*see Figure 8*). By contrast, for the high-speed near-straight (telegraphed) approach into a triple lutz, a three-revolution jump from the toe pick, the oscillation takes place over a distance measurable in hundreds of feet. (And for a motorcyclist, say, traveling on an interstate highway, the distance is measurable in thousands of feet.) Perfectly linear motion is a very difficult and underrated achievement.

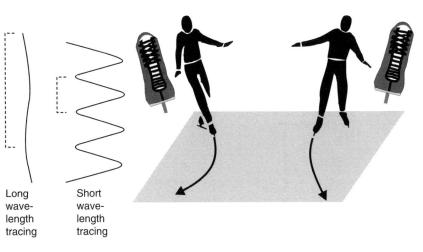

Long
wave-
length
tracing

Short
wave-
length
tracing

Figure 8. *There is no straight line in skating. Instead, skill means the ability to achieve a single-edge equilibrium.*

Presteering

To start a turn, a skater often needs to "presteer" by momentarily leaning in the opposite direction. To make a right turn, a skater first turns a little left, thereby starting to fall to the right. Then, after falling to the correct rightward tilt, the skater can execute the right turn. A similar phenomenon occurs in cycling. When traveling in a straight line too close to the edge of the sidewalk, a cyclist cannot avoid falling off the curb, because there is not enough sidewalk on which to make the necessary swerve in the wrong direction to initiate the turn away from the edge.

Since normal skating is on a curved, or arcuate, path at speed, balance is maintained by leaning into the circle. Except during the process of starting a turn, the skater's COG is never vertically above the contact point (*see sidebar, "Presteering"*).

Because a cyclist can maintain a fairly constant velocity, cyclists are able to navigate a truly circular path without any difficulty in steering, simply by leaning into the turn. This is called "passive steering." Leaning, in and of itself, can initiate a passively steered turn whether the athlete is on a bicycle, on skis, or on skates.

In skating, passive steering occurs when a centripetal force is applied to the skater's COG without any dynamic movement of body parts. After each push-off stroke, the skater slows down, mostly because of friction at the edge-ice interface. In addition, the path made by the skater's COG departs from the circular, and the angle of the lean into the turn tends more to the upright (*see Figure 9*). (This description assumes only leaning, with no attempt to actively steer.) The departure from the circular path, or wobble, of the COG occurs because the inertial tendency, or centrifugal force, acting on the skater—which is proportional to velocity squared—decreases. The skater no longer needs to lean as strongly into the turn to counterbalance the outward, or centrifugal, force. Because of the reduction in velocity, the skater can maintain equilibrium or balance only by making a gradual increase in orbital radius—the tracing on the ice will deviate outward from circular.

Equilibrium is achieved when the cross-sectional plane of the blade is parallel with the angle of lean, pointing in the direction of motion, and tangential to the curvature of the tracing. Much as the side cut of an alpine ski helps a skier carve turns in the snow, the curvature of the long edge of figure and hockey blades helps the skater make arcuate turns on ice (*refer back to Figure 7*).

The equilibrium angle of lean of the skater's COG can be determined for a given velocity and arc (*again, see Figure 9*). As friction between the blade and ice slow the skater, equilibrium must be maintained by adjusting the angle of lean, the radius, or both. Since the

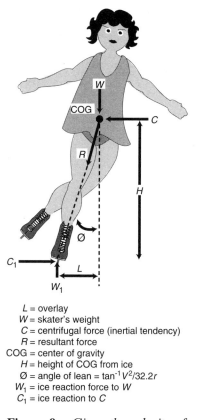

L = overlay
W = skater's weight
C = centrifugal force (inertial tendency)
R = resultant force
COG = center of gravity
H = height of COG from ice
Ø = angle of lean = $\tan^{-1} V^2/32.2r$
W_1 = ice reaction force to W
C_1 = ice reaction to C

Figure 9. *Given the velocity of a skater's COG and the radius of the arcuate path, it is possible to determine the equilibrium angle of lean: $W \times L = C \times H$. (Adapted from Broadbent, 1993)*

Figure 10. *Dynamic steering involves movement of the legs, hips, upper body, and arms. Here the leg kick, followed by the arms drawn in close to the body, initiates a spin.*

skater is perfectly poised on a stable path, this adjustment occurs without any conscious movement. This equilibrium-type glide is typical of figure skating and feasible because of the rockered skating surface of the blade. It involves some small additional friction from scuffing at the edge-ice interface because a flat (planar) blade is being forced into a curved path. The nonrockered, or flat, speed skate avoids this loss of efficiency, though at a cost: it has much poorer maneuverability. Maneuverability is of course a major concern of a figure skater, but it can easily be sacrificed by a speed skater for the sake of the greater speed of a longer, flatter blade.

How does a figure skater or a hockey player change the angle of lean when gliding on an inertially stable orbit? In an inertially stable orbit, a skater who is going fast enough cannot fall over sideways. To defy the earth's gravity, an object's inertially stable orbit around the circular earth requires a velocity of about 29,767 KPH (18,500 MPH). For the ice-bound skater, though, it takes a velocity of just a few kilometers per hour to maintain an inertially stable orbit. The objective of achieving an inertially stable orbit is to "fall around," rather than fall to, the earth (Armenti, 1992).

Two circumstances can preclude this, however: (1) the blade can fail to bite (because it is poorly sharpened, say); or (2) the strength of the ice may be exceeded by the centrifugal reaction C_1. In either case, the blade slips out from underneath the skater, who then falls to—rather than around—the earth.

An inertially stable orbit also demands that the skater hold a free-running edge. Any deviation from this constitutes dynamic steering—torsionally manipulating leg and ankle muscles to control the blade angle relative to the trajectory of the COG. This modifies the overlay dimension L (the distance between the point at which the blade meets the ice and the point over which the skater's gravity is centered). Angle of lean ø dimension H both change as well. Since the skater's weight W obviously remains unchanged, centrifugal force C must compensate to maintain equilibrium, resulting in a change in the COG radius of the skater's orbit. Lean and speed are the only variables the skater can control.

Dynamic Steering

Skaters can change direction through impulsive lateral body movements, or "dynamic steering" (*see Figure 10*). Most skating maneuvers require a combination of passive and dynamic steering. World-class skaters effortlessly use both explosive and subtle body movements to accomplish passive and dynamic steering.

Body movements aligned with the direction of motion; pivoting about the ankles, knees, or hips; and extending the arms all change the pressure on the blade forward and aft, but do not affect the path of the skater's COG. A skater's COG maintains its passively steered "orbital" relationship to the earth. The dynamics of the knee bend, or angle, have a somewhat different effect (*see Figure 11*). The skater's COG moves upward and downward along the angle of lean, increasing or decreas-

Figure 11. *The deep knee bend moves the skater's COG upward and downward along the angle of lean. It has only a minor effect on passive and dynamic steering but a major effect on control. Because the thigh muscles do most of the work in skating, instructors advise skaters to concentrate on controlling the thigh muscles—balancing body weight over the thigh. This control will naturally extend to the feet.*

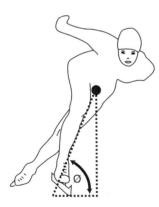

Figure 12. *Many skaters do not realize that they are using a nonequilibrium, or controlled-fall, technique to augment muscle power. During the stroking process, a skater "powers" from one edge to the next. Here the skater, navigating a curve, goes from a 75-degree angle of body lean on the outside edge of the left skate and then executes a controlled fall until the inside edge of the right skate comes down to catch him, at a 60- to 65-degree angle of lean (Ø).*

ing, respectively, the orbital radius. The upright skater follows a less curved path; the skater with a deeper knee bend follows a tighter curve. The dynamic steering effect caused by the knee bend is minimal because body mass is raised and lowcred but not extended laterally.

Lateral body movements in the direction of motion usually incur dynamic steering proportional to the impulse of that motion. For example, there is a much bigger impulse for dynamic steering when the free leg is kicked out to the side, or when the body sways about the hips, than when one arm (less mass) is extended outward (*see also ACROBATICS*).

Maintaining Momentum

Whereas figure skaters are greatly concerned with balance and "equilibrium glide," hockey and speed skaters are much more concerned with speed—obtained by maximizing power from the blade edges. Speed skaters and hockey players have tremendous leg strength and power, but they also use a nonequilibrium falling technique to augment muscle power (*see Figure 12*). Because speed skating involves no equilibrium-type glide, the nonequilibrium, or controlled, fall is very important. It is part of the stroking process, the "powering" from one edge of the blade to the next. These skaters augment muscle power by slowly leaning inward during the glide; before falling, however, they quickly swing the free skate under the body to start the next stroke. It takes time to master this technique, partly because the loss of equilibrium in a controlled fall is unnerving for novices until they become accustomed to it.

Controlled falling improves propulsion by reducing edge friction during stroke transition, and by adding the energy of actually falling onto the new edge to the muscular energy generated by pushing off from the former edge. In this way, the skater efficiently maximizes speed from total expended muscle energy. It is perhaps controlled falling, along with a smooth transition from one edge to the next, that most clearly distinguishes an accomplished world-class speed skater from a novice.

Directional Change Transitions

Figure skaters and hockey players must continually change modes of skating during the transition from forward to backward and from backward to forward. Transitions are categorized as either "mohawks" or "choctaws." A mohawk involves the change of foot from outside edge to outside edge, or from inside edge to inside edge; a choctaw involves the change of foot from outside edge to inside edge, or from inside edge to outside edge. These transitions can be executed with or without a controlled fall.

Upon completion of a transition, a figure skater is in either an open or a closed position. Open transitions leave the hips aligned with the direction of motion; closed transitions leave the hips at a right angle. In the open posture, no stroking action is possible, so the skater must focus on minimizing loss of momentum To accomplish this, open "mohawks" and open "choctaws" must be executed with the utmost smoothness. In the closed posture, when smoothness of execution is equally important, some stroking capability can be fluidly incorporated as the hips open up.

Hockey skaters make similar transitions, but for them the emphasis is on tactical expediency rather than aesthetics. The skater performs a controlled skid into these transitions, usually with some stroking action from the skidding foot as a controlled fall is made onto the other edge; this skill is often underappreciated. A hockey player makes a controlled fall by means of the "soft knee bend" technique. This soft-knee technique is the essence of stroking because it allows the skater to transfer body weight gradually. The gradual transfer is necessary to minimize the propulsive effort (force) to maintain or increase momentum. If the full weight of the skater is transferred immediately, the potential contribution of the fall to the stroking effort cannot be realized, and the potential to generate power onto the new edge drops considerably. This is a common problem among beginners.

Restoring a specific amount of momentum requires a specific amount of effort for a given weight, so the longer the thrusting period (in seconds; that is, time), the longer the length of thrusting (in linear units, such as feet). Thus, a lower average force is needed, which means that power is lower for the same result.

Stroking and High-Speed Turns

Stroking is the powered transition from one edge of the blade to the next: the skater is said to "stroke" from one edge to another.

A figure skater has two basic stroking techniques: the open stroke and the cross stroke. For the open stroke, the legs do not cross over; for the cross stroke, they do. Both strokes are unidirectional in that the skater "powers" from a forward edge to a forward edge or from a backward edge to a backward edge. These are powerful transitions not only muscularly but also because they can maximize the use of the controlled-fall technique.

In all short- and long-track speed-skating events, skaters use the cross stroke to contend with curves, or turns. Taking curves at speeds of up to 56 KPH (35 MPH) without tumbling is perhaps the most vivid example of the controlled-fall technique. Turns require the skater to push outward and to redirect some of the force normally used to accelerate forward. As a result, skaters cannot increase speed as much in turns as on straightaways.

When starting into a turn, a skater pushes on the ice in the direction opposite that of the curve. The ice exerts a horizontal force against the blade, toward the center of the circular path. This inward force on the skater is called a centripetal, or "center-seeking," force; the inward force works against the skater's inertia—the tendency to follow a straight path when moving. The inward force applied by the ice is the force that causes the change in direction around the turn.

From the point of view of the skater, a centrifugal force seems to pull the body outward. The skater compensates by leaning into the turn and pushing outward on the ice surface with the skates. However, in this situation cetrifugal force is only apparent: it does not really exist. Although the skater feels as if the body is being pushed outward, what is really happening is that the skates are being pushed inward, out from under the body, which is continuing in its straight-line path. To keep from falling, the skater must lean inward. The faster and tighter the turn, the greater the lean must be. A lean is also necessary whenever the skater accelerates. An object is said to accelerate whenever it changes the speed or the direction of its motion. Therefore, a skater rounding a turn accelerates even if speed remains constant (*see also FIELD ATHLETICS: THROWING*).

Determining how far to lean—finding the proper angle—is a major part of learning to skate around turns; it is critical particularly because ice is nearly frictionless. A skater who leans too little for any given turning speed will either fall outward or take the turn too wide (since the blades will generate too little centripetal force) and will, consequently, lose time. A skater who leans too much will fall inward either immediately (as COG shifts too far to the inside) or soon thereafter (as the blades slip to the outside because there is too little friction between them and the ice). This task is made more difficult by the fact that a skate's base of support is much smaller than that of a shoe—the blade is much narrower than a shoe sole—so the blade surface offers little support for executing the horizontal push necessary to change direction. Furthermore, speed skaters usually have only one blade on the ice at a time.

Experienced speed skaters develop a feel for how far to lean, but they must constantly fine-tune the angle of lean to suit weather and ice conditions. Here again, the American speed skater David Jansen can provide an example. Jansen was favored to win the gold medal in the 500-meter sprint in the Olympics of 1988 and 1994 but failed both times to get any medal at all: he tumbled in 1988 and slipped slightly in 1994. (In races decided by a hundredth of a second, even a slight slip can put a skater out of contention.) Some analysts believed that Jansen simply choked, but he may actually have pressed too hard, perhaps in an effort to get a little extra speed out of the last turn.

Mechanics of Speed Skating

This section examines several aspects of the mechanics involved in speed skating, which provide an interesting specific example of the mechanics of skating in general.

Air Resistance

One significant aspect of the mechanics of speed skating is air resistance—which is at least as important as ice-blade dynamics in affecting a speed skater's velocity. Air friction takes two forms: surface drag and pressure drag

In-Line Skating: Is It Different?

In-line skating is not a new phenomenon: it dates back to the early 1800s, when Robert John Tylers invented the Volito, a skate with five wheels in a single line. But it was in the 1980s and 1990s that the growth of in-line skating became explosive: in the mid-1990s it was one of the most popular participant sports; and from 1986 through 1992, sales of in-line skates had increased 6,000 percent.

One major reason for the growth of in-line skating is that it has solved a perplexing problem having to do with the wheels. Before the mid-1980s, each wheel of an in-line skate consisted of a bearing and a thick polyurethane wheel. As these wheels turned, they created friction at the

SALES OF SPORTS EQUIPMENT, BY CATEGORY

	Forecast for 1995 ($, millions)	Change from 1994 (%)
Firearms and hunting	$3,141	−10%
Exercise	$2,571	+5%
Golf	$1,436	+1%
Fishing tackle	$731	+2%
In-line skating	$662	+30%
Tennis	$244	−5%

bearings. This friction created heat at the bearing that would be transferred through to the hub of the wheel, and in turn to the polyurethane itself. "Hard-core" skaters—those who were able to generate a tremendous amount of work per stroke over an extended period—produced so much heat that the polyurethane would actually began to melt.

In-line racing skates come with five, rather than four, wheels.

Wheel manufacturers initially dealt with this problem by giving the wheel a spokelike core or midsection, between the hub and the polyurethane. This allowed air to circulate around and cool the bearing; moreover, the faster the wheel turned, the more effective the spokelike core became and the more heat was dissipated. As further ways were developed to reduce friction—and as manufacturers were able to lower costs by using less polyurethane—interest in in-line skating began to grow.

Another reason for the growing interest in in-line skating is its versatility. This is attributable to the efficiency, small size, and relative lightness of the skates. In-line skates are used for fitness, for racing, for tricks (quick turns and jumps), and even for commuting. Skaters can also use a single pair of skates for a variety of activities. When a skate blade is molded by the manufacturer, the rocker profile, or bottom surface, is not adjustable. By contrast, many manufacturers of in-line skates offer an adjustable profile angle, so that a skater can create different alignments for different applications—for tricks, for racing, for hockey, etc. It should be noted that setting the right rocker profile is important because shifting it in one direction moves the balance point approximately half the distance in the opposite direction. Not only is this important for specific applications; it also affects efficiency, comfort, and fatigue.

Many people are interested in the similarities and differences between ice skating and in-line skating. As might be expected, power skating with in-line skates is very similar to speed skating in terms of technique: both use a straight stroke, perpendicular to the direction of travel. Also, in effect, both use the same sources of muscle power. However, although data on

Surface drag occurs as the flow of air around the skater's body becomes turbulent. In speed skating, impressive steps have been taken to reduce surface drag: speed skaters wear a one-piece "skin" suit to create a streamlined body surface that will impede airflow as little as possible. These skin suits, which are tested in wind-tunnel conditions, are extremely thin and fit tightly around the contours of the body to minimize surface area. At a speed of 10 to 14 meters per second (25–32 MPH), a skin suit enables the wearer to skate 2 to 3 percent faster than would be possible with the one of the earlier woolen suits.

Adjusting the Rocker Angle
Unlike the fixed rocker angle of ice skates, the
rocker angle of in-line skates can be adjusted.

Trick skating. The front and rear spacers are
set in the high position, and the middle two
spacers are set in the low position. This
results in a large rocker angle, which is ideal
for quick turns and spins. This rocker angle
is much like that of a figure skating blade.

Racing. The three front spacers are in the
high position, with the rear spacer in the low
position. This position prolongs each stride,
maximizing work per stroke.

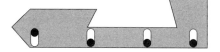

Roller hockey. The three rear spacers are in
the low position, with the front spacer in the
high position. The large front rocker and
small rear rocker make this a favorite setting
for roller hockey players.

"power per stroke" are not yet available, there are two compelling reasons to believe that in-line skaters generate greater work per stroke than speed skaters. First, ice is a nearly frictionless surface, which requires speed skaters to carefully plant and push; in in-line skating, there is more friction between wheels and surface, allowing in-line skaters to push off perpendicularly. Second, the in-line skater uses a slightly longer push stroke. In-line skaters plant their skates almost directly beneath the center of gravity. They (1) begin the push-off on the outside edge, (2) roll over to the cen-

ter, and then (3) extend outward on the inside edge. Because of the nature of a speed-skate blade, the speed skater's stroke includes only movements 2 and 3.

This additional potential for work per stroke may explain the quick success of Eric Flaim and K. C. Boutiette as crossover athletes in the early and mid-1990s. Both were accomplished in-line skaters who successfully made the transition to speed skating, winning medals at numerous World Cup events. In the early 1990s, speed-skating coaches had wanted to make them concentrate solely on speed

skating. However, many coaches came to realize that competing in both arenas could be a benefit, not a liability. (This was a leap of faith for most coaches, since the dominant trend in sports has been specialization.) Thus speed-skating coaches of the mid-1990s began to encourage in-line skaters to continue their usual in-line training as a foundation for training for speed skating. Given the success of Flaim and Boutiette, it is perhaps safe to say that the destinies of in-line racing and speed skating are intertwined.

John Zumerchik

Perhaps surprisingly, however, the rough woolen suit actually performs better than the skin suit at slower speeds (6–7 m/sec., or 13–16 MPH; van Ingen Schenau, 1982). This is because at moderate speeds *pressure drag* becomes more significant than surface drag. Pressure drag occurs as a region of low air pressure develops behind a moving object, tending to suck the object backward. In other words, because pressure is lower behind the skater than in front of the skater, the difference in pressure creates a net force backward on the skater. The more turbulent the airflow around an object, the less the air pressure behind it will drop and the lower the pressure drag will be. The rough surface of the woolen suit acts like the dimples on a golf ball (*see GOLF*), disrupting the smooth airflow, making it turbulent, and reducing the pressure drag on the skater. When a skater's speed reaches a certain threshold—approximately 7 meters per second (16 MPH), though this will depend on the geometry of each skater's body position—the air dynamics change; at and above this threshold speed, the advantages of wearing a skin suit to reduce surface drag far outweigh the advantages of wearing the woolen suit to reduce pressure drag.

However, the aerodynamic profile, or profile drag, of a speed skater has a much greater effect than clothing on overall drag. As in cycling, the greater the frontal surface area encountering air, the greater the muscle power needed to overcome surface drag. In skating, additional churning motions of the arms and legs create more drag than gliding without such movements. As frontal surface area increases, drag increases proportionately. Thus skaters devote much training time to learning to minimize drag by maintaining an aerodynamic profile.

In turn, with regard to drag, speed is even more important than aerodynamic profile. As noted, drag increases proportionally to frontal area, but it increases as the square of the speed—that is, expontentially. In other words, when a skater's speed doubles, four times as much drag is experienced, and thus a fourfold increase in power is required to sustain the new speed.

Scientific research has identified an important trade-off: the most biomechanically efficient technique does not produce the best aerodynamic profile. Increasing power output without improving the aerodynamic profile to reduce drag will hasten fatigue while yielding only a marginal increase in speed. A skater's choice between increasing power output and improving profile is, therefore, highly dependent on the length of a race. In relatively short races, where fatigue is less of a concern, power output is maximized at the cost of a less efficient profile; in longer races, power output is sacrificed to improve profile and reduce drag in order to minimize fatigue.

To reduce drag, speed skaters make several adjustments. First, they flex the trunk forward, as parallel to the ice as possible. This reduces both frontal area and pressure drag. The long blade of the speed skate helps: it not only gives greater speed—because of its greater surface area—but also permits skaters to lean forward without losing balance. Second, skaters keep the arms tucked flat against the back to keep frontal area low. In wind-tunnel tests of skiers, it was discovered that extension of the arms can double the surface drag force (Lind, 1996). In speed skating, the drag associated with arm swing must be weighed against the contribution of arm swing for propulsion.

Through straightaways, a speed skater can either keep both arms behind the body, presenting an efficient aerodynamic foil, or pump the arms back and forth to counter each leg drive. In running and jumping sports, arm pumping is almost a necessity, for it increases support, balance, and propulsion in countering the leg drives. But because speed skating is a gliding sport in which a horizontal, rather than a vertical, leg motion is used, it is not as vital for speed skaters to use the arms to create a lateral force countering the leg drive.

Films of speed skaters reveal that in short races the trunk of the body is slightly above the horizontal plane, allowing more powerful skating; in longer races, the body remains horizontal, reducing air resistance at the cost of some power in each stroke. The reason for this difference is quite simple. In the 500-meter event, where power is the major concern, a skater assumes a more upright position and pumps the arms through both the straightaways and the curves. In the 5,000-meter event, where minimizing air resistance is the major concern, a slight deviation is made from the most biomechanically efficient form—the form producing maximal power—to improve the aerodynamic foil of the skater (*see Figure 13*). Although studies find differences in trunk position and in arm action for different distance events, the optimal leg-drive motion remains the same at all distances.

Because the number of different factors involved in speed skating makes analysis complex, scientists have yet to develop an optimization model that quantifies—at a number of different distances and speeds—precisely where the benefits of added support, balance, and propulsion from arm pumping are canceled out by increased air resistance. As a general rule, however, arm-swing energy is used in short races and in sprints to the finish.

The dynamics of arm pumping are even more complex in turns. When negotiating a turn, a skater pushes toward the outside of the curve with both legs. Pumping with the inner arm significantly increases drag, and because the pumping can only be outward, it adds almost nothing to propulsion. World-class skaters, therefore, keep the inner arm tucked tightly behind the body in turns, to substantially decrease drag.

Muscle Power

In addition to air resistance, a second significant apect of the mechanics of speed skating is muscle power. Because speed skating is a gliding sport, the elasticity of the muscles and joints gives the body some of the qualities of a spring, and these springlike qualities are important for good skating rhythm. Rhythmically pumping the arms in conjunction with leg drives helps maintain balance and generate power for the next stroke. One stroke should lead smoothly into the next, so that each stroke adds to the power of the previous one and keeps the skater moving in a straight line. To add more power to each stroke, the skater uses a deep knee bend to maximize the length of each stroke and to create a good push-off across the full length of the blade.

The lower-body development of a world-class speed skater suggests the tremendous muscle power that speed skaters are capable of generating. To create power, skaters obviously need strong muscles in the buttocks and legs (particularly the thighs), but the muscles of the midsection are also important. Strong abdominal and back muscles

Figure 13. *Aerodynamics play an important part in speed skating. In the 5,000-meter event, skaters use a more horizontal torso position.*

keep the body in an aerodynamically efficient position while the arms and the legs generate the force to move forward. Muscles of the midsection help maximize leg power while minimizing work and extraneous body motion.

To maximize power, it is necessary for the leg to uncoil quickly to reach full extension. In speed skating, power production represents only 10 to 20 percent of the total sequence of phases in the "stroke," or stride—far less than in a rhythmic sport like bicycling, in which power is being produced approximately 80 percent of the time (*see CYCLING*). However, average power output is higher in speed skating than in cycling; in fact, the peak power of a speed skater is approximately three times greater than that of a cyclist. Thus a speed skater's short bursts of energy during the push-off are quite explosive. This difference in the pattern of power production may explain, in part, why Eric Heiden, a speed skater who had won five gold medals in the 1980 Winter Olympics (*see the essay "Accomplishing a Physiological Impossibility?"*), did not excel as a cyclist after retiring from skating. His ability to generate short, explosive blasts of muscle power as a speed skater did not serve him as well in cycling, which requires a more consistent power output.

The Start

Further aspects of the biomechanics of speed skating have to do with the start of a race and skating on straightaways and curves.

Many coaches argue, correctly, that the majority of short-distance races are won in the start. In addition to the obvious direct advantages of a quick start, there are major indirect, psychological advantages. As noted above, long-track speed skaters race against the clock, rather than head to head. They may be competing against thirty or more skaters, but in each heat only two skaters race. A skater who gets off to a bad start knows that at least one or two of those most favored to win will get a better start. The uncertainty that arises from not competing side by side with the entire field of competitors tends to make skaters press, or become overly aggressive, in trying to make up for lost time. This, in turn, often results in tumbles from turning too tightly in curves.

To start a race, a skater waits for the starter's gun with skates staggered at shoulder distance apart. At one time, all skaters used a starting style in which both skates would be aligned at an angle of approximately 40 degrees to the starting line. Most world-class skaters have since adopted a style in which the rear foot is parallel to the line and the front foot perpendicular (at a 90° angle). Because only one leg at a time can create propulsion, having the front foot pointed forward saves time: it does not need to be lifted and turned to take the first step. Considering that many speed-skating competitions are decided by 1/100 second, this becomes critical.

At the firing of the starting pistol, the skater lowers the center of gravity and shifts it to the rear foot. Then the skater begins a series of three or four very quick strides, with each stride slightly increasing in length over the previous stride. Much as in track sprinting, quick-fir-

Short versus Tall Skaters

Although a taller, heavier skater can produce more power, this ability is counterbalanced by increased ice friction and air resistance. In short sprints, therefore, smaller skaters are favored: they can more easily make tight turns at high speeds, because their center of gravity is lower, giving them better stability. On the other hand, in longer races short skaters have more difficulty than taller skaters when it comes to increasing speed in turns; this is because a shorter skater's muscles are correspondingly shorter and therefore less powerful.

ing stride turnover is essential for an explosive start (*see also RUN-NING AND HURDLING*). Each stride push has a sideward as well as a backward component. Although it may seem counterintuitive to use a sideward motion to create forward speed, the technique works because as the skater's COG comes over the striding foot, taking more weight, the sideward component is quickly minimized, with the skate blade taking a more forward profile.

Skating on Straightaways

The speed a skater can achieve depends heavily on good body mechanics. Muscle forces need to be applied as smoothly and as simultaneously as possible. Although the stride of a world-class speed skater may appear incredibly fluid, the "stroke cycle" can be broken into four distinct phases: (1) windup, (2) push-off, (3) lift-off, and (4) return.

In phase 1, windup—that is, preparation—the skater prepares for the push by digging the inside of the blade edge into the ice. A shift in the center of gravity transfers body mass down and over the inside of the blade edge. The greatest power is generated when a skater's feet form a V—heels together and toes apart—where the blade edges dig into the ice at an optimal angle (approximately 45°). A speed skater who is trying to accelerate may therefore waddle like a duck.

Next comes phase 2, push-off. Leg thrust, primarily generated by the thigh muscles, actually creates power by driving against the inside blade edge at an angle perpendicular to the gliding direction of the other skate. In almost all sports, effective propulsion takes place in a forward-aft manner because force is created against a fixed point (foot to ground). But in speed skating a forward-backward push-off is impossible because speed skating is mainly a gliding activity, and because ice is a low-friction surface. (Note that figure skating differs from speed skating in this regard: figure skates—unlike speed skates— have teeth that allow the skater to push off forward or at a right angle to the gliding direction.) If a speed skater tried to use a straight forward-to-back motion, the skate would slip backward, since there is no friction to push it forward; like someone using a treadmill or walking up a down escalator, the skater would not go anywhere.

In speed skating, friction increases significantly when a skater attempts to generate force from a fixed point, rather than along a significant segment of the length of a tracing. From a study of blade-ice dynamics, scientists have determined that at all velocities greater than 7 meters per second, the push-off cannot occur against a fixed point on the ice. At high speeds, an attempt to push off against a fixed point dramatically increases ice friction (van Ingen Shenau, 1989). Skating is unique in that propulsion occurs by generating force over an extended segment of the surface: the distance along the tracing is 2 feet. (By contrast, a sprinter creates propulsion in a 2-inch area: the area of contact between the ball of the foot and the ground.)

To make a push-off possible, the supporting leg must remain flexed, or bent, to increase the time and the distance of each propulsive stride, or glide. It is important that the flex occur at the knee and not the ankle. The skater tries to keep COG directly over the ankle

Eric Heiden: Accomplishing a Physiological Impossibility?

In the Winter Olympics, speed-skating events encompass a tremendous range of distances: 500 meters (547 yd., the length of about four football fields); 1,000 meters (1,094 yd.); 1,500 meters (1,641 yd.); 3,000 meters (3,296 yd., or 1.9 mi.); 10,000 meters (10,940 yd., or slightly over 6 miles). Much like the distance events in track or swimming, these distances require different combinations of aerobic power (endurance) and anaerobic power (speed). One predominant sprint speed skater of the 1990s was Bonnie Blair, who won gold medals in the 500-meter sprint in the 1988, 1992, and 1994 Winter Olympics, and a gold in the 1,000-meter race at the 1992 Winter Olympics. Her world record time of 39.1 seconds for the 500-meter sprint, set at the 1988 Calgary Winter Olympics, still stood as recently as 1996. During her reign, she was virtually unbeatable in the 500-meter sprint

and very competitive in the 1,000-meter race. But as gifted as she was, it seemed futile for her to try to compete at the longer distances. Her tremendous anaerobic power, which served her so well for shorter distances, was of little use in long-distance events, which require great aerobic power.

It is a unique athlete who can excel at short- and middle-distance races, or at middle- as well as at long-distance events. To excel in all three distances is almost physiologically impossible; however, it does occur, albeit rarely. When Eric Heiden swept all five speed-skating events at the 1980 Lake Placid Olympics, he achieved what many believed to have been physiologically impossible: he not only won the gold in all five events but set also an Olympic record in each event.

Heiden had a fine physique: he was 6 feet 1 inch (1.8 m) tall, and in 1980, when he was 21 and at the peak of his

career, he weighed 190 pounds (86 kg) and had powerful 29-inch (72.5-cm) thighs and a waist measurement of only 32 inches (80 cm). In addition to his physical endowment, he was a uniquely gifted athlete; and there is no disputing his acheivement. Nevertheless, some observers drew an unwarranted analogy, saying that his sweep of the five events was tantamount to a track athlete's winning all events from the 100-meter to the 10,000-meter.

In making any physiological comparison across sports, it is far more accurate to consider the events in terms of durations rather than in terms of distances. The time over which an event occurs more closely reflects the energy sources required—anaerobic or aerobic. For example, men's track, swimming, and speed-skating events can be listed in order of duration, with the approximate contribution from each energy source (*see the table*).

joint (*see Figure 14*). Any movement forward necessitates an inefficient countering pull backward by the calf muscle to maintain balance. A skater is trained to sit, or balance, on the skate and to push off from the rear of the skate.

Push-off ends and phase 3—lift-off—begins when the lower body parts can no longer accelerate against the surface with the push-off. For lift-off, the skater must learn to flex forward on the ankle joint. The ankle must be flexed enough so that the skate does not scrape the ice, since scraping causes a large increase in friction. This entire movement is difficult to master because it is counter to the way a person runs.

Phase 4 is the return. An effective return is a critical part of the stride cycle. After lift-off, the leg is in an outstretched position and must be returned quickly by remaining close to the ice surface, with the toes and knees pointing to the side. By keeping the feet close to the ice surface, a skater keeps the center of gravity lower to reduce drag and can progress in a straighter line, rather than in the inefficient waddling style. While a straight-line path has some obvious ben-

Skating event (m)	Track event (m)	Swimmimg event (m)	Approx. time of event	Anaerobic system	Aerobic system
500	400	100	0:38–0:45	90–95%	5–10%
1,000	500		1:00–1:15	80–90%	10–20%
1,500	800	200	1:42–1:55	60–75%	25–40%
5,000	3,000	800	7:35–8:00	30–45%	55–70%
10,000	5,000		13:08–14:28	15–35%	65–85%

Skating, track, and swimming events are compared by time of performance and approximate energy source. (Source: Morris, 1981).

Using duration as the basis for comparison suggests more appropriate analogies for Heiden's accomplishment—that it was the equivalent of an track athlete's winning all events from 400 to 5,000, or of a swimmer's winning all events from 100 to 1,600 meters. To repeat, though: Heiden's performance ranks among the greatest of all time and was a virtual physiological miracle. (It is true that the swimmer Mark Spitz was able to win seven gold medals at the 1972 Olympics, but these were all in sprint events.)

One factor in Heiden's amazing performance was the nature of speed-skating competition. In speed skating, there are no qualifying heats. As a result, the five events in which Heiden competed in 1980 were spaced over 8 days, and at his age (as noted, he was only 21), this gave him ample time to recover between competitions. It takes anywhere from 24 to 48 hours for the body to completely replenish muscle glycogen (the body's carbohydrate storage): this time is closer to 24 hours for younger athletes and closer to 48 hours for older athletes). Thus Heiden was given a physiological "window of opportunity" (*see also ENERGY AND METABOLISM*). This also allowed him to recover from another kind of muscle fatigue: the longer-lasting fatigue associated with sports in which there are prolonged periods of cyclical activity. In such activities, changes occur in the activity of various muscle proteins—calcium channels, troponin, tropomyosin, actin, and myosin. The number of active "bridges" between different muscle fibers decreases, as does the amount of force generated by each bridge. Considering the slim margin of victory among the top speed skaters, had Heiden been forced to compete on successive days or to compete in qualifying heats for each event, his chance of making a sweep would have been been very slim indeed (*see also SKELETAL MUSCLE*).

John Zumerchik

efits, films show that a perpendicular push-off does slightly change the skater's direction. Even for a top world-class skater, some side-to-side motion is unavoidable on a straightaway.

During each stride cycle, a skater alternates between periods of single-leg support and periods of double-leg support. Single-leg support occurs during the glide phase, whereas propulsion occurs during the double-leg support stage. To maintain horizontal momentum, a skater strives to keep velocity as consistent as possible over the entire stroke cycle. Each time there is a decrease in velocity, additional energy is required to accelerate. Because of aerodynamic drag and friction, however, a skater tends to accelerate during the propulsive stage and to decelerate during the glide phase. Speed skaters, like track sprinters, want to develop higher stroke frequency and a longer stride. However, frequency is of greater importance in that it ensures a more consistent velocity throughout the stroke cycle and is not as dependent on greater work per stroke. This makes push-off technique all the more important.

Not all top world-class skaters have the highest possible stroke fre-

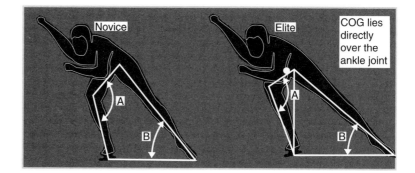

Figure 14. *It is useful to compare (left) a novice speed skater and (right) an elite speed skater. The elite speed skater has a larger flex at the right knee (angle A is smaller); this means that the left leg (where angle B is smaller) can generate more power, or more work per stroke. When angle A is smaller, the push-off is more effective because rotation of COG is prevented. Elite skaters concentrate on executing a push-off that maximizes forward movement and minimizes upward movement (minimizes straightening at the knee—angle B). (Adapted from van Ingen Shenau, 1989)*

Distinguishing the Best

- Smaller knee angle before the stroke, mostly from a more horizontal thigh position (and not flexing at the ankle)
- More work per stroke
- Higher stroke frequency
- More horizontally directed push-off (Source: van Ingen Shenau, 1989)

quency. However, they all consistently attain the highest output of work per stroke. Better "work per stroke" is a function of push-off power and efficiency, which (through training) can increase capacity—the skater's power potential. The skater's performance improves when less energy is used to sustain the same given velocity. This can be illustrated by comparing a long-distance skater to an automobile engine. Increasing stroke frequency is like pushing down on a car's accelerator: the engine does not increase in size, but it runs at a speed closer to peak velocity. Note, though, that this leaves the skater with less potential to accelerate further and that running at a higher speed requires more fuel—more energy. Sprinters debate the merits of increasing stride rate (*see RUNNING AND HURDLING*), but speed skaters all try to increase push-off efficiency by improving work per stroke.

Skating through Curves

For straightaways, speed skaters depend on a relatively natural locomotive technique; for turns, they rely on the considerably more difficult cross stroke. In the cross stroke, the left leg moves from out to in; since turns are made only to the left, speed skaters need to learn only a counterclockwise cross stroke. For each turn, a skater works through a series of cross strokes using the inside edge of the right skate and the outside edge of the left skate. The left skate generates most of the power as the right skate comes across the left in a scissor-like motion.

There is a great deal of controversy among coaches as to how a skater should navigate and create power through turns. Some coaches argue that an all-out approach should be taken in curves as well as straightaways. Others train skaters to maximize work in curves, saving straightaways for more relaxed and controlled extended gliding; these coaches claim that the best skaters accelerate like a slingshot out of turns. One of the major differences between turns and straightaways is the shorter stroke time and the lower peak force at the end of the push-off. Perhaps surprisingly, average "work per stroke" remains the same. However, stroke frequency is higher, because the push-off is abbreviated in turns—the first part of the gliding phase gets bypassed—allowing plenty of time for greater frequency.

Another major difference is the path the skater takes. In straightaways, skaters wobble from side to side as they move forward; by contrast, in turns the skater takes a smooth, controlled-radius path. This distinct difference alone gives some validity to the coaching theory that turns should be used to accelerate the skater into straightaways. It is more efficient to generate power when one's center of gravity follows a smooth radius—the smooth, continuous, controlled-falling technique—than when it wobbles. Considerable energy is wasted switching from a left lean to a right lean on straightaways.

Skaters try to map a turn course to minimize the radius while optimizing work per stroke. Too tight a course requires an adjustment of lean that steals power; too wide a course requires the skater to cover a greater distance. Both cost the skater time. In running around a curve on a track, each stride covers only a few feet; but in speed skating, each glide covers three or four times that distance, though the actual distance will itself vary with speed, ice conditions, and wind conditions. No matter how adept and well-practiced the speed skater, environmental conditions often make it difficult to execute cross strokes consistently around a curve.

Sidney Broadbent, James D. White, and John Zumerchik

References

Armenti, A. *The Physics of Sports*. New York: American Institute of Physics, 1992.

Adrian, M., and J. Cooper. *Biomechanics of Human Movement*. Dubuque, Iowa: Benchmark, 1989.

Amateur Skating Union. *Speedskating on Ice*. Glenn Ellyn, Illinois: Amateur Skating Union, 1993.

Bowden, F. "Friction on Snow and Ice." *Proceedings of the Royal Society*, A 217 (1953): 462ff.

Broadbent, S. *Skateology: Skates, Skating Fundamentals, Skate Sharpening, Ice Skating Conditioning Equipment*. Littleton, Colorado: Self-published, 1993.

Dash, J. G. "Surface Melting." *Contemporary Physics* 30 (1989): 89ff.

Gilpin, R. "Wire Regelation at Low Temperatures." *Journal of Colloid Interface Science* 77 (1980): 435ff.

Goodfellow, A. *The Skating Scene: The Factbook of Skating*. Tucson, Arizona: A. and T. Goodfellow, 1981.

Jones, D. "The Stability of the Bicycle." *Physics Today* 23, no. 4 (1970): 34–40.

Kobayashi, T. "Studies of the Properties of Ice in Speed Skating Rinks." *Ashrae Journal* (January 1973): 51–56.

Lind, David. *The Physics of Skiing*. Woodbury, New York: American Institute of Physics, 1996.

Mendelson, K. "Why Is Ice So Slippery?" *American Journal of Physics* 53, no. 5 (1985): 393–394.

Morris, A. "A Scientific Explanation for Eric Heiden's Unique Olympic Performance." *Journal of Sports Medicine* 21(1981): 156–159.

Swinson, D. "The Physics of Skiing." *Physics Teacher* 30, no. 8 (1992): 458–463.

van Ingen Shenau, G. "The Influence of Air Friction on Speed Skating." *Journal of Biomechanics* 15 (1982): 449ff.

van Ingen Shenau, G. "Speed Skating." In C. Vaugham (ed.), *Biomechanics of Sports*. Orlando: Florida: CRC, 1989.

White, James D. "The Role of Surface Melting in Ice Skating." *Physics Teacher* 30, no. 11 (1992): 495–497.

Skiing

OVER THE LAST FEW DECADES, the range of snow sports has rapidly expanded beyond the traditional Olympic events of ski jumping, downhill (Alpine) skiing, and cross-country (Nordic) skiing. Borrowing from other sports, growing numbers of young enthusiasts have developed the new sports of snowboarding and freestyle (aerial and mogul) skiing—often practiced on special slopes. The design for one such slope, aptly named "half-pipe," was in large part borrowed from skateboarding.

Today's expanding world of snow sports is a far cry from skiing's humble roots as a means of transportation. Thousands of years ago, Scandinavians crossed their snow-covered lands by strapping long, thin wooden boards to their feet. The oldest recorded evidence of skiing is a petroglyph, dated approximately 2000 B.C.E., found on a rock wall of a Norwegian island. It features the faded image of a person on narrow skis that were, in length, nearly twice the person's height. Other archaeological discoveries in Russia and the mountainous regions of China confirm the geographically widespread embrace of skiing. Considering that snow cover exists for over 6 months of the year in large portions of Scandinavia and Russia, it seems natural that their populations would develop skiing as a practical means of transportation.

Around A.D. 1200, skiing began to play a major military role as well. When the warring Swedish and Norwegian armies were bogged down by deep snow, King Sverre of Sweden sent out scouts on skis to determine the enemy's position. The strategy proved effective; by the 1500s, all Swedish soldiers were trained and equipped with skis, and the armies of Norway and Finland followed suit.

Although skiing had existed for centuries as transportation and for military purposes, it was not until 1767 that the first skiing competitions were held, by soldiers near Oslo. Setting a precedent for what is today called slalom, these soldiers staged an event in which they skied down a slope while working their way around several bushes. The first ski jumping competition was held in 1840 and the first Nordic ski race in 1866.

Skiing was not introduced to the United States until the 1840s, when Norwegian and Swedish immigrants began skiing the snow-covered terrain of New England. In 1872, Scandinavian immigrants established the first U.S. ski club in Berlin, New Hampshire.

International interest in skiing as a sport grew gradually in the early twentieth century but has rapidly increased over the last few decades. This is, in large part, attributable to the many options available to snow lovers. Snowboarders spend their days coasting up and down "pipes", downhill skiers can choose between jump, mogul, slalom, and speed runs; and Nordic skiers can decide between the traditional technique and the new "skating" technique. It is interesting to note, however, that some of the newer techniques have deep roots. The Nordic skating method, for example, may be considered a rediscovery and refinement of ancient techniques. One of the oldest ski sports, telemarking, has also reemerged. Telemarking is a hybrid skiing technique that borrows from both downhill and cross-country. Telemarking's deep-knee-bending style of downhill turning, the oldest known method of ski turning, existed for nearly 4,000 years, faded into obscurity during the surge of interest in downhill skiing in the 1960s and 1970s, and experienced a rebirth in the 1990s.

Named for a region of Norway, telemarking is popular there, as are most other snow sports. This small, sparsely populated country regularly wins more Winter Olympic medals, and more skiing medals, than any other country. At the 1994 Lillehammer Winter Olympics, Norway won 26 out of the 61 medals awarded, including 14 in skiing events.

Skiing is an exhilarating experience in which the participant has the opportunity to both enjoy and challenge nature. Meeting the challenges of the snow conditions and terrain—whatever the ski equipment or the technique—requires a skier to have an understanding of certain basic principles. This article presents the principles of physics that operate within the world of snow sports.

Surface Conditions: Physics of Snow

Unlike the consistent hardwood playing surface of basketball or the fairly constant surface of natural grass, snow—the surface medium of skiing—is dynamic and constantly changing. When the temperature drops below freezing, liquid fog droplets do not freeze, but actually evaporate to provide the moisture for snowflakes. Atmospheric snowflakes grow by vapor condensation on foreign particulates (e.g., dust particles). These particulates provide the core around which snowflakes form. The size and shape of snowflakes depend upon both the amount of precipitation in the air and the temperature. Generally, large amounts of moisture and temperatures just below freezing generate large snow crystals, while very cold temperatures and minimal moisture result in small snow crystals.

Each snow crystal forms a uniquely featured hexagonal shape. As snow crystals fall, their shape changes as they are worn down and rounded by the wind; the smaller the crystals and the colder the temperature, the smaller the effect of the wind on their shape.

Once the snow crystals reach the ground, a process of change begins that depends on weather conditions. Snow crystals pile upon

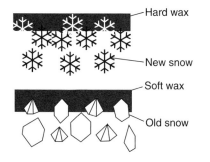

Hard wax

New snow

Soft wax

Old snow

Figure 1. *Because of the evolving nature of ground cover snow, the older the snow, the softer the wax needed for good traction.*

each other, getting broken down into smaller and finer grains. After a few days, the dazzling, brilliant snow crystals usually no longer exist, having been replaced by coarse "corn" snow. A process of thawing and refreezing turns this soft "corn" snow into coarse, rounded ice crystals—crusty snow often referred to as "skare." With time, after a series of thaws and refreezes, this snow changes to rounded crystals only a few millimeters wide. Fine-grained snow "marbles" result in slick, glassy, and dangerous ski trails, which most skiers try to avoid.

Another variable is the water content of the snow, which is largely a function of the temperature. At an air temperature below freezing, the temperature in the upper layer of the snow is about the same as the air temperature. At or above the freezing point, the temperature of the snow is below that of the air. A good way to judge the moisture content of snow is to pick up a handful. If it does not pack—if it falls apart when squeezed—it is considered dry snow. If the snow clumps together or water drips from it, it is considered wet snow.

Only after the age, nature, and moisture content of the snow are taken into consideration can a skier accurately select the proper wax for the skiing conditions. Selecting a wax that has the right hardness, stickiness, porosity, and thickness of application can have a dramatic affect on performance (*see Figure 1*).

Resistive Forces in Skiing

As a world-class skier descends a hazardous trail, he shifts his weight from one side to another, carving geometric patterns in the snow. His movements seem subtle, simple, and natural—far different from the movements involved in other sports. In most sports, competitors exert muscle power to run, jump, throw a ball, or swing a racket. Tremendous power is not the key attribute of top skiers, however. They rely more on subtle techniques, letting gravity supply most of the power. Instead of trying to speed things up, Alpine skiers direct most of their energy to slow things down.

In addition to gravity, skiers must contend with snow resistance and air resistance. Skiing has much in common with cycling, as cyclists and skiers share similar objectives: both try to minimize surface and air resistance and to harness as much speed from the force of gravity as possible. This array of factors affecting performance makes skiing both exhilarating and dangerous—a flirtation with the forces of nature that many skiers find addictive.

Gravity

Whether it is achieved by an Alpine skier who takes a chairlift to the peak, or a Nordic skier who works her way up a slope, a skier's magnificent mountain vista comes by virtue of attaining a certain altitude. The skier then possesses gravitational potential energy—energy due to her position. Perched high atop a peak, she is in a position to convert altitude into speed.

Gravity is the earthbound force that attracts a skier and all other objects toward its center, thereby giving the objects weight. Since the accelerating force of gravity is 9.8 meters/second^2 (32 ft./ sec.^{2}), the gravitational potential energy is the propulsive force upon which Alpine skiers rely. Although a negligible force on a level surface, gravity is the major force encountered by a skier whether looking up or down a steep grade. Body weight helps velocity on the downhill but creates an equal amount of hindrance for progress on the uphill. And the greater the hill grade, the greater the gravitational potential energy, and the greater the help or hindrance of gravity.

As long as the skier remains perched atop the mountain, she possesses the same amount of gravitational potential energy as another skier in the same position. But once she pushes off and sets off down the slope, her stored potential energy converts to kinetic energy—the energy a body has by virtue of its motion. The kinetic energy of an object is one-half the product of its mass and the square of its speed, which means that speed is far more responsible for a person's kinetic energy than is mass.

It is theoretically possible to start with the amount of time it took a skier to get down a slope and work backward to figure out the course and the maneuvers used. According to the principle of conservation of energy, the total amount of energy—the skier's kinetic and gravitational potential energy—must remain constant as she works her way down the slope. Energy can be lost or "wasted" only if the skier does work (force × distance) against a force, for example, digging the ski edges perpendicularly into the side of the mountain. If the skier encounters no friction or skidding forces, the total amount of energy will be the same from the top of the mountain to the bottom. At the top of the mountain, potential energy is great and kinetic energy is small, but near the bottom, kinetic energy is great and gravitational potential energy is minimal.

Since gravity is the sole force propelling a skier down the slope, Alpine skiing is far from an extended leisurely and effortless glide downhill (*see Figure 2*). A 90-kilogram (198-lb.) skier (including clothing and equipment), perched at a height of 1,000 meters (3,247 ft.) above the bottom, would possess a potential energy of 882,000 joules (210,500 calories). If he "cannonballs" straight down the 1,000-meter slope, he certainly reaches a high velocity and ends up with tremendous kinetic energy; he would never reach 882,000 joules of kinetic energy, however. Because he creates and encounters resistance on the way down, the gravitational potential energy of the skier and equipment will always be far greater at the top of the mountain than the kinetic energy of the skier near the bottom. The difference is primarily attributable to a large energy expenditure as he exerts considerable effort to descend the mountain safely at a moderate pace. He combats and controls the force of gravity by "working the slope," carving turns back and forth across the mountain on his way down. Thus, he reaches the bottom at a moderate velocity—and, perhaps more important, in one piece (*see also FIELD ATHLETICS: THROWING*).

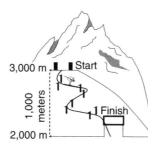

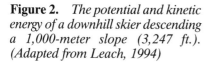

Mass of skier + equipment = 90 kilogram
Force of gravity = 9.80 m/sec² x 90 = 882 newtons
Vertical drop = 1,000 meters
Potential energy skier + equipment =
882N x 1,000m = 882,000 joules = 210,500 calories

Figure 2. *The potential and kinetic energy of a downhill skier descending a 1,000-meter slope (3,247 ft.). (Adapted from Leach, 1994)*

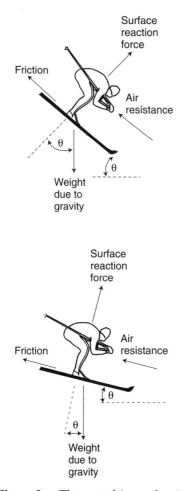

Figure 3. *The propulsive and resistive forces on a skier. The skier's weight, due to gravity, creates a force acting straight down. Anytime the straight line of weight falls along a plane different from the surface reaction force, the skier accelerates down the hill. On a steep 12-degree slope (above), the angle of the slope (θ) is great, so the skier accelerates much more quickly than on a gentle 6-degree slope (below).*

Snow Drag

The interaction taking place between the skis gliding along on snow is a major source of resistance to forward motion, and therefore a major determinant of the skier's velocity. Two components of snow drag exist: friction, and snow compression and displacement. Snow friction accounts for about one-third of the total snow drag, with the remaining two-thirds coming from snow compression and displacement. Whenever two solid objects slide across each other, there exists a resistance to motion, called friction.

The amount of friction depends on the surface properties of the two objects and the existence or nonexistence of lubrication. Friction between these two objects is greatest when both surfaces are dry. Once a layer of fluid develops between the surfaces, a dramatic drop in the amount of friction occurs. Just how dramatic a drop this is will depend on the thickness of the fluid layer and the size and frequency of the microscopic surface irregularities.

When the fluid layer is thin, the skis' microscopic surface irregularities become a far greater retarding factor than when the fluid layer is thick. At some point of fluid thickness, no direct contact occurs between the two surfaces. The more ski surface irregularities that exist, the thicker the lubricating layer must be before friction reaches the minimal coefficient of friction value, around 0.03 to 0.07 (Shimbo, 1971). The coefficient of friction of snow (0 being no friction and 1 extremely high) depends on the snow conditions, but usually falls within 0.1 and 0.2. Derek Swinson, a physicist and skier, estimates that a minimal grade slope of only 6 to 12 degrees allows a skier to pick up speed when the coefficient of friction falls between 0.1 and 0.2 (*see also* BOWLING).

The only way that the fluid layer can develop is by surface melting as a result of frictional heating. As the ski moves forward, passing over the snow, small droplets of water are produced by the friction between the base of the ski and the topmost layer of snow crystals. This thin film, forming along the entire surface of the ski, enables the ski to glide.

Despite the fact that surface melting is a function of temperature, frictional heating changes the dynamics. Although the freezing point is 0 degrees C (32° F), frictional heating raises the snow temperature and the ski's base to 0 degrees C, thus enlarging the liquid layer by melting more snow. If the snow is extremely cold, insufficient heat is

Snow Drag

1. Conditions of the slope or trail.
2. Force applied by the skier to the ski.
3. Pressure profile beneath the ski.
4. Weather conditions effecting ski-snow friction.

created by frictional heating, making the ski drag, not glide. At the other extreme, when temperatures are above freezing, the snow retains considerable moisture and sometimes begins to stick to the ski, a serious impediment to gliding.

It was long believed that pressure from the weight of the skier plus equipment also played a major role in lowering the melting point, but research has found that pressure is a negligible factor. Assuming a 75-kilogram (165-lb.) skier, evenly distributed pressure, and an average ski surface area of 0.0810 meters^2 (125.55 in.^{2}), the pressure necessary to lower the melting point of snow 1 degree from 0 to –1 degrees C would be 11 times the skier's body weight (Casey, 1990). Unless a skier straps 825 kilograms (1,817 lb.) of weight to his body, pressure cannot be much of a factor.

As mentioned, the liquid layer is thickest in warmer temperatures and thins as the temperature drops. Under extremely cold conditions, the ski often makes a crunching noise as it carves its way through the snow. A thick water layer minimizes the amount of snow crystals making contact with the ski surface, which consequently minimizes friction. Colder conditions, in which the liquid layer thins, allow more contact to be made between the snow crystals. Under these conditions, the coefficient of friction can increase two- or threefold.

These dynamics create several paradoxes for the Nordic skier, all of which are contingent on temperature. Cold temperatures provide excellent traction for hill climbing but come at the cost of greater resistance to gliding. In extremely warm conditions—above freezing—the ample liquid film provides excellent glide but makes traction on the uphill climb difficult. Temperatures near the freezing point, between these two extremes, provide the best of two worlds: fair traction and minimal resistance. Nordic skiers carefully select a ski wax that suits the conditions of the day. They try to select a wax that will give them good traction for the uphills, extended glide on the flats, and excellent speed on the downhill run. Wax allows traditional Nordic skis to grip the snow, overcoming inertia, so that they can accelerate yet at the same time glide over the snow. They can then maintain their momentum, a product of mass × velocity. Inertia is a property of mass, the steady state of a body or object. The inertia of a skier at rest tends to keep her at rest; the inertia of a skier in motion tends to keep her in motion.

Nordic skiers use wax for optimum grip and glide. Figure 4 demonstrates the ideal configuration: gripping wax at the midsection and gliding wax at the tip and tail of the skis. A sticky wax is used in the midzone so that snow sticks for traction. A properly selected midzone wax is one to which the snow crystals adhere when pressure is applied, yet which is not overly sticky. The snow should drop from the ski when the ski is lifted as the skier moves forward. During execution of all the simple and complex techniques employed by Nordic skiers, pressure is rarely evenly distributed along the entire length of the ski. Because the layers of snow crystals compress to varying degrees and do not melt uniformly from frictional heating, choosing the right wax is difficult. More important, correct application of wax

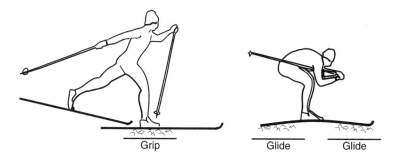

Grip   Glide   Glide

Figure 4. *Because skis are cambered (bowed), exerting the majority of the skier's weight over the midsection of one ski gives better traction (left). More evenly distributing weight over both skis creates relatively greater pressure on the glide-waxed tips and tails, which increases glide speed (right). Weight distribution between skis, and not the camber itself, primarily affects the snow force on the ski.*

allows the skier to glide and grip by applying pressure to the different parts of the ski. When a skier wants grip, she applies pressure directly underfoot. When she wants glide, she tries to apply pressure uniformly along the entire length of the ski.

Typically, the sharp edges of the snow crystals press into the base of the ski. When the base is treated with the right kind of wax, the snow crystals penetrate into the base wax and provide adequate grip (*see Figure 5*). When the wax is too hard, the skier can get little traction: the ski slips back without propelling her forward. Too soft a wax is not good, either. The snow crystals penetrate too deeply and stick to the base, not allowing the ski to glide well in either direction. An ideal wax equally matches the hardness of the snow base surface.

Snow Compression and Displacement

Although ski-snow friction is responsible for a considerable amount of the retarding forces facing the skier, snow compression and displacement account for much more. As the ski glides over the snow, it applies a force to the snow. The snow, in return, exerts an

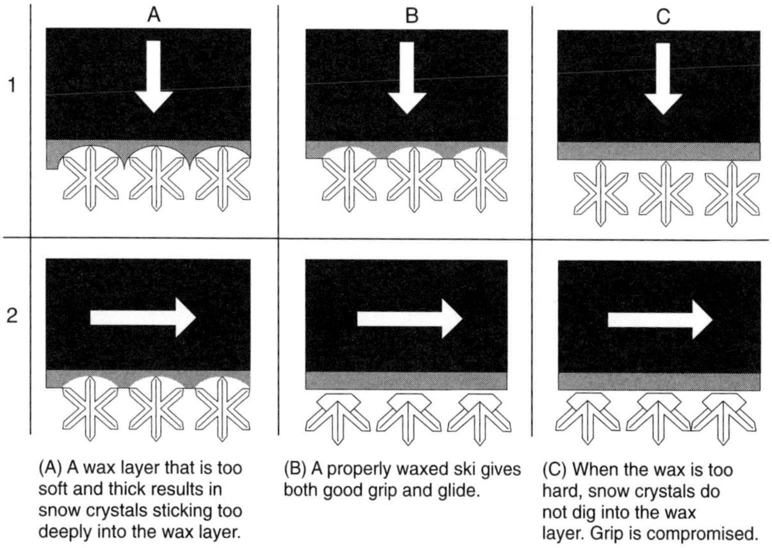

Figure 5. *The choice of ski wax depends on the temperature, age, and nature of the snow: (1) the kick (gripping) properties and (2) the gliding properties. Usually the glide wax on the tip and tail is a much harder wax that smooths the surface to limit friction and increase speed. For telemarking and "skating" Nordic skis, a glide wax is the only wax used and is applied from tip to tail. A wax layer that is too soft and thick (A) creates excessive friction, and in severe cases, snow sticks to the base, severely impeding the glide in both directions.*

A   B   C

1

2

(A) A wax layer that is too soft and thick results in snow crystals sticking too deeply into the wax layer.

(B) A properly waxed ski gives both good grip and glide.

(C) When the wax is too hard, snow crystals do not dig into the wax layer. Grip is compromised.

equal and opposite reaction force on the ski. Most of this force occurs directly upward against the downward force of the ski, but part of this reaction force occurs in the direction opposite that in which the skier is traveling. This element of snow compression and displacement contributes to the snow drag that hinders a skier's progress.

Several factors influence the amount of snow compression and displacement. The most critical is the condition of the slope or trail. A slope of densely packed snow compresses and displaces less, so the ski experiences less snow drag. The process of thawing and refreezing that creates an icy surface results in a surface condition of minimal, if any, displacement and compression, creating the least snow drag. Loosely packed snow and cold crystalline snow (e.g., following a snowstorm) create the greatest resistance. Ski slope and trail grooming equipment is used to firmly pack the snow so that conditions remain fairly uniform for skiing competitions.

A secondary factor in compression and displacement is the action of the skier. If a skier exerts significant muscle force in carving a turn, compression and displacement will be much greater than with a "softer" turn. Another factor is the design of the skis. Every ski is designed with a certain stiffness or flex to help maintain the proper pressure or weight distribution.

Air Drag

Air drag is the primary retarding force that slows the skier. It is proportional to the area of the body and primarily varies with the velocity. Air drag always exerts a force in the direction opposite that in which the skier is traveling, and it exists regardless of the wind direction. If a headwind or tailwind exists, it only respectively enhances or minimizes the amount of air drag encountered.

Air drag is a complex force because a combination of several fac-

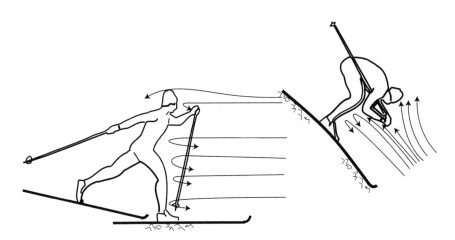

Figure 6. *The relationship of the air movement past the skier's body to the amount of air drag encountered in a standing and tucked position is depicted here. Uphill, speed is minimal; therefore, there is minimal air resistance. Downhill, an aerodynamic position becomes extremely important because, as flow velocity doubles at these greater ski speeds, the air drag increases fourfold. Air drag is approximately cut in half when a skier goes from a standing to a tucked position.*

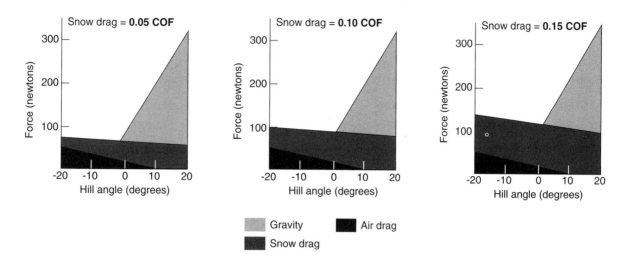

Figure 7. *The three resistive forces in skiing—gravity, snow drag, and air drag—vary depending on snow conditions, and on whether one is going uphill or downhill. The chart at the left illustrates icy conditions (COF = 0.05); the chart at the right shows slow conditions (COF = 0.15). (Adapted from Street, 1990)*

tors determine the total amount of air drag. The major contributing factors are the frontal profile of the skier and surface drag, which depends on the clothing worn. Skiers minimize the air drag from frontal profile by assuming a tucked position, thereby cutting air drag in half. In the 1990s, skiers have been wearing tight-fitting hooded stretch suits to minimize surface drag. Although the amount of energy saved is relatively small, any means of cutting air drag helps to increase skiing speed. As a skier moves along, air molecules apply a force on the skier because they are in motion relative to the skier's movement. If the airflow around the skier's body is smooth and unchanging, it is said to flow in streamlines, predictable straight-line or smoothly curved paths. Streamlined flow efficiently uses the skier's kinetic energy; little is wasted in the form of heat. When air bounces against the oncoming skier, airflow becomes turbulent. The air molecules start to bounce around in other directions, creating whirlpools of air that dissipate much of the skier's kinetic energy. The more streamlined the airflow around the skier's body, the greater proportion of the skier's potential energy gets converted to kinetic energy (*see also CYCLING and RUNNING AND HURDLING*).

The Mechanics of Alpine Skiing

Most sports require the generation of power to run, jump, throw, or swing. Alpine skiing is quite different. Instead of using power to speed up, the skier is required to exert power to slow down—much as in riding a bicycle downhill. Except for subtle movements of the body when leaning into turns, riding a bike downhill requires little effort by the rider. Almost all the power in cycling—as in Alpine skiing—is supplied by gravity.

Is It Possible for a Speed Skier to Outspeed a Skydiver?

Vertical fall

Side view

Front view

The frontal area of a "tucked" speed skier on a downhill slope (right) is about half that of a sky-diver in a "spread-eagle" position (left). Air resistance is such a major factor for speed skiers that hours are spent in wind tunnels testing "tucks" to find positions that mini-mize wind resistance on the skier and his equipment.

A never-ending pursuit of speed, an addiction for many sports enthusiasts, is probably the leading force behind the growing popularity of a new sport: speed skiing. As of 1996, the speed skiing record was an incredible 145.1 MPH, set by Phillipe Goitchel in 1993 at Les Arcs, France. Speed skiers reach such astonishing speeds by equipping themselves with extra-long (240 cm, or 93.6 in.), heavy (11.34 kg, or 25 lb.), wide skis. These skis whisk racers down the mountain by spreading their weight over the widest possible area to reduce snow friction. To reduce air resistance, they assume a tucked position wearing skintight suits custom-fitted for the racer's pose.

Since the speed skier and skydiver are propelled solely by the 9.8 meters/second^2 (32 ft./sec.^{2}) force of gravity, how can a speed skier gliding along on a snow-packed surface reach a terminal velocity 40.22 KPH (25 MPH) higher than that for a typical skydiver in free fall 193.08 KPH (120 MPH)?

Terminal velocity is the maximum free-falling velocity of an object, which is determined by the amount of air resistance that it encounters. It is a function of the cross-sectional area and mass of the object. Because the given mass for a skydiver and speed skier can be equalized, the greater terminal speed of the speed skier is a function of a smaller cross-sectional area. A skydiver's "spread-eagle" position presents about twice the frontal area to air resistance as that of a speed skier in a "tucked" position (*see figure*).

Despite this advantage, the sky-diver contends with air resistance only in free fall, while the speed skier descends on a grade, with his falling rate determined largely by the steep-ness of the mountain. He outspeeds the skydiver despite the fact that the downhill force on the skier—unlike the skydiver—is only a fraction of the skier's weight downhill (limited by slope grade), not his entire weight. Of course, the steeper the mountain, the greater the potential speed; neverthe-less, the majority of speed skiing

Gravity acts on a skier through the skier's center of gravity. The center of gravity is an imaginary point usually within the body (it is found outside the body during certain maneuvers) around which all body parts balance and rotate. Whereas the center of gravity is usually located just below the navel, a skier's center of gravity lies in the lower pelvic region because it includes the skier, the boots, and the skis.

By lowering her center of gravity, a skier not only reduces air resistance, but can react to conditions more quickly when executing

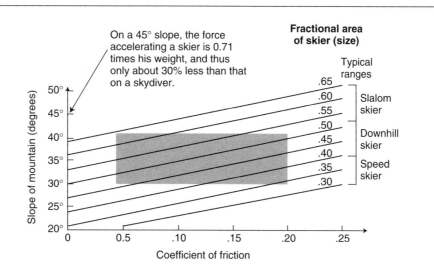

On a 45° slope, the force accelerating a skier is 0.71 times his weight, and thus only about 30% less than that on a skydiver.

A combination of factors makes it possible for a speed skier to exceed the speed of a skydiver: the slope of the mountain, the coefficient of friction of the snow, and the far smaller fractional area of the skier compared with the skydiver. The rectangular area, denoted by shading, represents the conditions under which the feat is possible. By reducing fractional area to only 0.3 of the skydiver's, the skier can reach a velocity faster than 120 MPH even on a moderate slope (35°) with unfavorable snow conditions (0.15 coefficient of friction).

courses are not as extreme as one might expect. Most courses average a slope in the 35- to 40-degree range. In effect, this is less than half the vertical dropping angle experienced by skidivers.

An additional concern for the skier is the type of snow cover, which determines the amount of snow drag. Snow drag values usually vary, depending on conditions, between a low of 0.04 and a very significant 0.2. Therefore, to reach or exceed the speed of a skydiver, the speed skier need only find the right combination of slope, ski-snow friction, and frontal air resistance area. This combination

is signified by the shaded box in the figure.

The shaded rectangle shows that a skier can reach higher speeds than a skydiver under a wide range of conditions. The factor that makes this possible is the much smaller fractional area of the skier. It more than compensates for the skier's handicap of descending a 30-degree slope, as opposed to a direct vertical drop, and the snow drag encountered on the way down. Of course, if the skydiver assumed a very aerodynamic position, like that of the speed skier, his terminal speed would be at least twice that of the speed skier. A skydiver can free fall at over

321.8 KPH (200 MPH), yet by changing her body position can also slow down to around 193.08 KPM (120 MPH).

The wide range of free-fall speeds that a skydiver attains by assuming a variety of positions indicates just how critical a factor air resistance is. Undoubtedly, this is the reason participants in high-speed sport—from running and cycling to bobsledding, Alpine skiing, and speed skating—continually dream up and devise ways to reduce air resistance.

**John Zumerchik
and Angelo Armenti**

turns. A lower center of gravity does not necessarily mean better balance, however. It actually is much easier for a tall skier to remain balanced than it is for a short skier—just as it is easier to balance a pool cue on end than a pencil. When falling, the pencil topples to the ground in a split second while the pool stick takes a few seconds. In all, the advantages of a lower center of gravity—less air resistance and quicker reaction speed—are somewhat offset by this balance disadvantage (*see also ACROBATICS*).

One Common Skiing Injury

Surprisingly, injuries to the ulnar collateral ligament in the thumb may account for up to 20 percent of all reported ski injuries (Leach, 1994). This injury usually occurs when the hand, holding a pole, is outstretched and sinks into the snow to brace a fall. The pole lands across the snow surface, so it forces the thumb to bend back and rotate at its joint, the metacarpophalangeal (MCP) joint. This injury can also occur without a pole in hand as a skier or snowboarder outstretches his or her hand to brace a fall. The severity of injury ranges from a slight sprain to a severely torn ligament, with surgery often necessary to repair the latter. Many people believe it is the design of poles and pole straps that causes this injury, but no evidence exists relating a reduced injury rate to the use of strapless poles or poles with molded grips.

Forces Involved in Turning

In its most simple form, Alpine skiing consists of making turns to control speed and to avoid obstacles while sliding downhill. In competitive Alpine skiing, the speed and the number of obstacles, or gates, vary according to the event. The downhill event entails high speeds, fewer gates, and very wide-radius turns. At the other extreme, the slalom event involves slower speeds, many gates, and very sharp-radius turns. The "super G" and the giant slalom fall between these two extremes. Technique also varies depending on weather, snow conditions, and course variations, such as slope steepness, radius of turns, and terrain.

All these events require Alpine skiers to execute a series of turns, most of which require them to engage in "edging"—balancing on the inside and outside edges of the skis. The steeper the slope, the more important it is to turn and edge to control speed. An edging turn is one in which the skier tilts and digs either the inside or outside ski edge into the slope. For a turn to the right, the skier turns primarily with the application of pressure on the inside edge of the left ski and the outside edge of the right ski. Hard, icy snow requires edging with firm pressure; with soft and fresh snow, a lighter touch is possible because there is greater resistance from snow compression and displacement. Hip and knee bend alone are adequate for slow and wide-radius turns; for high-speed, sharp-angle turns, however, the skier must place the skis on edge.

Turning is in essence a controlled fall. Skiers exert a centripetal (inward) force by leaning or falling inward. A skier leans on the outside edge of one ski and the inside edge of the other and increases the pressure on the skis by increasing the muscle force exerted by the legs. This is necessary to counterbalance the outward and downward force, an inertial centrifugal force created by inertia and gravity. When the skier turns, the body's inertial tendency is to keep going straight down the hill. Without the exertion of centripetal force, inertia naturally results in the skiers traveling in a straight-line course, following the "fall line" of the slope (*see Figure 8*). The most graceful skiers are those who most efficiently apply a centripetal force in executing the turn, developing a well-timed rhythm to match the steepness and terrain of the slope.

Much in the way an acrobatic figure skater brings her arms tightly into her body to lower her moment of inertia in order to spin at an accelerated rate, the skier roughly doubles his initial rotational velocity by moving from a squatting position to a standing position. Then, as he comes out of the turn, the skier can cut his rotational velocity in about half by bending lower and spreading his arms. To maintain a good aerodynamic profile, it would make sense for a slalom skier always to keep his arms at his sides as he rounds each gate, but he cannot because his arms must help in slowing his body's rotational velocity. He also tries to maximize the time he spends tucked and minimize the time his body is extended, because breaking out of a tuck nearly triples the aerodynamic forces the skier encounters.

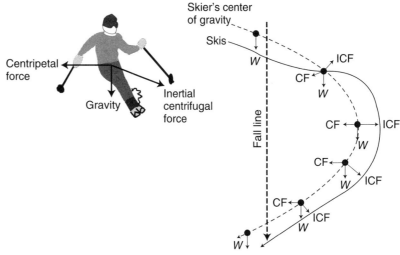

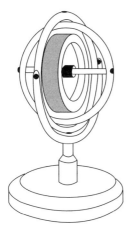

Figure 8. *The forces at play in the execution of a turn are the inertial centrifugal force (ICF) and gravity (W) acting on the skier, and the countering centripetal force (CF) of the skier. The dotted line indicates the shorter path of the body's center of gravity, as opposed to the skis, from the pronounced lean used to create the centripetal force.*

Figure 9. *A gyroscope is a disk mounted in gimbals that allow it to spin freely. If the base is tilted, the spinning disk still maintains its orientation in space (its axis remains fixed). As an Alpine skier leans left or right, she is "passively steering" to execute a turn. The physicist Derek Swinson experimented with "gyroskiing." By tilting the gyroscope axis clockwise, he was able to initiate a turn to the right. This passive gyroscopic action (body lean), along with unweighting and dynamic body movements, contributes to the turning action.*

Many turns in skiing require sideslipping, in which the skis are somewhat parallel to the fall line of the slope. The skier changes the effective ski-snow coefficient of friction by changing the angle base of the ski and the snow surface. When the uphill edges of the skis dig into the snow, they create considerable resistance to motion as they sideslip down the slope. When the skis are flattened against the surface, sideslipping becomes considerably easier. A combination of flattening and edging the ski against the snow to sideslip down the slope is the easiest way to learn to turn.

More advanced turning techniques require something that ski instructors call unweighting. Unweighting is necessary so that the skis can be repositioned to transfer weight from the outside ski of the previous turn to the outside ski of the forthcoming turn. Unweighting can be accomplished by either straightening the legs upward or bending them downward. In upward unweighting, the skier starts from a crouched position and pushes upward; in downward unweighting, the skier starts from a high position and goes to a low position, bringing the knees up and trunk down. The upward extension is the more natural and common way, yet downward bending is often the better choice for split-second maneuvering on steep slopes and bumpy terrain, where unweighting needs to happen more quickly.

A basic bathroom scale demonstrates this point. If one stands erect on a bathroom scale and unweights downward—lowering the trunk and bending the knees—the movement momentarily results in a reading that is less than one's weight. From this position, an upward unweighting—extending the knees and straightening the trunk—produces an initial scale reading that is greater than one's weight. Most recreational skiers use upward unweighting. Ski racers and mogul skiers, on the other hand, rely mostly on downward unweighting because the unweighting occurs almost instantaneously, allowing them to initiate turns exactly when and where they want.

The flexed posture of the downward unweighted skier also allows

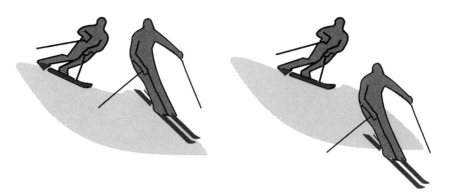

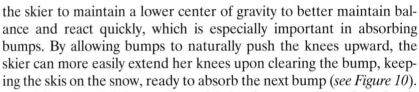

Figure 10. *Mogul technique. Flexion (bending) toward the top of one bump, followed by extension after clearing the bump, keeps the skis on the snow and ready to absorb the next bump. On the left, preemptive upward and downward unweighting (prejumping) keeps her center of gravity lower as she clears the top of each bump. Prejumping reduces the time and distance airborne, and reduces the impact force on landing. Unweighting nearer the mogul top results in a landing farther down the mountain (right). Notice how she extends her hands forward to counterbalance her center of gravity as it drops behind her boots.*

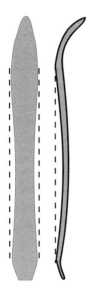

Figure 11. *On the left is a top view showing the sidecut; on the right is a side view showing the camber. The ski camber primarily aids the distribution of the ski-edge forces to the tip and tail for control and stability. Although Nordic and Alpine skis are constructed of very similar honeycombed cores and composite materials, there is a major difference in weight. A fully equipped Nordic skier carries less than one-quarter the weight of his Alpine counterpart. Because Alpine skiing is strictly a gravity-based downhill activity, heavier equipment is actually a plus. For the Nordic skier, heavier equipment brings a disadvantage on the uphill that outweighs the slight advantage it would bring on the downhill.*

the skier to maintain a lower center of gravity to better maintain balance and react quickly, which is especially important in absorbing bumps. By allowing bumps to naturally push the knees upward, the skier can more easily extend her knees upon clearing the bump, keeping the skis on the snow, ready to absorb the next bump (*see Figure 10*).

Although weighting and unweighting from one ski to the other is the major way that skiers execute turns, the skis play a role as well (*see Figure 11*). Subtle design characteristics make skis more responsive for turning. Alpine skis are manufactured wider at the tip and tail and narrower at the midsection, called the sidecut. If tilted on one edge, the edge forms an arc of a circle. This means that if a ski is just tilted on an edge, it naturally carves a circular path as it is pushed forward along the snow surface. It also means that in addition to unweighting, carving, and forward sideslipping, turns can be executed strictly by edging, by leaning into the ski's side cut to ride it through the curve. Edge turning while in forward motion is similar to the movement of a cyclist who executes a lean turn without actually turning the wheel.

The ski's flexible arch, called the camber, is just as helpful to good skiing mechanics as the sidecut. The ski's camber works like the elastic energy exhibited by a spring, so that when the leg's muscular force is correctly applied, the unweighting necessary to execute a turn is more easily achieved. Once the ski gets bent back in a reverse camber, the ski stores elastic potential energy. As the skier comes out of a turn, the ski rebounds back to its normal shape, converting its elastic potential energy into kinetic energy. This rebounding unweighting next aids the skier during the crucial unweighting phase of the turn. If the skier is too heavy for the ski, the result is poor edge control and a chattering noise as the skis vibrate off the snow. At the other extreme, underloading, turning becomes very difficult, especially in

Wide-Body Skis

To make the sport less punishing and easier, ski manufacturers have developed "wide-body" skis with a larger sidecut. The typical 63-millimeter width has been expanded to 79 to 114 millimeters at the waist and 104 to 134 millimeters near the tip and tail. These wider skis are a plus for those who ski off the beaten path, allowing easier edging in both powder and "mashed potato" snow.

soft and deep snow. Skis are designed with seemingly contradictory goals: good longitudinal rigidity to properly distribute pressure, yet good flexibility to traverse different snow packs and terrains. Until the 1990s, manufacturers developed two different lines of skis to address these conflicting goals: a soft, flexing ski for soft and deep snow, and a stiff, rigid racing ski for the packed snow on which most competitions take place. Because of newly designed composite skis, the great majority of skiers need only one set of skis. These new composites have ample rigidity and flexibility to perform well under almost all conditions.

The pole plant is also important in the unweighting phase of the turn. The pole is planted slightly downhill and in front of the skier. For sharp-radius turns and on steep slopes, it holds back the upper-body and hips, permitting the legs to twist into the next turn.

Muscle Action

Most recreational skiers are all too familiar with muscle soreness. Eight to twelve hours after a full day on the slopes, these skiers wake up with extreme stiffness and soreness of their upper leg muscles. When they return to the slopes, throughout the next day's skiing they often experience burning pain in the thighs. This comes as a surprise to those who pride themselves at staying in shape. However, Alpine skiing is unique in that it demands extended periods of high force and power from the leg muscles. Unfortunately, few people engage in adequate off-season strength training before heading to the slopes.

It is believed that these inadequately conditioned skiers suffer pain caused by microscopic injuries to their muscles cells. This pain subsides in a few days, but relief comes too late for many skiers, who regretfully admit to spending more of their ski vacations in the lodge than on the slopes.

Overworked upper leg muscles cause this muscle pain. From the moment the skier begins her downward descent to the moment she comes to rest at the bottom of the mountain, the upper leg muscles are in action. Muscle activity falls under two categories: static and dynamic. Static, or isometric, muscle activity entails the development of a force, but because there is no movement, no work is being performed. In skiing, an isometric force is required for good ski form, to keep the knees bent in a slight tuck with no upward or downward motion (*see Figure 12a*). Dynamic muscle forces—concentric (shortening) and eccentric (lengthening) muscle actions—take place when the skier wants to shift her center of gravity upward or downward (*see Figure 12b and c*).

These three muscle forces are evident when a skier executes any type of turning action. The crouch or tuck (a) requires a significant isometric muscle action. Next the skier uses a concentric muscle action to produce an upward movement of the body's center of gravity. This concentric muscle action helps unweight the skier from the surface and allows for the rotation of the body and the shift of weight from the right ski to the left (b). Weight shifts predominately or

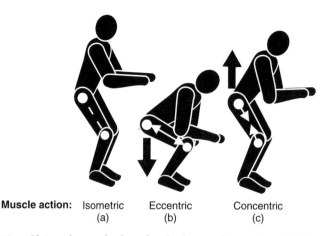

Muscle action: Isometric   Eccentric   Concentric
                        (a)   (b)   (c)

Figure 12. *Skiing demands that the thigh muscles exert a high level of force and power for an extended period of time. The isometric muscle force (a) maintains a good "steady state" ski form; the eccentric muscle force (b) lowers the body's center of gravity; and the concentric muscle force (c) raises the center of gravity.*

totally to the left ski as a controlled lowering of the body's center of gravity takes place with the following eccentric muscle action (c). In addition to the powerful action of the upper leg muscles, the lower leg muscles play a significant role. But while the demands on the upper leg muscles are for power and strength, the lower leg muscles are used for quick, fine-tuned actions. They are called upon extensively for precision edge control, and for shifting the body's weight backward and forward.

Nordic Skiing Techniques

Nordic ski mechanics fall within two categories: classic and skating. In many areas, and for all competitions, Nordic trail grooming machines pack two parallel tracks in the snow, one track for each ski. All three classical techniques depend on maintaining the skis within these tracks. Classical technique is entirely adequate except for sharp corners, steep uphill sections, and some difficult downhill runs.

Nordic skiing changed forever in 1971, because of highly variable snow conditions during a 50-meter race in Norway. Racers stopped repeatedly along the course to rewax or change skis. The one exception was the East German skier Gerhard Grimmer. He abandoned the classic technique and began "skating" by pushing off the inside edge of his weight-bearing ski. He won the race by a full 7 minutes, and since then skating has gradually become the style of choice. Although skating techniques were first used for corners and uphills, because they afforded easier creation of ski-snow forces necessary for difficult terrains, they have proved to be superior in many instances on the flat as well.

Snowboarding: More Than a Fad?

To the chagrin of many skiers, the ranks of snowboarders continue to grow. According to the National Sporting Goods Association, a national trade group, there were 10.5 million skiers and 1.8 million snowboarders in 1994. And though the majority of snowboarders were teenagers, the demographics were changing. The National Ski Areas Association reported a 64.7 percent increase in use of snowboards from 1992 through 1994 among people over age 16. By the year 2000, some observers expect that 40 percent of all lift tickets will be purchased by snowboarders.

Skiers are not necessarily being lured away to snowboards. Rather, youngsters heading to the slopes start out on snowboards and stay with snowboards instead of switching over to skis. This trend may continue, as snowboarding has much in common with some popular summer activities, such as surfing, windsurfing, slalom water-skiing, and skateboarding.

The biggest difference between snowboarding and skiing is in the size, shape, and weight of the equipment. Because the snowboard is lighter and takes up more area than two skis, it rides more easily over deep snow—the force per unit area is less. Because it does not compress the snow as much, turning a snowboard is easier than turning two skis. Moment of inertia, which reflects turning acceleration and velocity, is determined by the mass of the person plus equipment and by the distance from the axis of rotation. The snowboard, both lighter and closer to the rider's axis of rotation, turns more quickly and sharply because of its much lower moment of inertia.

Another significant difference is in the foot-binding placement. Unlike the ski-binding placement, the placement of the snowboarder's feet is to the rear and to the heel side of the center of gravity of the board. Because the feet are behind the board's center of gravity, the board rides more easily over, not through, the surface of deep snow. Further, the distance between the feet makes it possible for the boarder to have more control over his turns by shifting his weight and leaning forward or backward. A skier, whose two feet are rather close together, cannot generate as much torque as a snowboarder, whose feet are farther apart. Snowboards are perhaps the ultimate carving tools, since they can be shaped to large angles with much higher edge forces than skis.

Skiers must also develop a feel for a different type of turn. For the most part, skiing involves firmly carved turns. This is rarely the case for snowboarders, for most of their turns involve a combination of sliding and carving. Snowboard sliding turns are commonplace because the frictional resistance to sliding is distributed over a shorter distance (owing to the shorter board length), making it more predictable and easier to overcome.

Finally, snowboarding body mechanics are far different. Because skiers ski straight down the fall line, their movements involve symmetrical weighting with respect to the fall line—equal weighting on each side of the fall line. On the other hand, the bindings on a snowboard require a stance perpendicular to the long axis of the snowboard, which results in asymmetrical weighting toward the heel side. A noncentered stance is used because the trunk can more quickly and easily flex forward than extend backward. Snowboarders can easily compensate for this imbalance by using a much more pronounced lean for a toe-side turn than for a heel-side turn. Switching from the symmetrical mechanics of skiing to the initially uncomfortable nonsymmetrical mechanics of snowboarding is far too frustrating an experience for many adult skiers to endure. Most young skiers, on the other hand, are less set in their ways and quickly pick up the nonsymmetrical skills of snowboarding.

Despite the growing numbers taking up snowboarding, it will probably always remain the domain of the young and the short. Why? Try balancing a yardstick, then a pencil, on your finger. Notice how much easier it is to balance the yardstick. Likewise, it is much easier for a tall skier to maintain balance than it is for a short skier. The narrow base of support—feet fairly close together—favors the taller skier. On the other hand, the wider base assumed by snowboarders gives short snowboarders a distinct advantage: they can quickly shift their weight and lower their center of gravity.

The many distinct differences bode well for the future of the sport. Skiers had better get accustomed to sharing their slopes with brash boarders, for snowboarding shows no sign of fading.

Skating techniques borrow from the gliding technique employed by speed skaters: a right-angle push-off from the forward direction traveled (*see also SKATING*). Considering the negligible difference in the coefficient of friction encountered by skaters and skiers on, respectively, ice and packed snow, it should come as little surprise that Nordic skiers have widely adopted skating techniques.

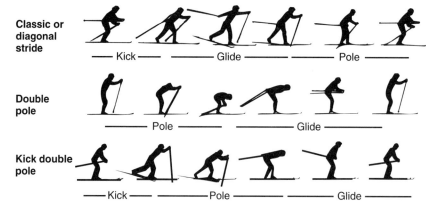

Classic or diagonal stride
— Kick — — Glide — — Pole —

Double pole
— Pole — — Glide —

Kick double pole
— Kick — — Pole — — Glide —

Figure 13. *The three classical Nordic ski techniques: diagonal stride, double pole, and kick double pole.*

Diagonal stride. The best-known and by far the dominant technique until the early 1980s was the diagonal stride, a natural motion that mimics walking. The term *diagonal* refers to the naturally opposing actions of the arms and legs. To be effective, this technique requires a well-coordinated push-off when the feet are side by side. Unless this occurs, one ski tends to "slip" as the other one "slaps" against the snow. It is important not to overextend the rear leg; this reduces the ability to balance on the forward gliding ski.

Double poling. This versatile technique is used in both categories: classical and skating. It requires a lean forward, moving the hips ahead of the feet, so that full power goes into the simultaneous push of the planted poles. The upper body follows the arms downward and back to generate extra pushing power. The deeper the compression of the skier, the longer the poling phase, which in turn generates more power.

Kick double pole. This graceful technique usually follows the double pole as the skier begins to lose his momentum. It usually allows the skier to maintain momentum, but at a cost: it requires significantly more energy expenditure, as all four limbs are recruited into action. The kick occurs when the feet are under the skier's body and the arms start forward after poling. The pushing leg moves backward and off the snow naturally to counterbalance the arms and upper body, which are moving forward to begin the double pole action. The kicking or extension of the rear leg should occur naturally; it should not be a forced lifting of the leg.

No-pole skating. At a fairly fast pace, no-pole skating is the best technique for moving across flat terrain or down small hills. It is the method of propulsion most similar to the one employed by speed skaters. A skier refrains from poling because she is moving too quickly to pole effectively. By the time she plants her pole, her significant speed has already carried her well beyond the point where she can generate an appreciable amount of force (*see also PADDLE*

When to Skate?

Although a skating technique is often superior, the skier must often make a critical decision: whether to remain in the tracks using classical technique or to opt for the superior skating technique. She must weigh whether the skating technique is fast enough to make up for, say, the fourfold increase in snow drag because of greater ski-snow compression and displacement outside the tracks. To make these critical decisions, skiers spend considerable time familiarizing themselves with the course and snow conditions.

SPORTS). Poling may even be detrimental, disrupting rhythm and balance. Faster than any of the classical techniques, no-pole skating requires more effort and better ski edge design.

Marathon skate. This technique was introduced by Bill Koch, a legendary Vermont Nordic skier who captured a silver medal at the 1976 Winter Olympics. A "half-skate action," it combines double poling with an extra push from a ski angled across the track. As the upper body adds power through double poling, it gets a simultaneous boost of power through the one leg generating forward power. Very effective on slight uphill grades, this advanced technique requires a subtle back-and-forth weight transfer from the gliding ski to the skating ski—a precarious type of balance. With weight transferred to the skating ski, an effective push-off is possible. This, in turn, naturally brings the body over the gliding ski in position for a strong stable double-pole action. The skier is almost always balanced over just one ski.

V1. When the legs alone cannot generate enough power to climb a steep slope, Nordic skiers must rely on some poling to supplement the skating technique. The skis function in a much fuller V-position for this steep uphill technique, and for every two skating strides, the skier double poles once. Pole planting is asymmetrical, though, with one hand higher than the other, so that an extended push-off occurs. It is efficient for the same reason that a horse's front and back legs, working together, employ an asymmetrical push-off when galloping.

V2. This technique is also familiar to Alpine skiers as a means of gaining speed on flat terrain at the top of slopes or for exploding out of the gate at the start of a race. It requires a double pole over each skating ski, and for every two skating steps, double poling occurs twice. What makes this technique unusual is the nonsynchronous

Figure 14. *The three modern Nordic techniques: marathon skate, V1, and V2.*

action of the poling with the skating technique: it occurs after the skier glides, but prior to push-off.

Despite the growing popularity of skating techniques, conditions often dictate the use of classical techniques. Skiers are presented with a perplexing decision: whether to remain in the groomed tracks using a classical technique or to venture out from the tracks using a skating technique. They must weigh whether the skating technique is fast enough to make up for, say, the fourfold increase in snow drag because of greater ski-snow compression and displacement outside the tracks. To make these critical decisions skiers spend considerable time familiarizing themselves with the course and snow conditions. It is neither an easy decision nor a small matter. A slower skier who selects a better wax—the one best tuned to the day's snow conditions—often triumphs over far more skilled competitors.

John Zumerchik and David Lind

References

Dane, A. "The Mechanics of Skiing." *Popular Mechanics*, February 1992, 34.

Dillman, C., and P. Martin. "Biomechanics of Cross-country Skiing." *Ski Patrol Magazine*, Fall 1984, 20ff.

Easterling, K. *Advanced Materials for Sports Equipment*. New York: Chapman and Hall, 1993.

Gullion, Laurie. *The Cross Country Primer*. New York: Lyons and Burford, 1990.

Hignell, R., and C. Terry. "Why Do Downhill Racers Pre-Jump?" *Physics Teacher*, no. 23 (1985): 487ff.

Howe, J. *Ski Mechanics*. LaPorte, Colorado: Poudre, 1983.

Leach, R. *Alpine Skiing*. Boston: Blackwell Scientific, 1994.

Lind, David. *The Physics of Skiing*. Woodbury, New York: American Institute of Physics, 1996.

Lloyd, B. "Snowboard Parks Have Roots in Geometry Class." *New York Times*, 19 January 1995.

McCluggage, D. *The Centered Skier*. Waitsfield, Vermont: Vermont Crossroads, 1977.

Plueddemann, C. "The Mechanics of Speed Skiing." *Popular Mechanics*, February 1994, 27ff.

Shimbo, M. "Friction on Snow of Ski Soles, Unwaxed and Waxed." In *Scientific Study of Skiing in Japan*. Tokyo: Hitachi, 1971.

Shonle, J., and D. Nordick. "The Physics of Ski Turns." *Physics Teacher*, no. 10 (1972): 491ff.

Street, G. "Biomechanics of Cross-Country Skiing." In M. Casey, C. Foster, and E. Hixson (eds.), *Winter Sports Medicine*, 284. Philadelphia: Davis, 1990.

Swinson, D. "Physics and Skiing." *Physics Teacher*, no. 30 (1992): 458ff.

Swinson, D. "Physics and Snowboarding." *Physics Teacher*, no. 32 (1994): 530ff.

Soccer

AS WITH A NUMBER of other sports, tracing the origins of soccer is a daunting task. Soccer (which is called football in most countries) seems to be the forerunner of all ball games, including cricket, croquet, golf, hockey, and tennis, and it may date back as far as ancient China. Around 1697 B.C.E., Emperor Huang-Ti devised a game called *tsu-chu*, based on military strategy, in which warriors kicked a leather ball stuffed with cork and hair between two bamboo posts; this vaguely resembled the soccer of the 1990s.

The Romans developed team games like the one called *harpastum*, a violent mass contest involving teams of up to 500 players who fought over an animal bladder. *Harpastum* was meant as a training exercise for battle; and as the empire expanded, Roman soldiers introduced it throughout the newly conquered lands, including England, where it reached Derby and Chester around 217 C.E. The English version evolved somewhat differently: each team would attempt to kick an object—originally a human skull but later an inflated animal bladder encased in leather—to the center of the opposing team's town. According to English legend, the skull of a captured Dane served as the first soccer ball.

It seems probable that soccer, like many sports, was developed as a way of preparing for war; and in its early days, when there were few or no rules, games were quite similar to military battles. There were no restrictions on the number of participants on a side or on the size of the playing field, and the game even involved bloodshed. In England, the lord mayor of London eventually attempted to forbid it. He issued an order in 1314, in the name of the king, referring to a "great uproar in the City, through certain tumult arising from great footballs in the fields of the public, from which many evils perchance may arise" and threatening participants with the "pain of imprisonment" (Marples, 1954).

As soccer evolved, it became less violent, crude, and brutal; lost its function as a military exercise; and began to emerge as a highly skilled strategic sport. The standardization of soccer rules in 1873 accelerated the movement toward the modern game.

In the 1990s, soccer is widely acknowledged to be the world's favorite game, both for players and as a spectator sport. Around the world, it is played by over 200 million people on more than 4.1 million teams in more than 20 million organized games—and these figures are projected to grow even larger. In almost every country in Europe, South America, Asia, and Africa, it is by far the most popular national sport. Although in the United States the World Series and the Super Bowl draw impressive crowds and television audiences, they are dwarfed in comparison with the huge number of soccer fans who passionately follow the World Cup—a monthlong tournament that takes place once every 4 years. In 1982, the World Cup drew more than 1.5 billion television viewers as Italy defeated West Germany in the finals. In 1994, when the finals culminated in an exciting victory by Brazil over Italy, the number of viewers was estimated at 2 billion.

Probably nowhere is the fervor surrounding soccer greater than in South America. Players in South America often have more to fear from their fans than from their opponents; and to protect referees and players from the wrath of disgruntled spectators, many soccer stadiums are built like fortresses, with a moat surrounding the playing field. At the first World Cup final in 1930, Argentinian fans incessantly chanted "Victory or death!" (Fortunately, their team won.) Passions run so deep that soccer once served as a pretext for an international war: in 1969, after several hotly contested World Cup qualifying matches between Honduras and El Salvador, El Salvador bombed and then invaded Honduras, killing 2,000 people. This conflict is actually known as the *Fútbol* ("Soccer") War.

There are several reasons why soccer is so popular. First, soccer—virtually uniquely among sports—consists of 90 minutes of almost nonstop action: two 45-minute periods, with only a short break between. Second, it is intended as a game of precision and endurance, rather than brute force: the players move in what seem to be smoothly choreographed patterns. Third, it requires no unusual physical characteristics and no expensive equipment: it is a sport anyone can play. Soccer does not discriminate between rich and poor or tall and short. A few people leisurely kicking a makeshift ball around on a beach will quickly draw a crowd ready for a game.

The Soccer Ball

The official ball used in modern soccer is of course far different from the original animal bladder or the makeshift stuffed rags used for pickup games all over the world. The present ball, the Questra, is a high-tech mixture of plastic, rubber, and fabric (*see Figure 1*). It is approximately spherical, with a multifaceted, seamed surface (the faces are called panels). Internally, it consists of a latex rubber bladder surrounded by five layers of material. Layers one through three (from the bladder outward) are woven fabrics that help the ball keep its shape when it receives an impact (unlike, say, a volleyball, which takes on an out-of-round shape). Layers four and five are made of a synthetic material, polyurethane: layer four is a highly compressive polyethelene foam that is very responsive in shooting and dribbling;

Indoor Natural Grass

On 18 June 1994, Michigan's Pontiac Silverdome laid claim to a first—the first indoor World Cup games. Because international soccer is played only on natural turf, the stadium officials had to bring natural grass indoors.

Actually, that had been done once before: in the 1960s, when the Houston Astrodome was first opened, it had a natural grass surface. This was possible because its roof consisted of 4,800 skylights that let in plenty of sunlight, the full spectrum of light needed for grass to grow. However, this natural turf was very soon replaced with artificial turf—not because of any problem with growing grass indoors, but because ballplayers were blinded by the sunlight penetrating the roof, which made it extremely difficult to track the ball.

The Silverdome, like most indoor stadiums, has a Teflon-coated fiberglass dome. This allows only 10 percent of the available sunlight to penetrate—not nearly enough to support healthy grass. As a temporary solution, scientists at Michigan State University designed a series of interlocking hexagonal (six-sided) trays of sod to serve as a portable natural grass playing surface. The hexagonal shape was chosen because its sides could be made thinner and lighter and would fit more snugly together, since there are three points at each corner instead of four. Each tray was 225 centimeters (7.5 ft.) wide, weighed 1,590 kilograms (3,500 lb.), and could hold 15 centimeters (6 in.) of topsoil.

First, grass (sod) was grown and maintained outdoors. When it was ready, the trays were carted into the stadium for assembly. For the Silverdome, 1,988 trays were needed in all. They were positioned 7.5 centimeters (3 in.) above the Silverdome's cement floor to allow drainage. During the 11 days of the World Cup, this makeshift soccer field worked so well that none of the players complained about it—for example, no one complained about poor footing, as might have happened if the turf had moved under the players. Moreover, this temporary turf would have worked far longer than the 11 days of the World Cup; in theory, it could last for 60 days.

On the other hand, this portable grass field did not represent a permanent solution, because the grass would need to be brought outside periodically to receive the proper amount of sunshine. Given that it takes 2 or 3 days and more than 1,000 hours of work to move the trays in or out, maintaining such a field would be prohibitively expensive. The logical long-term solution, therefore, is to develop a way to grow grass indoors. This is easier said than done, though; in fact, it is a tremendous technological challenge. The problem is to find a material for the dome that will provide an appropriate overhead background for ball games but still let in enough sunlight for the grass. In addition, the material would have to be just as strong, durable, and cost-effective as the Teflon-coated fiberglass of the 1990s.

The ideal solution may come from a convergence of advances in turf science and in materials science. Genetics researchers and engineers continue to make progress in developing hybrid grasses that need less and less light. Undoubtedly, materials scientists will eventually solve their side of this perplexing problem as well.

John Zumerchik

layer five, the outermost layer, is flexible but durable. Finally, a slick coating is applied to the surface so that the ball will meet less resistance as it sails through the air.

This new ball, introduced for the 1994 World Cup, looks like the two-layer ball it replaced, but responds much better in terms of both power and control. As noted, the additional layers are designed to help the new ball keep its shape when kicked—become less out-of-round—so that it will follow a truer flight path (*see also VOLLEYBALL*).

Equally important, the new ball is designed to maintain a more consistent coefficient of restitution over a range of kicking velocities. The coefficient of restitution measures rebound: if a ball has a coefficient of restitution of 0.6, for example, this means that when it is dropped from a height of 10 feet (300 cm), it will rebound up to a height of 6 feet (180 cm). For low-velocity kicks, the coefficient of restitution is probably about the same for the new ball as the old one;

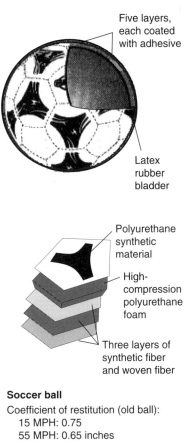

Five layers, each coated with adhesive

Latex rubber bladder

Polyurethane synthetic material

High-compression polyurethane foam

Three layers of synthetic fiber and woven fiber

Soccer ball

Coefficient of restitution (old ball):
15 MPH: 0.75
55 MPH: 0.65 inches

Ball circumference: 27 to 28 inches

Mass: 0.425 kilograms

Figure 1. *The new high-tech soccer ball has five layers and is more responsive than the two-layer ball (an outer layer of nonwoven taijin cordley, and an inner layer of backing fabrics) it replaced. (Source: Adidas)*

but with the new ball, the coefficient of restitution for high-velocity kicks shows less drop-off.

The biomechanist Stanley Plagenhoef found that the old ball had a 15 percent lower coefficient of restitution when struck at 88 KPH (55 MPH) than when struck at 24 KPH (15 MPH) (Plagenhoef, 1971; *see Table 1*). This large a change in the coefficient of restitution at higher impacts put the old soccer ball midway between a baseball and a tennis ball. The new soccer ball is intended to limit this kind of variability in the way the ball comes off the foot when kicked at different velocities: thus it is easier to control, pass, trap, and shoot.

Aerodynamics and the "Banana Kick"

The flight of a soccer ball is significantly affected by the air encountered along its path. Air resists the passage of the ball, imparting a force that slows the ball down. Consider a soccer ball kicked without spin in an evacuated chamber—that is, in a condition without air resistance. If the ball was kicked at 35 meters (115.5 ft.) per second at a trajectory angle of 45 degrees, it would travel 125 meters (412.5 ft.). In air, assuming no wind, the same ball would travel little more than half that distance: 66 meters (217.8 ft.).

Air not only impedes the flight of a soccer ball but also can alter its flight path tremendously, and this is important with regard to the "banana kick." Good soccer players are proficient at executing a banana kick to "bend" or curve the flight of the ball—a particularly effective strategy when the defenders form a wall by lining up shoulder to shoulder to block a free kick (*see Figure 2*).

A right-footed player typically executes a banana kick by striking the ball on its right side and slightly below its center; this off-center contact puts a counterclockwise spin on the ball that helps the ball curve from right to left. However, some highly skilled players can also strike the left side of the ball with the outside of the foot to give a clockwise spin and bend the flight path from left to right.

The ball—bear in mind that it is not smooth but multipaneled, with seams—curves because spin creates a dramatic imbalance in air

COEFFICIENT OF RESTITUTION OF VARIOUS BALLS AT 15 AND 55 MPH (24 AND 88 KPH)

Ball	15-MPH impact	55-MPH impact	Difference
Super	0.90	0.85	6%
Baseball	0.57	0.55	3.6%
Soccer	0.75	0.65	15%
Tennis	0.70	0.50	40%
Softball	0.55	0.40	37%

Table 1. *Coefficient of restitution drops as striking velocity increases. In this regard the old soccer ball fell between the baseball and the tennis ball. The new soccer ball is designed to have a more consistent coefficient of restitution—less variation at higher impact velocities. (Adapted from Plagenhoef, 1971)*

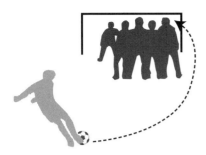

Figure 2. *A banana kick is a very effective way to score off a free kick. When defenders form a wall by lining up shoulder to shoulder, the only way to score is by bending or curving the kick around them.*

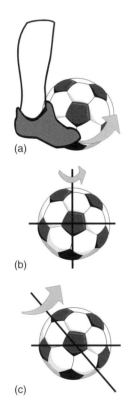

(a)

(b)

(c)

Figure 3. *The Magnus effect occurs when a kicking motion (a) creates an imbalance of air pressure on opposite sides of the ball and thus causes it to curve. The curve, or deflection, is greatest when the spin axis and the direction of airflow are at right angles to each other (b) rather than (c).*

pressure on opposite sides of it. This in turn creates an imbalance in drag, or air resistance. The imbalance—called the Magnus effect—is at a maximum when the ball's axis of spin and the direction of airflow are at right angles to each other. As the spin axis tilts and begins to converge with the direction of airflow, the Magnus effect declines: it reaches zero when the two axes meet (*see Figure 3*).

It should be noted that these descriptions assume windless conditions. In reality, head-, tail-, and crosswinds can help or hinder the Magnus effect by changing the dynamics of spin axis versus airflow. A headwind increases the deflection of the ball—the curve—because it increases the velocity of airflow (drag) past the ball. A tailwind decreases the curve because it decreases the velocity of airflow past the ball. In Figure 3, a right-to-left crosswind would increase the Magnus effect but a left-to-right crosswind would decrease it (*see also FIELD ATHLETICS: THROWING*).

Corner Kick

The corner kick is one of the most exciting plays in soccer. With opposing players remaining at least 10 yards away, the ball is put into play by kicking it from the quarter circle at the corner flag. Although the player is a long way from the goal and at an angle that makes it nearly impossible to kick the ball into the goal, a well-placed corner kick can put his or her teammates in an excellent position to score from a header or side volley (a ball hit while airborne).

There are two major types of corner kicks: outswinger and inswinger. These are both curved passes, and they are popular because the ball moves quite unpredictably: it is very difficult for the goalkeeper to judge how much the Magnus effect will alter the ball's flight path.

In an outswinger kick, the ball swerves away from the goalkeeper and toward the incoming forwards on the kicker's team. One advantage of the outswinger is that it gives the kicker's teammates a chance to create greater force for a header or side volley. Another advantage is that the ball moves away from the goalkeeper; this is important because the goalkeeper can jump much higher to catch the ball with the hands than another player can jump to kick or head the ball into the net. Usually four or five of the kicker's teammates are positioned near the goal and will try to kick or head the ball into it.

Although the inswinger kick is used less often than the outswinger, it is particularly effective in gusty winds. It curves the ball toward the goal, so if the goalkeeper misjudges the ball's flight path, the ball has a good chance of reaching the head or foot of a teammate or even of finding its way into the goal by itself.

Penalty Kicks

In the 1994 World Cup (as noted above), the finalists were Italy and Brazil, two teams with very different styles. The very talented Brazilian team was freewheeling and improvisational and played with high flair—affectionately called *ginga*. The Italian team, led by Roberto Baggio (who had been the World Player of the Year in 1993), played an all-field attacking game. The game ended in a tie—to the dismay of soccer purists, because the World Cup uses a much-criticized tiebreaker. To break a tie in the World Cup, the rule is that the winner will be decided by a "shoot-out": each team chooses five players to take one penalty kick each against the opponents' goalkeeper.

For mainly psychological reasons, coaches usually designate the players who are mentally toughest to lead off and anchor a shoot-out. The Italians chose the veteran Franco Baresi to lead off, and their star, Roberto Baggio, to anchor. After the Italians' fourth attempt, they were trailing Brazil by 1, and the game came down to a moment of great drama—Baggio's kick. Perhaps the pressure was too much for Baggio, or perhaps his nagging hamstring injury was bothering him, but his kick was too high, sailing far over the bar (*see also PELVIS, HIP, AND THIGH*).

Penalty kicks (as the term implies) are mainly awarded after a major violation within the penalty area. Most purists acknowledge the need for penalty kicks but are adamantly opposed to shoot-outs; it is held that the shoot-out highlights individuals and thus detracts from the team concept of soccer. Nevertheless, the one-on-one confrontation between kicker and goalie is theatrical and thrilling.

People sometimes wonder who has the advantage in a penalty kick. In the shoot-out between Italy and Brazil, the Italian team converted on only two of their five attempts; statistically, however, a penalty clearly favors the kicker: a goal is scored about 75 to 80 percent of the time. In a shoot-out, the kick is taken only 11 meters (36 ft.) out from the center of the goal, giving the kicker a target 7.2 meters (24 ft.) wide and 2.4 meters (8 ft.) high. This is not only a very large target for the kicker but also a very large area for the goalkeeper to defend.

Furthermore, professional soccer players can kick the ball at a velocity of 30 to 35 meters (99–115 ft.) per second (108–125 KPH; about 68–78 MPH; Ekblom, 1994). This means that in a shoot-out the ball will reach the top or bottom corner of the goal in about 0.38 to 0.45 second. According to calculations by Sam Williamson, a physicist at the Center for Neural Science in New York, the best theoretical human reaction time for a complex visual pattern is 0.26 second (Griffing, 1987). After this, it takes some additional time for the goalkeeper's brain to send the muscles signals to hurl the body across the "goal mouth" in an explosive movement. Thus it is questionable whether even a highly trained goalkeeper can react quickly enough to stop a kick beyond arms' reach. And even a goalkeeper who could react that quickly would have no time to take the one or two steps necessary to dive to cover the corner (*see Figure 4*).

When a penalty kick is well placed, the odds that the goalkeeper can stop it are low; therefore, coaches instruct goalies not to wait for the kicker but rather to "fake" one way and then lunge off the mark the other way—the direction in which they actually believe the kick will be going. The outcome depends on the goalie's ability to guess, anticipate, or, if possible, read where the ball is going. Ideally, goalkeepers widen the "window of opportunity" to stop a kick if they can

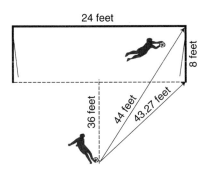

Figure 4. *Mathematics of a penalty kick in a shoot-out are shown. From 11 meters (36 ft.), the kicker has a target 7.3 meters (24 ft.) wide and 2.4 meters (8 ft.) high. At a velocity of 30 to 35 meters (98–115 ft.) per second, the ball arrives in the bottom corner of the net in about 0.38 to 0.45 second. A goalkeeper can reach the ball only if reaction time approaches the shortest possible. However, goalkeepers still manage to stop the ball about 20 to 25 percent of the time—through anticipation, guesswork, effective muscle recruitment, and timing.*

be off the mark at the moment the kicker "commits": 0.1 or 0.2 second before ball contact.

There is a subtle, and often overlooked, aspect of anticipation and reaction. A goalkeeper's movements actually begin well before ball contact, and even well before any feinting. In preparation for the kick, the goalkeeper's brain sends rhythmic signals to the leg muscles—excitatory synaptic input to the motor neurons—readying them for explosive movement (*see also SKELETAL MUSCLE*).

Three types of muscles are "recruited" in this way; in ascending order of speed of recruitment, they are: (1) slow-oxidative, (2) fast-oxidative, and (3) fast-glycolytic fibers. The trick is to recruit all three as quickly and as nearly simultaneously as possible. There is considerable potential for speeding up all three, particularly the fast-oxidative and fast-glycolytic fibers.

To improve muscle recruitment and thus shorten reaction time, goalkeepers try to coordinate their rhythmic motor-neuron signals with the approach of the kicker. A goalkeeper bounces rhythmically on the balls of the feet so that the propulsive muscles of the legs become stretched. When stretched and "excited," these muscles can contract rapidly, improving reaction time (*see also MOTOR CONTROL*). A similar phenomenon takes place in American football, when defensive linemen bounce about before the snap of the ball, trying to time their explosive takeoff to the snap. Studies have found that linemen's reaction times to rhythmic signals were quicker than their reaction times to nonrhythmic signals, and were quickest with the shortest snap counts (2–4 seconds hold time; Paige, 1973; *see also FOOTBALL*).

Stopping a penalty shot takes experience as well as superior reflexes and fast reactions; for this reason, most World Cup goalkeepers tend to be older than other players. These experienced goalkeepers do much better than their younger counterparts at reading and anticipating a kicker's intention during an approach.

Nevertheless, regardless of a goalkeeper's abilities, a well-placed kick into the top corners of the net scores almost every time; and kickers may be able to increase their chances even beyond the 75 to 80 percent average. For one thing, a kicker can take a nonrhythmic approach to the ball (e.g., stop-and-go). For another, the kicker can refrain from striking the ball at full force. (This is analogous to the very effective hesitation dribble used in basketball to freeze defenders; *see BASKETBALL*.) Giving the ball a higher velocity comes at the expense of losing some control, and velocity is not critical; thus the kicker is better off striking the ball with less force. In fact, researchers found that kickers were most accurate when the ball remained at 75 to 80 percent of maximal velocity (Asami, 1976). At three-quarters speed, the goalkeeper still cannot reach a well-placed kick simply by reacting fast enough. As a result, assuming a margin of error of a few feet within either post, a kick of three-quarters force (that is, a velocity of about a 80 KPH; 50 MPH) has a much better chance of scoring than a full-force kick.

Stop-and-Go Sports and the Mystery of Fatigue

Every fan has seen favorite players make an all-out effort but then slow down—or even take themselves out of the game—to avert serious fatigue. It is common in many ball sports to see players pacing themselves to avoid burnout.

Soccer, like basketball, tennis, or ice hockey, requires what physiologists call intermittent work: the players must generate frequent short bursts of intense effort interspersed with periods of rest. Soccer players often go for a long period in which they mostly stand around or walk, and then in the next moment are required to engage in a series of all-out sprints. The accompanying table shows the approximate percentages of time spent in various modes of motion in soccer.

Participants in sports requiring intermittent work rely on a combination of energy sources: anaerobic energy for short-term needs, and aerobic (oxygen-based) energy for long-term needs. Aerobic energy is produced

TIME SPENT IN VARIOUS MODES OF MOTION DURING A SOCCER GAME

Walking	49%
Jogging	36%
Running	7%
Standing	5%
Sprinting	3%

(Source: Ekbloom, 1994)

in the mitochondria, a special compartment of the muscle cells. High-energy phosphates—mainly adenosine triphosphate (ATP)—are responsible for transferring energy from caloric foods like sugar to the cells, allowing them to perform work. In soccer (as in other such sports), the rate at which ATP is utilized seldom exceeds the rate at which it is produced. For the most part, the rapid anaerobic process, coupled with an efficient aerobic system, allows well-conditioned soccer players to maintain ATP at a high level during the game.

In terms of their demands and effects on the body, intermittent ("stop-and-go") sports are very different from endurance sports. Intermittent sports do not call for the kind of physical staying power or aerobic power that is needed in events involving continuous, long-lasting effort at a higher level of intensity, such as long-distance running and cross-country skiing. In this regard, it is useful to consider the athlete's heart rate—although heart rate is an indirect measure of aerobic energy and therefore is not foolproof. In an endurance sport, an athlete's heart rate may remain near the individual's maximum from start to finish; by contrast, a soccer player's heart rate experiences a series of peaks and troughs, and usually remains well below the maximum. These peaks and troughs of the heart rate are shown in the accompanying

figure. Note that for a soccer player, the heart rate may may drop by as much as 50 beats a minute in a trough. In cross-country skiing, on the other hand, the skier's heart rate reaches maximal levels on uphill runs and drops by only about 20 beats a minute on level and downhill runs (*see also SKIING*).

Another useful indicator of aerobic energy is oxygen uptake. Aerobic performance depends on the ability of the lungs, heart, and circulatory system to maximize the delivery of oxygen to the working muscles. A ballplayer, especially in a team sport, has a lower maximum oxygen uptake than a trained endurance athlete. For example, the mean maximal oxygen uptake of top Swedish soccer, ice hockey, and basketball players is 25 to 33 percent less than the range found among top

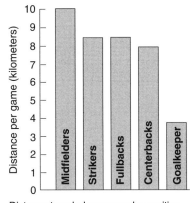

Distance traveled per game by position

Soccer Technique

Soccer is a sport that emphasizes speed, quickness, and coordination, not brute strength. It can be enjoyed equally by boys and girls, men and women, the very tall and the very short, the stout and the thin.

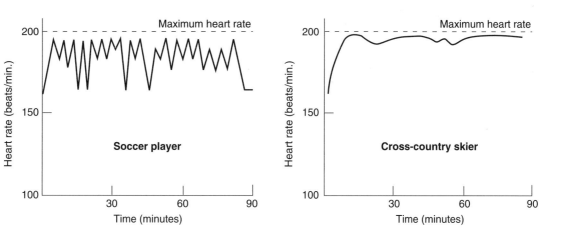

Heart rate for a cross-country skier and a soccer player during a 90-minute workout. The soccer player's heart rate bounces from around 160 to 200; the skier's heart rate rises rather smoothly to near-maximum and stays there. Because cross-country skiing engages all the major muscle groups, top cross-country skiers develop exceedingly high maximal oxygen uptake, even higher than that of runners; in fact, the readings for cross-country skiers are among the highest values ever recorded. (Adapted from Astrand, 1986)

Swedish cross-country skiers (Astrand, 1986).

Thus although soccer and other intermittent-work sports are excellent for developing and maintaining physical fitness, it is imperative for the players to have cross-training in endurance sports, such as long distance running and cross-country skiing, to increase their endurance and their maximal aerobic capacity. Endurance training forces the body to work harder and more continuously, and this is far more beneficial—and far quicker—than simply trying to play one's way into shape.

Stop-and-go team sports also cause many athletes to experience bouts of fatigue during intense parts of a game. Contrary to popular belief, though, this fatigue is not necessarily caused by a buildup of lactic acid (a metabolic byproduct). Nor is it caused by a lack of ATP: the concentration of ATP is only slightly lower in a fatigued muscle than in a resting muscle (Vander, 1994).

Actually, fatigue is a complex phenomenon with several causes, and the most prominent factor probably has to do with defects in the central nervous system. There is some evidence that fatigue can result from ion disturbances over the muscle fiber membranes or an inability of the nervous system to activate muscle fibers (Ekblom, 1994). Elevated potassium around the muscle fibers may gradually cut off sensory input. This in turn inhibits signals from the spinal motor nerves, decreasing the ability of muscle to generate force. When enough muscle fiber is "cut off" from the nerves—deprived of sensory input—motor activity decreases: the muscles are unable to perform a certain motor skill because they are unable to produce the target force. For a soccer player, a drop-off in production of force means a drop-off in running speed.

Fortunately, episodes of fatigue are usually short, rarely lasting more than a few minutes: the athlete quickly recovers and returns to action. The degree of fatigue depends on the intensity and duration of the exercise that caused it, the athlete's fitness, and the level of activity during the recovery period.

During the late stages of a game, however, the nature of fatigue is somewhat different. The muscles fibers most frequently recruited for running have the least capacity to rebuild glycogen during rest periods, and so they can become completely depleted of glycogen—the major form in which the body stores carbohydrates. When this happens, less fiber can be recruited to generate muscle force. The result is impaired performance: regardless of the athlete's competitive drive and "will to win," a glycogen-depleted body simply cannot perform the way the brain tells it to. As athletes try to grapple psychologically with this phenomenon, the commentator—sitting on the sidelines—loves to point out that fatigue can humble even the most competitive player (*see also ENERGY AND METABOLISM; MOTOR CONTROL; and SKELETAL MUSCLE*).

Individual offensive skills range from fundamental ball control—trapping, dribbling and so on—to kicking and heading for passing and scoring. The skills a soccer player develops are highly interdependent. Good players can switch quickly from walking to sprinting and from dribbling to passing and kicking, sometimes in a matter of only a few milliseconds. Thus all the skills should complement one another. Dribbling and trapping, for instance, are considered finesse or "touch" skills; good players know how to integrate these finesse skills with the power or striking skills: kicking and heading.

Dribbling and Trapping

Dribbling is defined as propelling the ball with the feet, though for highly skilled players it actually entails much more. With a colorful dribbler like Pelé, it amounts to an art form. Body contortions, stop-and-go motions, and short-stride shifts of the feet are just a few of the ways dribblers fake out defenders. Very adept dribblers use all these techniques to form gaps between defenders, which they then try to knife through, avoiding the opponents' lunging legs.

Before a player can begin to dribble, it is often necessary to control the ball by trapping it. Trapping involves reducing the velocity of the ball and then redirecting the ball (*see Figure 5*). The player can trap the ball with the chest, a thigh, or—the most popular means—the lower leg.

Kicking

Kicking is the most widely recognized skill in soccer; and the ability to kick the ball accurately and powerfully is often what distinguishes the best players.

Because of the fast and furious pace of the game, it is important for a player to become equally proficient at kicking with the dominant and the recessive foot. Being able to kick with only one foot would be analogous to being able to dribble with one only one hand in basketball. A one-sided player is only "half a player" because a defender can "cheat" by "shading" the dominant side. Many experts believe that the earlier children begin playing soccer, the easier it is for them to become proficient with both feet.

A soccer kick, much like throwing, uses a very natural diagonal-

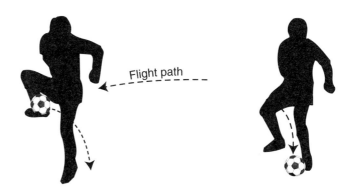

Figure 5. *Trapping an airborne ball is an important advanced skill that has much in common with catching a ball in other sports. For a foot trap, the player brings the receiving leg up into the flight path of the ball. At impact, the leg is pulled back along the line of flight. The ball and leg ride back as a unit until ball velocity decreases enough so that the ball can be redirected to the ground for a quick pass or dribble upfield.*

plane motion. The hip joint, like the shoulder joint, is multiaxial; and it has an added advantage: it is surrounded by several of the body's most powerful muscles. But it is also "handicapped," in a sense, because its range of motion is more limited than that of the shoulder. Stretching exercises that improve range of motion, especially at the hip joint, greatly improve a player's kicking ability (*see also PELVIS, HIP, AND THIGH*). Many factors affect the ability to kick, but for simplicity the focus here is on three distinct steps: (1) approach and plant, (2) leg swing, and (3) impact and follow-through.

Approach and plant. Surprisingly, the supporting leg is more important than the kicking leg. Moreover, the contact point of foot and ball is more important than the velocity of the foot in imparting velocity to the ball. One of the most critical variables determining this contact point is the way the kicker approaches the ball and plants the foot. For example—and this is true even with the best players—if the kicker plants the opposite foot too far ahead of the ball or too far behind it, the ball is likely to leave the foot weakly and off course.

A soccer kick is in many ways analogous to a golf swing: both are like a pendulum; and in both the player is trying to attain maximum velocity at the lowest point of the swing, at the placement of the ball (near the supporting foot). In soccer, if the plant foot is too far forward, most of the kinetic (motion) energy of the kick goes into the ground. If the plant foot is too far back, less kinetic energy is imparted to the ball because the velocity of the kicking foot decreases before contact is made, and the contact period is reduced.

The secret to making good contact with the ball is to plant nearly perpendicular to the ball in the intended kicking direction, and to lean slightly to the side opposite the kicking foot. This allows greater rotational momentum (momentum about a fixed axis) around the supporting foot as the kicking leg swings in an arc that brings it downward into the ball. Because the soccer ball is round, it gives a chance of making good contact with many plant positions.

Leg swing. The purpose of the leg swing is to transfer as much of the body's momentum to the ball as possible. The total momentum that can be transferred to the ball is a product of the mass of the leg and foot times the velocity of the foot, which includes approach velocity. How much momentum is actually transferred depends on motor coordination and the strength of the legs.

The kicking motion is an example of a kinetic chain event: each body segment helps propel the following body segment. The most powerful kicking chain action entails developing rotational and linear momentum. The hip drives the thigh, which drives the lower leg, which then drives the ankle and foot into the ball. The muscles "fire," not simultaneously, but immediately after one another. Muscles work in pairs, so that as one group (agonist) contracts, the other group (antagonist) relaxes. The major difference between the best soccer players and all the rest is that the top players have a better-than-aver-

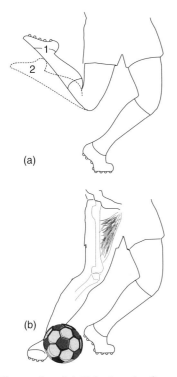

(a)

(b)

Figure 6. *(a) Bringing the foot up closer to the buttocks—(1) rather than (2)—lets a kicker generate greater leg velocity because it lowers the moment of inertia of the leg: the rotational force necessary to set the leg and foot in motion. (b) Studies have found that the hip flexor muscles, rather than the knee, are most responsible for generating rotational leg velocity during the leg swing.*

age ability to relax the antagonistic muscles during the swinging phase, which is of great importance for fluidity (Ekblom, 1994).

As the hips rotate about the planted foot, the hip flexor (bending) muscles start accelerating the leg forward. Then as hip flexor acceleration declines, the hip straighteners (hamstrings) and knee straighteners (the quadriceps group) provide more of foot's momentum before contact with the ball.

At the start of the leg swing, the knee joint should be fully flexed to allow a full swing of the lower leg. Flexing the knee completely brings more body mass near the axis of rotation—the hip joint. It lowers the moment of inertia (the force necessary to develop rotational motion) of the leg so that the angular velocity of the striking leg can be increased (*see Figure 6; see also ACROBATICS*).

Hip muscles play the most important part in the leg swing: they start the kinetic chain; they supply 90 percent of the work done by the leg muscles; and they are responsible for the motion of the thigh and the extensors (straighteners) of the knee (Robertson, 1985). Many experts believe that working on the strength of the hip flexors does much more to improve a player's kicking power than concentrating on the knee extensors.

Impact and follow-through. It has been found that just before impact, the knee flexors (benders) become more dominant than its extensors, actually reducing knee extension (Ekblom, 1994). At first, this finding seemed surprising: logically, the kinetic chain would dictate that just before impact the knee should be extended at full speed. But it is now believed that the kinetic chain does not completely apply to the knee action in kicking, because the hamstring group must start

BALL VELOCITIES RESULTING FROM STRAIGHT AND SIDE APPROACHES IN FOOTBALL AND SOCCER

Kicking style	Foot velocity before impact (ft./sec.)	Average foot striking mass (lb.)	Ball velocity (ft./sec.)
Football instep: side approach	79.2	5.7	95.5
Football toe kick: straight approach	78.1	5.3	82.0
Soccer rolling: straight approach	70.7	5.7	87.6
Football instep: straight approach	66.7	8.6	82.0
Soccer rolling: side approach	65.0	7.0	95.5
Soccer stationary: straight approach	65.0	7.0	78.2
Soccer stationary: side approach	64.2	8.6	91.7

Table 2. *Notice that the three greatest ball velocities (shaded) are achieved with the side approach. The critical factors in a soccer kick are the way the support foot is planted and the extreme backswing of the kicking leg. Although good players can boom the ball off at a variety of different angles, a low drive with full instep is the most efficient shot in the game. It transfers to the ball most of the momentum generated during the approach and leg swing. This is true for the same reason that it is easier to throw a ball faster and farther in a horizontal than a vertical direction. (Source: Plagenhoef, 1971)*

Figure 7. *Action-reaction dynamics in a jump header. As the back bends forward and the body begins to rotate forward, the legs must come up to counter, or cancel, this rotation.*

Activity	Time (milliseconds)
Soccer header	23.0
Handball serve	12.5
Volleyball serve	10.0
Soccer kick	8.0
Football kick	8.0
Tennis forehand	5.0
Softball (hit off tee)	3.5
Baseball (hit off tee)	1.3
Badminton	1.25
Golf ball (hit by driver)	1.0

Table 3. *Contact time of head and ball in soccer is more than 4 times that for racket and ball in tennis and 17 times that for bat and ball in baseball. But contact time in a header can be affected by how much hair and what kind of hair the player has. (Source: Plagenhoef, 1971)*

bending the knee early, before the follow-through—a "pulling back" to prevent hyperextension and possible damage to the knee.

At the actual point of impact, the kicker wants to have the swinging leg extended as fully as possible so that the velocity at the end of the foot is high. High ball velocity depends on maximizing the angular velocities of the thigh and shank. A comparison of various kicking styles shows that the three highest velocities of the ball are achieved with a side-approach instep kick (*see Table 2*).

Heading

Kicking a ball is a skill soccer shares with many other sports, but using the head to pass the ball, redirect it, or fire it at the goal is unique to soccer. To execute a header, the player must have excellent timing, accuracy, and power, since it involves gauging the speed of an oncoming ball and then coordinating the effort of the head and the trunk.

With regard to biomechanics, headers can be divided into three categories: (1) standing; (2) a vertical jump from a stationary position, and (3) a jump with both a horizontal and a vertical component, developed from an approach run. Given the same ball velocity at impact, the force delivered will be greatest for category 3 because of the run-up; therefore, muscle action is particularly important in categories 1 and 2—the stationary positions. In a header, muscle power comes mainly from the abdomen and the small of the back. To develop the action-reaction dynamics that will produce the greatest momentum before the impact, the back should be arched (trunk flexors), the thighs brought back (hip flexors), and the knees bent (knee extensors; *see Figure 7*). Because the time of contact between head and ball is considerable, much of the trunk motion takes place in the follow-through, after the first impact. At impact, it is important for the player to remain as rigid as possible, so that energy is transferred to the ball rather than being wasted by dissipating into the body (bear in mind that muscles and tendons can absorb energy).

Although creating muscle power is important, how much is actually needed depends entirely on the situation. The velocity of the ball after impact is, logically enough, a function of the momentum of the head and the momentum of the ball. The player must impart much more linear and angular momentum to a ball that arrives slowly than to a ball arriving faster.

In striking the ball, the head has a limited range of motion; thus the head itself plays a rather limited role in sending the ball off at a high velocity. What is critical here is the action at the hip, just as in kicking—although the velocity is far less because the levers involved in heading (hip through neck) are far shorter and have far less range of motion than those involved in kicking (hip through foot). This does not mean, however, that a header cannot be hit hard. Because the relatively large mass of the ball allows a prolonged contact (*see Table 3*), and because the ball has a considerable coefficient of restitution, a player can head the ball with surprising speed and accuracy. It is noteworthy that baldness can be an advantage in soccer. A player who is naturally bald or has a shaved head can expect a higher coefficient of restitution on impact with the ball than a player with a full head of hair—especially long, bushy, or wiry hair—because hair wastes, or "damps," some impact energy.

John Zumerchik

References

Asami, T. "Energy Efficiency of Ball Kicking." In P. Komi (ed.), *Biomechanics V-B*. Baltimore: University Park Press, 1976.

Asami, T., and V. Nolte. "Analysis of Powerful Ball Kicking." In M. Matsui and K. Kobayashi (eds.), *Biomechanics VIII-B*. Champaign, Illinois: Human Kinetics, 1983.

Astrand, P., and K. Rodahl. *Textbook of Work Physiology: Physiological Bases of Exercise*. New York: McGraw-Hill, 1986.

Dunn, E., and C. Putnam. "The Influence of the Lower Leg Motion on Thigh Deceleration in Kicking." In G. de Groot, A. Hollander, and P. Huijing (eds.), *Biomechanics XI-B*. Amsterdam: Free University Press, 1986.

Ekblom, B. *Football (Soccer)*. Boston: Blackwell Scientific, 1994.

Ghista, D. *Human Body Dynamics*. New York: Oxford University Press, 1982.

Griffing, D. *The Dynamics of Sports*. Oxford, Ohio: Dalog, 1987.

Marples, M. *History of Football*. London: Secker and Warburg, 1954.

Paige, R. "What Research Tells the Coach about Football." (Pamphlet.) Washington, D. C.: American Association for Health, Physical Education, and Recreation, 1973.

Plagenhoef, S. *Patterns of Human Motion*. Englewood Cliffs, New Jersey: Prentice Hall, 1971.

Reilly, T., et al. (eds.) *Science and Football*. London: Spon, 1988.

Robertson, D., and R. Mosher. "Work and Power of the Leg Muscles in Soccer Kicking." In D. Winter et al. (eds.), *Biomechanics X-B*. Champaign, Illinois: Human Kinetics, 1985.

Vander, A., et al. *Human Physiology*, 6th ed. New York: McGraw-Hill, 1994.

Statistics

STATISTICS IS ABOUT HISTORY. It is the process of collecting, analyzing, and interpreting numerical data through mathematical techniques to understand the past, and sometimes to make predictions about the future. Statistical analyses are used to advance knowledge in almost all imaginable fields—economics, business, and government being the most prominent among them. Political candidates devise campaign strategies based on statistics, and governments use statistics when making trade agreements. Statistics provide valuable information about the past that can enable individuals, groups, and governments to make informed, and often crucial, decisions about the future.

Statistics are used in sports by fans, athletes, and coaches alike. For fans, statistics have developed into a widespread pastime. Some people first learn about statistics as children by tracking the batting averages of major league baseball heroes, many of whom are admitted to the Hall of Fame almost solely because their career numbers are high above a statistical average. Fans often argue with each other and defend their favorite players by referring to statistics as proof of a player's superior talents. For players, goals are established and personal achievements are expressed in terms of statistics. A major league hitter may strive to beat his own previous year's batting average or to hit in the top 10 percent of his team. For coaches and managers, sophisticated statistical analyses are used for many purposes, such as to scout for new players and to devise strategies to use against opponents. For most people, newspapers serve as the primary source of statistics. Newspapers are packed with statistics from many fields of study, but perhaps no section contains more facts and statistics than the sports section, where page upon page of statistics are presented daily.

With such vast amounts of data available, and because of the tremendous public appetite for sports analyses, sportswriters as well as fans often take liberties with statistics; for example, they often draw conclusions based on selective use of statistics. In fact, one serious problem with statistics is that they may be presented or manipulated in such a way as to support unfounded conclusions. They are often used to sensationalize, inflate, confuse, and oversimplify. In many cases, inaccurate or misleading use of statistics is intentional—

that is, it is meant to decieve. But in many other cases, people misuse statistics unintentionally, because they do not fully understand how to analyze data. It is therefore important to learn to critically appraise data, and the claims made in analyses.

Statistics are numbers that mean something, but exactly what they mean is open to interpretation. People compare and compile numbers in various combinations to identify compelling relationships, although correlations between numbers often mean little or nothing at all. Statistical analysis is not an end in itself, but a tool to facilitate thinking and questioning.

This article covers some of the tools and techniques used in probability and statistics, and it applies these techniques to examples from sports. As one learns the basics of statistical analysis, one will become better at scrutinizing probabilities and statistics to distinguish between good and poor statistical reasoning and to decipher valid evidence without being misled by irrelevancies.

Statistical Issues

This section will consider two prominent aspects of statistics in sports, involving labor disputes and baseball batting averages.

Labor Disputes: Whose Average?

The year 1994 was perhaps the most bizarre and tumultuous in the history of sports labor: strikes—often cantankerous—delayed the completion of the National Hockey League (NHL) season and prematurely ended the major league baseball season. During these strikes, both the team owners and the players' unions tossed statistics around to support their case.

In baseball, for example, the owners pleaded poverty, or impending poverty, claiming that the future would bring them huge financial losses and thus that the future of the major league sport was threatened. The players challenged this assertion: if the owners were losing so much money, why were they spending millions of dollars more each year on players' salaries? If team ownership entailed such grave financial dangers, why had the price of a baseball franchise more than doubled from 1989 to 1994? For the owners, it was imperative to demonstrate financial hardship in order to achieve their objectives: a salary cap (how much each team could spend annually for players' salaries) and restrictions on free agency (each player's freedom to change teams). The owners believed that the players should help them achieve revenue redistribution and some type of "shared sacrifice." The players, on the other hand, wanted their salaries to continue to be determined by the competitive free market. Because each side felt that its position was very strong, the impasse was difficult to break.

To a considerable extent, these strikes were a public-relations

ESCALATING REVENUE AND SALARIES IN THE NHL

Year	Teams	Revenue	Mean player salary
1989–1990	21	$398 million	$232,000
1993–1994	26	$717 million	$558,000

Table 1. *Over four seasons, NHL revenues increased 80 percent while players' salaries increased 140 percent. If this trend continues at the same rates of growth, NHL hockey may be in jeopardy.*

battle—a battle for the support of the ticket-buying public. One problem in such a dispute is definition. For instance, the NHL claimed that the "average" team was losing $1.5 million a year. Such a statement is meaningless, however, unless it specifies to which of the common averages, or central tendencies, it refers—the mean, the median, or the mode. A *mean* is an arithmetic average. To arrive at the mean in this situation, one would add the profits and the losses of all 26 teams and divide the total by 26. A *median* is a midpoint. In this case, the median would be the team in the financial middle, the mean of the thirteenth and fourteenth of the teams ranked in order of income: half of the teams would post a greater profit (or less loss) than the median, and half a lesser profit (or greater loss). *Mode* refers to the most likely outcome, the measurement that occurs most frequently in a data set. For the numbers 1, 2, 2, 4, 5, and 20, for example, the mean is 5.6, the median is 3, and the mode is 2. In this example, if the highest number, 20, is replaced by 1,000, only the mean will change; the median and the mode remain the same. Thus because the term *average* can take different meanings, one must be cautious when encountering claims about averages.

Figure 1 presents a hypothetical example of the NHL labor dispute and shows how the word *average* can be used—correctly—to make the case for each side. Because the mean is more sensitive to extremely large and small numbers occurring in a data set, owners are likely to use this measure as the "average" ($615,384 loss). Although 22 teams turned a profit, the 4 financially troubled teams dragged down the average (the mean). Players, by contrast, would use the median or the mode as the "average." Focusing on the median teams, the players can show that a profitable franchise is very achievable. The situation looks even more promising when the mode is used. Because 8 teams generated a yearly profit of $2 million, that is the most frequently occurring outcome—and the players can claim that the league is in fact in very good shape; the few owners who are losing money need only change their business practices in order to turn a profit.

In the high-stakes negotiations in professional sports, then—as in many other situations—the term *average* can have many meanings, and it is often used selectively to influence opinion. Therefore, one should always ask for specifics: which average?

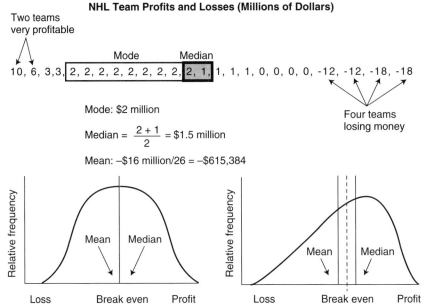

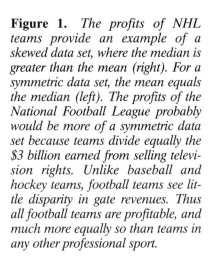

Figure 1. *The profits of NHL teams provide an example of a skewed data set, where the median is greater than the mean (right). For a symmetric data set, the mean equals the median (left). The profits of the National Football League probably would be more of a symmetric data set because teams divide equally the $3 billion earned from selling television rights. Unlike baseball and hockey teams, football teams see little disparity in gate revenues. Thus all football teams are profitable, and much more equally so than teams in any other professional sport.*

Batting Averages: An All-Time Great?

Comparisons between players and between teams are common in all sports, but they are especially common in baseball because baseball players produce a plethora of hard numbers that serve as measures of performance. The most widely cited measure of comparison is probably the batting average, and one of the sharpest debates among baseball fans is who—of all hitters, past and present—had the all-time best single-season batting average. Some people focus nostalgically on Ty Cobb's "seasons of glory," when he hit .420 (1911) and .410 (1912). Others point to Ted Williams's averages of .406 (in the 1941 season) and .388 (in 1957). It is often said that even the best players of the 1990s could never attain numbers like these.

When raw mean scores for batting are compared, one can indeed conclude that the feats of old-time players outshine those of their modern-day counterparts. However, there may be other considerations in calculating batting averages. Richard Cramer, for example, argues that the best way to compare hitters across eras is by calculating each player's "batter win average" (BWA)—the number of runs produced above the average (mean), divided by the player's total number of times at bat (Cramer, 1980) For example, in 1979, Fred Lynn's standard batting average was .333; but Cramer calculated a score of +.120 for Lynn during that season, giving him an impressive "corrected" batting average of .390. The difference between .390 and .333 was accounted for by Lynn's extra-base slugging. When Cramer converted his BWA into a predicted batting average, he came up with extremely low corrected batting averages for the stars of yesteryear. According to this measure, Honus Wagner, whose batting average was .354 for the 1908 season, actually had a very unimpressive corrected batting average of only .289—well below that of the top stars of the 1990s.

Actually, neither of these conclusions—nor the statistics used to buttress it—seems satisfactory. The nostalgists' analyses fail to consider that the "average athlete" improves over time, as is illustrated by the decreasing world-record times in all swimming and running events. As recently as the early 1960s, for example, many people still thought that no one would ever run 1 mile in less than 4 minutes. By the 1990s, the 4-minute barrier had long since been broken, and the world record was continuing to fall. (As of 1996, the world record was 3:44.39, set by Noureddine Morceli of Algeria on 5 September 1993 in Reiti, Italy.) Because athletes continue to improve, it is futile to compare past records against present achievements. Better training, better nutrition, and better conditioning give modern athletes an enormous advantage.

Baseball is, of course, very different from running. Baseball hitters compete against pitchers, not against the clock; and if batters' skills have improved over the years, it is probable that pitchers' skills have also improved. Also, batting averages have been dramatically affected by changes in the rules—such as outlawing the spitball, raising and lowering the height of the pitcher's mound, altering the "liveliness" of the ball, changing field conditions and dimensions, and adjusting the size of the strike zone. Most such changes were instituted to balance the advantages gained by pitchers or by hitters, and this further distorts comparisons across time.

However, Cramer's innovative comparison is not much of an improvement. He fails to take into account that the pool of players is much larger in the 1990s than it was in the early twentieth century. His table of "corrections" is based on the entire league in a given season, rather than on any individual player. In the 1990s, the larger pool of players had narrowed the gap between the average league batting average and the leading league batting average. Rogers Hornsby's league-leading batting average of .424 in 1924 was 129 points above the league average of .295. By the 1990s, it was rare for a league-leading hitter to exceed the league average by more than 70 or 80 points. Therefore, applying Cramer's corrections to all players of the past is a dubious exercise, and it is particularly inaccurate to apply these corrections to elite players.

There were simply more good players in professional baseball in the 1990s. Although the number of teams had increased significantly over the years, the talent pool had increased far more. An expanding talent pool in the United States—particularly with the gradual integration of black players beginning in 1947—as well as an increasing number of players from the Caribbean, and from South and Central America, resulted in a steady improvement in the ability of players, a larger pool of players of "average" skill. It is not surprising, therefore, that batting averages of the 1990s were much closer to the mean batting average than were the averages of the 1920s,

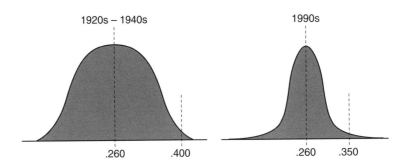

Figure 2. *Although the mean major league batting average has remained very close to means of the early 1900s, there has been an overall improvement among players. That is, there are more average players, as shown by the bell curve. Batting averages form a thin-humped bell curve for players in the 1990s (right) and a wide bell curve for the 1920s through the 1940s (left). As Stephen Jay Gould points out, the fact that there are fewer .400 hitters is due to improvements which indicate that the average batter's performance (.260) is approaching closer and closer to human limitations. Great players of the past, on this analysis, simply stood out from their peers and were no better than the greats of the 1990s. (Adapted from Gould, 1986)*

1930s, or 1940s. To put this another way, the bell-shaped curve for players' batting averages in the 1920s is much flatter than the curve for the 1990s (*see Figure 2*). Cramer's comparison does not take this into account.

Given these and many other factors, it may be impossible to make an accurate comparison between superstars of different eras. If Ty Cobb were to enter the major leagues in the 1990s, would he be a superstar? Would Wade Boggs have produced even better numbers if he had played in the 1920s? Such comparisons are tricky, and any conclusions are easily discredited. A much better—though less ambitious—approach is to compare players with their own peers to determine just how exceptional an individual performance is, in a given year and in terms of league performance as a whole.

Perhaps the must useful comparisons of hitters' batting averages through the decades have been done in separate analyses by the scientist Stephen Jay Gould of Harvard and by two engineers, Robert Watts and Terry Bahill—all of whom are baseball fans (Gould, 1986; Watts and Bahill, 1990). According to these scholars, the greater talent pool of the 1990s ensured that the majority of players were much better than players of bygone years; but the best contemporary players were neither appreciably better nor appreciably worse than the best earlier players. Because of the difficulties of comparing players across decades, they believe that any such comparison must be flawed. However, if one insists on making the comparison, perhaps the best way is to measure performace in terms of number of standard deviations above the league average.

Standard deviation is a statistical tool that assigns a numerical value to any random outcome—in this case, a batting average—as it relates to the average (mean). The probable deviation from the mean

MEAN: 260

Outcomes	258	253	262	267
Deviations	–2	–7	2	7
Square quantities	4	49	4	49

Variance = (4+49+4+49)/4 = 106/4 = 26.5

Standard deviation = $\sqrt{26.5}$ = 5.15

Table 2.

of a random event, a statistical measure of variance, is called the sum of squares or the mean square. Variance is a measure of how much outcomes are spread out. To come up with a variance, one first must determine the deviation of the sets of values from the mean. If the mean is 260, for instance, and there were only four outcomes (258, 253, 262, and 267), the deviations would be –2, –7, 2, and 7. Next, these quantities are squared: 4, 49, 4, and 49, respectively. The variance is the mean of these 4 quantities, and the standard deviation is the square root of that mean (*see Table 2*).

In the case of batting averages, the standard deviation is the square of the difference between a given batting average and the mean batting average. As Gould calculated the standard deviation for each year, he discovered a trend. Standard deviations declined rather sharply until 1940, and then began to level off in the 1940s. A standard deviation can be visualized as a certain distance along the baseline of the curve from the mean, or middle, of the baseline out to the left or right to the point where the curve rises (*see Figure 3*).

Standard deviations break down so that about 68 percent of hitters' averages (or of any data under consideration) will fall within 1 standard deviation of the mean, 96 percent within 2 standard deviations, and 99 percent or more within 3 standard deviations. Table 3 lists all the single-season performances by major league stars from 1900 to 1987 that were 3 standard deviations or more above the mean. Regardless of the year, a hitter who bats even 2 standard deviations above the mean is having a superb season. Season performances of 3 standard deviations above the mean are extremely rare: this happened only 38 times from 1900 to 1987. Interestingly, Ty Cobb's best season, 1911—when he hit .420—was not quite 3 standard deviations (2.920) above the league average, because the league average was .293 and the standard deviation was considerable (0.0326). Nevertheless, Cobb's career achievement of 2.372 standard deviations above the league average puts him at the top of all career hitters (*see Table 4*). "Shoeless" Joe Jackson, although he is only fifth on this list, had averages of .408 in 1911 and .395 in 1912 and was a model of consistent excellence.

Whatever the statistical considerations, however, sports fans will probably continue to argue passionately about the comparative merits of past and present players. Therefore it seems fitting to end this

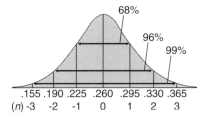

Figure 3. *Each number (n = –3, –2, –1, 0, +1, +2, +3) indicates number of standard deviations from the mean. Of all hitters, 68 percent fall within 1 standard deviation of the mean (they bat between .225 and .295) Great hitters approach 3 standard deviations above the mean. The worst hitters approach 3 standard deviations below the mean.*

EXCEPTIONAL SINGLE-SEASON EFFORTS

Player	League	Year	Batting average	Mean batting average	Standard deviation	n (+3 or better)
N. Lajoie	AL	1901	.422	.290	.0336	3.934
R. Hornsby	NL	1924	.424	.295	.0338	3.925
W. Boggs	AL	1985	.368	.268	.0264	3.808
G. Brett	AL	1980	.390	.278	.0297	3.787
R. Carew	AL	1977	.388	.272	.0312	3.710
T. Cobb	AL	1910	.385	.262	.0337	3.656
T. Williams	AL	1941	.406	.282	.0340	3.648
N. Lajoie	AL	1910	.384	.262	.0337	3.627
N. Lajoie	AL	1904	.381	.256	.0346	3.616
R. Carew	AL	1974	.364	.265	.0276	3.600
T. Gwynn	NL	1987	.370	.279	.0262	3.497
T. Williams	AL	1957	.388	.270	.0344	3.426
T. Speaker	AL	1916	.386	.263	.0363	3.391
S. Musial	NL	1948	.376	.276	.0297	3.381
G. Sisler	AL	1922	.420	.300	.0358	3.352
W. McGee	NL	1985	.353	.268	.0253	3.350
R. Carew	AL	1975	.359	.266	.0282	3.292
N. Cash	AL	1961	.361	.273	.0267	3.284
S. Musial	NL	1946	.365	.271	.0287	3.272
H. Walker	NL	1947	.363	.281	.0251	3.258
H. Wagner	NL	1908	.354	.257	.0293	3.235
T. Cobb	AL	1912	.410	.280	.0410	3.171
T. Cobb	AL	1909	.377	.260	.0369	3.154
T. Gwynn	NL	1984	.351	.269	.0261	3.151
H. Wagner	NL	1907	.350	.257	.0293	3.149
R. Carew	AL	1973	.350	.267	.0265	3.129
W. Boggs	AL	1986	.357	.269	.0283	3.118
T. Cobb	AL	1917	.383	.261	.0395	3.095
R. Garr	AL	1974	.353	.265	.0276	3.086
R. Hornsby	NL	1921	.397	.305	.0299	3.076
T. Cobb	AL	1922	.401	.300	.0358	3.073
A. Vaughn	NL	1935	.385	.291	.0306	3.067
R. Hornsby	NL	1922	.401	.305	.0312	3.063
J. DiMaggio	AL	1939	.381	.295	.0280	3.056
H. Zimmerman	NL	1912	.372	.288	.0275	3.049
W. Boggs	AL	1983	.361	.271	.0296	3.044
T. Cobb	AL	1907	.350	.261	.0292	3.037
W. Boggs	AL	1987	.363	.272	.0300	3.035

Table 3. *Truly exceptional single-season efforts are listed by the number of standard deviations (3 or more) above the average for that year. (Data adapted from Watts, 1990)*

section with an ancedote about Ty Cobb. After a major league old-timers' game in 1959, a reporter asked him, "How would you hit today, under modern conditions?" "About .305 to .310," Cobb replied. The reporter was puzzled: "But you hit over .400 three times. Why would you hit only .305 or .310 now?" After a pause, Cobb said, "Well, you have to remember that I'm 72 years old now."

**THE BEST CAREER BATTING AVERAGE PERFORMANCES
AS MEASURED BY STANDARD DEVIATIONS ABOVE THE MEAN**

Player	Seasons	Career batting average	n
Ty Cobb	23	.367	2.372
Roger Hornsby	13	.358	2.230
Ted Williams	16	.344	2.137
Rod Carew	17	.328	2.125
Joe Jackson	9	.356	2.054

Table 4. *Note that if Wade Boggs (1982–) and Tony Gwynn (1982–) ended their careers after the 1995 season, their number of standard deviations above the average for a career would place them in this elite group. (Data adapted from Watts, 1990)*

Issues of Probability

Whereas statistics is concerned with making inferences about a population from a sample, probability works in the opposite direction. Because the population is known, predictions can be made about obtaining various samples from the population. Probability is the ratio of the number of times an outcome occurs to the total number of trials. All outcome probabilities must lie between 0 and 1, and the probabilities of all potential outcomes must sum to 1. An event expected to occur every time a trial is repeated has a probability of 1, indicating certainty; an event expected never to occur has a probability of 0, indicating impossibility.

Most phenomena, of course, lie somewhere between certainty and impossibility; they have a degree of randomness. When scientists use the term *random*, they do not mean the common definition—haphazard, accidental, or without aim or direction. In statistics, *random* refers to an inability to predict the outcome of individual events. In other words, carried out under identical circumstances, a random event may yield different outcomes. The ubiquitous examples used in textbooks to illustrate randomness are tossing coins and throwing dice. The outcome of each successive throw of a die is completely independent of the previous throws. For instance, even if a 6 comes up 20 times in a row, the probability of getting a 6 on the next throw stays the same: it is always 1 in 6.

Are Seven-Game Playoff Series Fixed?

Although the outcome of individual ball games may depend in part of the players' talent and on which team is "hot," there is nevertheless some degree of randomness; a "lucky bounce" or changes in playing conditions, for example, may favor one team or the other. Nevertheless, many fans believe that a there is conspiracy to ensure that seven-game championship series will last six or seven games, because the longer a series runs, the more money will be made by ball clubs, broadcasters, advertisers, and others. The longer a series continues, the more revenue it produces for the league, the team owners, and the television networks. Teams benefit by packing their stadiums with fans who have paid premium ticket prices. Leagues make money from selling the broadcast rights. Networks pay a high price for broadcast rights, because they know that they will more than regain their investment from advertising. All these revenues have the greatest future value if every playoff series goes a full seven games (4 games to 3), and the least value if the playoff series ends up being a sweep (4 to 0). According to the conspiracy theories, then, network television executives and sports officials—the National Basketball Association (NBA) and major league baseball (MLB)—bend the rules to favor the trailing team, so that the series will last at least six games, or the full seven games.

A consideration of probability and randomness, however, shows that these conspiracy theories are rather far-fetched. Final playoffs usually involve the two best teams in the league, so it is reasonable to assume that each team has an equal chance (a 1-in-2 expected probability) of winning any one game. In practice, of course, it is often the case that one team is slightly better than the other; but this assumption is justifiable because few athletes or teams achieve their full potential on every outing.

The size of the sample is also important for probability. When a coin is tossed, for example, the law of large numbers applies: as more and more tosses are made, the actual outcome (heads and tails) will

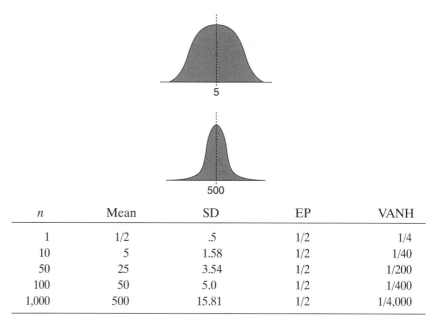

n	Mean	SD	EP	VANH
1	1/2	.5	1/2	1/4
10	5	1.58	1/2	1/40
50	25	3.54	1/2	1/200
100	50	5.0	1/2	1/400
1,000	500	15.81	1/2	1/4,000

Table 5. *For given number of coin tosses (n), the mean, standard deviation (SD), expected probability (EP), and variance of the average number of heads (VANH) are shown.*

come closer and closer to the expected probability. In other words, provided that samples are drawn independently, the larger the sample, the closer the outcome will come to the expected probability, even on the first trial. In the case of a coin toss, the expected probability that the coin will turn up heads is 1 in 2. This expected probability is always the same—always 1 in 2—but as the size of the sample increases, the "variance of the average number of heads" (VANH) gradually decreases (*see Table 5*). In other words, 9 out of 10 tosses may come up heads, but it is extremely improbable that 900 out of 1,000 tosses could turn up heads. Therefore, the larger the sample, the more closely VANH begins to approach the expected probability of 1 in 2. The bell-shaped standard-deviation curve illustrates the concentration around the mean as the sample increases—a skinny bell.

In a playoff series, the expected probability for each individual game—1 in 2—is the same as that of a coin toss. But the expected probability of the *length* of a best-of-seven series entails four differ-

EXPECTED PROBABILITY AND ACTUAL OUTCOMES OF SEVEN-GAME SERIES THROUGH 1994

Series finish	Expected probability	Baseball outcome (total)	Baseball outcome (last 20 years)
4–0	1/8 = 12.5%	15/90 = 17%	3/20 = 15%
4–1	1/4 = 25%	21/90 = 23%	4/20 = 20%
4–2	5/16 = 31.25%	20/90 = 22%	6/20 = 30%
4–3	5/16 = 31.25%	34/90 = 38%	7/20 = 35%
Comeback 0–3	6.25%	Never	Never
Comeback 0–2	15.625%	Ten times	Three times
Comeback 1–3	12.5%	Six times	Twice

Series Finish	Expected probability	Basketball outcome (total)	Basketball outcome (last 20 years)
4–0	1/8 = 12.5%	5/48 = 10%	3/20 = 15%
4–1	1/4 = 25%	11/48 = 23%	3/20 = 15%
4–2	5/16 = 31.25%	16/48 = 33%	10/20 = 50%
4–3	5/16 = 31.25%	14/48 = 29%	4/20 = 20%
Comeback 0–3	6.25%	Never	Never
Comeback 0–2	15.625%	Twice	Twice
Comeback 1–3	12.5%	Never	Never

Table 6. *Expected probability closely matches actual outcomes, overall as well as over the last 20 years, for both the World Series in baseball and the NBA finals in basketball. Because baseball is a more random game than basketball, its outcomes more closely match the expected probabilities. The expected probability assumes that the two teams are evenly matched, although in reality one team is often somewhat better. Outcomes are also skewed by home-team advantages. Comebacks from far behind are so rare that outcomes can be listed only under expected probability. Although a 0–3 comeback had not occurred in basketball or baseball as of 1996, it did happen once in hockey, in 1942, when the Toronto Maple Leafs overcame the Detroit Red Wings.*

ent possible outcomes: 4–0, 4–1, 4–2, 4–3. Table 6 shows the expected probability, the expected mean length of the series, of various outcomes, as well as the actual outcome of MLB and NBA series over a 20-year period.

The expected probability of a 4–0 outcome (a series sweep) is 1 in 8; the expected probability of a 4–2 outcome (a six-game series) or a 4–3 outcome (a seven-game series) is higher: 5 in 16. (*Table 7 shows how the expected probability is calculated.*)

The expected mean length of a seven-game series, then, is 5.81. Of course, expected probability differs from actual occurrence, but this expected mean length, 5.81, is very close to the mean actual length of seven-games series: 5.7 games. Mean actual length is the ratio of the total number of all NBA and MBL playoff series games played (787) to the number of series (138), that is: 787/138 = 5.7 games. The fact that actual mean length is a somewhat smaller figure than expected mean length makes the conspiracy theory unlikely. If

PROBABILITY OF A SERIES LASTING 5 GAMES

There are four ways a team can win in 5 games. (5th game must be a win.)

	1	2	3	4	5
1	L	W	W	W	W
2	W	L	W	W	W
3	W	W	L	W	W
4	W	W	W	L	W

Probability of each outcome = 1/2 × 1/2 × 1/2 × 1/2 × 1/2 = 1/32
Total probability for each team = 4 × 1/32 = 1/8
Total probability for both teams = 2 × 1/8 = 1/4 = 25%

PROBABILITY OF A COMEBACK FROM DOWN 0–2

There are 4 ways this can happen: win the next 4 games in a row or lose game 4, 5, or 6, while winning the rest. (Game 3 must be a win or it would be considered a comeback from down 0–3.)

	1	2	3	4	5	6	7
1	L	L	W	W	W	W	
2	L	L	W	L	W	W	W
3	L	L	W	W	L	W	W
4	L	L	W	W	W	L	W

Probability
Outcome 1: 1/2 × 1/2 × 1/2 × 1/2 = 1/16
Outcome 2: 1/2 × 1/2 × 1/2 × 1/2 × 1/2 = 1/32
Outcome 3: 1/2 × 1/2 × 1/2 × 1/2 × 1/2 = 1/32
Outcome 3: 1/2 × 1/2 × 1/2 × 1/2 × 1/2 = 1/32

Total probability
1/16 + 3/32 = 2 +3/32 = 5/32 = 15.625%

Table 7. *These calculations outline the expected probability of a five-game series (4–1) and the possibility of a comeback from down 0–2.*

this theory had any basis in fact, these results should be the other way around: actual mean length would be greater than expected mean length. It seems clear that most series last six or seven games not because of a conspiracy, but simply because the likelihood is greatest (62.5%).

Note that the the outcomes in baseball match the expected probability more closely than those in basketball. This is because baseball is the more random game. A game is considered very random if there is an equal probability of winning and losing. A game becomes less random the more the outcome depends on the talents of the players rather than on factors beyond their control.

There are a number of reasons why baseball is more random than basketball. First of all, in the NBA, the average field-goal percentage is about 50 percent (a probability of 1 in 2) and the free-throw average is around 75 percent (3 in 4); in comparison, the average MLB batting average is only around .250 (the probability of a hit is 1 in 4). This is a general probability, though. In individual cases, a hit depends not only on the batter's skill but also on who is pitching: a batter must react to a variety of pitches (e.g., curveballs and split-finger fastballs) and to a variety of pitchers, whose change-ups, for example, all break differently. Thus, the probability of getting a hit varies widely from one "at bat" to another. In basketball, by contrast, shooters decide what shot to use on the basis of their knowledge of their own accuracy in various situations. Also, a shooter who is being guarded tightly by a defender—a situation in which the probability of scoring may be well below 1 in 2—can choose to pass the ball to an open teammate. A hitter in baseball does not have that luxury.

Second, baseball is a more random game because the outcome depends solely on runs, not on hits. Thus luck becomes more of a factor. Team X can have have 12 singles in a game and not produce any runs, while team Y wins the game with one "lucky" hit that does produce a run. A grand-slam home run (4 runs) can also be "lucky," since the bases can become loaded from walks, errors, and hits that take a bad bounce. A weak hitter can be fooled by an off-speed pitch and still adjust the swing enough to pull the ball just inside the foul pole. During the course of the game, a team might produce 20 well-tagged line drives, yet if most of them are hit at fielders, they can come to nothing. A team might make many hits that come to nothing because they are not bunched—that is, are not in the same inning..

A third reason why baseball is more random is that the number of runs—the number of points—is small. If a baseball game could produce over 200 points, as a basketball game does, luck or chance would be much less of a factor. This is also true of soccer, where the margin of victory is more often than not one goal.

Golf: Breaking 80?

Many golfers are obsessed with the goal of shooting par or breaking 80. For golfers of limited ability, this goal is clearly elusive, but they pursue it anyway; and it is interesting to analyze their quest in terms of probability.

These players' reasoning is somewhat as follows. A golfer frequently plays one hole or another exceptionally well. Thus a golfer who plays a course enough times will eventually have played each hole well at least once. The golfer's mean score for the course may be, say, 95; but if the best scores for all the holes over the last twenty to thirty rounds are combined, the total score might be well under 80 or even well under par—perhaps as low as 68. The conclusion follows that if the score derived from all the "best holes" is 68, the goal of breaking 80 is attainable.

This logic may look plausible. However, there are some problems with it. To begin with, selective memory is a factor. Few golfers keep all their scorecards, and most remember only their best efforts and try to forget their worst ones. Second, the logic fails to consider the limits of control: for even the best golfers, it is, physically, nearly impossible to exert perfect control over 80 shots in a row; and the slightest error at impact can significantly alter the flight of the ball. Even professional golfers, many of whom practice for hours each day, consider it lucky to hit 18 shots in a row down the middle of the fairway. Third, the reasoning disregards external factors: how the ball lies, what the weather is like, how the course is laid out, what condition the course is in.

With all this in mind. the physicist Ted Jorgensen looked at the scorecards of one of his own golfing companions in order to calculate the probability that this man could attain the goal of breaking 80 (Jorgensen, 1994). For one particular par-4 hole, the friend's scores over the last 22 rounds had been: two birdies (3 strokes), three pars (4), fourteen bogies (5), two double bogies (6), and one triple bogey (7). From these numbers, Jorgensen calculated the probability of his friend's shooting a par on this hole as 3 in 22 (0.136, or 13.6%). This must be considered a very rough estimate, because the sample (22) is too small to satisfy the law of large numbers. Nevertheless, the sample is large enough to project this player's long-term chance of breaking 80.

Jorgensen went on to calculate the probable scores for the remaining 17 holes. Because the variability and the range of scores for the other holes were quite similar to those for the first hole Jorgensen had calculated, the probability that his companion could break 80 turned out to be very slim indeed: less than 3 in 100,000. To be certain of breaking 80 three times, therefore, his friend would need to play one game a week for 2,000 years. Of course, the friend could score 80 at any time, but given his past scores, such an extreme variation would be extremely unlikely (assuming, of course, that his skill did not improve appreciably). Jorgensen does not mention in his study whether he conveyed these results to his friend. Perhaps they were better left unsaid: few things can be more disheartening than calculations of probability.

Prediction:
Trends in Future Athletic Performance

Throughout history and across many cultures, people have been fascinated with the idea of seeing into the future; in fact, many ancient methods for trying to predict the future are still practiced. Modern methods, however, extend beyond the crystal ball or tarot cards; they include scientific and mathematical tools that are reliable, sophisticated, and scientific. These modern tools are applied to a wide range of topics and problems. For example, scientists are developing sophisticated mathematical models to forecast the impact of human activity on the fragile ecosystem of the earth. Considering the wide range of variables involved, this is no easy task. Some study global warming and the link between the greenhouse effect and the use of fossil fuels; some monitor and project the destruction of the ozone layer from the use of chlorofluorocarbons. The United Nations also uses statistical models to project world population growth, with an eye toward the impact of growing populations on the need for fossil fuels, the release of airborne chlorofluorocarbons, and global weather changes. At the height of the cold war, American national laboratories used supercomputers to consider the implications for the ecosystem of human-made catastrophes, such as the "nuclear winter" that might follow atomic warfare.

The worlds of business and finance are perhaps even more preoccupied with predicting the future. The stakes involved in predicting future market conditions are enormous: a correct decision can send a company's profits soaring; an erroneous decision can mean bankruptcy. The ability to predict future market demands may be the single most important factor in the success of small and big businesses alike. On Wall Street, billions of dollars are won and lost in a matter of seconds. The fortunes of several huge investment banks "evaporated" in a day as a result of dubious trading decisions made by a single analyst.

One modern statistical tool used to predict future values of a variable is called *regression analysis*. This term was first coined in 1886, in a research paper by Francis Galton. Galton found that the average height of sons whose fathers were tall was less than the fathers' height, and that the average height of sons whose fathers were short was greater than the fathers' height. He concluded that the sons of both tall and short men "regressed" toward the average height of all men.

The modern theory of regression analysis is somewhat more complex. Suppose, for example, that a variable under consideration—this is called the dependent variable—is altered only according to changes in a single independent variable. For instance, many scientists studying changes in climate are tracking the increase in temperature (the dependent variable) over time (a single independent variable). Regression deals with relations between variables, and the "traffic" usually flows in only one direction, from the independent variable to the dependent variable. For the scientists in this example, the question is how weather changes over time.

If the time plot of a dependent variable shows a definite trend, one that can be approximated by a mathematical curve, then the "best fit" of the actual data points is first obtained by finding the curve that most closely approximates the trend. The curve is called the least-square curve because the squares of the errors, or deviations, of the data points from the curve are minimal. (Deviations are the vertical distances between observed and predicted values.) The best-fit curve can then be extended forward in time to predict the most probable values of the dependent variable in the future.

Arjun Tan, a physicist and a fan of track and field, applied regression analysis to athletes' performance in several Olympic events (Tan, 1989). His model finds that gold medal performances in the shot put and in the discus throw have increased steadily with time and show no sign of leveling off. The throwing distances in both events have more than doubled since the first modern Olympics, held in 1896. Similar trends have also been observed in the high jump and in the pole vault. Future performances in these events, Tan concludes, will lie around the least-square straight lines extended in time, at least for the next several Olympics.

However, these linear increases in throwing and jumping records cannot be sustained indefinitely. At some point, human limitations will dictate that the rate of increase must level off. The trend may still be upward, but the rate of increase will be slower and slower. When a new trend emerges, a different least-square curve—most likely an asymptotic curve, that is, one that eventually flattens out—will replace the straight line as a predictor of future athletic performances. One study that failed to take this leveling-off phenomenon into account predicted that women's times would rival men's in the 400-meter and the marathon by the year 2000 and in the 800-meter and the 1,500-meter by 2060. Exercise physiologists, citing physiological differences, considered these predictions ludicrous (Angiers, 1992).

In fact, for Olympic running events (beginning in 1896 and still continuing as of the 1996 Olympics), the trend is already becoming asymptotic. Running times continue to improve, but at an increasingly slower rate. For example, it took only 4 years (1896–1900) for the men's time in the 100-meter to fall from 12 to 11 seconds, but it took 64 years (1900–1964) for the time to drop from 11 seconds to 10 seconds. Similar trends can be seen in sprint, relay, hurdle, and long-distance events.

Figure 4 shows actual and projected times (the latter are based on regression analysis) for the women's and men's 100-meter sprint. The model predicts that men will break the 9.5-second barrier by the year 2020; the 9-second barrier by 2060, and the 8.5-second barrier by the turn of the twenty-first century. Women's record times will improve at a faster rate, so that by 2036, the women's time will be faster than

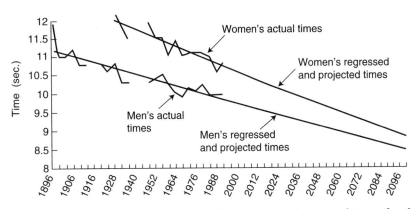

Figure 4. *This graph shows actual and regressed and projected times for the women's and men's Olympic 100-meter sprint. According to this model, the trend for men is to break the 9-second mark by the year 2060 and for women to break the 10-second mark by 2032. Drug-aided performances could change the curve. If Ben Johnson's drug-aided performance in 1988—9.79 seconds—had been allowed to stand (as of 1996, it was still faster than the official world record), followed by record performances in 1992 and 1996, the curve would be steeper, with less of an asymptotic regression.*

the men's current Olympic and world record, which was 9.84 seconds as of 1996. The real-time gap between men and women in the 100-meter sprint will continue to close, though women's times will still remain slower than men's.

Regression analysis is a useful a tool for projections in sports, as in other areas; but it is important to note that any historical trend in data should never be projected too far into the future. The key to a good prediction depends on the least-square curve chosen

John Zumerchik and Arjun Tan

References

Angiers, N. "Two Experts Say Women Who Run May Overtake Men." *New York Times*, 7 January 1992.

Cramer, R. "Average Batting Skill through Major League History." *Baseball Research Journal* (1980): 167–192.

Dyer, K. "Catching Up to the Men: A Statistical Look at the Progression of World Records in Sports Shows that Women are Closing the Gender Gap. Can the Trend Continue?" *New Scientist*, 2 August 1984.

Galton, F. "Family Likeness in Stature." *Proceedings of Royal Society* (London) 40 (1886): 42–72.

Gould, S. "Why No One Hits .400 Anymore." *Discover*, 7 August 1986.

Huff, D. *How to Lie with Statistics*. New York: Norton, 1982.

Jaffe, A. *Misused Statistics: Straight Talk for Twisted Numbers*. New York: Dekker, 1987.

Jaeger, R. *Statistics: A Spectator Sport*. Beverly Hills, California: Sage, 1983.

Jorgenson, T. *The Physics of Golf*. New York: American Institute of Physics, 1994.

Kitson, Trevor. "The Ultimate Mile: A Mathematical Analysis of the Record-Breaking Runs of the Past Suggests We May Already Be within One Second of the Fastest Mile Possible." *New Scientist*, 2 August 1984.

Krane, K. "Probability, Statistics, and the World Series of Baseball." *American Journal of Physics* 49, no.7 (1981): 696–697.

Runyon, R. *How Numbers Lie: A Consumer's Guide to the Fine Art of Numerical Deception*. Brattleboro, Vermont: Lewis, 1981.

Runyon, R. *Winning with Statistics*. Reading, Massachusetts: Addison-Wesley, 1977.

Sprent, P. *Statistics in Action*. New York: Penguin, 1977.

Tan, A. "Athletic Performance Trends in Olympics." *Mathematical Spectrum* 21 (1988–89): 78–84.

Watts R., and A. Bahill. *Keep Your Eye on the Ball: The Science and Folklore of Baseball*. New York: Freeman, 1990.